Workforce Restructuring in Europe

Workforce Restructuring in Europe

General Editors

Edzard Clifton-Dey
Solicitor and Rechtsanwalt (Germany), ebl miller rosenfalck

Pia Dalziel
Solicitor and Advokat (Denmark), ebl miller rosenfalck

Sara Kennedy
Solicitor, ebl miller rosenfalck

Emmanuelle Ries
Solicitor, ebl miller rosenfalck

With contributions from European practitioners

Bloomsbury Professional

Bloomsbury Professional Ltd, Maxwelton House, 41–43 Boltro Road, Haywards Heath, West Sussex, RH16 1BJ

Bloomsbury Professional is an imprint of Bloomsbury Publishing plc

A CIP Catalogue record for this book is available from the British Library.

ISBN 978 1 84766 700 7

Typeset by Phoenix Photosetting, Chatham, Kent
Printed and bound in Great Britain by CPI (UK) Ltd, Croydon, CR0 4YY

Foreword

Workforce restructuring is a reality of modern business and economic life. What do we mean by restructuring? It might be a reorganisation of a workplace or group of companies, in extreme cases a downsizing or closure, sometimes a relocation, at other times outsourcing is being considered. Whichever of these, the chances are that the employer has to consider not only what it is doing but how, including possible timing, consultation, cost and morale implications and processes.

Those businesses which deal with the human reality and the required legal processes with due care and sensitivity can avoid many pitfalls awaiting the unwary. But even in this era of apparent harmonisation of laws internationally (for example, the European Union's Single Market), it has transpired to be easier to make substantive rights (eg discrimination) turn on common laws and principles than it has been to develop common ways or mechanisms to enforce such rights. Taking that EU example, whilst we may have a single source of rules on discrimination or workforce consultation, the well informed reader will be aware that each EU Member State has its own traditions, its own ways of giving effect to those rules – in effect, creating a different terrain on which the rules are built. The EU retains a diverse cultural and legal heritage with only a limited amount of harmonised employment and labour laws but a long tradition of employee co-determination across many jurisdictions. So this book focuses on *how* to approach the issue of workforce restructuring in various countries – and as such, it aims squarely at making that terrain easier to read, understand and negotiate.

This book seeks to offer some practical insights for how the law works locally, what might be the legal drivers for local processes, all in a format that permits comparison of one country with another.

The typical reader of this book will be an HR director or manager or team member, or in-house or external counsel – any of whom might have the task of managing one of the most sensitive tasks in the corporate life cycle. It is a book for the planners of such change.

This book conveys one message above all: that the key to success is to plan carefully any European workforce restructuring, so as to get it right from the very beginning and ensure that any collateral damage in respect of unnecessary litigation, labour relations, reputational damage and costs is avoided. I warmly commend it as an invaluable planning aide towards these goals.

Michelle Taylor
HR Director – EMEAR
Epson Europe BV
Hemel Hempstead, United Kingdom

Introduction

THE HR DELIVERY MODEL

The HR function in many internationally operating corporates has undergone significant change over the last two decades. Key drivers – apart from costs considerations – were (and continue to be) the desire to develop the HR function into a strategic business role that is fully aligned with and supportive of overall business objectives at group level (taking the view from the top) rather than being limited to a local HR perspective in any particular jurisdiction within which the corporation happens to be active. In practice the delivery model is often therefore characterised by a shared central HR service hub that is then supported by local HR in country where that is required for day to day HR service delivery and/or project implementation or HR transactional support.

In Europe, one HR delivery model that is frequently chosen is that of centralised European HR function (or the even geographically broader area of EMEA (Europe Middle East and Africa) HR function) which typically sits with the European group company that carries an oversight function in respect of European country entities.

The strategic initiatives that any such central HR function drives forward typically covers a broad range of matters: from an integrated talent management and recruitment process through to an aligned reward structure, generally applicable policies, an integrated performance management process across the region, strategic planning of and support in respect of transactional change projects (including but not limited to mergers and acquisitions, off shoring and outsourcing and other efficiency restructuring and change projects) etc. One of the key functions here is hence to ensure that any strategic initiative also works 'downstream', ie is capable (from a legal and cultural perspective as well as an employee relations perspective) of being implemented seamlessly at local level in all relevant jurisdictions.

There is one element to success of any such initiative, one vital ingredient, both at the planning stage (when it comes to considering the feasibility and cost benefit ratio of initiatives) and at the project management and implementation stage: local knowledge.

The typical HR delivery model struggles, almost by definition, to meet the need for in-depth country expertise and detailed local knowledge which is crucial not just at the planning and feasibility stage but also at the point of roll-out where country-specific HR specialists and/or employment lawyers are required. Whilst this publication cannot replace the need for specialist local support it seeks to fill in for the lack of hands-on practical documentation of employment regulations across the 28 EU Member States (and Norway and Switzerland) on the key employment law concepts governing workforce restructuring projects in and across the region.

THE CHALLENGE OF DIVERSITY

Operating across the 28 EU Member States (and Norway and Switzerland) means to operate across a region that is in both cultural and linguistic terms, extremely diverse. Whilst English is seen as the 'lingua franca' across the region, language barriers continue to be an obstacle on a day-to-day basis when it comes to efficient communication and access to local HR guidelines and employment law sources. There is then the immense economic and fiscal diversity of this region which, of course, impacts on many of the strategic initiatives and provides a further challenge to the HR delivery model.

Most importantly though: there is a legal diversity across Europe. Frequently there are common themes that apply across the region and the European Union has consistently worked towards establishing some minimum ground rules in respect of working conditions across the region but all this was never meant to create absolutely identical conditions. For the purposes of the subject matter of this publication it is therefore of some relevance to consider closely the European law-making process and instruments and how these instruments then filter through to the level of the individual Member State laws.

INTERACTION BETWEEN EUROPEAN AND NATIONAL LAWS AND REGULATIONS

European Union law is divided into primary and secondary legislation. The various EU treaties (primary legislation) are the basis and the 'club rules' for all legislative measure taken at EU level. Secondary legislation – which includes European Directives and European Regulations as the most relevant instruments of the secondary legislation process – then provide the 'meat on the bone' flowing from the principles and objectives set out in the treaties.

European Directives

A European Directive is a legislative act that sets aims that all EU Member States must achieve within a particular time frame. Directives do not apply directly in any of the Member States but what is required is a process whereby each Member State implements the Directive into local law. In other words an EU Directive is a form of legislation that is addressed at Member State level. Whilst a Directive will set out the objective to be achieved, each of the

Member States must then pass the relevant domestic legislation to give effect to the terms of the Directive within a time frame that is also then set in the Directive.

It is a decision at Member State level to decide exactly how to do this, ie how to implement the Directive into local law. In most civil law jurisdictions (with a tradition of codified law) this is frequently done by amending pre-existing legislation as necessary to reflect the aims and objectives of the relevant directive.

In common law jurisdictions the Directive is frequently adopted in its original form as a piece of domestic legislation.

What is noteworthy (and this often creates practical complexities in multi-jurisdictional projects) is that Member States are not required to limit implementation of a Directive to the minimum standard set out in the Directive but that a Member State can – and often will – go further. It may also be the case that certain Member States already have in place a pre-existing standard that is equivalent or goes beyond the requirements of a particular Directive.

Whilst all EU Directives are available in all official European Union languages and are hence easily accessible without any language barriers (see http://eur-lex.europa.eu/homepage.html) the text of any Directive in itself will not provide the reader with a definitive insight as to how any Member State has chosen to achieve the prescribed aims and whether any Member State has decided to go beyond the requirements of a Directive (and if so, in what way this has been done). It will hence always be necessary to consider the relevant Member State implementation legislation (which is frequently not readily available in English but often only in the relevant local language).

European Regulations

A European Regulation is a binding legislative act. It is directly applicable in its entirety across the EU and hence no implementation process at Member State level is required. There is, however, no exclusive competence for the European Union in the area of social policy and employment but – within the scope of the Lisbon Treaty, there is an element of shared competence between the Member States and the EU. Consequently there is no room for Regulations in this area but the legislative instrument to be adopted for EU law making is primarily the Directive.

EUROPEAN LAW IMPACTING ON WORKFORCE RESTRUCTURING PROJECTS IN EUROPE

EU employment law principally covers two areas:

- **working conditions** – this includes (but is not limited to) working hours, part-time and fixed-term work, posting of workers; and

- **information and consultation of workers** in respect of transfers of businesses and collective redundancies as well relevant measures of a transnational nature

In respect of these areas the EU complements policy initiatives taken by individual Member States by setting **minimum standards**. The legal basis for such law making process is primarily set out in Article 151 and 153 of the 2007 Lisbon Treaty as the current constitutional basis of the EU[1] (similar provisions can be found in the predecessor treaties):

> 'Article 151
>
> The Union and the Member States, having in mind fundamental social rights such as those set out in the European Social Charter signed at Turin on 18 October 1961 and in the 1989 Community Charter of the Fundamental Social Rights of Workers, shall have as their objectives the promotion of employment, improved living and working conditions, so as to make possible their harmonisation while the improvement is being maintained, proper social protection, dialogue between management and labour, the development of human resources with a view to lasting high employment and the combating of exclusion.
>
> To this end the Union and the Member States shall implement measures which take account of the diverse forms of national practices, in particular in the field of contractual relations, and the need to maintain the competitiveness of the Union economy.
>
> They believe that such a development will ensue not only from the functioning of the internal market, which will favour the harmonisation of social systems, but also from the procedures provided for in the Treaties and from the approximation of provisions laid down by law, regulation or administrative action.
>
> [...]
>
> Article 153
>
> 1. With a view to achieving the objectives of Article 151, the Union shall support and complement the activities of the Member States in the following fields:
>
>   (a) improvement in particular of the working environment to protect workers' health and safety;
>
>   (b) working conditions;

1 See Consolidated versions of the Treaty on European Union and the Treaty on the Functioning of the European Union – Consolidated version of the Treaty on the Functioning of the European Union - Protocols – Annexes – Declarations annexed to the Final Act of the Intergovernmental Conference which adopted the Treaty of Lisbon, signed on 13 December 2007, Official Journal C 326 , 26/10/2012 P. 0001 – 0390, http://eur-lex.europa.eu/legal-content/EN/TXT/?uri=CELEX:12012E/TXT.

(c) social security and social protection of workers;

(d) protection of workers where their employment contract is terminated;

(e) the information and consultation of workers;

(f) representation and collective defence of the interests of workers and employers, including co-determination, subject to paragraph 5;

(g) conditions of employment for third-country nationals legally residing in Union territory;

(h) the integration of persons excluded from the labour market, without prejudice to Article 166;

(i) equality between men and women with regard to labour market opportunities and treatment at work;

(j) the combating of social exclusion;

(k) the modernisation of social protection systems without prejudice to point (c).

2. To this end, the European Parliament and the Council:

(a) may adopt measures designed to encourage cooperation between Member States through initiatives aimed at improving knowledge, developing exchanges of information and best practices, promoting innovative approaches and evaluating experiences, excluding any harmonisation of the laws and regulations of the Member States;

(b may adopt, in the fields referred to in paragraph 1(a) to (i), by means of directives, minimum requirements for gradual implementation, having regard to the conditions and technical rules obtaining in each of the Member States. Such directives shall avoid imposing administrative, financial and legal constraints in a way which would hold back the creation and development of small and medium-sized undertakings.

[....]'

In accordance with the Lisbon Treaty – particularly Article 153 – the means of achieving the aims set out in Article 151 are Directives (rather than Regulations), see Article 153 (2) b, above.

Over the years the EU has adopted three key Directives that are of particular relevance in the context of any workforce restructuring project impacting on the workforce in one or more of the Member States; these key Directives are considered in more detail below.

The Acquired Rights Directive

Commonly referred to as the 'Acquired Rights Directive', the official name of the Directive is 'Council Directive 2001/23/EC of 12 March 2001 on the approximation of the laws of the Member States relating to the safeguarding of employees' rights in the event of transfers of undertakings, businesses or parts of undertakings or businesses'. The Directive stipulates that its aim (see preamble) is 'to provide for the protection of employees in the event of a change of employer, in particular, to ensure that their rights are safeguarded.'

To achieve this aim, the Directive provides:

(a) that the transferor's (seller, outsourcer etc.) rights and obligations arising from an employment relationship existing on the date of a transfer are transferred to the transferee (buyer, service provider etc.);
(b) that the transfer is not in itself to constitute grounds for dismissal by the transferor or the transferee; and
(c) that workers' representatives have certain rights to be informed and consulted.

Some of the key provisions of the Directive have been set out below to illustrate the far-reaching impact in the context of a business asset sale, and potentially also the outsourcing or offshoring of business functions.

Scope and definitions

'Article 1

1.

(a) This Directive shall apply to any transfer of an undertaking, business, or part of an undertaking or business to another employer as a result of a legal transfer or merger.

(b) Subject to subparagraph (a) and the following provisions of this Article, there is a transfer within the meaning of this Directive where there is a transfer of an economic entity which retains its identity, meaning an organised grouping of resources which has the objective of pursuing an economic activity, whether or not that activity is central or ancillary.

[....]

Article 3

1. The transferor's rights and obligations arising from a contract of employment or from an employment relationship existing on the date of a transfer shall, by reason of such transfer, be transferred to the transferee.

Member States may provide that, after the date of transfer, the transferor and the transferee shall be jointly and severally liable in respect of obligations which arose before the date of transfer from a contract of employment or an employment relationship existing on the date of the transfer.

[....]

Article 4

1. The transfer of the undertaking, business or part of the undertaking or business shall not in itself constitute grounds for dismissal by the transferor or the transferee. This provision shall not stand in the way of dismissals that may take place for economic, technical or organisational reasons entailing changes in the workforce.

[....]'

As is evident from the above extract from the Directive, there are qualifying hurdles to be met; notably the Directive applies (only) 'where there is a transfer of an economic entity which retains its identity, meaning an organised grouping of resources which has the objective of pursuing an economic activity, whether or not that activity is central or ancillary.' (Article 1(1) b, above).

There is a complex, occasionally contradictory, body of relevant case law, both at Member State level and EU level, relating to the scope and in particular the interpretation of what constitutes an economic entity and maintenance of identity before and after the transfer. This is also true in respect of the consequences of a transfer. Here the issues are frequently linked to what is, and what is not, 'in scope' of terms and conditions that transfer over to the new employer. Last but not least, there are onerous information and consultation obligations to be complied with for both the transferor and the transferee, including the following set out in Article 7 of the Acquired Rights Directive:

Information and consultation

'Article 7

1. The transferor and transferee shall be required to inform the representatives of their respective employees affected by the transfer of the following:

   – the date or proposed date of the transfer,

   – the reasons for the transfer,

   – the legal, economic and social implications of the transfer for the employees,

   – any measures envisaged in relation to the employees.

   The transferor must give such information to the representatives of his employees in good time, before the transfer is carried out.

   The transferee must give such information to the representatives of his employees in good time, and in any event before his employees are directly affected by the transfer as regards their conditions of work and employment.

2. Where the transferor or the transferee envisages measures in relation to his employees, he shall consult the representatives of this employees in good time on such measures with a view to reaching an agreement.

   [...]

4. The obligations laid down in this Article shall apply irrespective of whether the decision resulting in the transfer is taken by the employer or an undertaking controlling the employer.'

Article 7(4) in particular is of relevance in group organisations where the decision-making process is 'top down' and the management of the local employing legal entity is not part and parcel of the actual decision-making process. Depending on how exactly Member States have decided to implement the aims of the Directive, decision making at controlling parent company level may be sufficient to trigger local information and consultation obligations (or the allegation of failure to inform and consult in a timely fashion or at all).

Offshoring and the Acquired Rights Directive

The Acquired Rights Directive in its form as implemented into the national laws of each of the Member States applies to a transfer where the relevant economic entity that is transferred is situated before the transfer and post transfer in one and the same Member State.

However, the Acquired Rights Directive does not expressly address the issue of cross border transfers other than by stipulating in its Article 1(2) that this 'Directive shall apply where and in so far as the undertaking, business or part of the undertaking or business to be transferred is situated within the territorial scope of the Treaty.' The key to the application is hence the location of the actual undertaking or business to be transferred (rather than the location of the legal entity controlling such undertaking or business).

Whilst there seems to be consensus in principle that a cross border transfer is capable of falling within the scope of the Acquired Rights Directive the practical approach often adopted in relation to a transfer across borders in that of redundancy. Whilst the Acquired Rights Directive may have the consequence of transferring the employment relationship to the new employer, the employees will remain in the location (in the country) that has also previously been the work location. As the new employer will arguably not have any use for the employees in that location (and employees often have no desire to relocate), they are then treated as redundant. Whilst arguably a practical approach, such strategy will always need to be considered carefully and in light of the relevant local laws by way of which the Acquired Rights Directive was implemented in all impacted jurisdictions. Only this exercise will filter out the feasibility – in costs and risk terms – of such an approach.

European Works Council Directive

Information, consultation and, particularly in civil law jurisdictions, co-determination rights of employee representative bodies at national level have a long tradition that pre-dates the establishment of the European Union (or its predecessor organisations).

European law (in the form of Directives) changed the landscape in 1994 with the result that certain corporates (community scale undertakings) became subject to information and consultation obligations at European level through a European Works Council.

Recast in 2009, the latest incarnation of the Directive[2] was implemented by Member States on or before 5 June 2011. The Directive requires the establishment of a European Works Council for the purpose of information and consultation with European employee representatives on transnational issues, but only where such European Works Council formation is requested by a sufficient number of employees or their representatives (at least 100 employees, or representatives of 100 employees, from two or more Member States). Only employers with over 1,000 employees within the European Economic Ares (the 'EEA') and at least 150 employees in two separate EEA states are within scope of the obligations. The relevant Directives are addressed by Member States and these, in turn have provided, by way of local implementation laws, for the right to establish European Works Councils and the process to be followed. Whilst implementation laws are broadly similar there are differences, not only in respect of the enforcement and sanctions for non-compliance, but also in respect of how European Works Council information and consultations then links into relevant local employee representative information consultation (both in terms of substance and timing). As a general rule, the law of the Member State where the company has its headquarters is the one that will apply when setting up and operating a European Works Council.

Particularly for larger organisations and/or those operating with integrated teams across legal entities and across borders, projects involving change will frequently trigger legal and HR issues in more than one jurisdiction at the same time. Where that is the case, ie where the issues are of a transnational nature, and where a European Works Council is already in place, it is key to assess if, and at what time, relevant information is to be shared with the European Works Council. This strategy will also then need to seamlessly link in and sit with local employee representative information and consultation (and co-determination obligations) in relevant Member States.

2 Directive 2009/38/EC of the European Parliament and of the Council of 6 May 2009 on the establishment of a European Works Council or a procedure in Community-scale undertakings and Community-scale groups of undertakings for the purposes of informing and consulting employees, http://eur-lex.europa.eu/legal-content/EN/TXT/?uri=celex:32009L0038.

The Collective Redundancy Directive

Council Directive 98/59/EC of 20 July 1998 on the approximation of the laws of the Member States relating to collective redundancies (commonly referred to as the 'Collective Redundancy Directive') requires employers to consult employee representatives in the event of collective redundancies. The Directive provides a definition of what constitutes a 'collective redundancy' (see Article 1 of the directive below) but it will always be necessary to cross-check against local implementation legislation in relevant Member States as these may provide for consultation to be triggered at lower threshold numbers of affected employees (please see relevant country chapters for details).

Definitions and scope

'Article 1

1. For the purposes of this Directive:

    (a) 'collective redundancies` means dismissals effected by an employer for one or more reasons not related to the individual workers concerned where, according to the choice of the Member States, the number of redundancies is:

    (i) either, over a period of 30 days:

    – at least 10 in establishments normally employing more than 20 and less than 100 workers,

    – at least 10% of the number of workers in establishments normally employing at least 100 but less than 300 workers,

    – at least 30 in establishments normally employing 300 workers or more,

    (ii) or, over a period of 90 days, at least 20, whatever the number of workers normally employed in the establishments in question;

    (b) 'workers' representatives` means the workers' representatives provided for by the laws or practices of the Member States.

    For the purpose of calculating the number of redundancies provided for in the first subparagraph of point (a), terminations of an employment contract which occur on the employer's initiative for one or more reasons not related to the individual workers concerned shall be assimilated to redundancies, provided that there are at least five redundancies.'

Information and Consultation

The Directive sets out what kind of information is to be provided and establishes a consultation process framework. Article 2 of the Directive provides as follows:

'Article 2

1. Where an employer is contemplating collective redundancies, he shall begin consultations with the workers' representatives in good time with a view to reaching an agreement.
2. These consultations shall, at least, cover ways and means of avoiding collective redundancies or reducing the number of workers affected, and of mitigating the consequences by recourse to accompanying social measures aimed, inter alia, at aid for redeploying or retraining workers made redundant.

   Member States may provide that the workers' representatives may call on the services of experts in accordance with national legislation and/or practice.
3. To enable workers' representatives to make constructive proposals, the employers shall in good time during the course of the consultations:

   (a) supply them with all relevant information and

   (b) in any event notify them in writing of:

   (i) the reasons for the projected redundancies;

   (ii) the number of categories of workers to be made redundant;

   (iii) the number and categories of workers normally employed;

   (iv) the period over which the projected redundancies are to be effected;

   (v) the criteria proposed for the selection of the workers to be made redundant in so far as national legislation and/or practice confers the power therefor upon the employer;

   (vi) the method for calculating any redundancy payments other than those arising out of national legislation and/or practice.

   The employer shall forward to the competent public authority a copy of, at least, the elements of the written communication which are provided for in the first subparagraph, point (b), subpoints (i) to (v).
4. The obligations laid down in paragraphs 1, 2 and 3 shall apply irrespective of whether the decision regarding collective

redundancies is being taken by the employer or by an undertaking controlling the employer.

In considering alleged breaches of the information, consultation and notification requirements laid down by this Directive, account shall not be taken of any defence on the part of the employer on the ground that the necessary information has not been provided to the employer by the undertaking which took the decision leading to collective redundancies.'

As before, the above only sets out minimum ground rules and many (continental) European jurisdictions have a framework of co-determination in place that goes considerably beyond the scope of the above minimum standard with a requirement to negotiate an agreement with the local employee representative body on the proposed measures (if, how and when these are implemented) and an associated severance package for affected employees. Therefore jumping to the conclusion (on the basis of the wording of the Directive) at the planning stage that all that is required is to 'begin consultations with the workers' representatives in good time with a view to reaching an agreement' (Article 2(1), above) is misleading – local requirements and the consequential potential impact on the restructuring costs should always be assessed carefully at an early stage and together with local advisers.

PLANNING AND COORDINATING MULTI-JURISDICTIONAL EUROPEAN RESTRUCTURING PROJECTS

Any centralised HR team will need to understand and be aware of the employment legislation of each of the jurisdictions in which it has an oversight role. This appears to be a self-evident statement but in practice many projects involving change are drawn up either without any such detailed understanding or simply with assumptions in respect of the legal landscape that later turn out to be incorrect.

Either way, any such planning errors will frequently either delay implementation or, as worst case scenario, derail a project in its entirety. What is required at an early (feasibility) stage is to obtain high level country by country advice to form an understanding of the key practical and legal issues involved.

For example:

- Will it be a requirement to agree a proposed measure with a local employee representative body or is information and/or consultation sufficient?
- If so, what is the likely timeline to comply with such local requirements and, equally important, when will the local employee representative body need to be informed of the measure to still make subsequent consultation meaningful?

- Do timelines in different affected Member States align?
- Who are the parties to local consultation (which inevitably takes place in the local language) and have the local entity representatives sufficient understanding of the subject matter to deal with either collective or individual consultation obligations?
- How will language barriers be dealt with (all local consultation will arguably require any documentation and presentations given to the local employee representative body to be in the local language)?

It is the purpose of this publication to assist at this stage (not as an academic text but as a practical country-by-country aide memoire) such that a multi-jurisdictional project plan can be reassessed in light of the country guidance provided in the publication.

COUNTRY CHAPTERS

This publication provides guidance on the relevant laws impacting on workforce restructuring projects in all 28 EU Member States and in Norway and Switzerland. Every reasonable efforts have been made to state the law in this first edition of Workforce Restructuring consistently across the country chapters as at 1 August 2015. The reader should note though that this text is neither intended to be a fully comprehensive guide nor an academic text. Rather, it is intended to provide a practical starting point for those who need to understand the key legal issues on a local level swiftly for any initial planning exercise. Detailed bespoke legal advice should then always be obtained from local HR and local employment lawyers.

Edzard Clifton-Dey, Pia Dalziel,
Sara Kennedy and Emmanuelle Ries
ebl miller rosenfalck, London

Contents

List of contributors

GENERAL EDITORS

The General Editors of Workforce Restructuring in Europe are all employment lawyers at ebl miller rosenfalck in London.

Edzard Clifton-Dey is a dual-qualified (Anglo-German) employment law specialist and a partner in the Employment Team of ebl miller rosenfalck in London. He has a particular expertise in managing multi-jurisdictional workforce restructuring projects and he frequently advises corporate clients on boardroom disputes, executive recruitments and senior management exits.

Edzard is a regular speaker at seminars on international employment matters. He is one of the General Editors and a co-author of *Employment Law in Europe* (Bloomsbury Professional, 2009). He is recognised for his experience of counselling clients on cross-border employment issues (*Chambers Global 2013* directory). He is also recognised in the *Chambers Global 2014* directory as a leader is his field of expertise.

Pia Dalziel is a dual-qualified (Anglo-Danish) corporate/commercial lawyer with ebl miller rosenfalck in London. In addition to her corporate/commercial work Pia regularly assists corporate clients with drafting and reviewing employment contracts subject to Danish law, advises on options when an employee dispute arises including negotiating exits and/or advising on dismissals of senior employees.

Pia's particular expertise in relation to cross border tax matters is recognised in *Chambers Global 2014.*

Sara Kennedy is an Associate Solicitor at ebl miller rosenfalck in London and advises businesses on both contentious and non-contentious legal matters ranging from the recruitment of staff, contract and policy drafting, issues surrounding the management of performance and obligations under the Working Time Regulations to terminations, business restructuring and Tribunal and High Court claims.

Recognised as a 'UK-qualified Danish national who often assists Denmark based clients, or companies with interests in Denmark' (*Chambers Global 2014*).

Emmanuelle Ries heads the employment team and the French desk at ebl miller rosenfalck in London. She advises a wide range of international clients on English employment law over the life of the employment relationship, mostly with an international element. She advises on HR documentation and incentive arrangements, senior executive contracts, international mobility issues, the employment aspects of corporate transactions, reorganisations, restructuring operations, outsourcing, collective redundancies, information and consultation with employee representatives at national and European level, restrictive covenant disputes, team moves and employment related litigation.

Emmanuelle is recognised by *Chambers Global 2014* as a Foreign Expert in UK employment law.

Producing this first edition of *Workforce Restructuring in Europe* would not have been possible without the excellent editing support received from Bloomsbury Professional, most notably Kiran Goss and Jane Bradford, and the enthusiastic support received from our colleagues Steen Rosenfalck, Stuart Miller and Ian Baker at ebl miller rosenfalck.

CONTRIBUTORS

Austria

Konstantin Fischer

Konstantin Fischer has been a partner in Zumtobel Kronberger Rechtsanwälte OG since 2004. He studied law in Graz and Salzburg and has a Master of Laws degree from the University of London in International Business Law. He advises on all areas of employment law and speaks German, English and Greek.

Zumtobel Kronberger Rechtsanwälte OG

Rainbergstraße 3 c,
5020 Salzburg
Austria
Tel: +43 662 624500
E-mail: fischer@eulaw.at
www.eulaw.at

Belgium

Theo Macours and Indra Veltjen

Theo Macours is a partner in Legalis advocaten in Tessenderlo (Belgium). He has been a member of the Hasselt Bar Association since 1987 and was appointed substitute Judge at the Court of Commerce of Antwerp for the Hasselt division in 2010. He focuses on company law, employment law and international litigation.

Indra Veltjen is a partner in Legalis advocaten in Tessenderlo (Belgium). She has been a member of the Hasselt Bar Association since 2006.

She primarily focuses on assisting companies in all matters regarding company law, including employment law and international law, and in litigation concerning these subjects.

Legalis advocaten

Vismarkt 26
3980 Tessenderlo
Belgium
Tel: +32 13 67 12 01
E-mail: theo.macours@legalis.be; indra.veltjen@legalis.be
www.legalis.be

Bulgaria

Iliana Ilieva

Iliana Ilieva is a qualified lawyer and a senior legal advisor in the Law Office Ivan Bojov. In her work at the Bulgarian law office she advises employers and/or employees on a broad range of contentions and non-contentious employment matters in connection with dismissals and claims for compensation.

Law Office Ivan Bojov

2nd floor, ap. 3
19, Dobri Voinikov Str.
Sofia 1164
Bulgaria
Tel: +359 2 865 03 61
E-mail: iliana@bojovlaw.com
Webpage: www.bojovlaw.bg

Croatia

Dora Gaži Kovačević, Ana Grubešć, Jelena Orlić and Ira Perić Ostojić

Dora Gaži Kovačevič heads the employment practice group and Wolf Theiss Split office. She has particular expertise in full workforce restructuring of domestic companies as well as restructuring at upper management level. She recently prepared best practices in labour law compliance and held a series of labour law related lectures.

Ana Grubešić joined Wolf Theiss after having been one of the youngest candidates ever admitted to the practice of law in Croatia. Ana has significant experience in employment matters across all economic sectors, mostly involving compliance and restructuring issues. She recently held a series of labour law related lectures.

Jelena Orlić speaks English, German, Italian and Croatian. With her knowledge of foreign languages, Jelena is of great assistance to international investors setting up their businesses in Croatia. Jelena regularly assists companies in compliance with the relevant labour law regulations and best practices.

Ira Perić Ostojić heads the Wolf Theiss Rijeka office. She has advised numerous companies in relation to employment compliance and restructuring matters across various industries, including retail, clothing, port, shipping, food and pharmaceuticals. She recently held a series of labour law related lectures.

Wolf Theiss

Ivana Lučića 2a
HR-10 000 Zagreb
Croatia
Tel: +385 1 4925 400
E-mail: dora.gazi@wolftheiss.com; ana.grubesic@wolftheiss.com; jelena.orlic@wolftheiss.com; ira.peric@wolftheiss.com
Webpage: www.wolftheiss.com

Cyprus

Charis Papachristodoulou

Charis Papachristodoulou, associate at Papadopoulos Lycourgos & Co, is a member of the Cyprus Bar and the Bar of England and Wales. He advises on both contentious and non-contentious legal matters and is actively engaged as counsel in civil litigation, with particular expertise in multi-jurisdictional commercial disputes and labour disputes.

Papadopoulos, Lycourgos & Co

2–4 Arch. Makarios III Avenue
Capital Center, 7th Floor
1065 Nicosia
Cyprus
Tel: +357 22 676126
E-mail: c.papachristodoulou@paplyclaw.com;
Webpage: www.paplyclaw.com

Czech Republic

Anna Diblíková and Jana Krautwurmová

Anna Diblíková is a corporate lawyer with a specialisation in labour law. She has substantial experience in restructurings, M&A, employee transfer and data protection. Anna got her Master degree from Charles University Law School, Prague in 2010 and a member of the Czech Bar Association since 2014.

Jana Krautwurmová specialises in corporate and labour law and has experience in collective dismissals. She also focuses on regulatory law. Jana graduated from Charles University Law School, Prague. During studies, Jana spent one year at the University of Nottingham Law School where she studied labour law and EU law.

WOLF THEISS

Pobřežní 12
186 00 Prague 8
Czech Republic
Tel: +420 234 765 221 and +420 234 765 246
E-mail: jana.krautwurmova@wolftheiss.com;
anna.diblikova@wien.wolftheiss.com
Webpage: www.wolftheiss.com

Denmark

Benjamin Lundström

Benjamin Lundström is a partner in SIRIUS Advokater and joint leader of the firm's Employment unit. He is a certified litigation lawyer and has been appointed by the Danish courts as a mediator and as an arbitrator by the Danish Arbitration Institute. Benjamin advises employers and employees in all matters relating to employment. He has assisted in many recruitment and termination proceedings relating to executives and key employees.

SIRIUS Advokater, Law Firm

Frederiksberggade 11
1459 Copenhagen
Denmark
Tel: +45 88 88 85 85
Mobile: +45 20 40 82 22
E-mail: bl@siriusadvokater.dk
Webpage: www.siriusadvokater.dk

England

Edzard Clifton-Dey, Sara Kennedy and Emmanuelle Ries

Edzard Clifton-Dey is a dual qualified (Anglo-German) employment law specialist and a partner in the Employment Team of ebl miller rosenfalck in London. He advises employers on a broad range of contentious and non-contentious employment matters. He has a particular expertise in managing multi-jurisdictional workforce restructuring projects.

Sara Kennedy is an associate at ebl miller rosenfalck in London and advises businesses on both contentious and non-contentious legal matters ranging from the recruitment of staff, contract and policy drafting, performance management to terminations, business restructuring and Tribunal and High Court claims.

Emmanuelle Ries heads the employment team and the French Desk at ebl miller rosenfalck in London. She primarily advises overseas clients on English employment law over the life of the employment relationship. She has a particular expertise in restrictive covenant disputes, team moves and employment related litigation.

ebl miller rosenfalck

Aylesbury House
17–18 Aylesbury Street
London
EC1R 0DB
England
Tel: +44 20 7553 9930
E-mail: ecd@millerrosenfalck.com; sk@millerrosenfalck.com;
er@millerrosenfalck.com
Webpage: www.millerrosenfalck.com
Webpage: www.ebl-legal.com

Estonia

Pirkko-Liis Harkmaa and Martin-Kaspar Sild

Pirkko-Liis Harkmaa is the Head of the Employment Law Team at LAWIN Tallinn. Pirkko-Liis has 16 years' experience in day-to-day employment related counselling and assisting in complex M&A transactions and restructuring projects, advising on matters related to transfer of employees, employee information and consultation procedures, noncompete and confidentiality issues.

Martin-Kaspar Sild is an associate in the Employment Law Team at LAWIN Tallinn. Martin-Kaspar advises clients on day-to-day employment related issues from drafting of employment contracts to handling of terminations. He also participates frequently in legal due diligence exercises focusing on employment related risks related to restructuring projects.

LAWIN

Niguliste 4
Tallinn, 10130
Estonia
Tel: +372 6306460
Fax: +372 6306463
Email: pirkko-liis.harkmaa@lawin.ee; martin-kaspar.sild@lawin.ee
Webpage: www.lawin.lt

Finland

Seppo Havia and Maiju-Juulia Jokinen

Seppo Havia heads Dittmar & Indrenius' Employment, Benefits and Pensions practice. He has extensive experience of Finnish and international employment and pensions law and advises corporate clients in all employment, pensions and employee benefits related issues, including reorganisations, M&A, outsourcing arrangements and dispute resolution.

Maiju-Juulia Jokinen is an associate in Dittmar & Indrenius' M&A & Private Equity, Employment, Benefits & Pensions and Real Estate, Construction & Environment teams. Her main practice areas are employment law as well as general contract and commercial law.

Dittmar & Indrenius
Pohjoisesplanadi 25 A
FI-00100 Helsinki
Finland
Tel: +358 9 681 700
E-mail: seppo.havia@dittmar.fi; maiju-juulia.jokinen@dittmar.fi
Webpage: www.dittmar.fi

France

Karine Clolus-Dupont and Daphné Rouchaud

Karine Clolus-Dupont is a founding partner of Lexington Avocats. She heads the Labour Relations department and advises employers on all contentious and non-contentious French employment law issues. She notably provides guidance to international companies in their daily management of their human resources and during large-scale projects (mass redundancies, restructuring, acquisitions, etc).

Daphné Rouchaud was admitted to the Paris Bar in 2012. She holds two masters' degrees in international business law (Paris-Sud XI University); and litigation and arbitration (Assas University). Daphné advises employers and employees with contentious and non-contentious employment law issues.

Lexington Avocats

72 Boulevard de Courcelles
75017 Paris
France
Tel: +33 1 83 75 41 41
E-mail: kcdupont@lxt-law.com; drouchaud@lxt-law.com
Webpage: www.lxt-law.com

Germany

Dagmar Dexheimer and Axel Weber (12.1–12.40)

Axel Weber has specialised in employment law since 1981, advising and representing employers and executives in both contentious and non-contentious employment matters. Axel has been a Fachanwalt für Arbeitsrecht (Employment Specialist) since 1986.

Dagmar Dexheimer is an associate lawyer at ebl factum rechtsanwälte, Frankfurt, Germany since April 2011. She was admitted to the Bar in 2008 and advises and represents companies and executives both in individual and collective labor law issues. In 2012 she became a licensed specialist in employment law (Fachanwältin für Arbeitsrecht).

ebl factum rechtsanwälte

Eschersheimer Landstr. 6
60322 Frankfurt am Main
Germany
Tel: +49(0)69 / 74 74 9 - 0
Email: d.dexheimer@factum-legal.com; a.weber@factum-legal.com
Webpage: www.factum-legal.com
Webpage: www.ebl-legal.com

Frank Engelhard and Tim Quintiliani (12.41–12.80)

Frank Engelhard is a partner in the employment and corporate law team of ebl esch & kramer in Düsseldorf and Wuppertal. He advises employers on a broad range of employment matters, both contentious and non-contentious.

Tim Felix Quintiliani is a professional support associate in the employment and corporate law team of ebl esch & kramer in Düsseldorf and Wuppertal.

ebl esch & kramer rechtsanwälte

Speditionsstr. 17
40221 Düsseldorf
Germany
Tel: +49 211 6022 40-0
E-mail: engelhard@eschkramer.de
Webpage: www.eschkramer.de
Webpage: www.ebl-legal.com

Greece

Fani Skartouli

Fani Skartouli is an associate at PotamitisVekris Law Partnership (Athens) and advises businesses on employment issues. She regularly drafts employment contracts, restrictive covenants and settlement agreements. She advises on the implementation of HR policies, pension funds and stock option plans and represents clients before Greek courts regarding employment disputes.

PotamitisVekris

9 Neofytou Vamva
Str. 10674 Athens
Greece
Tel: +30 210 33 80 049
E-mail: fani.skartouli@potamitisvekris.com
Webpage: www.potamitisvekris.com

Hungary

László Kenyeres and Buzási Barnabás

László Kenyeres is the partner heading the Employment practice group at Wolf Theiss. László has almost 20 years' experience in advising regarding contractual arrangements, conducting disciplinary investigations, the management of mass redundancy projects and collective labour law matters as well as handling employment issues arising from mergers & acquisitions.

Barnabás Buzási is an associate in the Employment practice group at Wolf Theiss. Barnabás has experience in employment restructuring, executive and general employment contracts drafting and advising in employment related litigation cases. Barnabás is currently in the final stages of a specialist Masters Course in Employment Law.

Wolf Theiss

Kálvin tér 12-13
Kálvin Center, 4th floor
1085 Budapest
Hungary
Tel: +36 1 4848 800
Email: laszlo.kenyeres@wolftheiss.com; barnabas.buzasi@wolftheiss.com
Webpage: www.wolftheiss.com

Republic of Ireland

Sinéad Grace and Ciara McLoughlin

Sinéad Grace is a professional support lawyer (PSL) on the Knowledge team at A&L Goodbody Solicitors. She supports the employment team exclusively. She is responsible for keeping the practice group updated on all developments in employment law and industrial relations in Ireland.

Ciara McLoughlin is a dual qualified (Anglo-Irish) employment law specialist with A&L Goodbody and a founding member of the firm's German group. She provides strategic advice to international and domestic clients on a wide range of employment issues including workforce restructuring, senior executive severances, managing performance and multi-jurisdictional transition projects.

A&L Goodbody

IFSC
North Wall Quay
Dublin 1
Ireland
Tel: +353 1 649 2000
E-mail: sgrace@algoodbody.com; cmcloughlin@algoodbody.com
Webpage: www.allgoodbody.com

Italy

Francesca Baldi

Francesca Baldi Attorney at law (Reggio Emilia Bar Association, since 1997); Professional Mediator (since 2010); Patrocinante in Cassazione Supreme Court (since 2012); Compliance Officer in many Italian companies.

Francesca's expertise is legal advice and assistance in companies' restructuring plans including employment issues, national and international M&A transactions, corporate law dealings, tender projects.

Studio Legale Baldi

Via G. Gutenberg 7,
42124 Reggio Emilia
Italy
Tel: +39 0522 232322
E-mail : f.baldi@baldilaw.it
Webpage: www.studiolegalebaldi.com

Latvia

Daiga Zivtina and Irina Kostina

Daiga Zivtina is a partner and Head of the Dispute Resolution practice group. With more than 20 years' experience, Daiga Zivtina represents clients in a broad range of employment matters, including contentious employment disputes, negotiations in out-of-court settlements and public institutions. Daiga advises employer clients on liability in actions brought by employees.

Irina Kostina is a Senior Associate in the Dispute Resolution practice group and is a leading expert of LAWIN Employment team. She has ten years' experience, specialising in all aspects of employment including dispute resolution. Irina assists clients in employment matters and regularly represents clients in court proceedings and state institutions.

Klavins Ellex

K. Valdemara 62
LV-1013
Riga
Latvia
Tel: +371 67814848
Fax: +371 67814849
E-mail: Daiga.Zivtina@klavinsellex.lv; Irina.Kostina@klavinsellex.lv
Webpage: www.klavinsellex.lv

Lithuania

Rimantas Stanevicius and Nerijus Patlabys

Rimantas Stanevičius is one of the leading members of the Valiunas Ellex employment team (Lithuanian). Rimantas has over ten years' experience in advising clients on all aspects of labour and employment matters. In addition, Rimantas also takes part in various governmental and non-governmental initiatives on improvement of employment legislation.

Nerijus Patlabys is a member of the Valiunas Ellex employment team (Lithuanian). Nerijus constantly takes part in providing employment advice and assisting clients in various employment-related matters. As a part of his day-to-day work, Nerijus prepares cases for representation in courts and other institutions for employment dispute resolution.

Valiunas Ellex

Jogailos 9
01116 Vilnius
Lithuania
Tel: +370 52681810
Email: rimantas.stanevicius@valiunasellex.lt; nerijus.patlabys@valiunasellex.lt
Webpage: www.valiunasellex.lt

Luxembourg

Anne Morel

Anne Morel heads Bonn Steichen & Partners' Employment, Compensation & Benefits department. She advises clients on a broad range of both contentious and non-contentious employment matters. Anne also has extensive experience in implementing restructuring and staff rationalisation measures for major manufacturing companies and banks.

Bonn Steichen & Partners

2, rue Peternelchen,
Immeuble C2
2370 Howald
Luxembourg
Tel: +352 26025-1
E-mail: amorel@bsp.lu
www.bsp.lu

Malta

Dr Josette Grech and Dr Mario de Marco

Dr Josette Grech is a senior associate at Guido de Marco & Associates and provides advice on a wide range of issues, ranging from the recruitment of staff, contract and handbook drafting to redundancies and business restructuring and assists in litigation concerning employment issues.

Dr Mario de Marco is a partner at Guido de Marco & Associates and provides advice on a wide range of employment issues, legal compliance, assistance in the resolution of employment disputes, and representation in litigation in the tribunals and courts.

Guido de Marco & Associates

9, Britannia House
Level 2
Old Bakery Street
Valletta
Malta
Tel: +356 21 255265/6/7
E-mail: jgrech@demarcoassociates.com; mdemarco@demarcoassociates.com
Webpage: www.demarcoassociates.com

The Netherlands

Frouke Vlaskamp

Frouke Vlaskamp has specialised in employment law since 1995. She is a partner and heads the employment team at Vlaskamp Advocaten. She advises mainly employers and executives on employment (policy) matters and has particular expertise in structuring the workforce (type of contracts and conditions).

Vlaskamp Advocaten

Regentesselaan 2
3818 HJ Amersfoort
Postbus 590
3800 AN Amersfoort
The Netherlands
Tel: +31 (0)33 462 79 20
E-mail: fv@vlaskampadvocaten.nl
Webpage: www.vlaskampadvocaten.nl

Norway

Merete Furesund and Lise Berntsen

Merete Furesund is a senior employment and pension lawyer at Kvale Advokatfirma DA. Merete has a Master's degree from the University of Oslo. Previously worked for an employers' association and admitted to practice in 2004. Clients include Norwegian and multinational companies requiring assistance with reorganisations/workforce reductions, transfers of undertakings, negotiations/legal proceedings and pensions.

Lise Berntsen is an associate at Kvale Advokatfirma DA and specialises in employment and pension law. She has a Master of law from the University of Oslo and was admitted to practice in 2013. Together with Merete, Lise has advised on several larger workforce reductions in the past.

Kvale Advokatfirma DA

Fridtjof Nansens Plass 4
Pb. 1752 Vika
0122 Oslo
Norway
Tel: +47 22 47 97 78
E-mail: mfu@kvale.no; lbe@kvale.no
Webpage: www.kvale.no

Poland

Renata Warchoł-Lewicka, Iwona Tomaszewska and Natalia Rutkowska

Renata Warchoł-Lewicka is a partner and specialist in all aspects of new technology and employment law. She advises national and international clients on various issues including employment matters and assists in drafting and negotiating of contracts and represents clients in court proceedings.

Iwona Tomaszewska is an advocate and associate. She specialises in commercial law, especially in the IT sector and assists with drafting and negotiating of contracts and in advising clients in business restructuring scenarios.

Natalia Rutkowska is a legal counsel and associate. She specialises in civil law, copyright law, labour law as well as commercial law and advises entrepreneurs on various legal issues related to business activities including employment Issues. She has broad experience in appearing before the courts in civil proceedings.

Gorazda, Świstuń, Wątroba i Partnerzy, adwokaci i radcowie prawni

Plac Szczepański 8
31-011 Kraków
Poland
Tel: +48 12 422 44 59
E-mail: renata.lewicka@gsw.com.pl; iwona.tomaszewska@gsw.com.pl; natalia.rutkowska@gsw.com.pl
Webpage: www.gsw.com.pl/

Portugal

João José Brito

João José Brito heads the employment department and the litigation team at Vaz Serra & Associados in Lisbon. Advises on recruitment, contract drafting, employment relationships including contentious and on-contentious issues and business restructuring.

Vaz Serra & Associados, Sociedade de Advogados, rl (vsa)

Av. Sidónio Pais 16 - 5°
D. 1050-215 Lisboa
Portugal
Tel: +351 213 840 086
E-mail: jjbrito@vsa-law.net
Webpage: www.vsa-law.net

Romania

Nicholas Hammond

Nicholas Hammond qualified in England as a solicitor and is a registered foreign lawyer in Romania. He advises clients in a wide spectrum of business sectors on corporate finance transactions, investment and mergers and tax planning. His areas of expertise are employment, aviation, banking & finance, corporate/M&A, taxation and energy.

BWSP Hammond Bogaru & Associates

61B Nicolae Caramfil
Sector 1
Bucuresti 014142
Romania
Tel: +40 21 326 6053
E-mail: nhammond@hbalaw.eu
Webpage: www.hbalaw.eu

Slovak Republic

Simona Haláková and Jana Černáková

Simona Haláková is a Partner at Čechová & Partners specializing in various fields of regulatory, corporate and M&A law, including transfers of enterprises, outsourcing and task/team moves. Simona assisted in a number of share and asset deals, business transfers and business reorganisations, advising on standard and strategic employment law related matters.

Jana Cernakova is an Associate Attorney at Čechová & Partners specializing in employment law and data protection. She advises businesses on day-to-day employment related business decisions as well as on strategic employment matters. She has been involved in multiple restructuring projects and is frequently assisting with the employment part of M&A.

Čechová & Partners

Štúrova 4
811 02 Bratislava
Slovakia
Tel: +421-2 54 41 44 41
E-Mail: simona.halakova@cechova.sk; jana.cernakova@cechova.sk
Webpage: www.cechova.sk

Slovenia

Klavdija Erjavec and Ana Lešnik Sitar

Klavdija Erjavec heads the employment-law department in Avbreht, Zajc & Partners, Ltd. She regularly attends as speaker at training seminars on employment law issues. Besides work in law office Klavdija Erjavec also acts mediator before the Labour court in Ljubljana. Klavdija Erjavec frequently supports clients during restructuring process.

Ana Lešnik Sitar has specialized in employment law from the start of her carrier with the firm. She advises in contentious and non-contentious employment matters including on relationships and disputes between management and other key personnel on the one hand and company on the other hand.

Avbreht, Zajc & Partners, Ltd.

Šestova Ulica 2
Ljubljana SI-1000
Slovenia
Tel: +386 1 434 54 00
E-mail: office1@azodvetniki.com
Webpage: www.azodvetniki.com

Spain

Sonia Cortés

Sonia Cortés is an employment law specialist and partner in the niche employment law firm Abdon Pedrajas & Molero. She advises employers on a broad range of matters and has particular expertise in restructuring projects and senior management matters. She is distinguished as a leading lawyer by most legal directories.

Abdón Pedrajas & Molero

Jorge Juan 35
28001 Madrid
Spain
Tel: +34 93 209 29 67
Email: sc@abdonpedrajas.com
Webpage: www.abdonpedrajas.com

Sweden

Anna Stenson

Anna Stenson is an Associate Attorney at Flood Herslow Holme in Stockholm, Sweden and a member of the Swedish Bar Association. She specialises in Employment law and advises and represents companies in a broad range of contentious and non-contentious employment matters. She also has particular expertise in representing executives.

Flood Herslow Holme

PO Box 7615
103 94 Stockholm
Sweden
Tel: +46 8 56 26 90 13
E-mail: anna.stenson@fhhlaw.se;
Webpage: www.fhhlaw.se

Switzerland

Marcel Aebischer and Manfred Küng

Marcel Aebischer, lawyer and notary public (Partner), specialises in all kinds of employment law. He advises both local and multi-jurisdictional employers on contract and employment law matters and represents them in court cases. He is deputy chairman of the arbitration board for employment law in the court district of St Gallen.

Manfred Küng (Senior Partner) advises and represents businesses in corporate and commercial legal matters including employment law. He was a visiting lecturer at the Universities of Zurich and St Gallen and lectured on commercial, business and capital market law. He is the author of several publications in the concerned areas of law.

Küng Lawyers

Haldenstrasse 10
9200 Gossau
Switzerland
T +41 (0) 71 380 07 50
E-mail: aebischer@kueng-law.ch
Webpage: www.kueng-law.ch

Küng Lawyers

Giesshübelstrasse 62d
8045 Zürich
Switzerland
T +41 (0) 44 217 40 00
E-mail: kueng@kueng-law.ch
Webpage: www.kueng-law.ch

Chapter 1
Workforce Restructuring in Austria

Konstantin Fischer
Zumtobel Kronberger Rechtsanwälte OG, Salzburg

INTRODUCTION

1.1 This chapter deals with the aspects of workforce reductions and restructurings in a company in Austria from a labour law perspective. Unless the parties (employer and employee) have agreed on any other governing law Austrian law will automatically apply to employment contracts where the employee habitually carries out his duties in Austria.

1.2 Provided the employment relationship is subject to Austrian law, various aspects need to be taken into account in human resources management.

To begin with, the provisions governing any restructuring, including the termination of the employment do not flow from statutory provisions (legislation) alone. The majority of businesses in Austria are subject to collective bargaining agreements entered into by the 'social partners' (eg the relevant trade union and the Federal Economic Chamber) for the relevant industry sector and these collective bargaining agreements define the minimum working conditions. Moreover, works council agreements are frequently entered into within a company between the workers' representatives (works council) and the company management to deal with a variety of matters, including (but not limited to), working time, overtime and overtime pay, general issues concerning discipline at the workplace and severance terms in the event of dismissals flowing from a reorganisation. Finally, individual terms and conditions agreed on an individual level between employer and employee also need to be considered. On a practical level it is hence important to obtain all relevant documentation upfront and to undertake a due diligence into the different and often interrelated provisions that govern any restructuring.

1.3 In respect of the provisions set out in those sources (statutory provisions, collective bargaining agreement, works council agreement, employment contract), the 'principle of favourability' applies.

Statutory provisions are the starting point, and provisions in collective bargaining agreements may only create a more favourable situation for the employee than those in the law (but may not 'undercut' the layer of minimum protection set out by law), shop agreements in turn may be more favourable than those of the collective bargaining agreement, and the employment contract may provide for more favourable terms than those set out in the works council agreement. Therefore, by way of an example, if a term of an employment contract is detrimental compared to the equivalent provision of a works council agreement, then this particular provision of the individual employment contract becomes void.

1.4 As a rule, a dismissal notice does not need to set out the dismissal reason. However, employees enjoy general protection against dismissal by way of a preliminary process during which the employer must involve the works council. In addition, certain categories of employees are subject to special dismissal protection.

Whether this general protection against dismissal applies will depend on the size of the company, as a works council can only have a say in respect of any such measures if such a council is in place. Only companies with more than five permanently employed members of staff are eligible for a works council.

Moreover, if several employees are made redundant at the same time, or within a short period of time, the early warning system of the Public Employment Service Austria (AMS) comes into effect. This will also depend on the size of the company and the overall number of employees, and of the number proposed to be made redundant.

The notification requirement is triggered if the employer proposes to make redundant:

- five or more employees in establishments with more than 20 and less than 100 employees;
- at least 5% of the employees in establishments with 100 to 600 employees;
- at least 30 employees in establishments with more than 600 employees; or
- at least five employees who are 50 years of age or older (exception: establishment for seasonal work).

The notification requirement is also applicable in the event of insolvency.

Note: There is a cooling off period of 30 days from the notification during which the employer may not implement any of the proposed redundancy dismissals. Any redundancy dismissal notices issued during the cooling off period will be void.

1.5 The representation of workers by the Federal Chamber of Labour (Bundesarbeiterkammer) and the unions is very strong in Austria. A system of compulsory membership is in place and consequently the majority of employees in Austria are members of the Federal Chamber of Labour. The latter offers advice and legal representation to its members and, if necessary, conducts lawsuits against employers on their behalf. Therefore, since action against a current or previous employer is possible without a cost risk for the employee, legal battles will very often ensue, especially in the case of terminations. Hence, it is all the more important strictly to comply with the provisions of the laws governing termination in Austria.

PREPARING FOR A RESTRUCTURING EXERCISE

1.6 Where restructuring measures are planned, the starting point is to assess whether a workforce reduction is generally required or whether the set commercial objectives can also be achieved by way of implementation of other measures.

As dismissals frequently result in termination-related claims by the affected employees it is necessary to carry out a precise cost benefit calculation prior to engaging in any such exercise.

1.7 The business unit or establishment where the restructuring measures will be implemented must be identified as well as the identity of employee and employer. Whilst this sounds like an obvious point to make, in practice it will be highly relevant to ensure that the individuals, who are authorised to act for and on behalf of the employing entity, are identified. For example, dismissal letters signed by an individual who is not so authorised are likely to be void.

1.8 In addition, a specific timetable should be determined for the implementation of the planned measures. In doing so, a distinction is generally made between short-term (operative), medium-term (tactical), and long-term (strategic) measures. A programme of measures should be determined for each of these phases.

1.9 From a practical point of view, it is advisable to maintain a good communication flow with the affected employees and the employee representatives. As a rule, measures that are communicated beforehand are met with less resistance from those affected.

COLLATING INFORMATION TO PLAN AND BUDGET FOR THE RESTRUCTURING EXERCISE

1.10 As regards the individual employees affected, it will be necessary to collect relevant data on their employment.

In the event of a proposed workforce reduction, the employer is obliged to select those employees for redundancy for whom the loss of employment will have a lesser social impact than on others. For this reason it is necessary to compare the relevant data of all potentially affected employees.

Practical Tip

The following data regarding the affected employees must necessarily be taken into account when planning restructuring measures, so as to be able to assess the cost and complexity of the measures, especially in the case of a workforce reduction:

- Name;
- Age;
- Activity;
- Place of work;
- Duration of employment with the company;
- Current remuneration;
- Severance pay claim;
- Maintenance support obligations (children, spouse);
- Term of employment contract (fixed term);
- Notice period, termination date (under the law, the collective bargaining agreement, or the employment contract); and
- Special protection against dismissal (maternity protection, disabled employees, trainees, etc).

EMPLOYMENT STATUS

1.11 For all labour law provisions in Austria to be applied to an employment relationship, the engagement must be one of genuine employment on the basis of an employment contract.

If an individual renders services on the basis of a freelance arrangement (freier Dienstvertrag) or on the basis of a contract for the provision or supply of works contract (Werkvertrag) most labour law provisions will not apply.

1.12 One speaks of a *genuine employment relationship* when an individual commits to rendering a service to another for a certain period of time. The critical distinction from other contract types is the personal dependence resulting from the fact that the service rendered benefits someone else and the employee yields to an organisational structure. A number of criteria suggest the existence of a personal dependence. For instance, the integration in the operation of the company, the obligation to follow the instructions of the employer, the employer's power of control, the obligation to deliver personal work, and the provision of work resources by the employer. These criteria must be used when assessing whether an employment relationship exists in an individual case. This will be determined by whether the essential attributes suggesting a personal dependence prevail. Relevant are only the content of the contract and any actual circumstances derogating from the same, while the label that is given to the contract is irrelevant.

A *freelance arrangement* means that an individual commits to providing his work to someone else without being personally dependent. Therefore, the essential element of personal dependence that would qualify it as an employment arrangement is not present. This constitutes an arrangement that sits between employment and a contractor arrangement. Though the individual is treated by the social insurance system as an employee, for the purposes of most employment protection rights the individual is considered self-employed.

A contract for the provision or supply of works or services is in place when someone undertakes to deliver specific works or services against remuneration. The difference to the above types of engagement is that the obligation here is to deliver a particular outcome rather than just be obliged to carry out certain tasks. As a rule, the contractual relationship will end upon completion of the works or services. The level of independence is the essential distinction from the employment contract, so in this case there is no personal dependence. The criteria pointing towards the existence of such a contract are, for instance, the right to use or be substituted by other individuals in providing the service, the lack of external influence on the place and time of the provision of services, the absence of the customer's right of instruction, no obligation to integrate into the work organisation, and the right and obligation to use one's own resources.

1.13 It is possible for one and the same company to engage individuals on the basis of different types of contracts. Therefore, it is important for the employer to classify the engagement status first, so as to be able to determine the legal provisions that apply.

White-collar workers and blue-collar workers

1.14 In Austria, a distinction is made between blue-collar workers (manual workers) and white-collar workers (salaried employees) according to their activity. Depending on the classification, different legal or collective bargaining agreement regulations will apply.

1.15 A white-collar worker is someone employed in the operation of a business to render professional trading services, professional non-trading services, or office work. Only certain activities of the employee are covered by the term white-collar worker. Professional trading services are understood as those typical activities of a business which require professional training (courses, etc) and certain skills, and which play a role in the management of a business.

Professional non-trading services are those requiring relevant knowledge and understanding of the task. Therefore, they require the corresponding prior knowledge, cogitation, creativity, familiarity with the tasks, authority to issue instructions, and an independent execution of the work tasks without continuous control by the employer. Purely manual work falls within the definition of blue-collar worker.

Office work involves activities that are typical for offices and are associated with a certain intellectual activity. These involve paperwork that goes beyond mere copying. Such activities are also carried out with a minimum of independence. Therefore, purely mechanical or manual activities are not considered office work.

1.16 The term blue-collar worker, however, is not defined by law. If an individual does not have the status of a white-collar worker, it is assumed that he can be considered a blue-collar worker.

In the case of mixed activities, one can assume the status of a white-collar worker if the time spent on such activities prevails. If manual work prevails, the individual is deemed to be a blue-collar worker.

Even if the time spent on manual activities prevails, one must nevertheless assume the status of a white-collar worker if the tasks requiring higher qualification are of essential importance to the employer.

1.17 The employer must classify the employee as a white-collar worker or blue-collar worker. Especially in connection with notice periods and termination dates and the reasons for dismissal, different rules apply to blue-collar and white-collar workers. Collective bargaining agreements also make a distinction between white-collar workers and blue-collar workers with regard to remuneration. Activities of blue-collar workers are in most cases classified in the lower wage groups; as a rule, the salary of white-collar workers is therefore higher. If an employee, for instance, is incorrectly classified as a blue-collar worker, he can claim compensation for any disadvantages, in particular any differences to the remuneration he is entitled to according to the collective bargaining agreement or the minimum wage rate.

GENERAL PROTECTION AGAINST DISMISSAL

1.18 In principle, employees in companies with a workforce of more than five staff can elect a works council. When a company has a works council in place, the latter is entitled to certain rights of co-determination. The works council also has a say in a dismissal proposed by the employer.

The employer must inform the works council one week prior to the notice of dismissal. The works council can deliver an opinion within a period of one week. It may agree or object to the dismissal. A third option for the works council is to remain silent over the issue, that is, refrain from issuing an opinion within the above period.

If this preliminary procedure is not complied with, i.e. the employer announces the dismissal prior to the expiry of the period or without any notification to the works council, the dismissal shall be invalid.

1.19 If the works council gives its approval to the dismissal in time, the employee may no longer challenge it for being socially unacceptable. The works council can no longer challenge the dismissal on such grounds either. In this case, the works council has a blocking right; a challenge to the dismissal is blocked by its approval. If, however, the dismissal is based on a proscribed reason, it can still be challenged by the employee himself despite its approval by the works council.

Such proscribed reasons include, for instance, the employee's participation in unions or in the works council, his position as a health and safety officer, safety expert or occupational physician, and the assertion of obviously not unjustified claims denied by the employer.

1.20 In the event of a challenge due to a proscribed reason, the employee only needs to substantiate that the dismissal was based on a proscribed reason. Although the employer has the opportunity to prove the existence of objective grounds for the dismissal, employers should avoid any indication of a proscribed reason when dismissing an employee. Such an indication may, for instance, be linked to the time of dismissal. If an employee asserts justified claims during his employment or even institutes proceedings before a labour court and the employer promptly announces his dismissal, this may lead to the impression that the dismissal was triggered by the assertion of claims under labour law, which is a proscribed reason.

If the works council has expressly objected to the intended dismissal, the requirements for challenging the dismissal for being socially unacceptable are also met (see paras **1.35** et seq). It is the responsibility of the works council to exercise the right to challenge the dismissal, provided that the employee demands this.

If the works council has refrained from issuing an opinion (modest objection), it will have no right to challenge the dismissal. The affected employee himself, however, can challenge the dismissal in court within two weeks of its receipt.

SPECIAL PROTECTION AGAINST DISMISSAL

1.21 Certain groups of employees enjoy special protection against dismissal. These groups of individuals include, for instance:

- Employees' representatives;
  members and alternate members of the works council, as well as candidates;
- New parents:
  from the beginning of pregnancy until four weeks after the end of the parental leave or part-time employment;
- Persons being drafted into compulsory military or civil service;
- Disabled workers; and
- Trainees.

Employees belonging to one of the above groups may only be dismissed for limited number reasons listed in the law, which must be particularly severe (eg persistent neglect of duties or (partial) discontinuation of business). Since these regulations can be found in various laws, they differ in the detail and must therefore be examined separately.

1.22 In this case, too, the legal effectiveness of the dismissal depends on compliance with a specific procedure. This will not, however, depend on the approval of the works council. Here, the requirement for an effective dismissal is the prior approval of the court. Therefore, the employer must institute proceedings for approval to the dismissal prior to the announcement of the dismissal. The dismissal may only be announced after approval by the competent court.

In case of violation against this special protection against dismissal, the dismissal shall be void. The employee can institute proceedings to establish the continued validity of the employment relationship, or allow the dismissal to take effect against him and then claim damages in the form of a termination compensation.

Special protection against dismissal for trainees

1.23 Trainees are subject to extensive protection regulations because they find themselves in a particular position of dependence toward the instructor (employer) and, in addition, they are still minors in most cases.

As a rule, a traineeship ends upon expiry of the training period that was agreed in the training contract. Following the end of the training period, however, the instructor is bound by a holding requirement. He is obliged to employ the trainee in the company for at least another three months in the position he was trained for.

The purpose of the holding period is to allow the trainee to consolidate the knowledge and skills acquired during training. For this reason, the employee may not be used for activities unrelated to his profession during the holding period.

As a rule, a fixed-term employment contract will be concluded for the holding period, which ends upon expiry of this period. If no fixed term is agreed and the employer wishes to terminate the employment relationship as soon as possible, he may give notice during the holding period so that the notice period will fall within the holding period.

1.24 During the training period, the traineeship may only be terminated by mutual agreement or for good cause. In principle, a dismissal is not possible.

A mutual agreement is possible only after the trainee has been informed about his rights by the competent labour court or the Federal Chamber of Labour. Reasons for a premature termination include:

- theft, embezzlement, or other criminal offences that render the trainee untrustworthy;
- serious insult or dangerous threat against the instructor, his fellow workers, or members of his household;
- violation or neglect of obligations under the law or the training contract despite repeated warnings;
- violation of trade of business secrets, or the pursuit of a damaging side business;

- unauthorised absence from the training site; or
- inability to learn the trade.

The premature termination of the traineeship must be made in writing; moreover, a dismissal letter must be addressed to the trainee. Where the trainee is a minor, the employer must also inform his parents about the termination of the traineeship. In addition, the employer must notify the responsible traineeship office of the Federal Chamber of Labour and the vocational school about the termination.

1.25 The dismissal will be ineffective unless these requirements are met. An unjustified dismissal does not terminate the traineeship. Therefore, proceedings can be initiated to establish the validity or continuation of the traineeship.

In principle, a dismissal during the period of training and the subsequent holding period is ruled out. In exceptional cases, the instructor may obtain approval by the Federal Economic Chamber for the dismissal if he is unable to meet the holding obligation for economic reasons.

1.26 There is also a possibility for an extraordinary termination of the traineeship. Such termination is possible with a notice of one month from the lapse of the last day of the 12th month of the training period and from the lapse of the last day of the 24th month of the training period.

The extraordinary termination shall only be deemed effective, however, if the instructor notifies the trainee, the responsible traineeship office of the Federal Chamber of Labour, the works council, and the young workers' council about the intended extraordinary termination and the planned commencement of a mediation procedure not later than at the end of the 9th or 21st training month, and a mediation procedure has been conducted and completed before the announcement of the extraordinary termination.

WORKFORCE REDUCTION

1.27 In Austria, a distinction is made between a dismissal (Kündigung), notice of which can be issued without stating any reason, and a summary dismissal without notice (Entlassung), which is only admissible where there are sufficiently serious grounds which render it unacceptable for the employer to continue the employment even for the period of notice. The dismissal without notice is typically linked to issues around gross misconduct and individual capability and as such is not typically directly relevant in the context of a workforce restructuring (although individual skills and capabilities may well play a role when selecting employees for a wider selection pool for redundancy).

1.28 Dismissal is the unilateral declaration of intent by one of the parties targeted at the discontinuation of the employment relationship on a specific date. A redundancy dismissal is a dismissal where the underlying reason and rationale for the exit is linked to operational reasons (betriebsbedingte Gründe) within the employing entity.

A dismissal is only an option if the employment contract was concluded for an indefinite term. In the case of fixed-term employments, these generally only end upon expiry of the fixed term. It is permissible to also agree a notice period in fixed term contracts but the lengths of the fixed term must then be of a reasonable duration to justify an agreement whereby the contract can be brought to an end prematurely on notice and before the expiry of the fixed term. What qualifies as 'reasonable duration' is to be determined on a case by case basis and on the basis of relevant principles developed by Austrian case law. Redundancy dismissals must, just as any other ordinary dismissal, be announced in a timely fashion so as to comply with the notice period from the time of the receipt of the notice by the employee to the termination date. Such dates and periods may result either from legal provisions or from the applicable collective bargaining agreement or the employment contract.

If the collective bargaining agreement or the employment contract does not contain provisions on the form of the redundancy dismissal notice it can be effected either in writing or verbally. For purposes of evidence, it is of course advisable to always notify redundancies in writing, and to have the receipt of notices confirmed by the employee.

Dismissal without notice

1.29 A dismissal by the employer without notice (Entlassung) or resignation (Austritt) by the employee without notice is possible only due to an 'important reason' (wichtiger Grund), as a result of which it seems no longer possible for either the employer or employee to continue the employment even for the period of notice. As such these dismissals without notice are not typically relevant in a restructuring scenario as the reasons justifying a dismissal without notice are linked to the individual employee rather than the business.

Such reasons include, for instance:

- Lack of trustworthiness:
  The employee behaves in a manner that severely breaches the employer's trust in the employee. Due to this behaviour, the employer is justifiably concerned that his interests and affairs are jeopardised by the employee.
- Acceptance of bribes:
  As part of his duties, the employee receives unauthorised benefits from third parties without the employer's knowledge or consent.
- Inability to render the services pledged or reasonably expected under the circumstances.
- The employee fails to meet the mental, physical, or legal requirements necessary to render the services for a significant period of time.
- Breach of a non-competition clause:
  Where the employee operates in an independent commercial company or commercial transactions in the employer's line of business in breach of a non-competition clause which prohibits such activity.

- Breach of the duty to work or of obligation to respect the employer's right of direction the employee persistently or repeatedly refuses to render the service or to follow justified instructions by the employer. At least one preceding warning is required in order to enforce this reason for dismissal, and it is advisable to issue it in writing for evidence reasons.
- Failure to render the service for a significant period without an objective justification:

  Inability to work for an extended period due to disease or accident cannot justify a dismissal. Dismissal is possible, however, if the employee's absence is due to his serving a prison sentence or other reasons.
- Acts of violence or indecency, or insults

This applies regardless of whether these actions are directed towards the employer himself, his family or other employees of the company.

This list is non-exhaustive. Therefore, an employee can also be dismissed for other similarly severe reasons.

Though separate reasons for dismissal apply to blue-collar workers, they mostly overlap with those for white-collar workers.

1.30 If there is such an important reason and the employer wishes to exercise his right to dismiss the employee, he must immediately announce the dismissal. If the employer is already aware of the reason for dismissal and nevertheless continues to accept the service rendered by the employee, he thus signals that a continuation of the relationship with the employee is not unacceptable and forfeits his right of dismissal without notice.

In case of such dismissal, the employee is not obliged to comply with any deadlines or notice periods. The dismissal becomes effective upon receipt of the notice by the employee, and the employment ends with immediate effect.

1.31 If a dismissal is mistakenly notified without an important reason, the employee must be treated as if he were properly terminated. Therefore, the employee must be paid the remuneration due to him in the form of termination compensation until the next possible termination date in compliance with the notice period. Nevertheless, the employment relationship remains terminated.

Protection against dismissal without notice

1.32 Even in the case of a dismissal without notice, both general and special protection against dismissal apply.

The works council must be informed prior to the employee being dismissed. Since the dismissal must take effect immediately, the information obligation merely constitutes a procedural rule. Therefore, even if the employer fails to inform the works council, the dismissal remains legally effective, but the period for the works council to deliver an opinion does not commence.

The works council can deliver an opinion within three days of being informed. Approval by the works council means that the dismissal cannot be challenged. In case of objection, the works council has a right to challenge the dismissal at the employee's request. If the works council fails to deliver an opinion within the above period, the employee himself shall have the right to challenge the dismissal on the basis of it being based on proscribed motives or being socially unacceptable.

Special protection against dismissal applies to particularly vulnerable groups. These basically overlap with those who enjoy a special protection against dismissal. Here, the court approval must be obtained beforehand. In these cases, the employer will often grant the employee leave of absence. Only in exceptional cases (such as criminal offences or insults against the owner of the company) it is possible to obtain the court's approval a posteriori.

Termination fee

1.33 For each termination of employment, the employer must pay a termination fee of €118 (2015). This obligation applies to all employment relationships that are subject to unemployment insurance contributions, and to freelance engagements terminated after 31 December 2012. The amount of the fee is adjusted on an annual basis.

Exceptions from this termination fee include cases in which the employment contract was for a fixed term of less than six months, the employee resigned or prematurely terminated the employment without a serious reason, or when the employee was justifiably dismissed.

DISMISSAL FOR OPERATIONAL REASONS (REDUNDANCY)

1.34 In Austria the employment relationship can be terminated at any time without a particular reason, operational reasons are not a requirement for a dismissal to be admissible.

Nevertheless, a company's operational requirements play a role: even if a dismissal were inadmissible due to the particular social impact on the employee, it can still be justified under exceptional operational circumstances (see below).

Socially unacceptable dismissal

1.35 A redundancy dismissal can also be challenged if it is socially unjust. The requirement for such an appeal is that the employee must have worked in the company for more than six months and, as a general rule, that the employees in the company are eligible to form a works council.

A redundancy dismissal is socially unacceptable if the dismissal tangibly and substantially affects the economic circumstances of the terminated employee, even if it does not present a threat to his very existence. In the case of older employees, for instance, this can be a lengthy period of unemployment or a significant loss of income.

If a redundancy dismissal is challenged on the grounds of being socially unacceptable, a 'social comparison' must take place in the event that the works council objected to the redundancy dismissal during the preliminary procedure. This process will examine whether, by way of a comparison of social aspects, the social impact for the employee proposed to be exited is more severe than for other employees employed by the same company and performing the same work (selection pool). On the part of the employee proposed to be exited, particular focus must be placed on his family situation, his maintenance obligations, his asset situation and, in the case of older employees, the years of continuous service in the company, as well as difficulties in connection with the employee's reintegration in the labour market due to increased age.

1.36 There are, of course, reasons that justify a termination despite the resulting social hardship for the employee. A distinction can be made between operational reasons and personal reasons attributable to the employee.

Such personal reasons include above all poor performance, frequent and/or long sick leave, or incompatibility with other employees. These reasons must therefore outweigh the social hardship that the termination would cause to the employee.

A dismissal for operational reasons (redundancy) is justified if the terminated employee cannot continue working for the company because of operational requirements. Such requirements include, above all:

- reduction of personnel costs;
- rationalisation measures; and
- production conversions, provided that these are necessary.

Operational requirements justifying a dismissal may also include a deterioration of the order situation and a noticeable decline in sales.

However, an operational reason for a redundancy dismissal is admissible only if the role of the terminated employee is eliminated and there is no possibility of continuing the employment of this individual in another role in the company. Therefore, a dismissal cannot be considered operationally required if the older employee is replaced by a younger one after his dismissal. In addition, the redundancy is only justified if, despite the employer's efforts, it was not possible to find alternative employment for the employee in another area of the company.

The employer is bound by an obligation to establish social protection for his employees. Therefore he must first offer such alternative employment where this is available, which corresponds with the employee's previous professional practice. If the employee rejects the alternative employment offered, the dismissal is considered operationally justified.

REDUNDANCY DISMISSAL PROCEDURES

Individual redundancy procedure

1.37 A redundancy dismissal for operational reasons must always be preceded by a consideration of the interests of both sides. Therefore, it must be established whether it is more acceptable for the employer to maintain the workplace than it is for the employee to be terminated.

If, in comparison, the redundancy will result in a far more severe social hardship for the terminated employee and there are no justifying operational reasons, the redundancy is socially unacceptable and can be revoked.

Therefore, especially in the case of a proposed redundancy dismissal of an older employee, the employer must assess beforehand if the redundancy dismissal of precisely this employee is absolutely necessary for operational reasons or whether other measures can be introduced instead in order to achieve the business objective. Otherwise, the redundancy dismissal can be challenged and the employee may have to be reinstated or reengaged. In that event the employment relationship will not have ended and the employer will then also have to make retrospective remuneration payments in respect of the time during which the redundancy dismissal was challenged. Therefore, balancing the mentioned interests beforehand is advisable.

INDIVIDUAL CONSULTATION

Involvement of employee representatives in individual redundancies

1.38 The works council has a say in case of a proposed termination of an employment contract (general protection against dismissal). The employer must inform the works council one week prior to the announcement of a proposed dismissal. The works council can issue an opinion on the dismissal proposal, either an approval or an objection, within a period of one week. The works council, however, may also remain silent, that is, refrain from issuing an opinion within that period. Depending on the opinion of the works council, there are different options for challenging the dismissal.

Such dismissal is in any case void if the preliminary procedure is not complied with, that is, if the employer gives notice of dismissal before expiry of that period or even without notifying the works council at all.

Employees working in a company with a workforce of less than five employees eligible to vote are excluded from the general protection against dismissal. The dismissal can be challenged, however, for being socially unacceptable if it affects employees of certain age groups (2014: year of birth 1935–1942 for men and 1940–1947 for women).

The general protection against dismissal does not apply in particular to (non-exhaustive list):

1 The individuals in management bodies of legal entities (board of directors etc) if these individuals are authorised to represent the legal entity vis-a-vis third parties;
2 Executive employees who have a significant influence on the management of the company;
3 Summer interns and other seasonal trainees who undergo a mandatory internship in a company to complete their school-based training.

COLLECTIVE REDUNDANCY PROCEDURE

Early warning system

1.39 If an employer intends to terminate several employment contracts during a short period of time, an 'early warning system' is in place, which needs to be taken into account for terminations to be lawful. An employer who intends to make several employees redundant within a period of 30 days must report this to the regional offices of the Public Employment Service Austria (Arbeitsmarktservice – AMS). The AMS is the responsible agency in Austria for unemployment insurance benefits.

The employer has an obligation to report if at least 5 employees are to be made redundant in a company with 20 to 100 employees, at least 5 in each 100 employees in companies with 100 to 600 employees, more than 30 employees in companies with more than 600 employees, or at least 5 employees above 50 years of age.

Such a report must be filed not later than 30 days before the first announcement of termination. If relevant dismissals are made without being reported to the AMS or they are made prior to approval by the AMS, these dismissals are void. The affected employee can then initiate proceedings to establish that the employment relationship continues to be in place.

The early warning system also covers mutually agreed terminations initiated by the employer, unjustified dismissals, or justified resignations. Hence, the employer must also report these terminations if the above thresholds are exceeded.

1.40 The report must contain precise information on the reasons for the intended terminations, the period, and the particulars of the affected employees (age, gender, qualification, duration of service, etc).

If the announcement of mass redundancies is required before expiry of the 30-day period for economic reasons, the employer may file a corresponding application with the AMS. The office in the respective Federal Province will then decide on the admissibility of these premature redundancies.

The employer must also notify the works council by sending a carbon copy of the report to the AMS. This information obligation, however, cannot replace the preliminary redundancy procedure within the company. This procedure must be separately implemented for the planned redundancies.

Involvement of employee representatives in collective redundancies: social plan

1.41 If a change in operations is to take place, the employer must under certain circumstances decide with the works council on certain preventive measures as part of a social plan.

A social plan is a works council agreement defining measures to prevent, remove, or mitigate the impact of a change in operations in case the latter results in a material detriment for all or significant parts of the workforce.

1.42 A change in operations involves:

- the limitation, relocation, and closure of the business as a whole, or of parts thereof;
- the termination of several employment contracts, triggering the obligation to report to the Public Employment Service;
- a merger with other businesses;
- changes in the objective, the facilities, the work and organisation of the business, and the organisation of its branch offices;
- an introduction of new working methods;
- the introduction of rationalisation and automation measures of material importance; or
- a change in the legal form or in the ownership structure of the company.

In the event of such a change, the employer must inform the works council about the planned changes in operation at a time and in a manner that allows the works council to assess the potential impact of the planned measures and to deliver an opinion. At the request of the works council, management must also carry out consultations with the works council on the organisation of these changes.

1.43 If the employer plans to terminate several employment contracts, requiring him to report to the AMS, the information provided to the works council must in any case include the following items:

- the reasons for the measure;
- the number and use of the employees who are likely to be affected, their qualification and duration of service, as well as the criteria for the selection of these employees;
- the number and use of the regularly employed workforce;
- the period in which the planned measure is to be implemented; and
- any planned accompanying measures aimed at avoiding any negative consequences for the affected employees.

1.44 The works council may present suggestions during the planning stage for the avoidance or mitigation of the expected negative impact. If such negative consequences cannot be avoided, a social plan must be devised, aimed at balancing the interests of both sides.

1.45 The requirement for the admissibility of a social plan is that at least 20 persons are permanently employed in the company. In addition, a social plan is admissible only if the change in operations will result in disadvantages for the entire workforce, or at least substantial parts thereof. Such disadvantages may include, for instance, lower wages, cuts in voluntary social benefits, longer travel to work, changes in working hours, transfers, or even a loss of the workplace.

1.46 The social plan can introduce a wide variety of measures.

In case of a discontinuation or limitation of operations, for instance, the employer may undertake not to carry out any redundancies, to make a voluntary severance payment or other payments to help bridge the time pending retirement, or introduce an early retirement scheme.

In the event of a workforce reduction, the social plan may provide for alternative workplaces, preferential re-employment for the employees to be terminated, or retraining and advanced training programmes financed by the employer.

In case the company operations are to be relocated, admissible measures as part of a social plan may include the introduction of a shuttle service, or financing of the relocation costs by the employer.

It is not possible to reach an agreement as part of a social plan in which the works council collectively approves the redundancies planned by the employer. Therefore, it will be in any case necessary to comply with the individual procedure for redundancies.

It is, however, possible, for instance, to make the benefits from a social plan conditional upon the consensual termination of employment. Hence, the employee will receive the envisaged benefits only if he agrees to a consensual termination.

1.47 Shop agreements like the social plan are entered between the company owner and the staff or the works council as their representative.

A social plan represents an enforceable shop agreement. This means that, upon the request of the works council or the company owner, the conciliation board will decide if the company owner and the works council fail to reach an agreement on the introduction, change, or suspension of a social plan.

The conciliation board will be established at the seat of the court of labour and social matters for the district in which the company is located. The board is composed of a chairman and three assessors, who must be nominated by the employer and the works council.

The conciliation board must reach its decision as soon as possible and in consideration of the interests of the company and the staff. Its decision may not be appealed. The decision of the conciliation board shall also be considered a shop agreement.

NOTICE

1.48 In case a redundancy is announced it will be necessary to comply with notice periods and termination dates stipulated under the law in collective bargaining agreements, or in individual employment contracts deviating therefrom. Different provisions apply to white-collar workers and blue-collar workers with regard to the notice periods and termination dates. If the employment is terminated within the first month – provided that this month was agreed as a probationary month, this can be done without notice and with an immediate effect.

MINIMUM NOTICE PERIOD

1.49 In the case of white-collar workers, the statutory notice period in case of dismissal by the employer is:

Term of service	Notice period
up to 2 years of service	6 weeks
up to 5 years of service	2 months
up to 15 years of service	3 months
up to 25 years of service	4 months
25 years of service or more	5 months

In case of a resignation by the employee, the statutory notice period is always one month.

1.50 The termination date is the date upon which the notice period must expire.

In the case of white-collar workers, the employer's statutory termination dates are at the end of each quarter. Individual employment contracts, however, may also provide for the last day or the 15th of each month.

In the case of resignation by the employee, the termination date is always the last day of the month.

1.51 A broad range of dates and periods apply to blue-collar workers.

According to the Austrian Trade Regulation Act, the notice period for a blue-collar worker is 14 days. This period, however, may be extended or reduced by a collective bargaining agreement, a shop agreement, or an individual contract. In principle, the notice periods for termination by the employer or by the employee must be equal. A more favourable regulation, however, may apply to the employee (shorter notice period). The law does not provide for a specific termination date, and the respective collective bargaining agreement may define special termination dates.

If a blue-collar worker is not subject to these provisions, the provisions of the Austrian Civil Code shall apply subsidiarily. Depending on the activity, different regulations apply in this respect.

According to these, a notice period of four weeks applies to blue-collar workers who render more sophisticated services. The termination must not be effected on a certain date.

Employment relationships in which remuneration is calculated on the basis of hours, days, or units can be terminated as of the following day.

If the blue-collar worker is employed in the company for more than three months or the remuneration is calculated on the basis of weeks, a redundancy can be announced not later than on the first working day of a calendar week for the end of that calendar week.

Other work agreements can be terminated with a notice period of at least 14 days.

1.52 Even if a redundancy is not in compliance with the notice period or termination date provisions, it still has a terminating effect. Hence, the employment relationship is terminated on the date even if the redundancy is not in compliance with the termination date provisions. The employee, however, shall be entitled to damages in the shape of a termination compensation. Therefore, the employee maintains his claim to remuneration until the next possible proper termination date.

GARDEN LEAVE

1.53 The employee is obliged to work even during the notice period pending the termination date.

Since any unused holiday must be paid in the form of holiday compensation in the case of termination, it is often agreed to use the holiday during the notice period. It must be noted, however, that the holiday will not be used unless such use is agreed upon between the employer and the employee. Moreover, the employee is not obliged to take leave during the notice period. Therefore, an employee cannot in any way be forced to take leave during the notice period.

The employee, however, may be put on leave of absence against his will during the notice period. This may prove necessary in order to prevent the employee from causing any damage or obtaining knowledge of more business secrets. In this case, the employer shall nevertheless be obliged to pay the full remuneration.

PAY IN LIEU OF NOTICE

1.54 The 'pay in lieu of notice' instrument as a unilateral right of the employer is not recognised in the Austrian legal system. Therefore, it is not possible to effect a dismissal without notice while paying the employee his accumulating due remuneration during the statutory notice period to be observed.

It is, however, possible to reach a consensus on such an arrangement with the employee. The employer will then terminate the employment with immediate effect with the employee's consent, but will still pay out the remaining remuneration.

Arguably though a notice of dismissal without a justified reason has the same effect. If the employment is terminated with immediate effect but without a justifying reason then the employee is entitled to damages. The damage consists of the loss of remuneration which would have been due in the event of a proper termination in compliance with a notice period. Since the employee will usually assert this claim in conjunction with other claims linked to the termination, and its enforcement often involves legal action, this type dismissal generally triggers further costs. From the employer's point of view, opting for this form of termination is not advisable.

SEVERANCE

1.55 Under certain circumstances, the employee is entitled to a severance when his employment is terminated. Two different systems may be applied in this case.

1.56 The 'old' claim to a severance payment applies to employment contracts concluded until and including 31 December 2002. Nevertheless, the employer can agree with the respective employee on a transfer to the new severance pay system.

To begin with, the requirement for such a claim is that the employment has lasted more than three years. Therefore, a claim to severance pay will only arise after three years of service with an employer.

Moreover, the nature of the termination of the employment is a determining factor. The cases in which an employee has a claim for severance pay includes:

- dismissal by the employer, including dismissal for redundancy;
- unjustified dismissal;
- justified premature resignation by the employee;
- consensual termination; and
- expiry of a fixed-term employment.

A claim to severance pay will also arise in other forms of termination, such as cases of retirement.

There is no entitlement to severance pay despite an employment period of more than three years in those cases in which the employee resigns, unjustifiably, leaves the company before expiry of his contract, or is culpable for his justified dismissal.

STATUTORY SEVERANCE PAY CALCULATION

1.57 The amount of the 'old' severance pay is based on the length of service.

Term of service	Amount of severance pay
after 3 years of service	2 monthly salaries
after 5 years of service	3 monthly salaries
after 10 years of service	4 monthly salaries
after 15 years of service	6 monthly salaries
after 20 years of service	9 monthly salaries
after 25 years of service	12 monthly salaries

1.58 For those employees whose employment began after 1 January 2003, the new severance pay legislation is applicable.

Under this legislation, the employer is obliged to pay ongoing contributions to a severance fund of his choice. The amount of these contributions will be based on the level of the remuneration. 1.53% of the monthly salary and of any bonuses must be paid to the severance fund.

In the case of a new employee, no contributions will be due for the first month of employment. Therefore, the employer's contribution obligation commences on the second month of employment.

No contributions should be paid during periods in which no remuneration is paid.

The obligation to pay contributions shall apply until the end of the obligation to pay remuneration under the employment contract. Therefore, the obligation to pay contributions shall expire after termination of the employment and payment of the termination-linked claims.

The employee retains his claim to severance pay against the severance fund in all types of termination; in the case of a resignation by the employee, a culpable dismissal, and an unjustified exit from the company, however, a blocking period comes into effect.

1.59 A transfer to the new severance pay legislation is possible for employment contracts that were concluded before 1 January 2003. Such a transfer, however, cannot be imposed.

Should the employer and employee wish to carry out such a transfer, a separate written agreement between them will be required. Moreover, they cannot agree on a transfer date before 1 January 2003 and after 31 December 2012.

It is possible to choose between a partial transfer and a full transfer.

In the case of the partial transfer, the existing entitlements obtained until the date of transfer will be frozen, ie they will not be transferred into the new system. As of the date of transfer, the new severance pay legislation will apply. Provided that the requirements are met, the employee shall have claims under the old and the new severance pay legislation upon termination of the employment.

In the case of a full transfer, however, the existing entitlements are transferred to the severance fund. The severance pay claim will therefore be entirely subject to the new severance pay legislation.

1.60 In case of a transfer of the company, the employment contract automatically passes over to the purchaser of the company. As of 1 January 2003, such transfer of an employment contract concluded until 31 December 2002 does not result in the application of the new severance pay legislation.

1.61 In principle, provisions may exist in collective bargaining agreements or individual employment contracts which provide for severance pay claims in excess of the statutory amount. Provided that these represent an improvement for the employee, such provisions can have precedence over the statutory provisions.

ENHANCED SEVERANCE PAYMENTS

1.62 Apart from the statutory 'old' severance pay, to which the employee is entitled under the law or the respective collective bargaining agreement, the employer can also contribute a voluntary severance pay. This is a voluntary contribution that relates to the termination of the employment. Such a voluntary severance pay is often agreed as part of a consensual termination.

TAXATION OF SEVERANCE PAYMENTS

1.63 In Austria, severance pay ('old' severance pay) to which an employee is entitled to under the law or the collective bargaining agreement is subject to final taxation at a rate of 6%. This is in any case a significantly more favourable tax rate than the progressive tax rate applied to the employee's current remuneration.

Voluntary severance pay is also taxed at 6%, provided it does not exceed a quarter of the current salary for the last 12 months. Since 1 March 2014, however, this favourable tax treatment only applies to the ceiling of nine times the maximum contribution basis as set forth in the General Social Insurance Act (2014: €4,530).

In the case of the 'new' severance pay, this favourable tax treatment no longer applies, since the employer pays into the severance fund. Based on this system, voluntary severance payments must be fully taxed like the current salary.

POST-TERMINATION RESTRICTIVE COVENANTS

1.64 During his employment, an employee is subject to a statutory prohibition of competition. Therefore, the employee may not independently operate a company or carry out commercial transactions in the same line of business. Failure to comply with this non-competition clause may result in a summary dismissal.

As a rule, the prohibition of competition no longer applies after termination of the employment. The employee will therefore be free to compete with his former employer.

If an employer wants to prevent competition by previous employees, he may agree in advance with the employee on a so-called competition clause in the employment contract. As a result, the employee will be contractually prohibited from carrying out certain activities after termination of his employment. Not every limitation is admissible, however. Such an imposed constraint may, on the one hand, only refer to activity in the employer's line of business, and on the other, it may not exceed a period of one year. Furthermore, the employee must be of legal age and, in the case of employment contracts concluded after 17 March 2006, his last earned salary must exceed the daily maximum contribution basis as set forth in the General Social Insurance Act (2014: gross €2,567) by a factor of 17. Taking into consideration the mutual interests of both sides, a competition clause may not present an unreasonable obstacle to the individual's professional advancement.

1.65 Non-competition clauses are legally invalid if they 'overshoot', ie become tantamount to a temporary occupational ban as a result. The employment limitations imposed in a non-competition clause must not force the employee to leave his knowledge and professional experience unused, to abandon a learned special trade and to change to a sector outside his profession with a lower income.

A non-competition clause does not constitute an inadmissible occupational ban if it is limited either geographically or even to individual companies. In this case, the employee has sufficient freedom to utilise his professional skills in the labour market.

A non-competition clause can only be agreed with employees of full age. The non-competition clause can also be agreed while the employment is ongoing.

1.66 The employer can only assert the rights resulting from an agreed non-competition clause if the employee has resigned, has given the employer reason for dismissal due to culpable conduct, his employment contract has expired, or the employment relationship is consensually terminated.

1.67 As part of the agreement on a non-competition clause, it is also possible to agree on a penalty in case of a violation. This penalty constitutes liquidated damages. Therefore, the employer is entitled to the compensation regardless of the actual extent of the damage. The penalty may be reduced by a court order. Therefore, the court may reduce the penalty if it considers it excessive according to the circumstances. The payment of the penalty by the new employer is unethical and represents a violation of competition rules.

If a penalty has been agreed, the employer may not file a lawsuit for injunctive relief. If no penalty has been agreed, the employer may file action to enforce the fulfilment of the admissibly agreed obligation by the employee, and for damages.

1.68 Therefore, when agreeing on an effective non-competition clause, one must take into account the temporal and geographical limitations, the qualification of the employee, and the line of business.

BUSINESS SALE, OUTSOURCING/INSOURCING AND OFFSHORING

1.69 In the event of the sale of a company, the employees of the company may not suffer any disadvantages as a result.

BUSINESS SALE

1.70 A transfer of business means that the person responsible for the company and who acts in the capacity of the employer changes, while maintaining the economic entity. Evidence for the preservation of the economic unity of the company include, for instance, the transfer of staff and customers, and continuation of activities in the same line of business.

The type of the underlying legal transaction for the transfer is irrelevant. Such transfer may be the result of a purchase, a lease, a donation, etc.

OUTSOURCING/INSOURCING

1.71 In situations where not the entire company but only part thereof is sold, the statutory provisions governing a transfer will nevertheless apply. The requirement for a partial transfer is that the part of the company is an economic entity the identity of which is preserved during the transfer. Therefore, the economic entity must continue to exist as under the previous owner. On that condition, even the outsourcing of individual departments constitutes a partial transfer of business.

Partial transfer of business means that the following criteria prevail:

- the economic entity is established on a permanent basis;
- the economic entity remains preserved during the change of ownership;

- the previous or similar business activities will be actually continued or resumed;
- transfer of resources, staff, customers.

1.72 On the other hand, if an activity is merely transferred, which does not constitute an economic entity, this does not constitute a partial business transfer but a mere transfer of function. In this case, the provisions governing the transfer of business do not apply.

Automatic transfer and protection of employment

1.73 When a company, a business, or partial business is transferred to a new owner, the latter automatically assumes the employment contracts existing at the time of transfer as an employer, including all rights and obligations. This is done ex-lege, ie neither the purchaser nor the employees need to approve it. Excluded from this transfer are only employer obligations which were agreed shortly before the transfer with an intent to cause damage to the new owner.

1.74 If the purchaser is subject to a collective bargaining agreement, the transfer will also result in a change of the collective bargaining agreement. This may not lead, however, to a reduction of the remuneration valid under the collective bargaining agreement prior to the transfer. A purchaser who is not subject to a collective bargaining agreement will fall within the scope of the collective bargaining agreement of the seller as a result of the transfer. This collective bargaining agreement will continue to apply after the transfer for an unlimited time.

If the company maintains its identity, existing shop agreements will also remain in place after the transfer. If a shop agreement is terminated as part of the transfer, it shall nevertheless remain in effect until the conclusion of a new shop agreement or its annulment.

Both seller and purchaser are jointly and severally liable for obligations from an employment contract concluded with the seller in the time before the transfer. The purchaser, however, is only liable for obligations he was or had to be aware of and which do not exceed the value of the company. The purchaser shall be unrestrictedly liable for new debt incurred after the transfer.

Objection to the transfer

1.75 Employees of the transferred company do not have a general right to object. In case of changes in fundamental provisions of the employment contract, however, the employee may object to the transfer. The deadline for such an objection is one month. In case of an objection by the employee, the employment relationship to the seller remains in place.

Protection from dismissal

1.76 A ban on transfer-related redundancies applies so as to protect the employees in the case of a business transfer. This ban applies to both the transferor and the transferee of the company. It prohibits dismissals issued within a short period of time before or after the transfer; this applies to employment contracts terminated within a period of one year before, and up to one year after, the transfer of business. The dismissal will nevertheless be admissible if it is carried out for other reasons, ie is not related to the transfer of business.

Protection of terms and conditions of employment

1.77 In the case of a transfer of business, the employees are to be protected against any material deterioration of their working conditions. For this purpose, each employee is given a right of objection, provided that the transfer results in changes to fundamental provisions of the employment contract. If an employee objects to the transfer within the above period, the employment relationship with the seller remains in place under the same conditions. From a practical point of view, however, the employment contract will be eventually terminated, since it will be no longer possible to meet the primary obligations.

WORKFORCE REDUCTION IN CONNECTION WITH SHARE SALE OR SHARE PURCHASE

1.78 As opposed to an asset deal, a share deal means that only the shares of a company are sold. These shares are transferred to a new holder, yet the legal entity, ie the company, remains the same. Therefore, there is no change of employer, since the employment relationship between the employees and the company continues to exist. For that reason, the provisions for a transfer of business do not apply in the case of a sale by way of a share deal.

CHANGING EMPLOYMENT TERMS AND CONDITIONS

1.79 If the operational changes require a change in the working conditions that were contractually agreed with the employees concerned, the contract terms must be amended. This can be done in different ways.

Mutually agreed changes

1.80 First, it is possible to reach a consensual amendment of the provisions through an express agreement between the employee and the employer. This, however, shall require the employee's consent.

From the employer's point of view, such a consensual amendment of the contract terms is probably the safest option, since amendments approved by the employee are most likely to be accepted and implemented by the same. Therefore, the top priority must be to try and establish a consensus with the employee.

Unilateral changes

1.81 Already when concluding the employment contract, the employer can reserve the right to amend contract terms to a certain extent. The employer can subsequently exercise this right without the need for a new agreement.

Dismissing and re-engaging employees on new terms

1.82 The termination of the employment relationship altogether and the subsequent conclusion of a new employment contract is not a usual practice in Austria.

1.83 Terminations with an offer of new contract terms, however, are admissible. Though the purpose of such termination is to amend contract terms, the entire employment contract is terminated. The termination, however, is subject to a condition. Such a termination is possible subject to a condition subsequent, that is, the notice of termination is issued and will be forfeited when the employee agrees to the amendment. A termination for purposes of amendment, however, can also be made subject to a condition precedent, meaning that a notice of termination is issued that will only come into effect if the employee fails to agree to a change in the working conditions.

As a rule, terminations may not be subject to any conditions, since the legal situation is unclear for the recipient. An exception to this, however, are conditions concerning the right of the employee to protest, the effectiveness of which exclusively depends on the recipient's will. In this case, the employee can prevent the termination from coming into effect through his own behaviour, and therefore terminations for the purpose of amendment are basically admissible.

Partial terminations are admissible in Austria only to a very limited extent. Such partial termination is in conformity with the law only when an additional agreement between the contracting parties, which can exist independently and is independently remunerated, is terminated.

1.84 Such a termination is also subject to protection against redundancy. Furthermore, attention must be paid to the protection against transfer, since an amendment of the contract terms may also result in a transfer. Not all transfers are admissible.

USE OF TEMPORARY STAFF

1.85 In certain economic sectors and in difficult financial times for a company, it may be beneficial to employ personnel who work only on a temporary basis and do not have a permanent employment contract with the company.

The advantage of this is that more personnel can be used on short notice to cope with peaks in the workload and which can subsequently be reduced quickly and without the need for elaborate labour law procedures. There are several ways of doing this.

AGENCY WORKERS

1.86 Individuals working for a temporary employment agency are obliged to render services to a third party. The temporary employment agency and the recipient company enter a personnel supply/service provision contract and the employees of the temporary employment agency are used to perform work tasks in the recipient company. In this case, the recipient company and the employee do not enter a contract.

Temporary employment agencies are subject to trade licensing requirements. An exception applies, however, to the temporary provision of staff to recipients operating in the same profession as the temporary employment agency up to a maximum period of six months per calendar year.

Also exempted from the laws governing employment agencies is the secondment of personnel by manufacturers, lessors, or vendors of technical facilities required for training, repair, or maintenance, by syndicates and in operation cooperation between companies, as well as the secondment of staff between companies within the same group.

1.87 Provision of personnel by a temporary employment agency means that pursuant to the truly intended contents of the pledge of performance between the employer and the third party, control over the labour of the employee is transferred to the third party for the pursuit of its operational purposes.

This type of temporary employment involves a division of employer obligations between the temporary employment agency and the recipient company.

The employment contract is concluded between the leased employee and the temporary employment agency. Therefore, the temporary employment agency is considered the contractual employer of the leased employee. The employee's work obligation toward the temporary employment agency is fulfilled by performing the agreed work in the company of the recipient. The recipient exercises his power to issue instructions to the employee within the framework of the employment contract.

From the point of view of employee protection, however, the recipient must be regarded as the employer. The employer's duty of care resides with the latter.

In principle, the temporary employment agency is subject to the collective bargaining agreement for employment agencies, though this only applies to blue-collar workers. Leased white-collar workers are subject to the collective bargaining agreement for trade employees. The claims of the leased employee under the employment contract must, however, be adjusted to the collective bargaining agreement applicable to the employees of the company to which he is leased.

1.88 In principle, the temporary employment agency can only lease staff upon conclusion of an agreement with the employee. This agreement must necessarily be made in writing. It must contain provisions on the level of remuneration, payment dates, vacation entitlements, extent of work performance, notice periods, type of work, etc. Regardless of this agreement, made at the beginning of the employment relationship, a separate notification must be sent prior to leasing an employee, containing the essential conditions of the leasing.

As a rule, remuneration is paid by the temporary employment agency. The recipient, however, shall be liable as guarantor for the employee's entitlement to remuneration and for contributions to the social insurance.

1.89 Leasing personnel to Austria from abroad is also subject to trade license requirements. This does not apply, however, to leasing from EEA countries.

Leasing of personnel from non-EEA countries shall nevertheless be subject to the limitations of the law on the employment of foreign nationals from Croatia until 30 June 2020.

If a company, in order to cope with peaks in the workload, uses several foreign nationals provided by another company who are integrated in the operations of the recipient and are subject to the recipient's control and power to issue instructions, and do not render any services other than those rendered by the company's own employees, this is regarded as temporary employment and as employment of foreign nationals subject to approval.

Since in this case the recipient company in Austria is considered an employer, it must apply for a permit for the leased staff. When such an application is submitted, the authorities must carry out a labour market review. The requirement for granting the permit is that the employment of specially qualified skilled workers is absolutely essential for labour market and economic reasons, that these workers are available from abroad exclusively by way of temporary employment, and that their employment does not threaten the wage and working conditions of Austrian employees.

During the period of temporary employment, the foreign employee shall be entitled to paid vacation, continued salary in case of sickness, compliance with the notice periods and termination dates, and to the application of the provisions of the collective bargaining agreement applicable to commercial temporary employment Austria.

FIXED-TERM CONTRACTS

1.90 As a rule, employment contracts in Austria can be concluded either for a fixed or an indefinite term.

Employment contracts entered into without an expiry date, ie that were concluded for an indefinite period, can normally be terminated by consensual agreement, notice of redundancy, or premature termination for good cause.

Fixed-term employment contracts entered for a limited period of time will basically end upon expiry. The duration can be defined either on the basis of a calendar year or be linked to a certain event. Making an employee under a fixed-term contract redundant is not possible. In case of a longer fixed term contract, however, the two parties can agree on a possibility of termination. The fixed-term employment relationship can be consensually terminated any time, or prematurely, for good cause (dismissal).

Renewal of fixed-term contracts

1.91 According to the EU directive on fixed-term contracts, which was also implemented on a national level, in principle employees under fixed-term contracts may not be disadvantaged as against those under contracts with indefinite duration, unless there are objective grounds justifying an unequal treatment. This discrimination prohibition also results in a ban on repeated fixed-term contracts.

If several fixed-term contracts are strung together so as to prevent the employee from obtaining rights such as protection against dismissal, notice periods and termination dates, to which he would be entitled to under a contract with indefinite duration, the result is a chain contract *contra bonos mores*. In such a case, the contract shall be considered a continuous employment contract of indefinite duration.

The reason for the inadmissibility of repeated fixed-term contracts is the risk of circumvention of mandatory legal provisions designed to protect the employee. If objective reasons exist for such fixed-term contracts, however, it is possible to have consecutive fixed-term contracts since their intended purpose is not to weaken the legal position of the employee in case of termination. Such objective reasons may include an unexpectedly large number of incoming orders, the unforeseen absence of an employee, the employee's express request to renew the contract, or a lengthier season in the case of seasonal contracts.

1.92 Fixed-term employment contracts will occasionally contain agreements on non-renewal statements. As a result, an employment contract originally entered for a fixed term is renewed for an indefinite period if none of the parties signifies to the other until a certain deadline that it does not intend to extend the employment relationship beyond the fixed term.

A non-renewal statement brings benefits for both sides of the employment relationship. Both sides are informed before the expiry of the fixed term whether the other party has any interest in extending the employment relationship beyond its term, or whether it will terminate by expiry. This gives both sides the possibility to make provisions earlier for the time after expiry of the fixed term.

According to the High Court's opinion, in Austria, however, such a non-renewal statement does not have the same quality as a dismissal. Therefore, not the same legal consequences are attached to such a statement as to a dismissal. In particular, it is not possible to challenge them on the grounds of being socially unacceptable.

EMPLOYMENT CLAIMS

1.93 In Austria, ordinary courts are called on to take decisions on labour matters.

Subject-matter jurisdiction

1.94 In first instance, subject-matter jurisdiction lies with the regional courts as courts of labour and social matters and, for Vienna, with the court of labour and social matters of Vienna. The Higher Regional Court decides in second instance, and the Supreme Court in the third instance.

As a rule, jurisdiction in labour and social matters is exercised in senates. These senates are composed of professional judges and competent lay judges. The meetings in the senate are chaired by a professional judge. In the exercise of their office, the competent lay judges act as judges with the guarantees of judicial independence.

Local jurisdiction

1.95 The parties can amend the mandatory court jurisdiction by concluding a jurisdiction agreement. The jurisdiction agreement must be an express agreement and refer to a specific legal dispute. The agreed court must either be expressly determined or at least be determinable.

Agreements on the local jurisdiction are basically admissible for individual labour law matters, though compulsory places of jurisdiction exist for other matters.

The Labour and Social Tribunal Act lists different connecting factors for the choice of places of jurisdiction in individual labour law matters. These include, for instance:

- the domicile or habitual residence of the employee during the employment relationship or at the time of the termination of employment;
- the company's registered offices;
- the place of performance;
- the place of remuneration.

Apart from these places of jurisdiction, the ones stipulated in other laws may also be used. These include, for instance, the place of jurisdiction where the damage was caused or where the main proceedings will take place.

When the employee makes a claim, he will in most cases choose the place of jurisdiction of his residence. Since the latter will not necessary coincide with that of the company's registered offices, additional costs may arise in case of legal proceedings (travel expenses, costs for a legal representative at the place of trial, etc).

UNFAIR DISMISSAL

1.96 An unfair dismissal means that it is based on a proscribed motive.

Such motives include, in particular, activities in unions, candidature to the works council, and the assertion of apparently not unjustified claims from the employment relationship.

1.97 If a dismissal is apparently based on such a reason, it can be challenged by the employee himself anytime. Even if the works council expressly declares its approval of the dismissal as part of the preliminary procedure, the affected employee himself can challenge the dismissal before court within a week after receiving the notice. In this case, the works council shall not have a blocking right. If the works council expressly objected to the dismissal, it shall have the right to challenge it, provided that the employee requests that it is challenged. If, however, the works council fails to comply with such a request, the right to challenge the dismissal is transferred to the employee.

If the works council has not issued an opinion on the dismissal, the employee himself can challenge a dismissal based on a proscribed motive before the court within two weeks.

1.98 An employee who works in a company for more than six months may also challenge the dismissal on the grounds that it is socially unfair. A dismissal is socially unfair if it compromises the material interests of the employee, unless the employer can prove that the dismissal is caused by circumstances attributable to the character of the employee and which have a detrimental impact on the interests of the company, or by operational requirements that render impossible a continued employment.

1.99 When assessing the material interests of the employee, the individual's entire economic situation must be taken into consideration. Essential factors include, for instance, their income, the assets, the spouse's income, maintenance obligations, etc. In the case of older employees, one must also take into account the duration of employment and the anticipated difficulties for integration into new work processes due to the greater age.

1.100 In the case of a dismissal for operational reasons (redundancy), it is possible to have a 'social comparison'. If a comparison of social aspects shows that the social impact for the affected employee is more severe than for other employees belonging to the same company, and the same line of work and whose work can also be performed by the terminated employee, the dismissal of the latter is considered socially unfair and can be challenged.

REMEDIES

1.101 If a dismissal is challenged for the above reasons and the court believes that the employee's request must be granted, the dismissal will be revoked as legally invalid.

If the court takes such a decision before expiry of the notice period, the employment relationship shall continue without interruption. If the dismissal is revoked after the expiry of the notice period, ie after the end of the employment relationship, it will be temporarily suspended, but will be retroactively resumed after the court's decision. The employee is entitled to compensation for the time after the end of the notice period during which the employer did not pay any remuneration. Therefore, the employer must pay the money due for this period in arrears, although he has not used the employee's services.

DISCRIMINATION

1.102 In the event of discrimination at work, a distinction is made between direct and indirect discrimination.

Direct discrimination means that an individual is discriminated against on the basis of certain protected characteristics, including gender, ethnicity, religion, belief, age, sexual orientation, etc.

Indirect discrimination, on the other hand is caused by rules that may superficially seem neutral, the effect of which, however, is to discriminate against certain groups of employees in relation to others.

Both direct and indirect discrimination are prohibited within the framework of an employment relationship. This prohibition covers in particular the establishment of the employment relationship (recruitment), the calculation of compensation and other benefits, the professional advancement (promotion), other working conditions, and the termination of the employment.

REMEDIES

1.103 If affected by such prohibited discrimination, the employee is entitled to certain claims which he can also assert in court.

1.104 If the recruitment procedure violates the principle of equal treatment so that an applicant is not hired despite objectively having the best qualifications, he shall be entitled to damages. The amount of this compensation shall correspond to at least two monthly salaries he would have received if he had been hired.

This claim can be asserted before a court or the Equal Treatment Commission within six months after the application was rejected.

1.105 If an employee belonging to a protected group of employees receives lower remuneration than others for the same or equivalent work without an objective justification on the basis of this attribute, he shall be entitled to the payment of the difference between his current and his due salary. In addition, he shall be entitled to a compensation for the personal impairment he suffered.

Such a claim can be asserted before a court or the Equal Treatment Commission within three years.

1.106 If an employee is hindered in his professional advancement in a company due to discrimination, he shall be entitled to damages. The compensation to be paid consists in the difference between the remuneration paid to him and the remuneration he would have been entitled to after a promotion. Compensation shall consist of the remuneration difference for at least three months.

This claim can be asserted before a court or the Equal Treatment Commission within six months after the promotion was rejected.

1.107 If an employee is sexually harassed at the workplace, he shall be entitled to damages both vis-à-vis the harasser himself (employer, colleagues, customers, etc) and vis-à-vis the company owner if the latter did not take appropriate remedial action despite being aware of the harassment by a third person.

The employee is therefore entitled to appropriate compensation for the violation of his personal dignity. He can assert this claim in court within three years after the harassment took place.

1.108 If an employment contract is terminated on the grounds of a characteristic protected under the Equal Treatment Act (gender, sexual orientation, age, religion, belief, and ethnicity), the employee can challenge the termination by invoking the Equal Treatment Act. This is known as individual protection against dismissal. In this case, the employee himself (but not the works council) has the right to challenge the dismissal. The employee has the possibility to challenge a dismissal on the grounds of discrimination regardless of the general protection against dismissal.

The affected employee, however, can also allow the termination to come into effect and claim damages. Such damage consists both in financial loss (loss of income) and in non-material damage.

The employee can assert this claim in court within three years after receipt of the notice of termination.

MUTUALLY AGREED TERMINATION

1.109 A consensual termination corresponds to a termination contract. In this case, the employer and the employee agree to terminate the employment on a certain date. As a result, they are not bound by any notice periods or deadlines. Such an agreement can be made in writing, orally, or by implication, and the law provides for a written form only in the case of particularly vulnerable groups of employees. The two sides may agree on further details in connection with the termination.

As a rule, a consensual termination is the best possible option for both sides, which explains why dismissals are often converted into consensual terminations.

Chapter 2
Workforce restructuring in Belgium

Theo Macours and Indra Veltjen
Legalis advocaten, Tessenderlo

INTRODUCTION

2.1 The Belgian legal system is a civil law system, which means that in principle, during law suits, emphasis is put on statute law.

In most cases, when initiating legal proceedings, the claimant will need to indicate what (written) legal clause has been breached.

However, during legal proceedings, every party can write down their point of view on the matter and also refer to jurisdiction of the Belgian courts in similar matters – this way there is some similarity to common law systems.

2.2 The fact that Belgium has three so-called 'language communities' (namely the Dutch speaking, the French speaking and the German speaking community) does complicate matters.

Every community has its own governments and of course there is a national government, all of which have competence (to a certain degree) to create new laws and regulations.

Furthermore, the King as well as a Minister can sign a special kind of decision which contains regulations.

2.3 Due to the fact that employment law can be found in a great number of documents, Belgian legislation contains an article that states which source of law takes precedence over another.

The hierarchy that is imposed on the different sources is the following one:

1 provisions of law from which one cannot deviate (meaning laws issued by one of the governments, the King or a Minister);
2 a collective labour agreement, hereafter referred to as 'CLA' (which is an agreement on a certain subject that has been negotiated between representatives of the employers and representatives of the employees), that has been declared binding and upon which agreement has been reached in:
   a the National Labour Council (a consultative body on the federal/national level which is composed of an equal number of representatives of employers organisations and trade-unionists);
   b the Joint Committee (a committee of employers and trade-unionists who are equally represented – most industrial branches have their own committee);
   c the Joint Subcommittee;
3 a CLA that has not been declared binding to everyone, but has been signed by the employer himself or by an organisation of which the employer is a member, and the agreement has been reached:
   a in the National Labour Council;
   b in the Joint Committee;
   c in the Joint Subcommittee;
   d outside one of the above;
4 the written individual employment agreement of an employee;
5 a CLA that does not meet the conditions as mentioned under 2 or 3;
6 corporate directives for employees;
7 provisions of law that one can deviate from;
8 the verbal individual employment agreement of an employee;
9 a custom.

2.4 Belgian employment law is quite strict and formal and is spread throughout numerous documents.

For instance, when dismissing an employee, for whatever reason, there are certain language requirements (due to the situation set out under paragraph 2) for the letter of dismissal.

It also needs to contain certain stipulations on the beginning and the duration of the term of notice.

Regarding restructuring/redundancy there are also certain procedures that have to be followed.

2.5 This contribution will summarise the general regulations that have to be followed by companies/employers in the private sector in their relationship to the employees with whom they have signed an employment agreement.

These regulations are often different from those in the public sector and for employees with posts governed by service regulations.

It is also possible that the regulations mentioned are not applicable or applicable in a different way to certain groups of employees with an employment agreement (eg different regulations can apply in certain sectors or to employees that only work part-time).

PREPARING FOR A RESTRUCTURING EXERCISE

2.6 When considering a restructuring of a company, it is important to gather all information that is of importance.

Not only will all information about the employees need to be collected, but it will also be necessary to get a cost estimate and, further on, to prepare a budget.

Identify the employing entity

2.7 It is always essential to identify which company is the employing entity.

In Belgium it is common for companies to mention their VAT number in any contract they enter into.

That way, by carefully examining the employment agreement, one should be able to identify the employer. Of course, it is also important to identify the exact group of employees of the employer.

The regulations on restructuring and redundancy, for instance will not apply to people working for the company as self-employed consultants, as posted workers, etc.

Collating information to plan and budget for the restructuring exercise

2.8 A lot of information can usually be found within the employing company itself (eg employment agreements kept by HR).

2.9 However, a lot of Belgian companies call in the help of a so-called Social Secretariat, hereafter 'SS'.

An SS is an organisation, recognised and supervised by the Belgian authorities, which will fulfil certain tasks for companies/employers with regard to the employment of personnel. It will also comply with all social and fiscal formalities.

Some of the tasks that an SS will take care of for an employer can be for instance:

- processing all data concerning wages and bonuses;
- calculating wages, paid leaves, indexations;
- taking care of all administration regarding the employment of personnel (registration for child benefits, unemployment benefits, disability benefits);
- filing the necessary declarations for taxes and social security (the SS can even be the proxy of the employer for the Social Security Service);
- composing different social documents for the employer (eg payslips, vacation certificates);
- everything concerning e-government (Dimona registration).

> **Practical Tip**
>
> Even though it is not mandatory, a company will benefit from using a Social Secretariat to take on certain tasks.
>
> Especially with regard to the calculation of wages, the SS can easily use a computer program which is up to date to all social and fiscal obligations.
>
> Preparing all calculations in house will take great effort, even more so when there is a high number of employees.
>
> The SS will charge the company/employer a monthly fee, but this will still be less than the costs of hiring an employee to take care of all of this.

EMPLOYMENT STATUS

2.10 Belgian employment law has a strict definition of an employment agreement. It is an agreement in which an employee commits to deliver (labour) output, under the authority of the employer, in return for the payment of wages.

Following this definition, there are three main components to every labour agreement:

- the employee delivers (labour) output;
- under the authority of the employer;
- in return for the payment of wages.

2.11 There is no definition on 'labour output', meaning that any kind of labour that is delivered will suffice.

Belgian employment law has been characterised for years by the difference in treatment between blue-collar and white-collar employees (with regard to, eg, the term of notice).

Because the Constitutional Court has deemed this difference to be unfair, there have been a lot of changes to the different statutes since the beginning of 2014 (see below paras 2.64 and 2.68).

2.12 For someone to be an employee and bound by a labour agreement, they will need to work under the authority of the employer.

It is this requirement that is most often a source of problems.

According to the jurisdiction of the Belgian Employment Courts, it is not necessary for an employer to actually exercise his authority over the employee in a permanent way, but it suffices if the employer has the ability to do so.

The employer will be able to give orders to the employee and examine and supervise his work, but this does not mean that the employee will not have any freedom whatsoever.

2.13 The fact that wages need to be paid in return for the output in order to constitute a labour agreement means that people that volunteer to deliver output, are not bound by a labour agreement. However, certain stipulations of Belgian employment law will still be applicable to them.

2.14 Only if a person is bound to an employer by a labour agreement, in principle, the entire range of regulations as set out below will apply to them.

GENERAL PROTECTION AGAINST DISMISSAL

2.15 Employment agreements can be for a fixed duration (or for a certain project) or for an undetermined duration (ie permanent).

2.16 Of course, when the end date is reached in employment agreements for a fixed duration, or the project is finished, the working relationship between the employer and the employee will come to an end.

2.17 Belgian employment law also has a number of ways to end an employment agreement which has an undetermined duration:

- by mutual agreement (see paras **2.145** et seq);
- by giving notice to the employee (see paras **2.58** et seq);
- because of the death of the employee (the death of the employer will not end the agreement);
- by force majeur;
- when a certain condition that is foreseen in the agreement is fulfilled (condition precedent);
- by judgment of an Employment Court (this is only possible in certain cases);
- in case the employer is declared bankrupt and the trustee does not want to keep on employing the employee; or
- because of an urgent cause.

An urgent cause is considered to be a severe shortcoming that renders it impossible, in an immediate and definitive way, for the employer and the employee to maintain a professional working relationship.

It will be up to the Employment Court to assess whether or not the cause that is invoked is urgent enough to end the employment agreement and bring about the dismissal of the employee.

When a contract is ended because of an urgent cause, there is a strict procedure that has to be followed (note that there is a special procedure in case one wants to dismiss employees that are a member of the Works Council, hereafter 'WC', or the Committee on Health and Safety and the Work floor, hereafter 'CHSW', because of an urgent cause, see paragraph **2.23**):

- the dismissal notice itself needs to be given within a three (working) day period, including Saturdays, following the event that established the urgent cause (or following the point in time when it has become certain the event has taken place – this enables the other party to investigate the event). The dismissal notice should be communicated by a letter, sent by registered mail or delivered by a bailiff;
- once the dismissal notice is given, a new three (working) day period starts to run. Within this period, the facts and reasons that constitute the urgent

cause need to be disclosed to the party that has been dismissed. All this needs to be described in a document, sent by registered mail, delivered by a bailiff or delivered by hand to the other party which has to sign for it.

A dismissal for an urgent cause can have very serious consequences for an employee because he will be out of employment immediately, without any notice period or a severance pay. He will also not have immediate access to any unemployment benefits.

The party that gives the dismissal can also claim damages.

2.18 When a permanent employment agreement is terminated without respecting the correct procedure, the employee will have a claim for a severance pay.

This severance pay generally equals the wages that would have been earned during the period of notice that should have been respected.

2.19 In case an employment agreement for a fixed duration or a certain project is ended early without following the correct procedure, the dismissing employer will have to pay the wages that were due until the end of the agreement (however, there is a cap that differs in every individual case).

2.20 When all procedures have been followed correctly in dismissing an employee, this employee can still claim an extra indemnity if he can prove that there was no valid reason to dismiss him.

Regulations concerning unfair dismissal ('seemingly unreasonable dismissal') will be set out below (see paras **2.141** et seq).

2.21 Due to the fact that the Belgian government noted an increasing number of older employees who were not able to find new employment after being dismissed, an obligation was created, in certain cases, for employers to offer the employees they were dismissing so-called 'outplacement'. This means that the employee will receive assistance from an outplacement agency in order to find a new employer or to become self-employed as fast as possible, following the dismissal.

Outplacement agencies will assist the dismissed employee on different levels: eg they will give psychological support if requested; they will help develop a plan of action; and they will offer logistic and administrative support.

Different laws and CLA's regulate the outplacement procedure.

In general, outplacement needs to be offered by the employer if the employee who is dismissed has a right to a term of notice of at least 30 weeks.

The outplacement does not need to be offered if the employee has been dismissed for an urgent cause.

The outplacement guidance will be provided for 60 hours (if the employee was working full time), spread out over a period of maximum 12 months.

Employees who are at least 45 years old and have at least one year of seniority at the time of their dismissal also need to be offered outplacement by the employer.

This will not be required if the employee is dismissed for an urgent cause or if he is able to retire.

All the costs concerning the outplacement will be met by the employer which has requested it.

SPECIAL PROTECTION AGAINST DISMISSAL

2.22 Certain categories of employees receive special protection against dismissal under Belgian employment law.

These categories are:

- pregnant employees;
- employees who are on paternity leave;
- employees who are on parental leave;
- employees who are breastfeeding a child;
- employees who are on leave in order to adopt;
- employees who are sick or had an accident;
- employees who reduce their schedule in order to work part-time;
- employees who are granted a leave of absence or so-called 'time credit';
- employees who are granted a leave of absence because of educational reasons;
- employees who have to work with new technologies;
- employees who are on political leave;
- employees who demand equal treatment (male – female);
- employees who demand equal wages (male – female);
- employees who have filed a complaint with regard to violence or (sexual) harassment on the work floor;
- employees who are so-called 'prevention advisors'.

All these categories of employees are protected against dismissal during a certain period of time. Should the employer dismiss them during this period, in most cases he will have to pay an additional indemnity on top of the severance pay.

2.23 A more elaborate protection against dismissal is imposed by law for the members of the WC and the CHSW.

Even those employees who do not get elected, but were candidates, will benefit from this special protection.

During the period of protection, this category of employees can only be dismissed for an urgent cause or for economic or technical reasons.

The duration of this protection can vary, depending on whether or not the employee has been elected and whether or not he was a first-time candidate.

In case of a dismissal for an urgent cause of one of these employees, the employer will have to inform the employee organisation that he is a member of, and consult with it.

If the employer wishes to go through with the dismissal, the Employment Court will have to recognise the employee's shortcoming(s) as being an urgent cause.

In case of a dismissal for economical or technical reasons, the employer will also need to follow a strict procedure.

WORKFORCE REDUCTION

2.24 In Belgium, an employer can – in principle – dismiss an employee at any time if the term of notice is respected and if it is not found to be a voluntary/seemingly unreasonable dismissal.

So if an individual employee is deemed to be redundant the employer will need to follow the general rules on dismissal.

There is no particular individual procedure that has to be followed.

2.25 In case there is a 'collective dismissal' however, the stipulations that are set out below need to be followed, except in a few very particular cases.

DISMISSALS ON GROUNDS OF REDUNDANCY

Redundancy procedures

2.26 As long as an employer is not giving a collective dismissal to a certain number of employees, there are no specific regulations that need to be followed if the reason for the dismissal is redundancy.

In these cases, the employer will have to respect all standard requirements (eg with regard to the letter of notice, the term of notice and the fact that the dismissal cannot be seemingly unreasonable) which apply to any dismissal (see paras **2.58** et seq).

2.27 However, as soon as the number of employees being dismissed makes it a collective dismissal, there are additional requirements that have to be met.

On the one hand there are requirements with regard to the individual employee and on the other hand there are those with regard to the collective dismissal itself.

2.28 An extra difficulty is created by the fact that, in Belgian employment law, the definition of 'collective dismissal' is different in the three procedures that deal with collective dismissal, namely the individual procedure, the collective procedure and the procedure concerning the calculation of the redundancy payment.

Individual redundancy procedures

2.29 As soon as an employer announces that he is making a collective dismissal, especially in case of a restructuring of the company, he will generally need to establish so-called 'employment cells'.

2.30 The law of 23 December 2005 on the Generation Pact has stipulated that these employment cells need to be established in case of a collective dismissal, meaning the dismissal of:

•	in companies with up to 11 employees:	half of all employees
•	in companies with 12 up to 20 employees:	6 employees
•	in companies with 21 up to 99 employees:	10 employees
•	in companies with at least 100 employees;	10% of all employees

2.31 The following procedure will apply to the employees who are employed by the employer at the time that the collective dismissal is announced and who are dismissed during the period of restructuring.

Requirements for the employer

Establishing the employment cell

2.32 As mentioned above, the employer should establish an employment cell at the moment he announces he will be making a collective dismissal.

In any case, the cell needs to be established before the first employee is dismissed in the collective dismissal.

2.33 The date of the final individual dismissal within the collective dismissal will determine for what period of time the cell will need to be operational.

The cell will need to be operational during three months following the final individual dismissal of an employee who is under 45 years of age and six months following the final individual dismissal of an employee who is at least 45 years old.

Composition of the employment cell

2.34 The cell will, in any case, be comprised of the employer, a delegation of employee representatives and the competent regional Service for Employment Mediation and Professional Education.

In case it exists within the business sector of the company, the sectoral Educational Fund will also be involved.

The cell will be presided over by the regional Service.

Consultation with the employee

2.35 The employer is obliged to invite the employee to an individual redundancy consultation before he can dismiss him.

During this consultation, the employer will inform the employee about the employment cell.

2.36 The invitation will need to be sent by registered mail and it will need to reach the employee at least seven working days prior to the consultation.

If the employee prefers, he can have an employee representative attend the consultation with him.

2.37 After the consultation, the employee has a seven working day period to let the employer know whether or not he will participate in the employment cell.

If the employer has not received an answer within this period, the employee will be supposed to have agreed.

Termination of the employment agreement

2.38 Once the decision made by the employee is clear, the employment agreement can be terminated and the date of termination will be communicated to the President of the employment cell.

The termination of the agreement can be immediate or after a term of notice, depending on the age and seniority of the employee.

Enrolling in the employment cell

2.39 When the employment agreement is terminated, the employee can be enrolled in the employment cell.

2.40 The most important task of the cell is to offer 'outplacement' to the employee (see para **2.21** – however the amount of hours and months of guidance is somewhat different).

Requirements for the employee

2.41 As mentioned before (see para **2.33**), an employee will be enrolled in the cell for at least a three or six-month period.

While the employee is enrolled, he is obligated to accept every offer of outplacement and he has to actively cooperate.

He also needs to enrol himself as being unemployed at the competent Service for Employment Mediation.

Compensation for activation

2.42 The employer will need to pay a compensation for activation to all employees who are enrolled in the employment cell and have at least one year of seniority.

The compensation is paid monthly for three months, if the employee is under 45 years of age, or for six months, if the employee is 45 years or older.
This compensation can be deducted from the severance pay the employer might have to pay the employee.

Collective redundancy procedure

2.43 Since the 1970s, collective dismissals in Belgium have been regulated by the collective labour agreement n° 24 and the Royal Decree of 24 May 1976.
On 27 February 1997 however, the Renault factory in Vilvoorde (near Brussels) announced its closure, which took everyone by surprise.
Most regulations of the CLA n° 24 were ignored by the management/mother company, which caused a social massacre for about 3,100 employees.
Due to these problems, a new law on collective redundancy procedures was passed. This law is complementary to the CLA n° 24 and is called the 'Renault Law'.

2.44 A dismissal is considered to be collective under this law when, within a 60-day period, for one or more reasons with no regard to the person (read: his competences and abilities) of the employee, at least the following number of employees of that company (read: technical company unit) is dismissed:

•	companies that have employed more than 20 and less than 100 employees in the calendar year before the dismissal:	10 employees
•	companies that have employed at least 100 and less than 300 employees in the calendar year before the dismissal:	10% of the employees
•	companies that have employed at least 300 employees on average in the calendar year before the dismissal:	30 employees

Involvement of employee representatives in collective dismissals

2.45 When a company has 50 employees or more (in certain cases there even has to be a minimum of 100 employees), a Works Council 'WC' as well as a Committee concerning Health and Safety on the Work floor 'CHSW' has to be installed.
The members of the WC are representatives of the employees (and chosen from among them) and representatives of the employer, which consult on certain matters with regard to the company.
The CHSW focuses on the wellbeing of the employees on the work floor.

2.46 Companies can also have employee representatives linked to certain trade unions.

2.47 It is possible that smaller companies do not have a WC or CHSW, nor any employee representatives or trade-unionists.

When there is a collective redundancy procedure in those companies, the employer will have to consult with the employees directly.

Information and consultation requirements

2.48 During a collective redundancy procedure, there are four stages that have to be run through in order for an employer to meet all the information and consultation requirements.

2.49 First, when the employer intends to make a collective dismissal, he needs to give all useful information on this subject to the employee representatives (WC, trade-unionists, CHSW or the employees themselves) and he has to submit a written document to them containing at least the following:

- the reasons for the dismissals;
- the number of employees involved, as well as the categories to which they belong;
- the number of employees and of categories that he generally employs;
- the period during which the dismissals will be made;
- the criteria that will be used to select the employees who face dismissal;
- the way in which enhanced redundancy payments will be calculated.

After sending this document to the employee representatives, the employer has a meeting with them during which he will explain the content of this document further. This way the employee representatives have the opportunity to give remarks and make suggestions.

The employer will then consult with the employee representatives about the possibilities of avoiding the collective dismissal or decreasing the number of dismissals.

The employee representatives will have the opportunity to ask questions and make remarks or suggestions again.

2.50 Secondly the employer will assess these remarks and suggestions and will answer the questions that were asked.

2.51 Thirdly the employer has to send a letter by registered mail to the Director of the Sub-regional Employment Service, hereafter 'SES', that is competent for the town the social seat of the company is situated in and to the President of the Committee of Directors of the Federal Service concerning Labour.

In this letter, the employer needs to inform these services about his decision to give a collective dismissal. This letter needs to contain the following information:

- the company information (name, address, activities, the Joint Committee the employees are subject to);

- the ordinary number of employees;
- the reasons behind the intended dismissals;
- the number of employees involved in the dismissals (divided in groups by sex, age, profession and company branch);
- the period during which the dismissals will take place.

The employer also needs to mention in this letter that he confirms that he has met the following four conditions:

- that the employee representatives were informed, in writing, about the intention to make a collective dismissal;
- that he has had a meeting with them about this intention;
- that the employee representatives have had the opportunity to ask questions about this intended collective dismissal, and have had the opportunity to make suggestions and proposals;
- that the employer has assessed the remarks and suggestions and has answered all questions.

He also needs to add proof of this.

On the same day as the employer sends this letter by registered mail, he will also have to distribute a copy of it within the company, send a copy of it to the employee representatives (so they can send their remarks to the Director of the SES) and send a copy of it (by registered mail) to the employees that have already been dismissed due to the collective dismissal.

During 30 days following the despatch of the above-mentioned letter by registered mail (and the distribution of copies of it to the employee representatives), the employee representatives have the opportunity to raise objections to the employer concerning him not following the procedure correctly.

This 30-day period can in certain circumstances be shortened and prolonged (to a maximum of 60 days) in certain specific cases.

The employer can file an appeal against this prolongation.

It is important to note that, during this 30-day period, the employer cannot give notice to employees who will be dismissed in the collective dismissal.

2.52 Finally, when this 30-day period is over, the employer can give notice to the employees who will be dismissed in the collective dismissal, except when the objections the employee representatives raised are found to be well-grounded.

If this is the case, the employer will have another opportunity to fulfil the above-mentioned four conditions. When these conditions are met, the employer will have to send another letter to the Director of the SES and another 30-day period will start (that can again be shortened or prolonged).

An employee who has been dismissed and has been given notice has his own (individual) 30-day period to inform the employer if he thinks not all four steps of the procedure were correctly followed. He has to do this by registered mail.

However, this employee cannot do this if the employee representatives have not made any objections during the 30-day period after the employer has sent the letter by registered mail.

Summary

An employer initiates the collective redundancies process (A). He draws up the necessary document and sends it to all parties involved.

The employer and the employee representatives have a meeting, after which the employer assesses all the remarks and suggestions and answers all questions.

If the employer still wants to go through with collective redundancies, he sends the letter by registered mail to the authorities and delivers the necessary copies (B).

The employee representatives have the opportunity to raise objections concerning the procedure that has been followed (in principle: B + 30 days).

Notice (C) can be given to the employee after this period (B + 30 days), or after a shortened period (B + less than 30 days), or after a prolonged period (B + 30 to maximum 60 days).

The employee has an individual right to file a complaint (C + 30 days), but only if the employee representatives have raised objections during B + 30 days.

Regulatory requirements

2.53 As mentioned above, when the employer intends to make collective redundancies, he informs the employee representatives about it.

When the employer wants to go through with the collective dismissal, he will also have to send a copy of his (written) decision containing the necessary data by registered mail to the Director of the Sub-regional Employment Service that is competent for the town where the company has its social seat and to the President of the Committee of Directors of the Federal Service concerning Labour.

Standard forms to give these notifications can be downloaded from the internet.

Sanctions

2.54 The 'Renault Law' has provided sanctions in case the provisions of CLA n° 24 are not followed. This law does not provide sanctions for breaches of the provisions of the Royal Decree.

2.55 With regard to the sanctioning, there are two possibilities that have to be taken into account:

The employee has been dismissed and a period of notice has been given

2.56 If an individual employee has been given notice, but he is of the opinion that the information and consultation requirements have not been met by the employer, he will need to send a letter by registered mail to the employer.

If the Employment Court agrees with the employee, the term of notice will be suspended from the third working day following the sending of the letter by registered mail until the moment in time that the employer proves that he has met all requirements.

This suspension will end in any case after a period of 60 days after the Director of the SES has been correctly informed.

It is only the period of notice that will be suspended in this case. This means that the employment agreement still exists and both parties still have to respect it and carry it out.

The employee has been dismissed and a severance pay has been granted

2.57 If the employment agreement of an individual employee has been terminated and he has already received a severance pay, but he is of the opinion that the information and consultation requirements have not been met by the employer, he will need to send a letter by registered mail to the employer. In this letter, he will specifically need to ask to be reinstated.

If the Employment Court declares that the employee is right, the employer needs to reinstate the employee within 30 days following the third day after sending the above-mentioned letter by registered mail.

If the employee is reinstated he will have to reimburse the severance pay to the employer. The employer needs to pay wages to the employee, starting the day of the wrongful termination.

However, if the employee is not reinstated, the employee will get to keep the severance pay and will be granted an additional compensation.

It has to be noted that judgments from Employment Courts regarding these types of cases are scarce.

NOTICE

2.58 Of all of the possible ways to end an employment agreement (see para 2.17), giving notice to the other party is the one that is most common.

2.59 It is important to note however that employment agreements for a fixed duration or for a certain project cannot be ended by giving notice before the end of the fixed duration or before the completion of the project.

Giving notice: form and content of the letter of notice

2.60 When ending an individual agreement, the dismissal needs to be given in writing to the individual employee.

2.61 The party which is giving notice can only deliver the letter of notice to the other party in one of the following three ways:

- the employee can give the letter to his employer (note that if the employer is the one that is giving the notice, he cannot use this form of delivery);
- the party giving the notice can send the letter by registered mail to the other party;
- the letter can be delivered to the other party by bailiff.

2.62 The letter of notice needs to state clearly that the party giving notice wants to end the employment agreement.

Furthermore, the letter needs to mention the starting date and the duration of the term of notice.

Finally the letter needs to be signed and dated by the party giving notice.

Giving notice: language of the letter of notice

2.63 Due to the fact that there are different language communities in Belgium (see para 2.2), it is important to use the correct language in the letter of notice.

The only criterion in determining the language of the letter of notice is the location of the seat of exploitation of the company.

This means that, for instance, the location of the social seat does not have any consequences.

Seeing as the territory of Brussels-Capital is considered to be bilingual, it is up to the employee to choose whether he wants Dutch or French to be used.

> **Practical Tip**
>
> When giving notice, always check carefully what language needs to be used in the letter of notice.
>
> For example, if the seat of exploitation of the company has moved, it is possible that at the time an employee signed his employment agreement it was in German (language requirements also apply at that point), but when he is given notice, the letter of notice needs to be in French.
>
> The party giving notice that uses the wrong language in the letter of notice, will be considered not to have given notice at all.

Reason for dismissal

2.64 In Belgium, it has always been easy for employers to dismiss (individual) employees.

Only when an urgent cause was invoked to dismiss an employee, it was deemed necessary for the employer to prove that there was an actual urgent cause.

It was also possible for an employee to start legal proceedings against the employer if the employee felt that had been dismissed voluntary. In that case the Employment Court would judge whether or not the reasons invoked to dismiss the employee were arbitrary.

2.65 Along with the modification of the terms of notice (see below), it was deemed necessary to add new regulations with regards to the reason an employer needs to give for any dismissal.

Since 1 April 2014, the new CLA n° 109 with regard to this subject has entered into force.

This CLA grants the employee the opportunity to request the employer to inform him about the actual reason(s) for the dismissal in case the employer has not informed him about this at the moment the dismissal was given.

2.66 The employee needs to send this request to the employer by registered mail within two months after the employment agreement has ended. However, this term cannot exceed a term of six months following the dismissal.

2.67 After receiving the request from the employee, the employer in turn has two months to answer the request by registered mail to the employee.

An employer who does not answer the request or does not answer it in time, will have to pay the employee an indemnity that equals two weeks of wages.

> **Summary**
>
> If an employee is dismissed (A), the employment agreement will end at a certain point in time (B).
>
> In case the employee was not informed about the reason for dismissal, he can send a request to the employer until B + 2 months, taking into account that this date cannot be later than A + 6 months.

Terms of notice

2.68 Belgian employment law strictly regulates all terms of notice.

For decades, there had been an enormous difference in the terms of notice of blue-collar workers and white-collar workers in Belgian law.

In 2011 the Belgian Constitutional Court deemed this difference in treatment to be unlawful.

Therefore, drastic adjustments had to be made.

2.69 Since 1 January 2014, the law states that the terms of notice for all employees are equal.

However, due to the fact that certain employees had gained a lot of seniority under the old system, it was decided to use both systems in case the employment agreement dates from before 1 January 2014.

2.70 The main criteria to determine the duration of the term of notice, under both systems, is the seniority of the employee that will be dismissed and the party that is giving the dismissal.

Terms until 31 December 2013

Blue-collar worker

2.71 If the employee is a blue-collar worker, the duration is stipulated in a law, a Royal Decree or a CLA.

However, if he has over six months of seniority, parties can deviate from this duration, as long as certain minima and maxima are respected.

Seniority	Notice by employer	Notice by employee
Less than 6 months	28 days (4 weeks)	14 days
6 months – less than 5 years	35 days (5 weeks)	14 days
5 years – less than 10 years	42 days (6 weeks)	14 days
10 years – less than 15 years	56 days (8 weeks)	14 days
15 years – less then 20 years	84 days (12 weeks)	14 days
20 years or more	112 days (16 weeks)	28 days

White-collar worker

2.72 When a white-collar worker is dismissed, his wages (yearly) will also be taken into account.

If the employee is a white-collar worker, the duration of the term of notice is the following:

Wages	Seniority	Notice by employer	Notice by employee
Up to 32.886 EUR	less than 5 years 5 to 10 years 10 to 15 years 15 to 20 years 20 to 25 years 25 to 30 years …	3 months 6 months 9 months 12 months 15 months 18 months …	1,5 months 3 months 3 months 3 months 3 months 3 months …

Wages	Seniority	Notice by employer	Notice by employee
Over 32.886 EUR up to 65.771 EUR	Parties will make an agreement on the term of notice. If no agreement can be reached, the Employment Court will have to determine the duration. (The Court will often use a specific formula, called the 'Claeys' formula, which takes into account the seniority, the wages and the age of the employee, as a guideline.)		
Over 65.771 EUR	In case the employer is giving notice, the duration may not be shorter than that given to an employee with the same seniority but with wages under 32.886 EUR. If the employee is giving notice, the duration can be 4, 5 months at maximum.		

Terms from 1 January 2014 onwards

2.73 If the employment agreement that has been concluded between an employer and an employee takes effect from 1 January 2014 onwards, the terms of notice that apply will be the following:

Seniority	Notice by employer	Notice by employee
< 3 months	2 weeks	1 week
3–6 months	4 weeks	2 weeks
6–9 months	6 weeks	3 weeks
9–12 months	7 weeks	3 weeks
12–15 months	8 weeks	4 weeks
15–18 months	9 weeks	4 weeks
18–21 months	10 weeks	5 weeks
21–24 months	11 weeks	5 weeks
2–3 years	12 weeks	6 weeks
3–4 years	13 weeks	6 weeks
4–5 years	15 weeks	7 weeks
5–6 years	18 weeks	9 weeks
6–7 years	21 weeks	10 weeks
7–8 years	24 weeks	12 weeks
8–9 years	27 weeks	13 weeks
9–10 years	30 weeks	13 weeks
10–11 years	33 weeks	13 weeks
11–12 years	36 weeks	13 weeks
12–13 years	39 weeks	13 weeks

Seniority	Notice by employer	Notice by employee
13–14 years	42 weeks	13 weeks
14–15 years	45 weeks	13 weeks
15–16 years	48 weeks	13 weeks
16–17 years	51 weeks	13 weeks
17–18 years	54 weeks	13 weeks
18–19 years	57 weeks	13 weeks
19–20 years	60 weeks	13 weeks
20–21 years	62 weeks	13 weeks
21–22 years	63 weeks	13 weeks
22–23 years	64 weeks	13 weeks
… (+1)	… (+1)	13 weeks

Notice given after 1 January 2014 if the employment agreement dates from before 1 January 2014

2.74 As mentioned above, if an employment agreement that started before January 1st 2014 is terminated after that date, both systems will need to be used.

2.75 First, the term of notice for the employee on 31 December 2013 will need to be calculated, as follows:

Blue-collar worker		terms foreseen by law (old system)
	wages under 32.254 EUR	notice by employer: 3 months per 5 years seniority
		notice by employee 1,5 months per 5 years seniority (with a 3 month maximum)
White-collar worker	wages from 32.254 EUR up to 64.508 EUR	notice by employer: 1 month per year of seniority (with a 3 month minimum)
		notice by employee: 1,5 months per 5 years seniority (with a 4,5 month maximum)
	wages over 64.508 EUR	notice by employer: 1 month per year of seniority (with a 3 month minimum)
		notice by employee: 1,5 months per 5 years seniority (with a 6 month maximum)

2.76 Secondly, the term of notice under the new system as set out above needs to be calculated.

2.77 Finally, in order to achieve the total term of notice, both terms will have to be added.

2.78 Please note that all amounts cited are these that apply for 2014. The amounts are adjusted every year.

Giving 'counter notice'

2.79 When an employee is given notice by his employer, the employee can end the employment relationship with the employer before the term of notice is over by giving a 'counter notice' (eg when he has already found a new job).

2.80 In case a 'counter notice' is given, the term of notice is shortened as follows:

Seniority	Term of 'counter notice'
< 3 months	1 week
3-6 months	2 weeks
6-12 months	3 weeks
over 12 months	4 weeks

Sanctions

2.81 When the above-mentioned requirements with regard to giving notice are not followed, the notice given may fail to have any consequences.

In that case, the employment agreement will continue to exist and will have to be carried out by both parties under the same conditions.

Consequences of notice given in conformity with all regulations.

2.82 A notice that is given while all regulations are taken into account will cause the term of notice to start. The term will start, in all cases, the Monday following the moment the notice has been given.

During this period, in principle, both parties need to keep on honouring their obligations set out by the employment agreement as before.

However, when an employee has been dismissed by his employer, he will be granted some paid leave in order to apply for a new job.

2.83 Should, for whatever reason, the employer not want the employee to keep on working for him during the term of notice, he can ask the employee not to return to the company, but he will need to pay the employee an amount of money that equals the wages he would have earned during the term of notice.

REDUNDANCY PAYMENT

2.84 CLA n° 10 provides an exceptional payment that is to be made by the employer in case of a collective dismissal.

2.85 It is important to note that the definition of a 'collective dismissal' is slightly different from the definitions mentioned above.

In this CLA a 'collective dismissal' is considered to be every dismissal for economical or technical reasons within a 60 day period that involves at least the following number of employees:

- in companies with 20 to 59 employees: 6 employees
- in companies with at least 60 employees: 10% of the average total number of employees during the calendar year before the dismissal.

2.86 Furthermore, this CLA is only applicable if the company has had an average of 20 employees during the calendar year before the dismissal.

On the other hand, this CLA is not applicable to certain categories of employees.

Statutory redundancy pay calculation

2.87 Employees that have been dismissed in a collective dismissal will receive this redundancy payment in addition to their unemployment benefits.

They will receive these payments for (maximum) four months, starting the day after the termination of the employment agreement or the day after the end of the term of notice.

2.88 The amount of the redundancy payment equals half of the difference between a reference amount and the unemployment benefits.

An employee's monthly wages, with an absolute maximum of 3.207,55 EUR (adjusted last on 1 December 2012), minus social security contributions and taxes, is used as the reference amount.

Enhanced redundancy payments

2.89 It is possible that within a company or a sector, enhanced redundancy payments are agreed upon.

All of these enhanced payments need to be subtracted from the amount that is due as a statutory redundancy payment.

Taxation of redundancy payments

2.90 In principle, redundancy payments will be taxed progressively. However, there are no social security contributions to be paid on these amounts.

Non-competition clause

2.91 During the duration of the employment agreement, an employee will not be allowed to practice any activities that compete with those of the employer. If the employee should do this, the employer will be able to dismiss him for an urgent cause.

However, once the employment agreement is terminated, the employee will, in principle, regain his 'freedom' on this point.

By inserting a non-competition clause in the employment agreement, the employer can restrict the activities of his (former) employee after the termination of the agreement for a certain period of time.

This kind of clause can only apply to employees that have enough knowhow to actually compete with the activities of the employer. These employees also need to earn an amount of at least 32.886,00 EUR per year.

The employer will have to abide by certain restrictions with regard to this clause:

- it has to relate to similar activities as those of the employer;
- it has to be geologically limited to the area the employer works in and in any case it is limited to the Belgian territory;
- it cannot apply for more than one year after the termination of the employment agreement;
- it has to provide a non-competition compensation that the employer has to pay the employee (the calculation of this compensation is regulated by law – it is generally half of the wages that the employee would have earned if he had still worked for the employer during the period of non-competition).

If the employer does not want to invoke his rights under this clause, he needs to inform the employee about this within a period of 15 days following the termination of the employment agreement.

If the employee does not respect his obligations under this clause (in case it is invoked by the employer), he will have to pay back the non-competition compensation, as well as an additional fine.

BUSINESS SALE, OUTSOURCING/INSOURCING AND OFFSHORING

2.92 Early on, the European Council wanted to ensure that, in case a company (or parts of it) was (were) transferred, the employees could maintain all their rights with regards to their employment.

Therefore, the European Council Directive 77/187/EEG was implemented in Belgian employment law by CLA n° 32, which was agreed upon in the National Labour Council.

2.93 Due to difficulties in the application of this CLA, CLA n° 32 was abolished and replaced by CLA n° 32bis.

In turn, CLA n° 32bis has been amended by CLA n° 32ter, 32quater and 32quinquies.

2.94 CLA n° 32bis contains regulations that have to be followed in case of:

- a transfer (sale) of a company or a part of it;
- the taking over of assets after a bankruptcy (which will not be discussed further in this contribution).

It also contains the information requirements an employer has to meet in case there is a transfer and there are no employee representatives in the company.

2.95 In any case it is important to note that CLA n° 32bis is only applicable to (most) private companies. In principle it will not be applied to companies in the public sector.

Business transfer (sale)

2.96 CLA n° 32bis is only applicable in case there is a business transfer by virtue of an agreement.

2.97 The CLA itself sets out a definition of this 'business transfer by virtue of an agreement'.

In any case, three conditions have to be met:

- there has to be a change of employer

  The person or company that was considered to be the employer of a certain employee now loses that capacity and another person or company gains the capacity of being their employer.

  This can occur, for instance, in case of a fusion of two companies or a division of a company.

- the company, or a part of it, needs to be transferred

The transfer that takes place can be that of an entire company but it can also be only a part of a company.

As long as that part is a technical company unit (with economic and social autonomy) or an economic company unit (with a minimal structural autonomy), CLA n° 32bis will apply.

In any case, the economical identity of the entity that is transferred, needs to be preserved and an ongoing exploitation of its activities has to be possible.

- there has to be an agreement

  This criterion has been greatly influenced by the jurisprudence of the European Court of Justice.

  The Court has stated that the term 'agreement' needs to be interpreted in a broad sense, meaning that it is enough if there is a meeting of wills between buyer and seller.

  The Directive will be applicable even if there is no written agreement.

Effects of CLA n° 32bis

Automatic transfer and protection of employment

2.98 If the CLA n° 32bis is applicable, the employment agreement closed between the employee and the transferor, will be transferred to the transferee.
That way the employee and the transferee will have to carry out their obligations under this agreement in the same way as before the transfer. No new employment agreement needs to be signed.
The transferee needs to respect all that has been agreed upon regarding work and wages. He cannot make any unilateral changes to this agreement.

2.99 Seeing as all this only applies to employees who were working for the transferor at the time of the transfer, this will not apply to employees whose agreement has been terminated before the transfer or employees who did not work in the part of the company that has been transferred.
If an employee has been given notice before the transfer and the term of notice is not over at the moment of the transfer, this employee will also be transferred to the transferee.

2.100 Following the jurisdiction of the European Court of Justice, the transferor and the transferee cannot agree that certain employees of the (part of the) company that is being transferred, will not be transferred with it.
These employees will only be able to stay on with the transferor if they agree to it and if they object their transfer to the transferee (see below).

Objection to the transfer

2.101 The fact that the employment agreement is automatically transferred from the transferor to the transferee implies that an employee cannot consider his employment to be terminated on account of the transfer itself.

2.102 However, this does not mean that the employee is obliged to work for the transferee. The employee still has the right to give notice.

If the transferee should unilaterally change one of the essential elements of the employment agreement, the employee will be able to claim that he has been unfairly dismissed (see paras **2.138** et seq).

If the employee should refuse to work for the transferee without giving notice, the transferee can give him notice or dismiss him (on the grounds of a so-called 'urgent cause').

Protection from dismissal

2.103 As stated above, the transfer itself cannot be invoked as a reason for either party to end the employment agreement.

This means that the employee cannot be dismissed by the transferor shortly before the transfer or by the transferee shortly after the transfer.

The CLA does not state during which period before and after the transfer the employee cannot be dismissed.

If an employee is dismissed and he argues that the reason for his dismissal is the company transfer, the Employment Court will have to decide whether or not the dismissal was related to the transfer itself.

2.104 All this does not mean that the employee is protected from dismissal in any eventuality. The CLA contains two exceptions:

- the employee can still be dismissed on the grounds of an urgent cause;
- the employee can still be dismissed on economical, technical or organisational grounds.

Protection of terms and conditions of employment

2.105 An employee, under Belgian law, has both individual and collective terms and conditions of employment.

These terms and conditions can only be altered by the transferee in case the transferor had the opportunity to alter them.

2.106 The individual terms and conditions can be found in:

- The individual employment agreement of the employee;
- The corporate directives as issued by the transferor; or

- CLA's if the stipulations thereof have been incorporated in the individual employment agreement.

2.107 The collective terms and conditions can be found in the CLA's that are applicable to the employees of the transferred company.

These CLA's can be concluded on a sectoral or a company level.

Outstanding debts to the employee

2.108 It is important to note that, in case there are certain amounts due to the employee at the moment of transfer (eg a severance pay), this employee can claim these amounts from both the transferor and the transferee.

Information and consultation requirements under CLA n° 32bis

2.109 It is important to emphasise that these requirements are directed towards both transferee and transferor.

Duty to inform

2.110 If the company has a Works Council, this Council will need to be informed about the transfer in good time and, in any case, before it is publicly announced.

The concept of 'in good time' is quite vague and will differ from company to company. The information has to be given to the Council as soon as possible and in time for the Council to discuss it. However, the duty to inform cannot restrict the employer/transferor to make decisions of an economical nature in any way and it may not influence any negotiations that may be ongoing.

2.111 If there is no Works Council in the company, the information has to be given to the trade-unionists.

2.112 The information that has to be given to these employee representatives is:

- an overview of the economic, financial or technical reasons that make the transfer necessary;
- the economic, financial and social repercussions.

2.113 If there are no employee representatives in the company, the employees themselves need to be informed about:

- the date of the transfer;
- the reason for the transfer;
- the legal, economic or social repercussions of the transfer; and
- the overview of measures that might be taken with regard to the employees.

Duty to consult

2.114 The employee representatives need to be consulted, among other things, on:

- all means that can be used to avoid dismissals;
- the social measures that have to be taken; and
- all measures with regard to the optimal use of all the potential of the employees.

Social measures

2.115 The employee representatives need to get the necessary opportunities to make sure that as many of the dismissed or transferred employees can get back to work, eg by retraining them.

European Works Council

2.116 If a European Works Council is established in the company, a special procedure on information and consultation will also need to be followed.

The employees who are members of this European Works Council will also receive special protection against dismissal.

Sanctions

2.117 Should an employee suspect that he has been wrongly dismissed during the course of a business transfer, this employee can start legal proceedings on the grounds of a seemingly unreasonable dismissal (see paras **2.138** et seq).

If the court rules in his favour, the employer will need to pay him a certain amount of money as compensation.

Failure to comply with the requirements of CLA 32bis

2.118 CLA 32bis does not provide a compensation that has to be paid by the employer to his employees in case he does not comply with all requirements set out under this CLA.

However, the employer may be penalised, in which case he will have to pay a fine.

WORKFORCE RESTRUCTURE IN CONNECTION WITH SHARE SALE OR SHARE PURCHASE

2.119 Since this does not affect the legal entity of the employer, this does not have any consequences with regard to the relationship between employer and employee.

CHANGING EMPLOYMENT TERMS AND CONDITIONS

Mutually agreed changes

2.120 Generally, under Belgian law, all contracting parties are free to stipulate whatever they want (to a certain degree) in an employment agreement.

2.121 However, there are a few clauses that are forbidden. For instance, parties are not allowed to make an employment agreement for life or to stipulate that the employer will have the right to unilaterally change the terms and conditions of the agreement (see below).

There are also some clauses, eg a non-competition clause (see para **2.91**), that are strictly regulated.

2.122 With regard to changes to the employment terms and conditions, the Court of Cassation has ruled that an employment agreement can state that the employer has the right to unilaterally change the non-essential terms and conditions.

If no such clause is imbedded in the employment agreement, however, these non-essential terms and conditions can only be altered if both parties agree.

It is generally understood that the employee's agreement with the changes that are made does not have to be given explicitly.

For instance, if the employee continues to execute the employment agreement, it will be assumed he has agreed to those changes.

Unilateral changes

2.123 As mentioned above, Belgian employment law states that the employer may not stipulate in the employment agreement that he will have the right to unilaterally change the employment terms and conditions.

However, the Belgian Court of Cassation has stated that this prohibition only applies to the so-called 'essential' terms and conditions of employment.

These essential terms and conditions are the following:

- the amount of the wages;
- the capacity/function within the company;
- the working schedule/time table;
- the work location (this can be a point of discussion).

If one, or more, of these terms and conditions are substantially and unilaterally altered by the employer, the employee can state that he has been unfairly dismissed, even if the changes made by the employer are only temporary.

USING TEMPORARY STAFF

2.124 An employer can find different solutions in order to resolve any issues he has regarding a temporary work overload.

Of course, these types of agreements are very strictly regulated.

Fixed-term contracts

2.125 If an employer wants to hire an employee for a fixed period of time, the employment agreement will need to meet certain formal requirements.

The agreement will need to be in writing, for every employee individually and it has to be drafted before the employee is actually employed.

The content will need to be clear and the duration needs to be clearly and explicitly mentioned.

Obviously, the agreement will also need to be drafted in the correct language.

2.126 Belgian employment law has always stated that, in principle, fixed-term agreements had to be carried out until the end date, without a possibility of early termination.

In principle, only a termination for an urgent cause was possible.

However, since 2014, for fixed-term employment agreements that come into force after 1 January 2014, the legislator has foreseen the potential for a unilateral termination of these agreements for both employer and employee.

The option of a unilateral termination can only be exercised during the first half of the duration of the employment agreement, with a maximum of six months after the beginning of the agreement.

When this option is used, the party using it will give notice and the terms of notice that apply to employment agreements for an indeterminate period (see para 2.73) will also apply.

In case of consecutive fixed-duration agreements, unilateral termination will only be possible during the duration the first employment agreement.

Renewal of fixed-term contracts

2.127 If parties enter into multiple fixed-term employment agreements, following each other without interruption due to the actions of the employee, the agreement will be assumed to have been agreed for an indeterminate duration, unless the employer can prove that these consecutive fixed-term agreements were justified by the nature of the work or by some other legitimate reason.

If there is any dispute about this between the parties, the Court will have to assess whether the reason is legitimate.

2.128 When the end date of the employment agreement has been reached, but both parties keep on working together under the same terms and conditions, the agreement will also be assumed to have been for an indeterminate duration.

2.129 An employer is allowed to close consecutive fixed-term agreements with the employee in two specific cases:

- If there are maximum four consecutive agreements closed, each with a duration no shorter than three months, and the total duration is not more than two years;
- If different consecutive agreements are closed, each with a duration no shorter than six months, and the total duration is not more than three years (in this case the employee will need to get a specific approval from the competent authorities).

Employment agreements for temporary labour

2.130 Belgian employment law gives an employer the possibility to hire (directly or through the Service for Employment Mediation) an employee for temporary labour in the following cases:

- The replacement of a permanent employee is needed (eg because of sickness or pregnancy);
- There is a temporary work overload;
- There is an exceptional labour/work that has to be carried out (eg doing inventory in a company);
- There is artistic labour/work that has to be carried out.

This type of agreement will, in most cases, be limited to a very short period of time.

2.131 With regard to temporary labour, the employer will be allowed to agree consecutive employment agreements, without the assumption that the parties have concluded an agreement for an indeterminate duration (as opposed to what is the case for fixed-term agreements).

Agency workers

2.132 An employer has the opportunity to use agency workers in the same cases as mentioned above (only in the first three mentioned however).

If an employer chooses to do so, he will invoke the intervention of a working agency.

However, in certain sectors the use of agency workers is prohibited (eg moving companies) or limited (eg construction).

The posting of workers

2.133 The posting of workers takes place when one employer 'lends' one of his employees to another employer that will have authority over that employee.

This can, for instance, be the case when a contractor enlists the help of a firm specialising in steel constructions. The specialist company will deliver a crane to the contractor, as well as an employee that knows how to work the crane. This employee will have to follow the directions given to him by the contractor.

2.134 In principle, this posting of workers is unlawful and will be penalised.

However, in exceptional cases, the posting of workers can be permitted. This is only the case when the employer that is doing the posting has other activities than only posting workers (only employment agencies are allowed to have the posting of workers as a sole activity) and the posting needs to be temporary.

Most cases of posting will also require the permission of the labour inspectorate.

EMPLOYMENT CLAIMS

2.135 All claims with regard to an employment agreement need to be filed at the regional Employment Court within one year after the end date of the employment agreement.

The competent Employment Court is that which is competent for the city the seat (of exploitation) of the company is located in.

2.136 Any appeal against a judgment from the Employment Court needs to be filed at the competent Employment Court of Appeal.

2.137 In case there are procedural issues that have arisen in a certain case, parties can try to file their case at the Court of Cassation. However, this Court will never review the actual content of the case.

UNFAIR DISMISSAL

Definition

2.138 The above-mentioned CLA n° 109 introduced the notion of a 'seemingly unreasonable dismissal'.

This is a new notion, although it is similar to an older notion that has been abolished by recent regulations (for most categories of employees).

A 'seemingly unreasonable dismissal' is considered to be a dismissal that is not related to the behaviour or the capability of the employee, nor to the necessities with regard to the activities of the company.

Furthermore, it is a dismissal that would not be given by a 'normal and reasonable' employer.

Remedy

2.139 Seeing as this notion is brand new in Belgian employment law, no jurisdiction regarding the amount of the compensation granted to an employee in this case is available.

However, it is predicted that the courts will grant employees an amount equal to 3 to 17 weeks of pay, depending on how unreasonable the dismissal is deemed to be.

DISCRIMINATION

2.140 In Belgium there are some specific anti-discrimination laws that have to be respected in all possible fields.

For example, if an employer is restructuring his company and he dismisses all employees over a certain age, he can be penalised for discrimination.

The employees concerned will of course be able to file proceedings against him for an unfair dismissal.

2.141 In Belgian employment law, there are CLAs with regard to anti-discrimination regulations covering the selection of employees.

An employer cannot make any distinction between employees based on age, sex, marital status, state of health, race, colour, ethnicity, political persuasion or membership of trade organisations.

MUTUALLY AGREED TERMINATION

2.142 One of the basic principles of Belgian law is the parties' freedom to enter into an agreement. This also implies that they are free to end their agreements without any formalities.

Parties can even verbally agree to terminate the agreement, although it is recommended to put such an agreement down in writing.

2.143 Mutually agreed terminations of employment agreements are quite common.

They are also quite easy, seeing as they can end any type of employment agreement, at any stage of the employment agreement and for any type of employee.

2.144 It is important to note that, if parties have not mutually agreed to terminate, but one of the parties has started legal proceedings, they still have the possibility to negotiate a settlement agreement as long as the case has not been ruled on by the court.

Chapter 3

Workforce Restructuring in Bulgaria

Iliana Ilieva
Law Office Ivan Bojov, Sofia

INTRODUCTION

3.1 This chapter is looking at the employment laws in Bulgaria as they operate in relation to the restructuring of the workforce. The law in Bulgaria is a continental European civil law system. Bulgarian employment law is codified comprehensively by statute, called the Labour Code (the 'Code'). The Code provides employment terms that apply automatically. The Code sets out the employment relationship between employees and employers in Bulgaria, as well as other relevant relationships. Its purpose is to ensure protection of labour, equitable employment conditions and social dialogue between the state, employees, employers and their organisations.

3.2 The purpose of this chapter is to consider the requirements under the Code in respect of termination of employment: what are the permissible reasons for termination of the employment by an employer and what procedure will the employer need to follow when relying on a particular legal reason for terminating the employment relationship.

PREPARING FOR A RESTRUCTURING EXERCISE

3.3 Different types of issues may arise when carrying out a restructuring exercise. These may include the need to reduce the workforce, change terms and conditions or outsourcing and offshoring.

The key issues to consider are set out below.

Identify the employer

3.4 An employment contract can be concluded between employee and employer. Bulgarian law provides a legal definition of term 'employer'. Accordingly, 'employer' is each individual, legal entity or its division and any other organisationally and economically self-contained entity (enterprise, institution, co-operation, farm, household and other similar entities) which independently hires employees under a contract of employment. The employee's employment can also be with a group of persons, either directly or through an authorised representative. In such a case, the rights and obligations which the employee has will be in respect of each individual of the group as if the employment contract had been concluded with each person. The business decision underlying the restructuring has to be approached and documented by the respective organisation who is identified as the 'employer' for the purposes of the Code.

Collating information to plan and budget for the restructuring exercise

3.5 Under the Code an employer has the right to select an employee for dismissal in a restructuring situation in three cases: (1) upon partial closure of an enterprise; (2) to reduce personnel when there is diminution of work; and (3) although no reduction in their work, but dismissal in order to keep other employees with higher qualifications and better performances. In all cases the employer has the 'right of estimation'. Criteria for qualification and level of performance of work (work quality) in these three cases are the basis on which reliably to plan and structure any restructuring exercise. Key data required initially in respect of any employee potentially impacted by a workforce reduction may include: level of qualification; quality of work, which can be estimated in light of employee's job description; or length of service. Such information, and information relevant to determine redundancy payments, will be necessary for estimating the overall costs of the restructuring exercise and for planning the appropriate timetable for executing dismissals.

EMPLOYMENT STATUS

3.6 There is no legal definition of 'employee' under Bulgarian law. The employee is the other party to an employment relationship supplying labour. Only individuals, who work under an employment relationship, are protected against unfair dismissal and need to be included in a redundancy procedure for workforce restructuring purposes. It will be a relevant fact finding exercise in any restructuring exercise to assess if, within the impacted business, there are individuals engaged who are not employees of the entity affected by the restructuring (for example self-employed freelancers or consultants).

GENERAL PROTECTION AGAINST DISMISSAL

3.7 All employees are entitled to a minimum notice period of 30 days and a maximum of three months when employed subject to a permanent employment contract. Where the employment is regulated by a collective bargaining agreement the notice period can be calculated with reference to an employee's continuous service with the same employer. The period of notice required for termination of a fixed-term employment contract is three months or no more than the remaining term of the contract.

3.8 An employment contract may be terminated without notice if terminated by mutual consent in writing. However, this can happen only if the party who receives the offer of termination by mutual consent accepts it within seven days of receiving it. There is a two-stage test to determine whether a dismissal has been legal.

3.9 Stage one: the employer must be able to show that one of the reasons for the dismissal is one of the legal reasons set out in the Code. 'Reduction of personnel' or 'Diminution of work', as defined by Bulgarian law, are lawful reasons for dismissal.

3.10 Stage two: the employer must then be able to show that it acted reasonably in all the circumstances in dismissing the employee for that reason and that a legal termination procedure was followed. A fair procedure will involve the employer having engaged in a meaningful consultation with the individual, a fair and objective selection process and offering the affected individual suitable alternative employment where this is available.

Special protection against dismissal

3.11 Bulgarian law provides for special dismissal protection to the following categories of employees:

- pregnant employees or employees in advanced stages of in-vitro treatment;
- female employees with children under the age of three;
- disabled employees;
- employees on leave permitted under the Code;
- employees, acting as an employee representative under health and safety legislation;
- employees who are members of a special negotiating body of a European Works Council or of a representative body of European trading or cooperative society;
- employees who are members of trade unions at the enterprise.

3.12 It should be noted that if an employer wishes to dismiss employees who enjoy special dismissal protection, as outlined above, advance permission from the General Labour Inspectorate must be obtained for each such employee in order for the dismissal to be lawful. The General Labour Inspectorate is an executive state agency, part of the Bulgarian Ministry of Labour and Social Policy, responsible for compliance with employment legislation.

WORKFORCE REDUCTION

3.13 An employer who wishes to dismiss employees must first establish the business rationale for the dismissal. Careful thought must also be given to which permissible legal reason the employer wishes to rely on for the dismissals as this will dictate the dismissal procedure which the employer must follow. Any dismissals proposed as part of a restructuring may be justified on the grounds of, for example, complete closure or closure of part of the enterprise or reduction of personnel, diminution of work or ceasing the work for more than 15 business days or other reason, expressly permitted by the Code.

3.14 Additionally, employers who plan to carry out redundancies affecting ten or more employees within a 30-day period also have to follow the consultation procedure as set out in the consultation procedure section.

Redundancy

3.15 No statutory definition of 'redundancy' exists in Bulgarian legislation. According to the Code, for an employee's dismissal to be permitted for redundancy, it must be connected with:

(a) a closure or part closure of the business; or
(b) reduction of personnel (reduced requirement for employees to carry out work); or
(c) diminution of work or ceasing of work for more than 15 business days; or
(d) lack of efficient capacity to execute the work; or
(e) relocation of the business and refusal of employee to follow the business; or
(f) change of requirements for a particular position if the employee does not satisfy the said requirements; or
(g) where performance of an employment contract is objectively impossible.

DISMISSALS ON GROUNDS OF REDUNDANCY

3.16 When companies are planning to dismiss employees on grounds of redundancy they must have regard to procedures established by the Code.

3.17 When planning to dismiss ten or more employees, employers are required to follow the collective redundancy procedure.

Redundancy procedures

3.18 These procedures for dismissing employees on grounds of redundancy are set out in the Labour Code. If a *legal* procedure is not followed then the dismissals will be regarded as unlawful. As part of the legal procedures, the employees who it is proposed to make redundant are selected. This right of selection is obligatory for the employer when redundancy affects employees who are working in the same positions. If redundancy affects an employee who has a unique position, then there is no obligation to select:

Example:

There is only one driver in the company. There are no other employees in such a position. This means that there will be no obligation on the employer to undergo a selection exercise.

3.19 The Code and the development of case law have established the following principles:

SELECTION

3.20 The starting point is for the employer to identify the group of employees from which it needs to select those who are to be made redundant.

3.21 An employer will need to be able to show that it has exercised its right of selection lawfully in accordance with the appropriate criteria established by law.

SELECTION CRITERIA

3.22 The employer must use appropriate selection criteria as determined by law. Selection criteria must be objective and the employer must make an effort to ensure that the selection criteria it uses cannot be said to be discriminatory. Criteria which are discriminatory could give rise to successful claims challenging the legality of the dismissal.

The basis on which selection should be made is set out in the Code. The selection should be made in the best interest of the company's production and service and it should allow employers to avoid dismissing those employees who have better qualifications and stronger performances.

3.23 The two main selection criteria are: professional qualification and level of work performance. The professional qualification criterion relates to education, knowledge, and skillsets that are relevant for a particular position. Current case law makes it clear that qualifications do not only relate to education, but that they are a combination of business and professional virtues and skills for performance of certain position.

Level of work performance includes complying with deadlines, quantity and quality of performance with reference to the job description in question. Length of service can also be used as one of the selection criteria.

3.24 Employers must be careful that what may appear as objective criteria do not inadvertently place groups of individuals with protected characteristics at a disadvantage (indirect discrimination).

3.25 In certain situations an employee may fall into a category protected by discrimination legislation. This could be because of religion, age or gender for instance. Where there is a risk that the employee may fall into a protected category, the employer must make sure that relevant evidence is in place to show that the real reason for the decision to dismiss is in fact legal and has nothing to do with the relevant protected characteristic.

3.26 The Code does not identify a procedure for how the selection has to be performed. In practice, the employer appoints a selection committee of three people in key positions who carry out the assessment to ensure that the criteria are applied lawfully.

Individual consultation

3.27 There is no obligation for the employer to consult individually with each affected employee. Employers are merely obliged to give 30 days' notice of termination to the affected employees unless the parties have agreed on a longer period although this cannot be longer than three months.

3.28 The following steps should be taken:

(1) the employer should send a notice of termination to each affected employee. The respective employment contract will be terminated upon expiry of the notice period with a confirmation of dismissal issued by the employer; and

(2) the employee has the right to challenge the legality of the dismissal. This may be done either to the employer or to the court and the employee may claim:
   - (a) that the dismissal is unlawful and ask for withdrawal of the dismissal;
   - (b) reinstatement of the previous employment;
   - (c) compensation for the period of unemployment due to the dismissal; or
   - (d) amendment of the stated grounds of dismissal.

3.29 The employer may at its own initiative withdraw its final decision to dismiss at any time up to the point at which the employee submits a claim to the court. In cases when advance permission from the Labour Inspectorate is a legal requirement for the dismissal to take effect (), and no such permission has been granted before the dismissal, the court will render the confirmation of dismissal as unlawful on this ground alone.

INVOLVEMENT OF EMPLOYEE REPRESENTATIVES

3.30 Enterprises with 50 employees or more as well as economically self-contained divisions of enterprises with 20 employees or more are required to inform and consult with employee representatives when considering carrying out redundancies.

ALTERNATIVE EMPLOYMENT

3.31 There is no general requirement for the employer offer alternative employment to employees affected by redundancies. However, employees who are disabled have special protection from redundancy and they have the right to be offered any other suitable, alternative employment under suitable conditions subject to health professionals' instruction. This instruction obliges the employer to stop the employee carrying out certain types of work and replace the tasks with other suitable work. The employer is obliged to transfer the employee to alternative, suitable employment pursuant to the health professionals' instructions within seven days of receipt of the instruction. An employer with more than 50 employees is obliged to assess on an annual basis which positions are suitable for disabled employees and must identify between 4% and 10% of positions out of the total number of employees depending on business sector.

OTHER CONSIDERATIONS

3.32 Companies should ensure that they also comply with any contractual provisions or any internal employment polices relating to redundancy.

Collective redundancy procedure

3.33 Under Bulgarian law a collective redundancy situation arises where an employer proposes to dismiss as redundant at least ten employees within a period of 30 days.

3.34 The regulation on collective redundancy under the Code complies with the requirements of EU Directive 75/129 and EU Directive 98/59 on the approximation of the laws of the Member States relating to collective redundancies.

3.35 In a collective redundancy situation, the employer has a duty to consult trade union representatives and employee representatives not later than 45 days before the collective dismissals are due to take effect with a view to reaching an agreement.

3.36 Where there is a collective redundancy, the employer must also notify the Employment Agency, part of the Bulgarian Ministry of labour and social policy.

INVOLVEMENT OF EMPLOYEE REPRESENTATIVES IN COLLECTIVE DISMISSALS

3.37 When dismissing employees it is important to establish whether there are any recognised trade unions and, if so, the scope of such recognition.

3.38 Employers may inform and consult with an existing body of employee representatives which has been elected by the employees to represent their common interests on issues connected with employment and social security relations, including issues in respect of collective redundancies.

ELECTION OF EMPLOYEE REPRESENTATIVES

3.39 Employee representatives are elected with a majority of more than two-thirds of the General Meeting's members. The General Meeting includes all employees in the enterprise. The General meeting is convened by the employer, or by the management of a trade union, and may also be called on the initiative of one-tenth of the employees in the enterprise. The meeting may go ahead if it is attended by more than half of the employees. Employee representatives are elected for a term of one to three years.

INFORMATION AND CONSULTATION REQUIREMENTS

3.40 The employer must provide the following information in writing to the trade union/employee representatives as part of the information stage:

(a) the reason(s) for the proposed redundancies;
(b) the number of employees to be dismissed and the principal economic activities, groups of professions and positions to which they belong;
(c) the number of employees employed in the principal economic activities, groups of professions and positions in the enterprise;
(d) the specific criteria for selecting employees proposed to be dismissed;
(e) the period over which the dismissals will take effect; and
(f) the redundancy payments that will be made to dismissed employees.

3.41 In all cases the employer is obliged to start consultation not later than 45 days before the dismissals takes effect and to try to reach agreement with the said representatives in order to avoid the proposed dismissals or reduce the numbers to be dismissed and mitigating the consequences of dismissal.

REGULATORY REQUIREMENTS

3.42 Where an employer intends to dismiss ten or more employees within a period of 30 days, a copy of the information provided during the consultations must be sent to the relevant department of the Employment Agency within three business days after providing the said information. The trade union/employee representatives may submit a written opinion to the relevant department of the Employment Agency, relating to the information provided in respect of collective redundancies. The proposed redundancies must not take effect any earlier than 30 days after notification of the Employment Agency regardless of the length of the required periods of notice. Failure to inform and consult on collective redundancies is an administrative offence punishable with a fine (currently a maximum of BGN 5,000).

SANCTIONS

3.43 If the employer fails to inform the Employment Agency on collective redundancies the trade union/employee representatives can complain to the General Labour Inspectorate. Failure to consult with appropriate representatives may also render a dismissal unlawful and entitle an individual employee to bring a claim for unlawful dismissal.

NOTICE

3.44 The Code sets out the required notice period. The notice period is the period of time between notifying the employee that his employment is coming to an end and the actual last day of employment.

Minimum notice period

3.45 The minimum required notice period under the Code is 30 days although the contract of employment may provide a longer notice period, but no more than three months in case of a permanent contract. In a collective bargaining agreement, in some cases the notice period may be determined in accordance with the employee's length service with the same employer. In case of termination of a fixed term contract, the notice period is three months but not more than the remaining term of the contract.

3.46 Employees have a right to work their notice period. The party entitled to terminate the contract with notice may terminate it before the expiry of the notice period subject to paying compensation to the other party for the amount of the employee's gross salary for the remaining term.

REDUNDANCY PAYMENT

3.47 Employees who are dismissed by reason of redundancy are entitled to a statutory redundancy payment. This payment is in addition to any notice pay or other statutory entitlement the employee may have under the Code.

Statutory redundancy

3.48 The amount of the redundancy payment, as specified by the Code, which is due to an employee is the employee's gross salary for the period of unemployment, up to one month. If the employee starts work during this month on a lower salary, then the employee shall be entitled to the difference for the same period. An act of the Council of Ministers, a collective bargaining agreement or employment contract may provide for a redundancy payment covering a longer period.

Payment for unused paid annual leave

3.49 Additional payment for unused paid annual leave is payable under the Code upon termination of employment contract regardless of the grounds of termination. Employees are entitled to payment for unused paid annual leave during a current calendar year in proportion to the length of employment service. In such case the employer pays to the employee a remuneration, calculated on the average daily gross salary received for the last calendar month during which the employee worked at least ten business days. If there is no month during which the employee has worked at least ten business days with the same employer then the payment shall be calculated on the basis of the gross monthly salary together with any additional permanent employment remunerations such as bonus.

Taxation of redundancy payments

3.50 Statutory redundancy payments are subject to tax under Taxes over Incomes of Individuals Law.

Post-termination restrictive covenants

3.51 The Code sets out the obligatory content required in employment contracts, which includes:

- workplace;
- position and type of work;
- date of its conclusion and beginning of its performance;
- term of contract;
- days of annual paid leave including any contractual paid annual leave in addition to statutory entitlement as per the Code
- equal length of notice period for both parties for termination of the contract;
- permanent basic and additional employment remunerations; and
- period for payment and working hours.

Other terms and conditions can be also negotiated under employment contracts which are not regulated by statutory provisions but purely contractual rights & obligations. Therefore, both parties may agree to include post-termination restrictive covenants for employees who could materially damage the employer's business by competing with the employer following termination of employment. The contents of such clauses depends on the will of parties who can determine what the restrictions after termination are and what the sanctions are if the employee breaches them.

BUSINESS SALE, OUTSOURCING/INSOURCING AND OFFSHORING

3.52 EC Directive 77/187 (as amended) aims to regulate the transfer of an undertaking by ensuring that terms and conditions of employment are maintained for the employees affected. This Directive has been implemented in the Bulgarian legislation. Another Directive which is implemented into the Bulgarian legislation is EC Directive 2001/23 on the approximation of the laws of the member states relating to the safeguarding of employee's rights in the event of transfers of undertakings, businesses or parts of undertakings or businesses. Under the Code, transfer of employment rights and obligations relating to transfer of staff to the new employer is possible in the following cases:

(a) merger of enterprises;
(b) merger by acquisition of one business by another;
(c) division of the activity of one enterprise into two or more separate entities;
(d) transfer of a self-contained part of business to another;
(e) change of legal form of business;
(f) change of business' owner; and
(g) transfer of activity from one business to another, including transfer of tangible assets.

In such cases of change of employer the employee's employment shall not be terminated.

RIGHT TO TERMINATE EMPLOYMENT CONTRACT WITHOUT NOTICE

3.53 In case of a business' reorganisation an employee is entitled to terminate the employment contract in writing without notice if working conditions with the new employer deteriorate substantially. In such case, where the employment contract is for an undefined term the employee is entitled to a payment of gross salary for the notice period; or in case of a fixed-term contract, the employee will be entitled to payment of damages for the actual loss suffered.

Information and consultation

3.54 Where employees are transferred from one employer to another, both the transferor and the transferee have duties to inform and consult with representatives of trade unions and employee representatives in relation to any of *either employers'* employees who may be affected by the transfer or by measures taken in relation to them.

DUTY TO INFORM

3.55 Employers are obliged to inform the representatives of their respective affected employees of:

(a) the proposed change and when the transfer is to take place;
(b) the reasons for the change;
(c) possible legal, economic and social implications of the transfer for the affected employees;

(d) the measures which the employer envisages to take, in relation to those affected employees, including such obligations to the employees in place before the transfer for which the transferee is liable in the event of merger or acquisition and change of legal form of business and in the remaining scenarios both the transferor and the transferee are jointly liable.

The employer-transferor and employer-transferee are obliged to provide this information in the two months before the transfer is to take place. If there are no trade unions and employee representatives, the employer must then provide the affected transferring employees with this information.

MEASURES AND DUTY TO CONSULT

3.56 Where any of the employers envisages any measures in relation to any affected transferring employees, the respective employer is obliged to start consultations in good time before the transfer takes effect and to make efforts to reach agreement with representatives of trade unions and employee representatives, concerning these measures. The Code sets out no definite timescale for consultation. The consultation must be notified 'in good time' to allow for any necessary consultation between the parties and the representatives to take place before the date of transfer.

EMPLOYER'S LIABILITY

3.57 The employer-transferor's rights and obligations connected with employment relationships, which arose before the transfer shall be transferred to the new employer-transferee.

Sanctions

Failure to inform and consult

3.58 If either employer fails to inform or consult in compliance with the statutory requirements, the trade union/employee representatives or the employees can file a complaint to the General Labour Inspectorate of a breach of employment legislation. Failure to inform on change of employer is an administrative offence punishable with a fine (currently a maximum of BGN 5,000).

WORKFORCE REDUCTION IN CONNECTION WITH SHARE SALE OR SHARE PURCHASE

3.59 If a sale of the shares of the business occurs then the identity of the employer does not change at all but only the identity of the shareholder changes.

3.60 In most cases such sale does not amount to a transfer as described above and employment relations are not affected at all. However, if the new owner (shareholder) wishes to restructure the workforce then any dismissals must fall under one of the lawful reasons permitted by the Code.

CHANGING EMPLOYMENT TERMS AND CONDITIONS

3.61 The Code generally prohibits the employer or employee from unilaterally changing the employment terms and conditions; however, there are exceptions (see 3.63). Where the employee is transferred to another job in the same enterprise without changing the specified place of work (for example: city location), position and amount of employee's gross salary this will not be considered as change of the employment contract. The Code sets out a legal definition of 'work place' which is a premise, room, facility or other territorially defined place in the enterprise where the employee performs its duties under the employment contract.

Mutually agreed changes

3.62 Pursuant to Bulgarian legislation the employment terms and conditions can be changed by mutual written consent between the employer and the employee for either a fixed term or permanently. From a legal point of view, any such amendment will only be contractually binding on the parties if there is a written agreement signed by both parties.

Unilateral changes

3.63 The Code sets out several exceptions where the employer unilaterally may change the terms and conditions of employment without an employee's agreement.

3.64 The employer may increase unilaterally the employee's wage. The Code allows such unilateral change because this is in employee's favour. However, the reverse action is prohibited per argument a contrario. The employer cannot unilaterally decrease the employee's salary.

3.65 The employer may change nature and place of work when the production so requires; in case of 'idle' and when insuperable reasons are in place.

(a) Lack of staff: If there are not enough resources for performance of important and/or urgent tasks in one part of the business, then the employer may temporarily assign employees from other parts of the business to perform such tasks, without their agreement, for a period of up to 45 days in a calendar year provided the affected department is located in the same town or area. In such cases, the temporary change must be in line with the employee's qualifications and regard must be had to any health conditions.

(b) In the event of a period of inactivity, where the workforce is in place but cannot work due to organisational or technical reasons (such as machine breakdown, lack of materials, problems with energy supply, etc.) the employer may temporarily assign the inactive employees to perform other work as outlined in the previous paragraph (a). The change must be effected subject to the employees' qualification and health condition.

(c) The employer may assign to the employees work of a different nature regardless of their qualification in case of insuperable reasons. These are the reasons beyond the employer's control. Such reasons can be natural disasters like fire, flood, earthquakes or industrial accidents, etc. The employer is allowed to make this change as long as it takes into account an employee's health condition.

3.66 If the needs of the business require it the employer may send the employee on a business trip outside of his permanent place of work but not for more than 30 calendar days continuously. In such a case the employer is entitled to send the employee to another town, different from the place of work initially negotiated in the employment contract. Business trips for periods longer than 30 calendar days are allowed only if mutual written consent of both parties is in place. The employer may only send pregnant employees, employees in advanced stage of in vitro treatment and mothers of children under three years of age on business trips *with their agreement.*

DISMISSING AND RE-ENGAGING EMPLOYEES ON NEW TERMS

3.67 Employers may dismiss the employees and offer re-employment on new terms if mutual consent to changes has not been achieved or where the employer is not entitled to unilaterally change the terms of employment. However, this approach carries with it an increased risk that the employees bring a claim for unlawful dismissal or the employees refuse to accept the new employment terms.

USING TEMPORARY STAFF

3.68 In a reorganisation situation the requirement for temporary staff may arise. Subject to the below restrictions, the employer may engage employees on fixed-term contracts.

Fixed-term contracts

3.69 Employers may decide to use fixed-term contracts only in the following cases:

(a) for a fixed period of three years for performance of temporary, seasonal or short-term work and activities, as well as for new employees of businesses in bankruptcy or in liquidation. As an exception, such a contract can be signed for a period of one year for works which have no temporary, seasonal or short-term nature. Such a contract can also be concluded for a shorter term upon the written request of the employee. The Code does not allow employers to use a fixed-term contract for other works and periods. In those cases, the contract shall be considered a permanent contract;
(b) when an individual is required for a specific project;
(c) for the replacement of an employee who is temporarily absent from work (for example an individual who replace employee on maternity leave);
(d) for working at a job through a tender , for the time until it is taken based on the competitive examination;
(e) for a defined mandate when such is stipulated by respective governmental body.

3.70 It should be noted that employees employed on fixed-term contracts have the same rights and obligations as, and are treated equally to, employees working on contracts for an undefined period. Accordingly, they cannot be put in a less favourable position than employees employed under permanent employment contracts.

RENEWAL OF FIXED-TERM CONTRACTS

3.71 Normally a fixed-term contract ends with expiry of the term or with completion of the specific work. A fixed-term contract will automatically be regarded as a permanent contract under the following conditions:

(a) the employee continues to work for five or more business days after the end of the term;
(b) there is no written opposition from the employer; and
(c) the position is otherwise vacant.

EMPLOYMENT CLAIMS

3.72 Employment claims are heard by a regional civil court within the local area of the defendant's registered residential address or the location where the employee usually works. Any appeals are made to a district civil court and then to the Supreme Court of Appeal. The Supreme Court of Appeal has certain limits in terms of the amount of claim which it may hear (over BGN 5,000 civil claim interest). Only in case of legal issues which contradicts the Supreme Court's case-law or decisions contradictory to the courts other decisions or related matters are considered important for the accurate application and development of the law can be appealed to the Supreme Court of Appeal.

3.73 The Code sets out one more option for the employee: to address the claim directly to the employer. In practice the employees tend to prefer to bring their claims to the competent court.

UNLAWFUL DISMISSAL

3.74 Under the Code employees are entitled to oppose the lawfulness of a dismissal and to claim:

(a) unlawful dismissal and annulment thereof;
(b) reinstatement to their previous positions;
(c) compensation for the period of unemployment due to dismissal; or
(d) revision of the grounds of dismissal which have been entered on the employee's service record or in other documents.

3.75 Employees have two months from the effective date of termination to bring a claim for unlawful dismissal to the competent court.

Remedies

3.76 If the competent court finds that the employee has been unfairly dismissed then it can order the employer to reinstate the individual and to revise the grounds of dismissal stated in his service record. The court also may order the employer to pay compensation.

3.77 Compensation for unlawful dismissal is made up of the amount of the employee's gross salary for a period of unemployment due to this dismissal but not for more than six months. If during the unemployment period the employee has worked in a lower-paid job then he will be entitled to be compensated for the difference between the wages. This right also applies to an employee who has been unlawfully transferred to another lower-paid job.

3.78 If an employee is reinstated into his old job by the courts but the employer refuses to allow him back into his job then the employer and any managers refusing him work will be jointly responsible and may face imprisonment of up to three years. Although the employee will be unable to carry out any work in such a case he will still be entitled to receive his gross salary from the day he makes himself available to re-start work and until the day the employer allows him to re-start his work.

The gross salary as the basis of calculation of compensation

3.79 The compensation is calculated based on the employee's gross salary received for the month preceding the month in which the grounds for claiming compensation have occurred *or* the last monthly gross wage was received by the employee. This amount of compensation shall apply unless an act of Council of Ministers, a collective bargaining agreement or the employment contract provide for a higher amount of compensation.

DISCRIMINATION

3.80 An employee may also bring a claim for discrimination in the Commission for Protection against Discrimination if he believes that the real reason for his selection for dismissal was because of one of the following protected characteristics: age; disability; gender reassignment; family status; race; religion or belief; sex; sexual orientation; personal and social status; education; citizenship; party affiliation; property status and any other characteristics, established in statute or in a treaty to which Republic of Bulgaria is a party. The Commission for Protection against Discrimination is an independent state authority responsible for ensuring compliance with protective legislation against discrimination.

3.81 Alternatively, the employee may address the discrimination claim directly to the regional civil court for a decision as to:

(a) whether there is discrimination;
(b) whether to order the defendant to stop the breach and to reinstate the situation before the breach, as well as to refrain from such breaches in the future;
(c) compensation for damages.

Remedies

3.82 Breaches of the legislation on protection against discrimination amount to administrative offences punishable with a fine (currently between BGN 250 and BGN 2,000).

3.83 The Commission for Protection against Discrimination may impose on the employer obligatory instructions for elimination of breaches of the discrimination legislation. Failure to comply with such instructions is an administrative offence punishable with a fine (currently between BGN 2,000 and BGN 10,000).

3.84 If the employee makes a claim in the competent court for compensation for injury to feelings then the court will determine such claim based on fairness. This determination depends on the facts, and usually involves an estimation of particular circumstances as to how serious the employer's discriminatory act is, which of the protected characteristics has been affected, etc.

MUTUALLY AGREED TERMINATION

3.85 An employer may wish to reach a mutually agreed termination with an employee rather than to dismiss the employee and risk employment court proceedings. The Code provides an opportunity for both parties to terminate the employment contract without a notice period by mutual consent in writing. Either party may offer to the other termination of the contract. The party receiving the offer is obliged to respond to the other within seven days of its receipt. Failure to inform the other party within that period will result in the offer being considered as rejected.

3.86 The Code states one more option for employers to terminate the employment contract subject to agreed compensation. In such cases only the employer may offer termination of the contract. If the employee fails to respond in writing within seven days then rejection of the offer shall be presumed. In case of agreement, the employer owes to the employee compensation for not less than the quadruple amount of the last received monthly gross salary, unless the parties agree on a higher amount of compensation. It should be noted that if the agreed compensation is not paid within one month of the date of termination of the employment contract, the termination grounds shall be presumed lapsed and the employee is entitled to recommence work on the same terms with entitlement to salary for the period which has passed in the meantime.

PRE-TERMINATION DISCUSSIONS

3.87 Pre-termination discussions initiated by the employer are possible during the process of termination. However, such discussions, their form, duration and influence on the overall termination process are not regulated by the Code. As a consequence such negotiations shall not be treated as binding and if the employee consents to termination during negotiations then he may still refuse to accept the written offer for termination of the employer.

Chapter 4

Workforce Restructuring in Croatia

Dora Gaži Kovačević, Ana Grubešić, Jelena Orlić and Ira Perić Ostojić
Wolf Theiss, Zagreb

INTRODUCTION

4.1 This chapter looks at the overall impact of restructuring under Croatian employment law, rules and practice. The legal system in Croatia is a civil law system and part of the European continental jurisdictions. The law is generally codified in a systematic way and fully harmonised with EU law. Employment law consists of a comprehensive employment act and secondary legislation. In addition, there is extensive case law offering interpretations of the codified law. There is a common principle equally applied in all cases that employment rules and terms of employment will predominantly be interpreted in favour of the employees. This principle represents somewhat slippery ground for employers, as it may lead to an unequal position in a dispute, with the employer often being viewed as the 'bad guy'.

4.2 Prior to making any decisions on individual or collective termination of employees in restructuring situations, the employer should always assess whether there is an additional layer of protection besides the one offered by the law. Generally, statutory provisions provide for default minimum employment protections that automatically apply unless there is a contractual agreement, an employer internal by-law or a collective agreement that offers more favourable terms for employees in respect of applicable notice periods, severance payments or any other termination right.

4.3 Under Croatian law there is no concept of 'employment at will' and an employer may unilaterally terminate an employment contract only if it has a legitimate reason under the law. In restructuring exercises it is considered that such a legitimate reason exists when the need for the performance of specific work ceases due to certain economic, technical or organisational reasons. In order to minimise the risk of employment tribunal claims, the employer also needs to follow the termination procedure set out by the law. All things considered, any business restructuring process should be carefully structured, budgeted and implemented in close cooperation with the employees and their representatives.

PREPARING FOR A RESTRUCTURING EXERCISE

4.4 The scope, budget and desired effects of any workforce restructuring exercise need to be carefully considered and planned in advance. This is to minimise the risk of different undesired issues that can come up along the way.

Identifying the employing entity

4.5 It is clear that the employer that entered into the employment contract is the one that can also terminate it.

4.6 Things may get confusing when we look at the structure of 'a group' that may involve several companies whose employees interlink in performing employment tasks. Although business decisions in such a scenario are usually delivered at the group level, any workforce restructuring and/or decision on dismissal has to be made and documented in each company separately.

Example

Company A is a parent company to companies B and C. Each of the companies have accounting departments that in company A consists of one senior accountant and in each of the companies B and C of 1 junior accountant. A business decision was passed at group level that only the accounting department in company A will be kept and that in addition to 1 senior accountant a junior accountant will be hired. The accountants in companies B and C were dismissed.

The accountants in companies B and C have a remedy only against their employing company. When hiring a junior accountant in company A, company A has no statutory obligation to consider or offer employment to the dismissed accountants from companies B and C.

IDENTIFYING THE EMPLOYEE

4.7 Only employees should be included in the workforce restructuring exercise.

4.8 Determination of individuals who fall within the legal definition of an 'employee' and thus enjoy protection against unlawful dismissal should not represent a difficult task. Generally, employees are employed under an employment contract while other non-employees are engaged by the company based on a service agreement (for example, translators and various other kinds of different advisors).

4.9 It is the content of the contract, rather than its name, that matters. An individual is considered to be an employee if the important elements of the employment relationship (such as monthly salary, permanent work tasks, work under the direction of an employer, entitlement to holidays) are included in a contract irrespective of what the parties call that contract (for instance, consultancy or service agreement).

4.10 Special attention should be given to the statutory directors. In general, statutory directors do not enjoy the same level of protection as the other employees unless their employment contracts specifically provide for such rights. In other words, protective termination provisions that also include the right to notice periods, severance payment and the prohibition of termination for no cause do not automatically apply to the employment contracts of statutory directors unless specifically agreed.

RESTRUCTURING PLAN AND BUDGET

4.11 At the outset of any restructuring exercise, it is important to collect all the data and to put together a restructuring plan that will determine the scope of the restructuring process. The restructuring plan should primarily include an analysis of the grounds for restructuring, indications of the work positions that will be affected by the restructuring, and information on the employees being considered for dismissal. Relevant information related to the impacted work positions and workforce is usually held by the HR or accounting department.

4.12 It is also important to gather relevant information regarding the involved costs in order to put together a realistic restructuring budget.

4.13 Budgeting may be time-consuming as it involves the creation of various scenarios and analysis of related costs. This is usually done by the HR department and external advisors with the significant involvement of the company's management or other decision makers. Employers should be aware of the 'golden rule' – the higher the budget, the lower the risk of employment tribunal claims.

4.14 In practice, a significant number of potential restructuring exercises end here. If a cost/benefit analysis is based on realistic assumptions including also a worst-case scenario, employers are often surprised that restructuring does not necessarily deliver the desired significant cost savings.

4.15 As any (more serious) restructuring should not happen too often, an analysis of the post-restructuring effects should also be included in the restructuring plan, including also the efficiency and productivity of the company's remaining workforce in the long run.

> **Practical Tip**
>
> The following data about the affected employees should be gathered:
>
> - place of work and work tasks;
> - length of service (overall and with the current employer);
> - age;
> - family support obligations (including number and age of children and other dependent family members);
> - contractual benefits;
> - relevant rules under the applicable work bylaws or collective agreement (if any); and
> - other information relevant to determine if the employee enjoys special protection against dismissal (see paras **4.38** and **4.46** below).

WORKFORCE REDUCTION BASED ON BUSINESS REASONS

4.16 The concept of 'employment at will' is not applicable under Croatian law. Generally, if a mutual termination is not reachable, the employer may only serve a termination notice for business reasons.

4.17 Our experience shows that in the restructuring process very few mutual termination agreements are reached. The majority of employment contracts are terminated by serving a termination notice due to business reasons.

4.18 Although entering into mutual termination agreements is the most flexible option, there are also certain drawbacks – employer's tax benefits and employee's unemployment benefits are lost, which makes the mutual termination more expensive and less attractive to both parties. For more information on mutual termination agreements please see the section starting at para **4.157** below.

4.19 In the structuring phase of restructuring, employers should especially be aware of the statutory prohibition against new employment for the same working position within six months following the service of a termination notice to an employee holding that position due to business reasons. If within the six-month time limit the need arises for employing an employee to perform the same work, the employer is under the obligation to offer the job to the dismissed employee. For failing to observe these rules the employer may be fined an amount ranging from HRK 31,000–60,000 (approx €4,000–8,000).

4.20 Fixed-term employment contracts may be terminated due to business reasons by the employer but only if early termination is provided for by the employment contract itself. For more information on fixed-term contracts please see the section starting at para **4.139** below.

DEFINITION OF A LEGITIMATE 'BUSINESS REASON' FOR DISMISSAL

4.21 In order to lawfully dismiss an employee in the restructuring scenario, the employer must be able to show the existence of legal reasons for dismissal. The statutory definition of 'a dismissal due to business reasons' provides that:

> 'The employer may terminate the employment contract if there is a justified reason such as a reduced need for the employee to perform certain work due to economic, technological or organisational reasons and subject to complying with statutory or contractual notice periods (ordinary dismissal).'

ECONOMIC REASONS

4.22 Dismissals due to economic reasons are generally caused by circumstances that the employer could not influence and that negatively affect the employer's business. Consequently, an employee's dismissal justified by economic reasons is usually attributable to closure of the entire business (or part thereof) or relocation of the business.

4.23 Examples of valid grounds for dismissals justified by economic reasons include:

- non-profitability of certain business activities due to the opening of the market to competitors;
- reduced business volume caused by a reduction in sales;
- loss of a licence resulting in the termination of operations conducted under licence.

4.24 We have seen in the past few years that most of the restructuring processes and related dismissals were successfully justified on the basis of the global financial crisis or the impact of Croatia's entry to the EU on the employer's business.

TECHNOLOGICAL REASONS

4.25 The introduction of more efficient equipment and technology in a company should result in a company's better performance. However, it also usually causes a number of workers to become redundant. Such reasons are recognised as technical reasons for dismissal.

ORGANISATIONAL REASONS

4.26 Dismissals due to organisational reasons are usually justified with the employer's right to improve the efficiency and productivity of the workforce, and to make certain organisational changes in the company that may include termination or reorganisation of certain work positions or departments. In practice, organisational changes in a company as a result of a merger of companies are recognised as legitimate reasons for dismissal.

Examples of dismissals due to business reasons

1 Exclusive Cars Limited was one of the market leaders in the sale of luxury vehicles. In 2009, sales dropped and Exclusive Cars Limited was forced to dismiss ten employees on economic grounds. Since the dismissals were challenged before the court, the court analysed the documentation provided by the company that clearly evidenced that a smaller number of cars had been sold and what impact that had on the company's profitability. Consequently, the dismissals were found to be lawful.

2 Watches Limited, a retail chain selling sports watches justified the dismissal given to an employee with economic arguments (financial difficulties). The court, however, found such dismissal to be unlawful as Watches Limited had employed three new employees shortly after the dismissal. One employment contract even indicated that a new employee was hired due to an increased amount of work.

OTHER REASONS IN A RESTRUCTURING SCENARIO

4.27 In addition to dismissal for business reasons, the opening of insolvency proceedings against the employer represents a separate valid reason for dismissal. No particular procedure, apart from applying a 30-day notice period, must be observed.

IMPLEMENTING THE RESTRUCTURING PLAN

4.28 When companies are planning to dismiss employees based on business reasons they must bear in mind two procedures: the Individual Dismissal Procedure and the Collective Dismissal Procedure. The Individual Dismissal Procedure must always be followed when dismissing employees on grounds of business reasons.

4.29 In addition, when planning to dismiss 20 or more employees within a 90-day period, and the dismissal of at least five of those employees is due to business reasons, employers are required to also follow the Collective Dismissal Procedure as set out in the section starting at para 4.50.

Individual Dismissal Procedure

4.30 Where a legitimate reason for dismissal exists, the employer must also follow a statutory termination procedure which mainly requires that the employees who are proposed to be dismissed due to business reasons are selected fairly, and that consultation is conducted or approval requested from the employee representatives, as the case may be.

DEFINING THE SELECTION POOL

4.31 After identifying the work positions that are no longer required, the employer needs to identify the group of employees who will be affected by the restructuring based on justifiable business-related reasons.

4.32 In situations where employers plan the closure of an entire business or department, identification of a selection pool is obvious. The challenge, however, is to make a selection pool in situations where the employer intends to reduce the number of the workforce that performs the same or a similar task. In practice, employees often challenge dismissals, claiming that the employer should have identified a wider selection pool. It is, therefore, vital that prior to making a decision on dismissal, the employer understands the tasks employees perform on a daily basis, instead of only reading job descriptions. Employers should carefully examine all similar work positions within the entire company. If there is an opening for a comparable work position in another department or even at another location within the company, the employer should offer that opening to the redundant employee.

Example:

A bank operates at two locations that are located close to one another. Each location employs two administrators. It was decided that one administrator per location would be dismissed.

Since a similar job is performed at both locations, the bank needs to include all four employees in the selection pool. The same reasoning would apply if the bank would decide to completely close down one location.

SELECTION CRITERIA

4.33 After determining the selection pool, the employer will need to evidence that each dismissal was based on rational and objective considerations by fairly applying specific criteria to all employees within the selection pool.

4.34 Certain social criteria are set out which the employer must apply if it employs more than 20 employees. These are:

- the duration of the employment contract (overall and with the current employer);
- the employee's age; and
- family support obligations.

4.35 In addition, the employer has a discretionary right to apply additional selection criteria, such as performance, experience, skills, quality of work, responsiveness, punctuality, etc.

4.36 Although the employer has an autonomous right to determine which of the above criteria it will give priority, its final decision should be based on objective criteria and not be influenced by its personal opinion. To the extent possible, the employer should be capable of backing up its decision with evidence, for example personnel records. This is especially important in case of dismissal of employees who are protected by anti-discrimination legislation (for example, belonging to a certain gender, religion or ethnic group).

Example:

Construction Limited employs two accountants. The Senior Accountant is 50 years old with 31 years of working experience, has one child and an ongoing divorce proceeding. The Junior Accountant is 42 years old with 15 years of working experience and no children. Construction Limited dismisses the Senior Accountant due to business reasons.

The court found that such dismissal was unlawful, as the employer did not consider (or at least did not prove that it considered) the mandatory social or any other criteria.

4.37 In order to easily document the fair and objective application of selection criteria, employers should use a score sheet to compare employees identified in the selection pool. Employees may also be given the opportunity to comment and challenge the scores. That may be an opportunity for the employer to rethink its decision and to timely prevent future court claims.

SCORING MATRIX FOR THE EMPLOYEES (EXAMPLE)

Name of employee	Criteria	Score	Weighting factor	Total	Notes by manager to justify scoring	Total score
	Years of service		*1*		This assessment should be verifiable on account of information held in the personnel file.	
	Employee's age		*1*		This assessment should be verifiable on account of information held in the personnel file.	
Employee 1	Family support obligations		*2*		This assessment should be verifiable on account of information held in the personnel file – number of children, age of children, number of household members, other family support obligations, etc.	*X*
	Skills/ qualification/ training		*3*		Set out details of employee's skills, qualifications and training necessary to be successful in the job long-term.	
	Performance Assessment (Year)		*3*		This assessment should be verifiable on account of previous performance reviews.	

SCORING OF LISTED CRITERIA

Employee's age				
1 = 18–30	*2 = 30–40*	*3 = 40–50*	*4 = 50–60*	*5 = > 60*
Years of service				
1 = < 5	*2 = 5–10*	*3 = 10–20*	*4 = 20–30*	*5 = > 30*
Other criteria				
1 = Poor	*2 = Below average*	*3 = Average*	*4 = Good*	*5 = Excellent*

PROHIBITION OF DISMISSAL

4.38 Certain categories of employees enjoy special protection against dismissal that includes a complete prohibition of dismissal. The following categories of employees may not be dismissed under any grounds whatsoever (except for business reasons in the case of a formal liquidation process of the employer):

- pregnant women;
- employees on maternity or parental leave;
- parents or adoptive parents exercising the statutory right to part-time working hours;
- employees on adoption leave or leave for taking care of a child with serious developmental disorders.

The protection of these employees extends to 15 days from the end of the pregnancy or from the completion of their exercising the other rights.

4.39 In addition, an employee who has suffered an injury at work or has contracted an occupational illness which affect their ability to work may not be dismissed for as long as he/she is temporarily unable to work due to medical treatment or recovery.

INVOLVEMENT OF EMPLOYEE REPRESENTATIVES IN INDIVIDUAL DISMISSALS

4.40 Before implementation of the restructuring exercise, the employer should determine if employee representatives (workers' council or trade union representative) have been nominated within the company. If so, the employer should always consult with the employee representatives prior to any dismissal and obtain prior approval in case of dismissal of certain categories of employees.

4.41 If the employer employs more than 20 employees, a workers' council may be established. Generally, employees are free to decide if they will establish a workers' council or not. If no workers' council has been established or if the employer employs less than 20 employees, a trade union, if active within the employer, may still appoint its representative in the company. Generally, employees are free to join any appropriate trade union and in that case, trade unions usually appoint one or more of their representatives working for the employer who assume the same rights and obligations as the workers' council.

DUTY TO CONSULT

4.42 The employer must consult the employee representatives about the planned dismissals in advance. Employee representatives should be presented with all relevant information regarding the restructuring plan and planned dismissals, including:

- reasons for the intended dismissals;
- total number of employees;
- number, qualifications, occupation and workplace of employees who are likely to be affected;
- criteria used when determining the selection pool;
- amount and method of calculation of the statutory severance payment and other additional benefits;
- measures and efforts taken in order to mitigate harmful consequences (such as practical efforts to introduce changes in technology and work organisation, reassignment of work positions, alternative employment, reduction of working hours, etc).

4.43 Consultations with the employee representatives should not be conducted as a mere formality, but as a constructive discussion in which the employer will evaluate the proposals of the employee representatives aimed at reducing the number of redundant employees and mitigating harmful consequences of dismissal.

4.44 In order for the consultation to be considered fair and meaningful, the employer should ensure that the consultation takes place when the proposal of dismissal due to business reasons is still at a formative stage. The employee representatives must be given sufficient information and time to respond to the proposal and the employer should carefully consider any response or suggestion which the workers' council or trade union representative puts forward.

4.45 The employee representatives should give their opinion within eight working days. However, a lack of response or a negative response will not prevent the employer from proceeding with the restructuring plan and planned dismissals.

DUTY TO OBTAIN PRIOR APPROVAL

4.46 The employer needs to request prior approval from the employee representatives in order to terminate the contract of the following individual employees:

- a member of the workers' council or trade union representative;
- a candidate for the workers' council who was not elected, or a member of the electoral committee, for a period of three months following the determination of the election results;
- an employee with an occupational disability to work or in immediate danger of disability;
- an employee over 60 years of age;
- an employee acting as an employee representative on the supervisory board.

4.47 If the employee representatives are silent on the employer's request for eight days, it shall be deemed they have consented to the employer's decision. In case the employee representatives deny their approval, the employer may, within 15 days from the receipt of the refusal, request that the approval process is replaced by arbitration.

FAILURE TO CONSULT OR OBTAIN PRIOR APPROVAL

4.48 Failure to consult or seek prior approval from the employee representatives on the contemplated dismissal may trigger a fine for the employer in the amount ranging from HRK 31,000–60,000 (€4,000–7,800).

4.49 In addition to fines, failure to inform and consult with the employee representative makes the decision on dismissal null and void.

Collective dismissal procedure

4.50 The collective dismissal procedure is triggered if the employer intends to terminate the employment contracts of more than 20 employees in a period of 90 days and at least five of such employees are terminated due to business reasons. In such a scenario, apart from the general obligation to consult the employee representatives or obtain their prior approval (for details please see paras **4.40–4.49** above), the employer needs to inform the Croatian Employment Service of the restructuring process.

4.51 Only employees whose employment is terminated based on mutual agreement initiated by the employer or due to business reasons are counted in the statutory threshold of 20 employees. All other forms of termination of the employment contract (such as alternative employment or termination for cause) do not count towards this threshold.

4.52 In practice, employers consider the following options when trying to avoid collective dismissal requirements:

- termination of less than 20 employees in any 90-day period; and
- termination of less than five employees due to business reasons (eg, by having employees terminated based on mutual agreement).

REGULATORY REQUIREMENTS

4.53 The employer needs to inform the Employment Service about the planned collective dismissal process. In addition to the documentation presented to the employee representatives, the employer must inform the Employment Service on the duration, results and conclusion of the performed consultations and the employee representatives' opinion on the collective dismissal procedure.

4.54 Another important deadline to bear in mind is the 30-day period (as from delivery of all the necessary information to the Employment Service) during which the employment contracts should not be terminated.

4.55 The Employment Service will closely examine the restructuring process and may make an order that implementation of the collective dismissal shall be postponed, either entirely or in part, but for a period not exceeding 30 days from the date of the order. In such case, the employer is not allowed to terminate the employment of any employee covered by the Employment Service's order. However, the Employment Service may not prohibit or object to the collective dismissal. In practice, the Employment Service rarely postpones the collective dismissal process if all the statutory requirements have been observed and complied with.

AVOIDING COMPULSORY DISMISSALS

4.56 As part of the restructuring exercise, employers should also consider alternatives to dismissal. However, such alternatives are possible only with the approval of employees as the terms and conditions of employment may be amended only by mutual agreement, ie, with the consent of both employer and employee.

4.57 In practice, the following restructuring alternatives have proven to be effective and economically feasible for employers:

- introduction of part-time work;
- reduction of salaries and bonuses;
- recruitment freezes;
- engagement of students and volunteers;
- unpaid vacation or sabbaticals;
- early retirements;
- inviting volunteers for termination;
- offering alternative employment to affected employees.

For more details on changing the terms of employment, please see the section starting at para **4.126**.

Alternative employment

4.58 As part of the restructuring process, the employer may also consider alternative employment within its organisation for the employee likely to be affected by the dismissals and offer the employee an amended employment contract. The employer, however, has no obligation to create alternative employment.

4.59 In case the employee is not willing to reach an agreement with the employer and accept the new employment conditions, he/she would still be considered for dismissal due to business reasons.

4.60 Alternatively, the employer may serve the employee with a termination notice for the existing job role, but also offer re-employment on new terms. The employer, however, should be particularly aware of the fact that even when the employee accepts a re-employment offer, he/she may still challenge the termination of his/her previous employment contract. Should the employee decide to challenge the dismissal from his/her previous employment, the court would not look into the appropriateness of the new employment, but would only examine the legitimate reasons for dismissal from the previous position.

4.61 By offering such alternative employment, the employer may reduce the number of dismissals due to business reasons. Employees who have accepted alternative employment are not taken into account when counting the required statutory minimum number of 20 redundant employees for triggering the requirement of a collective dismissal procedure.

4.62 Any offer of suitable alternative employment should be presented to the employee before the final decision as to the workforce to be dismissed due to business reasons is communicated. The employee should be made familiar with the differences between the employee's current rights and obligations and the proposed ones in a clear and unconditional way, and should be given a minimum eight-day period to consider the offer. If the employee declines the offer, he/she would still be entitled to the notice period, severance payment and other rights in case of dismissal as explained in the section starting at para **4.144**.

State Aid Schemes in Restructuring

4.63 New financial aid schemes have been introduced in order to preserve jobs and stimulate employment. Two different types of aid are available: aid for subsidising salary during a necessary reduction of working hours; and aid for education and training of employees. Both aids may be used by employers facing a temporary reduction in business activity and/or which have had a negative financial result in the previous financial year, provided that they have paid their taxes and contributions and adopted a job preservation plan in cooperation with the employee representatives.

4.64 The aid/subsidy available to fund a reduction in salary as a result of reduction in working hours enables employers to cut the standard total of 40 working hours per week by up to 16 hours. As a result, employees are still paid as if they work full time hours. Employers are subsidised in respect of the portion of the salary which represents the reduced hours, however capped at the minimum permitted monthly salary (€400). This aid can be used for up to 12 months within a three-year period. This solution represents a notable departure from the general framework for changing the duration of the work week set out by the labour regulation and provides a considerable margin of flexibility for employers to accommodate their business situation.

4.65 The aid available for supporting education and training of employees enables employers to, for what is called 'justified reasons', organise subsidised training sessions for up to 25% of their employees whose services in specific positions are no longer required. As these reasons are not specified, the competent authorities will have to establish the qualifying circumstances (the scheme was introduced recently so there is no available practice as yet). During the training, employees would be absent from work but would still receive their full salary from their employer. Employers would be subsidised for a portion of employees' salaries corresponding to the amount of aid paid by the state. As this amount is equal to regular unemployment aid, which is determined by a variable formula, the amount of aid payable by the state may be determined only by looking into the specific status of each employee. The employer may use this type of aid only once for up to six months per employee.

4.66 Using either type of aid imposes certain restrictions on the employer, who will not be allowed to: (i) hire new employees for work that can be performed by the employees for whom the aid is used; (ii) order overtime work for employees who perform the same duties in the same department as the employees for whom the aid is used; and (iii) pay bonuses or other types of incentives to management and supervisory board members.

4.67 Furthermore, employers applying for either type of aid must agree not to terminate the employees for whom they receive aid for a period of time equal to one half of the period for which the aid was provided (certain exceptions to the rule exist). Finally, both types of aid cannot be used at the same time for the same employees.

4.68 The authority for awarding the aid is the Employment Service and the application procedure is simple.

4.69 Interestingly, even if an employee has more favourable employment rights (such as additional benefits or extra days of holiday) than the minimum level provided for in the labour regulations (for instance, by employment contract, work by-laws, or a collective agreement), the use of these aids will replace the more favourable rights by the statutory minimum level. Not only is this provision in stark contrast with domestic case law which generally favours the employees, but it may also be used as a tool for employers to decrease the level of employment rights of their employees without their consent. If its use becomes widespread there will certainly be pressure to amend this provision in the future.

TERMINATION NOTICE

Notice period

4.70 The notice period describes the period of time between notifying the employee of his/her termination of employment and the actual last day of employment. The notice period must be observed and either worked by the employee or spent on garden leave. For details of garden leave please see paras 4.78–4.81 below.

Minimum notice period

4.71 The minimum notice period by law applies unless a more beneficial scheme to the employees is provided for under an employment contract, employer's bylaws or a collective agreement. The minimum statutory notice periods are set out below.

Length of Service	Notice period
Less than 1 year	2 weeks
1 year to 2 years	1 month
2 to 5 years	1 month and 2 weeks
5 to 10 years	2 months
10 to 20 years	2 months and 2 weeks
20 years and more	3 months – for employees under the age of 50
	3 months and 2 weeks – for employees aged 50 to 55
	4 months – for employees aged 55 or above

4.72 The notice period is deferred during:

(i) pregnancy;
(ii) maternal/parental/adoptive leave;
(iii) shorter working hours due to enhanced child care;
(iv) temporary inability to work due to receiving medical care or recovering from a work injury or occupational disease; or
(v) performing military defence duties.

4.73 The notice period is generally deferred during a temporary inability to work (on grounds other than under para 4.72(iv) above), but not unconditionally. If temporary inability to work occurred after the employee had been served with a termination notice, the employment will in any event terminate within six months following receipt of the termination notice at the latest. The temporary inability to work does not suspend the notice period at all if the employee is placed on garden leave after being served with a termination notice (unless otherwise agreed by collective agreement, an employment contract or the employer's bylaws).

4.74 During the notice period, employees are entitled to a four hours paid leave per week for the purposes of seeking new employment.

4.75 The employee may not waive the right to the notice period or agree with the employer to shorten the notice period in advance. He/she may do so only after being served with a termination notice.

4.76 Employers must carefully monitor the expiry of the notice period, as they are under the obligation to deregister the dismissed employees from the relevant pension and health care registries within a very short period of time, ie, within 24 hours from expiry of the notice period.

4.77 Employers must ensure the employees have used all of their holiday entitlement before the expiry of the notice period. Otherwise, unused holiday entitlement must be compensated. If not otherwise agreed, compensation amounts to the average salary during the last three months in proportion to the unused vacation days. As the notice period regularly runs during vacation, there is no obstacle for the employees to use their unused vacation even during the notice period.

Garden leave

4.78 Employers may prefer to have the employee leave the workplace immediately after dismissal so as to avoid or minimise further disruption to the workforce following a restructuring exercise. In such a situation the employer may place the employee on 'garden leave', meaning the employee does not attend work for the duration of the notice period. Pay in lieu of notice is not possible under Croatian law.

4.79 Garden leave does not affect the obligation of the employer to pay the salary and provide the employee with all other statutory and contractual benefits as if the employee had worked the entire notice period. If the employer decides to place an employee on garden leave, such a clause must be included in the termination notice. A garden leave clause does not need to be provided for in the employment contract.

4.80 The purpose of a garden leave clause is to prevent the employee from working for a competitor or setting up his/her own business (and in both cases taking the best customer contacts from the employer) by keeping the employee employed during the notice period, although he/she is kept away from the workplace and no work is given to him/her to perform. Garden leave is commonly used to prevent employees from gathering and using up-to-date information as well as to give the employee's successor (if any) or colleagues some time to contact customers and establish themselves before the employee sets himself/herself up with a competitor. Garden leave may also be used to prevent dismissed employees from encouraging other employees to leave.

4.81 In short, an employee remains employed during the notice period but is not allowed to work, attend the workplace or contact customers. A garden leave clause is often used together with post-termination restrictive covenant clauses to ensure maximum protection for the employer's business. For further information please see the post-termination restrictive covenants section below starting at para **4.88**.

Type of Notice Period	*Effective Date of Termination*	*Benefits*	*Disadvantages*
Employee working the notice period	Upon expiry of the notice period.	Employer gets value from the employee in terms of work during the notice period.	Employee may be disruptive to colleagues or may gather and copy confidential data from the workplace.
Garden Leave	Upon expiry of the notice period.	The employee is prevented from working elsewhere. Coupled with post-termination restrictive covenants, the employer has the maximum protection possible.	The employer gets no value in terms of work from the employee during the notice period. The employee remains entitled to a salary and all other statutory and contractual benefits.

SEVERANCE PAYMENT

4.82 An employee, whose employment contract is terminated by the employer due to business reasons after a minimum of two years of continuous service is entitled to a statutory severance payment. The amount of statutory severance payment depends on the length of service with that particular employer. The employee's collective length of service with the current and prior employers or years of age are of no relevance.

4.83 The employer is under no obligation to pay a severance payment if a contract is terminated for cause or under a mutual termination agreement.

Statutory severance pay calculation

4.84 The minimum statutory severance payment amounts to one third of an average monthly gross salary paid to the employee in the last three months of service, multiplied by the number of years working for the employer. The overall severance amount may not exceed an amount equal to six of such average monthly gross salaries, unless agreed differently in a collective agreement, an employment contract, the employer's by-laws or if it is imposed by the law.

Example:

Mr Horvat has been dismissed from Minas LLC. He was employed by the company for eight years and his average monthly gross salary, prior to the day he was dismissed due to business reasons, was HRK 9,000.

Mr Horvat is entitled to a minimum statutory severance pay in the amount of 1/3 of his average monthly gross salary in the last three months, which amounts to HRK 3,000.

Such amount is multiplied by the number of years Mr Horvat has worked for the company, eight years, which equals a statutory severance pay in the amount of HRK 24,000.

The calculated amount is tax free, since it does not surpass the statutory maximum amount of HRK 51,200 (HRK 6,400 per year). For further details on statutory severance pay taxation see paras **4.86** and **4.87** below.

Enhanced severance payments

4.85 A separate law, collective agreement, employment contract or the employer's bylaws may provide for a higher severance payment than the minimum statutory amounts.

Taxation of severance payments

4.86 Severance payments are subject to tax only to a certain extent. A severance payment up to HRK 6,400 (€850) multiplied by the number of years of service is tax free. The amount surpassing the above threshold is treated as salary from the tax perspective and thus subject to relevant contributions, tax and local surtax.

4.87 Severance payments agreed on and paid out under mutual termination agreements are fully taxed, regardless of the amount.

Post-termination restrictive covenants

4.88 The employer should consider contractual post–termination restrictive covenants for key employees who could cause material damage to the business by competing with the employer post-termination, either by working for a competitor or setting up his/her own business. Such non-compete clauses may be included in an employment contract or in a separate agreement. They may also be provided for under the mutual termination agreement.

4.89 The employer and employee may agree in writing on a certain period of time post-termination during which the employee may not be employed with another employer or undertake any business activities that are competitive with the employer. A maximum non-compete period is limited by the law to two years. Non-compete clauses must be tailored carefully to each business. They should only cover what is strictly necessary for the employer to protect its legitimate business interests and should not unreasonably limit the work and professional progress of the employee. Otherwise, the employer will not be able to enforce such a clause and will remain unprotected. As a result, restrictions are better drafted slightly narrower in scope to minimise the risk of them being unenforceable by the employer.

4.90 The employee is under an obligation to observe a non-compete clause if the employer pays compensation during the non-compete period. The minimum non-compete compensation amounts to one half of the average monthly salary paid to the employee in the last three months of the employee's service. In case of breach, the employer may enforce the non-compete clause against the employee (ie, request the non-compete clause to be observed) and request to be compensated for the full damages incurred.

4.91 As the enforcement of a non-compete clause may prove to be rather difficult, particularly given lengthy court proceedings are often a given, alternative of contractual penalty clauses are more commonly used in practice.

4.92 Payment of a monthly non-compete compensation may be avoided by agreeing to the alternative option of a contractual penalty in the event of a breach. In such case, the employer is restricted to demanding payment only in accordance with the agreed contractual penalty rate, even where the full amount of damage incurred exceeds that rate. Further the employer will be prevented from enforcing the non-compete clause against the employee.

4.93 The employer may decide to opt out from the non-compete clause at any time during the non-compete period by a written notification to the employee. The obligation of the employer to pay compensation to the employee remains for the period of three months following such notification.

4.94 Minors or employees receiving less than the average gross salary as per the published by the State Statistics Office of the Republic of Croatia are protected and may not be bound by such restrictive non-compete clauses.

4.95 Non-compete clauses are commonly used with garden leave which when combined provide the employer with maximum protection from possible negative consequences of dismissal.

Practical Tip

The amount of the contractual penalty must be set out carefully, in proportion to the value and effect of the non-compete clause. Otherwise, if set unreasonably high, the court may revise and reduce such amount.

BUSINESS SALE, OUTSOURCING/INSOURCING AND OFFSHORING

4.96 The Acquired Rights Directive ('ARD'), EC Directive 77/187 (as further amended), aims at 'the approximation of the laws of the Member States relating to the safeguarding of employee rights in the event of transfers of undertakings, businesses or parts of businesses'. The ARD is implemented into Croatian law by way of Article 137 of the Labour Act ('Article 137'). Article 137 essentially protects an individual's employment in the event that the undertaking for which he/she works is transferred to a new employer.

4.97 More practically, Article 137 may apply where a business or part of a business – as a going concern – is sold or otherwise transferred (by way of a corporate change or transaction), such may typically be the outsourcing or insourcing of a subsidiary activity of the company's main business. Article 137 does not apply to a change of ownership by way of a transfer of shares, limited assets and/or equipment to a different owner.

4.98 The key effects of Article 137 are:

- the employment of affected employees automatically transfers to the new employer;
- continuity of employment regardless of any change in ownership;
- the automatic transfer of employment rights, obligations and liabilities relating to transfer of employees to the new employer;
- the obligation to inform and consult with employee representatives; and
- protection of employees from dismissal due to such transfer.

Business sale

4.99 To determine whether or not a business sale constitutes a transfer of existing employees under Article 137, it should be assessed if an undertaking or, business activity or any part of such undertaking/business activity in whole or in part is affected by the transfer maintains its economic integrity post transfer. Due to the lack of Croatian case law, the ARD and relevant decisions of the European Court of Justice should apply as an interpretative guideline for the Croatian courts. The ARD defines the transfer of an economic entity as one which retains its identity, meaning an organised grouping of resources which has the objective of pursuing an economic activity, whether or not that activity is central or ancillary.

4.100 The key question is whether the economic entity still exists and is carrying out the same or similar activities post transfer. The assessment will depend on a number of factors. A useful guide is to see whether the core assets of the business have transferred to the new employer and are being used in essentially the same kind of business activity as previously. Other determining factors may include whether or not goodwill has been retained (ie, whether any customers have been transferred), whether or not tangible assets (such as buildings and movable property) have been transferred, the degree of similarity between the activities carried on before and after the transfer and the extent of any suspension of those activities.

4.101 Article 137 applies even in the events of business transfers within the same group of companies.

Outsourcing/insourcing

4.102 Outsourcing and insourcing are typical cases of legal transactions leading to the application of Article 137 where one business ceases to provide its services and another business takes them over. This frequently includes the outsourcing of a particular business activity (core or ancillary) to an external service provider. Alternatively, termination of an outsourcing arrangement where activities cease to be carried out by the external service provider and continue to be carried out by either another service provider or are taken back in-house (insourcing) will trigger the application of Article 137.

4.103 As for a business sale, the transferred business activities must be essentially the same before and post transfer. In addition, the existing employees should be assigned to carrying out the transferred activities. Article 137 should not be applied to a situation where one service contract is terminated and another service contract is entered into for the performance of the same or similar work if there is no simultaneous transfer of significant tangible or intangible assets or a major part of the workforce, in terms of their numbers and skills, assigned by the predecessor to the performance of the contract.

4.104 In some cases services may be divided and outsourced to more than one service provider. If the services in such a case become so fragmented that it is not possible to identify the services subject to transfer, then Article 137 may not apply.

Effect of Article 137

Automatic transfer and protection of employment

4.105 The employment of individuals employed in the transferring business will automatically transfer simultaneously with the business on existing terms and conditions, always provided they were working for the transferring undertaking or assigned to perform the transferring business activity. All outstanding rights of the employees (unpaid salary, remaining holiday entitlement, etc) will also be transferred. The employee's record of continuous service also transfers to the new employer.

Objection to the transfer

4.106 An employee is not entitled to object to his/her transfer under Article 137, as the transfer is conducted automatically and a new employment contract is not required. Thus, if an employee does not present himself/herself at the (new) workplace, this may be considered a breach of employment obligations and grounds for dismissal.

Protection from dismissal

4.107 The transfer of an undertaking or a business activity is not a valid reason for dismissal. Employers are not entitled to dismiss employees solely due to such a transfer. Dismissal may be justifiable only if a valid business (economic, technical or organisational) reason occurs, regardless of whether the dismissal occurs before or after the transfer. In practice, it is very challenging to successfully substantiate a valid dismissal due to business reasons prior to the transfer, as the transfer may appear as the underlying reason for such dismissal. A dismissal may be easier to substantiate post transfer, but it is of great importance to fully observe the dismissal procedure, applying the selection criteria equally to both the transferred employees as well as the existing employees (if any).

Protection of terms and conditions of employment

4.108 Similarly, the terms of employment are also protected. As a general rule, terms of employment may not be amended unilaterally, regardless of the transfer (see the section starting at para **4.126** below). In addition, if a collective agreement was in place prior to the transfer, such collective agreement will continue to apply until a new one is adopted, but in any event no longer than one year from the transfer.

4.109 To that end, the previous employer is under the obligation fully and accurately to inform the new employer of the rights of the transferring employees. Usually, the previous employer provides the new one with a list of affected employees, copies of their employment contracts, collective agreement, internal by-laws and agreement between the previous employer and employee representative (if any).

4.110 The rights of employees may be reduced when the transfer of an undertaking or part of an undertaking is conducted within insolvency or similar business recovery proceedings. However, such reduction of rights may be done only if contemplated under a collective agreement or an agreement between the workers' council and the previous employer.

4.111 The status and function of a workers' council established and elected with the previous employer remains unchanged post transfer with the new employer until the end of its elected term. However, if the autonomy of the transferred undertaking or business activity was not preserved, the employer must enable the transferred employees to continue to be properly represented during the period necessary for the reconstitution or reappointment of employee representatives in accordance with the regular statutory procedure.

Liability of employers

4.112 Article 137 provides for both the previous and the new employer to be jointly and severally liable for any obligations towards the transferred employees occurring prior to the transfer. This in practice enables the employees to bring a claim against either of the employers (whichever is more liquid), or even both, to secure his/her claims to be duly paid. However, the liability of the previous employer is limited to the value of the transferred assets.

> **Practical Tip**
> All changes in employment must be registered with the relevant health insurance and pension fund registries, including the change of employer. The previous employer must deregister the transferred employee, while the new employer must perform the new registration. This must all be done within 24 hours from when the transfer takes effect.

Information and consultation

Duty to inform

4.113 The transferor (previous employer) must inform both the employee representatives and the affected employees on the following:

- the fact that the transfer is to take place, date of transfer and reasons behind it;
- the legal, economic and social implications of the transfer for the affected employees (for example, change in work location); and
- measures envisaged in relation to the concerned employees, if any.

Duty to consult

4.114 The transferor has a general duty to consult the employee representatives prior to adopting any decision important to the position of employees. To that end, the employer must provide the employee representatives with all relevant data. This rule also applies to the contemplated transfer of an undertaking or business activity.

4.115 The consultation must be conducted as seeking the agreement of the employee representatives to the measures to be taken. However, there is no requirement to reach an agreement. Employee representatives are not even under the obligation to respond to the employer's notice (the usual timeframe for a response is eight days). In such case, it will be considered that the worker's council has no objections or comments.

4.116 Within the consultation process, the employer should:

- completely and accurately explain the contemplated transfer and the associated legal, economic and social implications for the affected employees;
- provide the employee representatives with all the associated data in writing;
- make itself available for any discussion on the topic; and
- give the employee representatives the opportunity to comment or make suggestions about the contemplated transfer.

4.117 The legislation sets out no definite overall timeframe for information and consultation. The duty to inform must be undertaken in a timely fashion to allow for any necessary consultations between the parties to take place before the date of transfer, considering the eight-day timeframe the employee representatives' have at their disposal to respond. The discharge of the formal duty to consult cannot properly begin until the employee representatives have been supplied with the requisite information in writing.

Sanctions

Unfair dismissal

4.118 Any dismissal will be considered unfair where the principal underlying reason of dismissal is the transfer itself. In practice, any dismissal due to business reasons given immediately prior to or after the transfer will be under heavy scrutiny, so as to avoid potential abuse of the business transfer rules. For further details on the remedy for unfair dismissal see the section starting at para **4.146** below.

4.119 As the new employer and old employer are jointly and severally liable for any obligations towards the transferred employees in place prior to the transfer, the new employer may be found liable for unfair dismissals made by the old employer. The underlying commercial agreements governing the transfer should commonly contain detailed indemnities in relation to the financial liability for acts and omissions relating to transferring employees. Such agreements will be valid and enforceable to the extent that they do not attempt to contract out of Article 137.

Failure to inform and consult

4.120 Failure to inform the affected employees on the contemplated transfer may trigger a fine to the previous employer in the amount ranging from HRK 61,000–100,000 HRK (€8,000–13,000).

4.121 The sanction for failure to inform and consult with the employee representative is more severe and makes the decision on transfer null and void.

Application of Article 137 to cross-border transactions/offshoring

4.122 Notwithstanding the provisions on territorial application, Croatian labour regulations do not make it clear whether they apply to international transfers (or outsourcings), either to a country within the EU or outside the EU. Arguably, the primacy of EU law and the underlying principle of uniform application of EU directives means that a cross-border transfer should be covered by the ARD, resulting in the automatic transfer of employees and their contracts. A detailed analysis should therefore be conducted in order to asses all the circumstances of the particular transfer, including the type of undertaking, the degree to which assets, employees and customers are being transferred and whether or not the same activities are being performed after the transfer. As a result of this ambiguity problems may be expected in determining which law applies to the transfer.

4.123 Provided there is a European Works Council established within the group of companies affected by a multi-jurisdictional restructuring, then there may be an obligation to inform and consult with the European Works Council prior to implementing any such exercise.

WORKFORCE REDUCTION IN CONNECTION WITH SHARE SALE OR SHARE PURCHASE

4.124 Article 137 does not apply to a share sale, as the employer does not change in such case, but only the identity of its shareholder changes.

4.125 Conversely, if the new shareholder (owner) wishes to restructure the business post acquisition, then any dismissals must follow the appropriate dismissal procedure set out above.

CHANGING EMPLOYMENT TERMS AND CONDITIONS

4.126 Once an employment contract is entered into, it may not be amended without the consent of both employer and employee.

4.127 An employer wishing to change the terms and conditions of an employment contract has the following options at its disposal:

(a) reaching an agreement with the employee; or
(b) dismissing and re-engaging the employees under new proposed terms and conditions.

4.128 Within the second option, the employer remains exposed to an unfair dismissal claim.

4.129 It should be noted that where there has been a relevant transfer of employment contracts under Article 137, no changes to the previous employees' terms and conditions are allowed unless such transfer is conducted within insolvency or similar business recovery proceedings (and permitted under a collective agreement or an agreement between the workers' council and the previous employer).

Mutually agreed changes

4.130 The easiest way to change an employee's terms and conditions is to specifically agree on them with the employee. It is recommended that an existing contract is changed through consultation and discussion with the employee.

4.131 The employee is not under an obligation to accept any changes to his/her current employment contract. Therefore, there may be certain negotiations required as the employee may insist on receiving some benefit in return for agreeing to the proposed changes (in addition to remaining in employment). Also, employees are more likely to accept changes if the underlying reasons are carefully explained to them and they have an opportunity to express their views. Such approach makes good business sense, as it contributes to an employee's sense of engagement and motivation.

4.132 The proposed amendments should be clear and concise. As the employer is proposing and presumably preparing the amendments to the contract, any vagueness will be interpreted in favour of the employee. Also, amendments to the contract must be agreed on in writing.

Dismissing and re-engaging employees on new terms

4.133 Employers may serve employees with a termination notice and offer re-employment on new terms. This approach is used when employees are not willing to voluntarily agree to the proposed changes. This path should be considered only after thorough consultations with the employees and be treated as a last resort. However, it does not insulate the employer from an unfair dismissal claim.

4.134 Employees may decide to accept or decline such offer. Either way, their right to challenge the termination decision is preserved. In such a scenario the employer will have to prove sufficient legal grounds for dismissal (these will usually be economic, technical or organisational reasons). Refusal to enter into an amended employment contract does not represent a valid reason for dismissal. The employer will also have to ensure that the appropriate dismissal procedure was observed. For further details of re-employment please see paras **4.60–4.62** above.

Unilateral changes

4.135 Employers have been known to impose changes to the terms and conditions of the employees without their agreement. It should be noted that such approach may lead to fines. In addition, subject to the scope and extent of such unilateral amendments, the employee may be entitled to resign and request adequate damage compensation or to claim adequate protection of his/her rights in court.

> **Practical Tips**
>
> The easiest and safest option for employers when it comes to varying an employee's terms and conditions is obtaining the employee's express agreement to the variation.
>
> Most organisations will carry out an annual review of salaries and employers may simultaneously, if possible, consider introducing a proposed change to the terms and conditions. This would allow employers to make any salary increase or introduce any benefit such as additional holiday allowance, conditional upon the employee agreeing to the proposed change.
>
> Depending on the financial situation of the organisation, employees may be prepared to accept changes to their terms and conditions if the alternative is a dismissal due to business reasons. In such a situation employees should be given the relevant information about the organisation's financial position so as to be able to make an informed decision either way.

USING TEMPORARY STAFF

4.136 A reorganisation situation may call for temporary staff. Options to be considered are using agency workers or directly engaging employees on fixed-term contracts.

Agency workers

4.137 Using agency workers may be a convenient option when an organisation is in need of some temporary help at short notice and wishes to avoid conducting an actual recruitment process. However, a minimum level of effective protection must be observed towards temporary workers not only by the agency but also by the hiring undertaking.

4.138 In line with the principle of equal treatment, agency workers are entitled to the same pay and other essential working and employment conditions as their permanently employed counterparts, for the entire duration of their assignment at a hiring undertaking. The hiring undertaking should keep temporary workers informed of any permanent vacancies. Temporary workers should also have equal access to amenities and collective services at work.

Fixed-term contracts

4.139 Entering into permanent contracts is the general rule. Fixed-term contracts may be used only exceptionally, for a working engagement previously defined by a deadline, completion of a project or occurrence of an event. Accordingly, a particular reason must be specified in the contract, except in the first fixed-term contract. Employers tend to use this option when covering for an employee on maternity leave or when uncertain of a long-term commitment and they start off with a fixed-term engagement to assess their further needs.

4.140 Whatever the reason for using fixed-term contracts, the same working conditions as for the permanent employees must be accorded to their fixed-term counterparts. Employers must inform fixed-term employees about vacancies which become available to ensure they have the same opportunity to secure permanent positions as other employees.

4.141 The duration of the fixed-term contract must be specified, either by stating an expiry date or by occurrence of a specified event. If the termination date is clearly specified, the contract automatically expires on the set date, without any further action on the employer's side. Conversely, if the termination date remains vague, the employer must, in a timely fashion, inform the employee of the precise termination date.

4.142 The expiry of a fixed-term contract is not treated as a 'termination' by the employer. The employer is not under obligation to say why a permanent employment or a renewal is not offered to the fixed-term employee. If a fixed-term employee continues working at the same position after expiry of the fixed-term contract, his/her contract will be automatically converted into a permanent one.

RENEWAL OF FIXED-TERM CONTRACTS

4.143 Employers may renew a fixed-term contract for an unlimited number of occasions (provided they can justify the need for a fixed-term contract as opposed to engaging the employee under a permanent contract) within the set timeframe. The duration of a first fixed-term contract is not limited, but if executed for a period longer than three years it may only be renewed as a permanent engagement. If executed for a period shorter than three years, the maximum total duration of successive fixed-term contracts may not exceed three years, unless necessary as a replacement for a temporarily absent employee or expressly allowed under the law or a collective agreement. If the fixed-term contracts exceed the above timeframes, the contracts will automatically be regarded as permanent.

Practical Tips

A fixed-term contract may be terminated by an ordinary termination prior to its expiry only if such an option is expressly included in the contract. Failure to include such an early termination clause may lead to a well-founded unfair dismissal claim. An early termination could be successfully challenged on the basis that the employer was not entitled to serve a termination notice.

Despite having automatic expiry in place, employers are encouraged to shortly before the anticipated expiry date send a written notice to fixed-term employees confirming the exact expiry date and notifying them to stop coming to work after that date. This should prevent the possible conversion to a permanent contract if the employee simply continues coming to work regardless of the expiry of his/her contract.

EMPLOYMENT CLAIMS

4.144 Employment claims are brought before municipal, first instance courts of general jurisdiction (*Općinski sudovi*) within the location of the employee's place of work or an employer's headquarters (if different). The exception is Zagreb, where a specialised labour court is established (*Općinski radni sud u Zagrebu*) and deals with claims brought within its jurisdiction. Any appeals are filed in the regional, second instance courts of general jurisdiction (*Županijski sudovi*).

4.145 Employment proceedings are considered urgent and the intention is for first instance proceedings to be resolved within six months. However, it is rarely so in practice as such proceedings usually take much longer and can span several years.

UNFAIR DISMISSAL

4.146 Employees may file a claim for unfair dismissal if they believe there were no valid grounds for the dismissal (in a workforce restructuring this would be dismissal due to business reasons) or the appropriate dismissal procedures were not followed by the employer. Length of previous service with the same employer is not a prerequisite for filing such a claim.

4.147 Employees have only a rather limited window of time in which to react and must observe a strict procedure for complaining against unfair dismissal. As a first step, employees must issue a formal request for protection of their rights (a 'Request') to the employer within 15 days from receiving the termination notice. In termination cases, the employee Requests that the employer withdraws the termination notice and reinstates him/her to their previous position. If the employer fails to respond or refuses to comply with their request (in this case, cancelling the termination notice) within 15 days, the employee has a further 15 days to file a claim to the court. Failure to observe the above procedure and deadlines usually results in the claim being dismissed on procedural grounds.

Remedies

4.148 If the court finds that the employee has been unfairly dismissed then it will order the employer to reinstate the individual. Alternatively, at the request of either employer or employee, the court may terminate the contract (judicial termination) and may order damages if such have been claimed

4.149 If the employee is reinstated, the employee is also entitled to his/her salary accrued between the unfair dismissal and such reinstatement. However, the court will only order such payment to be made by the employer to the employee if specifically requested by the employee.

4.150 Judicial termination may be ordered at the request of either party. Employees' requests for judicial termination are adopted without any further justification. Conversely, employers must substantiate why the employment relationship should not be continued considering the interests of both parties. Courts are generally not inclined to adopt an employer's request for judicial termination and have done so only in situations where trust has been severely breached by the employee (fraud, theft, etc). Judicial termination orders are rare and the usual remedy for unfair dismissal is reinstatement.

4.151 A termination date must be specified when making an order for termination of a contract. The court is at liberty to set the termination date to any day from the date of notice of unfair dismissal onwards, depending on the particular circumstances of each case. For instance, if an employee gets a new job during the unfair dismissal proceedings, the termination date will usually be set immediately prior to commencement of his/her new employment.

4.152 In the event of judicial termination, the employee is entitled to compensation for unfair dismissal. The amount of compensation may range from the equivalent of three up to eight months' salary. The exact amount is at the court's sole discretion and depends on the length of service, prior working experience and family support obligations. In addition to the compensation, the employee is also entitled to the salary accrued between the date of the unfair dismissal taking effect and date of judicial termination (but the employer will be ordered to pay accrued salary only if specifically requested by the employee).

4.153 The amount of compensation in case of a judicial termination was recently lowered from the equivalent of 18 average months' salary to eight. The maximum amount has never been awarded and the highest award for compensation for employees with very long service amounted to 12 average months' salary.

DISCRIMINATION

4.154 An employee may also file a discrimination claim if he/she believes that the real reason behind his/her selection for dismissal was because of one of the following protected characteristics: race, ethnicity or colour, gender, language, religion, political or other beliefs, national or social origin, assets, trade union membership, education, social status, marital or family status, age, health condition, disability, genetic heritage, native identity, expression or sexual orientation.

Remedies

4.155 If an employee is successful in a claim for discrimination he/she is likely to be awarded a payment representing compensation. Such compensation is calculated with reference to the employee's actual loss (for example, lost earnings) and extent of non-material damage (for example, damage to his/her injury to feelings). Compensation for non-material damage is generally between €500 and €10,000 depending on how serious the court considers the employer's discriminatory act to be. There is no set amount

4.156 As an alternative to filing a separate discrimination claim, an employee may file a regular unfair dismissal claim on discrimination grounds. In such a scenario, an employee may request reinstatement to the previous position, payment of accrued salaries and, in addition, compensation due to discrimination.

MUTUALLY AGREED TERMINATION

4.157 A termination agreement is always preferable and is the most flexible option for the employer. By reaching a consensual solution, the employer is protected from claims of unlawful dismissals, thus avoiding potentially complicated and time consuming termination procedures.

4.158 The statutory restrictions (valid reason for termination, notice periods, statutory severance payments, mitigation of termination consequences) do not apply in this case. In this way, potentially complicated and time consuming procedures regarding the dismissal social outline, involving the employees themselves, the employee representatives and the Employment Service, would be avoided. The parties would be free to agree on the terms and conditions of termination (including the notice period or damage compensation), and the employee would normally not challenge the termination.

4.159 There are important drawbacks: in the event of a termination agreement, certain tax benefits applicable to the statutory severance payment would be lost. As employees tend to be aware of this, the employer would have to make up for the loss of the tax benefits. This increases the termination costs. Employees would also most likely expect to receive a higher voluntary severance payment as an incentive to enter into mutual agreements on termination. Finally, employees would lose their right to unemployment benefits which makes the mutual termination less attractive (or more expensive).

4.160 Employers should therefore be aware that offering a termination agreement is often viewed by employees as an invitation to negotiate a termination package and it is therefore important to ensure that the employer is in as good a negotiating position as possible. This could for instance be achieved by having started the appropriate dismissal procedure so that this can be resumed if severance terms cannot be agreed by the parties. In practice this means that most employers will initially offer a termination agreement and indicate that, should the termination agreement not be negotiated, a termination notice will be served. Once the agreement is accepted by the employee the dismissal process can be discontinued, however, it is critical for the employer's bargaining position that it can resume the dismissal procedure if the employee refuses to accept the termination agreement on the terms offered.

Chapter 5

Workforce Restructuring in Cyprus

Charis Papachristodoulou
Papadopoulos, Lycourgos & Co, Nicosia

INTRODUCTION

5.1 This chapter deals with the legal considerations applicable before, during and after a workforce restructuring exercise in Cyprus.

5.2 As a former British colony, the legal system in Cyprus is at its core a common law system and, as such, it is substantially different from continental European (civil law) jurisdictions. As in the United Kingdom and other common law jurisdictions, the law is not always exhaustively codified in a systematic way. It should, however, be noted that various areas of Law, which are not traditionally codified in common law jurisdictions, such as the law of contract and the law of torts, have been codified and are governed by specific statutes. That said, the provisions of the relevant statutes are quite broad and are interpreted, and sometimes even extended, by case-law. In common law jurisdictions, a court's judgment is binding authority for similar cases decided by the same court or by lower courts within the same jurisdiction. In Cyprus there are only two tiers of courts, the first instance and the appeal.

5.3 Following the independence of Cyprus in 1960, the judgments of the courts of England and Wales are no longer binding on Cypriot courts. Nonetheless they are strongly persuasive authority and in practice, Cypriot courts will heavily rely on English case law for interpretative guidance in all areas of law including employment law.

5.4 Employment legislation in Cyprus mainly derives from legislation enacted by the Parliament. Employment law legislation in Cyprus has been enacted in a piecemeal manner, in that the relevant statutes are generally enacted reactively when a particular need for implementing relevant measures arises. The trigger for enacting employment law legislation is usually public policy, the need to implement European Directives, or the need to ratify and enact into domestic legislation the various multilateral treaties to which Cyprus becomes party.

5.5 In Cyprus, there is no single point of reference for employment legislation, a difficulty for practitioners which is further exacerbated by the fact that, to some extent, the effect of the relevant legislation can only be fully ascertained when read in conjunction with the precedent (binding case law) interpreting the provisions of the law.

5.6 The less pervasive nature of legislation in common law countries and the lack of an exhaustive code for Employment law means that under Cypriot employment law, there are no default employment terms which automatically apply in the absence of an express contract. Even though there are some basic minimum terms for the benefit of employees which are prescribed by statute (eg the maximum working hours, minimum leave entitlement etc), employers in Cyprus usually expressly and extensively set out the employment terms in the contract.

5.7 Under Cypriot Law, the employer has an obligation to at least notify the employee via their written employment contract (or a letter or other signed document) of the 'essential' details of their employment including, amongst others, the identity of the parties, the employee's position, the commencement and duration of the contract, the applicable notice periods, the salary and the work hours of the employee.

5.8 When assessing the entitlements and obligations an employee has following their dismissal, the first point of reference is always the employment contract. This is an exercise necessary to establish what the parties have agreed in respect of the applicable employment terms and the termination of employment. It is noted that the minimum statutory employee rights can never be waived and, as a result, an examination of the contract alone is not in itself sufficient to fully ascertain the entitlements of the employee.

5.9 Unlike other non-EU countries (the most prominent example being the USA), Cyprus does not endorse the concept of 'employment at will'. Therefore, when an employee qualifies for statutory protection, a dismissal will only be fair (and thus not incur any sanctions for the employer) if it is made for one of the fair reasons prescribed by statute.

PREPARING FOR A RESTRUCTURING EXERCISE

5.10 Various considerations need to be taken into account in order to ensure the lawfulness of a restructuring exercise in Cyprus. The most essential details of the workforce which should be available are the contractual terms and conditions, the position and the years of service of each employee. All of these factors can have a significant impact on the lawfulness of the restructuring and consequently and more importantly the financial cost of such an exercise for the employer.

Identifying the employing entity

5.11 Where the employer is a company it may belong to a 'Group of Companies', however, each legal entity is an independent employer and it should generally be dealt with as such for the purposes of a restructuring exercise. Any other connected entities are not a consideration at the first stage of a restructuring exercise. Particular caution should be exercised to uphold this principle, where the restructuring concerns employees employed with various entities of a 'Group' who regularly collaborate on projects or tasks for the purposes of a Group.

5.12 It should be stressed that for a dismissal to be fair, the Group may potentially be under an obligation to consider, and if appropriate offer, suitable alternative positions that may be available in other companies of the group.

Example

Company A and B both independently trading in selling mobile phones and operating at the same geographical area, belong to the same Group.

The Group decides to stop the operation of Company A due to the fact that Company B of the group already caters for that area.

The terminations of the employees of Company A will constitute valid redundancies, provided that Company A and B operate independently of each other. An employee of Company A whose contract of service is terminated on the ground of redundancy will not have any remedy against the Group or Company B.

Conversely, the Group cannot selectively make some employees from Company A and some from Company B redundant, in order to fuse the remaining personnel in Company B, as the termination of the services of employees working at Company B will not be effected on the ground of redundancy and may amount to an unfair dismissal.

Collating information to plan and budget for the restructuring exercise

5.13 A restructuring exercise generally requires careful planning in advance, so that the risk of employment tribunal claims is minimised or at least that the financial impact of the restructuring on the employer is minimised. The employing entity should already have all the data on the relevant employees needed to ascertain the financial cost of the exercise.

5.14 In the event that the personnel information is handled by a centralised human resource department, each company will need to ensure that it has lawful access to employee data, as data sharing of employee data across the group's companies requires employee consent. If human resources are handled by a central department, it is good practice for the group to obtain the employee's authorisation in advance, by expressly including an authorisation to this effect in the employment contract.

5.15 Ideally, a record of the employees and the relevant information should exist, and in the event of large organisations it is preferable that such a record be computerised in an appropriate form (usually in the form of a database).

5.16 A restructuring exercise is generally a time consuming task. An organised, easily accessible and well maintained record of employees and their details can dramatically reduce the time needed to plan for restructuring. The planning of the restructuring should only begin after all the relevant employee information has been made available to the human resources department and their advisers.

Practical Tip

Employee data which should be made available to the HR department prior to planning for workforce reduction or restructuring exercise includes:

- job description and actual duties of the employee;
- length of service;
- contractual benefits, including entitlement on termination of employment and any potential enhanced redundancy entitlement;
- age;
- place of work;
- any applicable collective agreement; and
- evaluations of performance.

EMPLOYMENT STATUS

5.17 The legislation which governs redundancies and dismissal of employees in Cyprus is the Termination of Employment Law of 1967 (Law 24/1967) with its relevant amendments. For an individual to be protected under the termination of employment law, they must firstly meet the legal definition of 'employee'.

5.18 The definition of 'employee' in the termination of employment law is: 'any person working for another person pursuant to a contract of employment or pupillage, or under such circumstances that it is possible to infer the existence of an employer and employee relationship'. The description provided by the law is not in itself very helpful in ascertaining who is an employee. Nonetheless, it has been established in case law that the most essential factors which are taken into consideration to determine whether an 'employer and employee relationship' exists are:

- the provision of paid services by a person.
- the express or implied agreement that during the execution of his duties the worker will be under the control of the employer.

5.19 Other factors are also generally taken into consideration, for example whether the employer is responsible for paying the social security insurance contributions of the employee, nonetheless, the 'control test' is arguably the decisive factor in determining whether an employment exists under common law.

5.20 The control test requires answering a series of questions such as:

- does the employer have the right to tell the person what to do, how, when, and where to do the job or task assigned?
- does the individual use the employer's equipment and premises in the performance of his duties?
- is there an obligation on each side to offer and perform work?
- what are the financial risks of the work performed?
- can any other worker do the job if the individual cannot?

5.21 It is noted that directors and shareholders of companies are not precluded from obtaining 'employee' status simply by virtue of such capacity. The control test will always be the decisive factor to ascertain whether any person is an employee of the company.

GENERAL PROTECTION AGAINST DISMISSAL

5.22 As previously mentioned the 'employment at will' notion is not recognised under Cypriot Law, but a worker is not statutorily protected against unfair dismissal immediately from the commencement of his employment. Such protection is only available to employees who have completed their 'probation period'.

5.23 The default position under the law is that the probation period is completed when the employee has been 'continuously' employed with an employer for at least 26 weeks. This 'probation period' can be extended for up to a maximum of 104 weeks of 'continuous employment' by written agreement, however, such agreement must be in writing and must have been concluded at the time that the employee was hired and this will not always coincide with the commencement of the employment, so care should be taken. What constitutes 'continuous employment' for the purposes of the law is set out below at para 5.26.

> **Practical Tip**
>
> The employment rights prescribed by statute are the *minimum* protection afforded to employees and the statutory rights do not act as a cap to any more favourable contractual rights.
>
> Even though an employer may under the law be entitled to fairly dismiss an employee, the dismissal may still be 'wrongful' if, for example, the employer does not comply with the contractually prescribed notice period. A claim in 'wrongful dismissal' is a conventional claim for breach of contract and as such it is unrelated to the statutory concept of fairness under Cypriot law.
>
> As a result employers need to honour both the statutory and the contractual obligations in order to avoid claims against them.

5.24 Once an employee has completed his 'probation period' he can only be fairly dismissed on one of the following grounds:

- the employee fails to perform his work in a reasonably satisfactory manner (underperformance);
- the employee is redundant;
- the termination is attributable to force majeure, war, civil uprising, act of god or the destruction of the employer's premises by fire which is not a result of an intentional action or inaction of the employer; or
- the employment is terminated at the end of a fixed term contract, or due to the fact that the employee has reached the retirement age based on law, custom, collective agreement, agreement, work regulation or otherwise. For further analysis of the considerations relating to this ground, see the analysis on fixed term contracts starting at para 0 below.
- employee shows such conduct as to make himself liable to dismissal without notice. The law includes the following non-exhaustive list of examples of such conduct:
  - conduct on the part of the employee which makes it clear that the employer employee relationship cannot reasonably be expected to continue,
  - the employee commits a serious offence during the performance of his duties,
  - the employee commits a criminal offence during the performance of his duties without the explicit or silent consent of his employer,
  - improper conduct of the employee during the performance of his duties.
  - serious or repeated breach or disregard for workplace regulations or other regulations related to the employment.

5.25 Case law has established that in addition to one of the grounds above, the employer must generally evidence that the procedure leading to the dismissal of the employee was reasonable. Furthermore, pursuant to the Termination of Employment Convention of 1982, which has been implemented with domestic legislation, where the employment of a worker is to be terminated for reasons related to the worker's conduct or performance, he must be provided with an opportunity to defend himself against the allegations made, unless the employer cannot reasonably be expected to provide this opportunity.

THE CALCULATION OF THE CONTINUOUS EMPLOYMENT PERIOD

5.26 For the calculation of the employee's period of employment, the following weeks count towards the 'continuous' nature of the employment:

- weeks during which the employee has worked for 18 hours or more;
- weeks during which the employee was;
  - rendered incapable of working due to illness, injury or childbirth;
  - absent from their work due to the temporary interruption of activities;
  - absent from their work due to such circumstances that the employee and employer relationship is considered as continuous under agreement or custom or law; or
  - absent from their work on parental leave.

5.27 The 'continuous' nature of the employment is not interrupted by the following:

- absence from work due to the employee's service in the armed forces of the republic;
- absence from work owing to an employment dispute;
- change of employer in the event of a 'Transfer of an Undertaking' or transfer of the employee to 'linked entity';
- absence from work due to illness, injury or childbirth;
- absence from work due to the temporary interruption of activities;
- absence from work due to such circumstances that the employee and employer relationship is considered as continuous under agreement or custom or law;
- absence from his work due to employment abroad to a business owned wholly or mainly by the employer;
- absence from work on paid leave;
- absence attributable to force majeure, war, civil uprising or Act of God; or
- absence from work on parental leave or leave for 'important unforeseen reasons' as per the relevant legislation (effectively leave for death or illness of close relatives).

SPECIAL PROTECTION AGAINST DISMISSAL

5.28 A dismissal on one of the following reasons is automatically unfair:

- union membership or participation in union activities outside working hours or, with the consent of the employer, during working hours or the

membership in a safety committee under the Safety at the Workplace Law of 1988;
- seeking office as, or acting or having acted in the capacity of, a workers' representative, or past acts under such capacity;
- the filing of a bona fide complaint or the participation in proceedings against an employer involving alleged violation of civil or criminal legislation or regulations, or the recourse to competent administrative authorities;
- race, colour, sex, marital status, family responsibilities, pregnancy, religion, political opinion, national extraction or social origin;
- pregnancy or parenthood; or
- taking parental leave or leave for 'important unforeseen reasons' as per the relevant legislation (effectively leave for death or illness of close relatives).

WORKFORCE REDUCTION

5.29 In order to ensure that the restructuring can be effected on the basis of fair dismissals, an employer should first identify the business objective sought to be achieved by the workforce reduction. Unless such an exercise is undertaken at the outset, some or even all of the related dismissals may be deemed as unfair, and will lead to an increased financial cost for the employer.

5.30 The extent of the restructuring itself should also be taken into consideration, as employers who will be making collective redundancies must give notice of their intention to the competent authority and additionally follow the collective redundancy consultation procedure, explained in the collective redundancy procedure section below starting at para 5.82.

DEFINITION OF REDUNDANCY

5.31 The statutory definition of redundancy (section 18) of the Termination of Employment Law provides that 'an employee is redundant when his employment is terminated'*:*

(a) Because the employer has ceased or intends to cease conducting the business in which the employee was employed.
(b) Because the employer has ceased or intends to cease conducting business in the place where the employee was so employed.
(c) Due to any of the following other reasons relating to the operation of the business:
    (i) Modernisation, mechanization or other change in the methods of production or organisation, which reduces the number of the employees required.

(ii) Changes in the products or the production methods or in the necessary specialisation of the employees.
(iii) Elimination of departments.
(iv) Difficulties in product placement or credit difficulties.
(v) Lack of orders or of raw materials.
(vi) Reduction of the volume of the work or of the business.'

5.32 The first two grounds of redundancy are rather self-explanatory as they concern either a closure of the business altogether, or the closure of a particular workplace. The third ground is broader and relates to the reorganisation of a business.

5.33 Note that where any work is being outsourced or offshored, it will be necessary to consider if it is covered by 'the safeguarding of employees' rights in the event of transfers of undertakings, businesses or parts of undertakings or businesses law of 2000', which protects an individual's employment in the event that the undertaking for which he works is transferred by an employer to a new owner. For further details see the business sale, outsourcing/insourcing and offshoring section starting at para **5.123**.

Examples of redundancy situations

Reduction of work

Apollo Shoes Limited is a company which makes leather shoes. It employs a total of 100 employees, of which 60 are employed in the production team. The production team employees operate two types of machinery which cut the sole and leather. The two parts are then glued together by hand.

Apollo Shoes, invests in new machines that perform all of the work required ie cut the sole, leather and glue the two together. With the arrival of the new machinery it will no longer be necessary to employ the full 60 person production team employees as only 20 employees will be required to maintain the same output capacity. 40 employees of the production team have been made redundant as the number of required employees has been reduced.

Workplace closure

Hephaestus Limited operates three hotels in Cyprus. The reservations for one of the three hotels have substantially diminished during the past year and the company has decided to close it down. The employees of the hotel are redundant on the basis that their workplace is closing down.

5.34 Reorganisation solely on economic/cost-saving grounds is not recognised under Cypriot law as a fair dismissal ground. Dismissals for this reason without a concurrent valid redundancy ground (usually reduction in turnover or overall reorganisation)) have consistently been disapproved and deemed unfair by Employment Tribunals.

DISMISSALS ON GROUNDS OF REDUNDANCY

5.35 When companies are planning to dismiss employees on grounds of redundancy they must have regard to two redundancy procedures:

- the individual redundancy procedure; and
- the collective redundancy procedure.

5.36 The individual redundancy procedure must always be followed when dismissing employees on grounds of redundancy, even where a collective redundancy is taking place.

5.37 Companies are required to also follow the collective redundancy procedure where a particular of dismissals is effected within a period of 30 days. As explained below in the relevant section, the exact number of dismissals which trigger the collective redundancy protection is contingent on the number of employed employees.

Redundancy procedures

5.38 Although it is not a condition imposed by statute, case law in Cyprus has established that even where the conditions for redundancy are satisfied, the employer may still be liable for unfair dismissal, if the procedure followed to select the redundant employee(s) is not fair and objective. Employers therefore need to be guided by the guidelines established by case law to ascertain what amounts to a fair redundancy selection.

5.39 Larger organisations generally include the applicable redundancy procedure in their policy or staff handbook. In some professions, it is customary for collective agreements to provide for the 'applicable' redundancy policy and procedure. Provisions on the applicable redundancy procedure and compliance with such provisions will generally create a strong presumption of a fair procedure, especially where the applicable procedure has been negotiated with representatives of the employees in advance. Nevertheless, employers must be aware that the potential fairness of the redundancy selection procedure will ultimately always be decided by the Employment Tribunal. As a result, in addition to complying with the agreed or established procedure, employers should always ensure that the procedure followed is 'objectively' fair.

5.40 The overriding principles established by the Employment tribunal are that the employees who will be made redundant are fairly selected, all alternatives to a dismissal must first be assessed and there must have been meaningful consultation with each of the affected employees.

Individual redundancy procedure

5.41 Case law has established the principles outlined below regarding the fairness of an individual redundancy procedure:

Defining the selection pool

5.42 At the first stage of a fair selection process, the employer will need to identify the group of employees from which those who are to be made redundant will be selected. This group of employees is usually referred to as the redundancy selection pool.

5.43 The employer must be able to evidence that the redundant employees have been selected from the correct selection pool and that the decision is based on rational and objective considerations.

5.44 Where the first two grounds of redundancy under the Termination of Employment Law are concerned, the identification of the selection pool is generally an easy task. If the closure of an entire business or a particular workplace is contemplated, then the selection pool will generally be the entire workforce of the business or the entire workforce of the closing workplace respectively.

5.45 Where, however, a redundancy on the third ground is under consideration ie a reorganisation of the business is taking place, the pool will have to be more carefully considered. In this event all the employees who perform the particular kind of work should be pooled together.

5.46 The fairness of each selection pool will be decided by the Employment Tribunal and the employer will need to be able to justify its decision objectively. Where a specific position is no longer necessary for the running of the business, the employee in that post will effectively be in a selection pool of one.

Example of specific position redundancies.

Hydra Limited has an HR department consisting of three employees; two administrators and a manager who oversees the administrators. Due to an overall reduction in the workforce of Hydra, two of the employees of the HR Department are no longer necessary. Hydra should not automatically decide that the HR Manager must be dismissed because they will no longer have any administrators to oversee. If the HR Manager's job description includes performing the tasks of the administrator, the selection pool should be all three employees of the HR department.

5.47 It should also be noted that if the employer has more than one workplace within the same locality, it will generally be necessary to aggregate employees from both locations in one pool, if the work performed at both locations is similar in nature. This holds true even where the employer is proposing to only close down one location completely.

Example closure of one of two nearby workplaces.

Off-license Limited operates two kiosks on the high street within a 50-metre distance and has decided to completely shut down one of the two kiosks. The selection pool should generally include the employees from both kiosks.

Selection criteria

5.48 When the selection pool has been ascertained, the employer must thereafter apply objective evaluation criteria to determine which employees from the pool will be made redundant. The employer's opinion of the employee cannot be a criterion, but objective reasons which have led the employer to form that opinion, provided they are relevant to the employee's position, such as punctuality or communication skills (for a customer facing position) can be included.

5.49 The employer must ensure that they can document and objectively justify the reason for the decision to make a particular employee redundant is fair. Where a person in a 'protected category' is selected for redundancy the employer risks a further award against him for the discrimination claim in addition to any unfair dismissal award. It should also be noted that selecting the higher earners of the pool for dismissal on the basis of their salary has conclusively been held by the employment tribunal and the Supreme Court to be unacceptable and will amount to a manifestly unfair dismissal. As a result the need for extensively documented objective criteria is paramount, where the employees who are ultimately selected for redundancy are the highest earners of the pool or fall under a 'protected category'.

5.50 It is best practice to have a constant evaluation scheme and if such a scheme is in place, the selection of employees from the pool will be much easier as performance will usually be an overriding criterion.

5.51 Attention must always be paid to the formulation or even the inclusion of certain criteria to avoid a presumption of discrimination in the selection. Indeed, even prior to the enactment of equal treatment legislation, case law had recognised that dismissals were unfair, if the redundancy criteria involved characteristics inherent to an employee.

5.52 Criteria which lead to a direct discrimination are easily caught by the employer. Nonetheless, the employer must be cautious not to introduce any criteria which amount to an indirect discrimination. For example a 'Last in First Out' (LIFO) rule used to be a common method for selecting the employees who would be made redundant. In Cyprus, LIFO was even expressed to be as the overriding criterion in some Employment Tribunal cases, even though subsequent case law recognised that the weight which should be attributed to the years of service varies, according to the particular circumstances of the selection. Nonetheless, in light of the enactment of the Equal Treatment in Employment and Occupation Law of 2004 (which implements Directives 2000/43/EC and 2000/78/EC), it is submitted that a LIFO formula may now amount to indirect age discrimination.

5.53 Particular care should be taken to ensure that, what appears to be an objective criterion does not amount to indirect discrimination to groups of individuals with protected characteristics, or at least that the employer provides 'compensatory' credits to protected individuals who are inherently disadvantaged by the specific criterion. For example, if an attendance record is part of the evaluation, the employer should ensure that any absences due to maternity leave, illness or serving in the armed forces are excluded from consideration and will not affect the employees score.

5.54 Ratification of the selection criteria by a recognised and relevant trade union or employee representatives is undoubtedly desirable, especially where a collective agreement covers the employees in the pool. Nevertheless, such ratification will only strengthen an employers' case in an unfair dismissal claim, but it will not bar claims of unfairness against the employer, even when they are advanced by employees who are members of the trade union in question.

5.55 The most important part of the procedure is to apply the selection criteria fairly and consistently to all staff in the selection pool. The usual, and arguably the best, way to achieve this is by using a score sheet system for each employee with an evaluation of the skills, ability and individual performance of the pool employees.

5.56 It should be noted that the Protection of Maternity Law of 1997 prohibits the dismissal of women who have notified their employer that they are pregnant or will be adopting, during the period starting on the day that notice is given to employer and ending three months after the end of the maternity leave (the 'protected period'). The Law provides that during the protected period, the employer can only dismiss an employee on grounds of gross misconduct, the closure of the business or at the end of the employee's fixed term contract. The said provision seems to imply that an employer cannot include a woman in the redundancy pool during the protected period unless the entire business is closing down. There is, however, Employment Tribunal case-law suggesting that if the dismissal is effected on other grounds of redundancy the dismissal is effective and fair and it is submitted that this is the correct position. It is, however, stressed that there is no binding Supreme Court precedent on the matter, and as a result, employers should exercise caution when considering for redundancy employees within the protected period.

5.57 The score sheet generally contains the relevant criteria, the weight given to each criterion (applied as a multiplier to the score of each criterion) and the comments of the evaluation officers explaining why each score was awarded. It should be noted that the weighting of each criterion must also be objectively justified. For example, the experience criterion may warrant a substantial weighting in the case of a legal advisor, whereas in the case of a messenger it would generally be much lower.

5.58 Furthermore, only criteria necessary to perform the job description in question should be included. For example, communication skills and clarity of speech are generally unnecessary for back-office operations but are extremely important to customer facing posts.

Example of the scoring matrix for sales staff

Criteria	Score	Weighting	Total	Justification of the score awarded
Performance Assessment (past six months) • Number of Sales Concluded • Customer Feedback		4		1.1 *This assessment should be verifiable on account of invoices issued, other accounting records and customer feedback documents.*
Performance Assessment (six months prior to the past six months) • Number of Sales Concluded • Customer Feedback		3		1.1
Performance Assessment (Previous Year(s) before the past 12 months) • Customer Feedback		2		
Attendance		1		*The score should accord with the attendance record held on the employees file. Any periods of absence which are as a result of a protected characteristic must not be included (eg maternity leave, days off work for armed forces duty etc).*

Criteria	Score	Weighting	Total	Justification of the score awarded
Skills/Qualification/ Training		1		*Details of employee's skills, qualification and training which are necessary or desirable for the job.*
Punctuality		1		*Must agree with time keeping records. Any relevant warning letters should be taken into consideration in the absence of detailed time keeping.*
Disciplinary record		1		*This assessment should be verifiable on account of information held on the personnel file and can only account for misconducts which have been proven or acknowledged - not simply imputed misconduct.*
Experience		1		*Provide details of the employee's experience*
Total score				

Scoring

1 = Poor	2 = Below average	3 = Average	4 = Good	5 = Excellent

5.59 Ideally two or more competent persons will carry out the assessment in order to reduce the possibility of bias. Where the score for a particular candidate significantly differs between the two evaluation officers, an additional evaluation of the employee by a different evaluation officer should be conducted where possible. The additional evaluation of the same employee will usually be unnecessary when more than two evaluation officers are used. To reduce the impact of subjectivity on the evaluation, all candidates of a pool should be evaluated by the same officers.

5.60 Finally, the evaluators should justify their score either relying on supporting documentation from past regular performance appraisals or by providing the grounds on which their score is based.

5.61 Prior to acting on the evaluation scores, the employer should bring the scores to the concerned employee's attention, explain how and why his score was awarded and give the employee the opportunity to challenge the scores or raise any issues or objections concerning the impartiality of the evaluating officer(s).

Bumping

5.62 'Bumping' describes a situation where an employee whose job is not redundant is dismissed to make way for an employee whose role has become redundant.

5.63 It is unclear whether bumping constitutes a genuine redundancy under the Termination of Employment Law in Cyprus, as the position has not yet been tested with Cypriot case law. However, the authors believe that it may be possible for bumping to constitute a genuine redundancy ground under Cypriot law, given that the Termination of Employment Law does not expressly prohibit the practice. The wording it employs makes it possible to justify bumping following the reasoning adopted in other common law jurisdictions. Given that there is currently no binding precedent on the matter, employers should be very careful when considering a 'bumping' scenario and only proceed with such an arrangement where the risk of being faced with a potential unfair dismissal claim is justified.

5.64 In jurisdictions where bumping has been approved there is no absolute obligation to bump, or to even consider bumping and, the fairness of a failure to consider bumping will turn on the specific factual background of each case. The test is what a reasonable employer would do in the particular circumstances and whether considering or applying a bumping scenario would be reasonable. The factors which are taken into account to determine whether the bumping of an employee is justified include:

- whether there is a vacancy;
- how different the two jobs are;
- the qualifications of the employee in danger of redundancy;
- the difference in remuneration between the two jobs; and
- the two employees' relative lengths of service;

Individual consultation

5.65 Individually consulting with each affected employee and taking the employee's views into account is the best practice. However, failure to consult individually will not on its own render a dismissal unfair, when the selection of the particular employee is objectively justified.

5.66 Even though employers not effecting 'collective redundancies' (see below at para 0) are not under a legal duty to 'warn' and 'consult' with individual employees, such consultation will be extremely valuable from an evidential point of view, in a potential unfair dismissal claim against the employer.

5.67 For an effective warning and consultation procedure the employer should take the following action when the decision for redundancies has been taken:

- Inform each potentially affected employee of the fact that they are at risk of being made redundant and why this is so.
- Set up a meeting with the affected employees to discuss and explain the proposed redundancy.
- At the first meeting the employer should:
  - Explain why the decision has been taken to make redundancies.
  - Outline what steps have been taken to avoid the redundancy situation.
  - Indicate the proposed selection pool.
  - Outline the criteria it will use to select the redundancy candidates and the weighting that will be applied to each criterion and justify its choices.
  - Give the proposed score sheet to the employees.
  - Invite the employees to comment on the proposed pool and selection criteria.
  - Minute the meeting and send a follow-up letter summarising the meeting and the comments made by the employees
- Where justified, revise the selection pool and/or the score sheet based on the employees' proposals or explain why any employee proposals for the revision of the pool or the selection criteria have been rejected.
- Score each employee and prepare the list of provisional redundant employees.
- Send a letter to each provisionally selected employee inviting them to a first individual redundancy consultation meeting.
- At the individual consultation meeting, explain to each employee:
  - Why he has been provisionally selected for redundancy.
  - What steps have been taken to avoid making this employee redundant.
  - Where applicable, discuss with the employee any opportunities for suitable alternative employment that may be available.
  - Invite the employee to express his views on the procedure and his selection.
- Select the redundant employees after taking the individually voiced views of each employee into consideration.
- Send a written letter to each selected employee:
  - Outlining what was discussed at the individual consultation meeting.
  - Informing them that they have been selected for redundancy.
  - Setting the time period within which the employee can request a meeting to make any further representations to the employer.
- Following the evaluation of any further representations made by the employee, take their final decision.
- Inform the employee of the decision to terminate his employment in writing, explaining the reasons and the procedure followed leading up to the selection of this employee.

5.68 In order for the consultation to carry evidential weight:

- It must be conducted before the redundancy procedure is finalised.
- The employee must be given sufficient information on the procedure and reasonable time to enable him to respond and make representations.
- The employer must carefully, and genuinely, consider any response, representation or suggestion which the employee advances.

INVOLVEMENT OF EMPLOYEE REPRESENTATIVES IN INDIVIDUAL DISMISSALS

5.69 The requirement for involving employee representatives in limited circumstances has been introduced into Cypriot law as a result of European legislation (Directive 2002/14/EC). The legislation only applies to undertakings employing at least 30 employees.

5.70 If employees are represented, it is usually by a trade union. Even though there is no legal duty on the employer to allow employee representatives during individual consultation, it is best practice for the employer to provide individual employees with the right to be accompanied by a colleague or a trade union representative, during any individual redundancy consultation procedure.

DUTY TO INFORM THE MINISTER

5.71 The employer also has a duty to notify the Ministry of Labour, Welfare and Social Insurance of *any* intended redundancies at least one month prior to the date the termination of employment of the affected employees is expected to take place. Failure to comply with this provision without reasonable cause, entails a small monetary fine.

5.72 This notice is in a standard form and contains the following information:

- the number of employees which will potentially be made redundant;
- the affected department or departments of the business;
- the professions and, where possible, the names and family obligations of the affected employees; and
- the reasons for the redundancies.

AVOIDING COMPULSORY REDUNDANCIES

5.73 Employers should consider all available less drastic alternatives to redundancy, including a switch to working part-time, salary reductions, provident fund or pension scheme contribution reductions, sabbaticals, benefits reduction or revocation, early retirement incentive schemes and revocation of bonus schemes. It should, however, be noted that a unilateral change of the employee's terms of employment can form the basis of a constructive dismissal claim against the employer. As a result, employers who offer less drastic alternatives to redundancy should extensively document the arrangement and minute all relevant consultation with the employee, to avoid being exposed to bad-faith constructive dismissal claims following such an arrangement.

5.74 Even though employers frequently consider inviting volunteers for redundancy before starting the consultation process, in light of the Redundancy Fund payment system in Cyprus (discussed below in the section starting at para 5.108) the position is more complicated. It is stressed that the employer is under no obligation to provide such a scheme or to even consider it. The incentive in Cyprus will typically be an enhanced redundancy payment offered in addition to the Redundancy Fund payment. However, an employer must exercise additional caution to ensure that a genuine redundancy scenario is in place, otherwise the Fund could potentially reject the employee's application, and if the court agrees that the redundancy was not genuine, the employer will be exposed to an unfair dismissal claim.

5.75 From a commercial point of view such schemes are not always desirable as usually the employees volunteering will be the most competent and productive given their increased employability thereafter. Consequently, employers should stress that the final decision is left entirely to the employer's discretion and that any voluntary redundancies are contingent on the employer's acceptance.

ALTERNATIVE EMPLOYMENT

5.76 Case law suggests that a fair and reasonable redundancy process requires the employer to consider and, where possible, offer suitable alternative employment to affected employees within its organisation. This includes consideration of employment at other locations and within any linked entities. However, the employer is not under a duty to create alternative employment or to exhaust all the means available in considering whether an alternative employment is available.

5.77 The employee is not entitled to a redundancy payment, if prior to the termination of his employment, the employer offers suitable alternative employment and the employee unreasonably refuses such an offer or if an employing business transfers the employee to a connected company.

5.78 In practice a Cypriot employer will generally be less incentivised to actively seek alternative employment for the employee, given that where there is a genuine redundancy situation the payment will be made by the Fund (discussed below in the section starting at para 5.108) and not the employer. In practice an employer will only actively seek to offer alternative employment to avoid a potential unfair dismissal claim, where a redundancy scenario is not clear and the employee's application could potentially be rejected by the Fund, thereby exposing the employer to a claim of unfair dismissal.

RIGHT TO RE-ENGAGEMENT

5.79 The Termination of Employment Law provides that:

> 'where an employer who has effected redundancies wishes, within eight months from the redundancy, to increase workforce of the same type or expertise as the redundant employees, during the hiring they must prioritise the employees affected by the redundancy, taking, however, into consideration the needs of operation of the business'.

5.80 No explicit sanction is imposed by the law for failure to comply with this article. However, case law has established that non-compliance with the said provision could 'convert' a genuine redundancy dismissal to a prima facie unfair dismissal, unless the employer can provide objective justification for not reengaging the redundant employee. If such an offer is made, the employee is not under any duty to accept the offer and as a result, the employee will be entitled to payment from the Fund even if they reject such an offer, provided that there was a genuine redundancy situation at the time they were dismissed.

OTHER CONSIDERATIONS

5.81 As previously mentioned, legislation establishes the minimum rights of employees. When effecting redundancies, any additional contractual arrangements between the parties must be honoured in addition to the statutory rights. As a result, care should be taken, to ensure that the redundancy complies with the employee's contract of employment, any applicable collective agreements and company policy and regulations which may be deemed incorporated into the employees contractual work terms.

COLLECTIVE REDUNDANCY PROCEDURE

5.82 Under Cypriot law a collective redundancy situation arises where dismissals are 'effected by an employer for one or more reasons not related to the individual workers concerned, where the number of redundancies effected over a period of 30 days, is:

- at least 10, in establishments normally employing more than 20 and less than 100 workers;
- at least 10 % of the number of workers, in establishments normally employing at least 100, but less than 300 workers;
- at least 30 in establishments normally employing 300 workers or more.

5.83 The law states that it does not cover collective redundancies effected on the basis of fixed terms contracts of employment, or contracts for limited work, unless those dismissals are made prior to the expiration or performance of those contracts. For the purposes of the Law, the number of employees who are to be dismissed includes any volunteers for redundancy.

5.84 Where the employer intends to proceed with collective redundancies, he has a duty to 'consult employee representatives in good time, with a view to reaching an agreement'. This collective consultation is in addition to any individual redundancy consultation outlined above under the relevant title.

5.85 The employer must also notify the 'competent authority' (currently the Ministry of Labour, Welfare and Social Insurance) of any planned collective redundancy, stating all relevant information and details regarding:

- the planned collective redundancy;
- the consultation with the representatives;
- the number of the employees to be made redundant;
- the number of employees regularly employed by the employer; and
- the period over which the redundancies will be effected.

INVOLVEMENT OF EMPLOYEE REPRESENTATIVES IN COLLECTIVE DISMISSALS

5.86 If there is a recognised trade union, it will usually be involved in the consultation as a body representative of employees. Notwithstanding this fact, experience indicates that, with the exception of some business, it is rare for all the affected employees to be members of a trade union. Where a pre-existing elected and duly authorised representative body does not exist, the employee representatives should be elected or authorised by all the affected employees.

5.87 The employer should never assume that a trade union is authorised to represent all potentially affected employees, by virtue of the fact that the majority of the said employees are union members. Even where employees are trade union members, the employer should verify that the trade union is in fact authorised to represent its members for the purposes of that specific collective redundancy.

ELECTION OF EMPLOYEE REPRESENTATIVES FOR COLLECTIVE CONSULTATION PURPOSES

5.88 The employer does not have a duty actively to arrange for the procedure leading to the election of representatives. Nonetheless, given that pursuant to the Law it is not a defence for the employer to later invoke the fact that no representatives had been elected, the employer should ideally ensure that arrangements are made for the nomination of candidates and for a fair election of representatives. The voting must take place in secret and the election process should be completed before the start of the information and consultation process.

INFORMATION AND CONSULTATION REQUIREMENTS

5.89 The law provides that consultation must take place 'in good time', 'to enable workers' representatives to make constructive proposals' and 'with a view to reaching an agreement'. It is established that the employer must never carry out the selection process prior to consulting with the employee representatives.

5.90 The regulations and the relevant EU case law establish that the employer must consult with the representatives, not just in respect of the timing and the implementation of the proposals, but on the substance of the matters leading to the decision of effecting redundancies in the first place. The consultation must, therefore, take place while the procedure is still at a 'formative stage', so that representatives can become involved and make representations, during the assessment of whether redundancies are in fact necessary, the assessment of ways to reduce the numbers of dismissals and the ways of mitigating the consequences of dismissal. Employee representatives must be given sufficient time properly to consider the information. As is the case with all employment consultations, the employer should enter into the consultation in good faith, without predispositions and with the intent of genuinely considering all proposed options.

5.91 The employer must, in good time, during the course of the consultations:

(a) supply the representatives with all relevant information; and
(b) in any event notify the representatives in writing of:
  (i) the reasons for the projected redundancies;
  (ii) the number and categories of workers to be made redundant;
  (iii) the number and categories of workers normally employed by the employer;
  (iv) the period over which the projected redundancies are to be effected;

(v) the criteria proposed for the selection of the workers to be made redundant defined as the responsibility of the employee based on legislation or practice; and
(vi) the method for calculating any redundancy payments other than the method prescribed in the Termination of Employment Law.

5.92 The consultation must cover at least the following matters:

- the possible ways and means of avoiding the collective redundancies or reducing the number of affected employees; and
- the ways and means of mitigating the consequences which arise from the collective redundancies by recourse to accompanying social measures aimed, inter alia, at aiding the redeployment or retraining of the workers made redundant.

SANCTIONS

5.93 Any collective redundancies are put into effect no sooner than 30 days from the date of the notification to the competent authority. This time period is in addition to the individual notice period applicable to each employee.

5.94 If an employer breaches the provisions of the legislation regarding their obligation to inform and consult on collective redundancies, or if they effect dismissals before the 30-day notice period has elapsed the employer is guilty of a criminal offence punishable with a fine.

NOTICE

5.95 The notice period describes the period of time between notifying the employee of the termination of his employment and the employment lawfully coming to an end. The Termination of Employment Law provides that the notice of termination must be given in writing. If the termination occurs within the probation period, the employee is not entitled to any notice. The Law creates a rebuttable presumption that the employment is not on a probationary basis.

5.96 Where the parties have agreed a notice period longer than the statutorily prescribed minimum, they should expressly and clearly set out the length of the applicable notice period in the contract. Where a notice period longer than the statutorily prescribed minimum notice has been agreed, it must be honoured, otherwise, if the contract provides for a notice period shorter than the statutory notice period, the latter will be applicable.

5.97 Where the parties wish to apply the statutorily prescribed minimum notice period, the contract should expressly state so. If the contract is silent on the issue of notice periods, then a reasonable notice period applies. The reasonable notice period is generally ascertained by reference to the notice period applicable to other staff holding a similar position within the said employer, or the usual notice period in force by custom or by collective agreement.

Minimum notice period

5.98 The minimum notice period which must be given by the employer to employees (who have completed their probation period) as prescribed in the Termination of Employment Law, is set out below:

Length of service (in weeks)	Minimum notice which must be given by the employer
26 – 51	1 week
52 – 103	2 weeks
104 – 155	4 weeks
156 – 207	5 weeks
208 – 259	6 weeks
260 – 311	7 weeks
312 and more	8 weeks

5.99 The minimum notice period under statute, given by employees to employers, is set out below:

Length of service (in weeks)	Minimum notice which must be given by the employee
26 – 51	1 week
52 – 259	2 weeks
260 and more	3 weeks

Rights of the parties during the notice period

5.100 During the notice period, the employee is entitled to paid 'absence' from work, in order to seek new employment. When exercising this right, the total time of absence cannot exceed eight hours a week and the total number of hours from the date of the notice until the date of the termination cannot exceed 40 hours. The employee must obtain the employer's consent prior to each period of absence but the employer cannot unreasonably withhold such consent.

5.101 If an employee, to whom notice has been given by the employer, receives a job offer from another employer within his notice period, they can leave the previous employment without giving any notice. When this right is exercised the employee relinquishes his right to payment for the rest of the notice period.

5.102 If during the employment period the employee is lawfully dismissed for gross misconduct then the employee is not entitled to any further payment for his notice period.

THE THIRD TABLE OF THE TERMINATION OF EMPLOYMENT LAW

5.103 The Termination of Employment Law states that, during the notice period, the rights of the parties are governed by the 'Third Table', which is an Appendix to the Act. The purpose of the Third Table is to ensure that the employer does not act in bad faith during the notice period, for example by artificially limiting the employee's work hours so that the salary is reduced. The most important provisions of the Third Table covering most employees are the following:

'1. Where the employee works for a fixed daily salary, he is entitled to this fixed salary for the entirety of the notice period, unless otherwise provided in this table.
2. When the employee's salary is based on the number of hours of work and it does not vary according to the amount of work performed, the employee is paid for the number of hours which he has worked during the notice period.
3.
   (1) Where an employee covered by paragraph 1 above is:
   - Ready and willing to work but the employer does not provide him with work; or
   - Rendered unable to work due to illness, disease, injury or childbirth; or
   - Absent on leave; or
   - Absent on parental leave.

   they receive salary as per paragraph 1.

   (2) Where an employee covered by paragraph 2 above is:
   - Ready and willing to work but the employer does not provide him with work; or
   - Rendered unable to work due to illness, disease, injury or childbirth; or
   - Absent on leave; or
   - Absent on parental leave.

   The salary for each week of the notice period can be no less than the average of the employee's weekly salary during the last 12 full weeks of work prior to the notice.

It is understood that no week is considered a full week for the purposes of this section unless the employee has worked for more than 18 hours during that week.

(3) Any payment made to the employer in the form of illness payment counts towards the obligations of the employer under this paragraph.

(4) Where the employee is paid on an hourly basis, his payment during the notice period is no less than the payment for the number of hours for which he has worked during the notice period on the basis of the average of an hourly fee during the last four full weeks prior to the notice.

No week of work is considered a full week for the purposes of this paragraph unless the employee has worked for more than 18 hours during that week.'

Payment in lieu of notice

5.104 When dismissing an employee it may sometimes be preferable to have the employee leave the workplace sooner rather than later to avoid or minimise disruption to the workforce. In such a situation the employer has the option of making a payment in lieu of giving the employee notice.

5.105 Under the Termination of Employment Law, an employer always has the right to give the employee a Payment In Lieu Of Notice (PILON). When the right is exercised, all applicable periods for the purposes of redundancy and unfair dismissal must be calculated as if the employee had worked for the entire of notice period and the payment must be calculated in accordance with the provisions of the Third Table of the Law.

Example of a payment in lieu of notice.

Ushuaia Travel ('UT') is a travel agency. Mr. Doe who works at the customer sales department has been underperforming and has consistently received poor customer feedback. Following the applicable disciplinary proceedings the management of UT has decided he must be dismissed.

UT does not want Mr. Doe to take company calls as he may damage the company's reputation and customer reviews. UT therefore decides to make a payment in lieu of notice to Mr. Doe. UT pays him all benefits as if he had worked for the entire period of the notice and instructs him to leave the workplace with immediate effect.

Garden leave

5.106 An employer may additionally wish to restrain an employee from working for a competitor during his notice period. In some jurisdictions this is achieved by putting the dismissed employee on 'garden leave' for his notice period. Garden leave describes the practice where an employee remains employed during his termination period and on the payroll but is instructed to stay away from work during the notice period and refrain from contacting customers.

5.107 'Garden leave' arrangements are not common in Cyprus and their enforceability has not been tested before the courts. Article 11(2) of the Termination of Employment Law states that 'when an employee, to whom notice has been given, receives a job offer from another employer within his notice period, he can abandon his previous employment without giving any notice'. The wording of this article suggests that garden leave clauses are unenforceable where new employment has been obtained. The article contains the following reservation 'It is understood that when this right is exercised the employee relinquishes his right to payment for the rest of the notice period'. It could be argued that the Law simply aims to relieve an employer from the obligation of paying the remaining notice period where the employee willingly abandons his past employment for a new job especially given the title of the Article ('abandonment of the right to notice'). Nonetheless, in the absence of binding precedent affirming such a proposition and in light of the wording of the reservation itself which explicitly states that it creates an employee right as well as the legal position in Cyprus against covenants in restraint of trade, it is submitted that garden leave arrangements are unenforceable in Cyprus.

Notice period comparison table

Type of Notice Period	Effective Date of Termination	Benefits	Disadvantages
Employee working the notice period	The expiry of the notice period	Employee works during his notice period which will generally give the business value for the salary paid.	Employee may be disruptive to colleagues, may underperform and hurt the good name of the business, may vindictively injure the business or may gather and copy confidential data from the work place.
Pay in lieu of notice	The expiry of the notice period.	The employee will not attend the office, (avoiding all the aforementioned disadvantages of working during the notice period)	The employer gets no value in terms of work from the employee during the notice period.

REDUNDANCY PAYMENT

5.108 Employees with 104 weeks of continuous employment who are made redundant are entitled to a statutory redundancy payment. For a definition of 'continuous employment' see the Second Table of the Law, above.

5.109 This redundancy payment is in addition to any notice period payment or other contractual entitlement the employee has under his employment contract for the termination of his employment.

5.110 It is important to note that under Cyprus law, when a genuine redundancy situation exists, the redundancy payment is not made by the Employer but by the Redundant Personnel Fund. Employers have a legal duty to make contributions to the Fund for each employee in their service. The formula of calculating the applicable contributions for each employee is defined in subsidiary legislation enacted by the Council of Ministers.

5.111 Employees do not have an entitlement to a statutory redundancy payment if:

- they have been offered suitable alternative employment with the same or a linked employer which they unreasonably refuse; or
- if prior to the termination of their employment they have completed the retirement age.

5.112 Where the employee is made redundant 12 months before the completion of the applicable retirement age, the amount of redundancy pay is reduced by 1/12 for each month up to the age of retirement. The age of the employee being made redundant does not otherwise have any impact on the amount of the redundancy payment.

Statutory redundancy pay calculation

5.113 The amount of the statutory redundancy payment is calculated using the following statutory formula:

- For the first four years of continuous employment, two weeks of salary for each 52-week period.
- From the fifth year up to the tenth year of continuous employment, two and a half weeks of salary for each 52-week period.
- From the 11th year up to the 15th year of continuous employment, three weeks of salary for each 52-week period.
- From the 16th year up to the 20th year of continuous employment, three and a half weeks of salary for each 52-week period.
- From the 21st year up to the 25th year of continuous employment, four weeks of salary for each 52-week period.

5.114 For the purposes of calculating the redundancy pay:

- Where the continuous employment period in years is not an integer, any period over 26 weeks is considered a full continuous year (ie the number is rounded). The 'continuous' of the employment is determined according to the Second Table of the law (see paras 0 and 0 above).
- The employee's weekly salary is:
  - Generally the amount that the employee would be entitled to during his last week of employment pursuant to the Third Table of the Law.
  - For port workers the weekly salary is the average of the employee salary for the last year prior to his dismissal.
- Any amount exceeding the quadruple of the 'basic weekly insurable salary' is not taken into consideration. The basic weekly insurable salary is decreed via subsidiary legislation. For the years 2013 to 2016 the basic weekly insurable salary is defined at €172.98 and thus the 'cap' of weekly salary for redundancy pay is currently €691.92.

Example of statutory redundancy calculation

Mr Doe and Ms. Roe have both been made redundant from the PTF Hair Transplant Centres Company ('PTF'). Mr Doe has been employed by the Company for three years with a weekly salary of €500. Ms Roe has been employed by the Company for 18 years and 8 months, with a weekly salary of €800.

Mr Doe is entitled to a statutory redundancy pay in the sum of €3.000 (€500 × (3 × 2)), ie two weeks-pay for each year worked.

Ms Roe's statutory redundancy pay will be calculated as follows:

1. Mr. Roe's period of service is 18 years and 8 months and must be rounded to 19 years as she has worked for more than 26 weeks during the final year of her employment.
2. The total number of weeks of redundancy pay is 52, calculated as follows: (4 × 2) + (6 × 2.5) + (5 × 3) + (4 × 3.5) = 52
3. As her salary exceeds the quadruple of the basic weekly insurable salary the applicable weekly salary multiplier is capped at the said amount which is €691.92.

   Mr. Roe's redundancy pay is thus 52 × €691.92 = €35.979.84

5.115 Finally, it should be noted that under Cyprus law, even shareholders who exercise control over the employing business are entitled to a reduced redundancy payment equivalent to 1% of the shareholders weekly salary multiplied by 52 and multiplied with the years of service. Shareholders who do not control the employing business are paid a normal redundancy payment by the Fund.

Enhanced redundancy payments

5.116 'Enhanced Redundancy payments' may be payable under contract, collective agreement or an employer's policy. Where a contractual redundancy payment clause exists, the Law provides that the employee will receive the statutory redundancy payment from the Fund and any remaining amount not covered by the fund, is covered by the employer. If the parties intend to provide a 'clear' sum in excess of the full statutory redundancy payment, they should expressly state it in the contract or adapt their contractual redundancy payment formula accordingly.

Taxation of redundancy payments

5.117 Statutory redundancy payments and enhanced redundancy payments do not fall under the categories of taxable sources of income.

5.118 The Supreme Court has clarified that a redundancy payment can be exempt from income tax even where the redundancy is not effected for a statutorily prescribed redundancy reason. The Supreme Court has established that the following factors should be taken into consideration for determining whether payment is a redundancy payment:

- Does the employee find himself without a job through circumstances over which he has no control?
- Does the dismissal not give rise to a right to compensation unless the employee has been employed for a minimum period?
- Does the right increase initially with the period of employment and then subsequently reduces until eventually the employee loses any right of payment on his reaching normal retirement age?
- Is the payment made to compensate or relieve an employee for the consequences of becoming unemployed?
- Is it payable after the employment has come to an end?
- Is the payment 'divorced' from the employment:
  - Does it relate to the services rendered under the contract?
  - Does the right to payment inevitably accrue at the end of the employment irrespective of the way the employment is terminated and even when the employee leaves the employment of his own accord?

Post-termination restrictive covenants

5.119 Employers usually include post-termination restrictive covenants in the employment contracts of key employees who could materially damage the employer's business, by competing with the employer following termination of employment.

5.120 Covenants in restraint of profession, trade or business of any nature are void under Cypriot law. The only exceptions where such covenants will be enforceable, are prescribed in the contract law and are the following:

- 'one who sells the good-will of a business may agree with the buyer to refrain from carrying on a similar business, within specified local limits so long as the buyer or any person deriving title to the good-will from him, carries on a like business therein, provided that such limits appear to the court reasonable, regard being had to the nature of the business.'
- 'partners may, upon or in anticipation of a dissolution of the partnership, agree that some or all of them will not carry on a business similar to that of the partnership within such local limits as are referred to in the paragraph above.'
- 'partners may agree that some one or all of them will not carry on any business, other than that of the partnership, during the continuance of the partnership.'

5.121 Even though post-termination covenants in restraint of trade are unenforceable under Cypriot law, non-solicitation clauses and covenants restricting an employee from disclosing trade secrets and confidential information are enforceable. Such covenants will survive the termination of the employment contract and may even be implied by the court on the rare occasion that this is appropriate.

5.122 It should be stressed that as a matter of contract law, the repudiating party cannot seek to enforce the contract, even those provisions which are meant to survive the contract's termination. As a result, employers cannot rely on post-termination restrictive covenants if the employer has breached the contract by unfairly or wrongfully dismissing the employee, and thus additional care should be taken to lawfully effect the dismissal of an employee who could damage an employer if they are no longer under an obligation to honour such covenants.

BUSINESS SALE, OUTSOURCING/INSOURCING AND OFFSHORING

5.123 'The safeguarding of employees' rights in the event of transfers of undertakings, businesses or parts of undertakings or businesses law of 2000' (referred to simply as the 'transfer law') implements via its subsequent amendments the similarly titled Directive 2001/23/EC (referred to simply as the 'transfer directive').

5.124 The transfer law ensures that terms and conditions of employment are maintained for employees affected by transfers of undertakings, businesses or parts of undertakings or businesses (referred to simply as 'transfers of undertakings'). In practical terms, the Transfer Law applies where the entire business or a specific identifiable part of the business is transferred to another employer.

5.125 The key protection provisions of the Transfer Law are:

- the employment of affected employees automatically transfers to the transferee;
- the employment rights, obligations and liabilities relating to transferring staff automatically become obligations of the transferee; and
- the transferor has a duty to inform and consult with affected employees individually and with elected employee representatives collectively.

Business sale

5.126 The Transfer Law applies to transfers where a 'stable economic entity' that retains its identity post transfer is transferred to another employer. The description of economic entity in the Transfer Law is identical to that of the Transfer Directive ie 'an organised grouping of resources which has the objective of pursuing an economic activity, whether or not that activity is central or ancillary.'

5.127 The question whether the economic entity still exists and is carrying out the same or similar activities post transfer is answered by taking into account a number of factors. The Supreme Court of Cyprus has adopted the following factors laid down by the European Court of Justice (ECJ) to determine whether a transfer of an undertaking within the meaning of the Law has taken place:

- the type of undertaking or business;
- whether or not its tangible assets, such as buildings and movable property, are transferred;
- the value of its intangible assets at the time of the transfer;
- if the assets are to be used by the purchaser with the intention of carrying on the same kind of 'business' as the seller;
- whether or not the majority of its employees are taken over by the new employer;
- whether or not its customers are transferred;
- the degree of similarity between the activities carried on before and after the transfer; and
- the period, if any, for which those activities were suspended.

5.128 These are merely single factors which must be taken into account for the overall assessment of the matter and cannot be considered in isolation.

Outsourcing/insourcing

5.129 It is safe to assume that a transfer of an undertaking within the meaning of the law occurs where for example a restaurant is taken over by another company and continues its operation on the same basis. Where, however, a 'service provision change' occurs, ie where one business ceases to provide the services and another business takes them over the answer to whether a transfer of undertaking has occurred will not always be clear.

5.130 Service provision changes commonly occur where a particular business function is outsourced to an external service provider. A service provision change could also arise on the termination of the previous outsourcing arrangement where activities cease to be carried out by the initial service provider and are subsequently assigned to either another contractor or brought back in-house by the business.

5.131 After a series of ECJ judgments, it has now been established that the outsourcing of a task or the mere loss of a service contract to a competitor does not, by itself, suffice to establish that a transfer of an undertaking within the meaning of the Transfer Directive has taken place. The principle arising out of European case law is that, where no assets or a minimal number of assets are transferred, the following questions should be answered in the affirmative in order for a service provision change to amount to a transfer of an undertaking within the meaning of the Transfer Directive:

- Are the activities performed fundamentally or essentially the same before and after the transfer?
- Is the activity based essentially on manpower?
- Are the employees an organised grouping of employees whose principal purpose is to carry out the relevant activities being transferred?
- Has the transferee employer taken on a significant number of employees?

Effect of the Transfer Law

Automatic transfer and protection of employment

5.132 When the Transfer Law applies all the rights and obligations of the transferring business are transferred to the transferee.

Objection to the transfer

5.133 The employee does not have a right to object to their transfer under the Transfer Law. The employee can always resign from the undertaking, however, in that event, the employee is not entitled to any compensation and will have no entitlement to notice (or a payment in lieu of notice), redundancy payment or any remedy for unfair dismissal.

Protection from dismissal

5.134 The transfer itself does not constitute a valid ground of dismissal and any dismissals not justified on an economic, technical or organisational (ETO) ground are unfair. It should be noted that this is an additional layer of protection and not a revocation of the provisions of the Termination of Employment Law. Consequently, if a dismissal is to be deemed as fair following the transfer of undertaking, it must have been effected on an ETO ground which is *also* a fair dismissal ground under the Termination of Employment Law.

5.135 The Transfer Law provides that if the contract of employment or the employment relationship is terminated because the transfer involves a substantial change in working conditions, to the detriment of the employee, the employer shall be regarded as having been responsible for termination of the contract of employment or of the employment relationship.

5.136 Pursuant to the Termination of Employment Law, the employee's continuous service length is not interrupted by a transfer.

Protection of terms and conditions of employment

5.137 Terms of employment are protected under the Transfer Law and may only be varied following a transfer if the principal reason for the change is unconnected with the transfer, or where it is for an ETO reason connected with the transfer. The Transfer Law does not in any way affect the operation of existing employment rights protections, thus any unilateral changes to employment terms can still form the basis of a constructive dismissal claim, even if they were justified for an ETO reason. As a result, transferee employers must always obtain the consent of the employees before making any changes to their employment terms as explained below in the section starting at para 5.157.

5.138 Any attempts to harmonise the terms and conditions of transferred employees with existing personnel will be void and will also justify a constructive dismissal claim, except in the unlikely event that the transferee employer decides to 'upgrade' the employment terms of less privileged employees.

5.139 Employers should also bear in mind that the date of payment and the composition of wages cannot be altered, even when the total amount of the wages remains the same, something which may increase the complexity of the employer's payroll system.

Information and consultation under the Transfer Law

5.140 Both the transferor and the transferee have a duty to inform the employees and their representatives of the following:

- the date or proposed date of the transfer;
- the reasons for the transfer;
- the legal, economic and social implications of the transfer for the employees; and
- any measures envisaged in relation to the employees;

DUTY TO INFORM AND CONSULT

5.141 The transferor must give the relevant information to the representatives of his employees in good time and in any event before the transfer is carried out or any employees are directly affected by the transfer.

5.142 Where the transferor or the transferee envisage measures in relation to the employees, they should consult the representatives of the employees in good time on such measures with a view to reaching an agreement. The information must be provided and consultations must take place in 'good time' before the transfer.

5.143 These obligations apply irrespective of whether the decision resulting in the transfer is taken by the employer or an undertaking controlling the employer. If this duty is breached, it is not a defence for the employer to allege that the breach occurred because the information was not provided by the controlling undertaking.

5.144 If the undertaking or business or part thereof preserves its autonomy, the status and function of the representatives or of the representation of the employees are preserved. Where the undertaking does not preserve its autonomy, the transferor and the transferee must ensure that employees are properly represented during the period necessary for the reconstitution or reappointment of the representation of employees.

5.145 Where there are no employee representatives through no fault of the employees, the employer must directly provide the employees affected by the transfer with the aforementioned information in advance.

5.146 In practice, the transfer itself will rarely have much effect on existing employees, especially where the undertaking will maintain its identity and operate at its established locality. The duty will usually simply be to inform employees that they will automatically transfer to their new employer. If, however, the transferee proposes to make redundancies after the transfer, then the obligation to inform and consult is triggered.

5.147 The duty to inform is not limited to the employees being transferred but all employees affected by the transfer. So if for example a restaurant franchise sells-off one of its stores, but the store's management personnel will not transfer and will be redeployed elsewhere within the transferor, the employer has a duty to inform them and their representatives of changes such as their potential relocation or changes to their day to day duties.

Bankruptcy of the transferee

5.148 Where the transferor is the subject of bankruptcy proceedings or any analogous insolvency proceedings which have been instituted with a view to the liquidation of the assets of the transferor and are under the supervision of a competent public authority, not all the provisions of the Law will apply. More specifically, the provisions for enhanced dismissal protection and the automatic transfer of rights and obligations will not apply. As a result, where the transferee is insolvent, the effect of Transfer Law is effectively limited to the duty of informing and consulting.

5.149 To prevent abuse of this provision, the Transfer Law states that where the transferor is the subject of insolvency proceedings which have been instituted with a view of depriving employees from their rights accruing from the Transfer Law, they are guilty of an offence punishable by a monetary fine and this is without prejudice to any additional rights of the affected employees.

Sanctions

Unfair dismissal

5.150 If an employee qualifies for protection under the Termination of Employment Law, a dismissal will be automatically unfair where the principal reason for the dismissal is the transfer itself or a non ETO reason connected with the transfer. For the remedies available for unfair dismissal see the section starting at para **5.196**.

5.151 Given that all employment liabilities transfer to the transferee under the Transfer Law, the transferee can find themselves liable for dismissals effected by the transferor. The transferor and the transferee can agree that after the transfer date they will be jointly and severally responsible for all obligations created prior to the transfer. This is expressly permitted by the Transfer Law and the Transfer Directive. In practice, properly drafted commercial agreements for the transfer of an undertaking will include intricate indemnities to regulate the obligations of the parties.

Practical Tip

Even if an unconditional indemnity is given by the transferor covering the full liability of the transferor towards the employees up to the transfer, such indemnity will be useless to the transferee in the event that the transferor is dissolved before a transferred employee advances their claim. In light of this, the transferee should be particularly vigilant when agreeing the commercial terms of the transfer and should conduct a 'due diligence' on the transferor's financial robustness so they factor the risk, of the transferor's potential future dissolution and the subsequent liability, in the 'purchase price'.

FAILURE TO INFORM AND CONSULT

5.152 Employers who fail to inform and consult with the employees and their representatives are guilty of an offence punishable with a fine.

Application of the Transfer Law to cross-border transactions

5.153 The Transfer Law itself does not contain any provisions, or provide any guidance regarding its territorial jurisdiction. As a result, guidance must be sought from the Transfer Directive, which states that it applies 'where and in so far as the undertaking, business or part of the undertaking or business to be transferred is situated within the territorial scope of the Treaty [of Rome]'.

5.154 The wording of the Transfer Directive makes it clear that the Transfer Law applies to all intra-EU cross-border transfers of undertakings and consequently transfers into Cyprus (onshoring) from a member state or transfers out of Cyprus (offshoring) to a member state. In such a scenario the employment of affected employees will automatically transfer from the transferor to the transferee on the existing terms and conditions of employment. The wording of the Transfer Directive also makes it clear that the Transfer Law will not apply where an undertaking is on-shored to Cyprus from a non-member state.

5.155 The position is slightly more complicated where the transfer of the undertaking is from Cyprus to a non-EU member state. The Transfer Law clearly applies to such a scenario, as it relates to an undertaking situated within EU territory. In this event it could be difficult to enforce the Transfer Law against a non-EU transferee. Employees may, therefore, be unable to enforce any judgments against the transferee and thus find themselves in a position worse than if the Transfer Law did not apply, where they could have claimed unfair dismissal against the transferor or apply for redundancy payment. Developments, either in the form of authoritative EU case law or even an amendment of the Transfer Directive itself, should be expected where offshoring is concerned, to remedy this potential shortcoming of the Transfer Directive.

WORKFORCE REDUCTION IN CONNECTION WITH SHARE SALE OR SHARE PURCHASE

5.156 The Transfer Law and the Transfer Directive do not apply where ownership of the employing entity changes by way of a share sale. In such a case, there is no need for special provisions as the employing entity remains unchanged. As a matter of company law the underlying ownership of the company does not concern persons dealing with it nor does it affect the rights or obligations of the company.

CHANGING EMPLOYMENT TERMS AND CONDITIONS

5.157 Once an employment contract is entered into, it is unlawful to unilaterally vary the employment terms without the employee's consent, unless the employment contract provides for such a right. Even then, any clauses purporting to allow sweeping unilateral changes to the employment terms will only be held enforceable, if the changes effected on the grounds of such clause are objectively justified. In light of this, clauses in the employment contract purporting to allow unilateral changes to the employment terms by the Employer:

- must explicitly be brought to the employee's attention and where practicable the employee must acknowledge the existence of the clause and the employer's right to vary the employment terms;
- should be confined in their scope to only allow changes dictated by the specific commercial needs;
- should be carefully drafted so that they:
  - explicitly set-out the specific conditions upon which a change can be effected;
  - specify what type of change each condition entitles the employer to make and the extent of such change; and
  - provide an objective commercial justification for the right to make each change.

5.158 In the absence of an express clause allowing unilateral employment term changes an employer wishing to modify the terms of existing employees has the following options:

(a) agreeing changes with the employees;
(b) seeking to unilaterally change the employment contract; or
(c) dismissing and re-engaging the employees on the new desired terms and conditions.

5.159 The last two options carry a significant risk of claims against the employer for breach of contract and constructive unfair dismissal.

Mutually agreed changes

5.160 The mutually agreed changes option effectively carries zero risk for the employer provided that the employer can prove that the contract was amended with the freely given agreement of the employees. A way to show that the employee had free will is by ensuring that employees have received independent legal advice, or that they have been represented and advised by their trade union. Where possible, a combination of the two is ideal. However, independent legal advice is arguably the more important of the two. It is good practice to include the fact that the employee has received independent advice in the amended contract (or the amending agreement) and to have such document attested by the lawyer who has provided the independent legal advice.

5.161 Under Cypriot contract law, any contract and any amendment to a contract is only binding on the parties if 'consideration' has been provided. 'Consideration' is the term of art used in common law jurisdictions to describe the benefit that each party derives or expects to derive in exchange for the detriment he suffers in the execution of the contract.

5.162 An existing contractual duty is never good consideration, and as a result, a mutually agreed change to the employment terms will only be effective and enforceable, if the employee obtains some other benefit in exchange for the changes to their terms of employment to their detriment. Typically, mutually agreed changes are made where restructuring is imminent, with a view to avoiding making employees redundant. In this case the employer will generally argue that the benefit for the employee is derived from the fact that the employee will retain his employment and does not run the risk of being made redundant. Nonetheless, simply remaining employed will not always amount to good consideration and thus thought must be given to ensure consideration exists when employment contract variations are mutually agreed.

Practical tips on changing terms and conditions

The easiest and safest option for employers is to always obtain the employee's express consent for the variation of the employment terms.

If the employer is facing financial problems most employees will usually be willing to agree to reductions, especially where the danger of redundancies (or bankruptcy) is imminent.

Another option where the employer is financially robust is to obtain employee consent *quid pro quo*, by providing new benefits (eg free medical insurance, provident fund schemes etc) to employees who agree to changes in the desired employment terms.

Unilateral changes

5.163 An employer may under certain circumstances choose to impose changes on the terms and conditions of the employees without an express clause allowing him to act in this manner and without first obtaining the consent of the employees.

5.164 This is not a safe approach, as the employer will be breaching the contract, thus potentially exposing themselves to constructive unfair dismissal claims and precluding them from enforcing any post termination covenants. Where a change to the terms is trivial, it will not always amount to a significant breach justifying a constructive dismissal claim.

5.165 If the employee continues to work after changes have been made, they must express an objection to the employment term changes within a reasonable amount of time. Otherwise, they will be estopped from claiming constructive dismissal and will be deemed to have accepted the new employment terms.

DISMISSING AND RE-ENGAGING EMPLOYEES ON NEW TERMS

5.166 Finally, employers may dismiss the employees and offer to re-employ them on the new terms.

5.167 As previously explained, in Cyprus a dismissal effected for purely cost-saving reasons can never amount to a genuine redundancy, thus, a dismissal and an immediate re-engagement on less favourable terms without the employee's consent will always amount to an unfair dismissal. In light of this, if one of the two unilateral options must necessarily be followed, it is submitted that the unilateral change of employment terms is preferable for employers because:

- The sanctions for unfair dismissal are identical to the sanctions for constructive dismissal.
- In a claim for constructive dismissal the burden of proof rests on the employee. In a claim for unfair dismissal, the employee only needs to prove that he was employed and that he was dismissed. The burden of proving a fair dismissal then shifts to the employer.
- The employee cannot be certain the court will agree that the changes to their terms of employment were indeed significant breaches of the contract justifying the employee's resignation.

USING TEMPORARY STAFF

5.168 Sometimes during the transitional period after the restructuring, the remaining personnel will be unable to handle the workload. In this event it is common for the employer to use temporary workers from an agency or to directly engage employees on fixed term contracts.

5.169 Both the Fund and the Court will generally view an immediate engagement of other persons to perform the tasks of redundant employees unfavourably. The employer should, thus, be very careful when implementing such an arrangement, especially where the redundancy ground being invoked is a reduction of the work in question.

5.170 Attention should be given to the rights of redundant employees to be re-engaged under certain conditions (see para 5.79 above) and the limitations to using agency workers after effecting redundancies discussed below in para 5.176.

Agency workers

5.171 Agency workers are workers on a contract of service with an agency, who are deployed to perform specific tasks for other business (which for the purposes of this section will be referred to as the 'third-party employer').

5.172 In the past the third-party employer was not concerned with the terms of employment of the agency worker; they were effectively buying services from the Agency. Following the enactment of the 'Corporations of Temporary Employment Law of 2012' (which also implements the Temporary Agency Directive 2008/104/EC) some responsibility has been placed on the third party employer. It should be noted that the provisions of the national legislation go beyond the scope of the relevant directive and more strictly regulate the deployment of agency workers.

5.173 Each period of deployment 'cannot exceed four months' which can be extended by a renewal in writing, but the total period of deployment cannot exceed 12 months.

5.174 Temporary Worker Agencies are strictly regulated in Cyprus and must deposit a bank guarantee with the competent regulatory authority before obtaining their license to operate.

5.175 The agency and the third-party employer are jointly and severally liable for an agency worker's salary rights. However, the third-party employer is relieved of this liability where the agency worker's rights can be satisfied by a forfeiture of the bank warranty deposited by the Agency.

5.176 The law specifically prohibits the deployment of an agency worker to a third-party employer where:

- The agency worker will be deployed to replace employees on strike.
- The employer had effected redundancies in the past 12 months for the same kind of personnel, unless, the deployment is to replace:
  - an ill employee; or
  - an employee whose contract has been suspended; or
  - an employee who has been made redundant and does not wish to be reengaged in the company or organisation.

5.177 The basic terms of the agency worker are at least the terms which would have applied during the time of their deployment, had the third-party employer directly employed them in that position.

5.178 The third-party employer has a duty of informing the agency workers of any vacancies but simply placing a general notice in a visible place in the workplace will suffice to dispense with this duty. Agency workers are also entitled to the right of representation.

Fixed-term contracts

5.179 Fixed-term contracts are used where an employer does not have an ongoing need for an employee. This is usually the case where the employer is faced with a non-recurring workload (eg the computerisation of old files), where a person with particular expertise is only required for a specific part of a project or where a replacement worker is required for employees on a maternity, parental or illness leave.

5.180 Following the adoption of the Fixed-term Work Directive 1999/70/EC and the enactment of the implementing 'Fixed-Term Employees (Prohibition of Less Favourable Treatment) Law of 2003', fixed-term employees now enjoy substantial protection.

5.181 A fixed-term contract will usually be drafted to terminate at a specific date or at the conclusion of a particular project or task. The termination of the contract at the end of the fixed term is a fair ground for dismissal under the Termination of Employment Law, subject to the powers of the Tribunal to 'convert' the fixed-term employment to a permanent employment discussed below.

5.182 Fixed-term workers cannot be treated less favourably than comparable permanent workers solely because they have a fixed-term contract or relation unless different treatment is justified on objective grounds. The equal treatment principle also applies to any period-of service qualifications relating to particular conditions of employment.

5.183 Fixed term employees have the same rights of being informed, consulted and represented as comparable permanent employees.

RENEWAL OF FIXED-TERM CONTRACTS

5.184 Employers may renew a fixed-term contract a number of times, provided that they can justify the need to conclude a fixed-term contract instead of engaging the employee on a permanent contract.

5.185 When a fixed-term employee is employed with the same employer for a total period 30 months or more, irrespective of any successive fixed term renewal contracts, the employment is deemed to be permanent and any fixed-term provisions become void unless the employer can prove that the fixed-term is justified on objective grounds. The law sets-out the following list of objective grounds which justify consecutive fixed-term contracts:

- The needs of the business for conducting of some type of work are temporary.
- The employee is replacing another employee.
- The particularity of the work in question justifies the fixed term.
- The fixed-term employee is under probation.
- The employment on a fixed-term is for the enforcement of a court judgment.
- The employment is for a particular category of 'five-year volunteer' army personnel.

5.186 It should be noted that even before the enactment of the relevant Fixed-term Employees Law of 2003, the Tribunal had the power to treat a fixed-term contract as a permanent contract. For the purposes of determining the fairness of a dismissal the Termination of Employment Law provides that 'Where the Employment tribunal considers that any fixed-term contract or any series of fixed term contract can be regarded either separately or jointly as a permanent contract, then such fixed-term contract or series of contracts is regarded as a permanent contract'.

5.187 Generally, a fixed-term employee, who has completed their probation period, will have a strong claim for unfair dismissal if:

- the employer terminates the fixed-term contract prior to the of the term;
- at the end of the fixed-term the employer does not renew the contract in bad faith with the sole intention of depriving the employee of his rights; or
- the employee has completed 30 months of employment with the same employer and the use of fixed-terms is not objectively justified.

5.188 A fixed-term employee who has not concluded his probation period or whose contract is not deemed by the Tribunal to be permanent can never claim unfair dismissal; they may, however, still have a claim against the employer for breach of contract. For this reason, the employer should always include a contractual provision, allowing them to terminate the contract before the expiry of the fixed-term.

5.189 If the employment is unlawfully terminated before the fixed-term, the employer will generally be liable to pay the employee their full salary for the duration of the contract. The full amount of the contract will be limited by the general duty of mitigating loss and it may potentially be further limited by an implied term of a 'reasonable' period of notice, usually where such a notice period would normally apply to this type of contract or work.

EMPLOYMENT CLAIMS

5.190 As a general rule, employment claims are heard by a regional employment tribunal within the district of the employee's place of work. The competent employment tribunal has exclusive jurisdiction over claims for the rights established by the Termination of Employment Law.

5.191 Employment tribunals were introduced to create a forum for employees and for employers to resolve their disputes quickly and inexpensively. The tribunal is composed from three members, a single judge presiding and two lay members; one 'representing' employees (usually a person from a major trade union) and one 'representing' employers (usually from the Cyprus Employers & Industrialists Federation). The judgment of the majority is binding on the parties, but in the event of a dissenting minority that judgment must also be handed down to the parties. Where a point of law is concerned, the decision of the single judge is binding on the other members.

5.192 Appeals from the employment tribunal's judgment are heard by the Supreme Court, but the appeal can only turn against findings of law.

5.193 In claims arising from the Termination of Employment Law, the Tribunal does not have jurisdiction to award any sum higher than two years of salary.

Limitation

5.194 Employees have 12 months from the date that the right accrued to bring a claim before the employment tribunal, or nine months from the receipt of the Redundancy fund's response to the employee's application for redundancy payment, where an application has been filed with the Redundancy fund.

5.195 Where an employment related claim for breach of contract claim is advanced in the district court the contractual limitation of six years period from the date of completion of the cause of action applies.

UNFAIR DISMISSAL

5.196 Employees who have completed their probation period can bring a claim for unfair dismissal if they believe that their dismissal was unfair.

Remedies

5.197 The usual remedy granted by the tribunal is compensation. Compensation for unfair dismissal is calculated pursuant to the First Table of the Termination of Employment law which lays down the following guidance:

- The compensation awarded for unfair dismissal shall in no event be lower than the sum which the employee would have received if he had been made redundant (see paras **5.113** and **5.114** above).
- The compensation cannot exceed the salary of two years.
- When making the award, the court should take into consideration, amongst other things, the following:
  - The salaries of the employee and any other remuneration.
  - The employee's period of service.
  - The loss of career of the employee.
  - The true circumstances of the termination of the employee's services.
  - The age of the employee.

5.198 When the employer employs more than 19 employees, the tribunal has the authority to order the employer to reinstate the employee, provided that the employee has sought such relief in his application. This power is entirely discretionary and will only be exercised where the surrounding circumstances justify the order. In practice, it is uncommon for the Tribunal to make such orders and indeed, employees will rarely seek such relief. If a reinstatement order is made, the tribunal can additionally order compensation for the damage actually sustained by the employee as a result of the dismissal, with a maximum cap of 12 months of salary.

Apportionment of the payment of the award

5.199 The compensation awarded by the Tribunal for unfair dismissal, is apportioned. The part of the amount up to one year's worth of salaries is paid by the employer and any amount awarded exceeding one year's salary is paid by the Fund.

> **Example of an unfair dismissal payment and its apportionment**
>
> Unreasonable Ltd has unfairly dismissed Mr. Doe who has worked with the company for 25 years. According to the statutory redundancy payment table Mr. Doe would be entitled to 75.5 weeks of salary if he had been made redundant so his unfair dismissal award can in no event be lower than the said amount.
>
> In light of Mr. Doe's old age, the loss of career and the unreasonableness of the decision of the employer to unfairly dismiss him, the Tribunal exercising its discretion, makes a compensation award for the equivalent of 92 weeks of Mr. Doe's salary.
>
> Unreasonable Ltd must pay Mr. Doe 52 weeks of salary to Mr. Doe. The remaining 40 weeks (92 minus 52) of salary will be paid by the Redundancy Fund.

DISCRIMINATION

5.200 An employee may also bring a claim for discrimination in the employment tribunals if they believe that the real reason for his selection for redundancy was because of one of the following protected characteristics:

- disability;
- gender reassignment;
- pregnancy and maternity;
- race;
- religion or belief;
- sex; or
- sexual orientation.

Remedies

5.201 If an employee is successful in a claim for discrimination the tribunal will award 'fair and reasonable compensation which covers at least the entire positive damage' to the claimant. This is a broad provision which allows flexibility in the quantum of the damages awarded. Cypriot courts have followed the CJEU guidance for the calculation of damages for such claims and thus any amount awarded must 'provide effective protection, be preventative of discriminative conduct and proportionate to the damage'.

5.202 An employee who has been discriminated by simply not being considered for a position which they would not have gotten in any event, will only have a 'punitive' amount awarded against the employer. Even though the directive allows it, Cyprus has not adopted a cap for such claims in national legislation.

5.203 Employees who would have taken the position, save for the discriminatory conduct of the employer, will generally be awarded a substantial sum equivalent to their full loss of earnings.

Practical Tip

Once a protected person adduces real facts establishing a prima facie case of discrimination, the burden of proof shifts to the employer who must evidence that the non-hire or the dismissal was not discriminatory. As a result, an employer should always document the reasons for hiring particular candidates or for selecting particular persons from a redundancy selection pool and should implement an objective scoring system.

MUTUALLY AGREED TERMINATION

5.204 An employer may wish to reach a mutually agreed termination with an employee. Under the terms of such an agreement, the employment is mutually terminated and thus there is no dismissal.

5.205 There are no statutorily prescribed formalities required for the validity of a settlement agreement for the mutual termination of the employment. However, case law has established that the employee must be fully informed of his rights, he must enter into such agreement with his free will and it is preferable if he has received independent legal advice on the terms of the agreement from a qualified lawyer.

5.206 As with all common law contracts, in order for a settlement agreement to be binding, it must have consideration. If the employee is simply getting what he would be entitled to under statute, the agreement will be void and the employee can advance an unfair dismissal claim.

5.207 It is good practice for the settlement agreement to be unequivocal and as detailed as possible. The agreement should set out the reasons of the parties for the mutual termination of the employment and the benefit that each party obtains from the agreement. It is usual to have the independent lawyer advising the employee attest the settlement document to show the free will of the employee.

Chapter 6

Workforce restructuring in the Czech Republic

Anna Diblíková and Jana Krautwurmová
Wolf Theiss, Prague

INTRODUCTION

6.1 This chapter considers workforce restructuring issues that may arise under Czech law with the aim of providing practical guidance for employers. The Czech Republic has a civil law system that is part of the European continental jurisdictions and is generally harmonised with EU law. Employment is regulated by a number of acts, decrees and regulations. The general framework is set out in the Civil Code which regulates Czech civil law, including labour law. The Civil Code was a key part of the recodification of Czech private law which took effect from 1 January 2014. In addition to the Civil Code, the Act on Business Corporations and the Act on Private International Law were also enacted. These acts replaced more than 250 pieces of legislation of private and public law. Labour law underwent fewer changes than other legal fields, primarily because it continues to be more closely and separately regulated by the Labour Code.

6.2 During the planning and execution of individual or collective termination of employees during a restructuring, it is essential to consider the layers of legal authority in the Czech Republic. The Labour Code is considered a *lex specialis* to the Civil Code; therefore, Labour Code provisions prevail if there is any conflict between the provisions of these two Codes.

6.3 Specific areas of labour law, such as labour office competences or collective bargaining, are governed by specific legislative acts, such as the Act No. 435/2004 Coll., on Employment, as amended, and the Act No 2/1991 Coll, on Collective Bargaining, as amended.

6.4 The majority of key issues that arise during a restructuring are addressed by the Labour Code, as it regulates, inter alia, the employment term and termination, working conditions, working hours, overtime work, salary and salary compensation, women's and minors' working conditions, and compensation for damages. Most labour law provisions are mandatory and cannot be carved out in employment contracts or modified in employers' internal regulations.

6.5 Employers need to be aware that the State Labour Inspection Office and its branches play a significant supervisory role. Generally, they control and monitor compliance with statutory duties regarding recruitment, working conditions, health and safety at work, female employees and minors. Its inspectors may apply sanctions against employers who are in breach of their duties in the regulated areas.

6.6 Similar to the other European jurisdictions covered in this publication, the Czech Republic does not recognise the concept of 'employment at will'. An employer may unilaterally terminate an employment agreement only for 'permissible reasons' listed in the Labour Code and only by following specific statutory termination procedures.

6.7 For the purposes of this chapter, 'restructuring', refers to organisational changes within the employer that result in workforce reductions, changes in employment terms, integration and harmonisation of workforces from different companies, the use of temporary staff, outsourcing, employee dismissals and reassignment of staff responsibilities.

PREPARING FOR A RESTRUCTURING EXERCISE

Identify the employing entity

6.8 Employment is always connected with a specific legal entity and never with a 'group of companies'. Business decisions on restructuring and/or any redundancies must be executed and documented separately for each company within the group. This is particularly important when teams of employees are working together for more than one company within a group, eg the HR manager for CEE region.

Example

The parent company decides to discontinue its Czech subsidiary's activities. Even though the group policy may require a global resolution on the department redundancy, as a matter of Czech law, an additional resolution must be adopted by the Czech subsidiary as the employer.

Further, the global policy may prescribe other obligations to consider, such as higher severance payments or, where appropriate, an offer of suitable alternative positions that may be available in other companies within the group.

Collating information to plan and budget for the restructuring exercise

6.9 Any restructuring requires careful planning. HR managers will need to establish their data requirements in order to budget for and undertake the restructuring. The planning and structuring stage can realistically begin only when appropriate data is available.

6.10 In a group structure, we recommend ensuring that a centralised HR department can obtain lawful access to employee personal data (such as name, date of birth, marital status). Sharing personal data outside of the European Union usually requires the employee's consent.

> **Practical Tip**
>
> Key data initially required in respect of any employee potentially impacted by restructuring include eg:
>
> - job description;
> - length of employment;
> - notice period;
> - contractual benefits and entitlements arising from the employment termination (such as severance payments);
> - age;
> - workplace;
> - maternity or parental leave;
> - collective agreement; and
> - non-competition clause.
>
> This information will be necessary for estimating the costs of the restructuring and for planning the appropriate timetable for dismissals.

EMPLOYMENT STATUS

6.11 In addition to the above listed data, employers may wish to assess whether there are any persons engaged in the impacted business who do not have the status of an employee. This would concern, for instance, self-employed contractors or consultants. As contractors do not benefit from labour law protection during the termination of their agreements, they need to be treated separately in the dismissal procedure during the restructuring.

6.12 Within certain restrictions, individuals can be engaged as contractors rather than employees during the restructuring. This choice lowers costs due to a different tax treatment of their payment and lowers the administrative burden (eg no registration obligation, no mandatory occupational medical exams). It should be noted, however, that under Czech law it is prohibited to engage staff as contractors by way of a civil/commercial law agreement in place of executing an employment contract when the nature of the work to be performed clearly falls under 'dependent work' as defined in the Labour Code and discussed below. Breach of this rule is subject to fine of up to CZK 10 million (approx €400,000).

Practical Tip

The main differences between an employee's position pursuant to labour law and position of a contractor pursuant to commercial law are the following:

- **nature of the relationship with the company**

Employee: The employees' work is considered *dependent work*. This means that employees:

(a) are subordinate to employers and have to follow their instructions;
(b) perform the work in the employers' name and on employers' responsibility; and
(c) have to perform the work for employers personally.

Contractors: Contrary to the employees, contractors are independent, they may choose their working hours and their work. Notably, contractors perform the work in their own name and take personal responsibility for it.

- **existence of labour law protection**

Employee: Employees are protected under the Labour Code, for instance:

(a) they are entitled to their monthly salary irrespective of amount of work performed;
(b) their employment can be terminated only for reasons stipulated in the Labour Code;
(c) they are entitled to severance payment in case of employment termination;
(d) they are entitled to paid annual leave;
(e) they are entitled to compensation of overtime work, work on public holidays; and
(f) they are entitled to financial compensation during their sickness.

Contractors: Contractors are not entitled to the labour law protection (as described above). Their rights and obligations arise out of the agreement and the Civil Code (agreement termination, remuneration, etc).

GENERAL PROTECTION AGAINST DISMISSAL

6.13 In the Czech Republic employees enjoy the benefit of a minimum notice period and, in addition, employees can be given a termination notice only on the grounds expressly specified in the Labour Code.

6.14 As a matter of Czech law, the employer may terminate employment relationships by:

(a) a termination notice on statutory grounds;
(b) an immediate termination on statutory grounds;
(c) a termination agreement between the employer and employee; or
(d) a termination during the probation period without any reason.

For more details on termination notices please see paras **6.55** et seq and on fixed-term contracts paras **6.124** et seq.

6.15 First, the employer must be able to show that there is a reason for termination stipulated in the Labour Code. Redundancy, as defined by the Labour Code, is one of the statutory reasons for dismissal.

6.16 Secondly, the employer must be able to show that he has acted properly during the dismissal process and that the statutory procedure was followed. In particular, it is necessary to ensure that:

- the termination documents are duly signed by both parties and, preferably, personally delivered to the employees at their workplace, at their home or another place where they can be reached. Only if this is not possible, the employer may deliver the termination documents via mail with a proof of receipt;
- the employee receives correctly calculated severance payments, bonuses and compensation for overtime work and spent holiday, if any;
- the employer has delivered to the employee a certificate of employment (in Czech *potvrzení o zaměstnání*), which is a document stating the length of employment, achieved qualification and salary deductions, if any; and
- the employee underwent a medical examination if required by law or requested by the employee.

SPECIAL PROTECTION AGAINST DISMISSAL

6.17 Czech law provides for special dismissal protection for certain categories of employees during their so-called 'protective period'. Employees may claim the termination notice was invalid if the notice was served to them during a protective period.

The protective period includes:

- the period when employees are found temporarily unfit to work;
- performance of a military service;
- the period when employees are appointed to a public office;
- the period when female employees are pregnant, on maternity leave or when female or male employees are on a parental leave; or
- the period when employees working at night are found temporarily unfit to perform night work based on a medical report issued by a corporate preventive healthcare facility.

6.18 In some cases it is objectively not possible to maintain certain employee positions. Here, the Labour Code provides for specific exceptions to the protective period rule. Namely, the employer may serve a termination notice to any employee even during the protective period on the grounds that the business or a part thereof is closed or relocated.

6.19 Additional obligations apply in relation to dismissal of employees, who are trade union representatives active at the employer, during their role as the trade union representative and within the period of one year after their role as the trade union representative. In such case, the employer must ask the trade union for its prior consent to the termination of employment. If the trade union refuses to grant such consent, the notice or immediate termination is invalid. However, if the trade union does not refuse to grant such consent within 15 days from the date of the request, it is presumed that the consent was given.

6.20 Dismissals based on age, marital/civil partnership status, race, religion or belief, sex or sexual orientation are considered discriminatory and are invalid.

WORKFORCE REDUCTION

6.21 Employers must carefully assess whether the number of planned dismissals could trigger a collective redundancy procedure. For more details about the collective redundancy procedure, see para **6.44**.

Statutory termination reasons

6.22 As stated above, the employer may give a termination notice to the employee only on the grounds stated in the Labour Code. These are as follows:

(a) closure of the employer in whole or in part;
(b) relocation of the employer in whole or in part;
(c) employee redundancy;
(d) employee work-related injury or illness;
(e) long-term loss of the employee's ability to continue performing his/her current work due to his/her medical condition;
(f) non-fulfilment of legal or statutory prerequisites for the performance of the agreed work by the employee or employee's unsatisfactory work results;
(g) serious breach or continuous less serious breaches of employee's obligations; and
(h) breach of the sick-leave conditions in a particularly gross manner by the employee.

Definition of redundancy

6.23 Redundancy is one of the most frequently used reasons for employment termination. Together with total or partial closure or relocation of the employer's business, redundancy also constitutes one of the '*organisational reasons*' justifying dismissal.

6.24 Generally, the employer may decide on:

- a change in its activity and technical equipment (eg switch to a new business activity);
- reduction of personnel for the purpose of increasing work efficiency (eg some employees are replaced by machines); or
- other organisational changes (eg merger of departments).

The selection of employees who will be made redundant and who will be given notice is in the employer's sole discretion. The employer is not bound by any restrictions and the selection cannot be reviewed by a court. However, the selection of the employees must not be discriminatory.

6.25 Under Czech law, it is typical in a redundancy that the employer is still able to assign work to the employees under their employment contracts even after execution of the organisational change. This is in contrast to the employer's closure or relocation where the employer is objectively not able to assign work to the employees under their employment contracts, because the employer either no longer exists or is inactive at the agreed workplace.

6.26 When work is outsourced or sent offshore or an organisational change includes a transfer of the employer's activity, it is crucial to determine whether the Acquired Rights Directive, Council Directive 2001/23/EC of 12 March 2001 applies to safeguard employee rights in such situations. For further details see the Business sale, outsourcing/insourcing and offshoring section starting in para **6.85**.

Examples of redundancies

A Czech limited liability company decides to redesign its CEE business unit due to its continued negative financial results and stagnating sales. The company's management may decide on the following resolutions to increase business:

First, the company may decide on the marketing and sales department's merger where marketing department employees take over sales responsibilities. In the end, the employees in the sales department will be dismissed on the grounds of redundancy.

Secondly, the company may decide to switch its focus from the CEE market to China where business competition in similar products is substantially lower. For this reason, it will be necessary to hire new sales representatives who are fluent in Chinese and have experience with the Chinese market. With the closure or decrease of the current CEE region sales activities, the current sales representatives will become redundant and can be served a termination notice.

DISMISSALS ON GROUNDS OF REDUNDANCY

6.27 Professional and qualification changes for employment may be the driving factor for redundancy. Consequently, the employer may still be hiring new employees while dismissing other employees on the grounds of their redundancy. The employer may of course recreate the cancelled work position if external factors and conditions have changed.

6.28 It should be noted, however, the employer may not pretend that there is an organisational change when the actual reason for the employee dismissal is different, eg the employer believes that the employee delivers insufficient work results.

6.29 In the event of a larger restructuring collective redundancy procedures may come into play. Please refer to para **6.44** for more details.

Redundancy procedures

6.30 It is essential to follow the procedure prescribed in the Labour Code to validly dismiss employees to minimise the risk of facing a successful lawsuit. We would note that wrongful termination lawsuits constitute a majority of labour law disputes in the Czech Republic.

Individual redundancy procedure

6.31 First, the employer must adopt a resolution on an organisational change ('Resolution'), which describes in sufficient detail the reasons for the redundancy. These may include, for example, a reorganisation following the elimination of a specific job role or a decrease in the number of employees in order to reduce costs.

6.32 Secondly, the employer should establish which employees are affected by the Resolution and ensure that there is a link between the Resolution and redundancy of the particular employee.

6.33 Thirdly, the Resolution and the notice of termination or termination agreement must be in writing and signed by a person authorised to act on behalf of the employer, ie the Czech company. The documents must be delivered to the employee in person by the employer as stated in para **6.16**.

6.34 Finally, the employer must not dismiss employees on the grounds of redundancy during the 'protective period', eg if the employees are temporarily unfit to work, pregnant, on maternity leave, or on parental leave (please see para **6.17**).

FORM OF THE RESOLUTION

6.35 The Resolution may be adopted in any form and is not required to be published or otherwise publicly announced. It is of course recommended to have the Resolution in writing for evidentiary purposes.

TIMING OF THE RESOLUTION

6.36 The Resolution must be executed prior to serving the notice of termination or entering into the termination agreement with the employee. The Resolution does not have to be effective immediately, eg to ensure a proper implementation of the organisational changes. Nevertheless, the Resolution has to be effective, at the latest, as of the day immediately following the date of the employment termination. Please refer to the below example for more details about the timing requirements.

Example

Following the scenario described above in *Examples of redundancies*, the Czech limited liability company has decided to merge its marketing and sales departments. After the company's lawyers drafted the Resolution on the organisational change for the department's merger, the company's managing directors executed the Resolution. The Resolution was executed on 1 June 2014 with deferred effectiveness to 1 September 2014 to ensure a proper implementation of the changes. In other words, the departments will merge on 1 September 2014.

Consequently, the employees working in the company's sales department will become redundant on the same date, ie on 1 September 2014.

In this scenario, the first day when the company may serve the termination notice to the employees is the same date when the Resolution was executed, ie on 1 June 2014.

Furthermore, the earliest day when their employment may terminate is the day immediately preceding the day of the Resolution's effectiveness, ie on 31 August 2014. Otherwise, it could not be argued that the employees were dismissed due to their redundancy as there would be no effective redundancy resolution.

INVOLVEMENT OF EMPLOYEE REPRESENTATIVES IN INDIVIDUAL DISMISSALS

6.37 The employer is obliged to consult with trade union representatives prior to every service of termination notice or immediate termination of employment. The purpose of this consultation process is to reach an agreement between the employer and the trade union representative with regard to the employment termination. Nevertheless, if the parties do not agree on the employment termination, the employer may still proceed.

6.38 Involvement of a trade union regarding the notice or immediate termination given to an employee who is a trade union representative is set out in the section 'Special protection against dismissal' starting at para **6.17**.

AVOIDING COMPULSORY REDUNDANCIES

6.39 Employers should consider alternatives to compulsory redundancies. Careful consideration should be given to the possibility of employees working part-time and the use of other strategies such as sabbaticals, early retirement and withdrawal of bonus schemes, amongst others, with a view to avoid or minimise the number of employees affected by a compulsory redundancy.

6.40 Employers also often ask for volunteers for redundancy before starting the consultation process although they are under no obligation to do so. In this case, an employer typically offers an increased severance payment to employees who volunteer to leave, in addition to the minimum amount prescribed in the Labour Code.

6.41 Employers should be clear with employees that whilst they are applying for voluntary redundancy there is no guarantee that employees who applied to participate will be selected for voluntary redundancy. This is to ensure that any key employees who are required for the continued success of the company are retained by the employer and not granted voluntary redundancy.

ALTERNATIVE EMPLOYMENT

6.42 Under Czech law, the employer is not obliged to offer suitable alternative employment to the dismissed employees. However, the employer may of course offer employees alternative employment in a subsidiary or other group company.

OTHER CONSIDERATIONS

6.43 The responsible HR managers should carefully review any collective agreements, contractual provisions or any group or subsidiary policies relating to redundancy as these may add an additional layer of protection for the dismissed employees. An increased amount in severance payment is usually one of the contractual provisions that should be taken into account.

Collective redundancy procedure

6.44 As mentioned above, under Czech law, a collective dismissal means the termination of employment by an employer due to organisational reasons, such as the redundancy of employees (please refer to para **6.23** for organisational reasons overview) by a termination notice within a period of 30 calendar days, if it affects at least:

- ten employees where the employer employs from 20 to 100 employees;
- 10% of employees where the employer employs from 101 to 300 employees; or
- thirty employees where the employer employs more than 300 employees.

The total number of employees should be calculated as on the day of giving the termination notice to the first employee.

6.45 If at least five employees were dismissed within the relevant thirty calendar days period by a termination notice, then the employees whose employment was terminated within such relevant period by a termination agreement must also be included when calculating the number of the dismissed employees (as stated in para **6.44**). In other words, employees whose employment was terminated by a mutual termination agreement (in contrast to the termination notice), would also be considered as employees affected by the collective dismissal provided that at least five other employment relationships were terminated by a termination notice within a period of 30 calendar days.

Example

A Czech limited liability company employs 250 employees in its three factories. Due to recent market development, its products do not sell well and the market demand is declining. As a result, the company's management has decided to reduce the workforce and dismiss 20% of all employees, ie 50 employees.

The management announced its decision and, without specifying the employees to be dismissed, offered a severance package to every employee, who voluntarily signed a termination agreement. Following this announcement, 15 employees volunteered and signed the termination agreement as they either found a new job or decided to take early retirement.

The company then had to select the remaining 35 employees to be dismissed by a termination notice.

Notwithstanding the different methods of employment termination, all 50 employees will be deemed to have been dismissed in the collective redundancy procedure.

INVOLVEMENT OF EMPLOYEE REPRESENTATIVES IN COLLECTIVE DISMISSALS

Information obligation

6.46 The employer should inform the trade union and the works council established at the employer in writing of its intention to conduct a collective dismissal. The written notification should be served on the trade union and the works council prior to giving a termination notice to individual employees no later than 30 days before serving the termination notice on the employees.

6.47 The following information should be included in the written notification:

(a) the reasons for the collective dismissal;
(b) the number and professional qualifications of the employees whose employment is to be terminated;
(c) the number and professional qualifications of all employees employed by the employer;
(d) the time period during which the collective dismissal is to occur;
(e) the criteria for selection of the employees whose employment is to be terminated; and
(f) the severance payments and, if relevant, any other rights of the employees whose employment is to be terminated.

Consultation obligation

6.48 In addition to the information obligation, the employer must also consult with the trade union and/or works council regarding a collective dismissal.

6.49 The 'consultation' within the meaning of the Labour Code means a prior negotiation between the employer and the trade union and/or the works council with an exchange of views and explanations with the aim of achieving an agreement. However, failure to achieve such agreement does not invalidate the collective dismissal and does not, in itself, constitute grounds for imposing fines on the employer by the State Labour Inspection Office.

6.50 The purpose of these mandatory negotiations is to identify appropriate measures which could limit the negative impact of the collective redundancy and explore the possibility to offer the employees who are otherwise to be made redundant another suitable position with the employer.

6.51 If there are no trade unions or a works council established at the employer, the employer is obliged to fulfil its information and consultation obligation as described above vis-à-vis each employee who will be directly affected by the collective dismissal.

INFORMATION OBLIGATION VIS-À-VIS THE LABOUR OFFICE

6.52 The employer should provide the relevant labour office, determined by the location of the employer's business, the following information in writing:

- information under para **6.47**(a)–(f);
- information about commencement of the consultations with the trade union and/or the works council; and
- the timing when the decision on the collective dismissal has been made, including a report on the decision on the collective dismissal and the outcome of the negotiations with the trade union and/or works council. The report should include details of the total number of employees as well as the amount and professional qualifications of the employees who are to be made redundant.

6.53 As stated below in para **6.56**, a statutory minimum of two months' notice period is generally applicable in the Czech Republic. However, the employment of the employee affected by the collective dismissal may not expire earlier than 30 days from the date of delivery of the written report on the decision on the collective dismissal to the relevant labour office as described above, even if the statutory minimum two months' period has already expired. This rule can however be modified by an agreement with the employee.

SANCTIONS

6.54 The State Labour Inspection Office may impose a fine up to CZK 200,000 (€8,000) if the employer does not fulfil its information obligation vis-à-vis the trade union and/or works council and a fine up to CZK 300,000 (€12,000) if the employer does not comply with its information obligation vis-à-vis the labour office.

NOTICE

6.55 Any termination notice given by either the employer or the employee must be in writing and properly delivered to the other party (as described in para **6.16**).

Minimum notice period

6.56 Czech law prescribes a minimum statutory notice period of two months. Its duration must be the same for both the employer and the employee. The employer and the employee may agree on a longer notice period in a written agreement. The notice period begins on the first day of the calendar month following the month in which the termination notice was given and ends on the last day of the relevant month. The employment ends with the expiration of the notice period.

> **Example**
>
> Ms Novakova lawfully received a termination notice from her employer, a Czech limited liability company, on 13 March 2014. Her employment contract provides for a notice period of two months. Ms Novakova's notice period starts on 1 April 1014 and ends on 31 May 2014. Ms Novakova's employment terminates on 31 May 2014. As of 1 June 2014, Ms Novakova is no longer employed by the company, regardless of the fact that the last day of the notice period was a Saturday.

6.57 Employment contracts customarily repeat the statutory notice period, although Czech law does not require it. A longer notice period is exceptional and, if agreed, then usually between an employer and a senior or management employee.

6.58 The employee's rights and obligations remain unchanged during the notice period. The employee must continue working as instructed by the employer until the end of the employment. As an alternative, the employee may spend the notice period on a so-called 'garden leave' or as individually agreed by the parties in case of a mutually agreed termination. For details on 'garden leave' and mutually agreed termination please see paras **6.60** and **6.138**.

6.59 The Labour Code prescribes the duration of the notice period if a termination notice is given by an employee in connection with an employment transfer (for more details on the employment transfer, please see para **6.85**). In such case, the employment ends no later than on the date preceding the effective date of the employment transfer. Consequently, the employee is not transferred to the new employer. In this scenario the notice period will therefore be shorter than the statutory minimum notice period of two months.

Garden leave

6.60 In order to maintain a good working environment, the employer may prefer to keep the dismissed employee out of the workplace. The concept of 'garden leave' ensures that whilst dismissed employees remain employed during the notice period they are excluded from the work place. During this period, no work is assigned to the dismissed employees. This concept was introduced to Czech employers by foreign parent companies, mainly from the United Kingdom, and has become quite common.

6.61 'Garden leave' is also a popular way to protect the employer's business data and knowhow as well as existing contacts and relationships with business partners and customers.

6.62 This concept is not expressly provided for in Czech law and there is not even have a proper Czech legal term for this. In practice, the concept of 'other impediments to work on the part of the employer' (in Czech *jiné překážky v práci na straně zaměstnavatele*) is used to justify the employer's instruction to a dismissed employee not to come to the workplace during the notice period.

6.63 Although the Labour Code does not specify the 'other impediments to work on the part of the employer', the impossibility of the employee to perform work because the employer does not assign work would constitute such impediment. Employees are not obliged to be present at the workplace if the employer is not instructing them to perform any work. More importantly, employees are entitled to salary compensation in the amount of their average earnings. Please see further para **6.70** on average earnings.

6.64 The State Labour Inspection Office and its branches are familiar with this practice. Based on our experience they do not impose any fines for garden leave as long as the employer pays the required salary compensation.

6.65 A non-competition clause is also often used in conjunction with garden leave to prevent damage to the company and unauthorised disclosure of confidential information and know-how. For further information please see the section *Non-competition clause* starting in para **6.76**.

REDUNDANCY PAYMENT

6.66 Employees who are dismissed on the grounds of so-called organisational reasons (one of them being redundancy), are entitled to a statutory severance payment. The specific procedure, as described in paras **6.31–6.36**, needs to be followed to proceed with a dismissal due to redundancy.

6.67 The severance payment must be paid regardless of whether the dismissed employee has immediately found a new job or started their own business. If the employment is terminated by a mutual agreement for organisational reasons, including redundancy, the employee is still entitled to the severance payment.

6.68 However, the dismissed employee must on request return the severance payment or its proportionate part, if they begin working for the same employer before the lapse of a number of months. Such repayment is determined by the number of average monthly earnings used for the calculation of the severance payment. Please see an example below.

> **Example**
>
> Employment was terminated by a termination agreement due to closure of one of the employer's departments and the employee received a severance payment in the amount of three times their average earnings. The employee would have to return the severance payment (or its part), if they started to work for the same employer again during the next three months after the end of the previous employment. Of course, it is in the employer's discretion to decide whether to request the return of the severance payment or not.

Statutory redundancy pay calculation

6.69 The amount of statutory severance payment entitlement is calculated with reference to each employee's length of employment as follows:

Length of employment	Severance payment, ie number of employee's average monthly earnings
Less than 1 year	one
At least 1 year and less than 2 years	two
2 years and more	three

6.70 The Labour Code prescribes a method for calculation of the average earnings, therefore 'average earnings' are not equivalent to an employee's monthly salary. Average earnings are calculated from an employee's gross salary (including bonuses) accounted for in the preceding quarter of the year and hours worked during the preceding quarter of the year.

6.71 The length of the employment must include the periods of any previous employment with the same employer if the period between termination of the first employment and commencement of the second employment was less than six months. Please see an example below.

Example of statutory redundancy calculation

Mr Maly and Mr Cech have both been made redundant from Manufaktura, a.s. (the 'Company'). Mr Maly has been employed by the Company for 2.5 years and his average monthly earnings are CZK 27,000 (approx. EUR 1,000). Mr Cech has been employed by the Company for half of the year and his employment started on 9 September 2013. His previous employment with the same employer, ie the Company, lasted one year and was terminated on 30 June 2013. His average monthly earnings are CZK 17,500 (€650).

Mr Maly is entitled to a statutory severance payment in the amount of CZK 81,000 (approx. €3,000), calculated as CZK 27,000 × 3, because he falls into the '2 years and more' category and is entitled to three average monthly earnings.

Mr Cech is entitled to a statutory severance payment in the amount of CZK 35,000 (€1,300). His last employment lasted only six months but his former employment must also be included when calculating the length of the employment. The period between the termination of the first employment and commencement of the second employment was not longer than six months (in the given example: only two months and eight days). For the purpose of calculation of the statutory severance payment, his employment lasted 1.5 years in total. Therefore he falls into the '1–2 years' category and his statutory severance payment is calculated as CZK 17,500 × 2.

Enhanced redundancy payments

6.72 Additional and/or higher severance payments may be payable under the employment contract, termination agreement, collective agreement or the employer's internal regulations. The employer needs to ensure that any additional or higher severance payments could not be considered discriminatory, that is, eg due to sex, age or any other type of discrimination.

Taxation of redundancy payments

6.73 Statutory severance payment is subject to personal income tax.

6.74 Conversely, it is not subject to social security tax (in Czech *pojistné na sociální zabezpečení a příspěvek na státní politiku zaměstnanosti*) and health insurance tax (in Czech *pojistné na všeobecné zdravotní pojištění*). Based on judicial interpretation, the same also applies to higher severance payments, if such compensation is paid in connection with employment termination due to organisational reasons. Thus, not each compensation paid in connection with the employment termination and designated by the parties as severance payment will benefit from this regime. If the employer and employee agree that the employer will pay compensation to the employee in connection with the employment termination without having actual organisational reasons for the employment termination, eg to motivate him/her to enter into the termination agreement, the compensation should be designated as, eg extraordinary bonus. Such extraordinary bonus has the same tax treatment as the employee salary, ie it does not have the beneficial treatment as the severance payment.

Practical Tip

An employer may consider offering employees a termination agreement during the first stage of the workforce redundancy procedure. To motivate the employees to accept the offer and reach an agreement the offer might include an increased severance payment. It is common for such dismissals to be resolved in a quicker and friendlier manner. The specific date of the employment termination may be agreed in the termination agreement. Therefore, the employment may end in a shorter period of time since the notice period will not be applicable in those circumstances. For more details on the mutually agreed termination please see para **6.138**.

Post-termination restrictive covenants

6.75 When a senior or other key employee is being laid off, one of the biggest concerns of the employer is to restrict the employee from competing with it by using acquired know-how. A non-competition clause may be used to manage the circumstances in which the employee can compete with the employer and thereby mitigate the risk that the dismissed employee could (immediately) establish himself as a new competitor.

NON-COMPETITION CLAUSE

6.76 Under Czech law, a non-competition clause is a contractual obligation of the employee to refrain from performance of a profitable activity that would be identical to or competing with the employer's scope of business for a certain period after the employment termination. Under this obligation the employee cannot perform the same job as well as conduct the same business as the employer on its own. The non-competition clause may be agreed for maximum of 12 months.

6.77 The employer may agree on a non-competition clause with its employee if it can be fairly requested from the employee considering the nature of information, findings and knowledge of working and technological procedures that the employee obtained in the course of the employment. Moreover, the use of the information must substantially hinder the employer's business. Therefore, the non-competition clause cannot be validly entered into with each and every employee. The employer must evaluate on a case-by-case basis whether the employee has obtained specific knowledge that may reasonably be protected pursuant to a non-competition clause.

6.78 In consideration for the non-competition undertaking, the employer is required to provide the employee with adequate financial compensation. The compensation has to be at least half of the average monthly earnings of the employee per month of compliance with the non-competition obligation.

6.79 The non-competition clause can be agreed either in the employment contract or in the termination agreement. In both cases the clause must be in writing.

6.80 It is possible to stipulate a contractual penalty for an employee's breach of the non-competition clause. Such contractual penalty must be proportionate to the possible damage which would be caused by use of the information and proportional to the amount of the employee's compensation.

6.81 To ensure the maximum protection possible, we recommend that the non-competition clause is combined with the concept of 'garden leave' as described in paras **6.60** and **6.65**.

PROTECTION OF BUSINESS SECRETS

6.82 Under Czech law, companies are protected against breaches of their business secrets (ie commercial, manufacturing and technological facts relating to its business). Violators may even face criminal prosecution. The employer is also protected by the general provisions of Czech law on protection against unfair competition practices.

6.83 The concept of 'protection against unfair competition' means that any actions which might be conflicting with fair competitive practices and could cause harm to other competitors or customers are prohibited by law.

6.84 If the employee breaches the non-competition clause or conducts unfair competition practices, the employer may apply for an injunction to stop the employee from continuing such behaviour. In addition, the employer may also claim damages including loss of profit and actual losses caused by the employee's unlawful conduct.

BUSINESS SALE, OUTSOURCING/INSOURCING AND OFFSHORING

6.85 The Transfers of Undertakings Directive 2001/23/EC has been implemented into Czech law, namely into Sections 338 and 345a of the Labour Code. However, Czech law provisions on employee transfers are brief and not very detailed. Only limited Czech case law is available. Accordingly, employers should take into account the case law of the Court of Justice of the EU ('ECJ') when considering whether an employee transfer is triggered.

6.86 Under Czech law, the automatic transfer of employees is generally triggered by: (i) a transfer of business or part of the business; (ii) a transfer of tasks and activities of the employer or part of the activities and tasks to another employer; and (iii) a merger and other statutory situations foreseen under the Civil Code and by the Act No 125/2008 Coll, Act on Transformations of Business Companies and Co-operatives, as amended.

6.87 Key consequences of the employee transfer regime are:

(i) employment of affected employees transfers automatically to the new employer;
(ii) existing employment rights and obligations are not affected by the employee transfer and remain unchanged; and
(iii) the current employer (transferor) and the new employer (transferee) have a duty to inform and consult with employees' representatives or in the absence of such with each of the individual employees.

Business sale

6.88 An employee transfer regime may apply if an employer's business is sold or leased and/or if the performance of activities currently undertaken by the employer is reorganised. Typically the employer wishes to outsource certain activities. All aspects of each particular transaction including the parties' intention need to be evaluated.

6.89 An employee transfer would generally be triggered if a 'stable economic unit' is transferred to another party. That is, the identity of the economic unit is maintained with the new employer and it continues or resumes the same or similar activities with the transferred personnel, tangible and intangible assets.

6.90 The assessment will depend on a number of factors that must be considered together. Such factors include, among others:

- whether any assets (such as real estate, software or equipment) are transferred;

- intention of the transferee;
- whether customers are transferred;
- whether key or 'ordinary' employees are transferred; and
- how the business is conducted prior to and after the transfer.

Outsourcing/insourcing

6.91 In the services industry an employee transfer will most likely be triggered by a change in the scope of services, either by outsourcing or by insourcing. In outsourcing, the current employer does not wish to continue providing certain services which are instead taken over by an external provider. On the other hand, with insourcing, the provision of services is taken back in-house.

6.92 Based on the ECJ case law, a stable economic unit is made up of a group of employees performing particular activities in an interlinked and organised manner. The transferee is required to continue performing the same activities as well as to take over a substantial part of the group of employees performing it prior to the transfer.

6.93 The employee transfer regime would not apply to a situation when a group of employees is not transferred as a whole to the new employer, ie when the transferred activity is divided into several parts and performed by several providers after closing of the transaction. For an assessment whether employee transfer regime applies it is necessary to consider the organisational structure of the group of employees prior to and after the transfer.

Effect of the employee transfer

Automatic transfer and protection of employment

6.94 As of the effective date of the transfer, the transferor's employees are automatically transferred to the transferee. All rights and obligations arising out of the employment contracts or under the Labour Code existing on the date of the transfer are transferred to the new employer as well.

6.95 In line with ECJ case law, employees of the transferor whose employment was unlawfully terminated before the transfer or whose dismissal is challenged and its validity is questionable at the time of the transfer, will be deemed to be employed by the transferor on the date of transfer and therefore, they will also be part of the transfer.

Objection to the transfer

6.96 Czech law does not entitle employees to object to the transfer. An employee's refusal to perform work assigned to them by the transferee, may be considered a breach of employee's obligations (ie work discipline) and can lead to dismissal.

6.97 However, an employee who does not agree with the transfer, may give a termination notice prior to the effective date of the transfer as described in para **6.59**. The employee would not be entitled to any compensation or severance payment.

6.98 Further, where the employee hands in a termination notice (or enters into a termination agreement) within two months after the effective date of the transfer, the employee may file a claim with the court that the employment was terminated due to substantial impairment of working conditions in connection with the transfer. If the court decides that the employee's claim is justified, the employee would be entitled to a severance payment.

Protection from dismissal

6.99 An employee transfer does not constitute a statutory reason for dismissal. If either the transferee or the transferor dismisses an employee in connection with the transfer, the employee may file a claim for invalid dismissal. If the claim is successful, he/she will be regarded as employed by the transferor and his/her employment will be deemed to have been transferred to the transferor. For more details please see para **6.129**.

Information and consultation duties

6.100 The Labour Code requires that both the transferor and the transferee inform and consult the trade union and the works council, if established at the employer, about the following issues:

(i) the proposed date of the transfer;
(ii) reasons for the proposed transfer;
(iii) legal, economic and social consequences of the proposed transfer; and
(iv) any contemplated measures affecting the employees.

6.101 If no trade unions or works councils are established at the transferor or the transferee, the employer is required to perform the information duty by informing each of the affected employees directly. Based on the prevailing interpretation of the law, there is no requirement for consultation with each of the affected employees in relation to their transfer unless there is a functioning trade union or works council in the work place.

6.102 In practice, the notification and consultation usually takes the form of a letter addressed to the trade union and/or works council or to the affected employees, followed by a meeting. Whilst reaching an agreement between the transferor, the transferee, the employees' representative and/or the affected employees is the aim, there is no requirement for such to be concluded during such process and its absence does not affect the validity of the transfer.

6.103 The information of and consultation with employees must take place at least 30 days prior to the effective transfer date. However, failure to comply with the information and consultation duties does not result in the invalidity of the transfer.

6.104 Where a European works council is established within the group of companies affected by a multi-jurisdictional redundancy process or cross-border employee transfer there may be an additional duty to inform and consult with the European works council about proposed steps and measures.

6.105 Whilst a breach of the information and consultation duties vis-à-vis employees' representatives does not impact on the validity of the transfer such breach may result in a fine up to the amount of CZK 200,000 (€7,500) imposed by the relevant branch of the State Labour Inspection Office.

Application of employee transfer regime to cross-border transactions/offshoring

6.106 Czech law does not expressly regulate a cross-border employee transfer. From a legal point of view, a detailed analysis to determine applicable law governing such employee transfer would have to be conducted. The above-described employee transfer regime would be applicable to employees, whose employment is governed by Czech law prior the transfer.

6.107 As stated above in para **6.87**, the rights and obligations of the employees are not affected by the transfer. Therefore the workplace of a particular employee also remain unchanged. If the transferred employee is to be relocated (including abroad) it will require his/her prior consent. In general, relocation of the employer constitutes a statutory ground for dismissal, in which case the employee is also entitled to a severance payment. Please see paras **6.22** and **6.66**.

WORKFORCE REDUCTION IN CONNECTION WITH SHARE SALE OR SHARE PURCHASE

6.108 In the event of a share sale the identity of the employer does not change (only the identity of the employer's shareholder changes) and therefore the employee transfer regime and corresponding employer's obligations as described above do not apply.

CHANGING EMPLOYMENT TERMS AND CONDITIONS

6.109 Once an employment contract is entered into between an employer and an employee, their rights and obligations may only be changed by an agreement (typically by amendment to the employment contract). However, a few statutory exemptions may also apply allowing the employer to change the employment contract unilaterally, eg the employer may change the employee's working position and assign a different type of work in the following circumstances: (i) if criminal proceedings were initiated against the employee; or (ii) to prevent damage caused by a natural disaster as necessary.

6.110 Each party may suggest changes to the rights and obligations of the other party at any time. Obviously, the other party does not have an obligation to accept such proposal. If the employer suggests a change of employee's rights and obligations, negotiation will most likely take place and the employee might request extra benefits or a pay rise in return.

6.111 The change of workplace or/and the working position of potentially affected employees may be used to avoid a redundancy situation, provided that the employee consents thereto and/or an agreement between the parties is reached.

Change of workplace

6.112 Any changes of the employee's workplace as stated in the employment contract are subject to the employee's approval. The employer's right to relocate the employee is restricted for certain categories of employees, eg pregnant employees and employees caring for children under the age of eight.

6.113 Under Czech law, the workplace may be identified quite broadly in the employment contract. A specific address is not required, a reference to a city, a region or a country would suffice, and/or the employment contract may contain a provision pursuant to which the employee grants his/her approval to a potential change of his/her workplace.

6.114 If the employer proposes a change of workplace and it is not accepted by the employee, and the employer is not able to continue employing the employee at the originally agreed workplace, the employer may dismiss such employee as it constitutes a statutory redundancy reason for dismissal.

Change of working position

6.115 Similar to the regulation of the change of the workplace, change of the working position (employee's role), ie transferring an employee to different type of work than agreed in the employment contract, can be made by agreement with the employee. Whether or not it is necessary to enter into such written agreement would depend on the description of the employee's position in the employment contract. No agreement is necessary if the newly assigned tasks are such which are already included under the description of the employee's position in the original employment contract.

6.116 The employer must ensure that the new scope of work is suitable for the employee with regard to his health, skills and qualification(s). Moreover, the Labour Code also stipulates reasons when the employer is obliged to change the employee's working position, eg for health conditions of the employee.

> **Practical Tips on changing terms and conditions**
>
> If the employer would like to maintain a higher degree of flexibility to change the employees' rights and obligations in the future, it should draft the employment contract broadly and include employees' approvals to such changes to the maximum extent possible under the mandatory provisions of the Labour Code.
>
> For example, it would be convenient for the employer to agree that the workplace will be 'Prague' instead of a particular address in Prague. If the employer changed its offices within Prague, it would not require the consent of the employee to relocate the employee to the new office.

USING TEMPORARY STAFF

6.117 During the restructuring employers may need employees with flexible arrangements who could easily and temporarily substitute the loss of workforce, cover a potential increase in demand for the employer's services and goods, and/or perform specific tasks relating to the restructuring. The employer has several options to meet its goals:

(i) use workers from an employment agency;
(ii) hire employees based on special types of agreements relating to work, ie, an 'agreement on work performance' (in Czech *dohoda o provedení práce*), please see more details in para **6.123**, and an 'agreement on working activity' (in Czech *dohoda o pracovní činnosti*), please see more details in para **6.122**; or
(iii) hire employees on fixed-term contracts.

Agency workers

6.118 Using agency workers may be a good solution when a company does not wish to employ permanent employees, but requires additional personnel.

Hiring workforce from an employment agency may lessen administrative burdens. Obviously, the employer and the employment agency enter into an agreement regarding the details.

6.119 The Labour Code provides, amongst others, that the employment agency must have a special permit for such activity and may temporarily allocate its employees (agency workers) to perform work for another employer based on specific arrangements to do so in their employment contracts or agreements on working activity. The employment agency undertakes to arrange for the temporary work to be carried out for another employer (in Czech legal terminology the 'user') by the agency worker and the agency worker undertakes to perform the work according to the user's instructions.

6.120 Agency workers are entitled to the same labour law protection enjoyed by 'comparable employees', meaning an employee of the user who performs or would perform the same work as the agency worker, taking into consideration the worker's qualifications and experience.

Special types of agreements relating to work

6.121 Special types of agreements relating to work are designed to enable employers to attain their business goals in circumstances when it may not be practical to recruit full-time employees. To a great extent, the employer can free itself from many obligations that apply to regular employment relationships, in particular those concerning the termination of employment.

Agreement on working activity

6.122 An agreement on working activity may be concluded with an employee if the average scope of work does not exceed one-half of ordinary weekly working hours, ie on average, 20 working hours per week. It can be unilaterally terminated for any reason or without a reason with a 15-day notice period starting on the day when the written termination notice is served on the other party.

The agreement on working activity is used eg for trainee positions.

Agreement on work performance

6.123 The agreement on work performance can be concluded for a maximum of 300 hours per calendar year and is generally used for a particular project (rather than an on-going work). The total number of working hours must include those hours performed by the employee for the same employer in one calendar year based on another agreement on work performance.

Fixed-term contracts

6.124 There are many good reasons to use fixed-term contracts including replacing an employee on maternity leave or study leave, or employing project specific personnel. In general, employees with fixed-term contracts have the same rights and obligations as permanent employees.

6.125 The use of successive fixed-term employment agreements is limited. A fixed-term contractual employment relationship between the same employer and the same employee is limited to a maximum of three years and subject to a limit of no more than two extensions. In other words, they may be prolonged only twice. However, the total duration may also be as little as three months with three contracts each for a period of one month. If there is a gap of at least three years between fixed-term employments, the above rule does not apply, ie the previous fixed-term employment are ignored for compliance purposes.

6.126 Unless terminated as described in para **6.14**, a fixed-term employment terminates with the expiration of the agreed period.

Example

Ms Vomackova has already entered into a fixed-term contract with her employer, the company Ceska s.r.o., three times. The first fixed-term contract was concluded for the period of three months starting from 1 January 2013 and ending on 31 March 2013, the second employment lasted from 1 June 2013 to 31 December 2013 (seven months) and the third employment was agreed for a period of 3 years (1 January 2014 to 31 December 2016). Ms Vomackova and Ceska s.r.o. might enter into another fixed-term contract at the earliest on 1 January 2020.

EMPLOYMENT CLAIMS

6.127 Any disputes between employers and employees are resolved in the ordinary courts. In the first instance the dispute would be heard by specialised labour law senates (one judge and two lay judges) in district courts. Local jurisdiction is determined by the defendant's place of residence or registered office. Arbitration proceedings are forbidden in all employment matters.

6.128 Fourteen per cent of employment disputes decided in Prague during the year 2013 concerned disputes where the termination notice was given by the employer and 63% of those concerned termination notices which were given on the grounds of redundancy. This indicates that employers should carefully assess the applicable regulations with respect to dismissals (and particular when citing redundancy as the reason). This shows that Czech employees are not reluctant to challenge a termination. Relatively low court fees of CZK 2,000 (€75) for commencing an action disputing the validity of an employment termination also encourage disgruntled employees to act.

UNFAIR DISMISSAL

6.129 A claim for invalid dismissal would typically be based on a lack of a statutory reason for dismissal (please see a list of statutory reasons in para 6.22) and/or failure of the employer to follow the procedure prescribed in the Labour Code.

6.130 The employer must prove that one of the statutory reasons existed at the time of the dismissal and that a fair and reasonable procedure has been followed in implementing the dismissal.

6.131 If an employee is found to have been dismissed without good cause and insists on continuing his/her employment, the employment continues to exist and the employee is entitled to salary compensation. This is subject to the employee having successfully filed a claim to that effect. The employee has to notify the employer in writing and file a claim for invalid dismissal within two months from the date the employment should have terminated based on the alleged invalid termination notice.

Remedies

6.132 If the employee's claim is successful he/she is entitled to compensation in the amount of salary and benefits which the employee would have received if employment had continued. The employer is entitled to ask the court to reduce the total amount of salary compensation for the invalid dismissal if the total amount of monthly salaries which should be compensated exceeds six monthly salaries.

6.133 If the court decides that the dismissal was invalid, the employment relationship is deemed to continue and treated as if it was never terminated. The employer is therefore obliged to again assign work to the employee (claimant) or find a valid reason for termination of the employment. Salary compensation should be paid until the employee is properly instructed and his/her employment is reinstated or it is validly terminated. If the employee was paid a severance payment, he/she must re-pay it to the employer as the basis for entitlement to the severance payment never existed.

DISCRIMINATION

6.134 Discrimination is prohibited in all labour law relationships. Protection against discrimination is governed by the Act No 189/2009 Coll, Anti-discrimination Act, as amended.

6.135 Discrimination is determined as a result of specific conduct or an omission when one person is treated less favourably than others in a comparable situation due to, among others, his/her race, ethnic origin, nationality, gender, sexual orientation, age, religion or faith.

6.136 The alleged victim of discrimination may bring a claim in court if the employee believe he/she was dismissed on the grounds of the above prohibited discriminatory reasons.

Remedies

6.137 The employee may seek an end to the discriminatory treatment and a remedy for its consequences to include adequate compensation (eg an apology and/or monetary compensation), compensation for non-monetary loss (for harm to reputation or dignity of the employee) and/or damages (lost salary). If an employee is successful, the court is likely to award both the apology and monetary compensation.

MUTUALLY AGREED TERMINATION

6.138 Conclusion of a mutual agreement between the employer and the employee is the preferred method for employment termination. Of course, not even the best termination agreement can guarantee that there will be no further disputes.

6.139 The termination agreement must be in writing and either party must receive one original each.

6.140 Parties can include a non-competition clause (or its waiver), the amount of severance payment and/or a confidentiality clause in the termination agreement. Moreover, the protective period as set out in the paragraphs on special protection against dismissal starting at para **6.17** above does not apply in respect of employment termination by termination agreement. It is also usual to include a provision confirming that the employee has received all due payments and do not have any other claims vis-à-vis the employer. Although, the employee cannot waive their entitlement to salary and severance payments.

6.141 The employment will end at the specified date in the termination agreement. The statutory notice period is not applicable to termination by the termination agreement.

6.142 Negotiation of the termination agreement is governed by general provisions of Czech law and contractual freedom is fully applicable. Therefore, the employee can refuse to accept the draft termination agreement and to some extent use their leverage to propose amendments (eg higher severance payment). Employers should ensure that they are in a good negotiation position and obtain a proper legal assessment of all options for dismissing the employee and/or any measures necessary and available if the employee does not accept the proposal.

Chapter 7

Workforce Restructuring in Denmark

Benjamin Lundström
Sirius Advokater, Law Firm, Copenhagen

INTRODUCTION

7.1 This chapter looks at the employment laws in Denmark. The Kingdom of Denmark includes Greenland and the Faroe Islands; however due to the extended autonomy of those areas different laws apply for them. Hence this chapter does not include the employment laws in Greenland and the Faroe Islands. The chapter focuses on workforce restructuring in the private sector.

7.2 As other continental European jurisdictions the legal system in Denmark is a civil law system. That said all employments are based on agreement. In terms of legal aspects the employment is first and foremost a contractual arrangement which is also reflected in the laws regulating the contract both the codified and the uncodified. As a starting principle the employment agreement is regulated by the general laws of obligation (contract law) which also apply to other contracts. In addition to this, however, there is of course a whole body of specific regulation that only applies to the employment contracts – some of these are mandatory to the extent that the rules can only be dispensed with if for the benefit of the employee.

7.3 The Danish labour market has three main features:

- bipartite/tripartite cooperation;
- influential employer and employee organisations; and
- collective agreements as one of the most important sources of law in labour law matters

This combination, which makes up the Danish Model, is a hybrid in the sense that it resembles the flexibility of the British labour market but at the same time gives the employees the Scandinavian security benefits.

7.4 Over the years, both Danish and international studies have established these characteristics of the Danish labour market. In EU terminology this is called 'flexicurity' due to its combination of flexibility and security. The flexicurity model is based on three elements: (1) flexible recruitment and termination; (2) an active labour market policy concerning the duty and right to participate in welfare to work programmes; and (3) a relatively high level of accessible benefits in case of unemployment. By combining flexibility and social security both employers and employees become more willing to take risks on the labour market. By increasing the security in connection with work change the employees become more willing to be mobile in the job market. The flexibility in connection with the recruitment and termination of employees makes the employers more willing to make ventures on unsafe grounds.

7.5 In terms of the flexible termination, the standard indicator is the average period of continuous employment with the same employer. In Denmark the average job duration is less than five years which is among the lowest in the EU.

7.6 In Denmark collective agreements have a significant position leaving the use of statute limited in comparison with other European jurisdictions. The main labour organisations which are the DA (The Confederation of Danish Employers) and LO (The Danish Confederation of Trade Unions) have agreed to regulate the labour market through collective agreements rather than through statute. The Danish Parliament has primarily regulated in accordance with needs established by the labour organisations and the principles they have agreed to. As a characteristic for Danish labour law there is no general Danish statutes on minimum wages, normal working hours, overtime pay, sick pay, salary during maternity leave, pension or termination of employment as these elements together with a number of other employment terms rest – to a large extent – on the collective parties' own agreement. Today 75–80% of the Danish labour market is covered by collective agreements.

7.7 In Denmark many principles and clarifications are derived from case law – such precedents play a significant role eg when deciding on industrial actions between unions and employers where no collective agreement applies but also in many other areas. In terms of legal system, the Danish system has some common features with common law systems. In Denmark there is extensive case law and no systematic codified employment law let alone a comprehensively codified statute book of law in this field. As in common law countries the statutes in Denmark are piecemeal in that they are mostly complementing the collective agreements or implementing European Directives. Only a few statutes passed during the last 20 years are purely national rooted – the statute on personal health information (1996), the statute on employee stock warrants (2004) and the statute on non-solicitation of employees (2008).

7.8 When assessing entitlements of employees in dismissal or any other restructuring scenario, one must first review the employment contract to ascertain what the parties have agreed upon. Next step is to clarify if the employment agreement is subject to a collective agreement. This is the case if the employer is a member of an employers' association or the employer has made a collective agreement with a union. Third step is to clarify the employee's work area to identify specific statutes that might apply.

7.9 The Danish Salaried Employees' Act ('SEA') plays an important role as it covers a large number of employees, including those not covered by a collective agreement. SEA makes a line between white-collar workers on one side (covered by SEA) and blue-collar workers on the other side (not covered by SEA). The tendency is that more and more workers move to the service sector, which is covered by SEA, to the extent that SEA now applies to approximately half of the workforce in Denmark.

7.10 Now, based on the above, looking at workforce restructuring in Denmark, including termination of employment or changing of the terms and conditions of employment, it will be necessary to consider the requirements under statutes and collective agreements. This is relevant both in respect to establishing what restructuring initiatives an employer can impose on the employees but also which procedure the employer should follow to comply with the law.

7.11 As mentioned in connection with the flexicurity model, compared to other European countries the Danish rules for termination of employment contracts are very liberal. Provided that the legal and agreed notices are respected, the employer is entitled to dismiss skilled and unskilled workers at any time, without paying compensation. This makes it easier for an individual business to adjust the size of its workforce in Denmark, compared to most other European countries.

PREPARING FOR A RESTRUCTURING EXERCISE

7.12 As a natural part of running and developing a business in an ever changing world with up and down turns and dynamic market opportunities there is a constant need for making adjustments in different aspects of the business. Those adjustments may call for different changes to the workforce. This may include a reduction of the workforce, change of the employment terms and conditions, integration and harmonisation of workforces, use of temporary staff, outsourcing and offshoring, or reassignment of functional and organisational responsibilities of staff.

7.13 In order to have an appropriate basis for decision making involving changes to the workforce it is important to gather relevant information in respect of the impacted workforce (such as their demographics and the existing contractual terms and conditions). Only with this information it will be possible to plan and structure the exercise and to outline a realistic budget.

The key issues to consider are set out below.

Identify the employing entity

7.14 A restructuring exercise can impact the employee both directly eg when the employing entity is involved and indirectly eg when specific tasks – sometimes across different group entities – are impacted. It is important however to note that in terms of identifying the duties owed and the privileges held between the employer and the employee as a main rule one need only focus on the particular legal entity in which the employee is formally employed. Therefore even if an organisation operates a group matrix structure the business decision underlying the restructuring and/or any redundancies has to be approached and documented separately in each company/legal entity.

Example

One company may decide to discontinue a certain function, making a certain department or a certain level of management redundant on the basis that another group company will in future fulfil this function.

Unless the companies are in reality run as one entity, the employee will only have a claim against the employing company. Even if there is a central HR function, the employing company is generally not under an obligation to consider or offer alternative positions available in other group companies even if these positions are suitable for the employee.

Collating information to plan and budget for the restructuring exercise

7.15 As mentioned in para **7.1** above and further outlined in para **8.6**, the restructuring exercise requires careful planning at the outset to optimise the end result including assessing the costs of the exercise and minimise the risk of claims from employees. Ideally the HR department has maintained an employee database (eg an ERP solution) comprising all relevant data such as contract terms, contact information, salary details, attendance, performance evaluation and promotion together with an organisational structure overview, staffing schedules and job descriptions.

7.16 If the employing entity does not already hold all the necessary data on the relevant employees it should be collected and analysed prior to decision making. The employing entity need to ensure that the registrations and processing of data comply with the law. According to the Danish Act on Processing of Personal Data ('APPD') (which implements EU Directive 95/46/EC) the registration and processing of 'normal' data does not require the employees' specific consent whereas 'sensitive' data requires the employees' prior consent. According to APPD an employer must usually report its processing of employee data (where it includes sensitive information) to the Danish Data Protection Agency and also obtain consent to processing from the employee. A well-drafted employment contract will usually provide for this.

'Normal' data

Normal data, which can be registered and processed without the employee's consent include, eg identification information such as the employee's name, address, phone number, date of birth, close relatives, education, references, previous employment, current position, job descriptions, work schedule, salary, tax, attendance, sick leave and other leave, pension arrangements, bank account details etc.

'Sensitive' data

Sensitive data, which can only be registered and processed with the employee's prior consent include, eg medical conditions, substance abuse problems, membership of union, criminal records and other offenses, personality tests etc.

It is prohibited for an employer to ask for, obtain, receive or use information on the employee's race, colour, religion or belief, political opinion, sexual preference or national, social or ethnical origin.

7.17 If an organisation has a central HR department, ie in a different legal entity than the employing company, the HR department would need to ensure that it has lawful access to any such data as data sharing of employee data across the group most often requires employee consent.

7.18 Even with a well-maintained and centralised employee database – and even more so without such a database – processing the relevant data and facts on the basis of which to reliably plan and structure any restructuring exercise can be very time consuming and should be considered at an early stage of the planning. Only with access to all relevant key data will the HR department and their advisers be able to provide the necessary basis for the business case in a restructuring plan.

> **Practical Tip**
>
> The following key data is often required initially for planning purposes in respect of any employee potentially impacted by a workforce reduction or restructuring exercise:
>
> - employing entity;
> - place of work;
> - job description;
> - employment status (ie freelance, salaried employee, executive director);
> - applicable collective agreement (if any);
> - seniority;
> - monthly salary;
> - accrued holiday;
> - contractual benefits and entitlements on termination of employment;
> - age;
> - information relevant to determine impact selection pool.

EMPLOYMENT STATUS

7.19 In Denmark it is a general legal principle that the managerial right rests with the employer. Derived from this, the main rule is that the employer has unrestricted access to restructure the workforce as required. This also concurs with the general laws of obligation which also applies to employment contracts (see para 7.1 above) and prescribes that either party to a contract can terminate the contract with agreed notice.

7.20 Since the 1960s certain limitations have been introduced with the result that today a dismissal of an employee covered by a collective agreement or SEA must be 'reasonable'/ 'fair'. For employments not covered by either a collective agreement or SEA the employer still enjoys an unlimited right to dismiss the employee and no claims can be made on grounds of unreasonableness. It is therefore key to identify the employment status of each employee.

7.21 In comparison to other EU countries it is relatively easy to dismiss employees in Denmark, which is partly due to the lack of general statutory dismissal protection and partly due to the comparatively high unemployment benefits and the easy access to these benefits.

Definition of salaried employee

7.22 As mentioned, SEA offers protection against unreasonable dismissals. Only those employees that meet the definition of a salaried employee enjoy the privileges under SEA. According to SEA a Salaried Employee is a typical white collar worker if the person concerned is employed by the employer for more than eight hours per week on average and occupies a position in which he works under the instructions of the employer.

Definition of Salaried Employee

In SEA Salaried Employees are defined as:

(a) shop assistants and office workers employed in buying and selling activities, in office work or equivalent warehouse operations;
(b) persons whose work takes the form of technical or clinical services (except handicraft work or factory work) and other assistants who carry out comparable work functions;
(c) persons whose job is to solely or mainly to manage or supervise the work of other persons on behalf of the employer; and
(d) persons whose work is mainly of the type specified in (a) and (b).

7.23 It should be noted that statutory directors of companies incorporated in Denmark who are engaged on the basis of an employment contract or director's service agreement are generally not considered to be employees as they are not considered to be working under the instruction of the employer. In international organisations that operate a matrix structure will often have a setup with local subsidiaries hosting the local representation and sales operation. The statutory directors of those subsidiaries will be considered salaried employees if they in reality perform the work of a salaried employee and do not hold the mandate to make executive top level decisions.

GENERAL PROTECTION AGAINST DISMISSAL

7.24 In Denmark only employees covered by a collective agreement or SEA enjoy a minimum notice period. In addition, all Salaried Employees who are over 18 years of age and who have been continuously employed in the enterprise concerned for at least 12 months prior to receipt of the notice of termination have a statutory protection against being dismissed without reasonable grounds. Also employees covered by a collective agreement enjoys protection against unreasonable dismissal, provided that they meet the seniority requirement set out in the collective agreement – nine months according to the main collective agreement between DA (The Confederation of Danish Employers) and LO (The Danish Confederation of Trade Unions).

7.25 It should be noted that an employer may *contractually* be entitled to terminate the contract of employment by complying with the contractual notice set out in the employment contract. However, this contractual entitlement is subject to compliance with the mandatory minimum requirements in SEA or the relevant collective agreement which prohibits deviation from the mandatory provisions of SEA by agreement between the parties where that deviation is to the detriment of the SEA Salaried Employee.

7.26 In Denmark the fairness test is mainly in one stage as opposed to the two-stage test applicable in other countries, eg England and Wales (see para **8.13**). The fairness test is normally independent of the procedure/process as the focus is mainly on testing whether the principal reason for the dismissal is one of the potentially fair reasons set out in the case law.

7.27 Neither SEA nor the collective agreements set out definitions or specific guidelines for a reasonable dismissal but leave it for the tribunals and courts to develop and define this through case law. That said both SEA and collective agreements permit that a fair reason can be established on the basis of either the employee's or the employer's circumstances, however the process for determination is very different in these two situations.

7.28 Generally a fair reason can be established if the dismissal is based on the rational operation of the employer's business or where the behaviour of the employee makes the continued cooperation impossible. As this shows the criteria differ from those ascribed to the question of fault in respect of breach of contract.

SPECIAL PROTECTION AGAINST DISMISSAL

7.29 Danish law provides for special dismissal protection for some categories of employees to the effect that it precludes certain reasons from constituting a fair dismissal regardless of age and seniority. Examples include (but are not limited to) reasons related to:

- pregnancy and adoption;
- maternity or parental leave;
- assertion of legal rights (for example maximum working hours, equal rights or health and safety regulation);
- joining or not joining an association (hereunder a trade union);
- gender, race, colour, religion or belief, political opinion, sexual preference, age, disability, or national, social or ethnical origin;
- making a protected disclosure (whistleblowing);
- being a part-time employee;
- transfer of undertaking; or
- listed as candidate for, or member of, a local council.

7.30 In order to avoid artificial reasons the obligation to show that a dismissal is fair is on the employer rather than the employee (or can be shared) when the employer is terminating employees from certain categories. This can result in making it much harder, and sometimes impossible, to prove that the dismissal was in fact reasonable. If for instance an employee is dismissed during pregnancy or parental leave the burden rests on the employer to prove that the dismissal is not because of the pregnancy or parental leave.

7.31 It should be noted that compulsory retirement on the grounds of age is permitted at the age of 70 if it is based on a contractual arrangement. It is also permitted – if provided by collective agreements – to terminate employment of young employees when they turn 18, as the only reason.

7.32 Other employees enjoy special protection from dismissal which is solely derived from the category they belong to regardless of the actual reason for the dismissal. Accordingly, trade union representatives and other employee representatives can only be dismissed on grounds that show a compelling necessity. In a work force reduction, this special group of employees can only be dismissed as the last among equals. Furthermore, a prolonged notice period and special procedures apply.

WORKFORCE REDUCTION

7.33 When an employer plans to dismiss employees as part of a restructuring of the workforce it is important to identify and document the business rationale behind the expected dismissals. Next, it is important to establish whether this business rationale is reasonable and therefore presents a justification for the dismissals. The employer should ensure that the business rationale is in fact the real and only reason for the actual dismissals and should observe that the dismissals are carried out in accordance with the identified business rationale for each employee. The employer should be aware that the onus rests on the employer if certain protected employees challenge the reason for their dismissal. This applies to pregnant employees, employees on maternity, paternity or parental leave or during adoption and to trade union representatives. In other situations the onus is shared but in all other cases, the general rule is that the onus rests on the employee challenging the fairness of a dismissal.

7.34 If the restructuring involves the dismissal of ten or more employees within a 30-day period the employer might be required to *also* follow the collective redundancy consultation procedure as set out in the collective redundancy procedure section starting at para **7.62**.

Reasonable dismissal – employer's situation

7.35 Neither SEA nor collective agreements define what reasonable dismissal is in connection with a workforce reduction based on grounds related to the employer's circumstances. The interpretation of what is 'reasonable' is subjective and will depend on the facts in each case. As mentioned above case law shows that a fair reason can generally be established if the dismissal is grounded in the rational operation of the employer's business. If the reason for the dismissal is that of a financial downturn and declining profits or lack of orders resulting in lack of work the dismissal will be considered reasonable and therefore legitimate except if the negative financial situation is of a very brief and temporary nature. The assessment is based on the factual circumstances at the time when the termination notice is given and the employer can – to a great extent – make a decision at its own discretion as to which employees to dismiss. This is so even if the work is taken over by another employee.

7.36 Also normal cost saving initiatives which are not due to a strained financial situation can be reasonable. It is a managerial prerogative to balance the business foundation and activities with the spending and to decide on the necessary adjustments in the workforce in this respect. Case law shows that the courts generally respect decision by the management of the employer as to the level of the labour costs and only set aside the management's assessment in case of deliberate misjudgement. This is also the case in respect to deciding which employees to dismiss.

7.37 If work is being outsourced or offshored or an undertaking is transferred to another entity one must assess whether the Danish Transfer of Undertakings Act (TUA) comes into play as the act awards protection to the employees affected by the transfer. This scenario is covered by sections stating at para **7.145** below.

Examples of reasonable dismissals

Company A provides core material kits to the windmill industry. It employs a total of around 150 employees in Denmark of which 100 are employed in the production team, manning four independent production lines which handles the individual orders from start to delivery. In order to reduce production costs Company A has invested in a number of new and more advanced machines which substitute traditional manual milling operations with new CNC machines, thereby reducing the need for manpower. With the new machinery there will no longer be enough work for all of the 100 employees. Company A has identified that, with the introduction of the new machines a reduction of around ten employees in the production team will be necessary. The requirement of the business for the number of employees to man the machinery has been reduced and work in the production team has diminished as a result. The dismissals will be reasonable.

Company B is a retail chain selling white goods in a number of locations around Denmark. It has 50 stores in Denmark but since sales have been slow in the past year it has decided to close five stores. The management has identified the five stores applying a geographical criterion. The criterion is to minimise the impact on the distance between the remaining stores. The five selected stores are not necessary the shops with the lowest performance or the highest decrease in sales in the past year. As a result Company B will dismiss all employees in the five stores on the basis that their workplace is closing down. The dismissals will be reasonable.

> Company C is an international IT company selling consultancy services and CMS software across the world. The management of the company has decided to restructure its operations by which number of roles will be reorganised into new positions. Additional skillsets will be required for these new positions and those employees who do not possess those additional skills will be dismissed. After the reorganisation the same number of roles will exist and some new employees will be hired to replace those, who do not have the required skillset for the new roles. The dismissals will be reasonable.

Reasonable dismissal – employee's situation

7.38 What amounts to a reasonable dismissal where the grounds are related to the employee neither SEA nor collective agreements give any definition or guidance. The interpretation of what is 'reasonable' is subjective and will depend on the facts in each case. In a restructuring scenario the reason for dismissal is always based on grounds related to the employer's business situation and this situation will not be covered in depth in this section. Generally speaking any failure (save for mere trifles) by the employee to fulfil his duties as an employee can constitute grounds for a reasonable dismissal. Unless it is a breach of a clear instruction or work place policy the employer will however usually be expected to issue a warning rather than dismiss the employee in order to allow the employee the opportunity to rectify his behaviour. Entitlement to dismiss will usually arise upon up to several warnings being issued without rectification. This is particularly so if the instruction or policy is not clear to the employee or if the instruction or policy has not been upheld consistently by the employer. Any gross negligence on the employee's side will always constitute a reasonable ground for dismissal without prior warning.

7.39 A reasonable dismissal, based on grounds related to the employee, might also occur if the employee's abilities and competences are insufficient or are no longer adequate for the position. In these situations there is normally no requirement for warnings as the employee cannot be blamed for the situation and have no means to rectify. Instead the employer is required to consider alternatives available to dismissal.

DISMISSAL PROCEDURES

7.40 When employers are planning to dismiss employees in a restructuring scenario they must have regard to two procedures: *the individual redundancy procedure* and *the collective redundancy procedure*. The individual redundancy procedure must always be followed when dismissing employees.

7.41 When planning to dismiss at least ten employees at *one establishment* over a period of 30 days or less the employer will be required consider the collective redundancy procedure in addition to the individual procedure.

7.42 In addition to the actual dismissal procedures the employer must consider the general information and consultation requirements pursuant to both the Danish Employees Information Act (EIA) (which implements Directive 2002/14/EC and only applies to employers with 35 employees or more) as well as any applicable collective agreements. Pursuant to these regulations the employer needs to inform and consult the employees in respect to: (a) recent and projected development of the employer's business activities and economic situation; (b) the situation, structure and future development of employment opportunities with the employer including any anticipated measures, in particular where there is a threat to employment and; (c) decisions likely to lead to substantial changes in organisation of work or in employment conditions.

7.43 Pursuant to EIA, information shall be given at such time, in such fashion and with such content as is appropriate to enable, in particular, employees' representatives to conduct an adequate study and, where necessary, prepare for consultation. Consultation shall take place: (a) while ensuring that the timing, method and content thereof is appropriate; (b) at the appropriate level of management and representation, depending on the subject under consideration; (c) on the basis of information supplied by the employer together with any written opinion by employees' representatives; (d) in such a way as to enable employees' representatives to meet the employer and obtain a reasoned response, to any opinion they might present; and (e) with a view for employer and employee representatives to reach agreement as to the required business decisions the employer must make.

7.44 Regulation under the EIA and the collective agreements in this respect does not limit the employer's right to make dismissals and under current case law failure to comply with these procedures does not appear to impact on the assessment of a fair dismissal.

Redundancy procedures

7.45 For a private sector employer who is not subject to collective agreements the procedural requirements do not generally have any impact on the assessment of whether a dismissal is reasonable or not. In other words there is no specific fair procedure requirements nor is there any generally applicable consultation requirement under Danish employment law. For public sector employers the administrative laws prescribe mandatory consultation procedures to be followed. Public sector employment, however, is outside the scope of this chapter.

7.46 If an employer provides for a redundancy policy and redundancy procedure in the staff handbook or in the employment contract the overarching guiding principle is that the employer shall comply with the procedures set out therein. If the employer fails to comply with such procedure and such is reasonable in the particular circumstances, the onus rest on the employer to prove that the failure to apply the procedure did not impact on the end result. Otherwise the failure to comply with the procedure could render the dismissal unreasonable.

Examples of unreasonable dismissal due to procedural approach

An employee, E, who is in the management of Company A, is dismissed for disloyal behaviour, since he had joined the subordinates in their criticism of the management of Company A. According to the employment contract Company A was obliged to convene a meeting with E before dismissing E in order to exchange views on the proposed dismissal. E is being dismissed without any prior meeting. E had been with Company A for 21 years and had never received any warnings during his employment. Company A is not able to prove that the meeting – if held – would not have resolved the situation. The dismissal is not considered reasonable.

Individual redundancy procedure

7.47 Application of specific individual redundancy procedure depends on whether or not the employee is covered by a collective agreement or is a trade union representative or employee representative. For all other employees there is no applicable redundancy procedure according to Danish law (other than the respective notice requirements, see the section starting at para 7.86).

7.48 That said if the employee proposed for dismissal belongs to a category of protected employees the employer need must show that the real reason for the decision to dismiss is a legitimate reason and not linked to the relevant protected characteristic, eg pregnancy, maternity, paternity or parental leave etc, see para 7.30.

7.49 Applying a process that supports the case that the dismissal is in fact based on fair reasons will ease the burden of proof for the employer. Often this is provided through a process where the employees are scored and compared. To do this a selection pool is identified and appropriate objective selection criteria are set out in order to score the relevant employees and identify the lowest scoring employee for dismissal.

7.50 With this process documented the employer will usually find it easier to show that the decision is based on legitimate reasons based on a commercial business rationale and that the dismissals are therefore reasonable.

> **Example**
>
> Employee, E, who became a father six months ago, works as an in-house lawyer. He informs his employer, that he will go on parental leave in three months. The employer has resolved to cut costs and reduce its staff which also involves dismissing three employees from the legal department. The employer also plans to put in post four new specialised positions after the redundancy process.
>
> To prevent claims for unfair dismissal and in order to show that the dismissals were based on legitimate operational considerations the employer applies a score sheet and compares each employee on personal and educational criteria including a performance assessment based on productiveness, efficiency, quality and initiative.
>
> If this shows that E should be selected based on his lower scores the employer will be able to show the score sheet as documentation if challenged and thereby be more likely to demonstrate that the decision to dismiss was fair and legitimate as part of cost-cutting measures by submitting the score sheet as documentation.

OBLIGATION TO SUBSTANTIATE A DISMISSAL

7.51 Pursuant to SEA the employee can demand that the employer substantiate the dismissal by providing written reasons. When an employer initially dismisses an employee the dismissal can be concise and concentrated to establishing the notice as there is no legal requirement to substantiate the dismissal notice termination until the employee makes such request. Not until the employee requests written reasons for the dismissal will the employer be required to explain in writing the reasons.

Collective agreements

7.52 Employers bound by collective agreements need to comply with specific procedures set out in the collective agreements. Many collective agreements set out rules for information, consultation and negotiation prior to dismissal. Failure to comply with these rules will generally not render a dismissal unfair but will entail penalty payments.

7.53 Each collective agreement will specify the type of dismissals which are subject to these rules.

7.54 Generally the duty to inform will only apply when the plan to reduce the workforce is somewhat firm however still allowing for the actual consultation and negotiations (if applicable) to take place before the final decision is made.

Employee representatives

7.55 With respect to dismissal of employee representatives (ie employee board members, health & safety representatives and union representatives) specific, mandatory procedures apply pursuant to most collective agreements. Depending on the actual wording of the applicable collective agreement the employee representative must not receive the dismissal notice before the union has been informed and the proposed dismissal has been tried in court or tribunal. The notice period will in these cases commence when the proposed dismissal has been approved by the court or tribunal. This process is subject to the union observing certain relevant deadlines as specified in the collective agreements.

Avoiding compulsory redundancies

7.56 As part of being a prudent and responsible employer, the employer should always consider alternatives to compulsory redundancies. Such alternatives could involve job-sharing and other strategies such as a salary sacrifice, withdrawal of benefits, work place cost reductions amongst others with a view avoid or minimise the number of employees affected by compulsory redundancy.

7.57 With regards to job-sharing this can only be applied if provided for by the applicable collective agreement or by an agreement between the employees and the employer. The job-sharing should involve either a reduction of the working hours to minimum two days a week or one week with full work schedule followed by one week off work. With a job-sharing arrangement of less than 13 weeks – or with the approval of the Regional Employment Council up till 30 weeks – the employee will be eligible for income support from the unemployment fund. A job-sharing arrangement must be notified to the local job centre.

7.58 Employers should also consider inviting the employees for voluntary redundancy before starting the compulsory redundancy process although this is not mandatory. Enhanced redundancy payment offered by the employer to the employees volunteering will typically provide an incentive to affected employees. In order to ensure that key employees are retained for the continued success of the company the employers should make it clear to the employees that there is no guarantee that the volunteers will be accepted for voluntary redundancy. The employer should also observe that the selection criteria are non-discriminatory.

7.59 When a volunteer has been accepted for voluntary redundancy the enhanced redundancy payment will often be made conditional on the employee signing up to a settlement agreement where the employee waives any claims against the employer. This should be carefully drafted to ensure adequate protection is put in place, see more in para **7.239**.

Alternative employment

7.60 In other jurisdictions the question of redeployment within an organisation subject to redundancies is often linked to the question of a fair and reasonable redundancy process. In Denmark the question of redeployment is viewed as an issues which is considered a question linked to the material protection against dismissal.

7.61 Danish law does not specify any specific statutory requirements on the part of an employer to offer suitable alternative employment to affected employees within its organisation in case of a work force reduction. Further the main collective agreements do not contain any provisions on redeployment. However, s local collective agreements might contain such provisions applicable to dismissals on grounds related to the employer's situation and in such cases the employer will need to comply with such provisions.

7.62 In employments which are not covered by collective agreements case law has developed providing an obligation to redeploy under certain circumstances. This case law shows that the employee has a right and an obligation to take up another position with the employer if there are any suitable, alternative roles at the time when the employee receives the termination notice. The relevant point in time where the possible redeployment possibilities must be addressed is the date when the employee receives the notice. Any vacancies emerging after this date are irrelevant in this respect.

7.63 Some legal commentators see this obligation purely as a natural element which ought to be included in any assessment of work shortage rather than as a separate issue. Also in some cases the redeployment is linked to or derived from the principle of proportionality which means that in some situations, where employees have long seniority or special protection rights, the employer will need to make an effort to search for and offer the employees suitable alternative employment within the organisation even if this will entail some retraining of staff.

7.64 If an alternative position involves material changes to the employee's current employment terms and conditions, an employer will generally not have an obligation to redeploy the employees to such vacancies.

7.65 Employees on maternity leave and union representatives have special protection and case law has established a right for these employees to be offered suitable, alternative employment as well as priority over other employees in respect of any available suitable, alternative employment.

7.66 If an employee transfers to a new position with the employer the employee retains her seniority and the employer will not be able to impose a probation period.

7.67 If an employee rejects an offer of alternative employment which is suitable or does not involve a material change to the employee's employment terms and condition the employee is considered the terminating party and no claims for unfair dismissal can be made.

OTHER CONSIDERATIONS

7.68 If the employment contract contains provisions on redundancy and redeployment or if the employer has created staff policies in this regard an employer must observe these and act in accordance. If so provided in the provisions herein the employer will have a duty to search for vacancies and investigate the possibilities for redeployment. However, the decision as to which employees will be redeployed is at the employer's discretion.

Collective redundancy procedure

7.69 According to the Danish Collective Redundancy Act ('CRA') (implementing Directive 98/59/EC) a collective redundancy situation arises where an employer proposes to dismiss over a period of 30 days or less: (a) 10 or more employees in a business with more than 20 employees but less than 100 employees; (b) 10% or more in a business with more than 100 employees but less than 300 employees; or (c) 30 or more employees in a business with more than 300 employees.

7.70 In respect to the application of the CRA it is irrelevant whether the staff reduction is decided by the employer or by someone else with a majority vote in the employer, eg an international parent company.

7.71 A secondary act (the Notification Act) was introduced in 2011 in order to define the term 'business' and to establish the principles for counting the employees. According to this act if a business comprises of separate local units, stores, garages, departments, stations, etc, these are all considered 'one' business if situated in one Employment Region. Denmark has four Employment Regions: Northern Jutland, Central Jutland, Southern Denmark and Copenhagen & Zealand. However, where the number of redundancies in one local unit meet one of the thresholds the local unit in itself shall be considered a 'business' in respect to CRA and shall therefore follow the rules laid down in CRA. It has been suggested that this definition is not in compliance with the EU directive and that it might give way if challenged.

Example

The company Happy Toys A/S with 220 employees (190 in the Employment Region of Copenhagen & Zealand) has 45 stores across Denmark. Five of the stores (the Nyborg, Korsør, Næstved, Slagelse and Sorø stores) are no longer as busy as they used to be. As a result the management has decided that there is not enough work for all of the 45 employees currently employed across the five stores and is proposing to reduce headcounts. The management has identified that 5 employees in each of the Nyborg, Korsør, Næstved, and Slagelse stores and 3 employees in the Sorø store are to be made redundant. Accordingly, the management will propose that a total of 23 employees are made redundant across the five stores; 18 in the Employment Region of Copenhagen & Zealand and 5 in the Employment Region of Southern Denmark.

With the five stores placed in two different Employment Regions and with the distribution of the proposed redundancies in the two Employment Regions, Happy Toys A/S will **not** be required to follow the collective redundancy procedure as each region is below the threshold.

However, if the Notification Act is in conflict with the Directive the redundancies proposed across all five stores must be considered together when deciding whether the collective redundancy procedure applies. In this scenario, Happy Toys A/S would be required to follow the collective redundancy procedure since it is proposing to dismiss 23 in total out of 220 employees which is '10% or more in a business with more than 100 employees but less than 300 employees'.

7.72 The number of employees who have volunteered for redundancy is included in the numbers above if at least five employees are proposed dismissed. However, those employees on fixed-term contracts whose dismissals take effect on the termination date or on the termination event stipulated in their employment contracts should be disregarded for the purposes of assessing whether the total number of employees proposed for redundancy meets the threshold.

7.73 When an employer is going through a collective redundancy situation, it is under a statutory duty to initiate consultation with the employees – or their representative – as early as possible. The purpose of the consultation is to reach an agreement to avoid or limit the proposed dismissals and to mitigate the consequences of the dismissals by activities especially aimed at redeploying or retraining workers made redundant.

7.74 For the purpose of the consultation the employer must provide the employees – or their representative – with all relevant information concerning the situation including, as a minimum, written information on

(i) the reasons for the proposed redundancies;
(ii) the number and categories of workers to be made redundant;

(iii) the period over which the proposed redundancies are to be effected;
(iv) the total number and categories of workers normally employed;
(v) selection criteria proposed for workers to be made redundant in so far as national legislation and/or practice confers the power therefore upon the employer; and
(vi) whether any of the projected redundancies are entitled to redundancy payments according to individual or collective agreement and the method for calculating the redundancy payments in such case.

7.75 When informing the employees in writing, as described, the employer must at the same time send a copy to the Regional Employment Council.

7.76 If the employer decides to carry out the redundancies after the consultation procedure the employer must notify the Regional Employment Council in writing. If the projected redundancies amounts to 50% of the employees in one 'workplace' and the 'workplace' normally employs 100 employees or more the notification can be issued no earlier than 21 days after the commencement of the consultation procedure.

7.77 If the employer operates workplaces in different geographic locations all locations within one municipality are considered one 'workplace' for the purpose of establishing the application of certain formalities pursuant to CRA.

7.78 As soon as possible after sending the first notice to the Regional Employment Council, and no later than ten days thereafter, the employer must inform the Regional Employment Council of the employees the employer will make redundant. The affected employees must be informed simultaneously.

7.79 The redundancies can take effect no earlier than 30 days after notifying the Regional Employment Council – or no earlier than eight weeks after this notification if the redundancies amounts to 50% of the employees in one 'workplace' and the 'workplace' normally employs 100 employees or more.

7.80 CRA does not modify the individual or statutory notice periods or those notice periods prescribed by collective agreement.

COLLECTIVE AGREEMENTS

7.81 CRA does not apply to the extent the employer carries equivalent responsibilities pursuant to a collective agreement. An employer should carefully consider such collective agreements as these often contain special rules on collective redundancies.

7.82 Where an employer does not recognise a trade union (or does not recognise the union as representative for some or all employees), an employer may inform and consult with an existing body of employee representatives which has been elected or appointed by the affected employees and authorised by such to act in this regard. Where there are no appropriate employee representatives, such election must be arranged. There are statutory rules for the election of employee representatives for the purpose of collective consultation and the onus is very much on the employer to ensure that the relevant requirements for the election process are complied with. However, such employee representatives do not replace a recognised trade union's rights to information and consultation in respect of collective redundancies. A recognised trade union must always be informed and consulted.

SANCTIONS

7.83 If the employer fails to inform and consult on collective redundancies or fails to notify the Regional Employment Council the employees are entitled to compensation amounting to payment equivalent to 30 days' salary. If the redundancies amounts to 50% of the employees in one 'workplace' and the 'workplace' normally employs 100 employees or more the compensation will amount to payment of a sum equivalent to eight weeks' salary. The compensation will be reduced by salary received during the notice period.

7.84 Furthermore failure to inform and consult on collective redundancies or failure to notify the Regional Employment Council is considered a criminal offence punishable with a fine.

7.85 Failure to comply with Danish Collective Redundancy Procedure has not yet been seen to render a dismissal unfair.

NOTICE

7.86 As mentioned at the beginning of this chapter, unlike some European countries, Denmark does not have one statute in place conferring certain minimum rights on all employees. Accordingly, there is no general rule in respect to length of notice periods. In order to establish the applicable notice period in each individual case one must initially clarify whether the employment relationship is governed by a collective agreement and/or whether the employee is covered by SEA (or other specific regulations) which provide for a minimum mandatory notice period. One should also consult the individual employment contract which of course must not take away employee rights flowing from statute and/or collective agreement to the detriment of the employee.

7.87 Pursuant to the Danish act implementing the Directive 91/533/EEC of 14 October 1991 (on an employer's duty to inform employees of the conditions applicable to the contract or employment relationship) the employment contract shall – among other important terms – include provisions on the notice periods. Employment contracts typically provide for an agreed contractual notice period. The notice period is the period of time between notifying the employee of his employment coming to an end and the actual last day of employment (the 'effective date of termination' or 'EDT'). The correct notice period must be observed by both parties and either worked by the employee, spent on suspension or on garden leave. For details of suspension and garden leave please see the section starting at para **7.101** below.

Minimum notice period pursuant to SEA

7.88 For those employees covered by SEA (see para **7.22** above] minimum notice periods apply to notice given by both the employer and the employee.

7.89 The length of notice period by the employer depends on the length of service with the employer ('seniority'). SEA minimum requirements will override shorter contractual notice periods where these are shorter than the statutory notice periods:

Employment period up to	Notice by Employer
5 months	1 month
2 years and 9 months	3 months
5 years and 8 months	4 months
8 years and 7 months	5 months
more than the above	6 months

7.90 If the employer can show that it has been agreed that the work is of a purely temporary nature and that the employment relationship does not exceed a period of one month, the notice periods above shall not apply.

7.91 The employee can terminate the employment by giving one month's notice irrespective of seniority.

7.92 The parties can agree to extend the statutory notice periods provided that the extension on the employer's part is at least identical to the employee's extension, ie 1:1. If, for example, the parties agree to extend the employees notice by one month the employer's notice should also be extended by at least one month. It is not a requirement that the extension is proportionally equal.

7.93 The notice periods above all expires with effect at the end of a calendar month. As an example if the employer dismisses a salaried employee with two years' seniority on 2 April, the notice is three months and the EDT will be on 31 July.

7.94 The parties may agree in writing on a probation period of up to three months during which the employer may terminate the employment by giving two weeks' notice. During a three months' probation period the employee can terminate the employment without notice or with an agreed notice of up to 14 days. If the probation period exceeds three months the normal notice periods will apply to any termination.

7.95 The parties may agree in writing that the employer has a right to dismiss the employee at the end of a month, where the employee has received salary during periods of illness for a total period of 120 days during a period of twelve consecutive months. The validity of the notice shall be dependent on it being given immediately after the expiry of the period of 120 days of illness and while the employee remains ill, whilst its validity shall not be affected by the fact that the employee has returned to work after the notice of dismissal has been given.

7.96 In terms of requirements as to form SEA requires a notice of termination to be given in writing. This requirement is however only a question of proof. If one of the parties claim that a verbal termination notice has been given the onus is on the party making the claim to show that the termination notice was in fact communicated to the other party.

7.97 Other than the requirement for a notice to be in writing, the legislation does not provide for any specific requirements in respect to form. The wording of the termination notice should however be clear and in definite terms. It is not a requirement that the other party accepts the notice of termination or acknowledges receipt hereof or that the other party has actually read the notice. It is however necessary – if challenged – that the terminating party can show that the termination notice has been delivered to the other party.

Minimum notice period pursuant to collective agreements

7.98 For employees covered by collective agreements the notice periods will be regulated by the collective agreement – often with the same seniority system as in SEA and sometimes by reference to those rules. Within the industry sector and for the typical blue collar workers the collective agreements often provide significantly shorter notice periods than those stipulated by SEA.

Minimum notice period for other employees

7.99 If the contract is silent on the issue of notice periods (which will often constitute a breach of the act on employers' obligation to inform employees of the employment conditions implementing the Directive 91/533/EEC) then termination will be subject to giving reasonable notice which in some instances will mean that no notice is required. The length of the notice period depends on what is common pursuant to the main collective agreement within the same or similar field of work. Factors such as employees education, seniority, the circumstances of the termination and the prospects for finding a new job will influence what will be considered a 'reasonable' notice period.

7.100 Unless the employer determines otherwise the employee is required to continue working as normal during the notice period. The employer should however consider whether it is better for the business to release the employee from the obligation to work. Often the employer will release an employee holding a managerial position or with close connections with customers in order to protect the interests of the business. In such a situation the employer may have two options. The first option is to place the employee on 'suspension' and the second option is to put the employee on 'garden leave'.

Suspension

7.101 Under Danish law an employer can decide to suspend the employee with pay at any time during the notice period. This is so even if the contract is silent on the matter.

7.102 If the employee is required to be at the employer's disposal during the notice period the employee is considered to be on suspension. When on suspension the employee is only temporarily released from his or her work duties and will have to return to work if required by the employer.

7.103 The employer can only uphold the suspension if there is a real and actual need for keeping the employee at the employer's disposal. If the employer has no real intention for the employee to return to work the employer will have to make a decision as to whether to release the employee, ie put the employee on garden leave.

7.104 A suspended employee is allowed to seek and take other employment as long as it does not compete with the employer's business and the employee remains at the employer's disposal. This would usually require agreement between the employee and the new employer that the employee can leave immediately if required by the former employer during the notice period. The employer is not entitled to reduce the salary with any additional income the employee might receive from such additional work.

Garden leave

7.105 Under Danish law an employer can decide to put the employee on garden leave (Danish term: 'Fritstilling') any time during the notice period. This is so even if the contract is silent on the matter.

7.106 An employee on garden leave remains employed by the employer during the notice period but is not given any work and is not allowed to attend the workplace or contact customers. As the employment continues during the garden leave the employee is bound by a duty of good faith and fidelity to the employer until the end of the garden leave period (ie the end of the notice period). This will prevent the employee from working for a competitor or setting up his own competing business.

7.107 The employee is however under an obligation to seek and take up another non-competing employment while he is on garden leave. The employer is entitled to set off any earnings of the employee during the garden leave period against the salary which is payable during the remaining notice period. If the employee is a salaried employee, and therefore covered by SEA, the employer will only be allowed to set off earnings made after three months' garden leave.

Example of suspension and garden leave

Clear Glass A/S ('CG A/S') is restructuring its business and has decided to dismiss, amongst others, a sales consultant Thomas Hald ('TH') with ten years' seniority and a controller, Casper Andersen ('CA') with nine years seniority. Under SEA both TH and CA are entitled to six months' notice.

TH has a close relationship with important costumers of CG A/S and CA has extensive knowledge of the business and future plans of CG A/S.

CG A/S is concerned that both employees, who are unhappy with the situation, will have a bad influence on the business if they are allowed to work during the notice period. CG A/S wants to minimise the risk of any damage, but at the same time reserve the right to call CA in again for work during the notice period if necessary in connection with the audit of the annual accounts. When handing the employees their notice on 31 February CG A/S therefore decides to place TH on garden leave and CA on suspension.

In the beginning of April CG A/S realise that it will not require CA to work during the remaining notice period and decides to put CA on garden leave as well.

TH manages to find a new job as of 1 May with a monthly salary of DKK 30,000–5,000 less than the salary from CG A/S.

Since mid-March CA has worked freelance with a chain of pet shops. When put on garden leave he is immediately employed full time by the pet shop's head quarter. From mid-March to end August CA received a total salary amount which was significantly higher than the salary from CG A/S.

CG A/S can set off TH's new salary of DKK 30,000 in the salary payment for June, July and August, thus paying TH only 15,000 in total for this period. CG A/S is not entitled to set off any amount in May as TH has not been on three month's garden leave in May. TH therefore attains double income in May.

Despite receiving a higher salary in the pet shop CG A/S is not entitled to set off any amount in CA's salary as CA's garden leave does not exceed three months. CA therefore receives double income in the full notice period.

Time off for seeking work

7.108 Pursuant to SEA, salaried employees have the right to take time off if necessary to seek new employment when they have received or handed in their notice of termination of employment. The employee shall however pay due consideration to the employer's reasonable preferences when planning time off for such efforts. The employee is entitled to receive full salary during necessary absence for his job search.

SEVERANCE PAYMENT

7.109 Employees, covered by SEA, with 12, 15 or 18 years' continuous service who are dismissed by their employer, are entitled to a statutory severance sum of respectively one, two or three months' salary. This is in addition to any notice pay or other contractual entitlement that the employees may be entitled to under their employment contract.

7.110 Pursuant to section 2a subsection (3) of SEA the employee is however not entitled to severance pay if, at the EDT, the employee receives retirement pension from a pension scheme financed by the employer, which the salaried employee has entered into before attaining the age of 50 years (unless otherwise prescribed by a collective agreement).

7.111 Pursuant to section 2a subsection(2) of SEA the employee is also not entitled to receive statutory severance pay if, at the EDT, the employee is entitled to receive state retirement pension – regardless of whether the employee at the EDT actually exercises his/her entitlement to receive such state retirement pension. Section 2a subsection (2) of SEA is however by many legal commentators considered to conflict with the directive on equal treatment, and the general EU principle to the same effect, thus constituting unlawful age discrimination. A similar construction was overturned by the ECJ in the Ole Andersen case (C-499/08) which led to a U-turn by the Danish courts. Section 2a subsection (2) is therefore by many legal commentators also expected to be overturned. On 1 October 2014 the Ministry of Employment has initiated a consultation procedure regarding a draft bill proposing to change the severance payment rules in SEA. The bill is expected to come into force as of 1 February 2015 if approved by parliament. Pursuant to the draft bill and subject to the bill being passed, salaried employees dismissed on or after 1 February 2015 with 12–17 years' continuous service will be entitled to a statutory severance payment of one month's salary while an employee with more than 17 years' seniority will be entitled to a statutory severance payment of three months' salary. The bill simplifies the current severance rules removing the references to being in receipt of retirement pension as having any influence on the right to receive severance pay.

Enhanced severance payments

7.112 Additional severance payment may be payable under contract, collective agreement or an employer's insurance policy. Employers need to take steps to avoid any enhancements that they may grant can be considered discriminatory under the age discrimination legislation.

Taxation of severance payments

7.113 Under current tax rules, severance payments of up to DKK 8,000 whether statutory or contractual are tax exempt if the employee's employment is terminated and the severance payment is paid in close connection with the EDT. This is further conditional on the severance payment being paid by the actual employing entity (and not a different group entity) and that the severance payment is not a substitute for remuneration entitlements.

POST-TERMINATION RESTRICTIVE COVENANTS

7.114 During the employment the employee is subject to a duty of good faith and fidelity towards the employer. Accordingly this will prevent the employee from engaging in any competing activities during the employment. As mentioned above under the section starting at para 7.101 this also applies during suspension and garden leave.

7.115 Once the employment relationship has ended, and unless otherwise agreed, a former employee is free to engage in competing activities as long as the employee does not use any of the former employer's trade secrets and does not selectively target the former employer's customers or business connections. For this reason, and to protect the employer's business interests, employers may include post-termination restrictive covenants in the employment contracts in the form of non-competition and non-solicitation clauses. Such clauses are permitted under Danish law with certain statutory limitations and under certain conditions.

Non-competition clause

7.116 A salaried employee can – where the employer wishes to restrict competition – commit himself not to carry on a trade or other business of a specified type, nor to accept employment within any such trade or business ('non-competition clause'). A non-competition clause will only be enforceable if the employee holds a post of special responsibility or has concluded an agreement with his employer on the right to use an invention created by the employee. When determining what constitutes a post of 'special responsibility', the Danish courts will look at the potential effect on competition that particular employee could impose on the employer if the employee was hired by a competitor.

7.117 A non-competition clause will only be enforceable if the salaried employee receives compensation for the period during which the non-competition clause is in force and only if the restriction and entitlement to compensation is included in a written contract. The compensation per month shall, as a minimum, amount to 50 per cent of the salary at the EDT. In this context, 'salary' includes all salary components, eg the taxable value of any company car, mobile phone and other benefits in kind as well as performance-based payments such as bonus schemes.

7.118 The compensation for the first three months shall be paid as a lump sum at the EDT and subsequently each month during the remaining period where the commitment is in force.

7.119 The right to compensation will lapse if the employer has summarily dismissed the salaried employee with good cause.

7.120 An employer may terminate a non-competition clause by giving one month's notice for expiry to the end of the following month. However, regardless of such notice being given by the employer the salaried employee shall be entitled to a minimum lump sum of three months' compensation if the employee departs within six months after the employer has given notice of termination of the non-competition clause.

7.121 If the salaried employee obtains other appropriate work, an amount equal to the salary earned during the period from such work may be deducted from his claim for compensation for the period that falls after the start of this employment relationship. However, a deduction shall not apply to the three months' lump sum compensation. 'Appropriate work' means work within the occupational field of the salaried employee for which he has been trained or in which he has been working to date. As a result of the right to deduct an amount equivalent to income earned from suitable alternative employment from the compensation, the employee must actively seek new employment. If not, the employee will lose the entitlement to receive compensation. Case law shows that for an employee to set up a business during the restricted period will not satisfy the employee's duty to mitigate losses.

7.122 Applicable non-competition agreements are not enforceable and no compensation will be due if the salaried employee has been employed for three months or less by the employer. If the salaried employee has been employed for more than three months but less than six months by the employer, the non-competition restriction is subject to limit of six months after the departure.

7.123 The above mentioned conditions and limitations pursuant to SEA do not apply to the extent other rules have been laid down by collective agreement concluded on 15 June 1999 or later. A non-competition clause in a collective agreement will however only be enforceable if the employee holds a position of special responsibility or has concluded an agreement with his employer on the right to use an invention created by the employee.

7.124 Special rules apply where a salaried employee accepted the non-compete clause before 15 June 1999.

7.125 The provisions of sections 36 and 38 of the Danish Contracts Act apply to non-competition clauses. Under section 38(1) of the Danish Contracts Act, a non-competition clause is not binding on the employee if the provisions concerning duration, territory and other terms go beyond what is necessary to avoid competition or if it restricts the employee's access to new employment in an unreasonable way.

7.126 Section 36 provides a general rule on the invalidity of modification of unfair or unreasonable agreements. An agreement may be modified or set aside in whole or in part if it would be unreasonable or contrary to the principles of good faith to enforce it. If the non-competition is wider than what is strictly necessary to protect the employer's legitimate business interests, the non-competition clause may be set aside by the Danish courts with reference to section 36 even though, according to current case law, this will only happen in extraordinary circumstances.

7.127 If a non-competition clause is set aside on the basis of section 36 or 38(1) of the Danish Contract Act the entitlement to receive compensation set out in the non-competition clause falls away.

7.128 Under section 38(2) of the Danish Contracts Act, a non-competition clause will become unenforceable if the employee is dismissed without having been given reasonable cause or resigns and the employer's failure to meet its obligations provides a valid cause for leaving. If the employee is dismissed by the employer, it is for the employer to prove that the employee has given reasonable cause for the dismissal. If the employee resigns, the starting point will be that the non-competition clause is operative unless the employee shows that the employer's breach of contract justifies termination of employment.

7.129 For employees not covered by SEA the only provisions regulating non-competition clauses agreed between employers and employees are sections 36 and 38 of the Danish Contracts Act.

Non-solicitation clause

7.130 An employee may agree to commit not to be employed by or to have any direct or indirect contact with the customers of his former employer or other business connections after his resignation by accepting a 'non-solicitation clause'. For salaried employees a non-solicitation clause may only be invoked if there has been a commercial relation with the customer or business connection concerned within the past 18 months before the date of the notice of termination. Furthermore, this commitment will only be valid in relation to customers and business contacts with whom the salaried employee has had personal business relationship during his employment with the former employer or so called list-customers. The list-costumers comprise of those customers who have been included under the non-solicitation clause by separate notice in writing prior to the notice of termination of the employment relationship.

7.131 According to case law 'commercial relation' means that the employer has bought, sold or delivered goods or services to the customer in question during the 18 months prior to the date when notice of termination was given.

7.132 A non-solicitation clause is only enforceable if the salaried employee receives compensation for the period during which the restriction is in force and only if a written contract has been drawn up including the commitment and the right to compensation. The compensation per month shall, as a minimum, correspond to 50 per cent of the salary at the EDT. The compensation shall be paid each month during the remaining period during which the non-solicitation clause is in force. If the salaried employee receives compensation for a non-competition clause, the employee will not have the right to compensation for the non-solicitation clause as well. As the employee is prevented from receiving 'double compensation' employers may decide to impose both a non-solicitation clause and a non-competition clause on the employee. As with the non-competition clause the right to compensation will lapse if the employee has been summarily dismissed with good cause by the employer.

7.133 If the former salaried employee secures other appropriate work, an amount equal to the salary from such employment may be set off in his claim for compensation which falls due in the period which follows the start of this new employment relationship.

7.134 Where the salaried employee has been employed for three months or less with the employer, a non-solicitation clause may not be invoked and the employee will not be entitled to compensation. If the salaried employee has been employed for more than three months but less than six months with the employer, the non-solicitation clause may not be invoked for a period exceeding six month after the departure.

7.135 An employer may terminate a non-solicitation clause by giving one month's notice for expiry at the end of the month.

7.136 The above mentioned conditions and limitations pursuant to SEA do not apply to the extent other rules have been laid down by collective agreement concluded on 15 June 1999 or later.

7.137 The provision of sections 36 of the Danish Contracts Act also apply to non-solicitation clauses (see to the description in para 7.126 above). Employees not covered by SEA can only rely on the provision of section 36 of the Danish Contracts Act to regulate the limitations that apply to non-solicitation clauses agreed between employers and employees.

Non-solicitation of employees/'no-hire'

7.138 In Denmark employers' use of non-solicitation clauses and 'no-hire' clauses have been subject to much debate. In 2008 the act on employers' use of non-solicitation of employees and no-hire clauses came into place and made it more or less impossible to invoke such clauses in practice due to the statutory requirements.

7.139 Agreements between two (or more) employers not to hire each other's employees (no-hire clauses) and agreements between an employer and an employee not to poach ex-colleagues after termination (non-poaching clauses) are now only valid if the employer and the employees affected by the clause have signed a written agreement which describes the limitation of the affected employees' job opportunities as a result of the non-poaching and no-hire clauses and the affected employees' entitlement to compensation.

7.140 The employer must pay compensation to the affected employees during the period in which the employees' job opportunities are limited as a result of the restrictive covenant. The affected employees' job opportunities are normally limited when their employment ends. The compensation must – as a minimum – amount to 50% of their pay on the EDT and the compensation must be paid on the same dates as salary payments under the employment contract. However, if the employee receive compensation for a non-competition clause or non-solicitation clause, he will not be entitled to further compensation.

7.141 The provisions entitling the employer to deduct an amount equivalent to income obtained by former employees from new employment and also the requirement for certain minimum service requirements are similar to the non-competition clauses and non-solicitation clauses pursuant to SEA as described above.

7.142 The requirements are somewhat relaxed in relation to temporary employment agencies and in the situation where negotiations have been initiated for the transfer of an undertaking.

Enforceability

7.143 If an employee breaches the post-termination restrictive covenants the employer may apply for an injunction to prevent the employee from any further breaches of the restrictions (this may for instance be to prevent the employee from competing or soliciting customers).

7.144 An employee who has engaged in activities in breach of the post-termination restrictive covenants, and in so doing has caused the employer financial loss, will be liable for any such loss in accordance with the general principles of damages under Danish law. It is however often quite a challenge for the employer to prove that he has incurred a loss and to present a proper estimate of the loss. It is also usually difficult to show the link between the breach and a decrease in turnover as the turnover is affected by many factors. To avoid these challenges employers often include a penalty clause in the contract. Penalty clauses are subject to adjustments by the Danish courts based on the actual breach and the circumstances involved including the resulting loss suffered by the employer. The penalty is normally settled to an amount of between DKK 100,000 and 250,000 per breach but case law shows that the actual penalty awarded rarely goes above DKK 250,000 in total. In a case where the author represented an employer against a key employee the court awarded the employer a total of DKK 750,000 (100,000) in penalty based on three proven activities in breach of the post-termination restrictive covenants each carrying a penalty of DKK 250,000. This seems to be the highest amount yet awarded in Denmark in an employment situation.

BUSINESS SALE, OUTSOURCING/INSOURCING AND OFFSHORING

7.145 When a business is sold or acquired questions arise in respect to the rights and obligations of the affected entities and employees. EU has regulated this area with the Acquired Rights Directive ('ARD'), Council Directive 2001/23/EC. ARD aims to regulate the transfer of an undertaking by ensuring that existing terms and conditions of employment are maintained for the affected employees.

7.146 ARD prescribes minimum requirements, and the national laws of the member states therefore vary from jurisdiction to jurisdiction. The ARD has been implemented in Denmark through the Transfer of Undertakings Act ('TUA'). In order to understand and apply the Danish rules correctly, it is essential to have a thorough knowledge of Danish case law in this area which is constantly developing.

7.147 TUA applies if there is: (1) a transfer; (2) of an undertaking or part of an undertaking; and (3) the undertaking is based in the EU and where the employees affected by the transfer are subject to Danish law. In other words TUA generally applies where a business is acquired and/or where a specific business activity is outsourced or insourced.

7.148 If there is a transfer under TUA the principle is simply that the transferee shall respect and comply with the obligations and rights of the previous owner towards the transferring employees. Also TUA confers an obligation on the transferor and the transferee to inform and consult with affected employees and provides protection to the employees from being dismissed for reason of a TUA transfer.

Transfer

7.149 According to case law 'a transfer' means a change of the person or legal entity responsible for the running of the business and carrying the employer's responsibility towards the employees insofar as the transferred business maintains its identity after the transfer. It is irrelevant whether the transfer entails a change of ownership and whether the transfer is based on a direct contractual relationship between the transferee and the previous owner. The decisive factor is whether there is a transfer of the de facto managerial authority from one legal entity or person to another.

7.150 A 'transfer' includes an acquisition of assets, including by way of acquisition of assets from a insolvent liquidation or probate, a gift, a merger or business transformation from personal to limited liability, a leasehold transfer, franchise or other situations where the business actually continues with a new holder, including privatisation through outsourcing. Normally a transfer is based on an agreement between the transferor and the transferee, but this is not always the case as shown with this example.

Example of transfer

Good Danish Hotel ('GDH') is a chain of Danish hotels. GDH is dissatisfied with its cleaning provider ('CP1') and has decided to cancel the contract with CP1. GDH enters into a 2 months' contract with a different cleaning provider ('CP2'). CP2 takes over 100 of CP1's cleaning employees all of whom have worked under the previous cleaning contract with GDH. The employees continue their employment with CP2 without any interruption of the cleaning service at GDH's hotels. They continue doing the same work as previously using the same operating equipment as previously. The operating equipment is owned by GDH. Even though there is no contractual agreements between CP1 and CP2 this is considered a 'transfer' of employees covered by TUA. The 100 employees therefore enjoy the protection of TUA.

7.151 While TUA applies regardless of the nature of the activities of the entity and regardless of whether the entity is a private or public undertaking TUA explicitly excludes transfers of administrative functions between public administrative authorities.

Undertaking

7.152 What constitutes an 'undertaking' is not defined in TUA or in the directive but is established through case law.

7.153 According to Danish case law as well as the ECJ an undertaking is defined as an autonomous economic entity with a minimum of organisational independence which retains its identity post transfer. Whilst applying the ECJ's case law the Danish courts use a broad application of the definition when deciding whether TUA applies to a specific transfer of an undertaking. In doing so the courts take into consideration factors such as the nature of the business, whether tangible assets are being transferred, the value of intellectual property rights at the time of transfer, whether the majority of the staff is being transferred, whether customers are transferred, to which extent the activities before and after the transfer have changed and for how long the activities have been suspended. None of these elements are decisive in their own right but are included in the overall assessment.

Outsourcing/insourcing

7.154 In an outsourcing/insourcing scenario where one entity ceases to provide services which are then taken over by another entity, such transfer of services will often constitute a 'transfer' under TUA. An outsourcing scenario frequently includes the transfer of a particular business function to an external service provider with the effect that TUA applies as the example above also shows.

Effect of TUA

Automatic transfer and protection of employment

7.155 According to TUA, all rights and obligations of the transferred employees will automatically be transferred with the business on existing terms and conditions. A person is considered an 'employee' under TUA as defined by Danish law in general. Generally this depends on whether the person reports to a manager of the employer and whether the employee is under an obligation to perform work without the option to transfer this responsibility to another person. If the transfer only involves part of the transferor's business the employees who spend the majority of their working hours for the transferred business are considered transferred 'employees' under TUA.

7.156 Employees who have received notice of dismissal but who are working their notice or who are on garden leave prior to the transfer will become transferred 'employees' under TUA.

7.157 The rights and obligations that are transferred may arise from: (1) a collective agreement; (2) terms relating to pay and working conditions laid down or approved by a public authority; and (3) an individual agreement concerning pay and working conditions. The employee seniority and benefits are therefore, among others, unaffected by the transfer. A material change to these rights will be construed as a dismissal and will be subject to the rules applicable for dismissals, see in para 7.40.

7.158 Outstanding claims and entitlements accrued prior to the transfer (unpaid remuneration, bonus entitlements, accrued holiday etc) will transfer with the employee. Pension contributions are considered part of the employee's remuneration and the employee's rights to pension contribution will therefore also transfer. The transferee is however not liable under TUA for the employee's entitlement to payments from a pension scheme. This right is established through other legislation.

Collective Agreements

7.159 As a general rule the transferor's rights and obligations pursuant to collective agreements will also transfer. If the transferee is opposed to a transfer of the collective agreements the transferee must notify the relevant trade union within three weeks from the transfer date or within five weeks after becoming (or should have become) aware of the existence of the collective agreements.

7.160 If the transferee has rejected a transfer of a collective agreement by due notice to the trade union, the employees' rights under the collective agreements will apply only as individual rights.

Objection to the transfer

7.161 An employee is not entitled to object to a transfer under TUA and is not entitled to refuse to work for the transferee unless – in exceptional cases – the employee has such a strong personal relationship with the transferor that the transfer in itself constitutes a material change to the employee's employment terms. Otherwise, if the employee is opposed to working for the new employer, the employee is entitled to terminate the employment in accordance with general rules and subject to adhering to the applicable notice period.

Protection from dismissal

7.162 TUA prescribes that a dismissal made on grounds of the transfer of an undertaking will be considered unfair unless the decision to dismiss is due to an economic, technical or organisational reason entailing changes in the workforce (referred to as an 'ETO reason').

7.163 As TUA does not provide for any specific sanctions for unfair dismissals the real protection for employees must be derived from other rules, eg collective agreements and SEA.

7.164 Salaried employees with at least one year's continuous service subject to this rule enjoy protection derived from the general rules on unfair dismissals, see para **7.35**. A dismissal made on grounds of the transfer itself or a reason – other than an ETO-reason – connected with the transfer will thus confer a right on the salaried employee to receive compensation, see para **7.234**. In many cases the transferee and the transferor will be held jointly and severally liable for such compensation claims.

Protection of terms and conditions of employment

7.165 Under Danish law an employer can always make non-material chances to the employment terms. This is part of the employer's managerial authority and is not affected by a transfer of undertaking on the other hand. With regards to material changes a notice of such is construed as a notice of dismissal if the employee does not agree to the material changes. The employee can therefore claim the protection against dismissal as described above in para 7.24.

7.166 Employers often ask when they can safely make changes – or dismissals – after a transfer. The answer is that there is no fixed 'safe time' in this regard. The onus is on the employer to show that the change – or dismissal – is justified, and the longer the timespan the less burdensome this onus becomes.

Information and consultation under TUA

7.167 According to the procedural rules of TUA both the transferor and the transferee have duties to inform and consult with their respective employee representatives or, in absence of such representatives being appointed, their respective employees affected by the transfer.

7.168 The information and consultation procedures shall take place in reasonable time, before the transfer is carried out, and – for the transferee – before the employees are directly affected by the transfer as regards their conditions of work and employment.

7.169 In terms of timing, 'reasonable time' has not been defined in TUA and is not a fixed standard. According to the preparatory works, considerations must be paid to both the employees and the transferee's and the transferor's circumstances in determining when to inform and consult. It will be relevant in this respect whether early disclosure of the transfer will have any negative effects on the transferring parties. It is up to the courts to determine the 'reasonable time' standard based on all the facts and issues in each case.

7.170 It is evident, however, that the information procedure shall be followed through prior to making the final decision. And it is also evident that the consultation shall be carried out with the purpose of reaching an agreement with the affected employees prior to making a final decision on the matter.

DUTY TO INFORM

7.171 According to TUA the following information shall be provided:

a) the transfer date or the proposed transfer date;
b) the reasons for the transfer;
c) the legal, economic and social implications of the transfer for the employees (for example, change in employer, change in work location); and
d) the possible changes relevant for the employees employment terms.

7.172 The information shall be detailed enough to allow the employees a real chance to assess the consequences of the transfer in relation to the effect on employees' employment terms. There is no requirement in respect to form so the information does not have to be in writing. It is however often recommended to do this in writing to avoid misunderstandings and to retain proof of compliance with the duty.

DUTY TO CONSULT

7.173 The transferor and the transferee only have a duty to consult if either person anticipates that it will make changes in relation to employment terms of any of its affected employees in connection with the transfer.

7.174 The obligation to consult does not apply to changes that the employer can implement on the basis of the employer's managerial authority such as non-material changes. Material changes which will trigger the consultation procedure include eg pay cuts, material limitations of the employees' responsibilities and authority, significant relocation of the workplace etc.

7.175 The consultation must be with the aim of seeking an agreement to the proposed changes. However, there is no requirement to actually reaching an agreement.

EUROPEAN WORKS COUNCILS

7.176 Provided there is a European Works Council ('EWC') established within the group of companies affected by a multi-jurisdictional restructuring or redundancy exercise then there may be an obligation to inform and consult with the EWC prior to implementing any such exercise.

Sanctions

Unfair dismissal

7.177 SEA and collective agreements provides rules concerning the sanction of unfair dismissals.

7.178 Pursuant to SEA if an employee has one year's continuous service, dismissal will be automatically unfair where the principal reason for the dismissal is the transfer itself or a reason connected with the transfer that is not an ETO reason. For further details on the remedy for unfair dismissal see the section starting at para 7.231 below. As all employment liabilities transfer to the transferee under TUA, the transferee can find themselves liable for dismissals by the transferor. Commercial agreements will commonly contain detailed indemnities in relation to the financial liability for acts and omissions relating to transferring employees. Such agreements will be valid and enforceable to the extent that they do not attempt to contract out of TUA.

7.179 In the absence of any indemnity agreement between the transferor and the transferee Danish case law sets out that the transferor shall nevertheless indemnify the transferee for any liabilities towards the employee which has accrued up and including the date of transfer.

Failure to inform and consult

7.180 If a transferor fails to comply with the information and consultation rules under TUA the transferee and transferor may be jointly and severally liable for claims by the relevant employees. However the only sanction that TUA provides in terms of breaching the information and consultation rules is in form of a fine to be paid to the state. The fine has no upper limit and so far there is no known example of this sanction actually being imposed.

Application of TUA to cross-border transactions/ offshoring

7.181 TUA only applies if the employees are covered by Danish law in general. It is therefore important to consider the laws of each jurisdiction that may apply to the employees in order to clarify to what extent the transfer or parts hereof is subject to Danish law.

7.182 Where Danish law applies and where the undertaking is offshored, the change of workplace will be a change which should be included in the information and consultation procedure. Any mandatory rules in the jurisdiction of the transferee might also impact on what must be included in the information and consultation procedure. If the employees refuse to accept these changes they can consider themselves dismissed on reasonable grounds and will thus not be transferred.

Practical Tip

Where a particular business function is being offshored to another jurisdiction, the transferee will typically ask the transferor to effectively terminate the employments with those employees that will not transfer to a new location. If the employees' EDT is before the transfer date, the employees' rights will not transfer to the transferee. The transferee will often, as part of the deal negotiation, request appropriate indemnities in respect to compliance with redundancy procedures and TUA procedures.

WORKFORCE REDUCTION IN CONNECTION WITH SHARE SALE OR SHARE PURCHASE

7.183 The application of TUA requires that there is a change of the person or legal entity responsible for the running of the business and carrying the employer's responsibility. A sale and/or purchase of shares in (limited liability) companies does not involve such changes. In these situations the employer remains the same legal person regardless of the transfer of shares and the subsequent change of the shareholder's identity. Thus TUA does not apply to a share sale.

7.184 If the new owner (shareholder) wishes to dismiss employees as part of a restructuring of the business, the normal dismissal rules apply.

CHANGING EMPLOYMENT TERMS AND CONDITIONS

7.185 An employment relationship often undergoes changes during its term. Some of these changes are automatic and natural following the employees personal development in their post or as a result of the general changes in the business environment or society. Other changes are immediate and direct as a result of sudden changes imposed by the employee or the employer, eg introduction of new technology, structural changes, physical moves etc.

7.186 As a starting point the employer can make changes to the employment and the employees' terms pursuant to the employer's managerial prerogative. Normally the employees will be entitled to proper notice so they can adjust to the changes in due time. Depending on the materiality, the changes can be effected with: (i) no notice; (ii) a reasonable notice (less than the termination notice); or (iii) the applicable termination notice, see the section starting at para **7.86** regarding notice.

7.187 If the employees accept a specific change, the parties may agree when such changes take effect and whether it should take immediate effect or within a certain time frame and thereby waiving other notice requirements.

Mutually agreed changes

7.188 Making unilateral changes to a contract always carries with it a risk of claims being brought against the employer for breach of contract and (constructive) unfair dismissal. Thus agreeing with the employee on the changes might be preferred if possible. Unlike other jurisdictions there is no a legal requirement in Danish law that the employee should receive some benefit in return for the proposed change, a so called 'consideration'. However, section 36 of the Danish Contracts Act applies to any agreement and offers general protection to the employee against unfair or unreasonable changes to the employee's employment terms. In this respect whether some form of 'consideration' has been offered will influence the assessment of the fairness of an agreed change.

Unilateral changes

7.189 An employer may decide to impose unilateral changes to the employment terms and conditions and it then becomes evident to apply the right procedure and notice subject to the materiality of the changes.

NO NOTICE

7.190 Changes that are insignificant and immaterial can be imposed by the employer without notice. In many situations it will be obvious whether a change is immaterial. In other situations, the qualification will cause difficulties.

7.191 In the assessment of whether a proposed change is immaterial and whether it can be imposed without notice – and without the employee's consent – one needs to understand the nature and limits of the employee's position. Sometimes the position will itself carry a prerequisite for the changes. Also the provisions of the employment contract have to be considered as an important factor. If the contract expressly permits changes subject to the limitation of any mandatory statutory provisions the employer will generally be allowed to make the changes without notice – or with a reasonable notice if the changes have some effect on the employee. Also the common understanding of the employment terms, the employee's length of service and the employee's known assumptions in regards to the employment terms will have an impact.

7.192 Minor changes to the employee's tasks and temporary changes to the employee's tasks in case of a co-worker's absence or in case of the employee's dismissal can normally be imposed without notice.

NOTICE – TERMINATION NOTICE

7.193 If an employee receives notice of a material change the employee is entitled to perceive the change notice as a dismissal and an offer of re-employment on new terms. As a result material changes to the employment can only be imposed by observing the applicable termination notice.

7.194 If the change implies that the employee is given a new position and therefore exceeds the reasonable expectations of the employee the change is considered material.

7.195 Any change in the remuneration, work time, special benefits and extended notice, will – as the general main rule – be considered a material change. The same applies to any introductions of new restrictive covenants.

7.196 Change of work place is considered a material change if – on an individual basis – it has a significant negative impact for the employee. There are examples in Danish case law showing that a 47 km move extending the employee's commuting time by 91 minutes was not a material change.

7.197 Any such changes have to be fair as the employee will otherwise be able to bring a claim for unfair dismissal. The employer will also have to comply with the appropriate dismissal procedure. This includes the collective redundancy consultation procedure as outlined in the section starting at para 7.62 above where the employer decides to take this approach in respect of a number of employees.

NOTICE – REASONABLE NOTICE

7.198 Between those situations where change can be imposed without notice and those situation where it requires notice equivalent to a termination notice, there are a number of changes that are neither immaterial nor material to the effect that failure to give reasonable notice amounts to a dismissal. These situations will require reasonable notice which is usually shorter than the applicable termination notice.

7.199 It is very difficult to make a general description of the changes that fall into this category. As an example though, even if a change of working hours or work place is a permitted change in the employment contract or in a collective agreement such will normally require reasonable notice prior to being imposed.

USING TEMPORARY STAFF

7.200 In a reorganisation the employer may be in a situation where using temporary staff should be considered. Temporary staff can be engaged directly on fixed term contracts or through an agency. Different rules apply in these situations.

Agency workers

7.201 If an employer is in need of some temporary cover at short notice and wishes to avoid engaging in a formal employment relationship the employer may instead engage agency workers.

7.202 As of 1 July 2013 agency workers engaged by a Danish user undertaking enjoys certain protections under the Danish Agency Workers' Act ('AWA'). AWA is an implementation of the directive on temporary agency work (2008/104/EC of 19 November 2008). The purpose of AWA is to ensure the protection of temporary agency workers and to improve the quality of temporary agency work. This is done by ensuring that the principle of equal treatment is applied to temporary agency workers, and by recognising temporary work agencies as employers.

AWA IMPOSES STATUTORY DUTIES ON BOTH THE AGENCY AND THE USER UNDERTAKING

Duties of the agency

7.203 The agency shall ensure that the basic working and employment conditions of temporary agency workers shall be, for the duration of their assignment at a user undertaking, at least those that would apply had they been recruited directly by that undertaking to occupy the same job. The 'basic working and employment conditions' means working and employment conditions laid down by legislation, regulations, administrative provisions, collective agreements and/or other binding general provisions in force and applying to the user undertaking. The conditions may relate to the duration of working hours, overtime, breaks, rest, periods, night work, holidays and public holidays and pay. The aforesaid also includes that the rules in force in the user undertaking on:

(a) protection of pregnant women and nursing mothers and protection of children and young people; and
(b) equal treatment for men and women and any action to combat any discrimination based on sex, race or ethnic origin, religion, beliefs, disabilities, age or sexual orientation;

must be complied with as established by legislation, regulations, administrative provisions, collective agreements and/or any other general provisions.

7.204 According to AWA, agency workers are entitled to receive information from the agency about the above mentioned employment terms that apply during the duration of their assignment at a user undertaking.

7.205 According to AWA, an agency is not entitled to make successive assignments to the same user undertaking without a fair reason. A fair reason is for instance that the agency worker is to finalise the assigned work or that the person, whom the agency worker was substituting for, prolongs her leave.

7.206 AWA prohibits use of any restrictive covenants that prohibit or have the effect of preventing the conclusion of a contract of employment or an employment relationship between the user undertaking and the agency worker after his assignment. However according to AWA this prohibition is without prejudice to provisions under which temporary agencies receive a reasonable level of recompense for services rendered to user undertakings for the assignment, recruitment and training of temporary agency workers.

7.207 AWA also sets out that agencies shall not charge workers any fees in exchange for arranging for them to be recruited by a user undertaking, or for concluding a contract of employment or an employment relationship with a user undertaking after carrying out an assignment in that undertaking.

Duties of the user

7.208 With regard to the user undertaking AWA also provides for some obligations. The user undertaking shall inform the agency workers of any vacant posts in the user undertaking to give them the same opportunity as other workers in that undertaking to find permanent employment.

7.209 Unless the difference in treatment is justified by objective reasons, the user undertaking shall ensure that the temporary agency workers is given access to the amenities or collective facilities in the user undertaking, in particular any canteen, child-care facilities and transport services, under the same conditions as workers employed directly by the undertaking.

7.210 The user undertaking is also obligated in most cases to provide suitable information on the use of agency workers to employees' representative.

7.211 AWA is generally superseded by collective agreements giving the agency worker the same minimum rights as AWA.

Fixed-term contracts

7.212 Fixed-term employment contracts can be useful if an employer wishes to engage work resources for a limited period of time or for a specific temporary project. The limited periods are often used when someone is required as maternity or sick cover. The use of fixed-term contracts is on the decrease in Denmark and it is estimated that less than 10% of the employments are on fixed-term contracts.

7.213 The common denominator for such employments is that the employment will terminate automatically without notice when the time or the project has lapsed. The fixed-term employee will not be able to challenge the fairness of the termination. Except from the pre-set termination date, the fixed-term employment is regulated by the same employment laws as other employments. It is established that an employer cannot circumvent the rights of the employees pursuant to collective agreement or SEA by entering into fixed-term contracts instead of permanent employment contracts.

7.214 When using fixed-term contracts certain specific rules apply pursuant to SEA and the Danish Fixed-term Employees Act ('FtEA'). The latter implements the Council Directive 1999/70/EC of 28 June 1999 concerning the framework agreement on fixed-term work.

7.215 According to SEA the employer and the salaried employee may agree in writing on a probation period of up to three-months during which the employer may terminate the employment by giving two weeks' notice. During a three-month probation period the employee can terminate the employment without notice or with an agreed notice of up to 14 days. If the probation period exceeds three months the normal notice periods will apply.

7.216 If the employer and the employee have agreed that the work is of a purely temporary nature and that the employment relationship does not exceed a period of one month SEA exempts the normal notice requirements and permit an immediate termination of such fixed-term employments.

7.217 FtEA applies to fixed-term employments and aims to improve the quality of fixed-term work by ensuring the application of the principle of non-discrimination and to establish a framework to prevent abuse arising from the use of successive fixed-term employment contracts. FtEA does not apply to employees that enjoy the same protection under collective agreements or agency workers covered by AWA.

7.218 According to FtEA, fixed-term workers shall not be treated in a less favourable manner than comparable permanent workers solely because they have a fixed-term contract unless different treatment is justified on objective grounds. When hiring people it remains the employer's decision – within the limitations of collective agreements – whether to offer the employee a fixed-term or a permanent employment.

7.219 FtEA sets out that the principle of *pro rata temporis* shall apply, where rights are accrued or obtained in proportion to the duration of the employment. If certain employment rights are accrued subject to certain seniority the same requirement shall apply to fixed-term employees and permanent employees unless different treatment is justified on objective grounds.

7.220 FtEA's other aim is to prevent abuse arising from the use of successive fixed-term employment contracts. According to FtEA the use of successive fixed-term employment contracts is only allowed where justified on objective grounds such as

(a) sudden absence due to illness, pregnancy, maternity, leave, public duty;
(b) time or project determined piecework;
(c) finalisation or modification of a specific temporary project; and
(d) certain teaching and scientific employments with government and independent institutions financed by the state (however limited to two successive renewals).

7.221 Pursuant to FtEA the employer shall inform fixed-term workers about vacancies which become available in the undertaking or establishment to ensure that they have the same opportunity to secure permanent positions as other workers.

7.222 The employer shall also, as far as possible, facilitate access by fixed-term workers to appropriate training opportunities to enhance their skills, career development and occupational mobility.

BREACH OF FTEA

7.223 If an employer breaches the rights of the fixed-term employee he will have to pay compensation to the employee. The same applies if the employee is dismissed because he claims his rights under the FtEA. Under current case law the compensation amounts to a one-off payment of DKK 15,000 in addition to any other compensation entitlements under other applicable rules. If the breach is committed by successive fixed-term employment contracts in conflict with FtEA the contract will automatically be regarded as a permanent contract.

EMPLOYMENT CLAIMS

7.224 The ordinary Danish courts of law consist of 24 district courts (and a Maritime & Commercial Court), two regional high courts and a Supreme Court. According to the Administration of Justice Act most cases are heard by a district court as a first instance; and the judicial system is based on the principle that most cases may be tried at two and only two instances.

7.225 Denmark has just one Labour Court. It is not part of the ordinary judicial system but has, according to the Labour Court Act, exclusive jurisdiction to deal with first of all disputes of rights, especially breaches of collective agreements on wages and working conditions, including industrial actions in contravention of collective agreements.

7.226 Cases involving individual employment contracts are heard by the ordinary courts of law or in some cases by arbitration pursuant to the Danish Arbitration Act. Cases concerning employment regulated by collective agreements may also be eligible for hearing in the ordinary system of law courts. Thus, if due to the interpretation of a statutory provision the Labour Court does not have exclusive jurisdiction or in the whole does not centre on areas that comes under the jurisdiction of the Labour Court, each of the parties is entitled to demand that the matter be dismissed by the Labour Court or, at least, be stayed pending the decision of the ordinary courts of law.

7.227 Individual employees cannot institute proceedings before the Labour Court. Meanwhile, if the relevant trade union is not inclined to issue proceedings on behalf of the employee before this court, the Labour Court Act grants the person in question permission to bring his own action for outstanding wages before the ordinary courts. The same applies to employees, who are not members of a trade union.

7.228 The Labour Court is not concerned with the interpretation of collective agreements. Instead, according to a special negotiation procedure, such disputes are brought before the industrial arbitration tribunals, set up by the relevant parties.

7.229 If the parties agree the industrial arbitration tribunals may also consider other matters, and some collective agreements, particularly those involving public bodies as employers and salaried employees contain provisions that completely dispense with the Labour Court for dispute-resolution. Similarly, the Labour Court hear cases that would otherwise be subject to industrial arbitration, if the parties so agree.

UNFAIR DISMISSAL

7.230 Salaried employees with more than 12 months of service, or employees, who are covered by a collective agreement and meet the seniority requirement therein (typically nine months), can bring a claim for unfair dismissal if they believe that the dismissal was unfair.

Collective agreements

7.231 If the claim is based on a collective agreement the procedure set out therein must be followed. Unless otherwise prescribed the employee's union can bring the claim for unfair dismissal to the Labour Court. The Labour Court is a special court with an independent legal framework and with the influence of employer and employee organisations.

7.232 Collective agreements often transfer certain cases to specific tribunals. Accordingly the main collective agreement between DA (The Confederation of Danish Employers) and LO (The Danish Confederation of Trade Unions) ('Main Agreement') transfers such claims to a labour tribunal. The Main Agreement provide the following procedure for such claims:

(a) In the case of dismissal of an employee who has been employed in a company for at least nine continuous months, the employee concerned is entitled to request the reason for his dismissal in writing.
(b) If the employee claims that the dismissal is unfair and not on grounds related to the employee the employee or the company, a request may be made for the dispute to be settled locally between representatives of management and employees. The local negotiations shall be completed within two weeks of notice being given.
(c) In case the employer has given flagrantly incorrect information about the reason for the dismissal and this is of considerable importance to the case, the above notice shall run from the time that the employee was or should have been given the correct information. The local negotiations, however, must be completed within three months of notice being given.
(d) In case agreement is not reached, and the relevant trade union (or central management) requests that the matter be taken further, negotiations shall immediately be initiated between the employee and employer organisations.
(e) If agreement is not reached, the relevant trade union (or central management) is entitled to submit a complaint to one of the central organisations' permanent Tribunals. The complaint shall be submitted to the Tribunal and to the opposing organisation within seven days of the conclusion of negotiations between employee and employer organisations.
(f) The Tribunal shall issue a reasoned award. If the Tribunal finds that a dismissal is unfair, it may, after a claim to that effect, decide to set aside the dismissal, unless there has been, or there is deemed to be, a breakdown in relationship between the employer and the employee, which prevent any further continuation of the employment relationship. If the Tribunal finds that the dismissal is unfair, but that the employment relationship should nevertheless be terminated, or if a claim is made for compensation for unfair dismissal, the Tribunal may decide that the company should pay compensation to the dismissed employee. The amount of compensation depends on the facts of the case and the seniority of the unfairly dismissed employee. Compensation may not exceed 52 weeks' pay, calculated on the basis of the average earnings during the preceding year.

Salaried employees

7.233 If the employment is not covered by a collective agreement the salaried employee may bring the claim in the ordinary courts, ie the district court in the first instance.

7.234 If the dismissal of a salaried employee over 18 years of age and who has been continuously employed in the relevant enterprise for at least 12 months prior to the notice of termination is not found to be reasonably justified on grounds related to the employee or the employer, the court shall award the employee compensation. The amount of such compensation shall be determined with due regard to the length of service of the employee and any other circumstances of the case, but it may not exceed the amount of salary of the employee for a period corresponding to half the notice paid to which the employee is entitled under SEA. However, if the employee is over 30 years of age at the time of notice of termination, the compensation may amount to up to three months' salary.

7.235 If a salaried employee has been continuously employed by the employer for at least ten years, the compensation of up to four months' salary may be awarded. After 15 years' continuous employment with the employer compensation of to up to six months' salary may be awarded.

DISCRIMINATION

7.236 An employee may also bring a claim for discrimination in the Labour Court, Tribunal or the courts as above, if she believes that the real reason for her dismissal was because of one of the following protected characteristics: age; disability; pregnancy, paternity, maternity; parental leave, race; colour; political opinion; national, social or ethnical origin; religion or belief; sex; or sexual orientation.

7.237 Discrimination claims can also be brought to the Board of Equal Treatment ('The Board'). The Board is an administrative quasi-judicial body that deals with complaints about discrimination based on gender, race, colour, religion or belief, political views, sexual orientation, age, disability or national, social or ethnic origin.

Remedies

7.238 If an employee is successful in a claim for discrimination he or she may be reinstated and/or be awarded compensation. Reinstatement is rarely used (if at all) and the majority of Danish anti-discriminatory statutes are not subject to a specific cap on the amount of compensation.

7.239 Under current case law, the amount of compensation awarded varies from case to case and also depends on the actual act of discrimination.

7.240 Under current case law the amount of compensation awarded when the reason for dismissal is as a result of the employee's pregnancy or maternity, paternity, or parental leave usually varies from six to twelve months' salary.

7.241 In case of age discrimination and dismissal on the grounds of disability, the amount of compensation varies from six to nine months' salary.

7.242 In terms of other protected grounds, in one case the Danish High Court awarded three months' salary in compensation to an employee who had been dismissed on the grounds of religious belief.

7.243 If a Danish court finds that a decision to dismiss is related to an employee's (non-) membership of a union or a particular organisation, the employee may be awarded a compensation of between one and twenty-four months' salary. If the employee has been employed more than two years, the amount of compensation will not be less than three months' salary.

> **Practical Tip**
>
> Even if an employee does not have the required one year of service (or nine months under collective agreements) at the time of termination and thus cannot bring a claim for unfair dismissal employers are still strongly advised to follow a minimum dismissal procedure and carefully document the reasons for the termination of employment so as to minimise the risk of employees claiming that the real reason for the dismissal was because of one of the protected characteristics.

MUTUALLY AGREED TERMINATION

7.244 The employer and employee may both wish to terminate the agreement on a mutual basis. This is often achieved by way of a severance or settlement agreement which will reduce the risk of claims proceedings and other uncertainties. Under the terms of such an agreement, the employee will often be required to agree not to enforce their employment rights by bringing a claim against the employer in exchange for a termination package – so called 'full and final' clauses.

Settlement agreements

7.245 Settlement agreements are regulated by the general laws of obligation and there are no specific requirements when it comes to such agreements. A settlement agreement is not binding on the employee if the employee has been forced or threatened to sign the agreement. Even though it is not required by law, an employer should always ensure that an employee receives independent legal advice on the terms of the settlement agreement before entering into the agreement.

7.246 The settlement agreement should as a minimum specify the purpose of the settlement agreement, the rights and obligations of the parties, and the practical details of ending the employment.

7.247 It is advisable to always specify whether the termination is caused by grounds of the employer or the employee as this can be relevant in respect to certain rights and obligations, eg the validity of a non-competition clause; the right to exercise and receive share warrants; unemployment benefits; and severance pay and compensation entitlements.

7.248 In terms of 'full and final' clauses Danish case law shows that these are not always approved by the courts as 'full and final'. These clauses are subject to interpretation by the courts, and case law shows that the following elements can influence the outcome of this interpretation:

(a) the purpose and reason for the settlement;
(b) the wording – content and consequence;
(c) who has drafted the agreement;
(d) the 'consideration' – ie some benefit in return;
(e) the claims are known to both parties; and
(f) fairness.

7.249 When considering whether a 'full and final' clause prevents the employee from bringing claims against the employer the courts seem to make an assessment which is based primarily on the background and the purpose of the settlement agreement. Next the court interprets the content and the consequences. Whether a waiver of rights is then contractually binding on the employee will depend on an overall assessment of the agreement including the fairness of the agreement, the parties professional level and bargaining power, the content of the negotiations, the sort of right being waived, the legal framework for the right (individual agreement, collective agreement, statutory right) and whether the employee is receiving proper consideration for the right waived.

7.250 To enhance the chances of full enforceability of a settlement agreement in Denmark it should therefore be carefully drafted and handled.

Chapter 8

Workforce Restructuring in England and Wales

Edzard Clifton-Dey, Sara Kennedy and Emmanuelle Ries
ebl miller rosenfalck, London

INTRODUCTION

8.1 This chapter is looking at the employment laws in England and Wales as the largest and economically most important jurisdiction in the United Kingdom (UK). Whilst the terms UK, Great Britain and England are frequently used – in day to day language – as interchangeable, it is worth noting that each term carries a distinct legal meaning. Broadly speaking, the term United Kingdom describes the area that is made up of England and Wales, Scotland and (Northern) Ireland. England and Wales, on the one hand, and Scotland on the other are jointly referred to as 'Great Britain'. The law in Northern Ireland and in Scotland differs from the law applicable in England and Wales and whilst these differences may well only be minimal in respect of employment law they nevertheless exist. However, for the purposes of this publication we have restricted the scope to the employment laws of England and Wales.

8.2 The legal system in England and Wales is a common law system and, as such, different from all continental European (civil law) jurisdictions. The law is not codified in a systematic way and in many ways it is more akin to the US legal system. Whilst employment statutes exist as Acts of Parliament such statutes are typically piecemeal in that they either compliment or correct case law (judge made law) or implement European Directives. The lack of an equivalent to a comprehensively codified statute book found in continental European jurisdictions means in practice that statute does not typically provide for default employment contract terms that automatically apply unless there is a contractual agreement to the contrary. Although there are some basic minimum terms for the benefit of employees, employers in England and Wales usually expressly set out in the employment contract all the terms which they wish to rely on for the protection of their business. As a consequence employment contracts in England and Wales tend to be substantially longer than in most other European countries since all terms, including definitions, are expressly set out in a well drafted contract of employment.

8.3 When assessing entitlements of employees in dismissal or any other restructuring scenario, the 'first port of call' is therefore the employment contract to ascertain what the parties have agreed upon in respect of applicable notice periods, post-termination covenants, garden leave, IP protection, and corporate change of control to name just a few.

8.4 Bearing in mind that none of the European jurisdictions covered in this publication accepts the concept of 'employment at will' it will then also be necessary to consider the requirements under statute in respect of the termination of employment: what are the accepted reasons for a termination of employment by the employer and what procedure will the employer need to follow when relying on any such accepted reason for termination. Even if the objective is not a downsizing of the workforce but perhaps limited to a harmonisation of terms and conditions across the workforce the very same issues need to be considered. Again, the lack of an 'employment at will' concept and the existence of certain statutory protections (most notably unfair dismissal protection and anti-discrimination legislation) will make it often very difficult – if not impossible – to unilaterally impose new terms and conditions of employment on employees.

PREPARING FOR A RESTRUCTURING EXERCISE

8.5 Different types of issues may arise when carrying out a restructuring exercise. This may include the need to reduce the workforce, change terms and conditions, integration and harmonisation of workforces, use of temporary staff, outsourcing and offshoring, or reassignment of functional and organisational responsibilities of staff.

8.6 At the outset of any restructuring exercise in England and Wales it is vital to gather relevant information in respect of the impacted workforce (such as their existing contractual terms and conditions, data concerning the demographics of the workforce) as this will be required to not only carefully plan and structure the exercise but to also put together a restructuring budget that is based on realistic assumptions. Whilst many restructuring exercises are started on the expectation of restructuring delivering significant costs-savings, this expectation is frequently not based on a detailed analysis as against the actual costs/benefit ratio of the restructuring but often no more than an overly optimistic 'guesstimate'.

The first key issues to consider are set out below.

Identify the employing entity

8.7 The employee's employment is always with a particular legal entity and never with 'the group' and therefore the business decision underlying the restructuring and/or any redundancies has to be approached and documented separately in each company. This is particularly important to bear in mind where an organisation operates a matrix structure where teams of employees are working together across the boundaries of employing entities.

> **Example**
>
> One company may decide to discontinue a certain activity, making a certain department or a certain level of management redundant on the basis that another group company will in future fulfil this function.
>
> Provided that the companies are run separately in practice, the employee will usually only have a remedy against the employing company. However, in looking at ways to mitigate the effect of redundancies, and particularly if the group organisation is such that there is a central HR function or a means of providing information about vacancies to the rest of the group, the employing company may be under an obligation to consider, and if appropriate offer, suitable alternative positions that may be available in other companies of the group.

Collating information to plan and budget for the restructuring exercise

8.8 A restructuring exercise involving one or more group companies, perhaps across a number of jurisdictions, requires careful planning at the outset as it will otherwise be impossible to assess the costs of the exercise or minimise the risk of employment tribunal claims. HR managers will therefore need to consider what they require in terms of data to run and budget for the restructuring exercise (see also para **8.1** Introduction, above).

8.9 The employing entity should already be holding all the necessary data on the relevant employees. A centralised HR department that sits with another group company will need to ensure that it has (lawful) access to any such data as data sharing of employee data across the group requires employee consent. A well drafted employment contract will usually provide for this.

8.10 Gathering the relevant data and facts on the basis of which to reliably plan and structure any restructuring exercise is in itself time consuming and it is essentially akin to a due diligence exercise. The planning and structuring stage can only realistically begin once such data and key facts are available to the HR team and its advisers.

Practical Tip

Key data required initially in respect of any employee potentially impacted by a workforce reduction or restructuring exercise includes (but is not limited to):

- job description;
- length of service;
- contractual benefits and entitlement on termination of employment;
- age;
- place of work;
- enhanced redundancy entitlement;
- applicable collective agreement (if any); and
- information relevant to determine redundancy selection pool.

This information will be necessary for estimating the overall costs of the restructuring exercise and for planning the appropriate timetable for executing any dismissals.

EMPLOYMENT STATUS

8.11 Only individuals, who meet the legal definition of 'employee', are protected against unfair dismissal and need to be included in a redundancy procedure for workforce restructuring purposes. It will be a relevant fact finding exercise in any restructuring to assess if, within the impacted business, there are individuals engaged that are not employees of the entity affected by the restructuring (for example agency workers, self-employed free lancers or consultants etc). Please note that statutory directors of companies incorporated in England and Wales who are engaged on the basis of an employment contract or director's service agreement are generally considered to be employees with just the same level of protection as any other employee in the business.

GENERAL PROTECTION AGAINST DISMISSAL

8.12 In England and Wales the concept of 'employment at will' is not applicable. All employees enjoy a minimum notice period and, in addition, all employees who have at least two year's continuous service at the effective date of termination have the statutory right not to be unfairly dismissed.

8.13 Please note that an employer may *contractually* be entitled to terminate the contract of employment by complying with the contractual notice set out in the employment contract. However, this contractual entitlement is entirely irrelevant to the statutory concept of fairness in English law. There is a two stage test to determine whether a dismissal has been fair.

8.14 Stage one: the employer must be able to evidence that the principal reason for the dismissal is one of the potentially fair reasons set out in statute. Redundancy, as defined by the relevant legislation, is a potentially fair reason for dismissal.

8.15 Stage two: the employer must then be able to evidence that it acted reasonably in all the circumstances in dismissing the employee for that reason and that a fair procedure/process was followed. A fair procedure/process will involve the employer having engaged in meaningful consultation with the individual, a fair and objective selection process and offering the affected individual suitable alternative employment where this is available.

SPECIAL PROTECTION AGAINST DISMISSAL

8.16 English law does not provide for special dismissal protection akin to the protection afforded to certain categories of employees (for example disabled employees, employees on parental leave, pregnant employees) in some continental European jurisdictions. However, dismissal for certain specified reasons is automatically unfair, regardless of length of service and procedure/process followed; Examples include (but are not limited to):

- joining or not joining a trade union or trade union activities/acting as an employee representative under statutory provisions;
- taking family related leave or requesting flexible working;
- assertion of legal rights (for example, under working time, minimum wage or health and safety legislation);
- a reason related to a protected characteristic (age, disability, gender reassignment, marital/civil partnership status, race, religion or belief, sex or sexual orientation);
- making a protected disclosure (whistleblowing):
- being a part-time or fixed-term employee;

Please note: Compulsory retirement on the grounds of age is unlawful unfair dismissal and age discriminatory unless it can be objectively justified (which is the exception rather than the norm).

WORKFORCE REDUCTION

8.17 An employer who wishes to dismiss employees as part of a workforce restructuring plan will need to carefully document the business rationale for the proposed dismissals at the outset so as to ensure that the dismissals are carried out on the grounds of the legal and potentially fair reasons permitted by statute. It is very important at this early stage to identify the business rationale and ascertain the legal reason on which the employer wishes to rely for the proposed dismissals as this will dictate the procedure the company will be required to follow. Depending on the factual scenario of a company's restructuring plan any dismissals proposed as part of the restructuring may be justified on the grounds of redundancy or some other substantial reason ('SOSR') of a kind so as to justify the dismissal.

8.18 Additionally, companies who plan to carry out redundancies affecting 20 or more employees within a 90-day period will be required to *also* follow the collective redundancy consultation procedure as set out in para **8.53** below.

Definition of Redundancy

8.19 The statutory definition of redundancy in section 139 of the Employment Rights Act provides that:

> 'an employee who is dismissed shall be taken to be dismissed by reason of redundancy if the dismissal is wholly or mainly attributable to
> (a) the fact that his employer has ceased or intends to cease-
> (i) to carry on the business for the purposes of which the employee was employed by him, or
> (ii) to carry on that business in the place where the employee was so employed, or
> (b) the fact that the requirements of that business-
> (i) for employees to carry out work of a particular kind, or
> (ii) for employees to carry out work of a particular kind in the place where the employee was employed by the employer,
> have ceased or diminished or are expected to cease or diminish.'

To fall within the above statutory definition of redundancy, an employee's dismissal must, broadly speaking, be wholly or mainly attributable to:

(a) a closure or part closure of the business; or
(b) a relocation of the business to another place or an otherwise reduced requirement for employees to carry out the work they were employed for.

A reduced requirement for employees to carry out work of a particular kind will include a situation where the employee's role disappears completely because of a lack of work. It may also cover situations where:

- the employee's role can be absorbed by other employees;
- technology means that some employees are replaced by machines; or
- the introduction of a more efficient IT-system has the consequence of fewer employees being required going forward;

Please note: where work is being outsourced or offshored it will be necessary to assess if this exercise is covered by the Transfer of Undertakings

(Protection of Employment) Regulations 2006 ('TUPE') which protect an individual's employment in the event that the undertaking for which he works is transferred by the employer to a new owner. Please see para **8.88** below for further details.

Examples of redundancy situations

Company A provides sheet metal to the aerospace and automobile industries. It employs a total of around 1,000 employees in the UK of which 400 are employed in the production team, manning two types of machinery which cut and treat the sheet metal before it is delivered to the customer. Company A has invested in a number of new and more advanced machines which cut and treat the sheet metal at the same time, thereby reducing the need for manpower as there will only be one type of machine going forward. With the arrival of the new machinery there will no longer be enough work for all of the 400 employees. Company A has identified that, with the introduction of the new machines, around 100 employees will no longer be needed in the production team. The requirement of the business for the number of employees to man the machinery has been reduced and work in the production team has diminished as a result.

Company B is a retail chain selling electronic equipment in a number of locations around the world. It has 50 stores across the UK but since sales have been slow in the past year it has decided to close five stores in areas where sales have diminished substantially. As a result Company B is proposing to make all employees in the five stores redundant on the basis that their workplace is closing down.

Definition of SOSR

8.20 If the reason for a workforce reduction does not amount to 'redundancy' under the definition as outlined above then the dismissals may still be fair if the company can show that the reason is 'for some other substantial reason' of a kind so as to justify the dismissal.

8.21 No statutory definition of SOSR exists, nor is there any statutory guidance. This can make it difficult for companies to rely on SOSR in practice as the reason for carrying out dismissals. Accordingly, the risk of employees challenging the fairness of the decision is likely to be greater when relying on SOSR as opposed to relying on 'redundancy' as the reason for dismissing the employees. Relevant case law makes it clear that to rely on SOSR the reason used to justify the dismissals must be substantial. The interpretation of what is substantial is subjective and will depend on the facts in each case.

8.22 SOSR will typically be used as the reason for dismissals where there is a reorganisation but where work is not diminishing and/or the overall headcount within the company is not being reduced. An example of this could be where there is no workplace or business closure and work is not diminishing but the employer still wishes to dismiss employees as part of a cost-saving exercise or as part of a reorganisation exercise where there is a reassignment of functional or organisational responsibilities of staff.

In practice it is more difficult to rely on SOSR to justify a dismissal and the circumstances should be carefully analysed with reference to the most recent case law.

Example of dismissals on grounds of SOSR

The management of pharmaceutical company Pharmandaleg Plc ('Pharma') has decided to restructure its operations by way of a business reorganisation. Although work is not diminishing, a number of roles will be reorganised into new positions as part of a global restructuring exercise across the group. Additional skillsets will be required in some of the new reorganised roles and those employees who do not possess those additional skills are proposed to be dismissed. This is not a standard redundancy situation as the same number of roles will exist after the business reorganisation and some new employees will be hired to replace those who do not have the required skillset for the new roles. The dismissals will be on grounds of Some Other Substantial Reason.

DISMISSALS ON GROUNDS OF REDUNDANCY

8.23 When companies are planning to dismiss employees on grounds of redundancy they must have regard to two redundancy procedures: *the individual redundancy procedure* and *the collective redundancy procedure*. The individual redundancy procedure must always be followed when dismissing employees on grounds of redundancy.

When planning to dismiss 20 or more employees companies are required to *also* follow the collective redundancy procedure in addition to the individual redundancy procedure.

Redundancy Procedures

8.24 Where a genuine redundancy situation exists this is not, in itself, sufficient to avoid unfair dismissal claims by employees. The employer must also follow a 'fair redundancy procedure'. What constitutes such a fair procedure is a frequently asked question: there is no mandatory procedure set out in statute in England and Wales for dismissing employees on grounds of redundancy. Nevertheless, statute provides that if a *fair* procedure is not followed then the dismissals will be regarded as unfair. Employers therefore need to be guided by case law to ascertain what amounts to a fair dismissal procedure and also by the (non-statutory) best practice redundancy guidance published by the Advisory, Conciliation and Arbitration Service ('ACAS') – see www.acas.org.uk for further details. Typically larger employers in England and Wales will also provide for a (non-contractual) redundancy policy and redundancy procedure in their staff handbook. The overarching guiding principle is that, as part of a fair procedure, the employees who are proposed to be made redundant are fairly selected and that there is a meaningful individual consultation period with each of the affected employees.

Individual redundancy procedure

Case law has established the following principles:

Defining the selection pool

8.25 As the first stage of a fair selection process, the employer will need to identify the group or pool of employees from which those who are to be made redundant will be selected.

8.26 Case law has established that an employer will need to be able to evidence that it has applied its mind to the question of the appropriate selection pool and that the decision is based on rational and objective considerations.

8.27 Identification of the selection pool may be obvious where there is an entire business or workplace closure contemplated but it is less straightforward where the proposition is for fewer employees to carry out work of a particular kind. In such a case, all employees who actually perform that kind of work should be pooled together. Occasionally where an employee carries out a unique role that is disappearing, they may be in a selection pool of one. However, an affected employee will often seek to argue an employer should have used a wider selection pool and an employer needs to be able to justify its decision. In particular, consideration needs to be given as to whether there are any other employees doing work which is sufficiently similar so as to make the roles comparable and effectively interchangeable, in which case a wider pool might be appropriate. In order to determine this, contracts, job descriptions and what employees actually do on a day-to-day basis should be compared rather than merely comparing job titles.

8.28 If the employer has more than one site within a reasonably close geographical area it may be necessary to include employees from both locations in the pool if the work done is similar at both locations. This is even so when the employer is proposing to close down one location completely.

Selection criteria

8.29 Once the selection pool has been determined, the employer must apply appropriate selection criteria. Selection criteria must be objective and should not merely reflect personal opinion. As far as possible, the selection criteria should be capable of being objectively verifiable, for example against personnel records.

8.30 The employer should ensure that the selection criteria used cannot be said to be tainted by any discrimination. As well as generally being deemed unfair, discriminatory criteria could give rise to successful discrimination claims. 'Last in and first out' used to be a common (and acceptable) formula for selecting those to be made redundant. However, there is a risk now that it may amount to age discrimination. Nevertheless, length of service may be used as part of a scoring matrix as one of the criteria which an employee is scored against.

8.31 In particular, care should be taken to ensure that apparently objective criteria do not place groups of individuals with protected characteristics at a disadvantage (indirect discrimination). For example, absences due to maternity leave or disability related illness should normally be discounted if the attendance record is a criterion for selection, in order to avoid claims for sex discrimination or disability discrimination. Additionally, employers should avoid using 'costs savings' (ie dismissing those employees with higher salaries) as a selection criteria as this has been held by the employment tribunals to be unfair. Where a trade union is recognised by the employer the employer should consult it on the proposed scoring criteria but it may also be prudent to consult on selection criteria is other cases.

8.32 There may be situations where an employee falls into a category protected by discrimination legislation, for example, by being a particular gender, belonging to a particular religion or racial group, being of a particular age or being a part-time or fixed-term employee. In such cases, the employer should ensure it is in a position to have in place contemporaneous documentary evidence that the true reason for the decision to dismiss is legitimate and not linked to the relevant protected characteristic.

8.33 The selection criteria should be fairly and consistently applied to all staff in the selection pool. The recommended method of selection is for an employer to use a score sheet or matrix to compare the skills, ability and individual performance of employees who are in the pool. Care should be taken when applying more subjective criteria because of the difficulty of assessing them fairly and objectively. To reduce the risk of a purely subjective assessment, it is preferable to have two managers carry out the assessment separately to ensure that the criteria were applied fairly. Ideally, there should be some supporting documentation for the evaluation given, such as performance appraisals from previous years.

Example

A scoring matrix could look like this:

Criteria	Score	Weighting factor	Total	Notes by manager to justify scoring
Skills/qualification/training		3		*Set out details of employee's skills, qualification and training necessary to be successful in the job long-term*
Experience		3		*Details of employee's experience*
Attendance		1		*This assessment should be verifiable on account of information held on the personnel file*
Length of service		1		
Time keeping		1		*Assessment ideally to be backed up with time keeping records*
Disciplinary record		1		*This assessment should be verifiable on account of information held on the personnel file*
Performance Assessment (Year) • Achievement of objectives • Customer Feedback Performance Assessment (Year) • Achievement of objectives • Customer Feedback		3		*This assessment should be verifiable on account of previous performance reviews*
Total score				

Scoring

1 = Poor	2 = Below average	3 = Average	4 = Good	5 = Excellent

The employer should consult the employees on their scores and must be able to explain how the scores were arrived at so that the employee is given the opportunity to challenge the scores. When scoring the score should be based on objective and verifiable factors if possible. Scoring should be measurable, rather than being based on someone's personal opinion and a note of the factors that have been taken into account should be made by the manager in the 'notes and queries' column.

Bumping

8.34 Bumping describes a situation where one employee's work is diminishing or disappearing ('Employee A') but instead of dismissing Employee A as redundant the company moves Employee A to another job to carry out another employee's work ('Employee B') and Employee B is made redundant as a result. Bumping is legal and can still amount to a fair dismissal.

> **Example**
>
> Interior Design Limited specialises in interior design projects and has two teams, one specialising in residential interior designs and the other specialising in commercial interior designs. The expertise and qualifications of the two teams are different. Interior Design Limited employs one employee in the residential team, namely a Senior Residential Interior Designer. The commercial team consists of one Senior Commercial Interior Designer, one Interior Designer and five Assistant Interior Designers.
>
> The commercial team is busy, however, work is diminishing in the residential interior design team and Interior Design Limited has recently decided to close down the residential team and only focus on commercial interior design projects.
>
> Interior Design Limited runs a redundancy exercise with the Senior Residential Interior Designer. As they would like to utilise the Senior Residential Interior Designer's skills and expertise they decide to offer him a position as Interior Designer in the commercial interior design team, even though this position is slightly more junior compared to his current role. As a result the current Interior Designer in the commercial team is made redundant.

Although there is no general requirement for employers to consider bumping when carrying out a redundancy exercise, case law suggests that a dismissal may be considered unfair if the employer has not considered bumping.

Individual consultation

8.35 Failure to consult individually with each affected employee and to take their views into account will generally render a dismissal unfair. Employers are under a duty to 'warn' and 'consult' employees about the proposed redundancies.

As a minimum the following steps should be taken:

(a) The employer should inform each affected employee of the fact that he is at risk of redundancy and the reasons for this. The employer should also outline the business rationale for proposing redundancies so that the employee understands the commercial business rationale and why it is proposed. The letter should also invite the employee to attend an information meeting to discuss the proposed redundancy.

(b) At the meeting, the employer must explain why the decision has been made to propose redundancies. The employer should explain the proposed selection pool and selection criteria it plans to use for identifying the employees that should be provisionally selected for redundancy. The employee should be invited to comment on the proposed pool and selection criteria. The employee should be given a copy of the selection criteria matrix and guidance notes on how the scoring will be carried out. A follow-up letter should then be sent to the employee outlining what was discussed at the meeting.

(c) The employer will now have the task of scoring each employee against the selection criteria and based on this send a letter to each of those employees who have been provisionally selected for redundancy inviting them to a first redundancy consultation meeting.

(d) At the meeting, the employer should explain why the particular employee has been provisionally selected for redundancy. This will generally involve providing details of the results of the assessment under the selection criteria. The employer should also explain what steps have been taken to avoid the redundancy, including details of any suitable alternative employment that may be available. The employee's views should be sought on the redundancy situation, his selection and any suitable alternative employment. It is important that no final decision has been made by the employer at this stage as the consultation must be carried out by the employer with an open mind. Otherwise the selection process may be considered to have been unfair.

(e) Once the employer has had an opportunity to fully consider any representations that the employee may have made including any proposals as to alternative employment, they should send a written invitation to the employee to a second redundancy consultation meeting to discuss the proposed dismissal. The invitation should summarise what was discussed at the first redundancy consultation meeting.

(f) At the second face to face redundancy consultation meeting with each employee the proposed dismissal is further discussed before a final decision to dismiss is taken. Any representations which have been made by the employee including any proposals as to alternative employment should be addressed having been fully considered.

(g) The employee should be informed of the decision to terminate the employment.

(h) The employee has the right to appeal against the decision. Should the employee decide to appeal the employer will have an opportunity to address any remaining issues at an appeal meeting.

In order for the consultation to be considered fair and meaningful the employer must ensure that the consultation takes place when the proposal of redundancy is still at a formative stage. The employee must be given sufficient information and time to allow him to properly respond to the proposal and the employer must carefully consider any response or suggestion which the employee puts forward. Failure to do this is likely to render the dismissal unfair even if there was a genuine redundancy situation.

Involvement of employee representatives in individual dismissals

8.36 The requirement information and consultation with employee representatives in limited circumstances has been introduced into English law as a result of European legislation. If employees are represented, it is usually by a trade union. Whether or not employee representatives have rights to information and consultation in the context of individual redundancies will depend on the specific agreements that are in place with the representative body. However, it is common (and best HR practice) for staff handbooks and policies to provide individuals with the right to be accompanied by a colleague or a trade union representative during any redundancy consultation procedure.

Avoiding compulsory redundancies

8.37 Employers should consider alternatives to compulsory redundancies. Careful consideration should be given to the possibility of employees working part-time and other strategies such as a recruitment freeze, sabbaticals, salary sacrifice, pension changes, early retirement and withdrawal of bonus schemes amongst others with a view to avoid or minimise the number of employees affected by compulsory redundancy.

Inviting volunteers for redundancy

8.38 Employers frequently also consider inviting volunteers for redundancy before starting the consultation process although there is no obligation to do this. The incentive will typically be an enhanced redundancy payment offered by the employer to the employees volunteering. Employers should make it clear to employees that they are applying for voluntary redundancy but that there is no guarantee that they will be selected for voluntary redundancy. This is to ensure that any key employees that are required for the continued success of the company are retained by the employer.

8.39 Employers should note that although an employee has volunteered for redundancy it may still be regarded as a dismissal by the employer on the grounds of redundancy. To minimise risk any enhanced redundancy payment made to a volunteering employee should ideally be made conditional on the employee signing up to a settlement agreement.

Alternative employment

8.40 As part of a fair and reasonable redundancy process, an employer must search for and, where possible, offer suitable alternative employment to affected employees within its organisation. This includes consideration of employment at other locations and within any associated companies. However, the employer is not obliged to create alternative employment.

8.41 Employees who are on maternity leave or adoption leave have special protection from redundancy in that they have an automatic right to be offered any suitable, alternative employment. They are not protected from being selected as redundant but they do have priority over other employees in respect of any available suitable, alternative employment.

8.42 The employer should continue to search for alternative employment for those employees who are provisionally selected for redundancy throughout the redundancy process up to the date on which the redundancy takes effect and the employment is terminated. All employees who are potentially redundant should be provided full details of any relevant alternative roles and the employer should not assume that because a vacancy for a role involves a lower salary, lower status or a change in working hours or change of workplace, that the employee would not be interested.

8.43 Where there is suitable, alternative employment but there is more than one potentially redundant employee, the employer needs to ensure that a fair and non-discriminatory selection process is undertaken. As set out above, employees who are on maternity or adoption leave have the right to be offered any suitable vacancies ahead of other potentially redundant employees. Employers should seek to fill any roles from the pool of potentially redundant employees before it offers such roles to the rest of the workforce or external candidates.

8.44 Any offer of suitable, alternative employment should be received by the employee before the employee's redundancy takes effect. The offer must be clear and must contain sufficient detail about the differences between the employee's current role and their proposed role and any material differences in terms and conditions of employment. If the employee is being given a choice of roles then they must be provided with sufficient details so as to be able to distinguish between them and make a choice.

8.45 In order to avoid any liability for redundancy, any alternative employment must commence no later than four weeks after the termination of the employee's existing role and the terms must be as per the offer that was made by the employer.

Probation periods

8.46 If the terms of the alternative employment differ wholly or in part from the employee's previous terms and conditions (including the nature of the role, place of work and any other terms) then the alternative employment will be subject to an automatic statutory four-week probation period. This probation period may be extended if retraining is required.

8.47 If an employee accepts an offer of alternative employment, subject to successful completion of a probation period if appropriate, they are treated as not having been dismissed.

8.48 If an employee unreasonably rejects an offer of alternative employment which was suitable or gives notice of resignation during the probation period they will lose their entitlement to a redundancy payment. Suitability of the employment for the employee is assessed objectively taking into account the nature of the job offered and the employee. Whether or not an employee has acted reasonably in rejecting a suitable job is assessed subjectively taking into account the employee's reasons and their circumstances. It is for the employer to prove at an unfair dismissal hearing, that the alternative employment offered to the employee was suitable and that the employee acted unreasonably in refusing it.

8.49 If the employer terminates the alternative employment during the probation period, subject to any further offer of alternative employment, the employee will be deemed to have been redundant as of the date on which their original employment contract terminated.

8.50 The employee may decide at the end of a probation period that the alternative employment is in fact not suitable. In such a situation the employee will also be deemed to have been dismissed as redundant as of the date on which their original contract terminated and will be entitled to a statutory redundancy pay.

8.51 Employers should be aware of the existence of both a statutory probation period and a common law probation period. The operations of these two types of probation periods differ slightly and, due to conflicting case law, there is currently some uncertainty as to the relationship between them and how they co-exist.

Other considerations

8.52 An employer must also act in accordance with any contractual provisions or any policies relating to redundancy and redeployment. HR Managers should be careful to review the employment contracts and policies as these may add an additional layer of protection for the employees in restructuring situations.

Collective redundancy procedure

8.53 Under English law a collective redundancy situation arises where an employer proposes to dismiss as redundant at least 20 employees at *one establishment* over a period of 90 days or less. For the purposes of an establishment, geographic location is not conclusive. There are situations where organisational factors, such as the inter-dependence and cohesion of employees, will mean that a grouping of employees at different sites will be deemed to be part of one establishment.

8.54 However, companies should be aware that the law on collective redundancy derives from an EU Directive and that there is currently uncertainty as to whether the terminology 'one establishment' should have effect in English law as there is no reference to this in the EU Directive. In practice, this means that the reference to *one establishment* should be disregarded for the time being even, though this makes the scope of the collective redundancy procedure much wider.

Example

The company Joyful Jewellery Limited has 54 stores across England. Five of the stores (the Leeds, Nottingham, Birmingham, Cambridge and Bristol stores) are no longer as busy as they used to be. As a result the Management has decided that there is not enough work for all of the 65 employees currently employed across the five stores and is proposing to reduce headcounts. The Management has identified that five employees in each of the Leeds, Nottingham, Birmingham and Cambridge stores and three employees in the Bristol store are redundant. Accordingly, the Management will propose that a total of 23 employees are made redundant across the five stores.

If each store is identified as *one establishment* Joyful Jewellery Limited will **not** be required to follow the collective redundancy procedure as each store is proposing to make less than 20 employees redundant. However, since recent case law suggests that the wording *one establishment* should be disregarded the redundancies proposed across all five stores must be considered together when deciding whether the collective redundancy procedure applies. In this scenario, Joyful Jewellery Limited would be required to follow the collective redundancy procedure since it is proposing to dismiss 23 employees in total.

8.55 Companies should also be aware that the definition of 'redundancy' for the purposes of the collective redundancy procedure is much wider than the definition used for unfair dismissal purposes as outlined at para **8.19** above. This means that often when a workforce restructuring exercise falls into the category of SOSR as the legal reason for the dismissals, the dismissals will still be regarded as 'redundancies' for the purposes of the collective redundancy procedure and will trigger the respective information and consultation requirements.

8.56 In calculating whether 20 or more employees are to be dismissed, any volunteers for redundancy must be included. However, those employees on fixed-term contracts whose dismissals occur on the termination date or termination event stipulated in their employment contracts should be disregarded for the purposes of assessing whether the total number of employees proposed for redundancy amounts to 20 or more.

8.57 In a collective redundancy situation, the employer has a duty to consult employee representatives in good time with a view to reaching an agreement. This collective consultation is in addition to, and must run concurrently with, individual consultation (as set out above).

8.58 Where there is a collective redundancy, the employer must also notify the Department of Business, Innovation & Skills (BIS).

Involvement of employee representatives in collective dismissals

8.59 In any restructuring exercise it is essential to establish whether there are any recognised trade unions and, if so, the scope of such recognition.

8.60 Where an employer does not recognise a trade union (or does not recognise the union in respect of all employees), an employer may inform and consult with an existing body of employee representatives which has been elected or appointed by the affected employees and has been authorised to act in this regard. Where there are no appropriate employee representatives, they must be elected. There are statutory rules for the election of employee representatives for the purpose of collective consultation and the onus is very much on the employer to ensure that the relevant requirements for the election are complied with. However, such employee representatives do not replace a recognised trade union's rights to information and consultation in respect of collective redundancies. A recognised trade union must always be informed and consulted.

Election of employee representatives for collective consultation purposes

8.61 Where there is no trade union and no pre-existing employee representatives it is the employer's duty to take steps to ensure that employee representatives are elected for the purposes of the information and consultation obligations under the collective redundancy procedure. The employer must ensure that arrangements are made for the nomination of candidates and for a fair election.

8.62 The voting itself must take place in secret and the election process as a whole should be structured so as ensure that it is completed before the planned start of the information and consultation process. The elected employee representatives and others who participated in the election process enjoy legal protection. Dismissing employee representatives on grounds related to the fact that the employees were representatives or put themselves forward as candidates will amount to automatically unfair dismissals.

Information and consultation requirements

Information stage

8.63 The employer must provide the following written information to the trade union/employee representatives:

(a) the reason(s) for the proposed redundancies;
(b) the number and description of employees proposed to be dismissed;
(c) the proposed method of selecting employees;
(d) the proposed method of carrying out the dismissals, including the period over which the dismissals will take effect (this may have been agreed with the relevant trade union or other employee representatives);
(e) the proposed method of calculating any redundancy payments, (over and above statutory entitlements), that will be made to dismissed employees; and
(f) Information about the company's use of agency workers.

Consultation stage

8.64 Consultation must be undertaken with a view to reaching agreement with the appropriate representatives and must include ways of avoiding the proposed dismissals; reducing the numbers proposed to be dismissed and mitigating the consequences of dismissal (such as offering severance payments or outplacement/careers guidance).

8.65 Consultation should take place when proposals are still at a formative stage, adequate information should be provided and employee representatives should be given sufficient time to properly consider that information. The employer should also fully consider and respond to any representations that may be made. Case law stipulates that an employer should enter into the consultations with an open mind and with a willingness to be persuaded.

8.66 A common mistake would be for an employer to carry out the selection process whilst purporting to consult with the trade union/employee representatives. Unless the union/representatives have, at that point, agreed to the selection criteria that are used then genuine consultation cannot be said to have taken place.

8.67 Where the employer is proposing to dismiss 100 or more employees, consultation should begin at least 45 days before the first of the dismissals takes effect. Where the employer is proposing to dismiss between 20 to 99 employees, consultation must commence at least 30 days before the first of the dismissals takes effect. Whilst an employer may give notice of termination to employees before the expiry of the 30 or 45-day period (subject to regulatory requirements having been met as set out below), in practice, an employer should obtain confirmation from the trade union or other appropriate representatives with whom it is consulting that consultation has been completed before serving any notices of termination of employment.

Regulatory requirements

8.68 Where an employer proposes to make 20 or more employees redundant at one establishment within a period of 90 days, notification of this intention must be made to the Department of Business, Innovation & Skills (BIS) using form HR1 which can be downloaded from the BIS webpage. Failure to notify BIS is a criminal offence punishable with a fine (currently a maximum of £5,000). Where 100 or more employees are to be made redundant within a period of 90 days, the notification must be made at least 45 days before the first dismissal takes effect, otherwise the notification must be made at least 30 days before the first dismissal takes effect. Affected employees must not be given notice of termination of employment until BIS has been notified.

Sanctions

8.69 If the employer fails to inform and consult on collective redundancies the 'appropriate representatives' (or an individual employee if there is neither a trade union nor employee representatives) can complain to an Employment Tribunal. If the complaint is upheld, the dismissals will still be valid but a 'protective award' of 90 days' gross pay for each affected employee may be made. Failure to consult with appropriate representatives may also render a dismissal unfair and therefore, in addition to protective awards, an individual employee may bring a complaint of unfair dismissal.

NOTICE

8.70 Employment contracts typically provide for the contractual notice period agreed between the parties. The notice period describes the period of time between notifying the employee of his employment coming to an end and the actual last day of employment (usually referred to as the 'effective date of termination or 'EDT'). Employment contracts often provide typically for notice periods of between four weeks and six months' notice to be observed by either party, depending on the seniority of the employee. The correct notice period should be observed (bearing in mind the minimum notice periods set out by statute) and either worked out by the employee, spent on garden leave or paid in lieu. For details of garden leave and payment in lieu of notice please see paras 8.75 and 8.78 below.

Minimum notice period

8.71 The minimum notice periods under statute are set out below. These will override contractual notice periods where these are shorter than the statutory notice periods:

Length of Service	Notice by Employer
Less than 1 month	no minimum period
1 month to 2 years	1 week
2 years and more	1 week for each year of service up to a maximum of 12 weeks

Note that unless the contract of employment provides for longer notice periods for the employee to comply with, the above prolonged statutory notice periods only apply to the employer.

8.72 If the contract is silent on the issue of notice periods then a reasonable notice period applies. How long that will be depends on what is common for this type of position both within the employer's organisation and within the specific industry sector.

8.73 As a starting point employees have a right to work during their notice period and an employer who refuses to provide the employee with work will be in breach of the employment contract unless the contract expressly allows the employer to withhold work from the employee.

8.74 When dismissing an employee it may sometimes be preferable to the business to have the employee leave the workplace sooner rather than later to avoid or minimise further disruption to the workforce following a restructuring exercise. In such a situation the employer may have two options (provided the employment contract is drafted to allow for this). The first option is to place the employee on 'garden leave' and the second option is to make a 'payment in lieu of notice'.

Garden Leave

8.75 Although an employer may be keen to ensure that the employee stays out of the workplace during the notice period to minimise disruption to the remaining workforce it may wish to ensure that the employee does not immediately start working for a competitor as this could cause damage to the employer's business.

8.76 The purpose of a garden leave clause is to prevent the employee from working for a competitor or setting up his own business by keeping the employee employed during the notice period, although no work is given to him to perform. The intention is that the information the employee has about the employer will be outdated by the time the notice period expires and the employee starts his new employment. The other purpose of a garden leave clause is to give the employee's successor (if any) or colleagues some time to contact customers and establish themselves before the employee sets himself up with a competitor.

8.77 In short, an employee remains employed by the employer during the notice period but is not given any work and is not allowed to attend the workplace or contact customers. A garden leave clause is often used together with post-termination restrictive covenant clauses to ensure maximum protection for the employer's business (see para **8.83** below on post-termination restrictive covenants).

Pay in lieu of notice

8.78 Employment can be terminated effectively with a payment in lieu of notice where there is an express provision in the contract of employment or where it is the employer's custom to always make such a payment. However, in the absence of a payment in lieu of notice provision in the contract of employment or a clear practice of doing so it would be in breach of contract and may not only lead to breach of contract claims but also to the employer losing the ability to enforce post termination obligations, such as restrictive covenants.

Examples of pay in lieu of notice ('PILON') and garden leave

Biscuit Wrapping Ltd ('BW') is restructuring its business and has decided to dismiss as redundant, amongst others, a Junior Wrapper Assistant (the 'Junior Wrapper') and a Master Wrapper Executive ('MW'). The Junior Wrapper is entitled to one month's notice under his employment contract and the MW is entitled to three months' notice.

BW makes a payment in lieu of notice to the Junior Wrapper and his employment terminates with effect from the date the payment in lieu is made. BW has decided to pay the Junior Wrapper his notice pay up front releasing him from his contract and allowing him to look for and start new work elsewhere immediately as this employee holds no key knowledge or information of the business of BW.

However, the MW has extensive knowledge of the business of BW, how it operates and of its future business plan. BW is concerned that if the MW applies this information to a role with a competitor it could damage BW's business. To minimise the risk of any such damage BW has decided to place the MW on garden leave so that he remains employed by BW for the duration of his notice period and thus is still under an implied duty of good faith and fidelity during this period and unable to work elsewhere.

Notice period comparison table

Type of Notice Period	*Effective Date of Termination*	*Benefits*	*Disadvantages*
Employee working the notice period	The expiry of the notice period.	Employee works for his salary which in theory gives the company value for the salary paid during the notice period.	Employee may be disruptive to colleagues or may gather and copy confidential data from the work place. The notice period may be that extra period which takes the employee beyond 2 years' of service entitling him to statutory redundancy pay or enabling him to bring a claim for unfair dismissal.
Garden Leave	The expiry of the notice period.	Employer has a degree of control over the situation as employee is prevented from attending the workplace but at the same time cannot work elsewhere either. Coupled with post-termination restrictive covenants the employer has maximum protection possible.	The employer gets no value in terms of work from the employee during the notice period. The employee remains employed during the notice period which means that he also remains entitled to any contractual company benefits such as permanent health care, pension contributions, bonuses, accrual of holidays etc. as entitled to under his contract.

Type of Notice Period	*Effective Date of Termination*	*Benefits*	*Disadvantages*
Pay in lieu of notice	When the notice period would otherwise have started (on the payment in lieu of notice).	The employee will not be an employee during what would have been the notice period. Accordingly, he will not attend the office, will not be entitled to any contractual benefits that would otherwise arise during the notice period. The termination date is moved forward which may prevent the employee from obtaining an additional complete year of service for redundancy pay and unfair dismissal claim purposes.	Employer has no control over the employee who could start work immediately elsewhere.

REDUNDANCY PAYMENT

8.79 Employees with two years' continuous service who are dismissed by reason of redundancy are entitled to a statutory redundancy payment. This is in addition to any notice pay or other contractual entitlement the employee may have under his employment contract. Employees do not have an entitlement to a statutory redundancy payment if they obtain suitable alternative employment with the same or an associated employer within four weeks of their redundancy or if they unreasonably refuse to accept or apply for such suitable alternative employment.

STATUTORY REDUNDANCY PAY CALCULATION

8.80 The amount of the statutory redundancy payment due to an employee is calculated with reference to each employee's age at the time of termination, weekly pay (capped at a statutory weekly maximum – currently (April 2015) £475) and length of service (up to a maximum of 20 years) using the following statutory formula:

Under the age of 22	0.5 week's pay for every complete year of employment
Aged 22 – 40	1 week's pay for every complete year of employment
Aged 41 or above	1.5 weeks' pay for every complete year of employment

Statutory Redundancy Calculation Example

Mr Smith and Mr Jones have both been made redundant from Global Painting Plc (the 'Company'). Mr Smith has been employed by the Company for 2.5 years and is 21 years old. Mr Jones is 52 years old and has been employed by the Company for 18 complete years.

Mr Smith is entitled to a statutory redundancy pay in the sum of £475 (£475 × 0.5 weeks × 2 years) because he falls into the 'under 22' category.

The calculation of Mr Jones' statutory redundancy pay will be done in two rounds as his employment from the age of 34 to the age of 40 (7 years) will entitle him to £475 × 1 week × 7 = £3,325 whilst the period from the age of 41 to 52 (11 years) will entitle him to £475 × 1.5 × 11 years = £7,837.50. This means that Mr Jones is entitled to a total statutory redundancy payment in the sum of £11,162.50

These calculations are on the basis that both employees' usual weekly salary at Global Painting Plc was no less than the statutory minimum.

Enhanced Redundancy Payments

8.81 'Enhanced redundancy payments' may be payable under contract, collective agreement or an employer's policy. Employers need to ensure that any enhancements that they may grant could not be considered discriminatory under the age discrimination legislation.

Taxation of Redundancy Payments

8.82 Statutory redundancy payments are tax free. Enhanced redundancy payments are normally tax free up to £30,000 (including the statutory redundancy payment) if they are genuinely payments for loss of employment.

Practical Tip

Employers may consider offering settlement agreements to the relevant employees at an early stage with an enhanced termination payment, especially if the time schedule is tight; with a view to cut short the redundancy consultation exercise. See the section on mutually agreed terminations and Without Prejudice discussions at para **8.150**.

However, employers should note that claims for failure to inform and consult on collective redundancies cannot be settled by way of the usual settlement agreement format but can only be settled by use of an ACAS settlement agreement (a COT3 agreement). ACAS is the Advisory, Conciliation and Arbitration Service and is an independent statutory body.

Post-termination restrictive covenants

8.83 Employers should ensure to include express post-termination restrictive covenants in the employment contracts for key employees who could materially damage the employer's business by competing with the employer following termination of employment.

8.84 As a starting point, all post-termination restrictive covenants are void under English law for being in restraint of trade and contrary to public policy. However, the courts will allow post-termination restrictive covenants where the employer can show that it has a legitimate business interest which it needs to protect and that the restrictions are no wider than what is strictly necessary to protect that interest. A legitimate business interest may be goodwill, trade connections or trade secrets for instance. There is no statutory default position so if the employer forgets to include restrictions in the contract there simply will be no protection for the employer's business although there will be a narrow implied (if not express) confidentiality obligation on the employee not to disclose confidential information.

8.85 Post-termination restrictions are most commonly used together with a garden leave clause which, when combined, will give the employer the maximum protection possible under English law.

8.86 As the restrictive covenants must be no wider in scope that what is strictly necessary for the employer to protect his legitimate business interest, post-termination restrictive covenants needs to be tailored carefully to each business and employee as they may otherwise be held to be too wide. The courts will not rewrite a restriction which is too wide in scope and so the employer will simply have no protection at all if the restriction, in its original form, is held to be void. As a result, restrictions are carefully drafted and, to err on the side of caution, are better drafted slightly narrower in scope to minimise the risk of them being unenforceable by the employer.

8.87 If an employee is in breach of the post-termination restrictive covenants the employer may apply for an injunction to prevent the employee from any further breaches of the restrictions (this may for instance be to prevent the employee from competing or soliciting customers). The employer may also claim for damages reflecting the direct financial loss caused to the business by the employee's breach of contract.

Practical Tips

Employers cannot rely on any post-termination restrictive covenants if the employer itself is in breach of contract. Making a payment in lieu of notice to an employee on the termination of employment where the contract contains no right for the employer to do so will constitute such a breach of contract by the employer.

> Accordingly, employers should always include a Pay in Lieu of Notice clause in the employment contract whenever post-termination restrictions are included so as to ensure that they are not in breach of contract by making such a payment in situations where it wishes to terminate the contract with immediate effect.

BUSINESS SALE, OUTSOURCING/INSOURCING AND OFFSHORING

8.88 The Acquired Rights Directive ('ARD') is the name given to the European Council Directive 77/187 of 14 February 1977 (as amended) which aims to regulate the transfer of an undertaking by ensuring that terms and conditions of employment are maintained for the employees affected. In England and Wales the ARD was implemented into the national law by way of the Transfer of Undertakings (Protection of Employment) Regulations 2006 ('TUPE'). In essence TUPE protects an individual's employment in the event that the undertaking for which he works is transferred by the employer to a new owner.

8.89 In practical terms this means that TUPE may apply where a business – as a going concern – is sold and/or where there is a 'service provision change', typically an outsourcing or insourcing of a subsidiary activity of the company's main business. TUPE does not apply to a situation where ownership of the employing entity changes by way of a share sale.

Key consequences of TUPE applying are:

- employment of affected employees automatically transfers to new owner;
- the automatic transfer of employment rights, obligations and liabilities relating to transferring staff to the new owner; and
- the obligation to inform and consult with affected employees individually and with (elected) employee representatives collectively.
- protection of employees from dismissal for reason of a TUPE transfer.

Business sale

8.90 To assess if a business sale constitutes a TUPE transfer of affected employees, the relevant definition in the regulations asks if there is a transfer of a stable economic entity that retains its identity post transfer. An economic entity is defined as an organised grouping of resources with the objective of pursuing an economic activity, whether or not that activity is central or just a supporting or ancillary function.

8.91 The key question is whether the economic entity still exists and is carrying out the same or similar activities post transfer. The assessment will depend on a number of factors, including whether the assets are sold as part of the transfer of a 'business' as a 'going concern' and if the assets are to be used by the purchaser with the intention of carrying on the same kind of 'business' as the seller (but not necessarily identical). Other determining factors may include whether or not goodwill has been retained (ie whether any customers have been transferred), the similarity of activities pre and post transfer and the extent of any disruption to those activities.

Outsourcing/insourcing

8.92 *Outsourcing/insourcing* may constitute a 'service provision change' (and therefore an automatic transfer of the employment of affected staff under TUPE) where one business ceases to provide the services and another business takes them over. This frequently includes the outsourcing of a particular business function to an external service provider. Alternatively, a service provision change could also arise on termination of an outsourcing arrangement where activities cease to be carried out by the initial service provider (1st generation service provider) and are carried out, going forward, by either a new incoming service provider (2nd generation service provider) or taken back in-house by the business (insourcing).

8.93 For there to be a service provision change case law has established that the activities must be fundamentally or essentially the same before and after the transfer. In addition, even if the activities remain fundamentally or essentially the same, an assessment must take place so to determine whether any employees are assigned to an *organised* grouping of employees whose principal purpose is to carry out the relevant activities for or on behalf of the customer.

8.94 Note that even if there is an organised grouping of employees the service provision change rules do not apply where the activity being carried out is wholly or mainly the supply of goods (rather than services) for the customer's use.

8.95 In some cases a fragmentation may take place in that services may be divided and outsourced to more than one service provider. In limited cases, if the services become so fragmented that it is not possible to identify the services which are being transferred, then TUPE may not apply.

Effect of TUPE

Automatic transfer and protection of employment

8.96 When TUPE applies the employment of those employees employed in the transferring business will automatically transfer with the business on existing terms and conditions, always provided they were wholly or mainly assigned to work for the transferring business or assigned to provide the relevant services. Outstanding liabilities (unpaid wages, untaken holiday etc) will transfer. There is, however, no requirement to provide transferring employees with access to an occupational pension scheme where this was a benefit prior to the transfer. The transferee will, however, need to provide certain minimum pension provisions if there were occupational pension benefits at the previous employer.

Objection to the transfer

8.97 An employee may object to their transfer under TUPE. Exercising the 'right to object' before transfer stops the otherwise automatic transfer. However, if an employee objects, his employment automatically terminates with effect from the transfer date. There are further harsh consequences which make it unlikely for an employee to exercise this right: the employee is not entitled to any compensation and will have no entitlement to notice or a payment in lieu of notice, a redundancy payment or a remedy for unfair dismissal purposes. This may only be different if the employee objected in anticipation of a fundamental breach of the terms of his contract of employment by the new employer.

Protection from dismissal

8.98 Employees enjoy an additional layer of protection from dismissal in the event of a TUPE transfer. If an employee has two years' continuous service, dismissal will be automatically unfair if the reason (or principal reason) for the dismissal was either

- the TUPE transfer itself; or
- a reason connected with the transfer but which was not an economic, technical or organisational reason entailing changes in the workforce (known as an 'ETO reason').

Note: this is the case whether the dismissal occurred before or after the transfer. Please also note that the employee's continuous service length transfers to the new owner under TUPE.

Protection of terms and conditions of employment

8.99 Similarly, terms of employment are also protected and may only be varied following a transfer if the principal reason for the change is unconnected with the transfer or where it is an ETO reason connected with the transfer. Any changes which are connected to the transfer and for which there is no

ETO reason will be void. This will include any attempts to harmonise terms and conditions of affected employees.

Information and Consultation

8.100 Where employees are transferred from one employer to another under TUPE, both the transferor and the transferee have duties to inform and potentially consult with appropriate representatives in relation to any of *their* employees who may be affected by the transfer or by measures taken in relation to them.

8.101 As with collective redundancy consultation, if the employer recognises a trade union, they must consult with that union; if not, employees must be given the opportunity to elect representatives if they do not already exist. There are strict rules as to election of representatives and it is important to factor in the necessary time to elect employee representatives.

Duty to inform

8.102 In practice, it is rare for the transfer to have much effect on existing employees of the new employer so usually the duty to inform rests primarily with the transferor in respect of the employees that will transfer. However, if the transferee proposes to make redundancies after the transfer which would affect the existing workforce, then the obligation to inform would be triggered. In addition, it is not simply the representatives of the transferring employees which the transferor will have to inform. If the transfer will affect the transferor's remaining employees (for example, if they will be relocated to a different site after the transfer) then the transferor must also inform the representatives of these remaining employees.

8.103 Employers are obliged to inform the representatives of their respective affected employees in writing of:-

- the fact that the transfer is to take place, when it is to take place and the reasons for it;
- the legal, economic and social implications of the transfer for the affected employees (for example, change in employer, change in work location, loss of future pension rights);
- the measures which the employer envisages it will take, in connection with the transfer, in relation to those affected employees or, if they envisage that no measures will be so taken, that fact.

Measures Letter

8.104 The transferee (new employer) is also obliged to inform the transferor in writing of any measures which it envisages it will take in relation to any affected transferring employees and sanctions may be applied to the new employer if it fails to comply (see further below). The transferor must then provide the appropriate employee representatives with this information.

8.105 In this context, 'measures' will include any action, step or arrangement in connection with the transfer which has been formulated as part of some definite plan or proposal. Examples include changes to terms and conditions, grading or other structures or proposed redundancies.

Employee Liability Information

8.106 The transferor must also provide information to the employee representatives about its use of agency workers, including the number of agency workers engaged, the type of work carried out by the agency workers and which parts of the business they work in.

8.107 In addition, the transferee is obliged to provide certain key information to the transferor about the employees who are in-scope to transfer no later than 14 days before the transfer date (so-called employee liability information).

Duty to consult

8.108 The transferor and the transferee only have a duty to consult the employee representatives if either anticipates that it will take measures in relation to any of its affected employees which are connected with the transfer.

8.109 As the obligation only arises in relation to measures which an employer envisages taking itself in relation to its own affected employees, there is actually no obligation on the transferee to consult representatives of the transferring employees about measures which it envisages taking in relation to them prior to the transfer. This is an unsatisfactory position and often, in practice, either the transferor or transferee will consult the transferring workforce on such measures in the interests of good employee relations.

8.110 The consultation must be with a view to seeking the agreement of the employee representatives to the measures to be taken. However, there is no requirement to reach agreement. At the very least, the employer should consider the following:-

- explain the measures which it proposes to take so that the representatives understand them fully;
- give the representatives the opportunity to make representations about the measures to be taken;
- consider those representations and respond to them in writing; and
- give reasons for any rejection of the representatives' representations.

The legislation sets out no definite timescale for information and consultation. The duty to inform must be undertaken 'in good time' to allow for any necessary consultation between the parties and the representatives to take place before the date of transfer. The discharge of the formal duty to consult cannot properly begin until the employee representatives have been supplied with the requisite information in writing.

European Works Councils

8.111 Provided there is a European Works Council ('EWC') established within the group of companies affected by a multi-jurisdictional restructuring or redundancy exercise then there may be an obligation to inform and consult with the EWC prior to implementing any such exercise. For further details please refer to the section on European Works Councils in the introductory chapter.

Sanctions

Unfair Dismissal

8.112 If an employee has two years' continuous service, dismissal will be automatically unfair where the principal reason for it is the transfer itself or a reason connected with the transfer that is not an ETO reason. For further details on the remedy for unfair dismissal see para **8.141** below. As all employment liabilities transfer to the transferee under TUPE, the transferee can find themselves liable for dismissals by the transferor. Commercial agreements will commonly contain detailed indemnities in relation to the financial liability for acts and omissions relating to transferring employees. Such agreements will be valid and enforceable to the extent that they do not attempt to contract out of TUPE.

Failure to inform and consult

8.113 The sanctions for failure to inform and consult under TUPE largely mirror the redundancy consultation rules. If either employer fails to inform and consult in compliance with TUPE, the employee representatives may present a complaint to an Employment Tribunal within three months of the date of the transfer. An affected employee's right to bring a claim themselves is very limited. He can only bring a claim where there is a defect relating to the election of employee representatives or where no representatives exist. The employer has a limited defence to the claim if it was not reasonably practicable to comply with the requirements.

8.114 If the Employment Tribunal declares that the complaint is well founded, it may order the employer who has failed to comply with the duty to pay appropriate compensation to affected employees. The amount of compensation will be that which the tribunal considers just and equitable having regard to the seriousness of the failure of the employer in question to comply with their duties, and will not exceed an amount equal to 13 weeks' gross pay per employee. There is no cap on what amounts to a week's pay in these circumstances. It has also been held that tribunals assessing compensation for failure to consult under TUPE should adopt the same approach to that for failure to consult in relation to collective redundancies meaning that the tribunal should always award the maximum 13 weeks' pay as compensation unless there are mitigating circumstances which justify a reduction in the award.

8.115 TUPE provides for both the transferor and the transferee to be jointly and severally liable for any award of compensation made by an Employment Tribunal for failure by the old employer to comply with its information and consultation requirements.

8.116 The transferor is also under an obligation to provide the transferee with certain information about transferring employees (employee liability information) no later than 14 days before the transfer and thereafter must notify any change to that information. Failure to provide the employee liability information can lead to a complaint by the transferee to the tribunal which can award compensation that must currently be no less than £500 per transferring employee unless the tribunal considers it just and equitable to award less.

Application of TUPE to Cross-Border Transactions/ Offshoring

8.117 TUPE is not limited geographically and this means that TUPE will apply to an outsourcing to a jurisdiction outside of England and Wales (offshoring) in a similar way as it would to an outsourcing scenario within England. TUPE will not, however, apply where a business or services transfers from overseas to England – often referred to as 'onshoring' – but please note that it will require a detailed analysis to determine if employees affected by such a transfer to England fall within the protective scope of any legislation implementing the Acquired Rights Directive in the jurisdiction where the business is located or the services are being provided immediately before the transfer.

8.118 Where TUPE applies, the employment of affected employees will automatically transfer from the transferor to the transferee on existing terms and conditions of employment. As terms and conditions relating to the place where the work is to be carried out are preserved, the affected employees will remain employed in England by the new (overseas) employer rather than their workplace automatically transferring overseas. If the overseas employer does not intend to employ staff in the UK then there will at this point (post-transfer) be a workplace closure redundancy situation. As part of such a redundancy exercise the overseas employer may offer alternative employment at the overseas location but would be under no statutory obligation to offer the same terms and conditions of employment at the overseas location. Consequently the overseas employment would be on local terms and conditions and it would most likely not be considered to be a suitable alternative by affected employees.

Practical Tip

Where a particular business function is being offshored to another jurisdiction where services can be provided at a lower costs base then the incoming service provider will typically ask the business for appropriate indemnities in respect of the redundancy costs concerning affected transferring staff in England. There is typically also a commercial discussion to be had concerning any redundancy costs on exit.

WORKFORCE REDUCTION IN CONNECTION WITH SHARE SALE OR SHARE PURCHASE

8.119 What is sold in share sale are the shares of the business, rather than its assets. Consequently the employer does not change at all but only the identity of the shareholder. TUPE does not apply to a share sale.

8.120 Of course, if the new owner (shareholder) wishes to restructure the business post acquisition then any dismissals must fall under one of the potentially fair reasons (redundancy and Some Other Substantial Reason being two of them) permitted by statute and follow the appropriate dismissal procedure set out above.

CHANGING EMPLOYMENT TERMS AND CONDITIONS

8.121 Once an employment contract is entered into it is generally difficult to vary the contract without the employee's consent. The exception is where the employer, at the time of entering into the contract, predicted that it would need to change a particular term in the future and ensured that the contract contains a clause expressly allowing the employer to change that particular term. A clause giving the employer wide flexibility to vary the contract in general may be accepted by the courts in terms of minor changes to the contract but not in respect of changes to the core terms of the contract.

8.122 A business wishing to change the terms and conditions of its employee's employment contracts, but no express clause allowing this exists in the contracts, has the option of:

(a) agreeing the changes with the employees;
(b) seeking to unilaterally change the contract; or
(c) dismissing and re-engaging the employees on the new proposed terms and conditions.

The last two options carry with them a higher risk of claims being brought against the employer for breach of contract and (constructive) unfair dismissal.

8.123 Employers should also remember that where there has been a relevant transfer under the TUPE regulations any change to the employees' terms and conditions, which is connected with the transfer and is not for an ETO reason (Economic, Technical or Organisational) will be void.

Mutually agreed changes

8.124 The easiest way to change an employee's terms and conditions is to get the employee's express agreement to do so. The employee may insist on receiving some benefit in return for the proposed change (other than the benefit of remaining in employment) and so it may be that some negotiation will take place.

8.125 From a legal point of view, any amendment will only be contractually binding on the parties if there is some form of 'consideration' – ie some benefit in return for the proposed change to the terms and conditions. However, it may sometimes be possible to argue that the fact that the employee remains in employment is a sufficient benefit (or 'consideration') to make the variation binding although this will not always be the case.

Unilateral changes

8.126 An employer may decide to impose changes to the terms and conditions on the employees without their agreement. If employees continue to work under the new terms and conditions then the employer could seek to argue that this amounts to an implied consent by the employees. Employers should be very careful if adopting this approach as they will be in breach of contract and the variation may also entitle the employee to resign and claim constructive unfair dismissal.

Dismissing and re-engaging employees on new terms

8.127 Finally employers may dismiss the employees and offer re-employment on new terms. This would prevent employees being able to bring a claim for breach of contract on the grounds that the employer varied the terms and conditions. However, this approach carries with it an increased risk that the employees bring a claim for unfair dismissal.

8.128 In such a scenario the employer will have to prove that the dismissal was for one of the potentially fair reason. Here the employer may be able to argue that the refusal to agree to the proposed change of terms and conditions entitled the employer to dismiss the employee for Some Other Substantial Reason, which is one of the five potentially fair reasons for dismissing an employee. The employer will also have to ensure that the appropriate dismissal procedure was followed. This includes the collective redundancy consultation procedure as outlined in para **8.53** above where the employer decides to take this approach in respect of 20 or more employees. Although the employer may be able to justify the dismissals themselves on the grounds of Some Other Substantial Reason – the collective redundancy consultation legislation is sufficiently wide to also, in certain circumstances, treat these types of dismissals as redundancies for collective consultation purposes.

Practical Tips on changing terms and conditions

The easiest and most 'safe' option for employers when it comes to varying an employee's terms and conditions is no doubt to get the employee's express agreement to the variation.

Most organisations will carry out an annual review of salaries and employers may therefore, if possible, consider introducing a proposed change to the terms and conditions at the same time as salary reviews take place. This would allow employers to make any salary increase or introduction of any benefit such as additional holidays or a new bonus scheme etc. conditional upon the employee agreeing to the proposed change.

Depending on the financial situation of the organisation employees may also be prepared to accept changes to their terms and conditions if the alternative is that a redundancy situation will become inevitable. In such a situation it is important that employees are given the relevant information about the organisation's financial position so as to be able to make an informed decision either way.

USING TEMPORARY STAFF

8.129 In a reorganisation situation the requirement for temporary staff may arise. The employer may consider the options of using workers from an agency or directly engaging employees on fixed term contracts.

Agency workers

8.130 Using agency workers can be a good solution when an organisation is in need of some temporary cover at short notice and wishes to avoid engaging in an actual recruitment process. However, Management should note that agency workers now have certain minimum rights and that not only the agency, but also the organisation hiring the agency workers, will have some responsibility for ensuring these.

8.131 The Agency Workers Regulations implement the EU Temporary Agency Workers Directive and provide, amongst others, that agency workers are entitled to the same pay as equivalent permanent staff after 12-weeks with the hiring organisation. Agency workers are also entitled to receive information from the hiring organisation about any employment vacancies which are available and to access collective facilities and amenities from the first day of starting work with the hiring organisation.

8.132 Agency workers are not entitled to the same protection that fixed-term employees enjoy (see para **8.133** below). This means that there is no obligation on the hiring organisation to treat a fixed-term agency worker the same as a comparable permanent employee.

Fixed-term contract

8.133 An organisation may decide to use fixed-term contracts when external funding is for a fixed period only or when an individual is required for a specific project for instance. It may also be that someone is required as maternity cover for a fixed period, or the organisation is not yet sure of the demand for a certain position and wishes to start with a fixed-term engagement to assess the requirements going forward. Whatever the reason for using fixed-term contracts, organisations should be aware that the EU Fixed-term Work Directive has been implemented by the Fixed-Term Employees (Prevention of Less Favourable Treatment) Regulations and that as a result fixed-term employees (but not workers) enjoy certain rights.

8.134 A fixed-term contract may be drafted to terminate at a specific date or at the conclusion of a particular project. The expiry of a fixed-term contract will be treated as 'termination' by the employer even though the expiry date was stipulated in the contract and agreed at the time it was entered into. This means that, unless the employer offers permanent employment to the fixed-term employee or offers renewal of the fixed-term contract, the employer must be able to justify the 'termination' (ie the non-renewal) of the fixed-term contract on the grounds of one of the five potentially fair reasons. The reason for non-renewal may be redundancy, in that there is no longer the need for the particular position, in which case the employer would have to follow the appropriate redundancy procedure as outlined in para **8.25** above.

8.135 Failure to justify the dismissal on the grounds of one of the five potentially fair reasons and follow the appropriate dismissal procedure would give the employee a strong claim for unfair dismissal. This is, however, provided the employee satisfies the relevant criteria for bringing such a claim, which includes two complete years of service with the employer (see para **8.139** on unfair dismissal).

Renewal of fixed-term contracts

8.136 Employers may renew a fixed-term contract on a number of occasions (provided it can justify the need for a fixed-term contract as opposed to engaging the employee on a permanent contract) but once engaged for four years or more the contract will automatically be regarded as a permanent contract. Moreover, employers should note that renewing a fixed-term contract beyond two years will qualify the employee for unfair dismissal protection and care must be taken when terminating the employment (including on the expiry of the contract).

Practical tips on Fixed-Term Contracts

Employers should ensure that contracts are drafted to include a right to terminate the employment before the expiry of the fixed-term contract. Failure to include such a clause can be expensive for employers as the employee will be entitled to receive payment for the full fixed-term period even if the contract is terminated earlier by the employer.

For instance an employer who employs someone on a fixed-term contract for a 15-month period and who decides to terminate the arrangement after three months would be in breach of contract unless the contract contains an express clause allowing for early termination. In such a situation the employer would have to pay the employee for the remainder of the 15-month period.

EMPLOYMENT CLAIMS

8.137 Employment claims are generally heard by a regional employment tribunal within the location of the employee's place of work. Any appeals are made to the Employment Appeal Tribunal and then to the Court of Appeal.

8.138 Employment Tribunals were introduced to create a forum for employees and employers to resolve their disputes. Employment tribunals have certain limits, not only in terms of jurisdiction but also in terms of the amount of financial compensation which they can award. This means that some employment related claims are preferably heard in the High Court. Employment Tribunals can award a maximum of up to £25,000 in respect of contract claims and up to a maximum of £78,335 in respect of unfair dismissal claims. Tribunals cannot order any other remedy such as an order for specific performance or injunction and any such action must be brought in the High Court.

Unfair dismissal

8.139 Employees with two or more years' service can bring a claim for unfair dismissal if they believe that the dismissal was unfair – either because the real reason for the dismissal was not one of the potentially fair reasons for the dismissal (in a workforce restructuring this would be either redundancy or SOSR) or because the appropriate dismissal procedures were not followed by the employer.

8.140 Employees have three months from the effective date of termination to bring a claim for unfair dismissal although this deadline can be extended by the Tribunal if it considers that it was not reasonably practicable to bring the claim within the three-month deadline.

Remedies

8.141 If the Employment Tribunal finds that the employee has been unfairly dismissed then it can order the employer to reinstate the individual or to re-engage the individual into an alternative role. However, such orders are rare and the normal remedy for unfair dismissal is compensation.

Compensation for unfair dismissal is made up of two parts:

- a basic award calculated according to age and length of service (in the same way as a statutory redundancy payment); and
- compensation for the losses (including potential future losses) suffered by the individual calculated according to what the Tribunal considers to be 'just and equitable' and the individual's duty to mitigate his losses.

Both the basic and compensatory awards are subject to a statutory cap which is reviewed annually. There is no cap on awards where an unfair dismissal is found to be connected to whistleblowing under the Public Interest Disclosure legislation or where dismissal is proved to be an act of unlawful discrimination. In such cases, an individual will also be eligible for an award for injury to feelings.

The Basic Award

8.142 The Basic Award is calculated based on the Employee's age, length of service and weekly pay (which is capped at £475 at the time of writing this chapter (July 2015) up to a maximum of £14,250) – the calculation is the same as that for statutory redundancy pay and if any SRP has been paid to the employee already then this will be offset.

The Compensatory Award

8.143 The Compensatory Award is calculated with reference to the employee's actual loss of earnings (and likely future loss of earnings) as a result of the termination of the employment. Employees have a duty to mitigate (take up new employment) so as to minimise the loss of earnings. The Compensatory Award may be reduced by the employment tribunal if the employer can show that the employee failed to take up reasonable employment that was made available to him. The Compensatory Award is currently capped at £78,335 or 52 weeks' gross pay (the employee's weekly gross pay at the time of the dismissal) whichever is the lower figure.

Discrimination

8.144 An employee may also bring a claim for discrimination in the employment tribunals if he believes that the real reason for his selection for redundancy (or his dismissal on grounds of SOSR) was because of one of the following protected characteristics: age, disability, gender reassignment, marriage and civil partnership, pregnancy and maternity, race, religion or belief, sex, sexual orientation,

Remedies

8.145 If an employee is successful in a claim for discrimination he is likely to be awarded a payment representing compensation for injury to feelings and a compensatory award. Compensation for injury to feelings is generally between £600 and £30,000 depending on how serious an employment tribunal considers the employer's discriminatory act to be.

8.146 The compensatory award is calculated in the same way as for unfair dismissal, namely with reference to the employee's actual loss of earnings and subject to mitigation, however there is no cap on the Compensatory Award, which means that employees can claim their full loss of earnings (subject to mitigation).

> **Practical Tips**
>
> Even if an employee does not have the required two years of service at the time of termination and thus cannot bring a claim for unfair dismissal employers are still strongly advised to follow a minimum dismissal procedure and carefully document the reasons for the termination of employment so as to minimise the risk of employees claiming that the real reason for the dismissal was because of one of the protected characteristics.
>
> If the employer plans to terminate the employment of 20 or more employees he will have to follow the collective dismissal procedure in any event even if the employees have less than two years' service. Failure to follow the collective redundancy procedure will entitle the employees to a Protective Award of up to 90 days' gross pay each (see para 8.69 above).

MUTUALLY-AGREED TERMINATION

8.147 An employer may wish to reach a mutually agreed termination with an employee by way of a severance or settlement agreement rather than to dismiss the employee and risk employment tribunal proceedings. Under the terms of such an agreement, the employee agrees not to enforce their employment rights by bringing a claim against the employer in exchange for a termination package.

Settlement agreements

8.148 In order to be valid, the agreement must comply with various statutory requirements. It is a statutory requirement that the employee must have received independent legal advice on the terms of the agreement from a qualified lawyer or, subject to certain conditions, a legal adviser from a voluntary organisation. It is also a requirement that the advice given must be covered by insurance or an indemnity provided for members of a profession or professional body.

8.149 It is common, although not mandatory, for the employer to pay for the employee's legal advice. The settlement agreement should specify the precise legal claims which the employee is waiving. An employer may include additional clauses in the agreement relating to the termination of employment such as provisions relating to confidentiality and references.

Without prejudice and 'pre-termination' discussions

8.150 If an employer wishes to offer a settlement agreement to an employee it should be done on a 'without prejudice' basis. A without prejudice offer is essentially an offer made 'off the record'. The legal purpose of a without prejudice offer is that the offer cannot later be used as evidence in a court of admission by the employer of any wrong-doing. This means that if the employee rejects the offer (and decides not to make a counter-offer) the employer's offer will be disregarded for legal purposes and it will be as if it was never made. The without prejudice rule exists so as to encourage settlement discussions between the parties and to reach a settlement out of court.

8.151 To be able to benefit from the without prejudice rule it is a requirement that there is a *pre-existing dispute* between the employer and the employee. Accordingly, in a redundancy situation, it is not possible, under the without prejudice rule, for employers to simply make an offer of settlement to a particular employee in confidence before the start of the redundancy procedure unless there is a genuine dispute in place between the two already. Under the without prejudice rule, employers would, therefore, always have to start the appropriate dismissal procedure before starting any discussions about possible exit terms. Otherwise such discussions would not be confidential and could be used against the employer in the tribunal.

Pre-termination discussions

8.152 In an attempt to make it easier to agree termination terms at an early stage, the government has recently introduced the concept of 'pre-termination discussions'. This new concept exists in parallel with the without prejudice rule but will allow the parties to discuss termination terms in confidence and 'off the record' without the need for a pre-existing dispute. Whilst this is a welcome development for employers, the pre-termination discussions are only protected in respect of unfair dismissal claims but not in respect of other claims, such as discrimination claims where the conversation can be disclosed to the tribunal as evidence against the employer. Employers should therefore take great care to record in detail the reason for the proposed termination so that it can show that the dismissal was not for one of the protected characteristics in case the employee seeks to argue this. Employers are advised to seek legal advice before entering into any pre-termination or without prejudice discussions with employees to minimise the risk that such discussions, which the employer thought were confidential, are legally disclosed to a tribunal and used as evidence against the employer.

8.153 Employers should be aware that offering a settlement agreement is often viewed by employees as an invitation to negotiate a termination package and it is therefore important to ensure the employer is in as good a negotiation position as possible – this would for instance be achieved by having started the appropriate dismissal procedure so that this can be resumed if severance terms cannot be agreed by the parties. A termination payment will usually be calculated with reference to the amount the employee may be able to claim in a tribunal if he issued a claim. In practice this means that most employers will start the appropriate dismissal procedure and then, in parallel offer a settlement agreement as part of the without prejudice discussion. Once the agreement is accepted by the employee the dismissal process can be discontinued, however, it is critical for the employer's bargaining position that it can resume the dismissal procedure if the employee refuses to accept the settlement agreement on the terms offered.

Chapter 9

Workforce Restructuring in Estonia

Pirkko-Liis Harkmaa and Martin-Kaspar Sild
LAWI, Tallinn

INTRODUCTION

9.1 The Estonian employment law system – indeed the legal system as a whole – is a civil law system. Estonia has joined all major international labour organisation's employment conventions and adopted all major EU employment Directives. Employment relations are governed mostly by the Employment Contracts Act, but also by other legislation. The central focus of current Estonian employment law is to provide flexibility and contractual freedom to both the employee and employer. Whilst the employee is protected by law with set of a reasonable minimum requirements for the employment relationship, the employer can make adjustments to, or reorganise, its work force more efficiently as and when the need arises.

9.2 Even so, Estonian employment law still maintains a considerable number of provisions aimed at protecting the employee as the weaker party to the agreement. One of the manifestations of this is that the concept of 'at-will employment' is not recognised by Estonian employment law, hence the employer – unlike the employee – can terminate an employment contract only if grounds exist as set out in the Employment Contracts Act.

9.3 In very broad terms, the legislation sets out two types of grounds for termination on the employer's initiative: (i) reasons pertinent to the employee's behaviour; and (ii) economic reasons. In the context of restructuring the reasons for termination would be driven by economic factors, accordingly we concentrate in our overview on termination due economic reasons, ie redundancy.

EMPLOYMENT STATUS

9.4 The Employment Contracts Act and the redundancy rules and procedures stipulated therein apply only to individuals who are employees. First, it is important to appreciate that the Employment Contracts Act explicitly excludes from the scope of its application the contracts of a member of the directing body of a legal person (members of the management or supervisory board) or a director of a branch of a foreign company. As members of the management or supervisory board of a company or a director of a branch office are not considered employees by law, they cannot have employment contracts for the performance of their managerial or supervisory duties and the redundancy rules and procedures in the Employment Contracts Act, do not apply to such individuals.

9.5 Secondly, the Employment Contracts Act provides that it shall not be applied to a contract where the person obligated to perform the work to a significant extent independently chooses the manner, time and place of performance of the work. Thus, sole proprietors acting as independent contractors, agents, or the like are also exempt from the regulation of employment law. However, this is so only on the condition that such a contractor is indeed independent in all the above-mentioned aspects – if this is not the case, then regardless of the formal set-up, the relationship could be redefined by the court as an employment relationship due to having the material characteristics thereof.

GENERAL PROTECTION AGAINST TERMINATION

9.6 In the most general sense, all employees enjoy protection against termination manifested in the fact that there needs to be actual reasons for the termination, eg in the case of redundancy, relevant economic reasons which give rise to the termination have to be present. Also, there are advance notice periods that have to be followed in the case of termination – the notice periods are progressively longer depending on the length of service of a particular employee. However, certain general protective rules may also be distinguished specifically in the context of redundancies.

9.7 Namely, in the case of termination due to economic reasons (except when termination occurs due to liquidation or bankruptcy of the employer) there are certain general restrictions for termination which serve to protect the employees concerned. If there are several persons employed in similar or comparable positions, then the employer has to follow the principles of equal treatment and justify objectively how he made the choice of employees to be made redundant and, while making the choice, the law requires the employer to give preference to remain employed to the employee who has a child under three years of age or who acts as an elected employee representative.

9.8 Also, prior to termination due to economic reasons (except when termination occurs due to liquidation or bankruptcy of the employer), the employer should offer the employees other vacant positions, if possible. The employer must, if necessary, organise the employee's in-service training or change the employee's working conditions, unless the changes cause disproportionately high costs for the employer. The Estonian Supreme Court has explained that the offer of vacant positions cannot be limited by the employee's professional qualifications. Any vacant position that the employee would be suitable for must be offered. The offering cannot be subject to the employee having to compete for the job.

SPECIAL PROTECTION AGAINST TERMINATION

9.9 Under Estonian employment law, there are only a very limited number of employee groups who enjoy special protection against termination. These mainly relate to termination due to economic reasons.

9.10 First, except when termination occurs due to liquidation or bankruptcy of the employer an employer is prevented from terminating the employment contract of an employee who is either pregnant or entitled to maternity leave or on parental leave on the basis of economic reasons. This prohibition only applies if the employee has notified the employer of her pregnancy or the right to use maternity leave before receiving the termination notice or within 14 days after receiving the termination notice,

9.11 Secondly, prior to terminating the employment contract of an elected employee representative, the employer must seek the opinion of the employees who elected the representative. Such opinion must be given within ten business days. The employer should take the opinion into account to the extent that it is reasonable. If the employees' opinion is not taken into account, the employer has to explain why it was rejected.

WORKFORCE REDUCTION

The definition and principal rules of redundancy

9.12 As one of the main duties of the employer *vis a vis* the employee is to provide the employee with work, it would be inconceivable for the employment relationship to continue where there is no more work for a particular employee. In that situation, the employer is given a 'way out' – in the form of entitlement to terminate the employment relationship on grounds of economic reasons.

9.13 Termination for economic reasons is justified in cases when continuance of employment relations on the agreed terms and conditions becomes impossible due to:

(a) decrease in volume of work;
(b) reorganisation of work;
(c) due to other reasons resulting in work ceasing;
(d) solvent winding up of the company; or
(e) insolvent winding up of the company.

9.14 Thus, the economic reasons which give grounds for redundancy may arise out of the employer's own decision to re-organise the business (eg to centralise or outsource certain functions, resulting in the employees in certain roles/functions being left without work, or to close down an entire business unit or even its whole business) or from more external factors, such as overall economic down turn leading to the decrease in volume of work or even to the insolvency of the employer.

9.15 A redundancy situation may arise when there is no longer any work at all for the employee or if no longer able to provide the employee with work on agreed conditions. However, according to the practice of the Estonian Supreme Court, an employee's refusal to accept modification of his or her employment conditions (including remuneration conditions) does not amount to an economic reason giving grounds for redundancy. The amendment of some terms of the employment contract does not necessarily mean that work on agreed terms has ceased.

9.16 When a situation of redundancy arises, the employer may have to make a choice between several employees in the affected positions. Thus, where a certain number of employees out of a group of employees are to be made redundant, the first step for the employer would be to define the relevant group of employees. The relevant group can be the group of employees associated with the relevant business unit of the employer, or a group of employees with similar duties or in a similar category, as the case may be. The employees must be comparable. When that group of comparable employees is selected, priority protection has to be given to the employees who have a child under three years of age or who act as an elected employee representative. Once the employer has filtered out such protected employees, then, according to the case law of the Estonian Supreme Court, the employer is absolutely free to decide whom from the remaining employees to make redundant. The employer can apply its own criteria for the selection as it sees fit – the selection does not necessarily have to be driven by the professional skill of the employees, but may also be based on, for example, social skills or other personal characteristics of the employees. In that stage, the employer is restricted in its choice only by anti-discrimination and fair treatment requirements.

9.17 However, if there is only one employee in the position that is to be made redundant, then he or she can be dismissed without any such selection – even if the employee in question has a child under three years of age or acts as an elected employee representative, ie an employee who otherwise would be protected if there were others to choose from. The same goes for the situation where an entire business unit is closed down and all employees who worked there have to be made redundant.

Collective dismissal

9.18 In the event certain thresholds are exceeded as to the number of employees to be made redundant, a collective dismissal may be established in which case certain additional procedural requirements would apply.

9.19 A collective dismissal occurs when during a period of 30 calendar days the employment contracts of a number of employees are to be dismissed, as follows:

Number of employees to be dismissed	Total number of employees per undertaking
5 employees	Up to 19 employees in average
10 employees	From 20 to 99 employees in average
10% of employees	From 100-299 employees in average
30 employees	At least 300 employees in average

9.20 Prior to deciding upon collective dismissal the employer must consult (as early as reasonably possible) with the employees or if they exist, the elected employee representative(s). The intention is to reach an agreement for prevention of the contemplated redundancies or reduction in the number planned redundancies and thereby mitigating the effects of redundancies, and also assist with finding new jobs for the employees being made redundant or re-training them.

9.21 In order to enable the employees or, if they exist, the elected employee representative(s) to make informed proposals during consultations, the employer should provide them as early as reasonably possible with all relevant information about the planned collective dismissals.

9.22 In particular, the employer must inform the employees at least of the following:

- the reasons for collective dismissals;
- the number of the employees whose contracts will be terminated, their job titles and the criteria for selecting the respective employees for redundancy;

- the number of employees working in the company and their job titles;
- the time span for terminating the contracts;
- the grounds for calculating and paying compensation to the employees, if any compensation is paid on top of the statutory compensation.

> **Practical Tip**
>
> The relevant employee notice letter must be either in written or electronic form. It is advisable to give the notice letter to each individual employee in writing and ensure acknowledgement of receipt by signature is provided.

9.23 At the same time, the employer is obliged to send a copy of the notice letter to the National Unemployment Insurance Fund.

9.24 During consultations employees have the right to meet with the management and make proposals with regard to the contemplated redundancies. Proposals have to be made in writing or in electronic form within 15 days of receiving the notice letter. The employees cannot veto the redundancies and the employer does not have to agree with any proposals made by the employees. However in the latter case, the employer has to provide reasons for refusing with the employees' proposals.

9.25 After the end of consultations, the employer has to once again provide the National Unemployment Insurance Fund with the same information that was contained in the employee notice letter (which may have been updated as a results of consultations) and also report on the outcome of the consultations. A copy of the documents sent to the National Unemployment Insurance Fund has to be provided to the employees or if they exist, the elected employee representative(s), who may provide their opinions regarding the collective dismissal to the National Unemployment Insurance Fund within seven days of receiving the said copy of documents.

9.26 Termination of employment contracts can only be effected after the end of the consultations and notification of the National Unemployment Insurance Fund as described above.

9.27 Collective dismissal comes into effect at the end of the termination notice period, but not earlier than 30 days from the date when the National Unemployment Insurance Fund has received the information regarding the redundancies and the report on the outcome of the consultations. During these 30 days the National Unemployment Insurance Fund will try to find solutions for re-employment of the redundant employees. If there are no problems finding new jobs for the redundant employees, the National Unemployment Insurance Fund may shorten the said 30 days' deadline or if finding new jobs is more complicated, the above deadline by be extended to 60 calendar days.

TERMINATION NOTICE AND SEVERANCE PAY

Notice letter

9.28 In order to terminate the employment contracts, the employees must be given notice.

> **Practical Tip**
>
> The notice letter can be in written or electronic form, but it would be preferable to use a written form notice letter and ensure that the employee signs for it. The notice letter has to explain why termination is necessary.

9.29 The notice letter becomes effective when the employee receives it and the employment contract ends on the date indicated in the notice letter without the need for any additional legal formalities, except payment of severance pay and final balance, as well as the handing over of any property and documents by the employee, if necessary.

Notice periods

9.30 The employees are normally entitled to prior notice graduated according to their length of employment. The relevant notice periods are as follows:

Length of employment	Notice period
Less than 1 year	15 calendar days
From 1 to 5 years	30 calendar days
From 5 to 10 years	60 calendar days
More than 10 years	90 calendar days

Payment in lieu of the notice period

9.31 During the notice period, the employer should let the employees continue working and pay their regular salary; however the employment contract can be also be terminated immediately without following the notice periods, but in such cases monetary compensation has to be paid in lieu of the notice period. The compensation is paid for each day of work that the employee would have worked if the employer had observed the notice period. The days of work are calculated from the actual date of termination until the date when the notice period would have ended if it had been applied. Compensation is paid on the basis of the average salary per day of work. The method of calculation of the average work day salary is laid down by a governmental regulation. As a rule, the remuneration earned by the employee within the six months before the month where the need to calculate the average salary arose have to be taken as basis for the calculation.

9.32 In addition, the employer has to give the employee sufficient time off during the notice period to look for a new job.

Final balance and severance pay

9.33 On the last day of employment, the employer must pay to the employee all amounts owed as at the last day of employment, including all outstanding salary and bonus amounts, as well as monetary compensation for accrued but unused holiday entitlement which has not expired.

9.34 The method for calculation of compensation for unused days of vacation is laid down by a governmental regulation. Holiday pay is calculated and paid on the basis of the employee's average calendar day salary.

9.35 Severance pay payable in the case of termination due to economic reasons amounts a payment of one month's average salary regardless of the length of employment of the employee. In the case of fixed term employment contracts, however, the employer should pay to the employee compensation equal to the salary that the employee would have received if he or she had worked until the end of the agreed term of the employment contract. However, the latter requirement does not apply in case the termination due to economic reasons occurs due to liquidation or bankruptcy of the employer.

9.36 Severance pay of one month is calculated on the basis of the employee's average daily salary. The method of calculation is laid down in governmental regulations. As a rule, the basis of the calculation should be the remuneration earned by the employee within the six months before the month in which the need to calculate the average salary arise.

9.37 In addition, depending on the length of employment (in case the length of employment is more than five years), the employee may receive extra compensation from the National Unemployment Insurance Fund. The relevant application to the National Unemployment Insurance Fund has to be submitted by the employer within five days of the date of termination. The compensation is paid directly to the employee's bank account.

GENERAL INFORMATION AND CONSULTATION OBLIGATION

9.38 There is a general information and consultation obligation for employers who employ at least 30 employees.

9.39 The employer has to inform and consult at least in relation to the following circumstances pertaining to employees:

(a) the structure of the employer, the staff, including the employees performing duties by way of temporary agency work, changes therein and planned decisions which significantly affect the structure of the employer and the staff;

(b) planned decisions which are likely to bring about substantial changes in the work organisation;

(c) planned decisions which are likely to bring about substantial changes in the employment contract relationships of employees, including termination of employment relationships.

9.40 Thus, if there are at least 30 employees employed and the planned reorganisation would bring about any significant or substantial changes for the employees, the employer needs to plan and carry out the applicable information and consultation procedures.

9.41 If there have not been elected any employee representatives, the information and consultation procedures are still triggered (as described above) but all employees will have to be informed and consulted individually instead.

9.42 The law does not set forth too many details or any very specific timelines for the information and consultation process.

9.43 An employer is required to provide employees with information in a manner which will enable them thoroughly to examine the information and, if necessary, prepare for consultations with the employer. The information has to be provided in writing or in a format which can be reproduced in writing, unless the parties agree otherwise. The law does not provide a mandatory timeline for starting the process.

9.44 After receiving the information regarding the planned changes, the employees or, if they exist, their elected representatives, have the right to present a written opinion or make a proposal concerning the information received from the employer or notify their intention to commence consultation within 15 working days from the receipt of the information. If the employer does not take their proposals into consideration, reasons have to be given at the earliest opportunity in writing or in a format which can be reproduced in writing. Thus, employees cannot veto the planned changes.

9.45 The employer has to start the consultation process within seven working days of the receipt of the request for consultation. The employer should explain the planned activities and the consequences for the employees. The parties are to seek an agreement on the planned activity. The law however does not set forth any minimum or maximum timeline for having the negotiations. Thus it depends on the employer and the employees, as well as on the circumstances.

9.46 As the information and consultation procedures are triggered by 'anticipated' decisions, the information and consultation procedures have to be completed prior to making and communicating any final decisions bringing about any significant and substantial changes affecting the employees.

RESTRICTIVE COVENANTS

9.47 If an employee is made redundant, the employer should always bear in mind whether, as a result of access to the employer's sensitive business information, the employee should be bound by confidentiality and/or non-compete obligations after the employment relationship terminates.

Confidentiality obligation

9.48 Under Estonian law, employees are automatically bound by a confidentiality obligation arising directly from the law, which is in effect during the employment relationship and, to the extent that it is justified by the employer's legitimate interests, also for an indefinite period thereafter. However, this confidentiality obligation will only apply if the employer has communicated to the employee (or all employees) in a clear and sufficiently detailed manner and in writing, what information is considered the employer's trade secrets that have to be kept confidential. Such definition of trade secrets may only encompass information that really is the employer's sensitive business information, eg information which is not publicly available and which has a certain commercial value for the employer due to its secrecy. As this can be communicated to employees unilaterally by the employer the confidentiality obligation does not necessarily have to be agreed upon by the employee. Consent from the employee is however required where the employer also wants to stipulate a contractual fine that could be imposed if the employee breaches the confidentiality obligation.

9.49 Hence, if the employee to be made redundant had access to the employer's trade secrets, the employer should check whether a valid confidentiality obligation binding the employee is already in place and, if not, whether reaching an additional agreement for these purposes should be considered (eg with a view to stipulating a contractual fine for the breach of the confidentiality obligation).

Non-compete obligation

9.50 The employer should also consider whether it would pose a risk if the employee were to begin working for a competitor immediately after the termination. This could be particularly important where the employee had access to the employer's trade secrets. In that case the employer could seek to reach an agreement with the exiting employee to restrict the employee with a non-compete obligation applicable after the termination.

9.51 The post-termination non-compete obligation can last for up to one year after the termination of employment. Specific requirements stipulated by the law have to be met for the agreement to be valid. Namely, the agreement has to be in writing and the restriction has to be clearly defined in the agreement and in sufficient detail, more particularly as to the restriction (who are the competitors, what activities are considered competitive), time (the period of validity of the restriction) and space (the territory where the restriction applies) of the restriction. Also, a just monthly compensation must be paid to the employee during the validity of the post-termination non-compete obligation, to compensate the employee for the loss of income due to the restriction of his or her freedom to find a new job. Usually, such compensation can be a reasonable percentage of the employee's remuneration.

9.52 If any of the above requirements are not met, the agreement will be unenforceable unless the employee duly adheres to the (void) agreement, in which case the employer is bound. The employer can terminate the post-termination non-compete agreement at any time by giving the employee an advance notice of 30 calendar days.

Practical Tip

It is recommendable to stipulate a contractual fine of a reasonable amount in the non-compete agreement, as it would ease the enforceability of the agreement should the employee fail to comply.

SUMMARY OF ACTIONS IN THE EVENT OF A WORKFORCE RESTRUCTURING EXERCISE

RECOGNISING A SITUATION OF REDUNDANCY AND DETERMINING ITS SCOPE	
Necessity of redundancy	The employer should ascertain whether a redundancy situation is present, ie whether there is no more work to be offered on agreed terms and conditions to certain employee(s), eg due to decrease in work volume, reorganisation of work, liquidation or bankruptcy.
Scope of redundancy	The employer should determine what positions are affected by the contemplated redundancy and: • whether the affected persons are employees (as opposed to board members or independent contractors). If not, the rules concerning redundancy do not apply; • whether one or several, but not all employees out of a group of employees in comparable positions have to be made redundant – meaning a choice has to be made between several employees; • whether any employees concerned are pregnant or entitled to maternity leave (provided the employee has already notified the employer). Such employees cannot be made redundant, except in the case of liquidation or bankruptcy of the employer.
	If a choice between several comparable employees has to be made • protected employees must initially be filtered out of the selection: these are employees who have a child under three years of age or who act as an elected employee representative; • selection criteria must be applied to the remaining comparable employees to select the ones to be made redundant. The employer is entitled to apply any criteria as it sees fit, being restricted in its choice only by anti-discrimination and fair treatment requirements. Nevertheless, the employer needs to be able to justify objectively how the choice was made.

Possibility to offer other vacant positions	The employer must ascertain whether it has any vacant positions that could be offered to the employee(s) to otherwise be made redundant. If yes, the positions have to be offered to the employee(s). If the employee(s) accept, a transfer to the other position should be carried out instead of termination.
COLLECTIVE DISMISSAL PROCEDURE / INFORMATION AND CONSULTATION	
Collective dismissal	*If numerous employees are to be made redundant within a period of 30 calendar days* The employer must check whether the thresholds for the application of the collective dismissal rules are met. If yes, then: • all relevant and required information concerning the planned collective dismissal must be provided to the employees as early as reasonably possible. Such information should be included in a written notice and given to each individual employee against signed acknowledgement of receipt; • a copy of the written notice regarding the collective dismissal must be submitted by the employer to the National Unemployment Insurance Fund; • consultation with employees has to be carried out; • the National Unemployment Insurance Fund must also be provided by the employer of the same information that was contained in the notice (which may have changed subject to the results of consultations) and also of the results of the consultations with employees. A copy of this notification must also be provided to employees; • termination of employment contracts may be initiated only after the end of the above mentioned consultations and notification of the National Unemployment Insurance Fund. Collective dismissal comes into force upon the end of the notice period of termination, but not earlier than 30 days from the date when the National Unemployment Insurance Fund has received the abovementioned notification. The deadline may be extended up to 60 calendar days.

General information and consultation obligation	*If the employer employs 30 employees or more* The general information and consultation obligations may have to be carried out prior to the redundancies being effected.
Specific information and consultation obligation in the case of elected employee representatives	*If an employee selected for redundancy is an elected employee representative* The opinion of the employees who elected the representative must be sought. The employees have 10 business days to give their opinion.
CARRYING OUT THE TERMINATION OF CONTRACTS	
A due diligence of employment contract terms	The employment contracts of the employees selected for redundancy have to be reviewed to check if they do contain any better terms in comparison to the statutory minimum as concerns termination notice periods, severance payments or other conditions relevant to the termination.
Delivery of termination notice letter	To effect the termination, a termination notice letter has to be delivered to the relevant employee(s). The notice letter must explain why termination is necessary. It is advisable to use a written form notice letter and hand it over to the employee and obtain an acknowledgement by signature on a copy straight away. The notice letter comes into force when it is received by the employee and the employment contract ends on the date indicated in the notice letter
Confidentiality and non-compete obligations	The employer should assess whether the employees made redundant should be bound by confidentiality and/or non-compete obligations after the employment relationship terminates. • *if a confidentiality obligation is necessary*: it should be ensured that the definition of the employer's trade secrets has been communicated to the employee or, alternatively, conclude a confidentiality agreement with the employee; • *if a non-compete obligation is necessary*: a post-termination non-compete agreement conforming to the requirements stipulated by the law must be concluded with the employee prior to or at termination. It is advisable to include a contractual fine in the non-compete agreement and, if concluded, the confidentiality agreement.

Settlement of final balance	On the last day of employment, the employer must pay to the employee all amounts owed as of the last day of employment, including the following: • outstanding salary and bonus amounts, • compensation for unused holiday entitlement, • severance pay of one months' remuneration. • *if the applicable notice period for termination was not adhered to*: compensation in lieu of notice period. Certain amounts have to be calculated pursuant to the method of calculation laid down by a governmental regulation.
Application to the National Unemployment Insurance Fund	*In the case the length of employment of the terminated employee is more than 5 years* The employee may be entitled to extra compensation from the National Unemployment Insurance Fund. The relevant application to the National Unemployment Insurance Fund has to be submitted by the employer within five days from the date of termination.

BUSINESS SALE, OUTSOURCING/INSOURCING

9.53 The Employment Contracts Act, in line with the European Union 'Acquired Rights Directive' (Directive 2001/23/EC of 12 March 2001 on the approximation of the laws of the Member States relating to the safeguarding of employees' rights in the event of transfers of undertakings, businesses or part of undertakings or businesses, codifies Directive 77/187/EC, as amended by Directive 98/50/EC), recognises the principle of automatic transfer of employment contracts on 'as is' basis as part of the transfer of enterprise, whereas termination of employment contracts due to transfer of enterprise is not allowed.

9.54 An enterprise is an economic unit through which a legal person operates and which consists of the things, rights and obligations relating to and being in the hands of the management of the enterprise, including contracts relating to the enterprise. A transfer of an enterprise is regarded to have taken place when the owner of the enterprise has changed, but the enterprise has maintained its identity so that that the acquirer of the enterprise can essentially continue the same activities as were conducted by the previous owner of the enterprise by the continuity of its workforce, its management staff, the way in which its work is organised, its operating methods or the operational resources available to it. In order to safeguard the interests of the employees as the weaker party the ECJ has numerous times found that the concept of transfer of enterprise has to be interpreted more widely in the context of employment relations and thus, in light of employment law, a transfer of enterprise may also take place in cases that do not strictly appear to be intended or planned as transfer of enterprise transactions (eg transfer of single assets or contracts). The Estonian courts have taken the same view.

Practical Tip

Both the old and the new employer are jointly liable to the employee for obligations which have arisen before the transfer of the enterprise and which, by the time of the transfer, have materialised or will materialise within five years after the transfer. This means that the employee has a right to choose against whom to file a claim; this right may not be signed away by the employee but it is possible for the two employers to agree on the allocation of liability.

9.55 The transferor and acquirer of an enterprise must submit, at least one month before the transfer of the enterprise, to the employees' representative or, in his or her absence to the individual employees in general a notice containing information on at least the planned date of transfer of the enterprise, the reasons for the transfer of the enterprise, the legal, economic and social consequences of the transfer of the enterprise for the employees and the measures planned with regard to the employees. Consultation with the employees must be initiated where there is an intention to make any changes affecting the employees as a result of the transfer of the enterprise. In the course of such consultations, the employees' representative or the employees can make proposals relating to the planned changes. Ultimately, the employees cannot veto the transfer of enterprise, but the employer should justify why the employees' proposals with regard to the transfer of enterprise are not taken into account.

WORKFORCE REDUCTION IN CONNECTION WITH SHARE SALE OR SHARE PURCHASE

9.56 In the event of a sale of the employer's shares, a transfer of enterprise does not occur and thus the rules on the transfer of employment contracts will not apply.

9.57 Still, if a workforce reduction is planned in connection with the share sale, the rules of terminating employment contracts due to economic reasons (including the rules of collective dismissal, if applicable) and possibly also the general information and consultation obligations will apply.

CHANGING EMPLOYMENT TERMS AND CONDITIONS

9.58 It has to be noted that agreed terms and conditions of the employment contract cannot be unilaterally changed by the employer, such changes require consent from the employee. Thus, the employee's consent must be sought in respect of any modification of the agreed employment terms and conditions.

9.59 There are exceptions where the remuneration of the employee can be unilaterally modified by the employer under extraordinary circumstances. One of these exceptions is where an employer, due to unforeseen economic circumstances beyond its control, fails to provide an employee with work to the agreed extent – in that case, the employer may, for up to three months over a period of 12 months, reduce the remuneration of the employee concerned by a reasonable amount (although in any case not below the minimum wage), if payment of the contractual remuneration could be considered to be unreasonably burdensome for the employer. Also, the employer could be entitled to reduce the remuneration for a particular instance where the employee has disregarded a reasonable, clear and timely instruction of the employer regarding his duties and has thus delivered work of insufficient quality.

9.60 However, any terms and conditions that have not been, and need not be, included in the employment contract, but are instead unilaterally communicated to the employee by the employer, can also be changed by the employer unilaterally. Thus, it should always be carefully considered by the employer, which terms to include in the contract and which to leave out. While some employment terms and conditions must always be agreed upon (eg remuneration, working hours, location of work and employment duties), including terms that could be communicated unilaterally by the employer in the employment contract will give them contractual effect, precluding later unilateral changes by the employer.

USING TEMPORARY STAFF

9.61 If a need for temporary staff arises, the employer has two options: either to hire temporary employees itself or instead engage the services of a temporary employment agency and rely on agency workers.

Agency workers

9.62 While the European Union Temporary Agency Workers Directive has been implemented in Estonian law, temporary agency work is still subject to limited regulation under Estonian employment law. The regulation pertaining to temporary agency workers mainly touches on anti-discrimination matters. Namely, temporary agency workers may not subjected to less favourable conditions in respect of occupational health and safety, working and rest periods and remuneration for work than those applied to comparable employees of the user undertaking. Also, temporary agency workers are entitled to use, during the period of performing their duties, the benefits of the user undertaking, eg meals, transportation and childcare services, on the same conditions as comparable employees of the user undertaking.

9.63 The terms and conditions in relation to engagement of temporary agency workers derive from the service agreement with the temporary employment agency. Whether or not temporary agency workers would be the preferable option for the employer in a specific situation depends on the circumstances: hiring agency workers could be prudent where the employer needs additional workforce on a short notice and flexible terms, without the need to worry about the legal conditions of employment of the said workforce. Agency workers could be necessary also where the employer cannot hire its own temporary employees due to the restrictions for concluding fixed-term employment contracts set forth by the law.

Concluding fixed-term employment contracts

9.64 If the employer decides to hire its own temporary employees, it has to comply with the restrictions of concluding fixed-term employment contracts as stipulated by the Employment Contract Act.

9.65 Namely, a fixed-term employment contract may be concluded only when it is justified by good reasons arising from the temporary fixed-term characteristics of the work. Foremost, the following reasons are accepted: a temporary increase in work volume, performance of seasonal work, participation in a project with a limited timeframe or the substitution of an employee who is temporarily absent. Fixed-term employment contracts may not be concluded to mitigate the employer's work organisation- or business related risks, eg the fixed term of the employer's activity license or supply- or customer agreements does not justify concluding fixed-term employment contracts with the associated employees.

9.66 It is imperative that the reason for concluding the fixed-term employment contract must be communicated to the employee in writing upon concluding the contract (eg it can be indicated in the employment contract). If this requirement is not complied with, the contract will be considered to be for an indefinite term. The burden of proof that there indeed was a good reason for concluding the fixed-term contract always lies with the employer and the employer's failure to show that results in the contract being considered to have been concluded for an indefinite term.

9.67 A fixed-term employment contract can be for a period not exceeding five years. The only exception is if the reason for the fixed term it is the need to substitute an absent employee – in that case, the term may be as long as necessary (ie until the employee returns). The deadline of the contract may be indicated as a specific date or instead tied to a certain event – eg the return of the substituted employee.

9.68 If a fixed-term employment contract for the performance of similar work has been concluded on more than two consecutive occasions, so that the time between the old and new employment contract is two months or less, it will be considered a contract for an indefinite term. Extension of a fixed-term contract more than once in five years has the same effect.

EMPLOYMENT CLAIMS

9.69 The employee may challenge a termination if he or she discovers that there was no legal ground for termination or the termination was not carried out according to the requirements of the law. In addition, the employee may challenge the termination in case he or she finds that the termination was against principles of good faith. The employee has to submit the respective claim within 30 calendar days as of receipt of the termination notice letter.

9.70 The employee may request reinstatement and demand unpaid salary that he or she would have received if still employed, but if the employer objects to it, then the court will not reinstate the employee and regard the employment contract as terminated as of the date indicated in the termination notice letter.

9.71 If the employee requests compensation for unlawful termination or if the court does not reinstate the employee, then the court may normally adjudicate compensation in the amount of up to three months' average salary of the employee (in case of pregnant employees up to six months' average salary). The severance pay amounts and compensation in lieu of notice period are in such case set off against such compensation.

MUTUALLY AGREED TERMINATION

9.72 Under the Employment Contracts Act, employment contracts can be terminated at any time also upon mutual agreement between the employer and the employee.

9.73 Termination by mutual agreement does not legally require giving of any prior notice or payment of severance, but the parties can agree upon prior notice term and severance amounts. Usually the employers offer a severance pay equal to the amount that the employee would have received if the contract had been terminated due to economic reasons on the initiative of the employer (ie one month's severance pay payable by the employer, severance pay received from the state, compensation in lieu of notice period and the final balance) and something on top of it in order to entice the employee to agree to termination by mutual agreement.

9.74 However, employees could still remain reluctant to agree with termination by mutual agreement, as it would deprive them of the right to further unemployment insurance benefit from the state (additional to the state paid severance pay in case of termination due to economic reasons). Thus sometimes the employers also offer to match the unemployment insurance benefit amounts as an incentive for termination on mutual agreement. Whether this is necessary, depends on the negotiations with the employees and on their attitude towards termination by mutual agreement – as with all other conditions of the termination by mutual agreement.

Chapter 10

Workforce Restructuring in Finland

Seppo Havia and Maiju-Juulia Jokinen
Dittmar & Indrenius, Helsinki

INTRODUCTION

10.1 The Finnish collective labour agreements and the extensive binding regulation of employment terms and conditions are built on a large and complicated structure of legislation. The fundamental provisions governing employment relationships are included in the Employment Contracts Act (2001, as amended), the Working Hours Act (1996, as amended) and the Annual Holidays Act (2005, as amended). The employees' collective right to information and consultation is regulated in the Act on Cooperation within Undertakings (2007, as amended) (the 'Cooperation Act'). The Personal Data Act (1999, as amended) and the Act on the Protection of Privacy in Working Life (2004, as amended) regulate data protection issues relating to employment.

10.2 The Finnish legal system is a civil law system. It is akin to the continental European systems in many respects. Employment statutes are provided in acts of Parliament, which implement Community law and form the ground for the interpretation of courts. Legal preparatory works and case law are of significance in respect of, for instance, the interpretation of undefined legal concepts.

10.3 Employment relationships in Finland are governed by statutes, collective agreements and individual employment contracts. The employer and the employee cannot agree on terms less beneficial to the employee than those provided by the law, and the strong philosophical starting point of the legislation is the protection of the employee. However, usually employers expressly set out all the terms which they wish to rely on for the protection of their business in the employment contract. The employment contracts are usually made in writing.

10.4 The Finnish labour market is characterised by a high level union organisation of employers and employees. Hence, the prevalence of collectively agreed terms and conditions of employment is important. If a collective labour agreement is generally binding, ie it is considered representative by a separate board in that particular industry, it applies to the whole trade or industry concerned. Otherwise, the collective agreement only binds the organisations which have concluded the collective agreement as well as their members and affiliates.

PREPARING FOR A RESTRUCTURING PROCEDURE

10.5 Restructuring of a company refers to, for instance, selling of business operations, outsourcing, restructuring without acquisition and transfer of business. These arrangements create changes that may lead to redundancy. When considering a restructuring procedure, the employer must take into account its obligation to provide work for employees even under changing circumstances.

10.6 Before decision-making in regard to restructuring and its effects on employees, it is important to gather relevant information in respect of the impacted employees. Employment contracts, applicable collective agreements and statutory obligations and entitlements are to be taken into account when planning the restructuring exercise.

10.7 Major issues such as changes in duties and working methods, arrangement of work, transfers from one duty to another and the effects of the intended changes must be negotiated with the employees. Prior to a consultation with the employees, the employer must provide the employees or their representatives with necessary information.

Identify the employing entity

10.8 The Employment Contracts Act defines 'employer' indirectly. 'Employer' generally refers to a legal person, yet a natural person or an economic combination may also be identified as an employer. An employer may appoint a representative to supervise and direct the work. However, the employer is liable for the actions of its representative. In general, the party to the employment contract is the official employer. However, in complicated structured group corporations, the right to supervise work may be applied by a company of the group which is not formally the employer.

10.9 According to the Cooperation Act, which applies to large companies regularly employing at least 20 employees, 'employer' generally refers to a corporation, foundation or natural person engaged in financial operations.

10.10 The obligation to carry out a consultation procedure in large companies arises despite of the fact that a Finnish company as a subsidiary would be a subject to final decisions made by its parent company. The consultation obligations have to be carried out in every company in Finland before a parent company can make a decision on reduction of workforce or a business decisions that may lead to redundancies.

Example

A parent company of a group corporation domiciled abroad (or in Finland) has decided upon reductions of workforce of its Finnish subsidiary. The parent company informs the Finnish subsidiary subsequently about the decision. This contravenes Finnish law.

The consultation obligations must be fulfilled in the company officially employing the employees. The subsidiary in Finland must carry out negotiations and end its consultation procedure fulfilling the statutory consultation obligations before the parent company and the subsidiary can make a decision on redundancies and/or business decisions that may lead to redundancies. The decision on redundancies can only be made after a consultation procedure has taken place.

Collating information to plan and budget for the restructuring

Exercise

10.11 In order to minimise the risks of claims of unlawful dismissals, avoid failure to comply with the statutory requirements on restructuring exercise and to assess the costs and alternatives for redundancies, the restructuring exercise requires careful planning. Especially if the restructuring exercise involves one or more group companies, it is important to clarify which data is needed, how it can be transferred and how the exercise must be carried out in each relevant jurisdiction.

10.12 If a company located in Finland is a subsidiary and acts as the employer, it must carry out its own statutory consultation procedure according to Finnish law. Generally, data requested on employees within the EU and the EEA may be transferred to the parent company if the subsidiary and the parent company are located in different countries and if the employees of the subsidiary may be under the threat of redundancy because of a restructuring procedure. However, the decision on workforce reduction can only be made after the consultation obligations have been fulfilled and the statutory negotiations have been carried out and completed in Finland.

10.13 Collecting the relevant data and facts as well as carrying out a due diligence process are important when planning the restructuring exercise. The planning of restructuring can only begin after relevant data is available to the team which is planning and assessing the potential strategies. The collected data helps with assessing alternatives when considering restructuring which may lead to dismissals or temporary layoffs. Furthermore, the consultation obligations and the final decisions based on such data may be easier to justify as fair and reasonable.

Practical Tips

Key data which may be required initially in respect of any employee potentially impacted by a workforce reduction or restructuring exercise includes (but is not limited to):

- pointing out the employees whose work would actually diminish or cease;
- job descriptions;
- duration of reduction of work;
- employees' skills;
- length of service;
- amount of dependants;
- special protection against redundancies and dismissals;
- possibilities to redeploy or retrain;
- contractual benefits and entitlement on termination of employment;
- gender;
- place of work;
- nationality;
- age; and
- applicable collective agreement (if any).

This information is necessary for estimating the overall costs and effects of the restructuring exercise and for planning the appropriate timetable for the consultation procedure and negotiations on potential redundancies or temporary layoffs.

EMPLOYMENT STATUS

10.14 The Employment Contracts Act defines an employee as a person who undertakes to perform a work task on the employer's behalf under the employer's supervision in return for consideration. All employees are equally protected in accordance with the law and no distinction is made between blue-collar and white-collar workers.

10.15 The protection of employees derives from the employment legislation, and thus self-employed persons are not protected by these provisions. A self-employed person is free to determine his activities, working hours, place of work and he is economically independent.

10.16 A managing director of a company is generally considered as a corporate body to which the employment legislation does not apply to the same extent as to regular employees. The position is seen as a position of trust, and the rights and obligations of the managing director are primarily based on a rather detailed contract.

10.17 Furthermore, the Employment Contracts Act imposes obligations on employees. As a general obligation employees must perform their work carefully and follow the instructions given by the employer.

GENERAL PROTECTION AGAINST DISMISSAL

10.18 The concept of 'employment at will' is not recognised in Finland. If an employment contract has been made for an indefinite period, it can be terminated by an employer only on legal grounds. However, an employer must usually observe a notice period. Generally, a fixed-term employment contract can only be terminated with immediate effect in case of a fundamental breach of the employment contract.

10.19 The grounds for termination have been divided into: (1) individual; and (2) collective grounds according to the Employment Contracts Act. Furthermore, an employment contract may be terminated with immediate effect, that is, without observing notice period if the employee fundamentally breaches of the employment contract.

10.20 If an employee challenges the termination of the employment contract, the employer has the burden of proof as to the grounds of termination. Characteristically, a legally valid ground for termination must be weighty and proper and of material importance.

INDIVIDUAL GROUNDS

10.21 Termination of employment on individual grounds relates to the conduct and performance of an individual employee. The employer might have legal grounds for termination if the employee neglects or seriously breaches the work tasks that relate fundamentally to his employment. Hence, the wording of the law emphasises employee's high level of protection against terminations. A termination typically requires that a prior warning has been issued to the employee and that the employee understands the seriousness of the situation.

10.22 The Finnish employment legislation does not specify the failures in performance and the conduct of an individual employee that may be considered serious enough to justify dismissal under certain circumstances. Instead, the Employment Contracts Act provides a list of circumstances that are not regarded as proper and weighty for termination, such as the employee's illness, disability or accident, participation in an industrial action, political or religious opinions and possible resorting to available legal means of protection.

10.23 If an employee is not able to carry out his work tasks due to an illness or disability, the employer has an obligation to redeploy and to provide training before considering dismissing the employee.

COLLECTIVE GROUNDS

10.24 Termination of employment on collective grounds relates to financial and production-related reasons or restructuring of the employing company. The employer has a strict obligation to provide work for its employees even under changing circumstances. However, in certain circumstances it is acceptable to lay off employees temporarily or terminate the employment. In general, the employer can make the employee redundant if the work has diminished or been materially reduced. The employer does not have to give a personal warning to the employee before making the employee redundant on collective grounds.

10.25 The reduction of work must exist throughout the notice period and until the day of the expiry of the employment contract. Furthermore, if possible, the employer is obligated to redeploy or retrain its employees. Notice of termination should be withdrawn if the circumstances change and the grounds for termination no longer exist. In most cases, labour shortage and hiring of new employees before or immediately after the dismissal discredits any alleged collective grounds for termination.

SPECIAL PROTECTION AGAINST DISMISSAL AND RETIREMENT AGE

10.26 The Finnish employment legislation provides for special dismissal protection to certain categories of employees. The right to dismiss shop stewards, industrial safety delegates and other personnel representatives is strictly limited. Furthermore, an employer has basically no right to dismiss an employee who is on maternity, paternity or child care leave. Unless otherwise proved by the employer, a dismissal of a pregnant employee is deemed to have taken place due to the pregnancy. In addition, employees who are performing their military service are subject to special protection in regard to dismissal.

10.27 Finnish employment legislation does not provide for any additional protection to employees who have reached the earliest possible retirement age. The employee is entitled to retire between the age 63 and 68, and during that time the employment contract cannot be terminated based on employee's statutory right to pension. An employee contract terminates automatically without a notice of termination at the end of the month in which the employee has his 68th birthday unless the employer and the employee have agreed otherwise.

WORKFORCE REDUCTION

10.28 External circumstances or business decisions made by the management of a company may create a need to reduce the workforce or to rearrange the employees' work. Employees may be transferred to new tasks, and workforce may be reduced temporarily or permanently. The statutory obligations ensure that the workforce reduction procedures are carried out fairly and justifiably as ruled by the employment legislation. Employers must plan the exercise carefully and not make decisions before the statutory consultation has ended. It is important to identify and ascertain the grounds for decisions regarding workforce restructuring.

10.29 The workforce reduction procedure varies depending on the size of the employer and grounds for termination. Small companies, which regularly employ less than 20 employees, are subject to the procedural provisions set out in the Employment Contracts Act. The Cooperation Act regulates the consultation obligations that must take place in companies regularly employing at least 20 employees when the employer considers measures which may lead to redundancy or temporary layoffs.

Definition of redundancy

10.30 The financial and production-related grounds for termination are defined in the Employment Contracts Act. The employer may terminate the employment contract if the work has diminished substantially and permanently for financial or production-related reasons, or for reasons arising out of reorganisation of the employer's operations. However, the employment contract may not be terminated if the employee can be redeployed to or trained for other duties.

10.31 If the employee could be given a notice of termination on grounds of redundancy, the employer may alternatively choose to temporary lay off the employee.

10.32 In general, the employer does not have a valid ground for termination if the employer has employed a new employee for similar duties either before or after the termination. Furthermore, there are no valid grounds for termination if work has not actually reduced due to the reorganisation of work.

10.33 Workforce reduction can be attributed to, for instance, decrease in the volume of orders, incorporation of certain functions, lack of work, including demised or materially reduced volume of work. As a general rule, in order for the reduction of work to be considered permanent, it must last more than 90 days. However, if the required notice period exceeds 90 days, the lack of work must exist during the whole notice period and at the time of the expiry of the employment contract.

10.34 In case workforce is reduced by outsourcing or through other assignments of personnel, Finnish transfer of business legislation may apply. Transfer of business legislation protects employees in case their employer changes due to, for instance, a business transfer. Transfer of business is covered in more detail in the business sale, outsourcing/insourcing and offshoring section below.

Temporary layoff as an alternative to dismissal

10.35 The employer can use temporary layoffs instead of making its employees redundant, if the employees could be given a notice of termination on financial and production-related grounds. Additionally, when work has been diminished temporarily and the employer cannot reasonably provide the employees with other suitable work or training, the employer can lay off its employees temporarily.

10.36 Temporary layoffs refer to interruption of work and payment of remuneration while most of the other entitlements and obligations of the employment contract maintain enforceable. An employee with a fixed-term employment contract can be subject to a temporary layoff only if he is working as a substitute for an employee with a permanent employment contract. The employees, who have been subjects to temporary layoffs, are entitled to take alternative work for the duration of the temporary layoff.

10.37 The employer must give the employee *an explanation* of the reasons for the temporary layoff as well as the estimated extent, implementation, commencement and duration of the layoff. If temporary layoffs concern a number of employees, the explanation can be given to the employees' representative following an opportunity to be heard concerning the explanation. However, an advance explanation is not necessary if the employer is otherwise required to negotiate the temporary layoff with the employees or with their representative.

10.38 The employer must notify all relevant employees 14 days prior to the commencement of the temporary layoff. However, collective agreements may contain provisions for a longer notification period. If the notice cannot be given in person, it may be given by letter or electronically. The notice must contain the same information as the explanation. Furthermore, the notice shall be given to the representative of the temporarily laid off employees and, if at least ten employees are being laid off also to the Employment Office.

10.39 If employees are dismissed during temporary layoffs, they are entitled to receive pay during the notice period as well as other additional payments depending on the contractual provisions and collective agreements. However, the employer may generally deduct a pay due for 14 days from the pay of the notice period if the employee has been laid off using a notification period of more than 14 days. An employee is entitled to terminate the employment contract without notice during the temporary layoffs. However, the employee does not have this right during the seven days preceding the end of the temporary layoff period if the employee is aware of the end date.

10.40 Reduction of working hours may typically take place if the employer would be entitled to terminate a full-time employment contract on financial and production-related grounds. The employment contract can be changed unilaterally by the employer using the statutory notice periods. The terms of employment must not be changed until the expiry of the notice period.

Examples of redundancy situations

Company A sells groceries and it employs around 100 employees of which 25 work in the cashier team cashing products collected by customers. The Company has identified that ten members of the cashier team would no longer be needed. The Company A has no opportunity to offer work to the ten cashiers in any other position and there is no need to retrain them either. The employer carries out a six week statutory co-operation procedure and consults with the employees' representative about the situation. After fulfilling the consultation obligations and concluding the negotiations no other alternative solution to the dismissals has been reached. Company A then dismisses ten employees on financial and production-related grounds.

Company B produces handicrafts and employs 15 employees. Since its sales have been decreasing during the past year, it has decided to restructure and reduce its workforce by two employees. There is no opportunity to offer work or any other positions to the affected employees, and Company B has informed its two employees about the situation. The two employees that the employer has selected for redundancy were given the reasons for termination in person as well as a written notice of termination. Company B fulfilled its statutory obligations when the employer explained the situation to the employees as early as possible.

Strict statutory requirements (No SOSR)

10.41 The employer can terminate an employment contract only on weighty and proper grounds. This is the fundamental principle of the Finnish employment legislation. Even though the legislation does not recognise the concept of 'some other substantial reason' the legislation does not specify all situations in which an employee can be dismissed either.

DISMISSALS ON GROUNDS OF REDUNDANCY

10.42 If a company is planning to dismiss employees on grounds of redundancy, the procedure must follow statutory requirements. Dismissals must be based on economic and production related grounds or on restructuring of the company. The Finnish cooperation ombudsman supervises compliance with the Cooperation Act. In addition, it is possible to obtain a statement from the Labour Council concerning whether the Cooperation Act is applicable to the company in question.

Redundancy procedures

10.43 The Finnish employment legislation recognises two statutory procedures regarding dismissals on grounds of redundancy: *redundancy procedure in small companies* and *redundancy procedure in large companies*. The termination of an employment contract may take place only if grounds for termination are weighty enough, proper and of material importance. If an employee challenges the termination, the employer has the burden of proof as to the existence of the grounds for termination.

DEFINING THE SELECTION POOL (THE EMPLOYEES SUBJECT TO DISMISSALS)

10.44 The starting point in defining the selection pool is to focus on the employees whose work has actually diminished or ceased. Collective agreements typically contain provisions which protect employees of the relevant field. Therefore, when operating in Finland, the employer should take into consideration that the statutory legal provisions may not provide all the necessary information required for defining the selection pool.

SELECTION CRITERIA

10.45 An employer must choose which employees are to be made redundant in accordance with the selection criteria. The selection must be objective, fair and non-discriminative and it must be carried out in accordance with the applicable collective agreements and statutory provisions on non-discrimination.

10.46 According to Finnish employment legislation, employees are protected against discrimination based on, for instance, gender, age, state of health, disability, nationality, sexual orientation, religion, trade union activity, political activity etc. It has been specifically stated in case law that an employer must not act inappropriately or discriminate when selecting employees for redundancy.

10.47 In many industry sectors the collective agreements contain provisions on protection against dismissal. When dismissals are carried out on financial and production-related grounds, skilled employees and the employees who have incurred a disability whilst at work for their current employer are typically the last to be dismissed. Furthermore, length of employment and number of dependants are considered.

10.48 Even though the law or collective agreements do not generally have requirements to collect data in a matrix or in a table on employees who may be subject to redundancy, a matrix may become of importance if a dismissed employee claims the dismissal was unlawful or without proper grounds. A matrix or a table displaying methods applied may help to show that a dismissal has been carried out on lawful grounds.

10.49 Furthermore, there are certain categories of employees who cannot be dismissed as they are protected beyond the permitted selection criteria. Shop stewards and elected employees' representatives can be dismissed only if the work ceases completely and the employer is unable to arrange work that corresponds to the person's professional skill-set, or if the employer is unable to train the person for some other work.

10.50 Pregnant employees and employees on family leave enjoy special protection against dismissals. Therefore, an employee on maternity, special maternity, paternity, parental or child care leave can only be dismissed on financial and production-related grounds or because of restructuring of a company, if the whole business of the employer is closed down.

TRANSFERRING WORK TASKS FROM ONE EMPLOYEE TO ANOTHER

10.51 As a starting point, if the amount of work has not actually diminished or ceased substantially and permanently, proper grounds for redundancy do not exist. However, case law indicates that if the work tasks of a certain employee diminish, the remaining tasks are imposed on other employees due to reorganisation and the employer cannot redeploy the employee who has been left without work thereafter, grounds for redundancy may exist. However, these kinds of situations are open to interpretations and depend on the facts.

AVOIDING COMPULSORY REDUNDANCIES

10.52 See paras **10.105–10.108** and **10.186–10.190**.

ALTERNATIVE EMPLOYMENT

10.53 An employer must not make an employee redundant if he can be reasonably redeployed or retained within the company or within other sites of the same company located in a different location. The redeployment obligation continues until the expiry of the employment contract throughout the notice period. Under certain circumstances, a parent company may also be liable for redeploying the employee at risk of redundancy to its subsidiary.

10.54 The employer must offer work to an employee instead of redundancy if the employer has work that is equivalent to that defined in the employment contract of the employee in question. If such work is not available, an employee can be offered other work that is suitable on the basis of his training, professional skills or experience. However, the redeployment must be reasonable from the employer's perspective. Thus, if the employee declines the offered position, the employer is not generally obliged to arrange other positions.

10.55 The company that reduces its workforce may be liable for redeploying the employees in other companies of the same group over which it has control on the basis of ownership, agreement or some other arrangement. If the employer, or another company in the group, cannot offer work that the employee could perform without training, the employer has to determine whether it is possible to train the employee to perform new tasks. In practice, the obligation to provide training means short-term on-the-job training.

PROBATIONARY PERIODS

10.56 At the beginning of the employment, the employer and the employee may agree on a maximum of four-month probationary period. A probationary period may last exceptionally for six months if the employer provides the employee with specific, work-related training that lasts for a continuous period of over four months. If the length of a fixed-term employment contract is shorter than eight months, the probationary period may not be longer than half of the length of the employment contract.

10.57 As a starting point, there can only be one probationary period, at the beginning of the employment. In practice, this means that when an employee is redeployed or retained within the company, he cannot have a second probationary period in addition to the one he has already had at the beginning of his employment. However, in certain exceptional situations a new probationary period may be acceptable.

OBLIGATION TO RE-EMPLOY

10.58 If an employer needs a new workforce to carry out same or similar tasks of a redundant employee within nine months after the termination of the employment contract, the employer must offer the work to any former employee who is still seeking work through the employment office. However, the employer is not obliged to offer the available position to a redundant employee if the position may be filled within the company. The company must give preference to an employee who has been laid off, and such employee must be called back to work before the re-employment obligation takes effect. In addition, possible part-time employees of the company should be offered additional work before re-employing redundant employees.

10.59 The obligation to re-employ refers work of the same, or similar, nature to that performed by the employee before the dismissal. The new work can be the same as before, work that resembles the employee's previous tasks or work for which the employee can be chosen without the employer being non-discriminative against other applicants.

10.60 An employer has fulfilled its statutory obligation to re-employ when it has contacted the local employment office and enquired whether any of the employees who have been made redundant are registered as job-seekers. The employer should not make a difference between an unemployed and newly employed former employee, if the latter is also still registered as a job seeker at the local employment office.

OTHER CONSIDERATIONS

10.61 The Finnish employment legislation is detailed and complicated. Most of the provisions are mandatory, and the trade and industry specified collective agreements contain additional stipulations that must be followed.

The HR team considering different alternatives must be aware of the Finnish employment legislation and should plan the consultation procedure and any possible terminations carefully. This helps the companies to identify and avoid possible pitfalls and to carry out the dismissals without unnecessary complications.

Redundancy procedures in small and large companies

10.62 The consultation procedure in connection with redundancy varies depending on the grounds for termination, size of the employer and the number of employees affected by the restructuring. The consultation procedure provided in the Employment Contracts Act applies to employers regularly employing less than 20 employees, and the Cooperation Act applies to the consultation procedure with regard to restructuring and possible terminations on financial and production-related grounds in companies regularly employing at least 20 employees.

Redundancy procedure in small companies

10.63 The redundancy procedure in small companies is carried out in accordance with the Employment Contracts Act. The consultation obligation in companies regularly employing less than 20 employees is simple. The employer planning to dismiss an employee on financial and production-related grounds has to clarify and explain the grounds for, and alternatives to the termination as well as the available employment services in the local employment office. The consultation between the employer and the employee and/or with the person assisting the employee should take place as early as possible.

INVOLVEMENT OF EMPLOYEE REPRESENTATIVES

10.64 When the consultation procedure takes place in small companies and involves several employees, the clarification about redundancies may be given to the employee representative or, if no such representative has been chosen, jointly to the employees concerned.

REQUIREMENTS TO NOTIFY THE EMPLOYMENT OFFICE

10.65 There is no obligation to inform the employment office about the redundancies unless at least ten employees are dismissed. When the employer is obliged to inform the employment office, the notification must be made without delay and it must contain the number and the professions of the employees as well as the effective date of dismissal.

10.66 The employer is obliged to inform the employees of their statutory right to an employment plan.

Redundancy procedure in large companies

10.67 Employers regularly employing at least 20 employees in Finland must comply with the Cooperation Act. Large companies are not entitled to make their decision on redundancies, or major business decisions resulting in redundancies, before they have fulfilled their statutory consultation obligations. Even if the outcome of the consultation procedure is not unanimous, the employer can decide on redundancies only after a statutory consultation procedure is completed.

10.68 In addition to the statutory consultation obligations, collective agreements may contain certain provisions on consultation obligations which must be given preference. In certain industries, the statutory consultation obligations may be less extensive than the consultation obligations in accordance with collective agreements. If statutory provisions are a part of a collective agreement, neglecting of statutory requirements means neglecting the provisions of the collective agreement as well.

10.69 The employer must give a written five days' prior notice of the consultation when it considers dismissals or business decisions resulting in dismissals. The employer must provide employees' representatives with the necessary information in connection with *an invitation* and *a proposal for negotiations*. The required information refers to, for instance, the commencement and place of the consultation. In addition, the employer should enclose an outline of the suggested agenda of the negotiations in the invitation and the proposal for negotiations.

10.70 If the employer is considering dismissing at least ten employees, the following information must be included, in writing, in the proposal for negotiations:

(a) the grounds for intended measures;
(b) initial estimate of the number of terminations, temporary lay offs, and reduction of working hours;
(c) report of the selection criteria used to determine which employees will be subject to dismissals, lay offs and/or reductions of working hours; and
(d) time estimate for implementation of the said terminations, temporary lay offs and reductions of working hours.

10.71 If the planned measures of the employer concern a possible redundancy of at least ten employees, the employer must present a written scheme with the help of the employment office supporting the re-employment of the redundant personnel.

10.72 If the intended terminations affect less than ten employees, the employer has to present principles of action according to which the employer supports the employees' applying for other work or education during the notice period.

10.73 The purpose of the consultation is to reach a unanimous result. The parties must discuss the grounds for, the effects of, and the alternatives to the planned redundancies in order to reduce the negative effects of the proposed change. Furthermore, the possibility to redeploy and retrain the employees who are under the threat of being made redundant must be discussed.

10.74 An employer cannot decide on redundancies before the consultation obligations have been fulfilled. The consultation must always be carried on until the statutory requirements have been fulfilled.

10.75 The minimum consultation period is two weeks. If ten or more employees are considered to be dismissed or laid off for a period of over 90 days, the period is six weeks. However, the consultation period is 14 days in companies regularly employing at least 20 but fewer than 30 employees.

10.76 The consultation period begins on the date of the first actual negotiation and the time period is calculated in calendar days. Furthermore, collective labour agreements may contain additional criteria on the schedule of the consultation.

10.77 Upon request, the employer must keep minutes of the negotiations. Additionally, the employer must ensure that the dates and names of participants to the negotiations, the outcome and possible dissenting opinions are entered into the minutes. The representatives of the personnel groups and the employer must inspect and confirm the minutes by signature unless otherwise agreed.

10.78 The employer makes the decision on dismissals only after the consultation obligations have been fulfilled and the negotiations have lasted the specified minimum period set forth in the law. The employer should observe that all the procedural requirements set forth in the law are followed.

Example

Company X has 32 stores across Finland. The operations of the company are loss-making and the Company is considering making the business more effective by closing down a store in Northern Finland. The company estimates that the closing down could lead to the redundancy of four employees. The number of employees within the whole company is 143. Therefore, the reduction of workforce on the grounds of redundancy must be handled in a co-operation consultation procedure.

The Company sends an invitation and a proposal for negotiations to the representative of the employees affected by the planned restructuring five days prior to the start of the negotiations and the consultation is carried out during 14 calendar days. The employer and the employees' representative discuss the statutory matters, including possible redeployments and dismissals. During the negotiations the Company informs the employees about the possibility to be repositioned to the flagship store of the Company in Southern Finland.

One of the employees under the threat of redundancy has relevant work experience and education. He is seen as such a valuable employee that he is offered a vacancy in the flagship store. He agrees to the redeployment. One of the three remaining employees has a child and according to the collective agreement of the relevant industry, employees with dependants should be given priority. Therefore, the employee with a child is offered a position, but he refuses. The employer is not able to offer him another vacancy and he is made redundant. The third and the fourth employee do not accept a position in the flagship store either and therefore they are also dismissed on financial and production-related grounds.

INVOLVEMENT OF EMPLOYEE REPRESENTATIVES

10.79 Parties to consultation negotiations are the employer and the employees' representative(s). If there are several personnel groups, the matters can be discussed in a joint meeting of the employer and all the employees' representatives. As a general rule, senior white collar employees, white collar employees and workers form the personnel groups of a company.

10.80 If the proposed dismissals concerns less than ten employees, the consultation primarily takes place between the employee and the employer. The matter concerning the employee must be handled between the employee's representative and the employer upon the employee's request.

REQUIREMENT TO NOTIFY THE EMPLOYMENT OFFICE

10.81 The employer must inform the local employment office about a consultation procedure which may lead to terminations or temporary lay offs. A copy of the prior notice of the consultation must be delivered in writing to the employment office no later than on the first day of the consultation, unless the said information has been provided earlier in some other context.

Election of employee representatives for collective consultation purposes

10.82 Shop stewards, who usually represent the employees in consultation procedures, are elected and their position is defined in the relevant collective agreement.

10.83 Employees may elect a representative from amongst themselves, if there is no shop steward referred to in the applicable collective agreement. Elected representatives are entitled to any information that is needed to assist them in representing employees of a company.

10.84 When a majority of any group of employees within the company is not entitled to participate in the election of a shop steward, the employees belonging to such majority shall be entitled to elect a cooperation representative from within their own group.

10.85 If the employees of a particular employee group have not elected a representative, the employer may fulfil this consultation obligation together with all the employees belonging to the said employee group. In these situations, the group of employees may give a power of attorney to one or more of its members.

Sanctions

10.86 If there have not been valid grounds for terminating an employment contract, the employees are entitled to claim compensation for unlawful dismissal. The maximum compensation equals to the salary of 24 months of the dismissed employee. Nevertheless, the maximum amount to be paid to either the shop stewards who are elected on the basis of a collective agreement or, where there is no shop steward, to representatives elected amongst employees is equivalent to the salary of 30 months. Primarily, the compensation ordered by the court depends on the length of the employment, the possibility to find new employment, judgment of the procedure carried out by the employer and the potential reason for dismissal given by the employee.

10.87 The company is liable for compensating the actual damage suffered by the employee if the employer fails to comply with its re-employment obligation.

10.88 When an employer is carrying out the consultation procedure because of possible redundancies or temporary layoffs but fails to comply with the statutory requirements set out in the Cooperation Act, the employer's negligence may results in liability towards the affected employees. The maximum individual compensation is €34.140 (January 2015). The compensation is not related to the damage suffered by the employee. Even if there were valid financial and production-related grounds for the redundancies and the consultation procedure would have resulted in the same decision, but the employer has not followed the provisions of the Cooperation Act on the consultation procedure, the employer is considered to have acted negligently and can be liable for compensating the employees.

NOTICE

10.89 Notice periods of employment relationships are generally determined in accordance with the applicable collective agreement. The employer and the employee may also agree on the notice periods in the employment contract. However, the provisions of an applicable collective agreement override contractual notice periods which differ from the provisions of the collective agreement to the detriment of the employee. If the employment contract or the applicable collective agreement does not include provisions regarding the issue, the statutory notice periods varying between 14 days and six months apply.

10.90 The employer is obliged to pay the employee's regular salary during the notice period and compensate the annual holiday entitlement the employee has accrued but not taken at the time of the expiry of his employment contract.

10.91 Basically the rights and obligations of the employer and the employee continue unchanged during the notice period. The employee is obliged to work and the employer is obliged to pay the salary during the notice period. However, it is rather usual that the employee has the accrued annual holidays during the notice period.

Statutory notice period

10.92 When the employer terminates the employment contract, the statutory notice periods depend on the length of employment as follows:

10.93 *Finland*

Length of Employment	Period of Notice
Up to 1 year	2 weeks
1 to 4 years	1 month
4 to 8 years	2 months
8 to 12 years	4 months
Over 12 years	6 months

10.93 The correspondingly fixed notice periods applied when the employee terminates the employment contract are:

Length of Employment	Period of Notice
Up to 5 years	2 weeks
Over 5 years	1 month

10.94 The maximum length of the notice period is six months. Accordingly, even if the parties have agreed on a longer notice period, the notice period is considered to be six months.

10.95 If an employment is not covered by any collective agreement, the parties may agree that that there is no notice period. However, the agreed notice period applicable to a termination by the employee shall not be longer that the notice period applied by the employer.

Time off – employee's right to employment leave

10.96 An employee who has been made redundant is entitled to have some time off during the notice period for seeking a new job, attending job interviews and re-assignment coaching and/or for participating in labour market training, related practical training or on-the-job learning. The maximum amounts for such time off are:

Period of Notice	Maximum time off
Up to 1 month	5 working days
1 to 4 months	10 working days
Over 4 months	20 working days

10.97 The employee has the right to take the time off as necessary and thus, the time off does not need to consist of full working days. The employee and the employer should agree on the use of the time off. However, if an agreement is not reached, the employee usually decides on the issue.

10.98 The employee must inform the employer on the grounds for leave as early as possible and, upon the employer's request, present a reliable account on the grounds for each leave.

Garden leave (relief from the obligation to work)

10.99 An employer can instruct its employee who has been made redundant not to come to work during the notice period. In that case, the employer pays the salary of such employee during the notice period either in parts or in advance as a one-off settlement.

10.100 The employer and the employee may agree that, irrespective of the relief from the obligation to work, the employee is responsible for answering the employer's questions relating to the work and that, if necessary, the employer is entitled to call the employee back to work.

10.101 Typically, the purpose of freeing an employee from the obligation to work is to prevent the employee from receiving further information about the employer's operations before possibly starting to work for a competitor.

Pay in lieu of notice

10.102 An employer may agree on the termination of the employment contract by making a payment to the employee instead of following the notice period. Such payment is actually a compensation that corresponds to the salary and the benefits the employee would have received if he had worked normally during the notice period. Pay in lieu of notice should be explicitly agreed upon between the employer and the employee.

Practical Tip:

When agreeing on pay in lieu of notice, the parties should state in writing that the employment contract will terminate with immediate effect and the payment will be made in lieu of notice. If the employer does not expressly notify the employee of the effect of the payment, the employment contract continues as normal until the expiry of the notice period irrespective of whether the employer has made the payment.

NOTICE PERIOD COMPARISON TABLE

Type of Notice Period	Effective Date of Termination	Benefits	Disadvantages
Employee working during the notice period	The expiry of the notice period	The employer benefits from the work the employee performs and gets the salary's worth.	The employee continues to receive potentially confidential company information. The employee's presence may delay and hinder the reorganisation of tasks at the workplace.
Garden leave *(relief from the obligation to work)*	The expiry of the notice period	The employee no longer has access to the company information and does not work for a competitor of the employer either. The employer can begin to reorganise the remaining work.	The employer has the obligation to pay the salary and other statutory benefits without benefiting from the work contribution of the employee.
Pay in lieu of notice	Agreed between the parties	The employment relationship terminates immediately and the employee is no longer at the service of the employer. The employer is not liable for paying employment benefits.	The employee may start working for a competitor immediately after the expiry of the employment contract.

REDUNDANCY PAYMENT

10.103 The employer is not obliged by law to pay any termination or severance compensation relating to legal termination of employment contracts.

Voluntary redundancy payments

10.104 In some cases employers establish voluntary redundancy packages which they offer to the employees who are under the threat of being made redundant. The redundancy package may be offered to all personnel or only to certain groups of personnel and it can contain, for example, premature retirement packages or additional training which improves the labour market prospects of the employees. An agreement regarding a redundancy payment may be made on the employee's initiative as well. The additional compensations do not, however, affect the employer's liability for a wrongful termination unless the employee concerned expressly waives his possible claims relating to the issue.

10.105 The employer may offer a redundancy package before, during or after a consultation procedure. The personnel and the employee representatives should be kept informed about the availability of the redundancy packages. It is essential that the redundancy packages offered before or during the consultation procedure are not presented to specific employees, since such conduct could contradict the objectives of the consultation procedure.

10.106 When an employee resigns voluntarily and receives a redundancy package the notice period is usually shorter than it would have been if the employer had made the employee redundant. Even if the severance compensation may be more expensive than dismissals, voluntary arrangements with the employees may avoid conducting consultations and redundancies. In addition, the business operations of the company may remain more efficient, and severance discussions with the employees in connection with unavoidable redundancies may improve the public image of the company.

Practical Tip

An employer should not actually *offer* voluntary redundancy packages to its employees. The better course of action would be encouraging the employees to discuss about termination arrangements themselves. This way the employer has the opportunity to decide itself whether it enters into an agreement with a certain employee and ensure that the key employees do not leave the service of the employer.

Taxation of redundancy payments

10.107 As a general rule, voluntary redundancy payments are subject to payroll tax. In respect of the employer's duty to make social security payments for the redundancy payment, the determining factor is whether the payment is considered to replace the employee's salary for the notice period.

Post-termination restrictive covenants

10.108 According to the Employment Contracts Act, an employer and an employee may agree that the employee refrains from conducting activities which compete with the employer after the expiry of the employment contract. Such prohibition has to be expressly agreed in the employment contract or in a separate agreement.

10.109 However, the law sets out certain criteria for the circumstances where a non-competition agreement can be validly concluded. Accordingly, the parties to an employment contract may agree on non-competition provided that the grounds for such restriction are based on the operations of the employer or on a particularly weighty reason relating to the employment relationship. When assessing the validity of the grounds, the nature of the employer's operations, the need to protect its business or trade secrets, the possible special training provided to the employee as well as the employee's status and duties shall be taken into consideration. A non-competition agreement which has been concluded without a particularly weighty reason is considered invalid.

10.110 Typically, a non-competition agreement is justified if the employee's duties relate to product development, research or other similar activity and the employee has access to information and know-how that is not in the public domain. Non-competition agreements are made for example in the following situations:

- sales representation, if the clientele is strongly committed to the company through a particular employee;
- protection of technical solutions developed in the company;
- protection of the confidentiality of the employer's customer agreements; and
- protection of the business and trade secrets of the employer's clients.

10.111 The non-competition agreement should clearly stipulate the kind of work the employee is not allowed to perform during the non-competition period. In certain situations, work for a competitor can also be prohibited in general, especially when there is a risk that trade secrets are revealed. The geographical area of the non-competition obligation should also be defined in order to avoid ambiguity between the parties.

10.112 In addition, it is possible to specify the competitors for whom the employee may not work and the customers to whom the employee may not, either personally or indirectly through a company, offer services or products during the validity of the non-competition agreement. Furthermore, a non-solicitation agreement prohibiting the solicitation of employees of the employer to another company established or represented by the employee may also be validly concluded.

10.113 The employee is not bound by the non-competition obligation if the employment relationship is terminated by the employer. In practice, this is the case in redundancy situations.

10.114 A non-competition agreement is in force for a maximum period of six months. The restricted period is calculated from the date of expiry of employment.

10.115 If the employee receives fair compensation, the non-competition obligation may be extended to one year. The amount of the compensation is not defined by law. However, compensating the employee with approximately 30–50% of his monthly salary for the restricted period is usually considered reasonable. The compensation amount is always determined on a case-by-case basis. It may also be agreed that the employee's earnings from another employer during the restricted period are reduced from the agreed compensation.

10.116 A violation of a non-competition obligation may result in an obligation to pay damages. Alternatively, the parties may have agreed on a contractual penalty. According to the Employment Contracts Act, the contractual penalty shall not exceed the employee's salary for the six months preceding the termination of his employment relationship.

10.117 The restrictions on the duration of a non-competition obligation and the amount of contractual penalty do not apply to employees who are considered to be engaged in the management of the business or to have an independent status comparable to director positions.

Example

The company X Technologies employs several engineers and a technical and commercial director. In addition, X Technologies has a managing director. The employment contracts of every employee include a non-competition clause in case of the termination of the employment relationship. However, the statutory restrictions relating to non-competition obligations do not apply to the employment contract of the technical and commercial director and thus, his non-competition obligation may be extended to over six months. The managing director is, due to his position, excluded from the applicability of restrictions deriving from the Employment Contracts Act.

BUSINESS SALE, OUTSOURCING/INSOURCING AND OFFSHORING

10.118 Employment issues relating to transfer of business are primarily governed by the Employment Contracts Act and the Cooperation Act.

The Acts implement the Council Directive 2001/23/EC on acquired rights of employees. They are interpreted in line with the judgments of the ECJ concerning the interpretation of the Directive. For the purposes of this section, 'transfer of business legislation' refers to national regulation concerning the protection of employment in the event work force is transferred from one employer to another in connection with a business transfer.

10.119 In general, 'transfer of business' refers to an assignment of an enterprise, business, corporate body, foundation or an operative part thereof to another employer. The assignment is considered as a transfer of business if the business or part thereof to be transferred, irrespective of whether it is a central or ancillary activity, remains the same or similar after the transfer.

10.120 All the employees engaged in the business concerned at the time of the transfer are automatically transferred to the acquirer. Correspondingly, the acquirer has an obligation to take over all such employees. The acquirer then has the same rights and obligations towards the transferred employees as the previous employer has had.

Business sale

10.121 The basic requirement for a transaction or arrangement to constitute a transfer of business is that the object of the transfer is an economic entity. 'Economic entity' refers to an organised grouping of resources which has the objective of pursuing an economic activity. The economic entity should retain these characteristics after the transfer. Whether the object of the transfer concerned is only a supporting function is not relevant as long as it can be considered as an economic entity as described above.

10.122 When evaluating whether a transaction constitutes a transfer of business, the following criteria are commonly considered. It should be noted that the transaction is reviewed as a whole and none of the below criteria is determining on its own:

- the nature of the business concerned;
- whether any tangible assets have been transferred;
- whether any intangible rights or assets have been transferred;
- whether the acquirer has recruited the larger part of the seller's personnel engaged in the business;
- whether the taking over of the business is based on a contract between the two companies;
- whether customers have been transferred;
- how similar the business operations are before and after the transaction; and
- for how long the business operations have been interrupted in connection with the transaction.

10.123 If a transaction constitutes a transfer of business within the meaning of employment legislation, all the employees engaged in the business concerned at the time of the transfer are automatically transferred to the acquirer of the business. New employment contracts or other forms of agreement by the transferring employees are not required. Correspondingly, the acquirer is obliged by law to take over all transferring employees.

10.124 Possible receivables of the transferring employees do not become due at the transfer of business, but the receivables transfer to the acquirer as the employment contracts of the transferring employees continue uninterrupted.

Outsourcing/insourcing

10.125 Outsourcing of a company's operations to an outside service provider or insourcing of certain services can be regarded as a transfer of business as defined in the Employment Contracts Act, if the above mentioned criteria are met. In addition, some collective agreements include provisions on outsourcing.

10.126 In principle, outsourcing or insourcing constitutes a transfer of business, if the transferring operation is considered an economic entity of its own. Typically companies outsource their support functions rather than actual production activities. Nevertheless, either situation may constitute a transfer of business. On the other hand, if a material amount of the assets or employees performing the outsourced service do not transfer, the transfer is unlikely to be considered as a transfer of business.

Effect of transfer of business legislation

Automatic transfer and protection of employment

10.127 Which employees transfer along with the acquired business depends on which of the employees are at the service of the business at the time of the transfer. The rule is based on mandatory law and thus, the seller and the acquirer cannot agree on the transferring employees. The employees serving the acquired business transfer with the business even if the acquirer would prefer to refuse to employ them or even if the acquirer is not aware of the existence of such employees. The seller's and the acquirer's wishes in relation to the transferring employees have no relevance.

10.128 Consequently, it is essential that the seller and the acquirer first determine the extent of business to be transferred. Which employees transfer can be determined only after that.

10.129 Whether an employee is considered to be at the service of a certain business is determined on the basis of whether the employee:

(a) has been assigned to work for the business concerned on other than a temporary basis; or
(b) performs more than 50 % of his work for the transferring business.

10.130 Both rules feature in Finnish case law. However, the first one carries more weight in the practice of the ECJ and therefore, it should be given priority.

10.131 The group of the transferring employees is determined at the time of the transfer. Consequently, an employee who has been transferred to another unit from the transferring business shortly before the transfer does not transfer to the acquirer. Similarly, an employee who has been assigned to the transferring business prior to the business transfer, transfers to the acquirer along with the business. Any prior reorganisation should, however, be based on valid business reasons. The purpose of the potential assignments must not be circumvention of the law.

10.132 Only employees with existing and valid employment contracts are transferred. Therefore, the transfer does not concern employees whose employment contracts expire before the transfer. If an employee who has resigned so that his employment contract expires before the transfer, does not transfer to the acquirer. If the notice period is still running at the time of the transfer, the employee transfers to the acquirer.

Practical Tip

Given the strict data protection regulation in Finland, personal information concerning the transferring employees and their employment terms should not be disclosed to the acquirer unless the transfer of business is very likely to take place. In respect of data protection of the employees, the general rule is that the acquirer will have the right to handle personal data of the transferring employees only from the moment it needs such information as a future employer of the employees.

Objection to the transfer

10.133 The transfer of business legislation does not grant the employees an option to validly object to their transfer. Instead, a transferring employee has a special right to terminate his employment contract prior to the transfer so that he does not enter the acquirer's service. Therefore, the seller cannot warrant to the acquirer that certain individuals transfer with the business.

Protection from dismissal

10.134 Terminations of employment contracts must not be caused by the transfer of business. The employees do not have any special protection against dismissal in connection with a transfer of business other than a claim for unfair dismissal.

Protection of terms and conditions of employment

10.135 As a general rule, the terms and conditions of employment of the transferring employees remain the same after the transfer. Consequently, the transferred employees do not have to sign new employment contracts or accept material changes to the terms and conditions of their employment contracts.

10.136 In general, the collective agreement(s) applicable to the employment contracts of the transferring employees binds the acquirer until the expiry of such collective agreement(s).

Information and consultation under the transfer of business legislation

10.137 As mentioned in above, the Cooperation Act is applied to employers regularly employing at least 20 persons. The Act regulates the information and consultation in connection with a transfer of business. Generally, only the employees working in Finland are taken into account for the purpose of the calculation.

10.138 The limit of 20 employees is determined separately for the entities of the seller and the acquirer. The number of actual transferred employees has no impact on the consultation procedure.

Smaller companies have a general duty to inform their employees in accordance with the Employment Contracts Act.

10.139 The personnel consultation procedure under the Cooperation Act in connection with a transfer of business is divided into two parts:

- informing the personnel prior to the transfer; and
- consulting with the personnel after the transfer.

DUTY TO INFORM

10.140 The acquirer and the seller have a joint obligation to inform the concerned employees or their representatives on issues relating to the transfer of business. According to the Cooperation Act, the purchaser and the seller must inform the affected personnel on

- the time or planned time of the transfer;
- the grounds for the transfer;

- the legal, financial and social consequences of the transfer to the employees; and
- the planned measures concerning the personnel.

10.141 The information should be provided in good time before the transaction. In practice, this means that the information must be given before the transfer of business has any effect on the personnel. The information is typically issued between the signing and the closing of the transaction.

DUTY TO CONSULT

10.142 Within one week after the execution of the transaction, the acquirer must organise a cooperation meeting with the transferred personnel or their representatives. The purpose of the meeting is to make sure the transferred employees have been provided with the necessary information, give the employees the opportunity to present specific questions on the transaction as well as to provide answers to these questions.

10.143 Additionally, the new employer should determine whether the transfer has such effects (eg redundancies) on the personnel that should be subject to discussion in full-scale cooperative consultations. If there are no such effects, the employer has no further transfer-related cooperative consultation obligations towards the personnel.

EUROPEAN WORKS COUNCILS

10.144 In Finland, the Directive 2009/38/EC regarding the establishment of a European Works Council has been implemented into the Act on Cooperation within Finnish and Community-wide Groups of Undertakings. The consultation obligations of the act apply to undertakings with at least 1,000 employees, including at least 150 employees in two or more member states.

10.145 In case a multi-jurisdictional restructuring affects the community-wide group of undertakings or at least two units of the group, and the concerned group has established a European Works Council, the Council should be informed and consulted prior to the planned restructuring.

Sanctions

Unfair dismissal

10.146 Transfer of business does not provide the employer any additional grounds for terminating employment contracts. Therefore, employment contracts can be terminated only if there is a legitimate individual or collective ground for termination. Dismissals should not have any connection to the transfer of business.

10.147 A dismissal due to a transfer of business is ineffective. However, the dismissal cannot be reversed. If an employee is dismissed without a valid individual or collective ground, the employer may become liable for paying damages due to unfair dismissal.

10.148 The acquirer is obliged to receive all the transferring employees. Furthermore, it is not allowed to materially change the terms of employment of the transferring employees. If the acquirer fails to fulfil these obligations, it will face liability for potential claims raised by the employees.

Failure to inform and consult

10.149 Should the employer or its representative fail to comply with its obligation to inform and consult with the personnel, it may also be subject to a fine. The fine could be imposed, for example, for giving inaccurate information to the personnel.

10.150 If as a result of inaccurate information given by the employer the employee suffers a loss, the employee can claim damages from the employer. The employer may, for instance, have failed to inform the transferring personnel of potential economic risks related to the transfer.

Application of the transfer of business legislation to cross-border transactions/offshoring

10.151 Offshoring and cross-border transactions may take place in various different forms. Finnish case law regarding offshoring is scarce, but as a general rule, national regulation of transfer of business is considered to have the same scope as the Council Directive on acquired rights of employees.

10.152 The transfer of business legislation applies primarily to employees who are employed by a Finnish employer and who are protected by Finnish employment regulation. Consequently, employees transferring to Finland due to a transfer of business are generally protected by the Finnish employment legislation when they are relocated to Finland. Application of the Finnish transfer of business legislation in cross-border transactions is less relevant in situations where the transfer is made within the EU, as the minimum standards prescribed by the Council Directive generally apply in all member states. In respect of third countries, Finnish legislation may apply if the business operations in the country of destination are clearly controlled by the (Finnish) seller. However, it is unusual for a relevant group of personnel to transfer in its entirety and thus, the applicability of Finnish transfer of business legislation in respect of transfers to third countries is open to interpretation.

WORKFORCE REDUCTION IN CONNECTION WITH SHARE SALE OR SHARE PURCHASE

10.153 The transfer of business legislation does not apply to sale of shares. Usually in share sales and purchases, the employer does not change and thus, the criteria for transfer of business are not met. However, other potential arrangements in connection with a share sale may affect this position.

CHANGING EMPLOYMENT TERMS AND CONDITIONS

10.154 The parties to an employment contract are bound by the conditions of the contract. Primarily, all amendments require the mutual consent of both parties. However, the terms and conditions of an employment contract may change in other ways during the course of the employment. The terms may alter due to a change in the applicable collective agreement or as a result of an established practice between the employer and the employee. The changing of conditions of an employment contract is not expressly regulated by law.

10.155 If an employment contract contains very specific terms and conditions, it could restrict the employers right to decide on the work arrangements. Therefore, employment contracts are often drafted in more general wording.

10.156 Changes in the conditions for the employment contract usually mean a significant change for the employee. Therefore, in companies subject to the Cooperation Act, material terms of employment may usually only be changed following a negotiation procedure.

Mutually agreed changes

10.157 An employer and an employee may, within the limits of mandatory employment legislation, agree on changing the conditions of the employment contract.

10.158 The parties to an employment contract are free to terminate the previous employment contract and agree on a new one regarding, eg different work assignments. The agreement has to be made with free will and with common accord. Some form of consideration as a result of the change is possible, but not obligatory under Finnish law.

Unilateral changes

10.159 According to Finnish case law, material conditions of employment contracts cannot be changed unilaterally by either of the parties without a legitimate reason. For example, the employer may not materially amend the work description of an employee without agreeing on the change with the employee.

10.160 An employer may make unilateral changes to employment contracts only if there would otherwise be a valid ground for dismissal. In addition, the changes can be adopted only after a transition period equivalent to the length of the applicable notice period. In practice, if the employer has the right to amend the employment contract unilaterally, new conditions are communicated to the employee and the previous contract terminates when the new conditions enter into force after the expiry of the notice period.

10.161 Minor changes are permitted under the employer's right to manage work.

DISMISSING AND RE-ENGAGING EMPLOYEES ON NEW TERMS

10.162 Re-engaging an employee on new terms is possible if the employer has a legitimate ground for dismissal as described above.

USING TEMPORARY STAFF

10.163 An employer might consider using temporary staff during a restructuring phase. Temporary workforce can be recruited directly or by using workers via an employment agency.

Agency workers

10.164 Use of agency workers is often a good way for an employer to recruit temporary staff, since certain standard employer obligations do not apply to use of agency workers. The employment agency carries most of the obligations and liabilities towards the agency worker.

10.165 Agency workers should be treated in the same way as regular employees. The employer should apply the same rules in respect of, for instance, working hours, breaks, holidays and pay. Furthermore, the employer should also inform the agency workers about any vacant positions arising in the company.

10.166 During restructuring phases, employers should consider carefully whether to use agency workers. If a company is considering dismissals or temporary lay offs of its permanent personnel, use of outside temporary workforce could prove problematic. Similarly, in situations where employees have been made redundant during the past nine months, the employer should pay attention to its potential obligation to re-employ its former employees before recruiting agency workers. See at paras **10.157–10.159**.

10.167 A company that regularly employs at least 20 persons has certain consultation obligations applying to the use of agency workers. According to the Cooperation Act, the employer should address the principles of using agency workers in a consultation negotiation. In addition, the employer should provide information on the use of agency workers to the representatives of the employees whom the agency work affects. Companies regularly employing at least 30 persons have an extended consultation obligation regarding the use of agency work.

Fixed-term contracts

10.168 Fixed-term employment is allowed only in situations where the employer has a justified reason to attach a fixed term to an employment contract. Usually, justified reasons relate to seasonal work, a certain project the employer carries out or to other temporary need for additional personnel. Employment contracts made for a fixed term on the employer's initiative without a justified reason are viewed as being in force indefinitely.

10.169 Fixed-term employment contracts terminate automatically without giving notice at the end of the agreed period. As a general rule, fixed-term employment contracts cannot be terminated earlier. However, employment contracts which are made for a fixed term of five years or more maybe terminated after the first five years on the same grounds as employment contracts made for an indefinite period.

10.170 Employers are not allowed to apply less favourable employment terms to fixed-term employment relationships than those applicable to other employment relationships merely based on the duration of the employment contract.

Renewal of fixed-term contracts

10.171 The employer may renew the employment contract of a fixed-term employee. However, it is prohibited to use consecutive fixed-term contracts when the amount or total duration of fixed-term contracts or the totality of such employment contracts indicates that the employer has a permanent need for additional staff.

EMPLOYMENT CLAIMS

10.172 Employment claims between employer and employee are usually heard in a general court of first instance. The procedure is similar to regular dispute resolution. The employment claim is filed with the competent district court, which then initiates the written proceedings. If the parties do not reach a settlement, the dispute proceeds to an verbal hearing.

10.173 In Finland, legal disputes arising out of the content or interpretation of collective agreements are heard by the Labour Court.

UNFAIR DISMISSAL

10.174 If the grounds for the termination are legitimate, the employer has no general obligation to pay a dismissed employee any compensation or severance.

10.175 However, when an employee has been dismissed without a legitimate reason, the court may make an order for payment of compensation for a wrongful dismissal. A court does not have the power to order an employer to reinstate or re-engage an employee.

Remedies

10.176 The maximum compensation for unfair dismissal is equal to 24 months' salary of the dismissed employee. Typically the compensation ordered would range from six to ten months' salary or wages. The amount of compensation ordered by the court depends primarily on the length of service of the dismissed employee, his chances of finding new employment and whether the employee has been given a reason for the dismissal.

10.177 In addition to the awarded compensation for unfair dismissal, the employer may have to pay the employee, for instance, damages for loss of income due to disregarding the notice period, damages for discrimination and damages due to disregarding its consultation obligations.

10.178 If the employer fails to comply with its re-employment obligation at a later stage, the company is liable for compensating for the actual damage suffered by the employee due to its failure.

10.179 The general civil procedure rules prescribe that the losing party in court shall indemnify the winning party's legal costs in full. However, if an employer wins a case against a previous employee, the loosing employee's obligation to compensate the company's legal costs is usually reduced.

DISCRIMINATION

10.180 An employer has an obligation to treat its employees equally. This means that an employer should not put an employee in a less favourable position than another on the basis of, for instance, gender, age or ethnic origin unless there is a legitimate reason to do so. When an employer is making decisions on redundancies, the decision should be based only on the characteristics of the work itself. In addition, an employer has a general statutory obligation to promote equality between men and women in working life.

Remedies

10.181 An employer may become liable for paying damages to an employee for economic losses caused by discrimination based on age, disability, nationality, sexual orientation etc. In addition, an employee may be entitled to damages for personal suffering even if the discrimination has not caused actual economic loss. The compensation is determined by court. Furthermore, an employer or its management may be fined or imprisoned for up to six months for work discrimination.

10.182 If an employee has been discriminated based on gender, the employee is entitled to compensation in accordance with the act on equality between men and women. The amount of compensation is determined on the facts of each case and depending on the extent of the violation. The court takes into account, issues such as severity, intention and frequency of the discriminating acts.

10.183 The above mentioned compensations do not prevent the employee from demanding and receiving damages based on general employment and tort law. A discrimination claim must be made within two years of the discriminating act.

MUTUALLY-AGREED TERMINATION

10.184 An employer and an employee may agree on the termination of the employment contract. In this case, the requirement for giving notice does not apply and the parties may agree on immediate termination of the employment relationship. In general, the employee cannot dispute a mutually agreed termination and the employer is free of consultation obligations.

Settlement agreements

10.185 The purpose of the settlement agreement is to settle the effects of the termination of the employment relationship. The most important aspect of the settlement agreement for the employer is to prevent the employee from bringing any claims against the employer. If some conditions of the termination are left open, it should be stated in the settlement agreement. Typically, a settlement agreement contains provisions on the period of notice, the remaining salary and benefits, non-competition and a potential severance due to the termination.

10.186 The content of the offered settlement agreement impacts on the employee's willingness to agree on the termination. For example, voluntary compensation and the timing of the termination may influence the employee's decision. It is important to determine whether the voluntary severance payment is classed as a golden handshake or compensation for damages as such affects, among others, the entitlement to unemployment benefits for the employee.

10.187 It is important to note that employees may not validly give up certain statutory rights whilst their employment contracts are in force. For example, the parties may not agree that the employee waives his right to the remaining salary. In order to ensure the validity of the settlement agreement, such agreement is usually concluded after the expiry of the employment relationship.

10.188 Mutually-agreed termination does not necessarily mean that the parties make an agreement on the termination. In some cases the employer offers certain benefits to the employee who then resigns on certain conditions, hence, the termination is in practice caused by the resignation of the employee.

Chapter 11

Workforce Restructuring in France

Karine Clolus-Dupont and Daphné Rouchaud
Lexington Avocats, Paris

INTRODUCTION

11.1 This chapter focuses on the consequences that a restructuring will have on employees pursuant to French law. French law has a strong civil tradition. In many respects, however, the rules of employment law constitute departures from the established principles of private law. A great many legal and regulatory provisions in employment law embody public policy in a way that precludes employees' rights of being waived, even if the parties agree to do so.

11.2 With the primary intent of protecting workers, French employment law is not known for its flexibility or its simplicity. Employment law with respect to restructurings provides a good illustration of the complexity and the variety of the procedures that must be followed. Company restructurings are generally motivated by economic or financial considerations have a huge bearing on issues of employment. Whenever they are frozen or cancelled, especially if the provisions about consulting the employees' representatives have not been observed, employment law becomes the main factor in hindering the restructuring.

11.3 French companies going into a restructuring will also have to consider the relevant provisions of collective agreements, both industry-wide and company-specific as under French employment law the parties in labour relations have the option to set standards that constitute the 'collective status' of the employees.

11.4 Naturally, the provisions of employment contracts are also reviewed when a company is restructured. In theory, employers and employees are free to adjust the terms of their relationship and to define the scope of their reciprocal obligations. However, if the provisions of law, or industry or company collective agreements turn out to be more favourable to the employee, then those are automatically substituted for what is in the employment contract. It is also advisable to consult the rulings of the *Cour de Cassation*, which regularly hands out decisions in this area of employment law.

11.5 Where redundancies are involved we will consider below which at how redundancies can be justified for economic reasons, at the procedures applicable and at the highly specific rules applicable to redundancies, such as reassignment, criteria for order of layoffs, information given to employees, etc.

11.6 Without necessarily leading to redundancies, restructurings often directly affect the terms of employment contracts currently in force. Should the legal status of the employer change, the laws in France allow employees to preserve the terms of their employment contracts. Employees' collective status may also be temporarily preserved. Moreover, specific rules also come into play when changes in an employment contract are planned.

What follows here will not touch on the effects on employment of restructurings carried out as part of an insolvency process. Such restructurings are covered by very particular rules of procedure.

GATHERING ESSENTIAL INFORMATION

11.7 Before going into a restructuring that will somehow impact, the employees working in a restructured entity, a certain amount of information needs to be gathered in order to: (i) identify the appropriate procedure; and (ii) put numbers on the costs involved.

11.8 To that end, both individual and collective data generally need to be assembled.

Individual information

- Hiring date and time in service, if different
- Type of contract
- Job category/classification
- Trial period in progress
- Notification period
- Age
- Compulsory training obtained
- Existence of a non-compete clause
- Fixed salary or wage
- Additional compensation
- Benefits in kind (housing, vehicle, etc)
- Work schedule (full-time, part time, hours/days per week/month/year, etc)
- Reimbursed expenses
- Accrued holidays
- Existence of a transfer clause
- Family situation
- Specific elements impacting the contract (level of training, parental leave, workplace accidents or occupational illness, whether jobholder is also a corporate officer, etc)
- Specific protections (elected employee representative, union representative, maternity leave, disability etc)

Collective information usually assembled

- Applicable collective agreement
- Company-specific collective agreements in force
- Description of implied terms and common practices, non-standard agreements or non-contractual arrangements found at the company
- Incentive and/or profit-sharing agreement
- Healthcare cost agreements and disability insurance
- Configuration of bodies that represent employees, etc.

EMPLOYEES PROTECTED

11.9 The French Labour Code protects certain employees whenever their personal or work-related situation calls for it. Thus, specific provisions protect the following from dismissal:

- employees who are pregnant;
- anyone with a work-related injury or an occupational illness while their employment contract has been suspended;
- an employee who is suing in a gender-parity case;

- employees who have been discriminated against (termination cannot be based on one's origin, gender, customs, sexual orientation, age, family situation, belonging or not to an ethnic group, nation or race, political opinions, religion, etc);
- an employee on strike; and
- an employee who has testified to the existence of sexual harassment which he or she experienced or refused to experience.

11.10 Furthermore, elected employee representatives and union delegates named by the unions represented in the company also receive special protection from dismissal, be it either for economic or for personal reasons. This protection is all the greater in that their employment contract cannot be terminated unless the plan to dismiss them has been submitted to the works council. Further, the inspection du travail (a French governmental unit concerned with labour matters, part of a broader agency with the French acronym DIRECCTE) must specifically examine the case of each protected worker, particularly the reason given by the employer to justify the planned dismissal, in order to approve the dismissal or not. Failing such approval, the employer is strictly forbidden from dismissing the employee.

11.11 This specific protection with respect to dismissals is also extended to candidates in employee elections, former employee representative whose term of office expired less than six months ago, etc. Any dismissal carried out without the authorisation of the DIRECCTE will allow the employee to either disregard his or her termination as null and void, or seek reinstatement and, in any event, to receive damages for the harm suffered.

11.12 These protections and special procedures are combined with the specific procedure applying to economic dismissals (see below). In situations where the employer's legal status has changed, when the transfers of employment contracts involve public policy, there are situations with respect to protected employees where no steps can be taken without governmental authorisation, as in the case of a partial transfer of assets entailing the transfer of some of the company's employment contracts to another legal entity.

GROUNDS FOR REDUNDANCY

11.13 The French Labour Code defines a redundancy (economic layoff) as dismissal for a reason or reasons unrelated to the employee as an individual and resulting in the elimination or transformation of a job or in the amendment, to which the employee does not agree, of an essential element of his or her employment contract, primarily as a consequence of economic difficulties or technological changes.

11.14 These points are not limited in number, and case law has added to the two aforementioned grounds (economic difficulties and technological changes) two other economic reasons for layoffs: reorganisation necessary for the company to remain competitive and the cessation of operations.

11.15 The grounds for redundancy have by definition nothing to do with the employee's performance. Where there are both personal and economic grounds for dismissal, the employer is obliged to choose between the two and to use:

- the cause that arose earlier, if the two causes are not connected; or
- the determining cause for the dismissal, if the personal and the economic are connected.

Economic difficulties

11.16 Neither the French Labour Code nor French jurisprudence has ever defined the notion of 'economic difficulties' each situation has to be reviewed case by case. The courts have nonetheless laid out a certain number of requirements that enable us to get an idea of this notion. It requires above all that the economic difficulties be real, significant and ongoing and that they have arisen after the employee(s) affected by the layoff was (were) hired. In practice, economic difficulties exist in the event of bankruptcy, cessation of payments, serious and not temporary cash flow problems, substantial, heavy losses of revenue persisting over several accounting periods, etc.

11.17 Conversely, simply wanting to generally lower expenses in order to rationalise the company's operating costs does not constitute economic difficulty. A one-time drop in revenues and profits that does not hamper business activity, the loss of a sales contract or a reduction or slowdown in sales are not enough to constitute economic difficulties. Generally speaking, any attempt to save money at the expense of job protection will be rejected.

11.18 Also, an economic justification will not be granted if the economic difficulties were caused by the employer's behaviour. Mismanagement, fraud or reckless decisions on the part of the employer will as a rule prevent the employer from citing economic difficulties that are of its own making. Such cases are, however, rarely encountered.

The date and severity of economic difficulties

11.19 Economic difficulties are deemed to exist as of the date that layoffs are announced. In the event of subsequent disputes, the employee may not use an improvement in the company's financial health after his or her layoff as an argument against the layoff.

11.20 If the company affected by economic difficulties is not part of a group of companies, the practice is to assess the difficulties at the company level, including all its facilities and locations and to do so even if only one location is experiencing difficulties. It is the situation of the company, the single legal entity that is considered. The difficulties of just one site, therefore, cannot constitute valid grounds for layoff unless they have a substantial and lasting impact on the financial health of the company (in that case, the employer will be able to take the position of 'reorganisation necessary to remain competitive'.

11.21 If the company is part of a national or international consolidated group, the difficulties are evaluated over the group's scope of businesses in that industry. The difficulties of a French subsidiary can therefore not suffice to justify a redundancy within that subsidiary if the business segment of the group it belongs to is not also facing serious, lasting difficulties. Conversely, and paradoxically, the fact that the group's businesses in that sector may be having real economic difficulties could justify layoffs at the French subsidiary even though it has been quite profitable.

Technological changes

11.22 These are grounds mentioned specifically in the Labour Code. The criterion of technological changes does not require that the company's competitiveness be threatened or that it be experiencing particular economic difficulties.

Thus, courts will accept grounds of technological changes as real if new computer hardware or new technologies have been adopted by the company. On the other hand, a mere change of computer model or of software is naturally not going to justify redundancies.

Reorganising the company to maintain its competitiveness

11.23 Reorganisation of the company to maintain competitiveness is a ground for layoffs that grew from case law. This ground must be proven by the necessity of preserving the competitiveness of the company in question. If the latter belongs to a consolidated group, it will be necessary to show the necessity of preserving the competitiveness of the business segment of the group of which the company is a part.

11.24 Though economic difficulties often go along with the necessity of reorganising the company to maintain its competitiveness, they are not required in order to justify layoffs on this basis. The preservation of competitiveness in fact allows the employer to prevent and anticipate risks and, very possibly, economic difficulties. Consequently, while the economic reason is generally evaluated as of the date that layoffs are announced, proving it in this particular case may be buttressed by, for example, subsequent changes in the market in which the company competes.

11.25 Thus an employer can use these grounds to carry out layoffs to deal with a new market pattern that will inescapably entail lower prices for its products and a corresponding sharp drop in revenues that cannot be made up for. An increase in raw materials prices with no prospect for near or medium term improvement and which makes it impossible for the firm to finance capital spending crucial to its continuation in business could justify the reorganisation.

11.26 In practice, these grounds for layoffs allow an employer to anticipate foreseeable economic difficulties and to take advantage of a still sound situation to reorganise its business under better conditions. It is thus able to preserve the interests of its business, which will then be able to continue when the already anticipated difficulties beset the market in which it competes.

11.27 In the event of litigation, the judge will verify that the reorganisation in question was indeed necessary to preserve the company's competitiveness. The courts, however, do not have the power to evaluate the appropriateness of the management decision made by the employer. Thus, once the real necessity of layoffs has been established by the employer, the judge will approve the stated grounds for them.

Final cessation of the company's operations

11.28 To justify redundancies, the company's cessation of operations must be complete and final. A strict definition of the finality of cessation of operations is used. The cessation of operations has to affect the entire company; the grounds have not been established if only one facility or site is shut down. Furthermore, in a consolidated group of companies, the courts have refused to grant these grounds if it appears that:

- Another company in the group may be in a position to co-employ the laid off workers. Such may be found in there is exists a mingling of interests, operations and management control between the company that had officially shut down and another company in the group. This is often the case, in practice, between a parent company and its subsidiary company. Should the subsidiary close its doors, the practice will be to see whether the parent company in not in a position to be a co-employer.
- The employer has behaved recklessly or been at fault in some way. For example, the shutdown of a company is not accepted as valid grounds for laying off workers if a company decides for no reason to cease its operations for the sole purpose of satisfying its shareholders when it had an ongoing business with good earnings and considerable ability to grow.
- The final shutdown of the company was decided on following a temporary shutdown announced after instances of industrial piracy or on account of the employer's mistake in not seeking the necessary government approvals to conduct its business activities.

PROCEDURES FOR REDUNDANCIES

11.29 There are two types of procedures for laying off employees: the procedure for laying off an individual and the one for laying off a group of people. Failure to observe these processes may prompt not only litigation by the employee but also sanctions against the employer. Once the employer has determined the economic grounds for the layoffs it is contemplating, it must then follow the particular procedure that pertains to its situation. Several criteria are in fact brought to bear in determining the procedure that applies:

- the number of employees affected by the layoff program;
- the size of the company; and,
- if there are elected employee representatives in the workforce.

THE RULES APPLYING TO ALL REDUNDANCIES

11.30 The shared set of rules described hereafter constitutes the procedural steps that are absolutely required. No matter the size of the company, the way in which its employees are officially represented or the number of employees affected by the layoffs, these steps are mandatory.

11.31 The employer is thus required:

- to identify the employees who will be in the layoff program based on the order of layoff criteria;
- to try to find a way to reassign the employees affected;
- to offer them formal assistance known as a *contrat de sécurisation professionnelle* ('occupational security contract') or, in certain cases, that known as a *congé de reclassement* ('leave for reassignment');
- and then, should reassignment prove to be impossible, to notify the employee(s) in precise terms of the grounds for their termination;
- to compensate workers monetarily for being laid off;
- and to observe all other legal duties arising from the termination. For instance, both the employer and the employee have a duty to meet their respective obligations under a non-compete clause.

Applying the order criteria

11.32 Once an economic layoff program has been decided on, whether it involves one or more than one employee, an order of layoffs (pool of selection) has to be drawn up. The employer will need to apply objective criteria to select from the pool of employees who hold identical jobs, those who have been identified as redundant. An order of layoffs will not be drawn up if all the employees of one category are affected by the layoff plan, if all the jobs in the company are eliminated (such as in a complete and final cessation of operations) or if the job category affected by the layoff plan includes only one employee.

11.33 The Labour Code sets a certain number of criteria which the employer must use in this respect, in the absence of any specific provisions that might lie in the bargaining collective agreement or the company-specific collective agreement. The criteria for the order are established after consulting with the company works council or, in its absence, employee representatives.

11.34 These criteria take account of the employees' personal and work-related situations. Thus, according to the Labour Code, the following must be considered in setting the order criteria:

- employees' family situations (single parents, number of children looked after, etc);
- employees' seniority;
- the personal situation of employees who face problems of social inclusion, especially the handicapped and the aged; and
- employees' work-related qualities (assessed by category).

11.35 The employer is entitled to stress one of these criteria over the others but must still see that all of them are applied. The employer thus may apply some sort of weighting.

Example of a weighting system: the more points an employee gets, the less likely he or she is to be laid off.

Family situation		**Seniority**	
Marital: married, civil union, living together			
Without children	0	Under 2 years	0
With 1 child	0.5	Between 2 and 4 years	1
With 2 children	1	Between 5 and 8 years	3
With 3 children	1.5	Between 8 and 10 years	5
With > 3 children	2	Over 10 years	7
Unmarried, widowed, divorced, single parent		**Age**	
Without children	0	Under 22 years old	0
With 1 child	1.5	Between 22 and 30	1
With 2 children	2	Between 30 and 40	2
With 3 children	2.5	Between 40 and 50	3
With > 3 children	3	Over 50	4
Disability		**Job ability (grade received at last annual review)**	
Disability<35%	1	A+	7
35%"Disability<50%	2	B or B+	5
Disability ≥50%	4	C or C+	2

Duty to look for alternative employment

11.36 The Labour Code will not allow redundancies to take effect unless the employer has met its duty to look for alternative employment. Thus the employer must, before any layoff is made, take all possible steps to avoid the layoffs or at the very least to reduce the number of them.

11.37 The attempts to reassign workers must be:

- first, to a job under the same category that employee now holds;
- failing that, to a job equivalent to the one the employee now holds; and
- failing that, finally, and provided the employee expressly agrees, to a job of a category below the one he or she now occupies.

11.38 The employee must be offered a position suitable for his or her qualifications and work experience. Nevertheless, the employer also bears a duty to retrain. It must offer employees in line for layoff any job that they might perform after receiving special training or after a period of supervised adjustment to the new position. Should the employee not be offered help through reassignment, the employer has to demonstrate, in the event of dispute, that it was impossible to make the employee such an offer. Otherwise, the layoff will be deemed to be without real or serious grounds.

11.39 The employer must put into writing personalised and detailed offers of reassignment. Each offer made will specify the features of the reassignment offered so that the employee can make his or her choice. The employee is not required to accept the position proposed under the duty to offer reassignment.

The scope of reassignment

11.40 The scope for reassigning is broad. The reassignment attempted has to be within the company but, also, if the latter is part of a group, in all of the group's entities.

11.41 In addition, if the group to which the company belongs has foreign locations, an attempt must be made to reassign employees in line for layoff to these as well. In that event, the reassignment follows a specific procedure, by which the employer must meet with each employee who might be laid off to find out whether he or she would agree to accept reassignment outside the national borders. In this connection a questionnaire is given to him or her that includes a complete listing of all the group's locations in the world. The employee has six days' time to indicate whether he or she agrees to accept a reassignment offer abroad.

11.42 Still, there is no duty to offer reassignment outside of the group. If such an arrangement can be made, however, it is generally laid out in the formal layoff plan termed in French the 'employment preservation plan' and known by the acronym PSE (see below.)

Length of reassignment

11.43 Efforts to reassign employees should in principle begin as soon as the plans to lay off workers have been made. Whenever conducting an informational or consultation process with employees is mandatory, the effort to provide reassignments must begin when that process has been completed. However, at companies obliged to implement a PSE that have a works council, the in-company reassignments can be carried out as soon as the works council has approved such a plan. Efforts to reassign people continue until employees have been given their layoff notices.

11.44 After these notices have been given, it is still possible to offer a job to a laid off employee. But such an offer is most often made in terms of a re-hiring priority. In the employee's dismissal letter it must be stated that for a one year period starting with the termination of his or her employment contract, the employee will have priority for re-hiring at the company. So any job that becomes available at the company and that matches his or her experience level (or the one he or she could have attained after the layoff) must first be offered to that employee. For this re-hiring priority to apply, the employee must, again, make the request. He or she must send the employer a registered letter with return receipt requested in order to confirm that he or she intends to take advantage of this specific right.

The 'contrat de sécurisation professionnelle' (CSP)

11.45 All employees in line to be laid off are entitled to the arrangement known as the '*contrat de sécurisation professionnelle*' or CSP. The CSP is a specific contract entered into by the redundant employee and the French job centre (unemployment insurance division). Its purpose is to offer specific assistance to the redundant employee and let him or her benefit from a set of measures meant to help him or her find new employment.

11.46 The employer is obliged to offer the CSP to the employee during the preliminary discussion, if one is held, and to let the employee know how to make use of the contract. If at the end of a 21-day consideration period the employee agrees to make use of the CSP, his or her employment contract is terminated 'by common accord,' with no need for prior notice to be given. The employer, however, is not exempt from all its procedural obligations. In particular, it remains obligated to send a dismissal letter in order to explain to the employee the grounds for the layoff.

11.47 Furthermore, the courts require the employer to provide full information pertaining to the economic reasons for the layoff before the 21-day consideration period is over. The practical consequences of this requirement are significant. It in fact obligates the employer to send along with the official documents describing the CSP a detailed note concerning the economic grounds for the layoff(s). This still does not relieve the employer of then giving the employee notice of the layoff by registered letter with return receipt requested, re-stating the same grounds already disclosed.

11.48 The beneficiary of a CSP is entitled to 12 months unemployment benefit (from unemployment insurance) in an amount greater than the allowances a person seeking work is normally entitled to receive. At the end of this 12-month period, if the laid off employee has still not found work, he or she may receive unemployment benefit under the usual terms and conditions.

The 'congé de reclassement'

11.49 The employer is exempt from the CSP and must offer employees in line to be laid off a 'reassignment leave' known as a '*congé de reclassement*' or 'CR in place of the CSP if:

- The company has at least 1,000 employees in France;
- The company is part of a group whose main headquarters is located on French territory and which employs at least 1,000 people, the headcount being calculated by adding together the employees of all the group, wherever in the world they may be;
- The company is a company or group of companies in the European Union whose corporate headquarters is in the European Union and has at least:
  - 1,000 employees in the EU member states or the European economic area (the 27 member states of the European Union plus Norway, Iceland and Liechtenstein); and
  - A facility employing 150 people or more in at least two of these member states.

11.50 The goal of the CR is similar to that of the CSP: to allow the redundant employee to have the optimal conditions in looking for work by assisting him or her with specific actions aimed at improving skills or qualifications, paid for by his or her employer for a period not to exceed 12 months.

11.51 During the reassignment leave, the employee remains on the company's payroll. He or she receives his or her normal wages for the time he or she has been put on notice; during the duration of the CR, he or she receives pay equal to at least 65% (almost free of social contributions) of his or her normal compensation (gross amount). The amount of this compensation and the duration of the CR are agreed during negotiations with the employee representatives. The works council is in fact required to be informed and consulted about how the CR will be carried out.

11.52 The employer must inform the affected employees that there is such a reassignment leave available. It is the letter of dismissal that formally proposes the CR, which the employee may accept or reject within eight days of the proposal (silence meaning rejection). If the employee wishes to take advantage of the CR, he or she must take the steps laid out by the employer. If the CR expires and the employee has not yet found a job, he or she receives normal unemployment benefits.

Notification of redundancy grounds

11.53 Any redundant employee must be formally notified of the grounds of redundancy. The dismissal letter sets the limits on claims that may be brought subsequently in the employment court known as the *conseil de prud'hommes (*industrial court*)*. This means that the employer cannot argue from grounds different than those cited. Accordingly, the dismissal letter has to be sufficiently substantiated and the all grounds cited must be demonstrable.

11.54 Besides sufficiently justifying the originating cause of the redundancies, the employer must also explain the consequences of the economic situation for the employee's job and especially the reasons for eliminating it. In the absence of a detailed, precise dismissal letter, the termination of the employment contract may be held to be without actual cause and not serious.

11.55 Lastly, the dismissal letter must include a certain number of required or recommended points concerning:

- The length of the prior notice and, if called for, whether the employer releases the employee from carrying it out;
- The efforts made to find alternative employment;
- The re-hiring priority the employee will have for one year after the layoff;
- The individual training to which the employee is entitled by law;
- The employee's option to dispute the validity of the layoff for a 12-month period from the time of the dismissal letter.

Compensating workers monetarily for being laid off

11.56 As it is the case for a dismissal for individual reasons, statutory severance pay is owed to any redundant employee. It is calculated based on his or her seniority and basis salary. This compensation is replaced by a contractual severance pay if the collective agreement in force at the company provides severance pay that is more advantageous than that defined by law.

The severance pay, the amount of which is set by statute or contract, is not subject to income tax from the employee. It also does not figure into the calculation of social security contributions.

Example of calculating the redundancy pay due to an employee

Calculation of statutory redundancy pay

The statutory redundancy pay is equal to 1/5th of monthly wages multiplied by the number of years of seniority the employee has. In addition, if the employee has over ten years of seniority, the law provides for paying an extra 2/15ths of a month's wages for every year of service over ten.

The average wage to be used is the highest of the average 3 or 12 months immediately preceding termination of the employment contract (bonuses included).

Thus for average wages of €2,000 the statutory severance pay will equal:

- With 2 years of seniority (2,000/5) × 2 = €800
- With 15 years of seniority [(2,000/5) × 15] + [(2,000 × 2/15) × 5] = 6,000 + 1,333.33 = €7,333.33

Calculation of the redundancy pay due to an engineer or supervisor pursuant to the national collective agreement of the French association of engineers and consultancies known as *bureaux d'études techniques, des cabinets d'ingénieurs-conseils et des sociétés de conseils* (syntec):

After two years of seniority, one third of a month per year of service by the engineer or supervisor, not to exceed 12 months calculated on the average wages received during the 12 months preceding the termination of the employment contract.

Thus for average wages of €2,000 the statutory severance pay will equal:

- *With 2 years of seniority* (2000/3) × 2 = €1,333.33
- *With 15 years of seniority* (2000/3) × 15 = €9,999.99

LAYING OFF ONE PERSON

11.57 Beyond the mandatory steps mentioned above, laying off a single individual remains rather simple. The following steps must be taken:

- *Inviting the employee to a preliminary meeting:* the company must invite the employee five working days before the interview. The invitation must also state that the employee can be accompanied by an outside advisor or by another company employee
- *The preliminary meeting:* the employee can choose to appear or not and to bring someone along or not. During this interview, the employer must reveal to the employee the economic grounds for the redundancy plan. At this point the employer must have made no final decision. The efforts to reassign the person are still under way and will continue up to the dismissal letter. During this interview and as stated above, the employer must also give the employee a note summarising the economic grounds and offer the employee the written material concerning the CSP if that arrangement applies. In practice, if the employee does not attend the preliminary discussion, the employer will, as a precaution, send him

(or her) these two documents by registered letter with return receipt requested.

- *Sending a dismissal letter:* this letter may not be sent less than seven days after the interview or less than 15 days after the interview if the employee is of a supervisory grade.
- *Informing government:* within eight days after the dismissal letter, the employer must inform the *inspection du travail* (see above) of the economic layoff that has occurred.

11.58 Supposedly, if there are employee representatives in the company there is no legal obligation to inform and consult with them about plan to lay off a single employee. Nonetheless, such informing and consulting becomes obligatory in the event that:

- the employer is obliged to establish criteria for the order of layoffs before identifying the job of the laid off employee; or
- the stated grounds for the payoff has an impact on work schedules.

11.59 At all events, and whatever be the case, it is strongly recommended to always consult the employee representatives about the layoff plans in order to avoid any disputes about the matter.

	To be done	Delay
1.	Invite to attend a preliminary individual meeting	D-5 minimum
2.	Preliminary and individual meeting before dismissal	D day
3.	Notice of redundancy	D+7 minimum (non-executive employees) D+15 minimum (executive employees)
4.	Information of the governmental organisation *(DIRECCTE)*	D+15 (non-executive employees) or D+22 (executive employees) maximum

COLLECTIVE REDUNDANCIES

11.60 Once the layoff plans involve more than one employee, specific rules come into play. One should draw a distinction between plans that involve fewer than ten people and those that involve more than ten in a single 30 days period.

Small group layoffs (fewer than ten employees)

11.61 To identify the procedure to follow when fewer than ten employees are affected by a layoff, one should classify the company by size:

In a company of fewer than 11 employees:

11.62 The procedure to follow is that of an individual layoff, with one exception: the mandatory consideration period imposed on the employer before sending the dismissal letter following the preliminary discussion is seven days regardless of the status of the employees involved (supervisory or not).

	To be done	Delays
1.	Notification to attend a preliminary individual meeting	D-5 minimum
2.	Preliminary and individual meeting before dismissal	D day
3.	Notice of redundancy	D+7 minimum
4.	Information of the inspection du travail (direccte)	D+15 maximum

In a company having between 11 and 49 employees:

11.63 Yet another distinction needs to be drawn depending on whether the company has employee representatives or not:

(i) *If there are no employee representatives:* the procedure will go through the same steps as those laid out for a layoff in a company of fewer than 11 employees. However, if the absence of employee representatives is due to some faults on the employer's part, the employee make argue from such fault to claim that his or her layoff be reclassified as a layoff without real and serious reason.

(ii) *If there are employee representatives (or a works council):* the procedure will go through the same steps as those laid out for a group layoff in a company of fewer than 11 employees. However, the employer will be obliged to inform and consult with the bodies that represent employees before inviting the employees to the preliminary meeting. At the time of the information and consulting process, the employer will provide the employee representatives with all useful information about the contemplated layoffs, especially about the economic grounds, and will in particular consult with the representatives about defining the criteria for the order of layoffs. Minutes of the information and consultation meetings held will be sent to the DIRECCTE (see above).

	To be done	Delays
1.	Notification of the employee's representatives to attend a meeting (information's transfer in view of their consultation)	D-9 minimum
2.	Meeting to inform and consul the employee's representatives	D-6 minimum
3.	Notification to attend a preliminary individual discussion	D-5 minimum
4.	Preliminary and individual discussion before dismissal	D Day
5.	Notice of redundancy	D+7 minimum
6.	Information of the inspection du travail (DIRECCTE)	D+15 maximum

In a company having at least 50 employees:

11.64 The procedure will go through the same steps as those laid out for a layoff of fewer than ten people in a company of fewer than 11 employees that has employee representation. The information and consultation with employee representatives will be replaced by a mandatory information and consulting sessions with the works council (and the health, safety and working conditions committee known by the French acronym CHSCT) This consultation will be held before any employees are called to the preliminary meeting.

Large group layoffs (over 10 employees) in a company having between 11 and 49 employees

11.65 In this case the procedure again is different depending on whether the company has employee representatives or not.

If the company has employee representation

11.66 The procedure to follow is strictly defined by the French Labour Code.
The employer must invite the employee representatives to an initial information and consultation meeting. The agenda of this meeting has to state that the purpose of the meeting is to review planned economic layoffs of a group of employees. All the information that might enable the employee representatives to be duly informed must be attached to the invitation, namely:

- complete information as to the layoff program (the nature of the economic grounds and in particular a description of the company's business condition, the company workforce at the time of the consultation, the number of employees in line for layoff, the occupational categories in which jobs would be eliminated, the criteria for layoff order contemplated by the employer and the projected calendar of layoffs); and
- the specific reassignments that might be offered to the employees.

11.67 The day after the first meeting, DIRECCTE is notified of the proposed layoffs. This notification will include all the information sent to the employee representatives as well as the minutes of the initial meeting. DIRECCTE has 21 days to check that the rules governing the economic layoff of a group are being followed.

11.68 A second meeting with the employee representatives must be held in the 14 days following the first meeting. The opinion of the employee representatives is supposed to be obtained at this second meeting. As a practical matter, the employer will often arrange one or two more meetings. This ensures that the employee representatives have all the information and explanations necessary to give their opinion and that they have, moreover, had enough time to do so.

11.69 The government, in the 21-day layoff notification period, must see that the employee representatives were duly informed and that the proper procedure is being followed.

In these circumstances the employer is not required to hold individual preliminary meetings with the employees. Employees may be notified of the layoffs after a period of 30 days.

	To be done	**Delays**
1.	Notification of the employee's representatives to attend a first meeting (information's transfer in view of their consultation regarding the redundancy project)	D-17 minimum
2.	First meeting of the employee's representatives and information of the *inspection du travail (DIRECCTE)*	D-14 maximum
3.	Final opinion of the employee's representative regarding the redundancy project (after 2 meetings at least) and information of the *inspection du travail (DIRECCTE)*	D Day
	Notification to attend a preliminary individual discussion	D-5 minimum
	Preliminary and individual discussion before dismissal	D Day

	To be done	Delays
4.	End of the delay granted to the *inspection du travail (DIRECCTE)* to check the regularity of the redundancy process	D+21 maximum
5.	Notice of redundancy	D+28 minimum
6.	Information of the inspection du travail (DIRECCTE)	D+36 maximum

If the company does not have employee representatives

11.70 In that case, the employer will invite the employees to individual preliminary meetings in order to present them with the grounds for layoffs in the manner provided by common law. Following the preliminary meetings, the employer will notify DIRECCTE of the layoff plans. It will have to send to the government agency, for verification:

- all the information that would have been sent to the employee representatives, had there been any, as well as a list of the names of the employees whose dismissal is planned;
- and the formal report that explains the absence of employee representatives.

11.71 Notifying the employees of the layoffs by registered letter with return receipt requested may not be done in less than 30 days after notifying DIRECCTE of the aforementioned information. In this situation, it is possible for the employer to draw up a PSE (see below) but that is merely an option.

	To be done	Delays
1.	Notification to attend a preliminary individual discussion	D-5 minimum
2.	Preliminary and individual discussion before dismissal	D Day
3.	Information of the French labour administration of the redundancy project	D Day
4.	End of the delay granted to the French labour administration to check the regularity of the redundancy process	D+21 maximum
5.	Notice of redundancy	D+30 minimum
6.	Information of the French labour administration	D+36 maximum

Large group layoffs (at least ten employees) in a company having at least 50 employees

When there is a works council

11.72 A company with over 50 employees finds itself with considerably greater obligations if it plans to lay off ten or more employees. In practice, it must:

- Consult the works council about the planned layoff and the planned PSE. At the initial meeting, the works council will decide whether to bring in an accounting expert, which will have a big effect on the development and length of the process,
- Keep DIRECCTE informed on a regular basis and incorporate any observations and suggestions the agency may have about the layoff program and the PSE. The government is in this way routinely informed of how the process is progressing from the first works council meeting forward. And it plays a stronger role.
- In addition, under these circumstances an employer can negotiate a company-specific collective agreement with the trade unions that will cover, in particular, the criteria for order of layoffs, the timing of the layoffs and all the general provisions contained in the PSE. At this point there are two levels of negotiation – one with the unions and the other with the works council.

The 'employment preservation plan' or PSE

11.73 Also, the employer is required to establish a so-called 'employment preservation plan' known by its French acronym PSE. As already indicated, this PSE can be negotiated with the union representatives. In that event, it must be submitted to DIRECCTE for validation. If the PSE is written unilaterally by the employer, it must also be submitted to DIRECCTE for approval.

11.74 The PSE must include:

- concrete, specific measures to assist the employees who are in line for layoff;
- serious, effective measures to reassign people;
- non-discriminatory measures, given that the PSE applies to all employees in the job categories affected by the redundancies; and
- measures that are in keeping with the resources of the company or consolidated group.

11.75 In practice, depending on the objectives that the employer has set, its resources and, when applicable, what the unions or the government are trying to achieve, the PSE may propose:

- measures to facilitate reassignment to a job located in another geographic area and therefore involving a geographic transfer (with transfer compensation, reimbursed relocation expenses, etc);
- measures involving fewer working hours (reduction in overtime, offer of partial unemployment, incentives to work part-time, a shortened work week for certain categories of employees, etc);
- measures favouring in-company or out-of-company reassignment of employees and adjustment of their job classification (creating a skills inventory, an assessment by the employer of possible future needs of the company for new job classifications);
- measures for turning around or starting up a company (help at board director level and with start-up costs);
- creating a special unit to assist employees in looking for a new job;
- paying, when appropriate, some amount of money above that legally required as compensation for some of the harm suffered by employees from losing their job;
- enhanced redundancy pay to encourage voluntary redundancies; or
- staggering the layoffs over time, etc.

11.76 Once the process of consulting with the employee representatives is over and the DIRECCTE validation or approval period has expired, the employer will then send out the layoff notices in the usual manner (there are no individual preliminary meetings). The measures in the PSE are then implemented.

When the company has no works council:

11.77 In this instance, the employer is required to establish a PSE. Throughout the procedure the employees must be kept apprised of the contents of the PSE and the comments made about it by the government, as well as the employer's replies. Because of the lack of employee representatives, the employees are required to be invited to an individual preliminary discussion. Naturally, if the lack of employee representation is in fact due to some faults on the part of the employer, the employee may claim that the layoff is without real and serious cause.

SANCTIONS

11.78 An employer that does not meet its obligations in the procedure for an economic layoff exposes itself to a challenge from the employee and certain number of both civil and criminal sanctions.

A challenge brought by the redundant employee

11.79 An employee laid off on economic grounds can challenge the validity of the layoff procedure, the economic grounds invoked or the validity of the PSE. The harm resulting from an absence of real and serious cause for dismissal made on economic grounds is compensated by damages. This compensation is a function of the harm suffered by the employee if the company has fewer than 11 employees or if the employee has fewer than two years of service in the company. When the company workforce is greater than eleven and if the employee has more than two years' seniority, his or her compensation cannot be less than six months' wages.

11.80 In the event that the layoff procedure and the PSE are voided, the employees have the option of requesting to be rehired at the company or receiving a special compensation of at least 12 months' wages.

The employee may also receive a special compensation if no employee representatives were consulted because none had been elected through some faults of the employer.

Sanctions

11.81 Carrying out a layoff without consulting the employee representatives or the works council is punished by a fine of €3.750 for each employee affected. Failure to meet and consult with the works council is a ground for trade unions to claim damages.

CHANGE IN THE EMPLOYER'S LEGAL STATUS: SALE OF THE COMPANY, MERGER, OUTSOURCING, ETC

11.82 Under French law, employees are protected on the transfer of a business. Thus, when a restructuring occurs (merger, sale, absorption, etc) their terms and conditions of employment are preserved. Please note however that their 'collective' situation is not necessarily preserved.

EMPLOYEES' INDIVIDUAL SITUATIONS

11.83 Article l. 1224-1 of the Labour Code provides that when there is some change in the employer's legal status – including by succession, sale, merger, breakup or incorporation – all the employment contracts in effect at the time of that change are transferred to the new employer.

11.84 The situations listed in article l. 1224-1 are merely suggestive. There may occur a great many situations, apart from those mentioned, in which the employment contracts in effect at the time of a change must be transferred (becoming a subsidiary, a takeover of business assets, letting a management contract, etc). The exact nature of the change is unimportant. According to case law, the implementation of article l. 1224-1 and the transfer of employment contracts require these two conditions:

- there must be an independent economic entity; and
- this entity must be preserved or continued once the transfer has been made.

An independent economic entity

11.85 There is no legal definition of an independent economic entity. According to the cour de cassation, the highest court in France, an independent economic entity consists of an organised set of individuals and of tangible or intangible assets enabling the conduct of an economic activity in pursuit of a specific objective (*cass. Soc., july 7, 1998 no. 96-21.451*). In practice, for each business for which a transfer is contemplated, it is advisable to list the set of elements, which, as a bundle of indicators, will support or not support the existence of an independent economic entity:

- *An organised set of individuals:* the presence of one or more employees directly and primarily attached to the transferred business is an indicator of its independent character. In certain cases, where there are no tangible or intangible elements, the existence of manpower directly attached to the business transferred is sufficient to find an independent economic entity.
- *Tangible assets:* equipment appropriate to the business, machinery, tools, premises used and so on are identified in order to ascertain the existence of an independent activity.
- *Intangible assets:* the existence of customers can suffice to find the presence of intangible assets; patents or more broadly industrial, literary or artistic rights of ownership directly related to the business constitute intangible assets.

11.86 To make up an independent economic entity, all these human or physical resources have to be organised and a specific objective has to be pursued.

Preservation or continuation of the entity after the transfer

11.87 Once an independent economic entity has been found to exist, the transfer of the employees' employment contracts will not be mandatory unless this entity is continued or preserved in the identical condition.

11.88 To check whether this requirement has been met, French courts, drawing on European community case law, looks for the effective continuation of the transferred business. To give an example, if the business continues with the identical operating assets (the same tools or equipment, the same manufacturing processes, the same customers, etc), the courts deem the business to have indeed been continued.

11.89 If there have been substantial alterations in how the business operates, then article l. 1224-1 of the French Labour Code cannot be made to apply. One of the most frequently cited cases to illustrate such an alteration in operations is the case decided on 18 July 1983. In that decision, the *cour de cassation* ruled that when an urban waste treatment operation previously in the hands of a company that destroyed the waste by pyrolysis, producing water vapour for industrial use, was put into the hands of a new company that destroyed it by incineration, producing hot water for heating buildings, the businesses did not operate in the identical way, and the differences there were between the technical processes used precluded finding a continuation of the entity (cass. Soc. 18 October 1983, no. 80-42060).

The situation of a partly transferred business or the transfer of an incidental business

11.90 The fact that a business has been partly transferred or that only the incidental assets of a business have been transferred is not enough to preclude the application of article l. 1224-1 of the Labour Code. So long as the business transferred, albeit partial or incidental, by itself constitutes an independent economic entity that preserves its business after the transfer, the article l. 1224-1 applies, and the employment contracts of the employees in question will be transferred to the new employer.

11.91 An EC directive (directive 77/187/EC amended by directives 98/50/EC and 2001/23/EC) supports this point in that it finds there is a transfer if an economic entity maintains its identity in order to continue a business activity, whether it is essential or incidental.

11.92 By way of example, the following were deemed transfers of business activity, though partial or incidental: the sale of one of three locations of the same legal entity (cass. Soc., 22 October 2003, no.01-44.710) and the IT department of a company that had 'special equipment and enjoyed management autonomy' and 'all of whose assets necessary to conduct its business had been transferred' (cass. Soc., 8 July 2009 no. 08-44.396).

11.93 The independence of an entity therefore has to be ascertained for every situation.

Examples:

Situations	Existence of an independent economic entity?
Operation of business assets taken over by a company, in the same premises and with the same customers	Yes
Transfer of the IT department of a company with special equipment and having true management autonomy	Yes
Transfer of the writing and editing of a newspaper without its own assets	No
Transfer of a contract for cleaning interiors with no transfer of operating assets	No

The automatic transfer of the employment contract of the employees in question

11.94 Once the conditions of article l. 1224-1 have all been met, the transfer takes place automatically, by operation of law.

Article l. 1224-1 applies regardless of the type of contract – be it a permanent employment contract, a fixed-term employment contract, a part-time employment contract, an apprenticeship contract, a work-from-home contract, a work-study contract, etc. Similarly, provided that it is effect at the time of the sale, merger, absorption, etc, the contract is transferred. So this will include employees on a probation period, employees during their notice, employees on sick leave, employees on maternity or parental leave, employees seconded to another entity and so forth.

11.95 The provisions of article l. 1224-1 are a matter of public policy, so that neither the employee in question nor the employers can opt out of them. Thus if the employee declines to continue to perform on his or her employment contract with the new employer, the latter can choose to impose sanctions. For instance, if the employee decides not to appear at his or her workplace after the change of employer, his or her attitude is considered to be non-attendance constituting serious misconduct. The new employer can dismiss the employee on those grounds. The employee's prior agreement to the transfer is not necessary. Under French law the employee does not have a right to contest the transfer of his or her employment contract in any way that might interfere with that transfer.

11.96 Neither may the employer opt out of article l. 1224-1 of the Labour Code. If the employer keeps its managerial authority over the employees transferred and accordingly decides to begin a procedure to dismiss them, it still has to cite just cause and not be making a manoeuvre the only aim of which is to thwart article l. 1224-1.

Likewise, any agreement entered into between the assignor and the assignee that would result in thwarting the provisions of article l. 1224-1 would be null and void.

Protection of working conditions and terms of employment

11.97 Transferred employment contracts must be maintained with the same terms and conditions. The new employer may choose to change some of the employee's working conditions after the transfer, but if so must observe the following:

- observing the specific procedure if the change is made for economic reasons;
- soliciting the employee's agreement if what is involved is a non-economic change in an essential element of his or her employment contract; or
- imposing the change on the employee only if it concerns a non-essential feature of his or her employment.

Informing and consulting with the employee representatives

11.98 If there is a works council or there are employee representatives, these must be consulted about any plans to change the legal status of the company. This means a consultation that is necessarily in advance of the actual change.

11.99 With regard to changes that might affect working conditions, the CHSCT (health, safety and working conditions committee) to be found in any entity with over 50 employees will also be consulted about the planned change.

11.100 Similarly, if there is a European Works Council whose remit would make it familiar with the entity to which some or all of the employees will be transferred, it may also be consulted about the plan.

11.101 In fact, at companies and groups with a European presence, the European works council will need to be consulted: (i) once a year concerning the activities of the company or the group and prospects for that company or group, (ii) each time a group layoff is contemplated and (iii) from time to time, if the council so wishes, concerning measures that significantly affect the workers' interest.

11.102 In practice, to facilitate the change in legal status, it is recommended that the employer arrange information meetings including the employee representatives and the assignor as well the assignee.

Informing transferred employees individually

11.103 Article l. 1224-1 does not require the former or the new employer to inform the employees affected by the transfer on an individual basis. Once the bodies that represent the employees have been duly informed and consulted, both of the employers have met their obligations.

11.104 It is recommended, however, that the collective information be supplemented by informing each employee individually. This will be especially useful if the transfer will include significant, immediate changes such as a change of workplace. Communicating with each employee individually will aid in the success of the transfer operation. Should there be no employee representatives in the entities affected by the transfer, it is also strongly recommended to make every effort to communicate with the affected employees on a regular basis.

COLLECTIVE STATUS OF THE EMPLOYEES

11.105 While article l. 1224-1 of the Labour Code makes strict provision for the individual consequences of a change in legal status, it does not, on the other hand, deal with the collective consequences of such a transaction. In principle, the collective agreements do not bind the new employer and are not assigned to it. And yet these agreements do not automatically disappear. Most of the time, it is advisable to adapt them so that they apply to the new employer, or to enter into new ones replacing those previously in force.

11.106 Indeed, though the transactions contemplated in article l. 1224-1 of the Labour Code entail an automatic voiding of the collective agreements in force at the time of the transaction, article l. 2261-4 of the Labour Code provides that whenever the application of an agreement is invalidated due to a merger, sale, spinoff or change of business activity, the agreement continues in effect until the agreement substituted for it becomes effective or, failing that, for one year from the expiration of the notice period.

11.107 As mentioned previously with regard to article l. 1224-1 of the Labour Code, the list of transactions referred to in article l. 2261-124 of the Labour Code is not exhaustive. Individual benefits also have to be dealt with. If no new agreement has been signed in place of the old ones within one year, the transferred employees keep the individual benefits that had vested to them pursuant to the collective agreements.

Temporary survival of the transferor collective agreements

11.108 Pursuant to article l. 2261-14 of the French Labour Code, the collective agreements therefore survive temporarily until they are replaced or, failing that, for a period of one year. A notice period usually set at three months is added to the one year period taken from the aforementioned article. In practice then, the transferred employees have 15 months in which they will be able to continue having the benefit of their old collective agreements so long as no substitute agreement has replaced them before the expiration of this period.

11.109 In practice, it frequently happens that during the survival period the transferred employees work under several collective agreements – those of their former employer and those of their new employer. Thus they can demand that all these agreements be applied. They are naturally not allowed to combine benefits of the same type having the same purpose. But they can choose to have applied the collective agreements that are the most favourable to them.

11.110 For this reason especially, it is in the new employer's interest to negotiate substitute agreements. These benefits apply only to employees transferred. The employees already working at the company are not affected by these terms. They can seek to apply only the collective agreements of their own company and may not use this situation to claim any breach for unequal treatment within the company.

When the 15-month period ends

11.111 When the aforementioned 15-month period comes to an end, the collective agreements of the former employer cease to apply to the transferred employees. If no substitute agreement of any kind has been negotiated, the benefits vested to the employees under these old collective agreements will remain in place with respect to these employees.

11.112 Case law holds that a vested individual benefit is one which gives the employee a benefit or entitlement that he or she enjoyed personally and that refers to a right already available and not merely potential. As an example, a seniority bonus paid to a transferred employee under a collective agreement will continue to be paid to him past the 15-month period in the absence of a substitute agreement. Assuming that the employee had not yet attained the seniority necessary for the seniority bonus to be paid past the 15-month period, on the other hand, this benefit would not be vested.

11.113 Similarly, in the case where an employee received extra days off from his former employer or a thirteenth month of pay or a vacation bonus, etc, he will keep these individual benefits past the 15-month period in the absence of a substitute agreement. By contrast, severance pay upon dismissal or retirement, monetary compensation for non-compete clauses, etc, will not be deemed vested individual benefits if the employee has never received them as of the date his or her employment contact was transferred.

Signing a substitute or adapted agreement

11.114 Pursuant to the Labour Code, when collective agreements have automatically been invalidated at the time of a restructuring, negotiations should be started by the transferee company within three months. The point of these negotiations is to enter into a new agreement for the purpose of adapting or replacing the former contractual provisions.

11.115 These negotiations are held in the manner prescribed by common law. Priority for negotiation is given to trade unions represented in the company (whether this involves unions of the transferor or the transferee companies.

11.116 The substitute agreement will allow the new employer to make the best possible adaptations of the previously existing provisions with respect to the transferred employees. The contents of the substitute agreement are freely negotiated; there is no duty to negotiate terms that are more favourable than or equivalent to those the employees enjoyed with their former employer.

Consequences for company practices and non-contractual arrangements

11.117 Article l. 2261-4 of the Labour Code does not deal with the consequences for company practices, non-contractual arrangements or 'non-standard' agreements as they are known. These are not automatically voided when the restructuring takes place. They survive at the new employer. It is up to the new employer to void them in the manner prescribed by common law: by informing the transferred employees and the employee representatives, and if appropriate, agreeing to negotiations to replace the practices and arrangements.

AMENDING THE EMPLOYMENT CONTRACT

11.118 Without necessarily entailing layoffs or the transfer of an independent economic entity, the restructurings contemplated within a legal entity may result in a simple change in working conditions or in an essential element of the contract.

Change in working conditions

11.119 Any change in working conditions presents very little problem under French law as long as it falls within the employer's managerial authority and is required of the employee. The employer must, however, undertake the change in working conditions in good faith. Can be considered as working conditions:

- Work schedules (if these are not contractual);
- Change in the division of labour among employees (if it does not include a change in responsibility);
- Change of place of work (within the same geographic area).

Amendment of an essential element of the employment contract

11.120 As opposed to general working conditions, the essential elements of an employment contract (pay structure, working hours, job description, occupational classification, etc) cannot be amended by the employer unilaterally. The express written consent of the employee affected by such an amendment must be obtained. No exceptions are permitted. In particular, the fact that a restructuring in progress requires the immediate amendment of an essential element of the employment contract would not justify an employer making such an amendment.

11.121 Should the employer impose such an amendment without the employee's consent, it would be exposed to the contract being terminated at the employee's initiative but at the sole fault of the company. This would have the same consequences as a layoff without real and serious cause, and would entitle the employee to damages.

Amendment of the employment contract on economic grounds

11.122 The employee should be notified by registered letter with return receipt, of an amendment of the employment contract which is contemplated for economic reasons. This letter states that the employee has one month to make known his or her rejection of this amendment and spells out the reasons why the amendment is being contemplated. If the employee fails to respond in that timeframe, he or she is deemed to have accepted the proposed amendment. If the employee rejects the amendment, the employer has a choice:

- withdraw the amendment, or
- begin a layoff procedure. In that event, the employer must observe every aspect of the appropriate layoff procedure.

11.123 In the case of an employment contract amended on economic grounds, it is only when and if at least ten employees have rejected the amendment of an essential element of their employment contract as proposed by their employer on economic grounds that their being laid off is subject to the provisions of law that apply to group layoffs, particularly the requirement for an employment preservation plan (pse).

THE USE OF TEMPORARY CONTRACTS

11.124 In the event of a reorganisation, a need may be felt to use temporary contracts. Using them, however, is complicated by legal requirements.

Fixed-term contracts

11.125 To be valid, a fixed-term contract (French acronym CDD) has to meet two conditions:

- have been signed in order to carry out a specific, temporary task; and
- not have the effect or purpose of filling a position related to the company's normal, ongoing business.

11.126 The CDD must also have been entered into for one of the specific purposes set forth by law:

- to replace an employee (off sick, on maternity leave, permanently hired but not yet on the job);
- to handle a surge in business (an unusual export order, an occasional task, urgent installation of safety equipment, cyclical variation in volume); or
- to perform work temporary by its nature (seasonal contracts).

11.127 The Labour Code prohibits signing a CDD on grounds of a surge in business that occurs after an economic layoff. This prohibition against CDDs lasts for the six months following the layoff and applies to all jobs where economic layoffs have occurred. The prohibition, however, only covers CDDs longer than three months and does not apply if the surge in business stems from unusual orders for export. Even in these exceptional circumstances, it will be necessary to consult the employee representatives before using a CDD.

11.128 The Labour Code authorises using a CDD in the very specific case of replacing an employee who has quit his or her job before it was eliminated. This refers to the somewhat rare situations in which, for example, an employee resigns while an economic layoff program is in progress. Once the company has planned as part of the layoff procedure to eliminate in the near future the job of the employee who has left the company, it is possible to replace him or her with an employee on a CDD. It will be necessary to consult the employee representatives on this point.

Use of temporary workers

11.129 It is possible to use temporary workers under French law: in this case, they will be hired by a temporary work agency that will execute a temporary mission. During the mission, the temporary work agency remains the employer.

11.130 To use temporary workers is highly regulated and shall stay exceptional. A company is allowed to use temporary workers for the execution of precise and temporary missions in case there is a need: (i) to replace an employee that is absent or on sick leave; (ii) to maintain a full time job when an employee is temporarily part time; (iii) to replace the company director; (iv) to replace an employee that left the company before his job is effectively being eliminated; (v) to wait for the arrival of a new employee hired; or (vi) to cope with a temporary increase of the activity.

11.131 Nevertheless, the French Labour Code prohibits that a company hire a temporary worker in order to compensate a temporary increase of the activity six months after the notification of redundancies for economic reasons. Such prohibition concerns jobs that were made redundant during the economic layoff program. If not, employees that were dismissed shall use such fact to prove that the economic reasons were neither consistent nor established to obtain damages.

OUTSOURCING

11.132 In order to reduce the cost incurred by hiring in a reorganisation context, companies can reduce their own headcount by entrusting a subcontractor with one or several missions. Case law considers that such outsourcing can constitute a fair reason to layoff an employee for economic reasons.

11.133 Such operation will be considered legal if the following conditions are met:

- a commercial contract is signed between the company and the subcontractor and such contract specifically details the mission(s) that the company does not want its employees to accomplish themselves because of technical specificities or because of an economic opportunity;
- the contract provides that the subcontractor will get a flat fee for the mission(s) to be executed regardless of the number of employees and the hours of works needed (the risk of the operation must be supported by the subcontractor);
- the subcontractor must be the only employer of the employees that accomplish the mission(s): it means that such employees must be pay and managed by the subcontractor only; in consequence their works conditions

will not be similar to the ones the employees of the company usually have; and

- the equipment used by the employees that accomplish the mission(s) shall be provided by the subcontractor only.

11.134 If not, such operation will be considered as an unlawful employee leasing, which is an offence punishable by a €150,000 fine for the company and a two-year prison sentence and a €30,000 fine for the company directors.

11.135 Outsourcing is never without risk before the *conseil de prud'hommes* (industrial court) for the company as the employee working for the subcontractor can challenge any further difficulties in the execution or termination of its employment contract and pretend that the company was his real employer to claim for damages.

OFFSHORING

11.136 The closure of an establishment in order to offshore its activities abroad can also be a fair reason to lay off employees if such offshoring is a solution that allows the company to save the competitiveness of the group sector economy. If not, any dismissal on such ground shall be void.

11.137 The offshoring does not, in principle, constitute a transfer of undertakings. Nevertheless if the conditions of the transfer of undertakings are met, the offshoring shall be consider as a modification of the employment contract that the employee can refuse before being made redundant for economic reasons.

MUTUAL TERMINATIONS

11.138 A mutual termination of the employment contract is a recent method of termination (law of 25 June 2008) which permits terminating a contract by mutual agreement and without specific grounds.

11.139 The mutual termination is formalised by the signature by the employer and the employee of a document which is sufficient to confirm their mutual consent to the separation. It is quite informal and involves a highly simplified procedure; the parties complete and sign a special, pre-filled out form, wait for a 15-day retraction period and then send the mutual termination form to the government, which has another 15 days to approve it.

In principle, the laws about economic layoffs pertain to any termination of an employment contract with the exception of mutual terminations.

11.140 However, mutual terminations may not be used with the aim of getting around an economic layoff. Though they are not ruled out in difficult economic circumstances or during an economic layoff procedure, it is prudent not to use them with an employee who falls under a job category directly affected by the economic layoff procedure. At that point, it might well be found that the mutual termination was used in place of an economic procedure in order to circumvent the rules that pertain to them.

The use of mutual terminations agreement within a restructuring exercise are therefore limited to those employees not at risk of redundancy.

Chapter 12

Workforce Restructuring in Germany

Dagmar Dexheimer and Axel Weber (12.1–12.40)
ebl factum rechtsanwälte, Frankfurt

Frank Engelhard and Tim Quintiliani (12.41–12.80)
ebl esch & kramer rechtsanwälte, Dusseldorf

INTRODUCTION

12.1 German employment law applies to employment relationships which are 'lived' in Germany (ie where the work is ordinarily or habitually carried out in Germany). Under certain conditions, it also applies to employment relationships where the employee was recruited in Germany but works abroad.

12.2 German employment law is codified in acts and regulations. There exists no uniform 'employment law code', which would govern all employment law aspects. Rather, German relevant statutory provisions are found in a wide variety of acts and regulations, both at a federal and state level. The most important statutory employment provisions are set out in the German Civil Code, the German General Equal Treatment Act, the German Act against Unfair Dismissal, the German Federal Holiday Entitlement Act, the German Continued Remuneration Act and the German Maternity Protection Act. Employment law is characterised, above all, by court decisions made in relation to the statutory provisions, by which employment law is construed, or complemented.

There exist pronounced rights of employee representation bodies (works councils), to which the German 'Labour-Management Relations Act' (*Betriebsverfassungsgesetz*) grants far-reaching rights of information, consultation and co-determination in relation to the structuring of the terms and conditions of employment at the business and company level. Works Councils do not form part of a trade union. The rights of the trade unions, which negotiate collective agreements with employers' associations for a specific region and industry, are normally limited to the definition of the framework conditions, especially in connection with collective wage agreements, which provide for the remuneration for their respective industry.

In practice, in connection with restructuring measures, an employer will have works councils as a counterpart for negotiations at a collective level, if a Works Council was established in the related business, which will mostly, but not always, be the case. In rare cases, however, trade unions are required to be involved.

12.3 In the event of a conflict between statutory provisions, a collective collective agreement and an employment contract, the 'principle of favourability' will apply. This means that the provision which is most favourable for the employee in the situation from time to time, ie, the provision which grants the most extensive rights to the employee, will apply. If, for example, the statutory provisions in the German Civil Code provide for a notice period of two months to expire at the end of a month, while the applicable collective agreement provides for a notice period of four months to expire at the end of a month, and the individual contracts provides for a notice period of four months to the end of a calendar quarter, the longest notice period will apply, ie, the notice period under the individual employment contract of four months to expire at the end of a quarter.

Therefore, in assessing any given situation, one must focus not only on the employment contract (this would, however, be the starting point), but also on the relevant works agreements (Betriebsvereinbarungen) entered into with the Works Council, any applicable collective agreements and, ultimately, also any statutory provisions.

12.4 In connection with restructuring measures, which will frequently result in a termination of employment relationships, or a fundamental change in the terms and conditions of the employment contracts (place of work, position etc), it must be noted that an 'employment at will' is not a concept recognised in German employment law. Unilateral changes to employment conditions by the employer and/or dismissal of the employee will also need to meet the requirements of the German Unfair Dismissal Act where the employee falls into the scope of this legislation (see for details of the protection scope below).

PREPARATION FOR A RESTRUCTURING EXERCISE

12.5 Employers restructuring their business may wish to meet a variety of objectives, including staff reductions, changing or harmonisation of contractual terms and conditions, the use of temporary workers (agency staff), outsourcing and off-shoring, as well as a reorganisation of staff hierarchies and staff reporting lines.

12.6 Regardless of the objectives and nature of the restructuring exercise, employers ought to gather the necessary information regarding the affected staff members at the beginning of the restructuring process. Only then can an employer carefully plan the restructuring and create a realistic basis for the costs of the exercise. Many restructuring measures are based on the expectation that the reorganisation will result in significant savings. However, that expectation is often not based on a detailed cost-benefit analysis but, rather, only a rough estimate.

Key legal issues which employers often face in implementing a restructuring are dealt with below:

12.7 First of all, it must be considered that employees are always employed by a specific legal unit, rather than with a group of companies. Therefore, the entrepreneurial decision on which the restructuring is based must be prepared and taken for each employing legal entity separately. This is of particular importance if a business enterprise is organised in a 'matrix structure', ie, if the employees cooperate beyond the boundaries of the individual business enterprises or where the HR function or certain managerial decision making is centralised in a European or Global parent company. In all these cases it will still require the management of employing entity to take and document the restructuring decision. Local management will therefore need to be involved from the beginning, not least as it will be local management that will have to inform and consult with the Works Council in a timely and meaningful manner and then also, where required, come to an agreement with the Works Council in respect of proposed measures.

Procurement of information

12.8 The restructuring process requires exact initial planning. Otherwise, it will be impossible to estimate the costs of the measure or to minimise the risk of claims before a labour court. HR staff must, therefore, consider what data they will need to implement and budget for the restructuring measure.

12.9 The employer will normally already be in possession of the necessary data of the affected employees on the basis of the employment relationship. If a centralised HR department allocated to a different group company wishes to access those data, it must, however, ensure the lawfulness of the access, as the legally independent group company is an independent third party in relation to the employing legal entity in terms of data protection. Therefore, the disclosure of employee data across the boundaries of legal entities within a group of companies constitutes a transmission of data to third parties and will require the employee's prior consent or a relevant Works Council agreement. This applies all the more if it is intended to transmit personal data to another country outside of the EU, such as the USA.

12.10 The collection of the data and facts on which the restructuring measure must be based is time-consuming. If the data and facts are not readily available to the HR department and its advisors it will be impossible to plan the restructuring and the consequential personnel measures in a definitive or reliable manner.

Practical Tip

The employee data required for a staff cut or a restructuring measure include (**not exhaustive**):

- Name, date of birth (age)
- Description of tasks
- Place of employment
- Date of joining (length of service)
- Maintenance obligations (ie actual legal obligations to support children, spouse etc.)
- Special protection against dismissal (eg, maternity protection in which case an exclusion of regular dismissal options applies)
- Severe disability
- Average monthly remuneration
- Notice period, proposed termination date
- Applicable reconciliation of interests, social compensation plan, collective collective agreement

That information is necessary to estimate the costs of the restructuring measure, to prepare a timetable for the dismissals to be effected, and to make the 'social selection'. In practice, it has proved effective to enter the information in an excel file.

EMPLOYMENT STATUS

12.11 The restructuring of an employer often makes it necessary to reduce staff. Only staff with the status of 'employee' enjoy general protection against dismissal in Germany. Therefore, it must be reviewed in the run-up to the restructuring what staff members qualify as employees. No statutory definition exists in that respect. Case law, however, defines an 'employee' as a person who is obliged under an agreement under private law to perform, in a relationship of personal dependency, work for another and subject to instructions. While 'executives' are also employees, they are treated differently to 'ordinary employees' in certain aspects. An employer's statutory representatives, ie, managing directors or board members (subject to the legal form), are not regarded as employees under German law for the purposes of dismissal protection rights.

GENERAL PROTECTION AGAINST DISMISSAL

12.12 The termination of the employment of all employees is subject to specific notice periods. However, since 1 January 2004, the German Act against Unfair Dismissal has limited the general protection against dismissal to employees employed for more than six months in businesses and administrations with *more than* 10 employees. Special provisions apply to employees whose employment relationship commenced on 31 December 2003 or earlier. Part-timers will not typically count as 'full employees' for these purposes, details depend on the contractual number of hours worked per week.

In accordance with the definition by the German Federal Labour Court, in that context, 'business' (*Betrieb*) means an organisational unit of a company within which the employer, alone or together with its employees, and by using material or immaterial means, continuously pursues specific procedural purposes which are not limited to the satisfaction of the employer's own requirements. Therefore, the terms 'business' (*Betrieb*) and 'company' (Unternehmen) are not identical under German employment law.

12.13 The application of the general protection against dismissal under the German Act against Unfair Dismissal is mandatory and may not be contracted out of to the detriment of the employee, neither by a collective collective agreement or works agreement nor by an individual employment contract. While a reason for the dismissal is not required to be stated in the letter of dismissal (German law requires written form for a dismissal; an e-mail, pdf attached to an email, SMS or fax transmission is not regarded as sufficient but an original letter with a 'wet ink' signature is required), the employer must, however, justify the dismissal before a court if the German Act against Unfair Dismissal applies and if the employee brings an action against the dismissal before the competent labour court within three weeks from the receipt of the letter of dismissal. A dismissal can only be 'justified' in that respect if it is either based on reasons related to the employee's personal circumstances or conduct, or on operational reasons. A dismissal for operational reasons, which is described in more detail below, is of particular relevance in business restructurings. Unjustified dismissals are ineffective, do not result in a termination of the employment relationship and will, therefore, result in a continuation of the employment relationship ('re-instatement' or 're-engagement').

12.14 A dismissal for operational reasons may be considered if urgent operational requirements conflict with the continued employment of the employee in the business. According to case law, any such operational requirements may result from internal circumstances (eg, an entrepreneurial decision regarding a rationalisation) or external circumstances (eg, a decline in sales). What is decisive in either case is whether the need to employ the dismissed employee ceased to exist at the time of the dismissal as a result of the operational requirements. It is not required that the employee's specific job ceases to exist, so long as the general need to employ is reduced. In addition, the operational reasons must be 'urgent', ie, the dismissal must be unavoidable for the employer. This reflects the 'principle of proportionality', which must be considered in relation to any dismissal.

12.15 If the dismissal is based on urgent operational reasons, it will nevertheless be socially unjustified if the employer did not, or did not adequately, consider the length of service, age, maintenance obligations or severe disability in the selection of the employee to be dismissed. Experience shows, that 'social selection procedure' is the biggest obstacle from an employer's perspective (see below for details).

SPECIAL PROTECTION AGAINST DISMISSAL

12.16 German employment law provides for special protection against dismissal for specific groups of employees. Therefore, when dismissing employees who enjoy special protection against dismissal, specific additional requirements must be observed, and the dismissal may require prior approval by the relevant state authority. The following categories of employees are, in particular, covered by that special protection against dismissal (the list is not exhaustive):

- employees who are pregnant or enjoy maternity protection,
- employees on parental leave,
- severely disabled employees,
- members of the Works Council,
- data protection officer,
- candidates or election committee members at elections for the Works Council,
- members of staff councils (in the civil service),
- candidates or election committee members at elections for the staff council,
- trainees/apprentices after the end of the probation period or members of committees for the representation of youths or trainees/apprentices,
- staff elected to parliament on federal or state level (in some federal states also on local council level);
- staff on nursing care leave or who have applied for the same.

WORKFORCE REDUCTION

12.17 Employers who wish to reduce staff in connection with a restructuring measure should document the underlying entrepreneurial decision in advance and should carefully compile the necessary employee data. The restructuring process which must be observed by the employer flows from an analysis of such data and the nature of the objective(s) and the underlying employer decision. In addition, this will facilitate at an early stage the review whether the envisaged dismissals meet with the legal requirements.

12.18 If a significant staff reduction is planned, employers will normally also be required to consider the rights of the Works Council, as employers are required (in companies with more than 20 employees entitled to vote) to inform the Works Council, in good time and comprehensively, of any planned operational changes which might have materially adverse effects for the staff, or a substantial part of the staff, and to consult on the planned operational changes with the Works Council(see below for details).

DISMISSAL FOR OPERATIONAL REASONS

12.19 The German Act against Unfair Dismissal does not contain a definition of 'urgent operational requirements', nor a definition as to when exactly those requirements justify a dismissal. The standard against which a dismissal for operational reasons must be measured is largely defined by case law, in particular, by case law of the German Federal Labour Court.

12.20 According to case law, a dismissal for operational reasons can be contemplated, in particular, in the following groups of cases (the list is not exhaustive):

- (partial) closure of a business;
- permanent decline in orders;
- outsourcing and offshoring;
- rationalisation;
- reassignment of existing workload to fewer staff;
- changes to the job requirement profile;
- cessation of employment opportunities as a result of technical developments.

The employer will need to be able to provide substantive evidence of the existence of any of those groups of cases the employer wishes to rely on.

12.21 Special caution must be exercised in the event of the sale of a business. If a business or business unit passes to another owner by way of an asset sale (as distinguished from a share sale), the provisions of section 613a of the German Civil Code, which implements the EU directive on safeguarding employees' rights in the event of a transfer of undertakings (the Acquired Rights Directive), must be observed. This includes, inter alia, the prohibition to dismiss an employee on account of the transfer of a business. In the event of outsourcing and offshoring, it must be carefully reviewed whether a relevant transfer of a business exists (see below for details).

Examples of a dismissal for operational reasons

Employer A manufactures sheet metal covers for the aerospace and automobile industry. It employs a total of 1,000 employees in Germany, of whom 400 are employed in a business in Frankfurt, where metal is cut and processed while using two special machines. Employer A made investments in new and more advanced machines capable of cutting and processing sheet metal simultaneously, so that one work step will cease to exist in Frankfurt in future. Following the introduction of the new machines, the work of 100 employees is no longer required, and Employer A has no longer any need to employ them.

Employer B is a retail chain which sells electric appliances at locations all over the world. It also operates 50 retail shops in Germany, the sales figures of which declined dramatically in the last few years. Employer B, therefore, takes the decision to close five of its German locations and to dismiss the employees there.

OTHER REASONS FOR A DISMISSAL

12.22 In addition to a dismissal for operational reasons, the German Act against Unfair Dismissal also provides for a dismissal based on personal circumstances or conduct. Those types of a dismissal hardly play a role, however, in connection with restructuring measures, and they are dealt with below for the purpose of completeness only.

12.23 In the event of a dismissal based on personal circumstances, the employer invokes reasons relating to an employee's personal circumstances, ie, reasons outside the employee's control. These include, for example, an illness which makes it impossible for the employee to perform the contractually owed activities.

12.24 A dismissal based on conduct relates to the conduct by an employee which can be voluntarily controlled and which constitutes a breach of the duties under the employment contract. Such a dismissal will normally only be possible if the employee has already been formally warned on account of a comparable breach of duty before effecting the dismissal.

12.25 In connection with a dismissal based on personal circumstances or conduct, the employer is also required to substantiate and, if applicable, furnish evidence of, the reason for the dismissal and the proportionality of the employer's actions.

REQUIREMENTS FOR A DISMISSAL FOR OPERATIONAL REASONS

12.26 If dismissals for operational reasons become necessary in connection with a restructuring measure, employers must observe both the standards under individual contracts and collective collective agreements.

12.27 While the establishment of a Works Council is not mandatory in Germany, the law allows employees to elect a Works Council where the business employs at least five employees. If a Works Council exists, it must be informed and consulted before effecting a dismissal for operational reasons, as well as a dismissal based on personal circumstances or conduct. In planning and implementing a restructuring measure, additional rights of participation must also be observed if the company (and not the business) has more than 20 employees (cf para **12.35**).

12.28 A dismissal for operational reasons must be based on an urgent operational requirement. This is the first, but not the only, requirement for the legal effectiveness of a dismissal. In addition, the employer must also carry out a legally effective 'social selection', observe the principle of proportionality, offer to the employee suitable alternative employment (if applicable) and hear the Works Council (if a Works Council exists) regarding the dismissal. If the employer regularly employs more than 20 employees, the employer must ensure that the German Federal Employment Agency is provided with a correct notice of a collective redundancy, if the thresholds for such collective redundancies are triggered. The thresholds for a collective redundancy are exactly specified in the German Act against Unfair Dismissal, please see para **12.36** below for details.

12.29 The individual requirements for an effective dismissal for operational reasons (except the urgent operational requirement already set out below) are dealt with below, in consideration of the current case law:

Selection pool and selection criteria

12.30 A dismissal for operational reasons normally requires a decision by the employer ('entrepreneurial decision') to eliminate a specific role. Even if urgent operational reasons exist for a dismissal, it will, however, be 'socially unacceptable' if the employer made a mistake in the selection of the employee to be dismissed, as the German Act against Unfair Dismissal requires the employer to make a 'social selection' at the level of the business.

This means that an employer must form a selection pool and compare employees who are comparable on the basis of the hierarchy level, scope of work, educational background and professional career. The criteria to be used for such comparison are set out in the German Act against Unfair Dismissal:

- length of service;
- age;
- maintenance obligations; and
- severe disability.

As a general rule, the youngest employee with the shortest length of service and with low, or no, maintenance obligations must be selected for dismissal, while older employees with a longer length of service and a large number of dependants will enjoy higher 'social protection' against a dismissal. In practice, a 'points system' will normally be set up, ie, points are awarded per year of age, every year of service, and in respect of every dependant entitled to maintenance, and the points will then be added. The employee with the highest score will enjoy the highest level of protection. While the German Federal Labour Court accepts points tables, it takes the view that an individual assessment of each case must also be made. Therefore, employers have a certain (limited) discretionary power in making the 'social selection'. Employers may also consider special knowledge, skills and performances of individual employees, ie, attributes which cannot be expressed in a points table. This proves difficult in practice. The law, however, does not require from an employer a mathematically exact selection but, rather, only that the aforementioned aspects of the length of service, age, and number of persons entitled to maintenance, are considered 'adequately'.

Example of a points table

	Calculation of points	Maximum points
Age	1 point per year of age	55
Length of service	1 point per year up to the 10th year of the length of service; 2 points per year from the 11th year of the length of service	70
Maintenance obligations	4 points per child entitled to maintenance; 8 points per spouse entitled to maintenance;	
Severe disability	5 points in the case of a degree of disability of up to 50%; 5 points + 1 point per degree of disability of 10% in the case of a degree of disability of more than 50%.	10

The Works Council must be heard before effecting any dismissal, not only a dismissal for operational reasons, while stating the relevant reasons for the dismissal. The Works Council must be notified of the employer's consideration regarding the 'social selection'. A dismissal effected without hearing the works council, or without a sufficient substantiation of the reasons, will be ineffective.

Principle of proportionality

12.31 When effecting a dismissal for operational reasons, employers must observe the 'principle of proportionality'. Therefore, employers must check whether the envisaged dismissal is suitable and necessary to reach the desired objective and whether the desired objective as such is not disproportionate to the impairments related to the dismissal. Therefore, employers should always consider alternatives to a dismissal such as short-time work, extensions of part-time work, early retirements, hiring freezes etc.

12.32 To avoid the uncertainty of the outcome of an unfair dismissal claim, it may be advisable to explore the feasibility of a termination of the employment relationship by mutual agreement (by way of a termination agreement) instead of a unilateral dismissal. An employee will not typically sign any such agreement without a (financial) consideration and will, therefore, expect and negotiate a severance payment. An alternative to a negotiated exit is a dismissal combined with the offer of a severance payment in accordance with section 1a of the German Act against Unfair Dismissal, according to which a claim of the employee to a severance payment of half the monthly remuneration per year of employment will arise if the employer dismissed for operational reasons and the employee did not bring an action against the dismissal within the applicable time limit. However, a reference in the letter of dismissal concerning the applicable severance must be set out by the employer such that is it clear that the severance payment turns automatically into an entitlement once the time limit for bringing a claim has expired.

Alternative employment

12.33 An 'urgent operational requirement' for a dismissal requires a lack of any suitable alternative employment. If, therefore, there exists an option within the employing entity to continue the employment at a different position, the relevant job must be offered to the employee. The following principles must, in particular, be observed in that respect:

- The employer is merely required to offer jobs on comparable or (if applicable, by way of a dismissal with the option of altered conditions of employment (*Änderungskündigung*)) on less favourable conditions. A duty to promote does not exist. The employer may, however, be obliged to accept a reasonable familiarisation or training period.
- When looking for options for suitable alternative employment, the employer is only obliged to consider vacancies. German law does not require the termination of an existing suitable job.
- If one job is eligible for several employees to be dismissed, the employer must undertake a 'social selection'. The offer for suitable alternative employment will then be made to the employee who enjoys the highest level of protection.

- Not only vacancies within the business must be considered; rather, vacancies within the company as a whole must also be considered. An extension to the group level will, however, only be considered in that context if the employer has legal and factual options to enforce the continued employment outside the employing legal entity, or if the employer undertook to do so in relation to the employee.
- What is relevant as a general rule is whether suitable alternative employment already existed at the time of the dismissal or came into existence during the notice period. If the employer knows, however, at the time when notice of the dismissal is given that a job will become vacant before the expiry of the notice period, that job must also be considered. Even if the option of alternative employment will only arise after the expiry of the notice period, it must be considered if the employer was aware of it at the time of giving notice or at the time of the effective date of termination if the employer can reasonably be expected to accept the bridging of the period of overstaffing.

12.34 If the employee does not accept a job on less favourable conditions offered to him, the employer may nevertheless not simply terminate the employment relationship by way of a dismissal, but is required to effect a dismissal combined with the offer to continue the employment on changed conditions. This will apply in particular in the event that the new conditions of employment are not completely 'inferior' or in the event that the employee did not unequivocally made it clear that he/she would under no circumstances accept the offer made.

A dismissal combined with the offer to continue the employment on changed conditions consists of two components: the termination of the existing employment relationship, along with the offer of a continuation of the employment relationship on changed (less favourable) conditions. The employee may react to that type of dismissal in three ways:

(a) the employee may accept the offer made; or
(b) the employee may reject the offer and take legal action against the dismissal combined with the offer to continue the employment on changed conditions. This option includes the risk for the employee of being unsuccessful with the claim and consequently be without employment; and
(c) the employee may accept the offer, provided that the change of the conditions of employment does not turn out to be socially unjustified within the meaning of the German Act against Unfair Dismissal.

In option (c), the dispute will be about the scope, rather than the existence, of the employment relationship.

INVOLVEMENT OF EMPLOYEE REPRESENTATIVES

12.35 If a Works Council exists in the business affected by the restructuring, it must be informed and given the opportunity for consultation before effecting a dismissal for operational reasons. A potential objection by the Works Council does not result in the proposed dismissal not being capable of being implemented. However, there are strict requirements concerning the information and consultation process with the Works Council, and a failure to comply with those requirements will render the dismissal void.

As part of the process, the employer must notify the Works Council of the reasons for the proposed dismissal. The duty to notify extends both to the 'urgent operational requirements' and the social selection, as well as the balancing of interests in the individual case. The employer is not obliged, however, to inform the Works Council of all facts which are objectively relevant for the dismissal but, rather, only of the reasons for the dismissal which are decisive for the employer in subjective terms.

If an employer considers a dismissal for operational reasons, the employer must provide the Works Council, in particular, with the following specific information (list is not exhaustive):

- personal data of the affected employee;
- type of the dismissal (here: dismissal for operational reasons in compliance with the respective notice period);
- the activities actually performed by the affected employee;
- notice period and date of the dismissal;
- cessation of the job as a result of the restructuring measure;
- no other employment option;
- if a social selection must be made: all relevant aspects (in particular, age, length of service, maintenance obligations and severe disability (if any) of the affected employee and the employees with a comparable job);
- balancing of interests in an individual case.

The detailed information to be provided to the Works Council, which also includes, in particular, the notification of the social data of the affected employees and all comparable employees, is also mandatory in the case of a collective dismissal. This process will be easier, however, if the Works Council has already been comprehensively informed of the reason for the dismissal in the context of the negotiations on a reconciliation of interests and social plan in the run-up to an operational change (see below for details). In those cases, it will be sufficient if the employer merely refers once more in general to the known reasons for the dismissal in connection with the information and consultation of the Works Council in respect of each individual dismissal.

After the notification of the relevant data by the employer, the Works Council has one week to comment in writing on the planned dismissal for operational reasons. If the Works Council does not provide comments during that time limit, the consent to the dismissal will be deemed granted. Comments may be provided within that time limit in the form of an express consent, a notification of concerns, or an objection. In that respect, neither a notification of concerns nor an objection will prevent the employer from effecting the proposed dismissal. If the Works Council, however, raised an objection in due form and within the time limit, the employee will have a special right to a continued employment for the duration of an action for unfair dismissal. If one of the reasons for an objection laid down in the German Labour-

Management Relations Act exists in addition, the effected dismissal will be deemed socially unjustified within the scope of application of the German Act against Unfair Dismissal, and the employer would then lose an action (if any) for unfair dismissal.

DEFINITION OF COLLECTIVE REDUNDANCY

12.36 Employers which regularly employ more than 20 employees in the company must also consider the following: if they effect a collective dismissal in connection with a restructuring, they must notify both the German Federal Employment Agency and the Works Council thereof in good time. The notification to the German Federal Employment Agency must be made in the form of a 'notification of a collective dismissal', which must also include comments by the works council. According to the German Act against Unfair Dismissal, a 'collective dismissal' exists if in businesses with:

more than 20 and fewer than 60 employees	more than 5 employees	
at least 60 and fewer than 500 employees	more than 25 employees, or	10% of the staff
at least 500 employees	at least 30 employees	

are dismissed within 30 calendar days. Terminations of employment relationships by way of mutually agreed termination agreements are treated as equivalent to a dismissal. According to the definition by the European Court of Justice, a 'dismissal' does not reference to the effective date of termination of an employment relationship but, rather, the date on which the letter of dismissal is issued. Therefore, the Works Council must be heard, and the notification of a collective dismissal to the German Federal Employment Agency must be made, before giving notice of dismissal, failing which the dismissals to be effected will be ineffective.

PARTICIPATION OF THE WORKS COUNCIL IN CASES OF OPERATIONAL CHANGE

12.37 In the case of an 'operational change', an employer employing more than 20 employees across its business and with a Works Council established must, before effecting any dismissals, enter into a consultation process (referred to in law as 'negotiations on a reconciliation of interests') with the Works Council in order to (in most cases simultaneously) agree a social compensation plan.

The German Labour-Management Relations Act considers the following as an 'operational change':

- the limitation and closure of the business as a whole, or of material parts thereof,
- the relocation of the business as a whole, or of material parts thereof,
- the merger with other businesses, or the splitting of businesses,
- fundamental changes to the organisation, objective or facilities of the business, and
- the introduction of fundamental new working methods and production processes.

The mere reduction of staff will also be considered to be an 'operational change' if, in businesses who regularly have:

fewer than 60 employees	20% of the regular employees	but at least 6 employees
at least 60 and fewer than 250 employees	20% of the regular employees	or at least 37 employees
at least 250 and fewer than 500 employees	15% of the regular employees	or at least 60 employees
at least 500 employees	10% of the regular employees,	or at least 60 employees

are to be dismissed for operational reasons.

When to inform the Works Council

12.38 The Works Council should have the possibility to influence the employer's decision. Therefore, it is mandatory that the negotiations on a reconciliation of interests take place before effecting any dismissals (or entering into termination agreements, respectively). If this is not done, and if the employer rather starts to effect dismissals without having completed negotiations, the Works Council may prohibit the employer from effecting such dismissals by filing an application for an interim injunction. The negotiations will end in a reconciliation of interests and, normally, in the conclusion of a social compensation plan, ie an agreement between the Works Council and the employer which provides for a compensation (severance payment, further training etc) for the employees affected by the termination.

12.39 The negotiations on a reconciliation of interests commence with a comprehensive notification of the Works Council; in business enterprises with more than 300 employees, the Works Council may also, in addition to a lawyer, call in a consultant (often business economists for an analysis of the employer's planning) at the employer's cost and expense. Statute does not define the term 'comprehensive notification', nor is there a definition of the concept of 'planning stage' at which the notification must commence.

Generally though Works Councils wish to be informed as early as possible, while employers often wish to wait until the completion of the planning. Disputes are inevitable here.

As a general rule, the Works Council must be notified of the names and data of the affected employees (and also of the unaffected employees because of the 'social selection'), as well as economic basic data of the company, including but not limited to, the planning etc. In relation to restructurings, this includes a detailed description of the planned measures (before and after view). If comprehensive information is provided to the Works Council at an early stage then this will reduce the risk of the Works Council having to request further information – if the employer provides information only on a limited basis or on a 'drip-feed'-basis then this is likely to delay the process. While the timeframe always depends on the individual circumstances, it is not unusual that negotiations continue over a period of between three to six months.

Practical Tip

All information that is provided to the Works Council should be provided in German or in a bi-lingual version. Even if the business language in the group is English this does not mean that the consultation process can be conducted in a foreign language. The result of any such process, ie a reconciliation of interests agreement (which covers the 'if, how and when' of the proposed restructuring measure) and the social plan (which deals primarily with the severance package for impacted employees) will be drafted in German by the supporting lawyers. It may be advisable though to have an English language version set out next to the German text to ensure that central HR or central legal team based in another jurisdiction can follow and influence the process.

In connection with the negotiations on a reconciliation of interests agreement, the employer may try to agree with the Works Council a 'list of names' which contains the names of those employees who are to be dismissed following a social selection (which may not be identical with the employees selected on the basis of the statutory selection criteria). If this is done (many works councils will refuse to do this or will try to 'sell' their agreement in the form of high severance payments for the employees), the social selection can only be reviewed by the courts for gross errors, and the operational reasons will be assumed to exist by operation of law. In practice, this means that the employee is subject to severe restrictions in its argumentation against the effectiveness of the dismissal in connection with the action for unfair dismissal.

If the negotiations on a reconciliation of interests and/or the social compensation plan do not come to a conclusion within a reasonable time period, then either the employer or the Works Council may apply to a 'conciliation committee' (*Einigungsstelle*), which will then, under the chairmanship of an independent third party (often an employment judge) continue the negotiations with an identical number of wing members (often two to four) from the employer and the Works Council side. The chairman of the conciliation committee and the external assessors (ie, the assessors who are not employed by the business) receive remuneration which must be negotiated for the chairman, while the external assessors will, subject to different remuneration based on the project or the time spent, receive 7/10 of that amount. The proceedings are no court proceedings but, rather, business-internal conciliation proceedings which may, however, make result in binding arrangements: Unless an agreement is reached during its meetings (which will mostly be the case), the conciliation committee will be authorised to determine in a binding manner the conditions of a social compensation plan, ie, the amount of severance payments to be made to dismissed employees. In that determination, the conciliation committee will be bound by specific criteria laid down un the German Labour-Management Relations Act such as the scope of financial disadvantages, the prospects of the affected employees on the labour market, but also any potential benefits granted by the state in that context. The total of the severance payments, ie, the financial scope of the social compensation plan, may not jeopardise the continued existence of the company, or the existence of the jobs which remain within the company.

Please note: Even if a reconciliation of interests agreement and a social compensation plan exists this does not necessarily mean that the individual employees selected for dismissal must accept their fate. Employees so affected by dismissal can nevertheless still challenge their dismissal by way of an (individual) unfair dismissal claim.

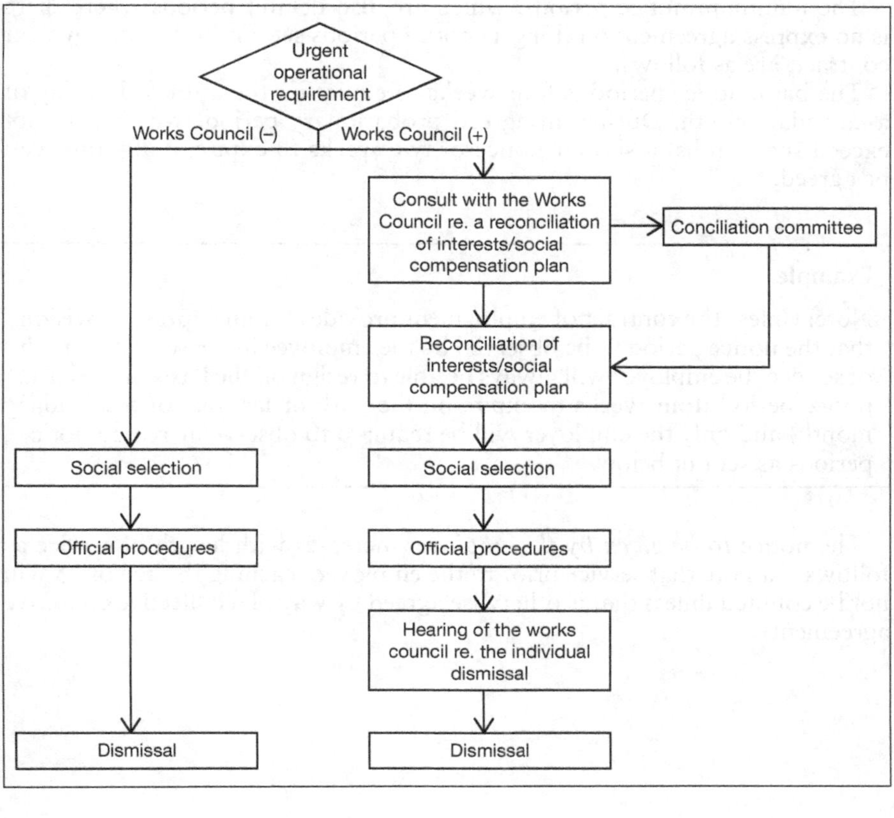

NOTICE

12.40 If the employment relationship is ended by dismissal notice by the employer or by resignation by the employee then, under normal circumstances, a notice period must be observed. This is the time between receipt of the dismissal notice or receipt of the resignation notice and the last day of the employment (termination date). Frequently German employees work out their notice period although the contract of employment may provide for the right of the employer to suspend the employee during the notice period (garden leave) or the employer may otherwise be able to establish a right to put the employee on garden leave during the notice period (see para **12.50** for details).

Minimum notice periods

12.41 The notice periods are largely addressed in section 622 of the Civil Code (*Bürgerliches Gesetzbuch*, BGB).

The minimum notice periods, which are also default periods where there is no express agreement on (longer) notice periods set out in the employment contract, are as follows:

The basic notice period is four weeks to expire on the 15th or last day of a calendar month. During an agreed probationary period (which may not exceed six months) a shorter notice of two weeks to expire at any time can be agreed.

Example

Note: Unless the contract of employment provides for an express provision that the notice period to be observed by the employee increases with length of service the employee will always be able to resign on the basis of the basic notice period (four weeks to expire on the 15th or last day of a calendar month) and only the employer will be required to observe increased notice periods as set out below.

The notice *to be given by the employer* increases with length of service as follows but note that service prior to the employee reaching the age of 25 will not be counted unless that is otherwise agreed by way of a collective collective agreement.

Period of completed continuous employment;	**Notice period**
Two years	one month to expire at the end of a calendar month
Five years	two months to expire at the end of a calendar month
Eight years	three months to expire at the end of a calendar month
Ten years	four months to expire at the end of a calendar month
Twelve years	five months to expire at the end of a calendar month
Fifteen years	six months to expire at the end of a calendar month
Twenty years	seven months to expire at the end of a calendar month.

Example

Employee A has a service length of two years and six months. The employer posts the letter with the dismissal notice to the employee on 31 March. The letter arrives the next day, 1 April. As the notice can only expire at the end of a calendar month the effective date of termination (last day of employment) will be the 30 June.

Had the letter arrived on 31 March the notice period would have come to an end on 31 May.

12.42 Fixed term contracts end automatically upon the expiry of the fixed term. The parties can agree that the contract can end sooner and upon either party giving notice.

12.43 Under the law of collective bargaining, binding arrangements in deviation from the foregoing may be established for the parties to the agreement with respect to duration of the notice period and termination dates.

Employers and employees that are not directly within scope of a relevant collective collective agreement can agree to apply the same.

12.44 In respect of the employment of temporary staff and locums (*Aushilfen*) who work in the company for no more than three months, shorter notice periods can be agreed, including no notice period at all. If the company has fewer than 20 employees – not including apprentices – an agreement on notice periods in deviation from section 622 of the Civil Code, eg effective at the end of a calendar week, is permissible, provided such notice period is no shorter than four weeks.

12.45 The parties can contractually agree longer notice periods. In addition, the parties are entitled to contractually agree on notice end dates that deviate from the statutory default. Under statute most notice periods expire at the end of a calendar month. The parties can contractually agree that the notice shall expire at, say, the end of the calendar quarter.

The agreed notice periods for a resignation by the employee or dismissal by the employer may differ. However, it is not permissible to require the employee to comply with a notice period that is longer than the notice period applicable to the employer.

Special notice arrangements

12.46 In some cases, the prevailing norm of section 622 of the Civil Code is superseded by special arrangements, such as in training/apprenticeship relationships (section 22 of the Vocational Training Act (*Berufsbildungsgesetz*, BBiG)), when employing disabled workers (section 86 of the Social Code (*Sozialgesetzbuch*, SGB), Book IX), and for fixed-term employment relationships under section 21, para. 4, sentence 1 of the Federal Act on Parental Benefits and Parental Leave (*Bundeselterngeld- und Elternzeitgesetz*, BEEG). In addition, there is a special right of termination in the event of insolvency of the employing company, where the notice period is limited to a maximum of three months (section 113 of the Insolvency Code (*Insolvenzordnung*, InsO)).

Termination without notice

12.47 An employment relationship may be terminated forthwith for an 'important reason' (*wichtiger Grund*) without complying with a notice period (section 626 of the Civil Code). Statute defines an 'important reason' as a set of factual circumstances against which either party cannot reasonably be expected to comply with a notice period. Most of the cases of summary dismissal that fall within this category are gross misconduct cases, including, but not limited to, theft or violence at the workplace. A summary dismissal is only possible within two weeks of becoming aware of the factual circumstances justifying such termination. In the context of workforce restructuring exercises such summary dismissal cases are hence not relevant as the dismissal is based on an operational reason on the employer's side rather than employee conduct reasons.

12.48 Notice of termination *must always be given in writing (excluding any electronic form (email, SMS, etc)*. The parties cannot agree otherwise. If this formal requirement is not complied with, the notice is ineffective in its entirety. This means that a hardcopy original with a 'wet ink' signature is required. The signatory or signatories will need to have authority to act for or on behalf of the employer, either by way of office (statutory director etc) or by way of a power of attorney (which would then need to be provided to the employee as well in an original hard copy form).

Giving of notice does not end the employment relationship until the effective termination date, meaning that it continues to exist unchanged in every respect until such time.

Leave and suspension during the notice period

12.49 In addition to typical forms of leave in an unterminated employment relationship, such as during holiday or a strike, German law recognises special types of leave for employment relationships during the notice period.

During the notice period, the employee has a statutory entitlement to be granted paid leave for the purposes of searching for new employment. Extended rights may exist under collective collective agreements.

12.50 Where the employer unilaterally suspends the employee (garden leave) during the notice period this conflicts with the employee's 'right to work' and it is therefore generally not permissible, even after notice of termination has been given.

By way of exception, this may be assessed differently where the employer has an overriding, protected interest in placing the employee on garden leave during the notice period.

Recognised circumstances include:

(a) elimination of the job due to the department being shut down during the termination notice period;
(b) other operationally related terminations, provided that placing employees on leave forms part of the agreed social compensation plan;
(c) conduct-related termination given with proper notice or termination based on the strong suspicion of a criminal act by the employee; and
(d) justified termination without notice.

In general, the parties are at liberty to agree contractually on both paid and unpaid leave and to also agree that the employer shall have a right to suspend the employee during the notice period (garden leave). However, any such clauses in German employment contracts are subject to the German Unfair Contract Terms provisions set out in the Civil Code.

SEVERANCE

12.51 Contrary to a widely held belief, the ending of an employment relationship does not in itself generally establish a claim to payment of severance. The parties are of course at liberty to agree on it by contract and collective agreements may also provide for severance entitlements.

In a restructuring exercise that involves mandatory Works Council involvement (by way of a balancing of interest agreement and social plan) an entitlement to severance pay will then flow from an agreed social plan. Severance can also be the result of employment litigation concerning the lawfulness of the dismissal.

In the event of a dismissal for operational reasons, the employer can agree with the employee to 'buy out' the employee's right to file an unfair dismissal action through payment of severance in the amount of half the employee's monthly remuneration per year of service. This arrangement is designed to offer the parties a simple, non-bureaucratic solution for handling dismissals for operational reasons and to help limit the uncertainty of a trial for unlawful dismissal. However, this is not usually a suitable instrument in cases where there is a requirement to negotiate a social plan with a Works Council. For such a severance claim to come into existence (a) the termination must be based on operational reasons and (b) the employee must be expressly informed that the severance claim arises if the employee does not file a claim for unlawful dismissal within the limitation period of three weeks. Indication of the amount of severance is not mandatory in the notice. Written form is required.

12.52 If there are changes in business operations within the meaning of section 111 of the Works Constitution Act, a social compensation plan is drawn up, either through voluntary agreement or through a ruling by the conciliation committee. The measures to be stipulated therein concerning 'compensation or mitigation of any financial detriments sustained by employees as a result of the proposed changes in business operations' (section 112, para. 1, sentence 2 of the Works Constitution Act) also include severance.

Severance claim under collective collective agreements

12.53 Severance entitlements can also be agreed in collective collective agreements. In this respect, alongside the creation of a social compensation plan within the company, unions have the possibility of working towards the conclusion of a so-called 'collectively bargained social compensation plan', ie a collective collective agreement, which picks up on the essential content of a potential social compensation plan and thus also on severance arrangements, whereby they can – in contrast to the Works Council – have resort to labour dispute tools, like strikes.

Taxation

12.54 Severance that is paid due to the dissolution of the employment relationship is, as a starting point, subject to income tax. There are no tax free elements and the severance is to be taxed at the employee's applicable tax rate in the fiscal year of receipt of the payment. As this may lead to an unfair income tax progression in the year of receipt, the so-called 'one-fifth rule' (section 34 of the Income Tax Act (*Einkommensteuergesetz*, EStG)) can be applied such that the tax burden is somewhat reduced in the year of receipt. Under this rule only one fifth of the severance will be added to the taxable income of the employee in the year of receipt and the marginal tax rate then be applied to the taxable income.

PROHIBITION OF COMPETITION

During an existing employment relationship

12.55 A prohibition of competition is expressly set forth in statute only for commercial clerks (*Handlungsgehilfen*) in sections 60 et seq. of the Commercial Code (*Handelsgesetzbuch*, Commercial Code). When interpreted in conformity with the constitution, it prohibits working in the employer's commercial branch and providing support for competing companies.

The prohibition of competition in section 60 Commercial Code constitutes a general legal concept, which leads to analogous applicability to other workers, provided they are not necessarily reliant on other work in order to make a living. A prohibition of this sort may also be derived from the principle of good faith (section 242 of the Civil Code (*Bürgerliches Gesetzbuch*, BGB)).

Post termination restrictions

12.56 While a post-contractual prohibition of competition can generally be agreed upon, it is subject to strict prerequisites.

Requirements

12.57 The basic principle must always be observed that a post-termination prohibition of competition may be agreed on only to protect the employer's justified interests and may not unreasonably hinder the employee's economic freedom. It must be agreed upon in writing, and an instrument signed by the employer must be handed over to the employee. In terms of scope, it may be concluded for a term of a maximum of two years, and it is mandatory that a so-called compensation payment (*Karenzentschädigung*) is agreed upon at the same time as the restrictions are put in place. This must amount to at least 50% of previous monthly remuneration for each month of the restricted period, whereby special payments like Christmas pay, holiday pay, and bonuses and commission payments are to be taken into account.

Compensation is generally payable at the end of each month. Whilst the statutory default position is that other remuneration that the employee earns through alternative work can be deducted, provided the same, together with the compensation, exceeds 110% of the original remuneration or 125%, where the employee has relocated, these off-set rules are often excluded by way of agreement between the parties.

Failure to meet requirements

12.58 A prohibition of competition that does not take into account the aforementioned basic principles or minimum substantive requirements is non-binding. In such case, the employee can free himself or herself of it by simple declaration.

If the agreement violates the stipulated form, or it if was concluded with minors or trainees, it is void.

In the case of effective termination by the employee without notice he or she can cause the prohibition of competition to become ineffective by making a written declaration within one month of termination He or she can also do so where he or she is terminated by the employer with notice and the reason for termination is not linked to the person of the employee. The employer can avert the latter by pledging to continue to pay the emoluments in full for the duration of the limitation on competition.

TRANSFER OF AN UNDERTAKING

12.59 In the event that a business is transferred the question arises if and on what terms the employees linked to the business transfer with the business to the new owner. This is dealt with in section 613a of the Civil Code (*Bürgerliches Gesetzbuch*, BGB) which implements the European Acquired Rights Directive into German law. The rules relate to asset deals only, not to share deals.

12.60 The core of the arrangement is the unchanged transfer of the employment relationship to the new owner. Continuous service is not interrupted by the transfer of business. Any collectively bargained arrangements are subject to status protection for one year. Status protection takes effect only insofar as the respective aspects have not been addressed by the new employer in a collective collective agreement or works agreement or the agreements have become ineffective in any event, eg through lapse of time.

12.61 The previous employer is jointly and severally liable together with the new owner for prior obligations to the employee, provided they are due within one year. Both parties to the purchase agreement must ensure that the employee is informed in writing about the planned transaction, its specific consequences for the employee, and the personnel measures planned for the future.

12.62 The transfer of business as such does not constitute a permissible reason for termination by the employer, but the transfer does not prevent termination for other unconnected reason. On the other hand, the employee may object to the transfer of the employment relationship within one month of receipt of the notification of the transfer (*Unterrichtungsschreiben*). In itself, the transfer of business does not necessarily constitute a change in business operations within the meaning of the Works Constitution Act (*Betriebsverfassungsgesetz*, Works Constitution Act) and is therefore, in itself, not subject to Works Council co-determination. However, typically a transfer goes hand in hand with operational changes which, in turn, are by and large subject to Works Council co-determination. Specific problems arise in cases in which a shut-down of operations was initially planned and partially implemented (social plans agreed and redundancy dismissal notices issued) and then, contrary to the original assumption, a purchaser does in fact emerge. In that scenario a dismissed employee whose notice period has not yet expired has a claim for reinstatement and continuation of the employment. Although the business basis for a potential social compensation plan generally no longer applies, the dismissed employee may have made arrangements in reliance on the dismissal, for which reason the employee is also entitled to let the employment relationship come to an end as was originally planned and rely on the terms of the agreed social compensation plan.

VARIATION OF CONTRACTUAL TERMS

12.63 The parties are at all times at liberty to mutually agree on new arrangements for an existing employment agreement. However, the modified agreement remains subject to the same substantive and formal requirements of a newly concluded employment agreement.

On the other hand, neither the employer nor the employee generally has the ability to retrospectively modify individual components of the agreement.

Part-time working requests

12.64 By way of exception, however, an employee working in a company with more than 15 employees can request that the contractually agreed working hours be reduced or extended (sections 8 and 9 of the Act on Part-Time Work and Fixed-Term Employment Agreements (*Gesetz über Teilzeitarbeit und befristete Arbeitsverträge*, TzBFG)).

12.65 The employer must comply with the employee's request to reduce working hours if: (a) the employment relationship has been in effect for at least six months; (b) the employee made the application not later than three months prior to the desired change; (c) no operational considerations stand in the way; and (d) during the past two years, no applications by the employee for reduction were approved or justifiably denied.

12.66 In addition, a part-time employee who is just as suited as other applicants has a claim to preferential consideration when filling a position with higher working hours, unless opposed by operational reasons or interests of other part-time employees that take priority.

Termination combined with the offer to reengage on new terms of employment

12.67 The employer may implement a modification of existing terms and conditions through termination combined with the offer to reengage on new terms of employment (*Änderungskündigung*).

Here the employer terminates the employee while at the same time offering to him or her that the employment relationship be continued under modified contractual conditions. In this regard, notice of termination may be given not only unconditionally but also subject to the condition subsequent of non-acceptance of the offer of continuation.

12.68 Since termination with the option of modified conditions of employment must also always contain a genuine termination, all requirements for effectiveness must be complied with, such as form, notice period, consultations, and social selection.

Applicable to this termination is also the labour-law principle of last resort, ie it must always be examined whether there is a method that is milder than and as equally effective as the offered change, such as offering other suitable alternative employment within the company.

In this regard, the employee can either accept the offer of modification and thus avert the ending of his or her employment relationship or acquiesce to termination through non-acceptance. The employee can also accept the offer subject to the proviso that termination was socially justified. In this way, the employee secures continuation of employment whilst retaining the possibility of judicial review.

TEMPORARY AGENCY WORKERS

12.69 Temporary agency workers (*Zeitarbeitnehmer*) are those who are provided by their employer to a customer on a temporary basis to perform operational tasks for and under the direction of the customer. This results in a triangular relationship between the provider undertaking (employer of the temporary agency workers), the user undertaking (customer), and the temporary agency worker: the right to give instruction is assigned to the user undertaking, and a statutory relationship based on an obligation to protect is established between it and the temporary agency worker, but the employment relationship continues to exist between the provider undertaking and the temporary agency worker.

Under a contract for temporary agency work, as opposed to a contract to produce a work, the employee is integrated into the user undertaking and is subject to its instructions. Although no rigid limits are placed on the duration of the assignment, it must generally aimed to be a non-permanent assignment.

Required permit

12.70 Temporary agency work is highly regulated in Germany. In order to assign workers on a commercial basis, a permit from the Federal Employment Agency (*Bundesagentur für Arbeit*) is required under sections 1 et seq. of the Act on the Assignment of Workers (*Arbeitnehmerüberlassungsgesetz*, AÜG). A failure to have in place in required permit creates a significant risk for the end user in that the temporary agency workers are then likely to be deemed employees of the end user rather than the provider.

Assignment of workers in the area of the construction industry is permissible to only a limited extent. Here, the prerequisite is that the user undertaking and the provider undertaking have a homogeneous rate structure, as well as that the provider undertaking has been covered by the applicability of the same framework and social insurance agreements for at least three years.

In addition, there are other exceptions to the permit requirement for other industry sectors.

EMPLOYMENT CLAIMS

Local jurisdiction

12.71 In the event of a dispute about the existence of rights and obligations under an employment relationship, both parties may take the dispute to the labour courts.

12.72 The labour court with locational jurisdiction is the one at the location at which the employee habitually performs his or her work.

12.73 There is also a place of jurisdiction at the location at which the contractual obligation is to be fulfilled. With employment relationships, this is usually the economic and technical centre of the work performance. A claim may also be brought at the respondent's place of residence. If more than one court has jurisdiction, the claimant can select the forum.

12.74 In the case of actions involving several claimants for compensation of damage under anti-discrimination legislation, the employer can request that the labour court at which the first claim was filed be exclusively competent for the other claims. In this case, the legal disputes are to be referred to this labour court and the trials joined together for simultaneous litigation and decision making.

12.75 Parties to a collective collective agreement can agree a different jurisdiction for the purposes of any disputes arising out of or in relation to the collective collective agreement. These jurisdiction arrangements also apply between employers and employees not bound by collective collective agreements if the applicability of the entire collective collective agreement was agreed to in the respective individual employment agreement.

Agreement on place of jurisdiction

12.76 An agreement on a place of jurisdiction in an individual employment agreement generally and prior to the arising of a legal dispute is generally void.

An agreement on a place of jurisdiction can be entered into *after* the dispute arises, with it being sufficient that although a claim has not yet been submitted, litigation is expected with some degree of certainty.

Limitation periods

12.77 A claim to protect the employee against unfair dismissal must be brought by the employee within three weeks of the employee having received the dismissal notice. This very short 'window of opportunity' frequently means that employees are advised to bring a claim in any event as the three week period is often not considered to be long enough for the employee's legal advisers to assess the case is full, let alone negotiate any kind of settlement agreement.

Remedies

12.78 The remedy that employees are primarily looking for are reengagement or reinstatement. German law does not provide for any other remedy to be requested as part of the litigation process. If the dismissal was not justified then the court generally finds that the employment relationship has not been terminated and that it continues: the dismissal will not just be unfair but simply void. However, if it is unreasonable to expect one or both parties to continue the employment relationship, the court will order the employer to pay severance rather than expect the employer to continue the relationship. In addition to such compensation (for the loss of employment) the employer may then also have to make a retrospective remuneration payment in respect of the time period from the end of employment as stipulated in the (void) dismissal notice and the point in time of the court ruling. Slightly modified rules apply to senior management employees.

Special arrangement in the Works Constitution Act (Betriebsverfassungsgesetz, Works Constitution Act)

12.79 Alongside the obligatory social compensation plan, a so-called reconciliation of interests (*Interessensausgleich*) can in addition be concluded in the event of a change in business operations (section 112 of the Works Constitution Act), which contains understandings between the Works Council and the employer on the 'whether', 'how', and 'when' of the measures to be implemented in connection with the change in business operations, whereby neither conclusion nor implementation of the understanding is mandatory. However, violation of a reconciliation of interests once adopted, as well as failing to negotiate, or failing to negotiate seriously, about the conclusion of the same, provides the affected employee under section 113 of the Works Constitution Act with the ability to bring a claim in court for payment of severance.

Termination Agreement

12.80 The ending of an employment may at any time be agreed upon by means of a termination agreement. Such agreements will usually include all-encompassing waiver clauses to the end that the agreement is in full and final settlement of all claims that the parties have or may have against each other.

The termination agreement must be in writing (within the meaning of German law). A standardised based waiver declaration will be regarded as 'general terms and conditions' (and as such subject to the scrutiny of the unfair contract terms legislation), and in the absence of compensation, it is ineffective as it would be regarded as unreasonably disadvantaging the employee. By contrast, an agreement that is entered into post dismissal and which deals only with the manner of the ending of an employment relationship, does not need to satisfy the form requirements of sections 623 and 125b of the Civil Code. If the prerequisites are present for a mass dismissal, a termination agreement and also the dismissal intended by it do not become effective until submission of a mass-dismissal notice with the labour office that meets the form requirements and obtaining of the latter's permission. However, participation by the Works Council is not necessary.

Content

12.81 The employer should make sure the employee is aware of the possible detriments following from voluntarily ending the employment by way of a termination agreement. This includes as possible suspension of the entitlement to unemployment benefits and the possibility of the occurrence of a disqualification period for unemployment benefit, as well as the possible reduction of state pension entitlements.

Chapter 13

Workforce Restructuring in Greece

Fani Skartouli
Potomitis Vekris, Athens

INTRODUCTION

13.1 The chapter looks at the employment laws of Greece as they relate to restructuring operations. Greece is a continental European jurisdiction, thus its law is codified. Greek employment law lacks a comprehensive and systematic codification, in the sense that there is no single Employment Law Code, as in some other European jurisdictions. The main sources of employment law may be found in the Greek Constitution, International Conventions, EU Regulations, Laws, Presidential Decrees and Ministerial Decisions, in collective labour agreements, national, sector or business-wide, arbitration decisions, business practices and individual employment contracts. Court rulings should also be consulted in order to understand how the above mentioned provisions are interpreted and applied by the courts. The employer's managerial rights also have an important impact on the employment relationship.

13.2 The contracting parties to an employment agreement are free to determine and adjust the content of their agreement, in accordance with the principle of freedom of contract, which governs Greek civil law in general. However, such freedom is significantly limited by regulatory restrictions. More precisely, numerous legal provisions are qualified as public policy rules which may not be circumvented, even if both parties to an employment relationship would be willing to do so. Greek employment law thus creates a social minimum, especially in terms of minimum payment conditions, working hours, annual leave entitlements, health and safety rules etc, which may not be arranged in a different way by the parties.

13.3 Besides this notion of social public policy, Greek employment law is traditionally governed by the principle of protection of employees. In this respect, when various provisions could apply to certain circumstances, the applicable provision will be the most favourable to the employee. For example, if an applicable collective agreement provides for a higher salary than the one which is set by statute, the collective agreement provision shall prevail. In the same sense, employment agreements may only provide for more protection than applicable collective agreement provisions, since the minima already set for an employee by statute or collective agreement may only be improved by individual agreements between the employer and the employee.

13.4 Due to the deep and ongoing recession that the Greek economy has encountered since 2008, unemployment has risen to unprecedented levels. As a consequence, significant changes have taken place with regard to the setting of minimum wages, the collective bargaining mechanism, the enforceability of collective agreements, the calculation of severance payments, the forms of flexible employment et al. For example, business-wide collective agreements have been liberated, meaning that they need not provide for more favourable treatment than sector-wide collective agreements, with a view to providing for more flexibility. Furthermore, the amount of statutory severance payment has fallen and in stark contrast with previous years, flexible forms of employment have been widely implemented by employers in Greece. The conversion of full-time employment to part-time or shift work is a striking example of this trend.

13.5 The following paragraphs will focus on the various legal aspects of restructuring operations in Greece, regardless of them leading to redundancies.

PREPARING FOR A RESTRUCTURING EXERCISE

Essential information

13.6 In order to assess the risks involved by a restructuring operation, the following information is considered necessary for outlining a restructuring plan.

- list of all current employees (including names, date of commencement of employment, date of birth, salaries and benefits);
- internal regulations;
- details on trade unions (if any) and other staff associations (eg works council) active in the company;
- template employment contracts usually signed by employees (or – if no such template exists – copies of all current individual employment contracts);

- calculation of severance pay owed to employees in case terminations are envisaged;
- information on any special termination arrangements;
- applicable collective labour agreement (sector or business-wide);
- summary of any threatened or pending labour disputes and any documentation relating thereto;
- information on fixed-term employees;
- information on staff loans, stock option plans and other profit sharing schemes;
- information on the group medical insurance policy;
- internal guidelines, employee handbooks, etc;
- information on collective redundancies or terminations for economic and technical reason during the last two years; and
- bonus schemes or salary policy in general

EMPLOYMENT STATUS

13.7 Greek employment legislation is applicable only to subordinate employment relationships. The main criterion to identify a subordinate employment is the criterion of dependence. According to the jurisprudential definition, the element of dependence exists when the employer has the right to direct the employee's work, to determine the place of work and the working hours and to control the employee's performance.

13.8 In this respect, dependent employees benefit from the protection granted by law and collective bargaining regarding base salaries, information agreements and consultation right, protection from dismissal, health and safety at work, working time, employee representation etc.

13.9 The distinction between subordinate employment and self-employment is often vague. The employment status of some subordinate employees is often disguised as a self-employment relationship, mostly in order to circumvent payment of social security contributions, application of fiscal law provisions and protection against dismissal.

13.10 However, according to relevant case law, self-employment may be qualified as subordinate employment, regardless of the qualification given by the contracting parties, to the extent that its particular characteristics relate closer to the characteristics of subordinate employment. More precisely, the main issues that a local court will look into if the qualification of self-employment is challenged are the instructions of the employer as to the time, the place and the method of provision of services

GENERAL PROTECTION AGAINST DISMISSAL

General information

13.11 According to Greek law, an employer may unilaterally terminate permanent employment agreements at any time, without any requirement to indicate the reasons for termination. In other words, the law does not require a 'serious cause' for the termination of indefinite-terms contracts. However, the employee may challenge the validity of the termination in the case of an abuse of the employer's rights to terminate. A typical case of such abuse would be the dismissal of an employee who performs well for non-justifiable reasons, such as victimisation by the employer, employee participation in industrial action, etc. Taking into consideration the above, in order to avoid any risks, the employer must be able to prove – with witnesses and documentation – that the employment agreement was terminated for justified reasons ie for breach of employee obligations, continuing underperformance, etc.

13.12 For the same purpose, dismissal must be the ultimate measure (*ultima ratio*) taken by the employer. In this respect, an employer must be in a position to prove that he has exhausted all alternatives before terminating an employment agreement.

13.13 According to Greek legislation, the termination of a permanent employment agreement is valid only if made in writing and upon a simultaneous payment of the exact amount of the statutory severance due to the employee. Payment may also be made in instalments, provided that an amount equal to two annualised monthly salaries is paid on the termination date. In addition, the termination document should be signed by the person who is legally authorised by the company to sign employee termination documents.

13.14 The only case where the employer is not obliged to pay the legal severance amount is when the employee has committed a criminal offence and the employer has filed criminal charges against him before termination

Notice

13.15 The employer is not obliged to terminate with prior notice; it remains at the employer's absolute discretion to give such notice. In other words, the employer has the option either to notify the employee (ie respecting the statutory notice period) before the dismissal or not to notify but terminate immediately. In the latter case the totality of the legal severance is due, whereas in case of termination with prior notice, half the amount of the statutory severance is due.

Statutory severance amount

13.16 Severance payments are calculated based on the monthly base salary of the employee on the termination date, multiplied by 14 (so as to take into account the Christmas and Easter bonus and the annual leave bonus, as per the Greek legislation), and divided by 12, in order to produce an annualised monthly average.

13.17 Such average salary is increased by all the fringe benefits the employee receives on a regular basis (such as car allowance, housing allowance, mobile telephone, insurance coverage, commissions – if the commission plan or variable pay scheme forms part of his/her individual agreement or is covered by a collective agreement, bonuses – if granted by the employer on a regular basis and without any disclaimer on the employer's side for the annulment of such bonus payment etc).

13.18 The following table provides the statutory notice periods and the respective severance amounts in case of termination with and without prior notice:

Years of service	Statutory Notice period (months)	Severance amount in case the statutory notice period is given (monthly salaries)	Severance amount in case no notice period is given (monthly salaries)
1–2	1	1	2
2–4	2	1	2
4–5	2	1.5	3
5–6	3	1.5	3
6–8	3	2	4
8–10	3	2.5	5
10	4	3	6
11	4	3.5	7
12	4	4	8
13	4	4.5	9
14	4	5	10
15	4	5.5	11
16 +	4	6	12

13.19 Paying the right amount of severance in case of termination is extremely important, since if the correct amount is not paid, the employee has the right to file a lawsuit contesting the validity of the termination, requesting the court to declare it abusive and invalid.

SPECIAL PROTECTION AGAINST DISMISSAL

Maternity Protection

13.20 Greek employment law prohibits the termination of employment of any employee who is pregnant or is the mother of a child under the age of 18 months. Therefore any termination during pregnancy, as well as during the first 18 months from the date of birth of the child is null and void, unless there is a serious cause for such termination. This protection is applicable only to permanent employment, whereas fixed term employment of pregnant employees or those who are mothers of infants ends automatically upon expiry of the fixed term.

13.21 In general serious cause for the termination of an employment agreement is defined as one or more acts which would objectively and in good faith render the continuation of the employment relationship unacceptable for the party who is entitled to terminate and regardless of the wilful misconduct of the other party. In the case of pregnant employees or those who are mothers of infants, such serious cause would be the employee's denial to comply with the employer's instructions, underperformance, repeated unjustified absence from work, significant fall of business activity, breach of faith by the employee, etc. Such serious reason may not be associated with underperformance caused by the pregnancy or motherhood. The onus of proof of the serious cause lies with the employer. Moreover, in terms of procedure, such serious cause must be clearly stated in the termination document which will be filed with the Labour Authority following termination.

Employee representatives

13.22 Employee representatives benefit from special protection regarding dismissal and performance of duties. More precisely, as far as dismissal of an employee representative is concerned, law 1264/1982 provides that any such dismissal will be considered as null and void. Exceptions are provided for by article 14 of law 1264/1982, but they depend on very strict conditions regarding the merits and the procedure to be followed.

13.23 More precisely, dismissal of union board members is allowed only for the following reasons:

- embezzlement upon hiring, eg submission of false certificates in view of being hired or paid with higher remuneration;
- disclosure of confidential business information;
- injure, threat or serious insult against the employer or the representative of the employing legal entity;
- constant and unjustifiable denial to provide services;

- unjustifiable absence from work; or
- participation in an illegal strike.

13.24 On the grounds of one of the above-mentioned reasons, the dismissal of a protected employee must be ratified by a Special Committee according to article 15 of law 1264/1982. Unless the Committee has given its permission, the employer may not proceed to the employee's dismissal and any dismissal contrary to the Committee's decision will be judged null and void.

Military service

13.25 Greece operates a system of a period of compulsory military service (currently nine months) for all men between the age of 18 and 45. Employees called to serve their military service are protected by mandatory legal provisions, as long as they have been employed for more than six months with the same employer. Upon completion of the employee's military service and following his expression of interest, the employer is obliged to reinstate the employee and termination of employment is forbidden for the next 12 months.

Employees hired by virtue of mandatory legal provisions

13.26 According to law 2643/1998 companies of more than 50 employees may be required by State order to hire people with disabilities who have limited access to employment due to lifelong health problems. Other categories protected by the same legal provisions are the children of victims of war or the children of members of the National Resistance. Employment agreements governed by these legal provisions are terminated only following a decision of the National Unemployment Authority or following an application filed by the employer to the relevant State Committee on the grounds of the employee's serious misconduct. The Committee will then render a mandatory decision ratifying or rejecting such demand for permission to terminate the employment agreement.

WORKFORCE REDUCTION

Dismissals for economic and technical reasons

Definition

13.27 The decision to downsize personnel in view of a restructuring and in general for economic and technical or organisational reasons, is not subject to judicial control. Greek courts do not query the underlying reason or business rationale for a restructuring. However, courts are entitled to look at the lawfulness of dismissals due to the restructuring. In these cases, the judicial control focuses on the following points: (a) if a restructuring actually took place and was not triggered with the sole purpose of terminating employment agreements; (b) if the employer had sought alternative solutions before proceeding to termination, eg removal from current role to another, part-time employment, negotiation of new employment terms and if such solutions were proved to be impossible or unproductive; and (c) if the employer respected the legal selection criteria when choosing the specific employees who were made redundant, and not others.

13.28 Of course, such judicial control does not take place at the court's own initiative, but only following the issue of legal action by the redundant employees, provided that such legal action has been initiated within three months as from the termination date.

General obligation of information and consultation with employee representatives

13.29 Restructuring operations are also subject to the current legislative framework for information and consultation rights of employee representatives in Greece. Presidential Decree 240/2006 (PD 240/2006) implemented Directive 2002/14 of the European Parliament and of the Council of 11 March 2002 establishing a general framework for informing and consulting employees in the European Community. According to PD 240/2006, an employer's obligation to inform and consult with employee representatives shall cover:

(a) information on the recent and probable development of the undertaking's or the establishment's activities and economic situation;
(b) information and consultation on the situation, structure and probable development of employment within the undertaking or establishment and on any anticipatory measures envisaged, in particular where there is a threat to employment; and
(c) information and consultation on decisions likely to lead to substantial changes in work organisation or in contractual relations, including those covered by provisions on collective redundancies (law 1387/1983) and transfer of undertakings (PD 178/2002)

13.30 Information and consultation with employee representatives is an obligation which may not be circumvented, especially since restructurings are operations directly affecting the employment conditions of the personnel. It should be noted that the employer is not obliged to reach an agreement with employee representatives, since consultation consists primarily in the exchange of points of view between the two parties.

Selection criteria

13.31 A 'selection process' should be followed each time an employer proceeds to redundancies for technical, organisational or economic reasons (ie closing, reorganisation, reduction of workforce, reorganisation of roles, etc), whether the intended restructuring includes collective redundancies (ie exceeding the thresholds mentioned hereunder) or not.

13.32 The comparison should be made between people belonging, or being able to belong, to the same category of employees, eg to people performing, or being able to perform, the same tasks

13.33 Although such 'selection criteria' are not enumerated by the law, the courts have found that the employer should take into consideration each and every social and/or financial criterion. In other words, the first to be made redundant should be those who: (a) enjoy the least protection compared to others in the selection pool; and (b) will have the least difficulties in finding a new job.

13.34 The employer should consider prior service (seniority) with the same employer ('last one in, first one out'), age ('the youngest should be made redundant before the oldest'), family maintenance obligations ('single employees should be made redundant before those who are married and have children'), health ('the healthy should be made redundant before the sick') etc.

13.35 Recently the courts have begun to accept the opinion that, in addition to such social and financial criteria the employer must also consider productivity, ie to first make redundant those who are less productive than their colleagues. In practice, since there is no ranking in the law of the social and financial criteria, their application should be made in the most objective way, however, it can be always challenged before the courts

13.36 A further complication may arise from a jurisprudential tendency to consider redundancies as '*ultima ratio*', ie 'last resort'. Thus, it is advisable that any and all conceivable means are employed in order to achieve the intended aim, *before* deciding to proceed to redundancies.

13.37 Finally, it goes without saying that any restrictions against dismissal (for example, protection to pregnant women and young mothers, mandatory hirings, employee representatives etc), also apply in this case

Collective redundancies

General information

13.38 The main law examined here is 1387/1983, as modified mainly by laws 2874/2000, 3488/2006 and 3863/2010.

The definition of collective redundancies

13.39 Collective redundancies are those which exceed 6 redundancies per calendar month for businesses employing from 20 to 150 employees, or the limit of 5% of the total workforce (and at most 30 employees) per calendar month for businesses employing more than 150 employees. In other words, the rules that are described hereunder *do not apply to redundancies where the above limits are not exceeded, and also do not apply to mutually agreed terminations*.

13.40 The workforce must be counted on the first day of the calendar month in question. Fixed term employment contracts terminated before the expiration of such fixed term should also be taken into consideration. The total number of dismissals which will take place during one calendar month is the critical element. For example, for a business employing less than 150 people, it is lawful to dismiss six people on 31 March and six more on 1 April. Only dismissals for economic and technical reasons (ie closing, reorganisation, reduction of workforce, economies of scale etc) shall be taken into account and not those occurring because of reasons which are particular to each employee (ie breach of contractual obligation etc).

13.41 Before proceeding to collective redundancies, the employer must consult with the representatives of the employees in an effort to avoid or reduce the number of collective dismissals and/or their negative consequences. Thus, such representatives must receive any and all useful information by the employer and most notably in writing on: (i) the reasons for proceeding to collective redundancies; (ii) the number and categories of the employees to be made redundant; (iii) the number of the employees who are usually employed; (iv) the time period during which redundancies will occur; and (v) the selection criteria. Copies of such information documents must be also addressed to the competent authorities.

13.42 The employer must first invite the employee representatives for consultation. A 20-day period follows, during which negotiations shall take place. The result of such negotiations is included in the minutes of such meetings, which are also sent to the competent authorities. If an agreement is reached, it shall be implemented as such. If not, the competent authorities may extend the consultation period for an additional period of 20 days. At the end of the 20- or 40-day period, the employer must obtain the permission of the

Ministry of Employment or of the competent Prefect in order to proceed to collective redundancies. Failure of the competent Authority to respond within ten days from receiving the aforementioned minutes means that the employer may proceed with the redundancies.

13.43 Given the above, the procedure for making collective redundancies is extremely complex and the validity of collective redundancies is conditional upon the Ministry's or the Prefecture's permission.

Business closure

13.44 According to an express provision of law no. 1387/1983 (which seeks to implement the European directive 75/129 on collective redundancies), the procedure of collective redundancies does not apply in closings of businesses, which are ordered by court rulings. This provision spurred controversy. Law no. 1387/1983 further provides in its article 5 (3) that the Prefect or Minister for Labour may, in the event of the parties to the collective consultation process not coming to an agreement, prolong the consultation by 20 days or to deny permission to go ahead with the proposed redundancies.

13.45 Greek law does not provide for a procedure, where a court will order the closure of a business. Thus, the courts have found that Greek law necessarily sets aside the prerequisite of a court ordering the closure.[1]

13.46 However, following decisions nos C-187/05 and C-190/05 of the European Court of Justice (ECJ), dated 7 September 2006, the Plenary Assembly of the Greek Supreme Court found that a failure to comply with the information and consultation procedure in relation to collective redundancies due to a business closure (but where such closure is not the result of a Court order), renders the redundancies null and void.[2]

13.47 Consequently, the crucial question is whether this would also happen in case of collective redundancies with a view to business closure, when the collective redundancies have not been ratified by the Minister's/Prefect's permission. It is clear that an employer must always follow the consultation process before proceeding to collective redundancies, even if a business is being shut down completely. However, the ECJ did not expressly find that a business cannot shut down and/or that it must always be wound down at a rhythm of up to 6 terminations per calendar month. Such limitation (up to six per month) does not result from the European Directives, but from Greek law no. 1387/191.83.

1 Because the law cannot require the impossible. Court of Appeal of Athens 8795-6/91, 5728/91, Court of Appeal of Thessalonica 2143/94, First Instance Court of Athens 3894/91.
2 Plenary Assembly of the Supreme Court 37, 38, 39 and 40/2007.

13.48 In fact, this matter was repeatedly raised with the ECJ, which made an interesting point in its decision dated 15/2/2007 on case C-270/05 (para. 37):

> '[…] Lastly, the Court notes that, in the context of proceedings before the Court, the issue of the compatibility of the intervention by the national public authorities, namely the prefect or the Minister for Labour, as provided for in Article 5(3) of Law 1387/1983, with Directive 98/59 and Article 43 EC has been raised with some insistence. That question was not, however, the subject of the present reference for a preliminary ruling […]'.

In other words, the ECJ refused to decide this matter because it was not asked this particular question by the Greek national courts, but at the same time indirectly invited such Greek courts to ask such a question.

13.49 Part of the legal theory stressed the opinion that in case of the closure of a business (not following a court order), if the employer has observed the information and consultation process, then the Minister is not entitled to prohibit the collective dismissals. It has also been pointed out that a finding to the contrary would infringe economic liberty, which is constitutionally protected.

13.50 Furthermore, according to Greek case law to date, the existence of a business is a necessary condition for the application of any and all legal protection against termination of an employment agreement. For example, Greek courts have repeatedly found that members of the Board of Directors of a Union cannot be lawfully terminated but for the few specific reasons restrictively enumerated in the law, yet that such protection does not apply in case of total closure of some business. For example, Greek courts have also rejected, as abusive, the claim of a Union Board member to be reinstated and paid by a business that no longer exists. Besides this, although a pregnant woman in principle cannot be terminated, Greek courts have accepted that such protection does not apply in case if a real and total closure of the employer's business.

13.51 In other words, there are many arguments to support the claim that, in case of business closure, the Minister's permission is not necessary. However there is no direct court decision on the matter.

BUSINESS SALE, OUTSOURCING/INSOURCING AND OFFSHORING

Main rule

13.52 The legal framework which applies to any transfer of business is set by the Presidential Decree 178/2002, implementing Directives 98/50 EC and 2001/23/EC. According to Greek case law, this legislation, the basic rules of which are examined hereunder, aims mainly at protecting employment and, thus, must always be interpreted accordingly.

13.53 It is important to note that the meaning of transfer of business is defined under the aforementioned legal provisions and it concerns any:

> 'transfer of an economic entity which retains its identity, meaning an organised grouping of resources which has the objective of pursuing an economic activity, whether or not that activity is central or ancillary'.

13.54 In the event of a transfer of a business, the employment contracts of all those employed in such business continue with the person or entity that acquires the business as the new employer. This practically means that the purchaser automatically becomes the employer of the employees working (ie dedicating at least 50% + of their activity to the undertaking, or part of, which is being transferred) or belonging in the transferred undertaking, on the same terms and conditions.

13.55 Such 'terms and conditions' may result from individual employment agreements and/or a collective labour agreement (national, sector or business-wide etc) and/or a business practice (general and/or of the particular business) and/or any other source of law.

13.56 The new employer's lack of awareness of the number of the workforce or the clauses and the exact content of their employment agreements (as they have been modified through time and practice) is of no relevance. The continuation of the aforementioned agreements is the result of the application of the law, no agreement (other than the transfer agreement) between the old and/or the new employer and/or the employee(s) to be transferred, nor any other formality are required.

13.57 The aforementioned obligation refers only to employees who provide their services under a subordinate employment agreement, on a fixed term or permanent basis, on a full or part-time basis, upon the time of the transfer. As such, this obligation includes also:

(a) employees who were mandatorily hired under Law 2643/1998;
(b) international staff hired by the employer (whether in Greece or abroad); only staff hired by the same employing entity that sells/transfer the undertaking are affected; employees hired by other legal entities, (eg seconded employees), are not included; and
(c) executive employees and directors who are providing their work under a subordinate employment agreement.

13.58 On the contrary, according to P.D. 178/2002, anyone not employed under a subordinate employment contract is excluded by the provisions of the 'automatic' transfer (ie the company's consultants, who provide their services under agreements of provision of independent services or project contracts).

13.59 The transfer of employees from the seller to the purchaser is mandatory law and the consequences of the transfer occur automatically, regardless of the will of the parties. Such consequences cannot be excluded or modified to the employees' detriment, not even by an agreement between the seller and the purchaser, or even between the seller and an employee to be transferred, as in such case there is the additional risk for the agreement to be found null and void. However, it goes without saying that if such modification is not to the employees' detriment, if for example an employee wishes to remain with the seller and the seller wishes to retain him/her, this can be achieved by an agreement.

13.60 It must be noted that, according to Greek law, the employees are not entitled to object to the transfer. There is no express provision for an employee to object to a transfer and the transfer takes place *ipso jure*, regardless of the employee's will. Therefore, by not appearing at his/her job post at the purchaser's, an employee is considered to have resigned.

Information and consultation process before the transfer

13.61 The purchaser has the obligation to inform (ideally in writing, ie by email, announcement, letter etc) all affected employees (including those whose employment will not transfer) of the following:

(a) that a transfer will take place (a transfer of what exactly);
(b) when it will take place (approximately, but ideally as precise as possible);
(c) the reasons for the transfer;
(d) the legal, economic and social implications/consequences of the transfer for the employees (and all affected employees in general); and
(e) any measures that the purchaser envisages to take in relation to those employees; and if the purchaser has the right to modify the level of employment and wants to do so, he must consult the union 'in due time', in order to try to reach an agreement.

13.62 The duty of the purchaser is to inform and consult with the employees' representatives for the above mentioned matters. If a Works Council exists, then by law it is the employees' representative. If a Works Council does not exist, but a trade union does, then the latter represents all the employees, even the employees who are not members of the relevant trade union. If neither exists, then the information must be addressed to all employees, who must elect representatives for the consultation.

13.63 Consultation must take place in 'good time' before the transfer. In practice, consultation can normally be completed in 1 month or even less. The employees have no right of objection to the transfer. There are no specific requirements for these meetings other than sharing the information set out above and exchanging views with the representatives. Minutes must be taken during consultation. These minutes should be signed at the very end of each meeting.

13.64 The most important part of the consultation process will be the details of any 'measures' that the purchaser intends to take (that is, whether it intends to change any working practices, replace any benefits, make redundancies etc). Of course the seller does not have any obligation to know the 'measures' the purchaser intends to take after the transfer. In practice the purchaser is called to participate in the consultation process or to inform the seller, even though the purchaser is not obliged to do so. The purchaser has a separate obligation to inform and consult with his employees' representatives on the measures he intends to take after the transfer that will affect his employees (including those transferred).

13.65 One should expect that the most sensitive issues will be possible redundancies, level of salary and benefits. In other words, the transferring employees are likely to be concerned that they may eventually lose their jobs, that their salary may be reduced (not unilaterally – there is no such right – but with immense pressure) and/or that their benefits may be cancelled. According to Greek Courts, only voluntary (ie conferred without obligation) benefits, not contractual ones (ie resulting from an agreement or practice) may be validly unilaterally amended or cancelled by the employer. The question of whether a benefit, which initially was voluntary, continues to be such or has become contractual, is entirely factual, and depends on proof.

13.66 If an employer fails to comply with the aforementioned obligations, he is liable to a fine of up to €8,804[3] or even €50,000.[4] However, in practical terms such employer will also cause serious unrest among his/her employees, their unions and, in addition, hostility from the part of the Ministry of Labour and other Authorities.

Medical and pension plans

13.67 As far as any existing additional plans (medical, pensions and insurance) are concerned:

(a) if the new employer accepts their continuation as they are, there is no problem;
(b) if the new employer accepts their continuation, but under different conditions, he shall have to inform the employees' representatives and consult with them, as well as with the old employer and the insurance company, in order to sign new contracts; and

3 Article 9 par. 1 of the presidential decree 178/2002.
4 Article 24 par. 1 of law 3996/2011.

(c) if the new employer does not want to continue such plans, the relevant funds shall be distributed following agreement between the old employer and the employees' representatives

13.68 Article 4 par. 3 of the President Decree 178/2002 provides that the 'automatic transfer' does not apply to the provisions of a group insurance plan related to any benefit (ie accident, disease, pension, lump sum etc). Thus, following strictly Greek law, all insurance benefits are excluded from the 'automatic transfer'.

13.69 However, according to article 3 par. 1 of Directive 98/50/EC and Directive 2001/23/EC, 'the transferor's rights and obligations arising from a contract of employment or from an employment relationship existing on the date of a transfer shall, by reason of such transfer, be transferred to the transferee'.

13.70 Article 3 par. 4 of Directive 98/50/EC and Directive 2001/23/EC introduces an exception from the abovementioned general rule. In particular, it provides that:

(a) unless Member States provide otherwise, paragraphs 1 and 3 shall not apply in relation to employees' rights to old-age, invalidity or survivors' benefits under supplementary company or intercompany pension schemes outside the statutory social security schemes in Member States;

(b) even where they do not provide in accordance with subparagraph (a) that paragraphs 1 and 3 apply in relation to such rights, Member States shall adopt the measures necessary to protect the interests of employees and of persons no longer employed in the transferor's business at the time of the transfer in respect of rights conferring on them immediate or prospective entitlement to old age benefits, including survivors' benefits, under supplementary schemes referred to in subparagraph (a)'.

13.71 Taking into account the above the EJC came in some cases[5] to the conclusion that the 'automatic transfer' does not apply to all insurance benefits, but only to those related to rights to old age, invalidity or survivor's benefit. According to the above assumption there is a risk that benefits related ie to life and medical insurance and/or early retirement may be considered as having been retained due to the transfer and that the purchaser has the obligation to provide similar benefits to the employees transferred.

TERMINATION OF EMPLOYMENT RELATED TO THE TRANSFER

13.72 The transfer of a business does not allow the termination of the employment contracts of those employed in such business. In fact, it is

5 In case C-164/2000 (*Beckman*) and in case C-4/2001 (*Martin*).

prohibited to proceed to terminations which are related with such transfer. As an exception, if specific reasons (economic, financial, technical, organisational etc 'impose modifications of the level of employment', ie reduction of the workforce), then terminations may be legal. But every single case needs to be separately examined.

13.73 Also, it must be noted that, if such 'prejudicial modification' occurs, it can only occur after the transfer of the business and, therefore, the employee concerned may claim the proper compensation/severance payment only from the new and not from the old employer, who is completely exonerated from all responsibility regarding the specific problem examined.

Liability of the transferor and the transferee

13.74 In order to distinguish which of the obligations arising from the employment contract concern the old employer and which the new one, the crucial point is the exact time of the transfer. As from the moment of the transfer, the purchaser is held liable for any and all employee claim as if the purchaser were the employer both before and after the transfer. The old employer remains jointly liable for any obligation that refers to the period before the transfer, but this is simply an additional guarantee for the employee, who may opt to file a lawsuit against either employer or even both of them.

WORKFORCE REDUCTION IN CONNECTION WITH SHARE SALE OR SHARE PURCHASE

13.75 As stressed before, the meaning of transfer of business is defined under the aforementioned legal provisions and it concerns any:

> 'transfer of an economic entity which retains its identity, meaning an organised grouping of resources which has the objective of pursuing an economic activity, whether or not that activity is central or ancillary'.

13.76 The aforementioned definition excludes from the scope of application of the legislation a share sale or share purchase deal, since such sale or purchase does not impact the legal entity itself, but the ownership of its share capital. This means that the legal entity continues to operate as prior to the sale of shares and there are no employment related consequences thereof.

13.77 Along similar lines, the legal provisions which apply to a transfer of business and will be presented hereunder are not applicable to a transfer of assets, as long as this concerns only assets and not the transfer of a going concern which retains its identity and has the objective to pursue an economic activity. Therefore:

(a) In the event of transfer of shares, the employees remain employed by the same legal entity, and nothing changes as far as employment terms and conditions are concerned.
(b) In the event of transfer of assets, and under the strict condition that this does not result in a transfer of undertaking/business (ie only some particular assets are transferred), the employees remain with the same entity, which no longer has some of its assets, and nothing changes as far as employment terms and conditions are concerned.

CHANGING EMPLOYMENT TERMS AND CONDITIONS

Change of employment conditions

13.78 During employment any change of the employment conditions must be agreed to by both parties and agreement may be expressly or tacitly stated. In the case of certain changes eg change from full-time to part-time work, an agreement of the parties in writing is mandatory.

13.79 The employer's right to amend employment terms, eg duties, place of work and the working hours is quite often already stipulated in employment agreements; however clauses which grant the employer a very wide power to change employment conditions according to the employer's free will could be found by courts as abusive and thus inapplicable.

13.80 Moreover, according to Greek employment legislation, in the event of any unilateral change of employment conditions, applied to the employee's detriment, eg removal from role, change of working hours, etc, the employee concerned is entitled to consider such change as a dismissal and claim a severance payment.

13.81 Given the above, the change of employment conditions may be lead to the following situations:

(a) The parties agree to the change of employment conditions by signing an amendment to the employment agreement in writing.
(b) The employer applies a change to the employment conditions and agreement is given tacitly, in the form of an absence of any discontent by the employee. The law does not provide for a specific duration during which the new employment conditions should be applied, in order for them to be considered as lawfully implemented. One should expect that a period of three months during which a change in the employment conditions has occurred and none of the parties has expressed its discontent, would be reasonable.
(c) The employee abides by the new employment conditions, but expresses his disagreement and reserves any right to challenge them and ask for

the retroactive application of the previous conditions. This would be especially applicable in the case of salary reductions and cutting down of benefits.

(d) The employee considers the change of employment conditions to be a dismissal, as covered by the abovementioned legal provision, and asks for severance payment.

Termination in view of change in employment conditions

13.82 An additional option is available to the contracting party wanting to change employment conditions. The party wanting to change the employment terms and conditions terminates the employment relationship, unless the other party accepts the suggested change. When initiated by the employer, it is advisable to suggest such an option in writing and grant the employee a reasonable time-limit in order to decide. If the employee rejects the suggested change, he is entitled to statutory severance, as in any other case of termination by the employer.

Using temporary staff

13.83 Temporary employment in Greece is governed by law 4052/2012 implementing Directive 2008/104/EC on temporary agency work. According to this, the use of temporary staff is prohibited in the following cases:

(a) if the user undertaking intends to replace employees on strike by using temporary employees;

(b) if the user undertaking has proceeded to the termination of employment agreements of the same position/category for economic and technical reasons over the last three months or has proceeded to collective redundancies over the last six months;

(c) if the user undertaking is subject to the legal provisions personnel selection of the public sector;

(d) if the nature of the activity of the user undertaking is particularly perilous for employee health and security, such activity being determined by Ministerial Decision; and

(e) if the employee is subject to the social security provisions of civil engineering labourers, although an exception is made regarding these employed for construction of more than €10,000,000, financed in whole or partly by state funds and in the name of institutions of the public or semi-public sector.

13.84 The basic employment conditions of temporary staff – including payment – for the duration of their assignment at a user undertaking shall be at least those that would apply if they had been recruited directly by the user undertaking to perform the same job. This means that the local legal framework incorporates the equal treatment principle of the directive on temporary agency work, including express reference to payment conditions.

13.85 Protection of pregnant and nursing women and protection of children and young people, as well as equal treatment for men and women and any action to combat discrimination on the grounds of sex, race, ethnic origin, religion, beliefs, disability, age or sexual orientation apply to temporary employees too.

13.86 The assignment of a temporary employee at a user undertaking, including any renewals which shall be agreed in writing, may not exceed 36 months. Where an assignment exceeds the limit of 36 months, the temporary employee is automatically qualified as a direct employee of the user undertaking under an employment agreement of indefinite duration. However, a new assignment may begin if there is an interval of 23 days between the end of the initial assignment, extended by any lawful renewals and the beginning of the new assignment with the same user undertaking.

EMPLOYMENT CLAIMS

13.87 In any case of termination, the employee is entitled to contest the validity of dismissal within three months of the termination date; in addition, he is entitled to claim additional severance amount within six months of the termination date, in case he claims that the severance amount paid to him was not correctly calculated. Where the court considers that the termination was invalid, then the employee will be entitled to receive salaries due as of the termination date, as well as compensation for moral damages; in addition, given that Greek employment law recognises the right to be employed, a Court may also order the employee's reinstatement to the same position, under the same working and payment conditions as before termination.

MUTUALLY AGREED TERMINATION

13.88 Mutually agreed termination is not regulated by specific employment law provisions, although such an option is a common practice, governed by the general principle of freedom of contract. Since it is not recognised by the law as a separate way to terminate the employment relationship, mutually agreed termination is materialised following signature by the parties, either as voluntary resignation or as a dismissal by the employer. This means that it shall be notified to the Labour Authorities as one of the latter forms of termination of employment. In most cases, the termination agreement will provide for a waiver of rights to challenge termination or in general a waiver of claims of any nature with regard to the employment relationship. For this purpose, mutually agreed terminations often provide for a severance payment which is significantly higher than statutory severance.

13.89 In case that a dispute has arisen between the employer and the employee, a settlement agreement may be executed at any point of the dispute. The settlement amount is negotiable and it depends on the circumstances of each dispute.

13.90 In view of restructuring operations and if a large scale downsizing is envisaged, the financing a Voluntary Redundancy Scheme may be the most preferable option. This has been the choice of the vast majority of foreign investors exiting a business in Greece in recent years. The launching of a VRS would probably call for higher severance amounts than the statutory severance indemnity, but terminations will take place upon conclusion of bilateral agreements for mutual separation with each employee. In this way, companies will avoid future litigation, which would be burdensome and time-consuming.

Chapter 14
Workforce Restructuring in Hungary

László Kenyeres and Buzási Barnabás
Wolf Theiss, Budapest

INTRODUCTION

14.1 This chapter examines the employment laws in Hungary with the emphasis on the rules of restructuring exercises, termination of employment relationships, different types of redundancies, relevant provisions regarding the transfer of undertakings and the possible temporary solutions.

14.2 The legal system in Hungary is a continental law system and, as such, different from the common law jurisdictions. The law is codified in a systematic way and applied and interpreted by the courts. The most important source of the labour law is Act I of 2012 on the Labour Code ('Labour Code'). The new Labour Code entered into force on 1 July 2012. The new act introduced conceptual changes in several key areas (eg liability for damages, unlawful termination). The aim of the new act was to make the employment relationship more flexible and thus increase the adaptability of employees to the changing needs of the labour market and support labour market transition.

The Labour Code changed the relationship between the statute and collective agreements radically. Collective agreements (and works council agreements) may derogate the provisions of the labour law to the detriment of employees as well. There are three types of provision in the Labour Code: (i) mandatory rules which regulate the important interests and fundamental rights of the employees; (ii) dispositive rules where derogation is allowed only in favour of the employees; and (iii) dispositive rules which may be derogated to the detriment of employees as well. The derogation can be regulated both in the employment contract and the collective agreement, however derogating to the detriment of the employee is allowed – bar a few exceptions – only within the framework of collective agreements and works council agreements.

14.3 When evaluating employee rights and entitlements during any kind of termination or restructuring, the importance of the Labour Code cannot be overemphasised. In the case where the provisions of the Labour Code may be derogated it is necessary to review the employment contract, the collective agreement or the works council agreement. Also in case of additional terms and benefits which are not regulated in the Labour Code, the employment agreement is the primary source of such information.

PREPARING FOR A RESTRUCTURING EXERCISE

14.4 Restructuring is a major issue in a company's life which raises a lot of important employment related questions, such as the reduction of workforce, reorganisation of the corporate structure and outsourcing of certain activities.

14.5 To prepare for restructuring in Hungary, it is essential to calculate the number of affected employees in order to find out which redundancy rules are applicable. Beside the number of the affected employees their unique contractual terms and protected status (such as pregnancy, fixed term employment, sick leave) must also be carefully examined. It is essential to calculate the financial consequences of the workforce restructuring precisely and collect all relevant data in respect of cost consequences in order to take all possible advantages of the changes.

The key issues to consider are set out below.

Identify the employing entity

14.6 In Hungary, each redundancy or any restructuring procedure should be conducted independently, taking into consideration that a given employee can be linked to one corporate entity (or in certain cases to more), even in cases where a number of companies operate in one group network or form task forces or when the employee receives instructions from different entities or where the employer has different types of employees such as temporary workers and disabled employees.

Collating information to plan and budget for the restructuring exercise

14.7 When restructuring an international group of companies, the financial and structural background should always be clear and any costs of future measures regarding the restructuring should be calculated to avoid unexpected surprises.

14.8 In order to have a clear picture of the employer's duties and risks in connection with the restructuring exercise the employer must hold the necessary data on the employees. Hungarian data protection law allows the employer to process the employees' personal data necessary for the fulfilment of obligations stemming from the employment relationship and in such cases it is even mandatory for the company to prepare and manage certain registers regarding employee data. Under the Labour Code the employer may disclose the data in two cases: (i) if it is permitted by the act; or (ii) if the employer receives the consent of the employee. Therefore, it is advisable to seek the employee's consent for various data controlling activities (eg intragroup data transfers, change of control scenarios, centralised performance evaluation) during the term of the contract.

Practical Tip

Key data required initially in respect of any employee potentially impacted by a workforce reduction or restructuring exercise includes (but is not limited to):

- job description;
- length of service;
- contractual benefits and entitlement on termination of employment;
- age;
- protected age;
- place of work;
- enhanced redundancy entitlement;
- applicable collective agreement, trade union agreement, works council agreement (if any); and
- data relating to protected status.

This information will be necessary for estimating the overall costs of the restructuring exercise and for planning the appropriate timetable for executing dismissals.

EMPLOYMENT STATUS

14.9 According to the Labour Code an employee is a natural person who works under an employment contract. Based on this only employees are protected against unlawful termination and receive certain benefits during a redundancy. Regarding the others who do not qualify as the employer's employees the general rules of the termination of the employment set out in the labour code are not applicable or a lower level of protection is applicable. The contractual relationship of such individuals may be terminated in accordance with the terms of the agreement or breach of it (civil law grounds in case of independent agents, freelancers etc). It is highlighted that managing directors may fulfil their duties on the basis of an employment contract or mandate agreement while company secretaries may only be engaged on the basis of an employment agreement. On one hand the responsibility of such executive employees are higher and on the other hand they have less protection by the law than regular employees.

GENERAL PROTECTION AGAINST DISMISSAL

14.10 The concept of 'employment at will' does not apply in Hungary. All employees are entitled to a minimum notice period after the expiration of the probation period which duration is maximum six months. In addition, all employees have the statutory right not to be unlawfully dismissed from the first day of employment.

14.11 The grounds and procedure for termination are regulated in the Labour Code. Parties may agree to deviate from the termination provisions of the Labour Code only in favour of employees. Pursuant to the Labour Code, an employment relationship may be terminated by either party: (i) by (ordinary) notice; (ii) with immediate effect with justification in case of serious breach of duties ; (iii) during the probationary period with immediate effect without justification; or (iv) by mutual agreement.

14.12 Termination by (ordinary) notice applies in case of a restructuring. The dismissal procedure must follow a two stage process to ensure that a dismissal is in accordance with the Labour Code.

14.13 Stage one: a clear, real and valid verifiable reason must be contained in the notice tailored to the current situation. The reasons justifying termination of an employment relationship may be related only to: (i) the abilities of the employee; (ii) his or her behaviour in relation to the employment; or (iii) the operations of the employer. Special reasons (for example breach of internal policies) set out in the employment contract are unlawful unless they are in line with the Labour Code and judicial practice. The fact of redundancy, which is regarded as a reason in connection with the employer's operation is an adequate reason to terminate an employee.

14.14 Stage two: the employer must follow the procedural steps of the Labour Code. A notice of termination issued by the employer must contain the employer's: (i) clear; (ii) real; and (iii) justified reasoning and it cannot result in an abuse of rights. Furthermore, in certain cases the employer is obliged to offer another suitable position to its employee (for example in case of single parents returning to work before the third birthday of their child).

SPECIAL PROTECTION AGAINST DISMISSAL

14.15 Certain types of employees have special protection against dismissal (for example employees on sick leave, pregnant employees and those enjoying pre-retirement status).

14.16 The Labour Code differentiates between periods during which the termination cannot be served to the employee at all (prohibition of termination), and periods during which the termination can be served but cannot be enforced (delay of the notice period). In the latter case, however, the notice period prescribed by law starts only after the expiry of the protection period (set). The employer must follow the rules regarding the notification, termination period and settlement. Furthermore, certain employees have an enhanced level of protection, where employment relationship may only be terminated for certain reasons (limitation of termination).

Prohibition on termination

14.17 The employment relationship cannot be terminated (ie the notice cannot be delivered) during the employee's:

- pregnancy;
- maternity leave;
- unpaid leave for nursing a child (up to three years, or up to ten years in the case of a permanently ill or seriously disabled child);
- military service; or
- treatment related to a human reproduction procedure (a maximum of six months from the commencement of such a procedure).

14.18 The consent of the works council is required for terminating the chairman of the works council and higher ranking trade union body's prior consent is required for the termination of the elected trade union officer.

14.19 As a consequence of a recent decision of the Hungarian Constitutional Court, prohibition on termination during pregnancy and human reproduction treatment applies even if the employer was not informed of the pregnancy or the ongoing reproduction procedure before the handover of the termination notice.

Delay of the notice period

14.20 The employment relationship may be terminated, thus the notice may be delivered, but the notice period may not commence during:

- sick leave,
- leave for the purpose of caring for a sick child; or
- unpaid leave for providing home care for a close relative.

Limitation on termination

14.21 Employees who: (i) have reached a protected age (ie they have five years until they reach their entitlement to old age pension); (ii) are mothers or single fathers with a child under the age of three; and (iii) are receiving rehabilitation treatment may be terminated with the following limitations. If the reason of termination is in connection with the employee's:

- behaviour – the level of breach must reach the threshold needed for termination with immediate effect;
- incapability, or operational reasons – the employer may terminate the employment relationship if the employer has no alternative, vacant position available suitable for the employee's skill, experience and education, or if the employee refuses the vacant position.

14.22 Employees receiving rehabilitation benefits can be terminated for health-related reasons only if no other appropriate position is available or if the employees refuse such an offer without a proper reason.

14.23 Certain types of protections are not applicable to the employment of executive employees. Therefore, for executive employees: (i) the employment relationship can be terminated during unpaid leave for nursing a child; (ii) the employer is not obliged to justify the termination with an exception of executives receiving rehabilitation treatment or rehabilitation benefits; and (iii) the termination period may start the day following the handover of the termination notice even during sick leave, leave for the purpose of caring for a sick child, or unpaid leave for providing home care for a close relative.

WORKFORCE REDUCTION

14.24 Planning the reduction of the workforce is a key point of the restructuring. The assets and business potential of the company, the exact workforce required for the new structure and other aspects should be evaluated and the help of certain experts (for example auditors, accountants, lawyers, other consultants) is also needed. During the planning stage, the company should prepare for any possibilities and have a stable monetary reserve for any hardship ahead.

14.25 According to Hungarian law it is necessary to distinguish between the individual and the collective redundancy. In case of collective redundancy the employer must follow additional procedural rules including negotiation and information duties towards the employee representatives. If a workforce restructuring is combined with a redundancy the reason for such termination is always in relation to the operation of the employer.

Definition of redundancy

14.26 There is no exact legal definition for redundancy. The Labour Code only states that an employee may be dismissed for reasons in connection with the employer's operation. The main features of the redundancy procedure were developed by case law.

14.27 Based on the reasons behind the decision of the employer, there are two types of redundancy: (i) downsizing; and (ii) restructuring. These are closely linked and the two types of redundancy typically occur at the same time.

14.28 In the case of downsizing the aim is to decrease the number of employees in the same or similar job roles. Typical reasons behind the downsizing are: (i) closure of the business/business line; (ii) decreased workload; and (iii) automation. On the other hand, in case of restructuring where the employee's job role ceases to exist (eg the employer has ceased or intends to cease to carry on the activity in which the employee was involved or outsource the particular tasks) or the employee's tasks are distributed between one or more employees (eg secretaries will take over the receptionists' tasks).

14.29 There is a third form of redundancy which is in connection with the employer's operation. It is called a 'quality replacement' where the purpose is the improvement of the quality of the work. In this case the number of employees remains the same, but the employer wishes to replace certain employees with other employees with higher qualifications in order to adapt to changed market conditions. The Labour Code does not define this concept. However it is a form of restructuring accepted by the courts. In this case if the employee challenges the decision during a court proceeding the employer will be obliged to prove that the qualification (not the performance) of the previous employee was not sufficient to carry out that specific type of work.

14.30 As a further aspect of the redundancy process is the applicability of rules of transfer of undertakings, especially where the work is outsourced.

Examples of redundancy situations

Company A provides sheet metal to the aerospace and automobile industries. It employs a total of around 1,000 employees in Hungary, of which 400 are employed in the production team, manning two types of machinery which cut and treat the sheet metal before it is delivered to the customer. Company A has invested in a number of new and more advanced machines which cut and treat the sheet metal at the same time, thereby reducing the need for manpower as there will only be one type of machine going forward. Company A has identified that the introduction of the new machines, around 100 employees will no longer be needed in the production team. The requirement of the business for the number of employees to operate the machinery has been reduced and work in the production team has diminished as a result.

Company B is a retail chain selling cars and boats in a number of locations around the world. It has ten car stores and five boat stores across Hungary but since sales have been shrunk in the past year it has decided to close the five boat stores in due to the decreased demand and the losses during the last three years. As a result Company B is proposing to make all employees in the five boat stores redundant on the basis that their workplace is closing down.

DISMISSALS ON GROUNDS OF REDUNDANCY

14.31 In general we can differentiate between two types of redundancies based on the number of affected employees: the individual and the collective redundancy procedure. The differences between the two types of redundancy are solely procedural.

Redundancy procedures

14.32 Every redundancy has to be conducted step-by-step in accordance with the law, taking into account all procedural provisions. Disregarding the mandatory notification and justification duties of the employer results in the unlawfulness of the termination and entails a greater risk of litigation and additional costs.

Individual redundancy procedure

Defining the selection pool/selection criteria

14.33 First selection criteria must be clearly determined by the employer to identify the group of employees to be included in the redundancy.

14.34 The court does not investigate whether the business decision of redundancy is based on rational and objective considerations. However, the implementation of the indicated changes in the operation of the employer will be examined. In order to defend the lawfulness of the redundancy the employer must show that the changes in the operation of the business which served as the reason behind the decision did occur.

14.35 The selection criteria must be linked to the business decision triggering the redundancy. The group of affected employees (the selection pool) must be defined on the basis of the level of job roles or business units. If the redundancy affects positions where only one employee is engaged the employer is not obliged to put other employees into the selection pool. It is always important to decide on the level of job roles first and only after the identification of the affected roles dismiss the affected employee(s).

14.36 In spite of the implemented redundancy, a dismissal based on restructuring will qualify as unlawful if the employer employs another employee instead of the dismissed one shortly after the dismissal in the same or similar individual position. In such case the terminated employee may argue that the actual aim of his termination was to replace him, and the aim of the restructuring was purely to terminate him and not his position.

14.37 If the employer hires a new employee for the same position (including by way of re-establishment of the previously terminated position) a few months after the termination, stating that the underlying business decision (which cannot be examined by the court) was inappropriate, redundancies which have been carried out may well be considered lawful where such takes place following a re-examination of the business decision. However, in this case the court will investigate the existence of the restructuring more profoundly if a claim is brought by the terminated employee.

14.38 Additionally, the employer is not obliged to consult the employees on the redundancy plan and the reasons behind the decision during of individual redundancy procedures.

Alternative employment

14.39 In the case of certain employees, offering alternative positions is a possibility and in some cases is a must for the employer. There is no general requirement to offer another job role in a redundancy procedure except for the employees specified in para **14.21**.

14.40 These employees may be terminated for reasons in connection with the employer's operation if no other suitable position is available at the employer in terms of skills, education and experience required for his previous position, or if the employee refuses the employment in the offered position.

Probation periods

14.41 Under the Labour Code the parties may stipulate in the employment contract a probationary period of no more than three months from the date of commencement of the employment relationship. In the event that a shorter probationary period has been stipulated the parties may extend the probationary period once. In either case, the duration of the probationary period may not exceed three months. The term of the probation period may not exceed six months as provided for in the collective agreement.

14.42 Hence the parties are not allowed to stipulate any probation period during the employment even if the terms of the alternative employment accepted or offered during a restructuring differ wholly or in part from the employee's previous terms and conditions.

14.43 However, if the employee is not able to carry out the tasks which are necessary to perform the amended terms of the employment due to the lack of his/her qualifications or abilities the employer has the right to terminate the employment relationship with notice. It is important to note, that in this case the termination is not in connection with the restructuring, but solely due to the employee's ability or behaviour.

> **Practical Tip**
>
> We recommend amending the relevant employment contract only for a definite period. If the employee is not able to perform the new tasks, the previous terms and conditions will be restored after the expiration date of the amendment or if the previous position is terminated during the restructuring process, the employee may be terminated for this reason.

Other considerations

14.44 Another aspect to consider is the internal policies and unilateral statements of the employer as well as the individual employment contracts of each employee. It is strongly advisable to review every potential employment document and even the practice of the employer in case of a redundancy or restructuring as the employee may state that his termination *pro forma* meets the requirements of the Labour Code but contradicts the internal policies of the employer or the employment agreement.

Collective redundancy procedure

14.45 Under Hungarian law a collective redundancy arises if the employer intends to terminate the employment relationship:

- of at least ten employees, when employing more than 20 and less than 100 employees,
- of at least 10 per cent of the employees, when employing 100 or more, but less than 300 employees,
- of at least 30 employees, when employing 300 or more employees within a period of 30 days

for reasons in connection with its operations.

14.46 If the employer has more than one place of business, the above criteria has to be examined separately for each place of business; however, the number of employees at various locations, but within the jurisdiction of the same local labour authority (for example Csongrád county), has to be calculated in aggregate. The place of business is an operational facility determined in the company's articles of association as a permanent and independent establishment that is located in a venue other than the company's registered office.

Example

The company Gorgeous Shoes Limited Liability Company has ten stores across Hungary. Three of the stores are no longer as busy as they used to be. As a result the management has decided that there is not enough work for all of the 63 employees currently employed across the three stores and is proposing to reduce headcounts. The management has identified that five employees in each of the Debrecen and Szolnok stores and four employees in the Pécs store are redundant. Accordingly, the management will propose that a total of 13 employees are made redundant across the five stores.

If each store is identified as *one place of business* Gorgeous Shoes Limited Liability Company will **not** be required to follow the collective redundancy procedure as each store is proposing to make fewer than ten employees redundant.

14.47 Companies should also be aware that the reason for the 'redundancy' has to fall into the category of the operation of the employer.

14.48 When calculating the number of employees affected, termination of fixed term employment relationships and terminations by mutual agreement initiated by the employer must be taken into consideration as well (during the relevant 30 days period).

14.49 In a collective redundancy (as opposed to an individual dismissal), a consultation procedure must be initiated and conducted between the employer and the employee representatives with the purpose of avoiding or mitigating the effects of the collective redundancy.

Involvement of employee representatives in collective dismissals

14.50 The Labour Code operates under the default scenario that there is an employee representation (works council) at the employer, in which case a consultation process is mandatory as part of the collective redundancy. If no organised employee representation operates at the employer; the Labour Code remains silent in connection with this scenario.

14.51 As a result, the conclusion can be inferred that if no works council operates at the employer, no consultation with the employee representatives is required (since there is no employee representation in the meaning of Art (b) Directive 98/59/EC). This means that the legal requirement is to decide on the mass redundancy and communicate the decision to the employees and the labour authorities.

14.52 However, according to several expert legal opinions it is advisable to maintain the previous practice and conduct a consultation process even when there is no works council at the employer. In the authors' experience it is in the best interests of the employer and it could carry numerous commercial benefits. Most significantly, a consultation process could greatly facilitate mutual terminations. By mutual termination, the employment of protected employees can also be terminated. Understandably, protected employees are only willing to agree to a termination if the associated package is sufficiently favourable, and an employee consultation process is the best way to assess what termination packages will be acceptable to the employees in order to agree the mutual termination.

14.53 In a case where there is no works council, the employer may conduct a consultation process as part of the collective redundancy with an ad hoc committee of the employees. The employer would subsequently conduct negotiations with this committee, as described in greater detail below. For the avoidance of doubt, in the event that the employer does not wish to proceed with the non-mandatory consultation, the employer's only obligations are to: (i) render a decision on the collective redundancy; and (ii) communicate this decision to the affected employees and the labour authorities.

14.54 A consultation process also gives employees the opportunity to start looking for other employment as soon as possible, which would also aid the redundancy process: employees who do find other employment generally leave peacefully and the practical risk of litigation in connection with these employees also decreases significantly. Those employees who are considering leaving the company may even volunteer for redundancy – this would also decrease litigation without any sort of added cost to the employer – a win-win scenario for all involved.

14.55 Finally, a bona fide consultation process (even when not mandatory) can also strengthen the employer's reputation as a responsible employer of good standing who makes efforts to take care of its employees, which would significantly decrease any reputational risks associated with a collective redundancy.

Information and consultation requirements

14.56 The employer informs in writing the works council or the ad hoc committee and the labour authority (a minimum of seven days before the consultation) about the following:

- the reasons for the planned workforce reduction;
- the exact number of affected employees broken down by job groups; or
- the six-month average number of the employees preceding the decision,
- criteria for reduction;
- conditions, rate and extra allowances not defined in the relevant legislation and/or collective agreement provided in connection with the collective redundancy;
- planned time scale and viewpoints of reduction;

14.57 Consultations must cover the possible ways and means of avoiding collective redundancies, the principles of the redundancy process, the means of mitigating the consequences and the possibilities of reducing the number of affected employees.

14.58 During the procedure the employer should consider the request of the employees, willingly focus on the mitigation of the effects of the redundancy and provide all information and options which helps reaching the above defined aims.

14.59 The employer is free to determine the selection criteria; however they must be in line with the justification of the redundancy process. Employee representatives are entitled to suggest alternative selection criteria and ask the employer to consider enlarging the selection pool in order to allow employees to decide themselves who will be dismissed.

14.60 Regardless of the number of employees made redundant the same timing applies. The employer should provide the information set out in para **14.56** at least seven days before the commencement of consultations. The commencement date of consultations with employee representatives must be at least 15 days prior to the decision on redundancy. The employer is not obliged to reach an agreement within the 15-day timeframe. However if the parties reach an agreement it must be made in writing and should be sent to the labour authority.

Regulatory requirements

14.61 The decision on the redundancy must include the number of affected employees broken down by job groups and the timeframe for implementing the redundancy.

14.62 The employer should notify the affected employees and the Labour Authority on the redundancy decision (even if it is formulated as an agreement of the parties) at least 30 days prior to serving the termination notices to the employees. Furthermore, a copy of the notification to the affected employees must be sent to the labour authority and the employee representatives. The notification to the labour authority shall contain:

- the personal data (including social security number);
- details of the last job role with the employer; and
- the professional qualification of the employees to be made redundant.

14.63 Based on the above and following a strict schedule, the employer may make its decision on the mass redundancy approximately three to four weeks after the initiation of the consultation process. Please note that the employer is strictly prohibited from making any final and binding decision on the redundancy prior to completing the consultation.

Sanctions

14.64 If the employer fails to notify the affected employees of the redundancy decision any notice of dismissal must be regarded as unlawful. If the employer breaches the above consultation duties the works council can complain to the labour court and ask that the consultation procedure be carried out.

NOTICE

14.65 Notice period is regarded as an additional time period after the communication of the notice, which theoretically provides the employee with time to find another job and for the employer to reorganise tasks associated with the terminated position. The starting date of the notice period is typically the date of the day the notice is handed to the employee and the last date is the actual last day of the employment. Employment contracts typically provide the statutory minimum for notice periods. As the minimum period is compulsory the parties may deviate from the Labour Code only in favour of the employee. If the contract remains silent on the notice period then the statutory minimum applies.

Minimum notice period

14.66 The maximum duration of the notice period is six months. The minimum notice period is 30 days; however it is extended in accordance with length of service as follows:

Length of service	Notice period extension
3 years	5 days
5 years	15 days
8 years	20 days
10 years	25 days
15 years	30 days
18 years	40 days
20 years	60 days

14.67 Note that unless the parties agreed otherwise the above periods only apply if the employment is terminated by the employer. When the employment is terminated by the employee, the notice period is 30 days notwithstanding the length of service, unless the parties agreed otherwise.

14.68 If the employment was terminated by the employee, he is obliged to work for the whole duration of the notice period unless the parties agreed otherwise in the employment contract or separately during the termination.

14.69 The employer is always entitled to exempt the employee from the obligation to work. Therefore it is an option for the employer to order the employee to not attend the workplace for the whole duration of the notice period.

14.70 In the event of the employer dismisses the employee, the employer must release the employee concerned from the duty to work for at least half of the notice period. The release from work should be allocated in not more than two parts, at the employee's discretion. For the period of being released from his duties the employee is entitled to receive absentee pay, except if he would not be eligible to any wages otherwise.

REDUNDANCY PAYMENT

14.71 The employee is entitled to a severance payment if his employment relationship is terminated for reasons related to the employer's business operation, to the termination of the employer without legal successor or to the ability of the employee in connection with a health condition. Collective redundancy is indisputably for reasons connected with the employer's business operation; accordingly severance payment is due to the employee in such circumstances. Severance payments are equal to the sum of the absentee pay (which includes base salary and regular wage supplements) due for:

Length of service	**Severance payment**
at least 3 years	1 month
at least 5 years	2 months
at least 10 years	3 months
at least 15 years	4 months
at least 20 years	5 months
at least 25 years	6 months

14.72 In the event of termination the employer is obliged to compensate for unused holiday entitlement. If the employee has unused holiday entitlement in the year of the termination he is entitled to financial compensation for this unused holiday entitlement. On the contrary if the employee took more holiday than his entitlement, he is not obliged to compensate the employer.

Enhanced redundancy payments

14.73 The amount of severance pay must be increased with the sum of the absentee pay in line with the below table if the termination takes place within the five-year period before the employee reaches the age limit for old-age pension.

Length of service	Additional payment
Between 3 and 10 years	1 month absentee pay
Between 10 and 20 years	2 months absentee pay
More than 20 years	3 months absentee pay

Taxation of redundancy payments

14.74 Redundancy payments are treated as employment income for Hungarian tax purposes. Therefore, under the current Hungarian tax rules, these payments should be subject to personal income tax and social taxes (eg, social tax, social security contribution). All taxes and charges should be withheld by the Hungarian employer.

Post-termination restrictive covenants

14.75 The Labour Code regulates post-termination restrictive covenants. It is advisable for employers to demand such covenants in the contracts of executive and other employees in key positions to prevent them from competing alone or jointly with others. Post-termination restrictions are always based on an agreement between the employer and the employee. This agreement can be part of the employment agreement or a separate agreement.

14.76 By agreement of the parties, the employee shall not engage in any conduct – for up to two years following the termination of the employment relationship – which infringes upon or jeopardises the rightful economic interests of the employer. The parties are entitled to agree the scope of restrictions. Typically the employee undertakes not to enter into an employment contract with a competitor, solicit employees from the employer or start his own business in the same line of business.

14.77 In exchange for this restriction on behalf of the employee, the employer must pay adequate compensation. In determining the amount of such compensation, the scope of restrictions and its impact on the employee's ability to find an appropriate position elsewhere – in the light of his professional skills and experience – should be taken into consideration. The Labour Code only sets out the compulsory minimum compensation. Accordingly the amount of compensation for the term of the agreement may not be less than one-third of the base salary due for the same period. The employee is entitled to withdraw from the agreement if he has lawfully terminated his employment with immediate effect. If stipulated in the agreement the employer is entitled to withdraw from the agreement anytime, without reasoning during the employment relationship.

14.78 Without a written agreement between the parties the employee is merely obliged to keep the business secrets of the employer for an unlimited period of time. Accordingly, it is advisable to include a detailed restriction in the employment contract right at the outset of the employment relationship particularly as the employer can reserve the right of withdrawal from the post-termination restrictions.

14.79 Post-termination restrictions can be used with a notice period without the obligation to work which extends the term of the restrictive period to maximum two and a half years. During the notice period the employee will be obliged not to damage the employer's business interests under the rules of the Labour Code without any specific agreement as the employment relationship is still in existence.

14.80 When drafting the restrictive covenant, considering each possible circumstance is essential. The compensation for the restriction must be proportionate to the undertakings of the employee. If the restrictions are too wide and the compensation is not commensurate with the restrictions the court may order the employer to increase the compensation or rules the restrictive covenant invalid.

14.81 In case of breach on the employee's side, damages may also be claimed by the employer in court. Furthermore, the employee may also be obliged to repay the full amount of the compensation received.

BUSINESS SALE, OUTSOURCING/INSOURCING AND OFFSHORING

14.82 The Acquired Rights Directive is the name of the European Council Directive 77/187 of 14 February 1977 which was replaced by the European Council Directive 2001/23 of 12 March 2001 ('Directive') which aims to protect employees in connection with business sales by preserving the original terms and conditions of the employment agreement. In Hungary the Directive was implemented into national law by way of the VI. Chapter of the Labour Code on the rules of the transfer of undertakings ('RTU'). In accordance with the Labour Code, the rights and the obligations of the employer are in general transferred to the acquirer of the business.

14.83 RTU rules apply where an economic entity (organised group of assets or other resources) – as a going concern – is sold, but cannot apply in situation where the employer's identity has not changed (for example in the case of a share sale where the employing entity itself has not changed, only its shareholders).

14.84 Key consequences of RTU applying are:

- the automatic transfer of the affected employees to the new employer;
- the automatic transfer of employment rights, obligations and liabilities relating to affected employees to the new employer;
- the legal obligation to consult with a works council or with the employee representative(s),
- the transfer of the undertaking may not serve as the sole reason behind the termination of the employment relationship, and
- joint and several liability of the employers in respect of obligations towards employees.

Business sale

14.85 A business sale falls under the RTU regime if the economic entity 'retains its identity' after the transfer. Key factors to determine include whether the material or immaterial assets have been transferred, whether there was any interruption of the activity, whether customers have been transferred, whether there are activities post-transfer similar to those carried prior to the transfer, whether key staff have been taken over by the new employer.

A transfer of assets to a subsidiary (by way of contributions in kind) – even if only certain part of the assets are provided in that way – qualifies as a transfer of undertaking and the RTU is applicable.

Outsourcing/insourcing

14.86 Outsourcing/insourcing may constitute a 'service provision change' (and therefore an automatic transfer of the employment of affected staff under RTU) where one business ceases to provide the services and another business takes them over. This frequently includes the outsourcing of a particular business function to an external service provider. Alternatively, a service provision change could also arise on termination of an outsourcing arrangement where activities cease to be carried out by the initial service provider (1st generation service provider) and are carried out, going forward, by either a new incoming service provider (2nd generation service provider) or taken back in-house by the business (insourcing).

Effect of RTU

Automatic transfer and protection of employment

14.87 Employees in job roles which are relevant from the viewpoint of the transfer are protected by the RTU. Affected employees are automatically transferred to the new employer and the provisions of their employment agreement remain unchanged. The employee's continuous service length transfers to the new owner under RTU. Conditions which are not regulated in the employment agreement can be modified unilaterally by the new employer to some extent.

14.88 The transferring business and the receiving employer shall be jointly and severally liable in respect of obligations towards employees existing before the date of transfer, subject to the employee submitting such claim within one year from the date of transfer.

Objection to the transfer

14.89 An employee may object to his transfer under RTU. The employee may terminate the employment relationship by giving notice if the transfer of his employment involves a substantial detrimental change to his working conditions and maintaining the employment relationship would entail unreasonable disadvantages or would be impossible. In this case the employee will be entitled to the mandatory notice period, absent fee and redundancy payment.

14.90 Employee may exercise the right to give notice within 30 days from the date of transfer of employment to the transferee. The employee must give reasons for giving notice of termination.

Protection from dismissal

14.91 In case of an RTU transfer, the dismissal is not regarded as lawful if the dismissal due to the RTU transfer itself. However, where the reason is connected with the transfer (eg redundancy or restructuring after the implementation of the transfer) the termination may be lawful.

Protection of terms and conditions of employment

14.92 Similarly, terms of employment are also protected and may not be varied if they are set out in the employment contract. However, the following terms and conditions can be modified if they are not regulated in the employment contract:

- the working hours and work schedule;
- salary elements above base wage, and other benefits;
- payroll calculations, the frequency of payment of wages, and the day of payment;
- tasks included in the job role;
- the number of holidays and the procedures for allocating and determining such leave;
- the rules governing the periods of notice to be observed by the employer and the employee;
- whether a collective agreement applies to the employer; and
- persons exercising employers rights (eg persons entitled to make binding decisions regarding the employment, such as terminating the employee, deciding on holidays, pay rise, etc).

14.93 The working conditions specified in the collective agreement covering the employment relationship existing at the time of transfer must be maintained for a period of one year after the date of transfer. However, this obligation shall not apply to the employer if the collective agreement expires within one year after the date of transfer, or if the employment relationship is covered by a collective agreement after the date of transfer.

Information and consultation under RTU

14.94 In case of transfer, either employers have certain information duties towards the employee representative(s) or –if there are no such representatives – towards the employees regarding the transfer.

Duty to inform

14.95 In general the duty to inform is regarded as a formal procedure but in some cases, especially if the new employer is planning major changes after the transfer, the duty to inform has a greater significance.

14.96 There are two levels of the duty to inform. First, before the time of transfer the transferor shall inform the transferee of the rights and obligations arising from transferred employment contracts, non-competition agreements (post-restriction covenants) and study contracts. Failure to provide such information does not prevent the enforcement of rights arising from such agreements against the transferee employer.

14.97 Secondly, the transferor and the transferee must, within 15 days before the effective date of transfer, inform the works council concerning:

- the transfer and its exact or its planned time;
- the reasons for the transfer; and
- the legal, economic and social implications of the transfer for the affected employees ;

14.98 Additionally, within 15 days after the date of transfer, the transferee shall inform in writing the affected employees of the transfer of employment as a result of the transfer of undertaking, providing the employees with details of the employer's identification data and any changes in the general working conditions.

POSSIBLE INFORMATION DUTY OF THE TRANSFEREE

14.99 If the transferor has no works council – due to lacking the number of employees – and no shop steward had been elected either, either the transferor or – if agreed amongst the employers – the transferee shall inform in writing the employees concerned not more than 15 days prior to the date of transfer of the following:

- the date or proposed date of the transfer;
- the reason for the transfer;
- the legal, economic and social implications of the transfer for the employees; and
- any measures envisaged in relation to the employees.

DUTY TO CONSULT

14.100 Within 15 days of the effective date of transfer the transferor and the transferee shall – with a view to conclude an agreement – enter into negotiations with the works council concerning other proposed actions affecting employees. The negotiations shall cover the principles of the actions, the ways and means of avoiding detrimental consequences as well as the means for mitigating such consequences.

14.101 As the transferee is only obliged to inform (and only if the transferor and the transferee agree) the transferring employees of the implications of the transfer and about the envisaged measures after the transfer there is no such duty towards the existing workforce. This means that the existing workforce may learn only on a later stage about the changing work conditions occasioned by the transfer.

14.102 The transferor and the transferee are considered to have met the obligation of information and negotiation once the decision underlying the transfer of employment with the transfer of enterprise has been adopted by the body or person exercising control over the employer. The employer shall not be excused regarding their failure to satisfy the obligation to supply information and hold talks on the grounds that the controlling organisation or person had failed to inform the employer concerning its decision.

Sanctions

Unlawful dismissal

14.103 Dismissal is unlawful if the reason therefore is the transfer or if the reason is related to the changes in the operation of the employer. The transferor and the transferee shall be jointly and severally liable in respect of obligations towards employees which existed before the date of transfer, if the employee submits the claim within one year from the date of transfer.

Failure to inform and consult

14.104 Before the time of transfer the transferor shall inform the transferee (new employer) of the employment relationships involved, and also on the rights and obligations arising out of non-competition agreements (post-termination restrictive covenants) and study contracts. Failure to provide the information shall have no bearing on the ability to enforce rights arising from such covenants on the receiving employer's part.

14.105 The works council or the trade union may bring an action within five days in the event of any violation of the provisions on information or consultation. The court shall hear such cases within 15 days in non-contentious proceedings. The decision of the court may be appealed within five days from the date of delivery of the decision. The court of the second instance shall deliver its decision within 15 days.

14.106 The affected employees also have the opportunity to bring a claim in the event of any violation of the provisions on information or consultation. However the right to bring a claim is very limited and the sanction is usually the performance of the information and consultation duty. It is rare that the court considers any amount of compensation or other payment obligation. Furthermore the court will not be obliged to follow the above rules regarding the short deadlines.

WORKFORCE REDUCTION IN CONNECTION WITH SHARE SALE OR SHARE PURCHASE

14.107 In the case of a share sale, the employer itself remains unchanged; only the ownership structure is changing. Therefore, the RTU does not cover situations where ownership of the employing entity changes by way of a share sale, but the employing entity remains intact.

14.108 In such a case, when the new shareholder decides to reorganise the structure of the company, the notice may be justified with a cause related to the operation of the employer.

CHANGING EMPLOYMENT TERMS AND CONDITIONS

14.109 Unless the employment contract contains a clause that expressly allows the employer to amend the contract unilaterally, the employee's consent is always required (eg after the occurrence of an event, such as the return of another employee, the employee will be employed in part-time).

Mutually agreed changes

14.110 If the employment agreement does not explicitly empower the employer to change the agreement unilaterally, a mutual agreement must be reached with the employee. It is advisable to combine the introduction of any proposed detrimental changes with the annual salary review of the employee as employees usually insist on receiving some benefit in return for accepting the proposed change (other than the benefit of remaining in employment).

14.111 If the necessity for the modification is related to the operation of the employer or the position of the employee cannot be maintained without this modification and the alternative of the employee's refusal is the redundancy, the refusal can serve as a lawful reason for the termination. For instance, if the employee's tasks are diminishing and the position can be maintained only with lower number of working hours or with some additional new tasks.

14.112 In compliance with the RTU, contracts can be changed on grounds of the transfer of economic organisation only to the extent allowed by the Labour Code. The Labour Code allows the employer to amend those working conditions which are not regulated in the employment agreement. Typically, these conditions are the following: number and calculation method of paid holiday; frequency of payment of wages; benefits not regulated in the agreement; and whether the employer is subject to any collective agreement.

Unilateral changes

14.113 Beside the mutually agreed modifications, under certain circumstances the employer has the opportunity to modify the contract unilaterally. A typical example for this situation is when the employer modifies the tasks and duties of the employee without modifying the actual job role.

14.114 Additionally, the employer shall be entitled to temporarily reassign their employees to jobs and workplaces other than what is contained in the employment contracts, or to another employer. This temporary period may not exceed a total of 44 working days or 352 scheduled hours during a calendar year. This shall proportionately apply if the employment relationship commenced during the year, if it was entered into for a fixed term or in the case of irregular daily working hours and part-time work. The employee affected shall be informed of the expected duration of work in derogation from the employment contract. If the employee refuses the offer of the change in employment contract it cannot serve as the basis for the termination of the employment.

Practical Tip

Under the Labour Code the employment contract shall contain only the base wage and the scope of the work. The employer is obliged to inform the employee of other important elements of the employment relationship (eg the daily working hours, wages above the base wage, and other benefits, payroll accounting, the frequency of payment of wages, and the day of payment, the functions of the job, the number of days of leave and the procedures for allocating and determining such leave etc) via a separate document within 15 days from the commencement date of the employment relationship. Therefore, we recommend to employers to carefully select the provisions of the contract as if a provision is included in the contract, it can be amended only with the parties mutual consent.

USING TEMPORARY STAFF

14.115 Employing a new workforce or a group of experts on fixed-term contract or hiring employees from agencies is a great opportunity for the employer especially in case of reorganisations.

Agency workers

14.116 Agency workers might be a quick and cost-efficient solution, but management should note that agency workers now have almost the same rights as regular employees and the agency and the hiring organisation is subject to joint and several liabilities for any damages caused to the agency workers.

14.117 The Agency Workers Directive is the name given to the European Council Directive 104/2008/EC of 19 November 2008 ('Directive') which aims to regulate the situation of the agency workers. In Hungary the Directive was implemented into the national law by way of the XVI. Chapter of the Labour Code on the rules of agency workers ('RAW').

14.118 The basic working and employment conditions of temporary agency workers shall be, for the duration of their assignment, at least those available to the workers employed by the hiring organisation under employment relationship. The basic working and employment conditions shall, in particular, cover: (i) the protection of pregnant women, nursing mothers and young workers; (ii) the protection of wages, including other benefits; and (iii) the provisions on equal treatment.

14.119 As regards the payment of wages and other benefits, the provisions on equal treatment shall apply after 184 days of employment at the hiring organisation with respect to any employee:

- who is engaged with a temporary-work agency in an employment relationship established for an indefinite duration, and who is receiving pay in the absence of any assignment to a user enterprise;
- who is recognised as a long-term absentee from the labour market
- who is working within the framework of temporary agency work at a business association under the majority control of a municipal government or public benefit organisation, and a registered public benefit organisation.

Fixed-term contracts

14.120 Employing fixed-term employees is an adequate solution when a workforce is only needed for a specific duration such as replacement for maternity leave, or for projects. Beside of its advantages it should be noted that the EU Fixed-term Work Directives were implemented into national law by way of the XV. Chapter of the Labour Code on the rules of fixed-term employment relationships. Fixed-term contracts might be profitable in certain situations but these workers enjoy some additional protection compared to regular employees.

14.121 The period of fixed-term employment shall be determined according to the calendar or by other appropriate means. If the duration of the employment relationship is not determined by the calendar, the date of termination of the employment relationship cannot be determined solely by one party's decision. In the latter case the employer is required to inform the employee of the expected duration of employment.

14.122 Employment established for a fixed term can also be terminated by notice (similar to the indefinite term employment contacts): (i) in case of the employer's bankruptcy or liquidation proceedings; (ii) on grounds based on the incapacity of the employee; and (iii) if the maintenance of the employment becomes impossible due to external reasons out of the parties' control.

14.123 Otherwise, fixed-term contracts can be terminated with immediate effect, without justification at any time by the employer. In this case the employee is entitled to his/her absentee fee due for 12 months, or if the period remaining from the fixed-term is less than 12 months, for the remaining period. Besides this payment such an employee is not entitled to further compensation in connection with the termination unless the parties agreed otherwise (eg within the framework of a social agreement concluded during the collective redundancy).

Renewal of fixed-term contracts

14.124 The duration of a fixed-term employment relationship may not exceed five years, including the duration of an extended relationship and that of another fixed-term employment relationship concluded within six months of the termination of the previous fixed-term employment relationship.

14.125 A fixed-term employment relationship may be extended or renewed within six months from the date of termination of the previous one upon the employer's legitimate interests. The agreement may not infringe the employee's legitimate interest.

EMPLOYMENT CLAIMS

14.126 Employment litigation is conducted at the regional administrative and labour courts ('Labour Court'). The competent Labour Court is determined according to the location of the employer, or according to the employer's permanent establishment, where the employee is or has been employed during his employment contract. The parties may apply to the Court of Appeal and then to the Curia.

14.127 Labour Courts operate to bring justice in the legal disputes between employees and employers. Labour Courts do not have limits on the amount of potential awards of compensation.

14.128 Employees may pursue their claims arising from the employment relationship or out of the Labour Code, and trade unions and works councils may pursue their claims arising out of the Labour Code or a collective agreement or a works agreement by judicial process. Additionally, employers may enforce their claims against employees arising from the employment relationship, if the claim amounts to less than three times the mandatory minimum wage by issuing a payment notice. The payment notice shall be made in writing.

Unfair dismissal

14.129 Employees may initiate a procedure at court regarding the notice under which they were dismissed – claiming the reason for the dismissal was either: (i) not genuine; (ii) not justified; or (iii) a result of an abuse of rights; or (iv) because the procedure to dismiss was not properly conducted. However, breaching certain procedural rules may not result in termination being considered unlawful (eg breaching the duty to inform the employee regarding the possibility of bringing a claim against the termination). These breaches may result in the extension of the time period during which the employee is entitled to bring a claim in the Labour Court.

14.130 Generally claims must be started within the limitation period which is three years. An action shall be brought within 30 days of notification of the employer's act, if it is in connection with:

- any amendment of the employment contract implemented by unilateral decision;
- wrongful termination of the employment relationship;
- the sanctions applied on account of a breach of obligation by the employee;
- a payment notice; and
- the provisions regarding the appraisal of the employee.

14.131 If the parties terminate the employment relationship with mutual agreement either party is entitled to bring an action but only after the claim was declined by the other party (failure of amicable settlement). The action shall be declined if the other party fails to respond within 15 days from the date of delivery, or refuses to accept it. In this case an action may be brought within 30 days from the date when the action was declared declined.

Remedies

14.132 If the Labour Court decides that the dismissal was not in accordance with the law then it can order the employer to reinstate the employee. However, such orders are applied only in limited cases (eg if the terminated employee was protected, see para **14.17**, or the employment relationship was terminated in breach of the principle of equal treatment). Usually there will be financial compensation for the unlawful dismissal.

14.133 The Labour Code does not provide for the possibility of an award of an average compensation. Under the Labour Code the employee is entitled to a compensation for the wrongful termination. Compensation for lost income is capped in the amount of employee's 12 months' absentee pay. The loss (non-pecuniary, income etc) must be shown by the employee, while the lawfulness of termination must be shown by the employer.

Discrimination

14.134 The employee may also start legal proceedings against the employer for unlawful termination based on discrimination, if the employee consider that either of the following protected characteristics were the true reason(s) behind the dismissal: age; disability; gender reassignment; marriage and civil partnership; pregnancy and maternity; race; religion or belief; sex; and sexual orientation. At the employee's request the court shall reinstate the employment relationship if it was terminated in violation of the principle of equal treatment.

MUTUALLY AGREED TERMINATION

14.135 The mutual termination agreement is widely preferred by employers because it has the lowest litigation risk. Signing such an agreement significantly reduces the risk of any claim in court against the employer.

Settlement agreements

14.136 In order to be valid, the agreement must comply with various statutory and other requirements developed under case law. According to case law, the employee must have had enough time to review and evaluate the offer and to receive advice from his legal adviser or other relevant person. The parties can agree on the termination of the employment relationship with immediate effect or at a specified time in the future. It is common practice that the parties agree on many additional points, such as the remunerations, confidentiality, notice period, etc.

14.137 The agreement should evidently contain the parties' unambiguous and mutual statement regarding the will to terminate the employment relationship and the date of the termination. It is advisable to be precise about the rights to be renounced by the employee. Parties may also specify obligations for the employee after the termination of the employment relationship or include other elements. A settlement agreement should not include any justification of the termination or information clause regarding the applicable remedies.

Pre-termination discussions

14.138 If an employer intends to offer such an agreement to its employee, it is important to inform the employee of the binding period, eg the timeframe during which the offer can be accepted. According to case law, the employer must provide enough time for consideration of the offer. Offers are typically made without any legal recording. This means that if the employee does not accept such offer (or leaves it unanswered within the binding period) the making of the offer will not legally bind the employer.

14.139 It is also permissible to combine the settlement offer with the redundancy procedure where the employer informs the employee of the lawful grounds of termination but, instead of serving the termination notice, offers him a settlement with the proviso that if the employee refuses the offer, the employer will terminate the employment relationship by way of notice. Making a settlement offer does not qualify as unlawful or as threatening to the employee as the lawful reason for the termination existed prior to the settlement offer being made by the employer.

14.140 A settlement offer will usually be calculated with reference to the amount the employee may receive during the (ordinary) termination of the employer. Usually the employer enhances this amount with additional benefits (extra severance payment, company equipment, etc) in order to make the severance offer more attractive. Once the employee accepts the offer there are very limited chances to successfully challenge the settlement agreement in the Labour Court.

Chapter 15

Workforce Restructuring in Ireland

Sinéad Grace and Ciara McLoughlin
A&L Goodbody, Dublin

INTRODUCTION

15.1 The recent economic climate has led many Irish employers to adopt a variety of measures to re-align their workforce in order to ensure the continued viability of their businesses. These measures can range from a reduction in workforce, changing terms and conditions of employment, outsourcing and offshoring or the use of atypical workers such as temporary agency staff. Many different types of issues arise when considering implementing such changes to an existing workforce. All of these options entail their own legal framework which must be considered prior to taking any steps to effect changes. This chapter provides guidance in relation to relevant employment law and best practice that applies in the Irish jurisdiction in the context of a workforce restructuring situation.

15.2 In order to understand the various legal obligations that may arise, it is necessary to look briefly at the Irish legal system. The legal system in Ireland is a common law system, similar to that of England and Wales. Much of our legislation, however, over the last number of years has been heavily influenced by our European obligations. Tort law has also imposed obligations on the employment relationship. An example of this is the duty employers owe employees for their safety, health and welfare whilst at work. In order to understand the scope of this legal framework, it is necessary to briefly outline the numerous sources from which employment law in Ireland derives. The main sources are as follows:

- Common law – this is law which has been developed by the courts or similar tribunals through the judiciary. The common law also implies terms into the contract of employment. Examples of such terms include the common law duty to maintain trust and confidence and the duty of good faith and loyalty;
- Statute Law – this is written law which is set down by the legislature in Ireland (the Oireachtas is the body responsible for promulgating legislation ('Acts'));
- Secondary legislation – (in the form of statutory instruments) such as regulations or orders made under Acts;
- The Irish Constitution (Bunreacht Na hÉireann) – there are a number of constitutional provisions which have application to employment relationships. An example of this is Article 40.1 which states that all citizens are to be treated equally before the law;
- Codes of Practice – these do not have binding legal application, however, they may be taken into account by a court or tribunal as best practice guidelines when reaching a decision;
- EU law – Legislation and EU case law have had a significant influence in Ireland. Regulations have direct application in Ireland and Directives are implemented into Irish law by way of primary legislation; and
- International Conventions – examples of this include the European Convention on Human Rights. This was implemented in Ireland by way of the European Convention on Human Rights Act 2003. The Convention imposes an array of rights and freedoms on contracting parties. From an employment law perspective, some of the key rights are the rights to privacy, fair procedures and freedom of association.

15.3 The judiciary is the branch tasked with compliance with the above sources of law. The recently enacted Workplace Relations Act 2015 reforms the institutional structure grounding employment law in Ireland. There will be a single body for matters of first instance, known as the Workplace Relations Commission, and the Labour Court will become a single appellate body.

15.4 There is no legal requirement to furnish a written contract of employment in Ireland however the Terms of Employment (Information) Acts 1994 to 2012 impose certain minimum obligations namely that employers furnish to employees, within two months of commencement of employment, certain terms and conditions in relation to the employment relationship. Notwithstanding the foregoing, most employers provide a contract of employment and incorporate the statutory obligations under the aforementioned legislation into the contract of employment. The document is generally headed 'Contract of Employment' including those particulars required to be given pursuant to the Terms of Employment (Information) Acts 1994 to 2012. On foot of this, the employment contract is the starting point for consideration of employees' rights in conducting a workforce restructuring.

PLANNING FOR A RESTRUCTURING EXERCISE

15.5 The first step in any restructuring exercise is identifying the employees at risk. This is important both from a strategic planning point of view but also from a cost perspective. All relevant information relating to such employees should be collated such as their job description, length of service, age, place/location of work and contractual benefits. Generally this information is available from the employees' contracts of employment and it is the task of the Human Resources department/team to ensure that this information is collated. Only individuals who qualify as employees are protected for the purposes of the unfair dismissals regime. Accordingly the HR team will need to examine carefully the status of any self-employed consultants, contractors or agency workers to consider whether they need to be considered for the purposes of any restructuring. Care should also be taken in identifying the employee's employer. This is particularly important in a group context and the employee's employing entity should hold all necessary data on the particular employee.

UNILATERAL VARIATION OF CONTRACT

15.6 One of the first options an employer often considers is making changes to an employee's contract of employment. This is not the most straightforward option available to an employer and is one that needs to be navigated carefully by an employer. The fact that 'employment at will' does not exist in this jurisdiction, coupled with strong statutory protection, often makes unilateral variation difficult. The general principle is that an employer is not entitled to unilaterally vary a contractual term of an employee's contract of employment. In order to vary a contract term the consent of the employee is necessary. An important consideration in relation to the issue of unilateral variation is whether or not the term is in fact a contractual term or whether it is simply a work practice. Employees do not have an indefinite right to preserve their working obligations completely unchanged from the time they start work. The courts have found that an employee is expected to adapt themselves to new methods and techniques introduced in the course of his or her employment. In this context identifying if it is a work practice or contractual term is crucial as changing a work practice does not usually require consent.

15.7 Fundamental terms of the contract include remuneration, job description, pension rights and other benefits. The unilateral withdrawal or variation of any component of a remuneration or benefits package without some compensation for the change that has been imposed could give rise to a challenge by an employee that there has been a breach of contract. There is also a risk that it could give rise to an industrial relations issue creating unrest and tension among staff and a significant demand on resources. An employer bears a risk if he decides to proceed to impose changes to the employees' terms and conditions without their consent. If an employee proceeds to work under the new terms and conditions then the employer could argue that the employees acquiesced in the change or that there was an implied consent to the change. Either way employers should proceed cautiously if adopting this approach as they may find themselves subject to a claim by the employee as outlined below.

15.8 Many employers insert a variation clause in the contract. Whilst it is helpful to have a clause to the effect that the employer has the right to vary the terms and conditions of employment, such a clause is not always successfully enforced. It is subject to the overriding caveat that any such discretion is exercised reasonably.

15.9 Unilateral variations of employees' terms and conditions of employment to the employees' detriment can give rise to the following:

- Breach of contract claim – the common law remedy for breach of contract is damages. This is designed to compensate the employee for the breach but not necessarily to punish the party who is in breach;
- Constructive dismissal claim – it is a well-established principle that neither party to the contract of employment is permitted to conduct himself or herself in such a way as to damage the trust and confidence which exists between the parties. An employee can only succeed in claiming that he is being constructively dismissed where he has terminated his employment because he was either entitled to at law without notice or because it was reasonable for him to do so given the employer's conduct. This means that the employer's conduct must be tantamount to a significant breach which goes to the root of the contract or which shows that the employer no longer intends to be bound by the contract. The employee is also bound to act reasonably and he is expected to pursue his grievance through internal procedures; and
- HR/IR Issues – the more practical problem which may arise in a situation of unilateral variation of contracts is the potential HR/IR issues for management. Insofar as possible if any compensatory gesture can be made, then this should be done.

The Irish courts have repeatedly emphasised that a mutual obligation of trust and confidence underlies the employment relationship. In circumstances where the employer proposes to withdraw a consistent element of the remuneration or benefits package, the employer should provide an explanation to the employee as to why this has occurred. Such an explanation should include the factors which have influenced the decision and the reasons why the decision was taken.

Practical Tips

- Conduct a thorough review of employees' contracts to see what may be changed with/without consent.
- Distinguish between contractual terms or work practices – if what is in issue is a work practice then, subject to the above, it may in certain circumstances be changed.
- Where possible, secure employees' written consent to any proposed change and provide reasonable notice for its implementation.

USE OF ATYPICAL WORKERS

15.10 One way of meeting the changing needs of the workforce, particularly where it is to address a short term need of the business, is to use temporary staff. This includes using agency workers and fixed-term workers.

Agency workers

15.11 Agency workers can be a useful means of filling a staffing crisis which arises at short notice. It also obviates the need for an employer to go through the recruitment process. Since 2012, agency workers have enjoyed significant statutory protection. Employers need to be aware of their obligations under the Protection of Employees (Agency Workers) Act 2012 including the entitlement of agency workers to the same basic pay as non-agency workers employed directly by the hirer. From the date of enactment (May 2012), all agency workers are entitled to the same basic working and employment conditions as an employee of the hirer who is engaged in the same or similar work.

'Pay' means:

Basic pay and pay in excess of 'basic pay' in respect of:

- shift work;
- piece work;
- overtime;
- unsocial hours worked; and
- hours worked on a Sunday.

It does not include:

- sick pay;
- payments under any pension scheme or arrangement; and
- payments under financial participation schemes.

15.12 In England and Northern Ireland the relevant legislation allows for a qualifying period of 12 weeks before the equal treatment entitlements relating to pay and other basic working conditions, such as annual leave and rest breaks, come into effect. The position in this jurisdiction differs significantly. The equal treatment entitlements and the right to access employer facilities such as canteen, childcare and transport facilities take effect from day one following the enactment of the legislation.

15.13 Basic working and employment conditions are terms and conditions required to be included in a contract of employment by virtue of any legislation or collective agreement or any arrangement relating to:

- pay;
- working time;
- rest periods;
- rest breaks during the day;
- night work;
- overtime;
- annual leave; and
- public holidays.

15.14 In addition to equal treatment in relation to basic working and employment conditions, the hirer of the agency worker is obliged to treat an agency worker no less favourably than an employee of the hirer, unless the difference in treatment can be objectively justified, in relation to access to collective facilities and amenities at a place of work including canteen or similar facilities, childcare facilities and transport services. This definition of 'collective facilities and amenities' is not exhaustive and it is anticipated that guidance in this regard will be published in due course.

Fixed-term workers

15.15 A business may decide to use fixed-term contracts when the demands of a business dictate a short term business need. A fixed-term contract includes any contract which is intended to have a definitive duration or is for a specific purpose. Generally such contracts can have great benefits for employers and can be particularly suitable for use in various situations including:

- temporarily replacing employees on leave such as maternity or parental leave; and
- engaging employees for specific temporary projects or to fulfil specific orders for limited periods.

15.16 The law regulating fixed-term employees in Ireland is the Protection of Employees (Fixed-Term Work) Act 2003. The protections contained in the Act are in addition to the provisions in the Unfair Dismissals Acts 1977–2007. The purpose of the legislation is to prevent abuse arising, in particular, from the use of successive fixed-term employment contracts. It does this by the application of the principle of non-discrimination combined with detailed rules in respect of the renewal of such contracts.

15.17 Fixed-term employees are not to be treated in a less favourable manner than comparable permanent employees in relation to their conditions of employment solely on the grounds that they are employed on a fixed-term basis unless the different treatment is justified on objective grounds. An objective ground has to be based on considerations other than the status of the employee. The less favourable treatment has to be for the purpose of achieving a legitimate objective of the employer and the means chosen to achieve the objective have to be appropriate and necessary for that purpose, ie are proportionate.

15.18 If, for example, as part of a restructuring, a company decides that it needs to cut back on expenditure that is a legitimate objective of the employer. The implementation of the objective determines whether the less favourable treatment is objectively justifiable.

15.19 To objectively justify less favourable treatment an employer needs to show that he has done this for a legitimate business reason, and that the measures he has taken are appropriate and necessary. This requires the employer to show that there was no alternative means having a less discriminatory effect by which the objective could have been achieved. It is important to remember that generalisations and unsubstantiated claims will not suffice to justify less favourable treatment.

15.20 It is useful to note that employers are entitled to consider the terms of a fixed-term employee's contract of employment in its entirety when comparing it with those of a comparable permanent worker. Provided that the 'basket of benefits', when taken as a whole, are at least as favourable as the terms of the permanent comparator, any specific less favourable terms set out in the fixed-term contract may be justified on objective grounds. Essentially this allows the employer to compare the contracts as a whole, rather than term by term.

PROTECTION AGAINST DISMISSAL IN IRELAND

15.21 In Ireland, similar to the other jurisdictions in this guide, the concept of 'at will' employment does not exist. An employee in Ireland is protected both at common law and by statute. As a matter of contract law, it is possible, where the contract so permits, to terminate a contract on giving the requisite notice, with or without a reason for the termination. This will have the effect of bringing the contract to an end. However depending on the circumstances, it may expose the employer to: (i) plenary High Court proceedings for breach of contract, eg failure to follow a contractually agreed procedure prior to termination, including an injunction to restrain the dismissal; or (ii) a statutory claim for unfair dismissal. An employee can bring a claim for wrongful dismissal where an employee is not given their full contractual notice, or is not given valid or proper notice, the employee is summarily dismissed in circumstances which do not justify dismissal or if fair procedures were not observed. In many instances employees bringing a claim for wrongful dismissal will also include additional claims flowing from the breach of contract, for example, consequential loss due to an inability to obtain future employment. There is no length of service requirement for employees bringing wrongful dismissal claims and such employees have six years within which to bring their claims before the courts.

STATUTORY UNFAIR DISMISSAL REGIME

15.22 There is a statutory presumption, under the Unfair Dismissals Acts 1977–2007, that a dismissal under Irish law is unfair. The burden is usually on the employer to show that the dismissal is fair. Under the statutory unfair dismissals regime, employees whose employment is terminated on specific grounds such as maternity related dismissals, dismissals related to parental or adoptive leave, an employee's race or age etc, are automatically unfair grounds. One year's service is not required for claims on this basis.

15.23 In certain limited circumstances a dismissal can be deemed to be fair where it is for one of the following reasons or for some other substantial reason:

- capability (relating to the employee's availability to perform the role);
- competence (relating to the employee's ability and skill to perform the role);
- conduct (relating to the employee's poor conduct in connection with his employment);
- redundancy; or
- the fact that continuation of the employment would contravene another statutory requirement.

15.24 Subject to specific exemptions, to be eligible to make a claim for unfair dismissal an employee must have one year's continuous service with the employer. This service qualification includes the individual's notice entitlement. The dismissed employee must lodge their claim within six months of the dismissal or in 'exceptional circumstances' within 12 months. Such claims are brought before a Rights Commissioner or the Employment Appeals Tribunal.

Fair procedures

15.25 If lawful grounds exist for a dismissal, then the employer must follow fair procedures before giving notice of termination. The employer must be able to demonstrate that it has acted reasonably in coming to the decision to dismiss and that the dismissal is within a range of reasonable responses open to the employer in the circumstances.

15.26 The employer must follow its own procedures in advance of a dismissal. Most employers will have a written disciplinary procedure which must be followed. It is, therefore, critical to have regard to the contractual documents, including an employee handbook, to determine the correct procedure to be followed.

Employees have a constitutional right to natural justice in addition to contractual rights, in situations where a charge of misconduct is put to them. The protection is enhanced where dismissal is a possible outcome from the disciplinary process. The constituent elements of constitutional justice include the right to know precisely what misconduct the employee is charged with, the right to respond, the right to be accompanied at any hearing, the right to cross examine witnesses, the right to appeal and the right to have the matter judged by someone who is unbiased. The precise scope of the right to natural justice depends on the circumstances of the case. A breach of any of these rights exposes the employer to a claim for statutory unfair dismissal or an employment injunction.

Remedies for unlawful dismissal

15.27 If there are no lawful grounds for terminating the employment or if fair procedures are not followed or if the penalty of dismissal is disproportionate in the circumstances, then the employer may be exposed to one or more of the routes of redress outlined below:

- compensation for statutory unfair dismissal up to a maximum of two years' gross remuneration (salary, bonus and benefits) calculated by reference to financial loss (ie if the employee finds new employment on similar terms immediately or soon after the dismissal, then the employee can only recover up to the amount of actual loss incurred or a token compensation of four weeks' pay at the Tribunal's discretion);
- re-instatement or re-engagement can be ordered by the Tribunal to compensate for a statutory unfair dismissal;
- damages may be awarded by the High Court in respect of wrongful dismissal proceedings which is an alternative to the claim for statutory unfair dismissal. Such damages are limited to the notice which the employer is obliged by statute or contract to pay;
- damages or the granting of interlocutory relief (the 'employment injunction') by the High Court in respect of breach of contract proceedings. A successful application for an employment injunction could include an order to restrain a dismissal, to restore and maintain pay in the interim, to lift a suspension, or to restrain the carrying out or completion of an employer's internal investigation or disciplinary process;
- damages may also be awarded by the High Court in respect of Personal Injury proceedings in circumstances where, for example, the employer is aware of an occupational stress complaint by the employee.

COMPROMISE AGREEMENTS

15.28 It is possible under Irish law for the parties to agree to compromise existing claims, to waive existing rights (both statutory and contractual) and to discharge the employer from all liability (except claims arising in the future). To be valid and enforceable, the compromise agreement must be entered into with the employee taking independent legal advice and for valuable consideration. By way of very general guidance, in the situation of a senior executive exiting a business on a 'no-fault' negotiated basis, the employee could expect a package calculated on the basis of between 12 and 18 months' remuneration, possibly in addition to payment in lieu of their notice entitlement and accrued benefits.

DISMISSAL BY WAY OF REDUNDANCY

15.29 Redundancy is broadly defined under Irish law and can occur in a number of situations but generally exists where there is a valid economic basis for termination of employment. It can include situations where:

- the employer ceases to carry on its business in part or entirely;
- work requirements have diminished;
- work is to be done in a different manner for which the affected employee is not qualified;
- work is to be done by a different person who already performs other work for which the affected employee is not qualified; or
- work is to be done at a different location.

The common denominator in relation to the above scenarios is change. Some form of change in the workplace is vital for a valid redundancy situation to arise. This can vary from a complete shutdown to reduction in numbers to a technological change in the way the business will operate.

15.30 The statutory definition is set out at section 7(2) of the Redundancy Payments Acts 1967–2014 (the 'RPA') as follows:

An employee shall be taken to be dismissed by reason of redundancy if the dismissal is attributable wholly or mainly to:-

- the fact that his employer has ceased or intends to cease to carry on the business for the purposes of which the employee was employed by him, or has ceased or intends to cease, to carry on that business in the place where the employee was so employed;
- the fact that the requirements of that business for employees to carry out work of a particular kind in the place where he was so employed have ceased or diminished or are expected to cease or diminish; or
- the fact that his employer has decided to carry on the business with fewer or no employees whether by requiring the work for which the employee has been employed (or had been doing before his dismissal) to be done by other employees or otherwise;

- the fact that his employer had decided that the work for which the employee has been employed (or had been doing before his dismissal) should henceforth be done in a different manner for which the employee is not sufficiently qualified or trained; or
- the fact that his employer has decided that the work for which the employee has been employed (or had been doing before his dismissal) should in the future be done by a person who is capable of doing other work for which the employee is not sufficiently qualified or trained.

15.31 There is no genuine redundancy situation if an employee:

- is employed on a fixed-term (or specific purpose) contract and is subsequently re-employed by the same employer within 3 months of the dismissal under the initial fixed-term contract and the nature of the employment is the same as or similar to that of the employment under the prior contract;
- is re-engaged under a new contract by the same employer and the new arrangement is to take effect immediately; or
- is re-employed following an offer in writing made by the employer before the ending of the current contract and the new contract takes effect immediately or no later than four weeks from the end of the previous contract.

15.32 As outlined above the key test to establishing that a valid redundancy situation exists is demonstrating that there is change in the workplace. In shut down situations, or where there are large scale redundancies, this test is more easily satisfied.

15.33 A second key consideration is ensuring that the redundancy process is impersonal – ie it is the position that is being made redundant, rather than the person. Accordingly, if the redundant employee is subsequently replaced, it is unlikely that his redundancy situation was genuine on the basis that his role continues to exist. Selection for redundancy purely on performance related or other 'personal' reasons are not valid redundancies.

EMPLOYEES' RIGHTS IN A REDUNDANCY SITUATION

15.34 Specific statutory redundancy rights exist for employees with at least two years' continuous service (although some of these obligations, especially consultation and notice, will also be owed to employees with less service). The rights in question relate to:

- consultation;
- notice of termination of employment;
- redundancy pay; and
- paid time off to look for alternative employment or arrange for training.

15.35 It should be remembered that where an employee has 12 months' service (inclusive of any notice period), every termination of employment is considered unfair until proven otherwise. A valid economic redundancy is a fair dismissal but the burden of proof is on the employer to show:

- the redundancy was valid and part of change in the workplace;
- objective criteria were applied in the decision making process;
- reasonable alternatives to redundancy were considered (such as suitable alternative employment, redeployment, re-training, pay cuts, pay freezes etc); and
- where a selection was necessary (where some employees were selected for redundancy from a larger group of similar employees), that the selection exercise was transparent, fair and reasonable.

INDIVIDUAL REDUNDANCY

15.36 Although in an individual redundancy scenario there is no need for a prescribed consultation process, such as in a collective redundancy situation, an employer should engage in reasonable consultation with those employees likely to be affected. An employer should consult appropriately with affected employees before making decisions on redundancy including in relation to any selection criteria to be applied.

15.37 An employer should, by way of a suggested timeline:

- inform employees of the possibility of redundancies and the business reasons as to why this is the case. This should be communicated as a proposal and not a final decision;
- employees should be advised that the employer has explored alternatives to the proposed redundancies and invite employees to put forward their own suggestions in this regard;
- at risk employees should be informed that they are in a pool from which selection for redundancies will be made and, in the event, that no suitable alternative positions are found, their role may be made redundant;
- a meeting should then be scheduled with affected employees. Such employees should be met on a one to one basis. Whilst consideration is to be given to alternative arrangements put forward by the employee, there is no obligation on the employer to adopt such arrangements or create new positions. An employer should, however, give due consideration to any suggestions put forward by an employee by way of an alternative to the redundancy of their role; and
- if there is to be a selection of employees then the selection process needs to be fair and transparent.

Defining the selection criteria

15.38 In redundancy selection exercises, the selection criteria can be set and allocated suitable weightings by the employer. It is important to spend some time establishing the most appropriate objective criteria to meet the business requirements. As a general guide, selection criteria often include a combination of the following:

- skills;
- qualifications;
- experience;
- flexibility;
- performance but only if previously objectively documented and relevant to the skills needed for the remaining roles/business objectives; and
- length of service (although use of a 'last in, first out' approach may give rise to a risk of discrimination claims on grounds of age, gender and family status).

15.39 Many employers, when approaching a redundancy selection exercise, use a detailed scoring based assessment system awarding marks under each category to the various employees who are being considered and those with the lowest marks are selected for redundancy. This method assists in showing that an objective method was applied in assessing which individuals should be made redundant. The employee in question should have an input in this process by having an opportunity to comment on the provisional marks in the individual meetings. Previous annual reviews or other assessments, if well documented, are normally objective sources of information in 'scoring' the redundancy selection. However, the redundancy selection process should not simply be based on performance-related criteria so as to avoid allegations of '*back door*' performance dismissals.

15.40 Discriminatory grounds such as gender, age, civil status, family status, disability, nationality, religious belief, sexual orientation and membership of the traveller community are automatically unfair grounds for redundancy selection. Likewise, employers need to be mindful of the provisions in many pieces of Irish employment legislation prohibiting victimisation. Therefore if, for example, an employee has referred a complaint under protective legislation including health and safety legislation or is involved in trade union activity, it is important to be able to demonstrate that his or her selection for redundancy was based solely on objective selection criteria fairly and reasonably applied to the relevant pool and that nothing else influenced the employer's decision in that regard.

15.41 Overall, an employer must be able to demonstrate that it has acted reasonably in relation to the selection of an employee for dismissal by reason of redundancy. Any deviation from this, such as by operating a subjective or non-transparent selection process, opens up the risk of claims for unfair or discriminatory dismissal and possibly a claim for victimisation.

Practical Tips

- Communication with affected employees is critical. There should be no sudden decisions and the timeline of events should be carefully choreographed so that no decision is presented as a *fait accompli*.
- Alternatives where possible should be offered by the employer and sought from 'at risk' employees.
- Whilst there is no statutory requirement to offer a right of appeal from the redundancy decision, it may be prudent to offer one where possible as this contributes to the requirement of reasonableness on the part of the employer.

COLLECTIVE REDUNDANCIES

15.42 Irish law imposes a number of information and consultation obligations on an employer where it is implementing a collective redundancy. A collective redundancy is triggered where the number of dismissals by reason of redundancy in a consecutive 30-day period meets or exceeds the thresholds set out in the table below:

Total workforce	Threshold number of redundancies
21 to 49	5 or more
50 to 99	10 or more
100 to 299	10% or more of the workforce
300 or more	30 or more

Consultation requirements

15.43 The employer is obliged to consult with employees' representatives on the proposed collective redundancies, with a view to reaching an agreement. Employees' representatives are either their trade union or staff association, or, where there is no recognised trade union or staff association, persons chosen by the employees likely to be affected to represent them.

15.44 The legislation stipulates that consultations must include discussions on the possibility of avoiding the proposed redundancies, reducing the numbers of employees affected by them or mitigating their consequences (eg by re-deployment to a different site, re-training employees or employment on different terms). Where a selection process is being carried out, consultations must also include the basis on which it will be decided which particular employees will be made redundant.

15.45 Notice of redundancy cannot be given before the conclusion of the consultation process (which can extend for up to 30 days). No notice of dismissal on the grounds of redundancy can take place before the expiry of 30 days from the start of the consultation period. A consultation process will typically involve at least three meetings together with individual meetings. At the conclusion of the consultation process, a decision is made as to whether the redundancy is confirmed and that is communicated to the employee. Irish employment legislation does not provide that an appeal mechanism is necessary but it is advisable in the interests of demonstrating reasonableness on the part of the employer.

Information requirements

15.46 The following information must be given to employee representatives in collective redundancy situations:

- the reasons for the proposed redundancies;
- the number and descriptions or categories of employees whom it is proposed to make redundant;
- the number and descriptions or categories of employees normally employed;
- the number (if any) of agency workers engaged by the employer;
- those parts of the employer's business in which these agency workers are for the time being working;
- the type of work that the agency workers (if any) are engaged to do;
- the period during which it is proposed to effect the redundancies;
- the criteria proposed for the selection of the workers to be made redundant; and
- the method proposed for calculating redundancy payments.

A copy of this information must also be sent to the Minister for Jobs, Enterprise and Innovation as soon as possible.

15.47 There is no obligation under Irish law to offer a voluntary redundancy programme before proceeding to compulsory redundancies. However, it is quite common in Ireland for employers to do so. It is particularly common in unionised businesses where it may be a term of a collective agreement that any compulsory process is preceded by a voluntary process. However, in a plant closure situation where all employees will be made redundant, there would be little merit in offering a voluntary redundancy programme, unless there was a plan to wind down the operation over a protracted period of time and redundancies were to be made on a phased basis. To maintain necessary skill and talent retention, employers should reserve the right to refuse certain applications for voluntary redundancy, provided this is not prohibited by, for example, a collective agreement.

Notification to the Minister for Jobs, Enterprise and Innovation

15.48 Employers who are implementing collective redundancies must give written notice of the proposed redundancies to the Minister for Jobs, Enterprise and Innovation. A copy of this notice must also be sent to the employees' representatives who may make observations to the Minister and must contain the following information:

- the name and address of the employer, indicating whether he is a sole trader, a partnership or a company;
- the address of the establishment where the collective redundancies are proposed;
- the total number of persons normally employed at that establishment;
- the number and descriptions or categories of employees whom it is proposed to make redundant;
- the period during which the collective redundancies are proposed to be affected, stating the dates on which the first and the final dismissals are expected to take effect;
- the reasons for the proposed collective redundancies;
- the names and addresses of the trade unions or staff associations representing employees affected by the proposed redundancies and with which it has been the practice of the employer to conduct collective bargaining negotiations; and
- the date on which consultations with each such trade union or staff association commenced and the progress achieved in those consultations to the date of the notification.

15.49 The Minister has power to make further enquiries and seek consultation with the employer about the situation and to carry out investigations if necessary. Such consultations are intended to seek solutions to any problems caused by the proposed redundancies. For the purposes of such consultations the employer must supply the Minister with information about the proposed redundancies as the Minister may reasonably require. This power has been relatively infrequently deployed to date.

15.50 The Minister should be notified at the earliest opportunity and, in any event, at least 30 days before the first dismissal takes effect. Failure to initiate consultation with the employees' representatives, or to notify the Minister, is an offence and an employer is liable on summary conviction to a fine not exceeding €5,000. Where collective redundancies are effected by an employer before the expiry of the 30 day period, the employer is guilty of an offence and liable on conviction on indictment to a fine not exceeding €250,000.

Initiating consultations

15.51 Irish legislation provides that consultations should be initiated 'at the earliest opportunity' and in any event at least 30 days before the first notice of dismissal is given. European Court decisions provide some clarity as to the point in time at which employers must commence the process in a collective redundancy scenario.

15.52 The European Directive from which the Irish legislation stems provides that, 'Where an employer is contemplating collective redundancies, he shall begin consultations with the workers' representatives in good time *with a view to reaching an agreement*.' [emphasis added]

A recent judgment of the Court of Justice of the European Union (CJEU) addressed this issue for the first time and its key rulings were that:

- the obligation to start consultations with employee representatives arises not when an employer plans to take measures as a consequence of which collective redundancies are to be expected, but upon the existence of an intention on the part of the employer to make collective redundancies or once the employer makes a strategic or commercial decision compelling it to contemplate or plan for redundancies within a group of companies. The obligation is, therefore, triggered on the existence of an intention to make collective redundancies;
- where the prospect of collective redundancies is not directly the choice of the employer but rather of the undertaking controlling the employer – and even though the employer might not have been immediately and properly informed of that decision – the obligation to start consultations arises upon the existence of an intention on the part of the controlling undertaking;
- consultations with workers' representatives can only commence if it is known in which undertaking within a group collective redundancies will be made. Therefore, if a parent company of a group of undertakings adopts decisions likely to have repercussions on the jobs of workers within that group, it is for the subsidiary whose employees might be affected by redundancies, in its capacity as their employer, to start consultations with the employees' representatives. It is, therefore, extremely important for employers who are part of a multinational group to be conscious of when any obligation to inform or consult may be triggered and that, once a decision has been made which contemplates redundancies affecting the subsidiary in question, consultation must commence;
- where all of the relevant information required to be furnished to employees/employee representatives may not be available at the commencement of the consultation process, the information could be provided during the consultation process and, therefore, the time at which consultations were to commence could not be dependent on whether the employer was able to supply the worker representatives with all of the necessary information; and
- the subsidiary employer should complete the collective consultation process before the parent confirms the final decision to make redundancies.

Selection

15.53 As mentioned previously, selection of employees does not normally arise in a shutdown situation where all employees are being made redundant on around the same date.

15.54 Where redundancy selection is necessary, it must be objective, transparent, fair and reasonable (this is outlined in detail at para **15.38** above). The selection process and proposed selection criteria should be discussed with the employees' representatives in the collective situation, and shared with the individuals in non-collective individual redundancy situations. In the context of collective redundancies, as the employer is expected to negotiate with a view to reaching agreement, the selection criteria will form part of that discussion. While an employer does not have to present the selection criteria in draft form, it should ensure that feedback on the selection criteria (be it from representatives, or individually affected employees) is properly considered.

15.55 Collective consultation in respect of the proposed selection criteria should also take place with individually affected employees before making final decisions. Care should be taken to ensure that documents are not created which indicate that final selection decisions were made before consultations with employees. Such documents may be subject to disclosure through data subject access requests or otherwise through a discovery process. Communications between the employer and its legal advisors are protected from disclosure on the basis of legal privilege.

15.56 An employer must be able to demonstrate that it has acted reasonably in relation to the selection of an employee for dismissal by reason of redundancy. Any deviation from this, such as by operating a subjective or non-transparent selection process, opens up the risk of an unfair dismissal claim or a potential claim for victimisation or discriminatory dismissal.

Notice of dismissal by reason of redundancy

15.57 Once consultation is concluded the affected employees can be given individual notice of redundancy. An employee who is being made redundant (and who has two years' continuous service) must be given at least two weeks' notice of the redundancy in writing.

Minimum notice

15.58 Employees however may be entitled to longer notice periods under statute, based on length of service, as set out below.

Length of service	Minimum notice
13 weeks to 2 years	1 week
2 to 5 years	2 weeks
5 to 10 years	4 weeks
10 to 15 years	6 weeks
15 years or more	8 weeks

15.59 Furthermore, employees may be entitled to even more notice under their contracts of employment. It is often commercial practice for employers to pay employees in lieu of notice (PILON) requirements and in most cases this does not lead to problems. The absence of a clear pay in lieu of notice provision in the contract of employment may expose an employer to a breach of contract claim if it seeks to pay employees in lieu of their notice entitlement without their agreement. An employer will also lose the ability to rely on post termination restrictions such as restrictive covenants if there is no express PILON clause. Employees with less than two years' continuous service are entitled to at least one weeks' notice or contractual notice if greater. All of these notice periods can run concurrently.

15.60 During the individual statutory two-week redundancy notice period, an employee is entitled to reasonable paid time-off to look for new employment, eg to attend interviews. An employer may request the employee to furnish it with evidence of arrangements made for these purposes.

PROTECTED LEAVE

15.61 Under maternity protection legislation, any notice of dismissal which is either given or due to take effect in a period of maternity leave, is void. There is no requirement to apply preferential treatment to those on maternity leave in terms of priority consideration for redeployment. Those on maternity leave should be consulted with in the normal manner.

15.62 It is important to identify whether employees are on any other type of protected leave such as carer's leave, parental leave or *force majeure* leave. Employees absent from the work-place on long-term sickness absence should be consulted with in the normal course.

GARDEN LEAVE

15.63 There are a number of reasons why an employer may seek to enforce a garden leave clause, including minimising disruption to the workplace and distancing the redundant employee from the marketplace for a specified period of time. During garden leave an employee remains employed by the employer but is not required to do work or attend the workplace (unless instructed to do do). The contractual relationship remains in place and they remain an employee (with the attendant duties and obligations of good faith etc) until the notice period expires.

POST-TERMINATION RESTRICTIVE COVENANTS

15.64 Many businesses try to restrain employees after they leave by imposing contractual restrictions preventing them from, for example:

- joining competitors for a defined period (usually 6–12 months post termination);
- soliciting customers or employees (again usually for 6–12 months post termination); and
- using confidential information or trade secrets (generally this restriction is indefinite in time).

Clauses covering the above scenarios are widely used in employment contracts particularly for middle to senior level employees and those that frequently have access to confidential information.

15.65 As there may be a question mark over the enforceability of restrictive covenants, careful and specific drafting of these clauses is paramount. While courts are more likely to enforce the continuing obligation of confidentiality, case-law has demonstrated a judicial resistance to curtail an employee's ability to work, albeit in competition with his or her former employer, for an unreasonably long period of time or in an unreasonably broad products/services field.

15.66 More recently the Irish courts have shown a greater willingness to enforce such restrictions and to protect legitimate business interests. This is encouraging although the courts have made it clear that for such clauses to work there must also be an identifiable business interest at stake and the contractual restriction itself must be both clear and reasonable in terms of:

- the geographical scope ie the restricted area of operation, for example all of Ireland or a province in Ireland, eg Munster or Leinster;
- duration; and
- the nature of the activity or business restricted.

Increasingly sophisticated forensic IT methods are identifying employees who try to download sensitive customer data for their private use and the courts have demonstrated a readiness to accept such evidence.

15.67 By way of practical guidance, the following principles should be noted:

- non-compete clauses should generally be no longer than six months and at a maximum 12 months depending on the seniority of the employee and the employee's access to confidential information and trade secrets;

- the restriction should be as specific and precise as possible in identifying the interest the employer is trying to protect – for example, expressly citing specified competitors or customers;
- 'boilerplate' or template clauses which give no description to the specific business will be very difficult to enforce;
- clauses should be reviewed regularly and updated to ensure accuracy and relevance. This could be done when promotions or salary reviews take place;
- it would be more difficult to justify restrictions on junior employees;
- non-solicitation clauses are generally easier to enforce; and
- if a payment is made in respect of the covenant by way of specific consideration, the courts may be more minded to enforce the relevant restriction.

The law on restrictive covenants is a difficult one to navigate. It requires that a balance be achieved as the law will still want to encourage competition whilst, on the other hand, acknowledging that an employer will want to safeguard the investment it has made to the employment relationship.

15.68 To seek to enforce restrictive covenants, an employer will likely apply for an injunction. Injunctions sought in relation to restrictive covenants are usually prohibitory or springboard in nature. While prohibitory relief simply stops unlawful action, springboard injunctions are sought where a departing employee is seeking to use or rely on trade secrets or confidential information belonging to the former employer as a '*springboard*' or an advantage in setting up his own competing business.

15.69 Damages may be awarded in circumstances where the employer can show loss of profit, for example, from the solicitation of customers.

REDUNDANCY PAY

15.70 There are two elements to redundancy pay: (i) statutory; and (ii) enhanced. An eligible employee with two or more year's continuous service is entitled to a statutory redundancy payment.

STATUTORY REDUNDANCY PAY

15.71 The amount of the statutory minimum lump-sum payment is calculated as follows: two normal weeks' pay for each year of continuous and reckonable employment; *plus* a bonus week's pay.

15.72 For the purposes of calculating a statutory redundancy lump sum payment, the value of a week's pay is capped at €600. A redundancy calculator is available on-line at http://www.djei.ie.

15.73 Employees must also be compensated for any accrued but unused rights as of the date of termination of employment. The best example of this is untaken annual leave which can be paid in lieu in such situations.

ENHANCED REDUNDANCY

15.74 Employers are not legally obliged to pay anything on top of the statutory entitlements. However, voluntary 'top-up'/'ex gratia' payments are common in Ireland and can often be quite significant. There are public relations, commercial and industrial relations advantages to making such payments to assist in a smooth restructuring process. The amount of any such enhanced payment is a matter for an employer to determine after consultation with the employees' representatives. However, that decision may be influenced by any existing collective agreement or policy in respect of severance packages, in addition to any custom and practice in the case of previous redundancies over the years in the wider business or custom and practice within the sector generally.

15.75 Enhanced redundancy payments in Ireland typically in the present climate tend to range from between two to six weeks' pay per year of service and this can either include or be in addition to the statutory redundancy lump sum payment set out above at paras **15.70–15.71**. Enhanced redundancy payments may also have the following features:

- multiplier of weeks' pay per year of service eg three weeks' pay per year of service;
- the amount may be capped to limit liability for long service;
- may be inclusive or exclusive of the statutory redundancy lump sum payment; and
- should be conditional upon a compromise agreement being executed by the employees, following independent legal advice, precluding them from taking any legal action against the employer in respect of their employment or its termination.

15.76 If deciding to make a payment an employer needs to be conscious of the IR, PR and general commercial risks that might result from offering lesser terms. If an enhanced payment is being offered it should be conditional on employees executing a waiver and discharge/compromise agreement in favour of the company. Such agreements usually provide that the employee must take independent legal advice on the content and purport of the waiver before signing it. This will assist the enforceability of the agreements but can slow down the process.

TAXATION OF REDUNDANCY PAYMENTS

15.77 The position in relation to the taxation of payments made to employees is as follows:

- statutory redundancy lump sum payments are paid tax-free;
- payments in lieu of accrued but untaken holidays are taxable in the normal course (ie as salary);
- payments in lieu of notice are taxable in the normal course (ie as salary) if the employee's contract provides for the possibility of such payments; and
- enhanced redundancy payments (and payments in lieu of notice where such are not provided for in the contract) are typically taxable on the basis set out below.

15.78 An employer is obliged to deduct applicable tax and pay that to the Revenue Commissioners. There are two ways of dealing with the taxation of enhanced redundancy payments and either can be used.

15.79 Firstly, an employer may apply the standard exemptions. Payments are exempt from tax on the first €10,160 and on an additional €765 for each year of the employee's service. The employee can also avail of an additional exemption of €10,000 if he/she has not benefited from such an additional exemption in the last 10 years. However, the application of the additional exemption must be approved in advance by the Revenue Commissioners.

15.80 The alternative (second) approach to calculating an employee's tax position is to calculate the Standard Capital Superannuation Benefit (SCSB) – which will be tax free. SCSB favours longer serving employees and is calculated in the following way:

(a) calculate the employee's average total remuneration over the last three years of their service;
(b) multiply that sum by the number of their complete years of service;
(c) divide the current total by 15; and
(d) subtract the value of any tax-free lump sum received or receivable under an approved superannuation scheme.

Practical Tip

Adhering to the requirements of the legislation is crucial in collective redundancy situations as there are significant penalties for employers for failing to comply with the information and notification requirements. This is particularly so in relation to consultation requirements and timelines etc.

STATUTORY ENTITLEMENT TO LAY-OFF/ SHORT TIME

15.81 There is statutory provision under the Redundancy Payments Acts 1967–2014 (the RPA) for an employer to place their workforce on lay-off or short time in circumstances where the employer is unable to provide work.

However, it should be noted that the employer is only entitled to do so where there is a reasonable belief by the employer that the lay-off or short time will not be permanent and the employer gives notice to that effect to the employee prior to them being laid off or placed on short-time. (Short time occurs where an employee's pay is less than one half of his normal weekly pay or his hours of work are reduced to less than one half of his normal weekly hours).

CLAIM FOR REDUNDANCY PAYMENT

15.82 While the RPA does not specify a maximum period of time for which an employee can be laid-off or kept on short time, where the period of lay-off or short time continues for four or more consecutive weeks, or within a period of 13 weeks for a series of six or more weeks of which not more than three weeks were consecutive, the employee will be entitled to give notice in writing to his employer of his intention to claim a redundancy payment. As such, this enables an employee to claim redundancy where he has been laid off or kept on short time for a specified period of time and prevents an employer from keeping an employee on lay-off or short time indefinitely without having to make a redundancy payment pursuant to the RPA.

COUNTER-CLAIM BY EMPLOYER

15.83 If such notice is received by the employer, the employer is entitled to file a counter-notice to the employee which must inform the employee that they will recommence employment not later than four weeks after the notification, and for a period of not less than 13 weeks during which time the employee will not be laid off or placed on short time. The lay-off period will only be determined by the receipt of notice by the employer that the employee intends to claim a redundancy payment. If an employee does not give his or her employer notice of their intention to seek redundancy, their lay-off period can arguably continue on for an indefinite period.

RIGHT TO DEDUCT WAGES

15.84 An interesting issue which arises and on which the legislation is silent is the right of an employer to deduct wages where employees are laid off or placed on short time. There is a technical argument that the employer is in breach of contract if he lays off an employee without pay or places an employee on short time, thereby reducing their pay, unless there is an express or implied contractual term permitting the employer to do so. There is no general right at common law to lay-off employees without pay or to place employees on short time. Such a right may, however, be established through custom and practice or general usage. Generally, where there is no contractual entitlement (either express or implied) for an employer to lay employees off without pay or to place them on short time. The safest approach from a legal perspective is for the company to seek the prior agreement of employees pursuant to the Payment of Wages Act 1991 to lawfully withhold wages during that time. From a commercial perspective, this approach is not always adopted by employers. An employee who normally works full-time but is placed on short-time or is temporarily laid off may be entitled to receive social welfare benefit. In the case of short time working, an employee would only be entitled to receive social welfare benefit in respect of the days he does not work, provided he meets any other conditions that may apply, for example, such an employee must not work more than three days per week.

15.85 On occasion other alternatives to redundancy are considered within a business. Examples of these include, but are not limited, to:

- unpaid or partially paid career breaks;
- paid career breaks;
- unpaid leave;
- retraining or redeployment;
- overtime ban;
- early retirement programme;
- non-renewal of fixed-term contracts; and
- termination of agreements with independent contractors.

EXCEPTIONAL COLLECTIVE REDUNDANCIES

15.86 A specific feature of Irish employment law is our exceptional collective redundancies legislation. An 'exceptional collective redundancy' arises in a situation where the employees have been replaced by other employees who are employed by the employer or whose services are to be provided to that employer to perform essentially the same functions as those previously dismissed and the terms and conditions of employment of those new persons are materially inferior to those of the dismissed employees.

15.87 In such a situation either the employer or the employee representative can refer the collective redundancy to the Redundancy Panel who will give a view as to whether or not the collective redundancy is in fact an 'exceptional collective redundancy'.

BUSINESS SALE/OUTSOURCING

15.88 A company restructuring can also arise where two businesses merge and after the merger there is a duplication of resources leading to the newly created entity taking steps to create efficiencies by optimising the use of new technologies or structures now available to them.

15.89 The law applicable to a situation outlined above is the Transfer of Undertakings Regulations. It is designed to safeguard employees' rights when businesses (or parts of businesses) are taken over by way of sale, outsourcing or otherwise. The various Directives have been transposed into Irish law by way of the European Communities (Protection of Employees on Transfer of Undertakings) Regulations 2003 (as amended) (the 'Transfer Regulations').

15.90 The Transfer Regulations apply to any legal transfer or merger of any undertaking, business, or part of an undertaking or business from one employer to another. A transfer can be by way of a lease or licence, franchise or other arrangement. There does not necessarily have to be a change of ownership.

THE TRANSFER REGULATIONS AND INSOLVENCY

15.91 There are various types of insolvency situations. The Transfer Regulations will apply in all such situations except a compulsory liquidation where the reason for the liquidation is the indebtedness of the company. A compulsory liquidation arises when company is wound up and a liquidator is appointed on foot of an order of the High Court under section 569(1) and (2) of the Companies Act 2014. A compulsory liquidation can be initiated by a petition to the High Court by the creditors or members of a company or by the company itself. In a compulsory liquidation, the Court supervises the liquidation of the Company. In such instance the Transfer Regulations will not apply.

Compulsory liquidation where reason for liquidation is indebtedness of company	**Transfer Regulations do not apply**
Compulsory liquidation where reason for liquidation other than indebtedness of company Members' voluntary liquidation Creditors' voluntary liquidation Receivership Examinership	Transfer Regulations apply

THE TRANSFER MUST INVOLVE A CHANGE OF EMPLOYER

15.92 It is essential to establish if there has been a change of employer: this is a fundamental pre-requisite to the application of the Transfer Regulations. A change of employer may occur in a contracting out or in situation. Similarly, a change of employer can, and generally does occur, within the context of an inter-group transfer. A share purchase alone may not attract the application of the Transfer Regulations as it does not necessarily involve a change of employer. In determining whether or not there has been a change of employer, the court will not be put off by devices such as service companies or by complicated group structures which conceal the true relationship such as a situation where, in a company belonging to a group, employees are in the formal employ of one company but working on a permanent basis for another. In those circumstances, if the company for whom the employee works on a permanent basis is transferred, that employee also transfers.

WHAT IS AN 'UNDERTAKING'?

15.93 The term 'undertaking' encompasses any entity engaged in economic activity regardless of the legal status of that entity and regardless of whether the entity is profit or non-profit making. This definition brings all the following within the scope of the Transfer Regulations: charities, local authorities, health boards, state and semi-state bodies, education establishments, medical establishments and foundations, trade associations and trade unions.

EMPLOYERS' OBLIGATION TO INFORM AND CONSULT

15.94 The Transfer Regulations impose an obligation on both a transferor and the transferee to inform their respective employees' representatives affected by the transfer or the impending transfer and, where measures are envisaged in relation to the employees, to consult with the employees' representatives in that regard. If there are no employees' representatives, the employer must facilitate the appointment of such representatives. It is only when this fails that the employer is able to notify the employees individually in writing. This information and consultation process has to be done at least 30 days before the transfer is carried out.

WHAT RIGHTS AND OBLIGATIONS TRANSFER?

15.95 The employees' rights and obligations arising from the contract of employment transfer to the transferee. The transferee is prevented from making changes to the employees' terms and conditions as a result of the transfer. There is an exception to this known as the *'economic, technical or organisational'* reasons (ETO). As this exception is not clearly defined in the legislation, a certain degree of flexibility to restructure post transfer may be envisaged. It is, however, commonly understood that redundancy situations and organisational changes post transfer may fall within the scope of the ETO exception.

15.96 The new employer is obliged to comply with any collective agreement in force at the time of the transfer. The transfer of an undertaking does not break an employee's continuity of service and the employee's length of service is, therefore, preserved. The liability to the old employer for personal injury and other potential employment claims transfers to the new employer on a transfer of undertakings.

15.97 The Transfer Regulations do not apply to employees' rights to old age, invalidity or survivors' benefits under supplementary or inter-company pension schemes falling outside the Social Welfare Acts. However, the Transfer Regulations do impose an obligation on a transferee to ensure that the interests of employees, and of persons no longer employed in the transferor's business, are protected in respect of rights conferring on them immediate or prospective entitlement to old age benefits, including survivors' benefits.

CAN EMPLOYEES OBJECT TO A TRANSFER?

15.98 The transfer of the employee from transferor to transferee is automatic, irrespective of the wishes of either party. This is subject only to the right of the employee to object to a transfer of their employment relationship. EU case law has found that employees are entitled to object to the transfer of their employment contract but the legal effect of this objection is a matter for each member state to determine. In the event that an employee objects to the transfer without cause there is no entitlement to a redundancy payment from either the transferor or the transferee.

REDRESS FOR BREACH OF THE REGULATIONS

15.99 Redress is generally to the Rights Commissioner and, on appeal, to the Labour Court. The Rights Commissioner is empowered to award compensation not exceeding two years' remuneration in the case of a breach of the Transfer Regulations. The maximum compensation that can be awarded for breach of Regulation 8 (the duty to inform and consult), is the equivalent of four weeks' remuneration per employee.

OUTSOURCING

15.100 There has also been an increase in businesses outsourcing certain non-core functions such as customer support and certain administrative functions. Typically, however, but not always outsourcing involves the transfer of employees and/or assets from one employer to another. While the historic motivation for outsourcing was to reduce costs, there is the added potential for a business efficiency that can result in an improvement in customer service in an area that has been difficult for the business to manage internally. There is usually a particular clause in an outsourcing contract to deal with the transfer of the employee from the employer to third party service provider. It is commonplace for the service provider to request an indemnity in relation to any employment risks prior to the transfer. The service provider may also be required to provide an indemnity against any and all employment risks and exposures during the lifespan of the outsourcing contract.

15.101 Typically the questions that arise for an outsourcing provider include the following:

- whether the outsourcing contract is subject to the Transfer Regulations;
- if it is decided that the Transfer Regulations don't apply, what are the protections that should be sought in the outsourcing contract;
- if it is the case that the Transfer Regulations do apply:
  - what rights and obligations transfer?
  - which employees have the right to transfer?
  - what protections should be sought in the outsourcing contract in relation to warranties and indemnities?
  - which employees are affected by the transfer for the purposes of information and consultation?
  - are there any measures envisaged post-transfer that may trigger consultation obligations? and
  - are there any economic, technical or organisational grounds to warrant the dismissal of any employees on transfer?

15.102 There is no express reference to outsourcing in the Transfer Regulations so careful consideration needs to be given to the above factors in determining the application of the Transfer Regulations in an outsourcing situation. Usually, particularly in relation to first generation outsourcing, the parties to the contract will often agree between themselves that the agreement is subject to the Transfer Regulations. However, in certain circumstances, for example, where the contract has been the subject of a formal tendering process it may be up to outsourcing providers themselves to decide if the Transfer Regulations apply.

Practical Tips

- Carefully analyse facts to determine whether the Transfer Regulations may apply to the particular restructuring.
- Ensure obligations and time limits regarding information and consultation are complied with.

CONCLUSION

15.103 Companies engaged in any form of restructuring need to be mindful of their wide ranging obligations under employment law, in particular under the collective redundancies legislation and the Transfer Regulations. On occasion, due to the need to implement changes speedily, consultation obligations may be abridged or circumvented, and this can expose the employer to liabilities.

Chapter 16

Workforce Restructuring in Italy

Francesca Baldi
Studio Legale Baldi, Reggio Emilio, Italy

INTRODUCTION

16.1 This chapter looks at the employment laws in Italy. The legal system in Italy is a civil law system, where law is codified: nevertheless, the number of provisions of the civil code, as well as the dissemination of the rules in other statutory and regulatory instruments makes the subject complicated to approach.

The following sources are the main sources of law and provisions governing the employment relationship including the creation, the existence and the termination of the employment contract in Italy:

- International and EU provisions;
- Italian Constitution;
- Statutes: labour market reform 'Biagi' (legge n. 276/2003) and labour market reform 'Fornero' (legge n. 92/2012);
- Applicable 'Contratto Collettivo Nazionale di Lavoro – CCNL' (National Collective Labour Agreement – sectors: Industry, Trade, Third Sector);
- Legge n. 300/1970 'Statuto dei Lavoratori' (Employees' Bill of Rights)…
- Company's employment contract;
- Individual employment contract;
- Company's practices.

16.2 Whereas the first document to be looked at when assessing the possibility of dismissing one or more employees is the employment contract, it may not be decisive and/or regulate the whole the employment relationship: it is common for the employee to sign a simple 'employment letter' in which the employer details the role assigned to the employee, the date of commencement of the employment relationship, the salary, and possibly indicates specific features of the employment relationship, referring, in respect of any other provisions to the applicable national labour collective agreement: Contratto Collettivo Nazionale di Lavoro – CCNL'.

EMPLOYMENT STATUS

16.3 Only individuals, who meet the legal definition of 'employee' (in article 2094 of the Italian Civil Code), are protected against unfair dismissal. It is therefore essential that: (i) any contracts with independent contractors i.e. individuals engaged by the company (eg agents, self-employed consultants and service providers) are drafted clearly and correctly, so to avoid the possibility of such contracts being deemed as employment contracts; and (ii) the way tasks are assigned to such individuals, and more generally any direction as to the performance of those tasks, does not present features (amongst whose, fixed working hours/place, hierarchic position inside the company) that could result in the relationship being deemed to amount to an employment relationship.

WORKFORCE REDUCTION

16.4 Depending on the reasons and the circumstances, the employer has the following options in order to reduce the number of its employees: individual dismissal(s) and collective dismissal(s) of employees.

Individual dismissals can be justified by subjective (disciplinary) or objective reasons: the employer will in any case have to follow a specific procedure, which is detailed in the following paragraphs.

Individual (disciplinary) dismissal procedure

16.5 The employer is entitled to use dismissal as a disciplinary measure for serious breach of the contractual duties imposed on the employee. In fact, the disciplinary measures which can be applied are:

- *verbal warning*: for minor violations;
- *written warning*: for more serious violations;
- *fine*: consists of the deduction, from the employee's salary, of an amount equal, at maximum, to four hours of the basic salary; said amount must then be paid by the employer to the welfare entities listed in the CCNL;
- *suspension*: suspension from the working activity implies the interruption of the payment of the salary for the whole duration, which cannot exceed ten days; or

- *disciplinary dismissal*: can be applied when the violation is so serious that the employment relationship cannot be continued.

For the correct application of the disciplinary power by the employer, two conditions have to be fulfilled, from the substantial and the procedural point of view. If one or both of these are lacking, the disciplinary measure is considered invalid.

The **substantial requirements** are:

- *existence of the illicit fact*: the presence of a culpable violation of the express or implied contractual duties imposed on the employee as a result of the employment relationship (diligence, obedience, loyalty); and
- *adequacy of the disciplinary measure*: the disciplinary measure must be proportionate to the violation which has been committed.

In any event, the employer cannot apply a disciplinary measure which is harsher than the one established by the applicable National Collective Labour Agreement (CCNL) for a specific breach.

The **procedural requirements** to comply with when imposing a disciplinary measure are:

- The preparation of a disciplinary code, ie a written document which details possible violations and the corresponding disciplinary measures.
- Displaying the disciplinary code in a place accessible to all employees. Failing this, the employer is prevented from imposing disciplinary measures on the employees to sanction their behaviour.
- The warning in respect of the wrong must be preventative, specific and immediate: the employer cannot impose a disciplinary measure on the employee without having previously reprimanded the behaviour and indicated the attributable facts with enough detail. The warning must be in writing, and must state the deadline for providing the motivation by way of disputing the warning by the employee (five days). If the employee considers the warning as illegitimate, within the term of 20 (twenty) days, he shall have the right to appeal the warning in front of the competent Court or in front of Direzione Territoriale del Lavoro or Commissione di Conciliazione specified in CCNL, requesting the suspension of the provision.
- The employee is granted right of defence: art. 7 of L. 300/70 (Employees' Bill of Rights) establishes that the employer following the warning letter has been issued has the duty to receive or hear the employee's defences, granting him/her a deadline of not less than 5 days from the moment when the employee received the warning letter.
- Following the employer's decision to impose a disciplinary measure, the applicable CCNL governing the employment relationship can decide to postpone the disciplinary measures taking effect until a certain number of days has passed from the date of receipt of the warning letter by the employee and a certain number of days from the receipt of the employee's motivation letter has passed. The decision to impose a disciplinary measure must be communicated to the employee by recorded delivery within a certain number of days from the expiry of the deadline granted

to the employee for the submission of his motivation, specifically stating the grounds and reasons of the disciplinary action which has been taken.

Individual dismissal procedure for justified objective reason

Legal requirements of dismissal for justified objective reason

16.6 Dismissal for justified objective reason is legitimate only when the employer:

- operates an actual (not fictitious) reorganisation of the company, based on true circumstances existing at the time of communication of the dismissal. Dismissal justified by a company reorganisation with the aim of improving efficiency is considered to be legitimate;
- despite attempts to relocate the employee (with similar tasks) within the company, concludes this is not possible within the whole company. In a multinational company, this operation has to be conducted not only with reference to the branch/office in which the employee is currently located, but with reference to the whole company. When a group of companies can be considered to be one single entity, in which the economic interests and the legal relationships are concentrated, this operation has to be conducted also with reference to the other companies of the group;
- selects the employee to be dismissed according the rules of good faith and fairness, and not arbitrarily;
- provides the required advance notice or pays the payment in lieu of notice;
- in the period following the dismissal (approximately six months), refrains from employing another person to perform the same tasks previously assigned to the dismissed employee, failing which the dismissal is automatically considered to having been unfair.

Attempt to Conciliation at the Direzione Territoriale del Lavoro's (Territorial Labour Division's) office

16.7 With the entry into force of the Labour Market Reform 'Fornero' in 2012, the procedural rules established by the previous legge n. 183/2010 have been significantly modified, providing that in case of dismissal for justified objective reason in companies employing more than 15 employees, an 'attempt to Conciliate at the Direzione Territoriale del Lavoro (Territorial Labour Division)'s office' is compulsory.

The employer therefore must initiate such pre-emptive procedure declaring to the representatives of the National Union in front of the Committee by the Direzione Territoriale del Lavoro his/her intention to proceed to dismissal, explaining the underlying reason.

During the meeting in front of the Committee the possible alternatives to the dismissal will be evaluated. The proceedings end 20 days after the date of the communication from the Direzione Territoriale del Lavoro summoning the parties to the meeting, unless the parties jointly declare that they have no intention to go ahead with the negotiations aimed to reach an agreement.

If such attempt fails, the employer can communicate the dismissal to the employee, who, in turn, can contest the dismissal with a formal (but extra-judiciary) letter in the following 60 days.

If an agreement is reached, and the mutual termination of the employment relationship is agreed upon, the rules on Assicurazione Sociale per l'impiego (ASPI) (Employment Social Security) will be applicable, and, in order to facilitate the employee in finding another job, he/she can be listed in the Employment Agencies' lists.

In summary, you will be allowed to proceed with the dismissal of the employee as soon as it becomes clear that the attempt to conciliate will be a negative result or after the expiry of the 20 days' deadline from date of the communication of the Direzione Territoriale del Lavoro summoning the parties to the meeting.

In case such procedural steps are not respected, according to Law n. 92/2012 the company will have to pay the employee compensation to be calculated on the basis of between 6 and 12 monthly salaries, whilst reinstatement of the employee in the workplace is not applicable in those circumstances.

Sanctions in case of unlawful dismissal for justified objective reason

16.8 The Labour Market Reform 'Fornero' has also significantly changed art. 18 of Law n. 300/1970 (Employees' Bill of rights), establishing that, when a dismissal is based on economic reasons, and the Labour Court decides the dismissal is unlawful due to lack of just cause or justified objective reason, reinstatement of the employee in the workplace is not possible, but the company will have to pay the employee compensation to be calculated on the basis of between 12 and 24 monthly salaries.

Specific provisions apply when the employee to be dismissed is a manager of the Company: in such a case, the dismissal is governed by the provisions of the Italian Civil Code, which establish that the employment contract can be terminated at any time, respecting the advance notice obligation, if not terminated immediately for just cause.

Such general regulation is, however, supplemented by additional, specific provisions where the manager's employment is governed by a collective agreement.

In fact, the collective agreements establish that the dismissal of a manager must in any case be justified: the idea of 'justification', nevertheless, is in this case different from just cause or justified reason, generally applicable to employment relationships, but it is significantly broader for managers.

The dismissal of a manager must be justified by reasons which are neither discriminatory, nor arbitrary, but objective and actually verifiable, or so serious to injure the peculiar bond of trust between manager and employer.

According to case law, the dismissal of a manager whose role had been made redundant further to a corporate restructuring, was considered to be justified because the dismissal of a manager on the basis of a business decision which is not arbitrary and based on reasonable grounds.

In all cases the dismissal must be communicated respecting the advance notice, calculated on the basis of the length of service of the employee.

Such advanced notice is to be calculated from the first day of the month following the date of receipt of the dismissal notice, but in case the employer dismisses the employee without notice, the employer must also pay an indemnity in lieu of notice.

Multiple individual dismissal procedure for justified objective reason

Collective dismissal and multiple (individual) dismissals for justified objective reason

16.9 When the legal conditions for adoption of the collective dismissal proceeding are not fulfilled (eg a reduction or a transformation of the business, or the closing of it) the only available instrument for an employer wishing to reduce the workforce is the process of multiple (individual) dismissals for justified objective reason.

The main limitation of this instrument is that it is not possible to dismiss more than 4 employees in 120 days.

In fact, further to the entry into force of legge n. 223/1991, all those situations which do not present all of the following features: five employees, to be dismissed in a period of 120 days by a company employing more than 15 employees are considered to be individual dismissals (governed by legge n. 604/1966).

The individual dismissal procedure for justified objective reason must be followed for each affected employee.

Company's crisis: social security cushions and collective redundancy procedure

16.10 The Italian legal system provides a complicated and intricate system of 'social security cushions' in order to mitigate the social effects of employment problems resulting from a serious business crisis, through direct actions – managed by the Institute of Social Security (INPS) – to support the salaries of employees of the companies in crisis or workers laid off from manufacturing processes.

The Italian legislation, which concerns and applies only to industrial companies with more than 15 employees, allows companies affected by structural crisis:

- to use the so called 'Cassa Integrazione' (temporary layoff), which can be ordinary or extraordinary depending from the causes that led to the crisis and depending on the consequences of the latter, if those companies believe to be able to maintain the existing employment levels, once the crisis is over. However, where the industrial company, after having benefited from a period of Cassa Integrazione, believes it is not able to ensure the reemployment of all the suspended employees and cannot put alternative measures in place, it has the right to initiate the procedure of collective redundancy under Law 223/1991, Article 4, paragraph 1.[1].The effect of the mobility procedure is to permanently terminate the employment relationship as opposed to the temporary layoff during periods where the employment relationship is only suspended;
- to directly use collective redundancy procedures by placing employees in mobility, so that they can perceive the applicable allowance, in the event companies cannot ensure the re-employment of suspended employees or offer alternative measures (CIGS).

The procedure explained in the two previous paragraphs does not start automatically, rather requires the implementation of specific proceedings, through a consultation with the Trade Union Representative's National Associations; or, failing this, with the majority of the represented associations nationwide.

CASSA INTEGRAZIONE GUADAGNI STRAORDINARIA (CIGS) – (TEMPORARY LAYOFF – EXTRAORDINARY SUPPLEMENTARY WAGE FUND)

16.11 Recourse to the extraordinary supplementary wage fund, CIGS, governed by Law 223/1991, may be sought by companies finding themselves in a serious 'business crisis' resulting in complex employment problems requiring prolonged intervention in the form of supplementary wages.

CONDITIONS FOR RECOURSE TO THE CIGS

16.12 The reasons which can justify financial assistance from the extraordinary redundancy fund (CIGS) are:

1 Law of July 23rd 1991 'rules of redundancy, mobility, unemployment benefit, implementation of the Directive of the European Community, job placement and other provisions relating to the labour market (Articles 1–24).

- **business crisis** (economic, sectorial or local) meant as a state of widespread and ongoing difficulty of the company in undertaking or continuing its business.
  In this sense, crisis, resulting from a sudden and unforeseeable event, due to situations arising out of the national or international setting, and which have led to a deterioration of production volume or activity, and consequently of the employment levels (for example, the reduction of exports or difficulties in accessing credit), are included. The maximum duration of the CIGS support is 12 consecutive months, with the possibility of a further period of intervention, after the expiry of a period of at least two/thirds of the period of the previous grant.
- **processes of corporate restructuring, conversion, re-organisation.** The duration of the CIGS is 24 consecutive months with the possibility of two further extensions of 12 months each, if required due to the complexity of the restructuring program.
  The parameter by which restructuring programs are approved, otherwise known as business plans, presented by companies that require the intervention of CIGS for corporate restructuring, are established by the Ministry of Labour.
  The term '**corporate restructuring**' refers to business situations in which industrial projects of renewal of the company characterised by provision of significant investment – aimed at technological upgrading of facilities or for organisational changes and/or modifications of production process. In these kinds of situations, the layoffs should be justified, with regard to the extent and to the timing of the same, by the present restructuring process and, in any case, the ratio of employees required to undertake a retraining and re-qualification process shall not be less than 30% of those covered by the CIGS support programme.
  The term '**reconversion**' refers to those processes aimed at recovering efficiency, either through the modification of the existing plants with a view to introducing new types of products in the company, or by updating the layout and processes of the plants, in order to make them more competitive.
  The '**reorganisation**' takes place where there is a necessity to face the inefficiencies of the management structure, due to imbalances between production, commercial and administrative equipment.
- **Insolvency**: pursuant to Article 3 of the Law no. 223/1991, financial support via the CIGS may be granted in cases of bankruptcy, compulsory liquidation, extraordinary administration (in circumstances where the company is not permitted to continue the activity); arrangements with creditors to assign goods; agreements on debt restructuring.

However, the author wish to point out that Law n. 92 of 28 June 2012[2] abolishes this Article 3 of Law n. 223/91, with effect from the year 2016, with the consequence that it will no longer be possible to apply support from the CIGS in cases in which the employment relationship appears terminated – as typically occurs in bankruptcy and in other insolvency procedures – or where

2 Law June 28th 2012 n. 92 'provisions on labour reform in a growth perspective'

the status of the company is such that there is no prospect of recovery at the end of the period of financial support.

In any case, there may be exceptions where financial support via the CIGS is granted subject to there being prospects for continuation or resumption of and safeguarding of employment levels, the valuation of such must be made on the basis of objective parameters issued by the Ministry of Labour.

DURATION OF CIGS IS 12 MONTHS

Submission of application

16.13 The CIGS applies to enterprises, including cooperatives of production and labour, which occupied more than 15 employees during in the 90 days preceding the filing of the application. For this purpose, apprentices, part-time workers, home workers and managers, are included in the count.

Companies, which have recourse to the CIGS, are required to pay a corporate contribution equal to 3% of entire amount of wages if they employ up to 50 employees or 4.5 % if they employ more than 50 employees. The contribution amount is doubled, starting from the 25th month following the commencement of treatment.

The categories of persons who may benefit from the extraordinary supplementary wage are the following: workers, employees, intermediate staff, managers with more than 90 days of continuous service, as at the date of submission of the application.

Managers, home workers and apprentices are only entitled to benefit if they are expressly included under the terms of the grant of the financial support via the CIGS.

Pursuant to Article 1, paragraph 8 of Law n. 223/1991, during a period of financial support the employer is obliged to rotate the workers who are either suspended or working part-time as a result of the difficulties encountered to ensure that the burden of having to take a reduction in hours and income is shared amongst all the employees and not just resting on a select few. . Failure to ensure that will result in heavy fines being applied to the company.

An employer, who does not comply with this duty of rotation, will be forced to pay additional contribution to the fund:

- with immediate effect and double the amount for each suspended employee;
- Increased by 150% and with effect from the first day of the 25th month following the act of granting the support via the CIGS. Where a company chooses not to adopt the system of 'rotation', for reasons connected with the maintenance of normal levels of efficiency, it must support such decision by provision of an adequate explanation. If the Ministry of Labour does not consider the reasons provided by the company to exclude the duty of rotation justified, the company is obliged to seek to reach an agreement with the Trade Union Representatives' National Associations.

If, within three months from the date of grant of support via the CIGS, such agreement has not been reached, the rotation mechanisms will be established by the Ministry of Labour.

Procedure for awarding support via the CIGS

16.14 The procedure to be applied in awarding support via the CIGS is divided into four phases, as detailed further below:

- notice by the company to the Trade Union Representatives' National Associations;
- joint assessment by the company and National Trade Union's representatives;
- on-line submission of the application for support via the CIGS to the Ministry of Labour ; and
- The procedure ends with the Decree of the Ministry of Labour granting the CIGS

1. *Notice by the company to the Trade Union Representatives' National Associations;*
   Companies that are interested in receiving support via the CIGS, must give an advance written notice, either directly or through the business association to which they belong, to the Trade Union Representatives (so called 'R.S.U. – Rappresentanze Sindacali Unitarie'), failing that, to the most represented trade union organisations of workers operating in the province.
   Under Article 1, paragraph 7, of the Law n. 223/1991, the notice shall include:
   1) the parameters for the selection of workers to be suspended;
   2) the rotation mode.
   It should be noted that a simple notice, in which the company express to have an ongoing contraction of the economic activity, is not sufficient to entitle employees to support via the CIGS. The employer must give the Trade Union Representatives the opportunity to evaluate the situation in advance, agree the parameters for selecting workers to be suspended, and justify the real possibility of being included into the rotation or not.
   Moreover, the Italian Supreme Court, by judgment of 10 May 2010 no. 11254 stated that, in the absence of certain information within the corporate communication, workers affected by the application of CIGS can obtain restoration of employment and payment of a full and unintegrated salary.
2. *Joint assessment*
   Within three days following issue of the above mentioned notice, the employer, or the Trade Union Representatives, must apply for a joint assessment of the company's situation. This request must be submitted to:

- the competent office of the Region, in whose territory the business units involved in the CIGS are located; and
- the General Direction for the protection of the working conditions of the Ministry of Labour, in the event the business units involved in the application of CIGS are located in different regions.

As confirmed by the Italian Supreme Court, in a judgment of 1 June 2011 n. 12103, the subject of the joint assessment is to evaluate the program that the company proposes to implement, together with information as to the duration and number of affected workers in the application of CIGS, any measures taken to manage any surplus, the parameters and the selection of workers to be suspended, the rotation mode, and the reasons where it is not possible to perform the rotation.

The entire consultation process ends within 25 days after the date on which the request of the joint assessment was filed; this term is reduced to 10 (ten) for companies which employ up to 50 employees.

Within 20 days after the conclusion of the consultation process, the region (or regions) express a reasoned opinion.

In letter n. 53 of 4 November 2002, the Ministry of Labour established that the procedure for applying for support via the CIGS continues, independently of the joint assessment, where 20 days elapses without any response.

It should be noted that failure to observe the abovementioned obligations to issue a notice and consult with the Trade Union Representatives, constitutes 'anti-union conduct' likely to be complemented by the corresponding protection process of repression provided by Article 28 of the Employees' Bill of Rights[3].

3. *Online submission of the application for support via the CIGS to the Ministry of Labour*

   Upon completion of the joint assessment, the company file an electronic application for support via the CIGS (the so called 'istanza di concessione'), which specifies a maximum period of support of 12 months, together with the necessary documentation provided for the different causes (crisis, restructuring, reorganisation), to the Ministry of Labour.

---

3 Article 28 of the Law n. 300 /1970 provides that: 'if the employer engages in conduct designed to prevent or limit the exercise of freedom and trade union activities and the right to strike, the local bodies of the National Trade Unions who have an interest may within two days appeal to the judge in the place, where the relevant behaviour takes place. Upon convening the parties, the judge will on the basis of the relevant information, decide if a violation has taken place and if so, issue a reasoned decree which is immediately enforceable against the employer, to cease the unlawful conduct and to remove the effects thereof. The enforceability of the decree cannot be revoked until a judgment of the Court of Employment, defines a lawsuit instituted pursuant to the following paragraph. The relevant parties may within 15 days of the notification of the decree appear in front of a judge of the Court of Employment, to oppose the decree. The judge will then decide whether the judgment is immediately enforceable. The provisions of Articles 413 as well as complying with the Code of Civil Procedure are binding. An employer who fails to comply with either the decree referred to in the first paragraph, or with the judgment following trial, is sanctioned under Article 650 of the Criminal Code. The judicial authorities shall order the publication of the criminal judgment of conviction in accordance with Article 36 of the Criminal Code'.

The application for support via the CIGS, as well as any later request for extension, must be submitted within 25 days (term reduced to 20 days in case of a request for direct payment of support to affected workers with CIGS) from the end of the month in which the suspension or reduction of the working hours takes effect. Failing that, the employer must estimate and pay a wage supplement to the entitled workers in addition to the payment of fees on that amount.

4. *Decree of the Ministry of Labour granting the CIGS*
   The process ends when the Ministry of Labour issues the decree granting the support via CIGS.
   it should be noted that, in case of restructuring, reorganisation or conversion, within 90 days from the commencement of financial support, investigations are carried out by the Inspection Services of the Territorial Direction of Labour and results are sent to the Ministry of Labour, before the end of the first 6 months.
   Following the expiration of the first 12 months of support via CIGS, a regular inspection check on the implementation of the program will take place within 20 days from the submission of the request by the company. In the event of programs of restructuring, reorganisation or conversion, of companies with more than 1,000 employees and with affected units located in two or more regions, a Technical Committee shall issue an opinion as to the basis for an extension within 20 days from the receipt of the inquiry documentation by the Ministry of Labour.
5. *Application to the National Institute of Social Security (INPS)*
   Within 25 days from the end of the current payment period in which the Decree of the Ministry of Labour granting support via the CIGS was issued the employer then submits an on-line request for payment to the National Institute of Social Security (so called 'INPS').

Granted application – payment

16.15 After having obtained the Decree granting support via the CIGS from the Ministry of Labour as well as the authorisation of INPS, financial support equivalent to 80% of the total remuneration for the hours employees are out of action (up to the contractual limit for each employee capped at a maximum of 40 hours per week per employee) is paid to the employer at the end of each month.

The above-mentioned payment by employer will later be reimbursed by INPS via the equalisation contributions.

In circumstances of serious financial difficulties, the Ministry of Labour may instruct INPS to make direct payment to the affected workers as opposed to paying to the employer.

The mobility (collective redundancies)

16.16 The Italian legislation provides two different circumstances where collective redundancies are permitted:

- collective redundancy as a result of the company undergoing reduction or transformation of the activity or termination of the same;
- collective redundancy when, following a period of support via CIGS, the company cannot guarantee the re-engage all suspended employees and has not managed to come with alternative measures.

Conditions

16.17 Collective redundancy procedures apply when the employer:

- occupies more than 15 employees;
- intends to effect at least five dismissals;
- during a period of time of 120 days.

According to Italian legislation, where either or both the temporal or of the quantitative requirement is absent, multiple redundancies will not be treated as collective redundancies but instead fall subject to the rules applicable to individual dismissals for objective fair cause.

Reasons

16.18 The reasons that justify the implementation of collective redundancies are:

- **reduction or transformation of the activity.** Corporate downsizing does not necessarily imply a corporate crisis and can be implemented without modifying or suppressing structures. By its decision of 21 October 1999 n. 11794, the Italian Supreme Court established that this is the case when a company proceeds with a change in the organisation of the production entailing the reduction of offices, departments, processes, or only in the presence of a shrinking workforce.
- **cessation of trading activity.** It is a requirement that the reduction of employees should flow from the production transformation. It follows from this, that a minor production transformation cannot justify a significant number of redundancies.

  Case law supports the use of the 'collective redundancy' procedure where the business plan was intended to reduce the workforce of the entire company in order to reduce labour costs provided that there is a causal link between the proposed 'corporate downsizing' and the reduction of the workforce (Supreme Court, 19 April 2003 n. 6385 and Supreme Court 6 May 2004 n. 8364).

The burden of proving the reality of a decrease in demand for labour falls on the employer, who, therefore, must refrain from filling staffing gaps arising from restructuring, and from extending the economic activity of the company in the aftermath of such measures (Supreme Civil Court, 20 January 2011, n. 1253).

Procedure

16.19 The procedure for reduction of employees is composed of the following steps:

1 **Make a contribution to the National Institute of Social Security (INPS)**
The employer must pay a contribution equal to one month gross maximum of CIGS support for each employee that the employer intends to dismiss and who is entitled to the mobility allowance (an unemployment benefit) to the INPS. The contribution is used to fund the mobility allowance.
A copy of the receipt of the payment must be attached to the notice, to be sent to the Trade Union Representatives.

2 **Communication to the Corporate Trade Union Representative (so called 'RSA' – Rappresentanze Sindacali Aziendali)**
According to Article 4, paragraph 2 and 4 of the Law 223/1991, the employer must give notice in writing of his intention to reduce the workforce and make employees redundant within seven days to the Corporate Trade Union Representatives and to the respective trade associations.
If there are no trade union representatives within the company, the notice shall be forwarded to the most representative associations nationwide.
The notice must contain:
- the reasons (technical, organisational, production) for making the redundancies including details of why the employer believes he cannot avoid the redundancy. In order to allow trade unions the accomplishments of an effective and substantial joint assessment and control, the employer must refer to the situation of the company at the point when the procedure was initiated (and not to prior situations or to restricting process dating back in time (Supreme Court, 13 July 2006, n. 159943);
- number, placement and professional profile of each redundant employee, and of the staff usually employed;
- the timing of the implementation of the redundancy program;
- any measures planned for contrasting the social consequences for the redundant employees;
- the method of calculation of all redundancy payments other than those already provided by the applicable law and by the collective agreements.

  A copy of the written notification must be forwarded to the competent regional office involved in the management of the labour market, or if identified to the provincial office.

3 **Joint examination**

After having received the above mentioned notice the Corporate Trade Union Representatives – RSA, can require a joint examination with the employer, with a view to identifying alternative solutions to the proposed dismissals. In the event a reduction of personnel cannot be avoided they can assist in establishing accompanying social measures aimed at facilitating the retraining of redundant employees.

Examination at the Territorial Directorate of Labour.

Once consultation with the unions is complete, the employer must notify the Territorial Directorate of Labour (DTL) of the outcome of the consultations and where agreement was not reached the reasons therefore. In the event of non-agreement, the DTL summons the employer and the trade unions for final negotiations with a view to reaching an agreement.

4 **Dismissing employees**

Having concluded the procedural stage, the employer can proceed to the dismissing redundant workers by applying precise criteria.

These criteria may be agreed between the employer and the trade unions during the consultation process. Where such criteria have not been agreed, those criteria established by law shall apply (Article 5 of the Law 223/1991):

- **agreed criteria**: the union agreement signed by the parties, may establish criteria for selection of persons for redundancy to be applied instead of those established by law. Such must have the character of objectivity and generality and must be consistent with the purpose of the redundancies;
- **criteria prescribed by law**: Statutory criteria apply in the absence of agreed criteria for selection. It follows from article 5 of Law n. 223/1991 prescribes that a list of the employees should be prepared taking into to account the technical requirements of production and organisation of the business, according to the following criteria in competition with each other:
  - family responsibilities;
  - seniority;
  - technical, productive and organisational needs. By judgment n. 17556/2004, the Supreme Court established that the business decision can be justified by the prospect of 'saving the costs of travel and mileage from the point of leaving the workplace'; therefore, a company is entitled to continue to employ employees available to render their services in sectors other than the habitual ones, as well as employees residing in the proximity of the workplace.

With regard to the selection of the employees to be dismissed, Article 5, paragraph 4 of Law n. 223/1991 prohibits the employer from dismissing a higher percentage of female workers than male workers in the company with regard to the tasks taken into consideration.

A comparison of the different positions of workers must be carried out in accordance with the principles of fairness and professionalism, and whilst taking the entire organisational and productivity context into consideration. In circumstances where the restructuring or the termination

of activity affects only part of the organisation ie. one sector or one business branch only the effects in this respect shall be considered.
The employees identified as redundant should be dismissed by written notice of dismissal in accordance with the contractual terms of notice.
At the same time as the employer gives notice of dismissal to the individual workers, he must also give notice to the trade unions and to the public bodies (Region, Province, Ministry) such notice shall include a detailed description of the method of application of the selection criteria.

Consequences of unlawful dismissal:

16.20

- In the event a dismissal does not comply with the collective dismissal procedure described in Article 4, paragraph 12 of the Law n. 223/1991, the protection established by Article 18, paragraph 7, as modified by the Law n. 92/2012 in respect of economic dismissals by employers with more than 15 employees will apply. Where re-integration in the workplace cannot take place, the court confirms the termination and makes an order for the employer to pay compensation to the employee equivalent to 12 to 24 months of the final total remuneration actually received by the employee.
- In the event that the selection criteria are not applied correctly, the Judge may annul the dismissal and order the employer to re-employ the employee and pay damages commensurate to the total remuneration from the date of dismissal up to the date of reinstatement, less any interim pay the employee has received or could have received by taking on a new job. In the latter case, the employer is obliged to pay contributions to social security and welfare from the date of dismissal up to the actual date employment is restored but only where the employee did not work for another company during this period. As an alternative to re-employment, the employee may request payment of an indemnity equivalent to 15 months' salary.

In conclusion, before taking steps to making staff redundant and in order to lawfully proceed with any required action, an employer must consider the following steps:

- In the first instance, the company should consider alternative and less traumatic action than collective redundancies such as using extraordinary temporary layoffs in order also to facilitate mandatory negotiations with the trade unions with a view to negotiate a solution to the employment problem.
- To assess, in the light of the consequences which sanctions might otherwise be applicable, whether there is an causal link and consistency between the planned restructuring or reduction and the dismissal of a large number of employees;
- Select the employees to be made redundant in compliance with the selection criteria set by statute and/or agreement with the unions.

MUTUALLY AGREED TERMINATION

16.21 Given the complexity of the subject matter, the employer may prefer to reach an out-of-court settlement agreement as an alternative to dismissing the employee, who might otherwise resort to challenge the basis for the dismissal by initiating civil proceedings before the employment division of the court. By such agreement, the employer may incentivise the employee to leave the company quietly, and obtain written confirmation from the employee that he or she has no additional claim whatsoever deriving from the employment relationship.

Settlement agreements

16.22

- Although there is no legal requirement for the employee (often considered to be the 'weak' party of the employment relationship) to be advised by a qualified legal professional or a representative of the trade unions, it is general practice that the employee and the employer are represented by their respective attorneys during the negotiations aimed to reach a settlement agreement.
- The settlement agreement (to be formalised and signed before the labour commission in the place where the employee resides, in a specific meeting fixed upon request of the parties), summarises the background of the agreement, includes details the financial arrangements, and generally contains the mutual renunciation of any further claims arising out of, or connected to the employment relationship, thereby making the settlement agreement a full and final agreement between the parties.
- If one party breaches the settlement agreement by not fulfilling the terms the non-defaulting party can take action to enforce the agreement.

Chapter 17

Workforce Restructuring in Latvia

Daiga Zivtina and Irina Kostina
Klavins Ellex, Latvia

INTRODUCTION

17.1 This chapter focuses on the Latvian law perspective on the consequences of a restructuring for employees.

17.2 European Union policies in recent decades have sought to achieve high employment and strong social protection, improve working conditions and protect social cohesion. As a member state of the European Union, Latvia has transposed all major European Union directives into its legal acts that in accordance with the Treaty on the Function of the European Union, article 153, have set minimum requirements for working and employment conditions, as well as informing and consulting workers.

17.3 In respect to the legal framework which governs employment relations, it must be emphasised that Latvia is also a member of international labour organisations and has ratified all eight fundamental conventions by 2006,[1] as well as four additional governance conventions that are considered as 'priority' instruments in labour law matters.[2]

17.4 In regards to the national law system, Latvian law is historically based on the civil legal system and has adopted a considerable part of mechanisms

1 See: http://www.ilo.org/dyn/normlex/en/f?p=NORMLEXPUB:10011:0::NO::P10011_DISPLAY_BY,P10011_CONVENTION_TYPE_CODE:1,F

2 See: http://ilo.org/global/standards/introduction-to-international-labour-standards/conventions-and-recommendations/lang--en/index.htm

from, in the main, German and French systems. The Labour Law of the Republic of Latvia regulates the main issues regarding workforce restructuring in Latvia; nevertheless, there are some areas that should be improved and specified.

17.5 We have prepared an overview focusing on the issues regulating workforce restructuring in Latvia, providing the reader with the applicable legal mechanism, case law and, where necessary, we have also added some practical tips and examples that help to illustrate the difficult issues.

17.6 In summary that the legal framework forms the base which creates a balance between the rights and obligations of both parties – employees and employers; nevertheless, the regulations set just the minimum standards, and measures can be applied in individual cases to increase the level of protection of the weakest party – the employee – in cases of restructuring and help employers to avoid employees' claims relating to restructuring procedures and consequences.

PREPARING FOR A RESTRUCTURING EXERCISE

17.7 Before the start of any restructuring exercise it is important to understand not only the legal background, but also the actual situation in each specific company as an individual legal entity in question. Extensive due diligence can reduce any potential risks and, in relation to workforce restructuring, there are several main issues which will be highlighted below.

17.8 First, the necessary information on the workforce of the particular target company must be gathered. Primarily, the information in regard of employment agreements (including supplements to employment agreements) must be collected and organised. The most relevant information in order to establish a brief profile of each employee would be the following: employees' job roles and description of their responsibilities; length of service; qualifications; age and other information relevant for collective redundancy purposes. It must be noted that the information regarding employee participation in trade unions cannot be gathered prior to the issuing of the employment termination notice, but the employee will disclose this information after receipt of relevant termination notice. Nevertheless, the employer is under an obligation to inform the respective trade union about the notice of termination if the employee is a member of trade union.

17.9 Secondly, an analysis of the collective agreement is recommended (if there is one in existence) to establish the rights of employees and employment conditions and other relevant obligations. There is no legal requirement for all companies to have internal collective agreements in place and this recommendation is optional.

17.10 Thirdly, a due diligence exercise on employment matters is an important step in establishing the actual situation concerning any disputes, disagreements or claims that are already initiated by employees or potential employment claims. Please note that all written and official correspondence between an employer and an employee can be relied on by either party to a potential dispute; therefore, it is important to be aware of all the facts and to have the necessary evidence in proper order. The employer has the burden of proof in employment disputes.

17.11 Finally, it must be decided whether the company has an authorised body that represents the employees. Pursuant to the Labour Law, the employees can exercise protection of their social, economic and occupational rights and interests, directly or indirectly, through the representation by employee representatives. Within the meaning of the applicable law, 'employee representatives' shall mean: (i) an employee trade union on behalf of which a trade union institution or an official, authorised by the articles of association of the trade union, acts on behalf of the employees; or (ii) authorised employee representatives who have been elected in accordance with the applicable laws and regulations. Authorised employee representatives may be elected if the company employs five or more employees. At the same time, there can be cases where the company has no authorised body that represents employees.

In workforce restructuring, honest communication with the employee representatives or all employees, if there are no representatives, can help to speed up the process and come to an agreement that is acceptable to both employer and employees, for example regarding social security package for the employees that will be affected by a workforce reduction.

17.12 The above-mentioned steps will help to organise and categorise the key information that will be helpful during the workforce restructuring process, and will help to establish the estimated costs.

EMPLOYMENT STATUS

17.13 Pursuant to article 3 of the Labour Law, an employee is a natural person who, on the basis of an employment agreement, for agreed remuneration, performs specific work under the guidance and supervision of an employer. There are four core elements relevant for determining if the person can be considered to be an employee: (i) the person is a natural person; (ii) an employment agreement is concluded; (iii) the person is receiving remuneration for the work; and (iv) the person performs the duties under the guidance of the employer. It should be noted that if there is no signed employment agreement this does not mean that the person could not be considered an employee if he/she has carried out work duties according to the instructions of the employer and received salary for their work.

17.14 The status of the member of the management board in the company must be reviewed individually. Pursuant to current applicable laws and regulations, there is no longer an obligation to enter into an employment agreement with an executive of the company. Historically an employment agreement with the members of executive bodies of companies had to be concluded, unless they were employed on the basis of some other contract governed by the Civil Law. Nevertheless, under current law, a company is now able to choose whether to establish a contractual relationship on the basis of an employment contract or alternatively, a management agreement.

17.15 It follows from case law, that the member of the management board renders services to the company and receives remuneration (especially where the member of the management board renders services that can be considered outside the scope of the duties of a typical member of the management board), an employment agreement should be concluded.[3] This position is supported by the State Revenue Service that has a relatively aggressive approach in developing interpretation and practice on this issue. For example, in cases where a member of the management board performs the duties of an accountant of the company, the State Revenue Service considers that it is necessary to conclude an employment agreement with the member of the management board for provision of accountancy services.

17.16 The fact that a person is a member of the management board and has not entered into an employment agreement does not automatically avoid the possibility that he/she can be considered as an 'employee'. The Court of Justice of the European Union has stated that 'it is necessary to consider the circumstances in which the member of the management board was recruited; the nature of the duties entrusted to that person; the context in which those duties were performed; the scope of the person's powers; the extent to which he or she was supervised within the company; and the circumstances under which the person could be removed.' Therefore if a dispute arises in the future, there is a risk that the court can conclude that an employment agreement exists between the parties and therefore, the Labour Law must be applied.[4]

17.17 In light of the above, it also must be emphasised that if the member of the management board is recalled from their position on the Board this automatically causes termination of the employment agreement where it was entered into with the member of the management board for fulfilment of their obligations as a member of the management board. Where the employment agreement was entered into with the member of the management board for fulfilment of any other additional obligations (for example, position of a chief financial officer), recalling him from the board position does not

---

3 Judgment of the Civil Department of the Senate of the Supreme Court of January 19, 2011 in the case SKC-1/2011 and Case No A42874509 of September 11, 2013 of the Supreme Court Senate Administrative case department.

4 The Court of justice of the European Union, case C–232/09, the judgement of November 11, 2010.

automatically mean that the employment agreement of the member of the management board is terminated regarding the additional position and work obligations. In order to remove the person from the status of a member of the management board, provisions of the Commercial Law are applicable, but in order to terminate the employment agreement, the regular procedure stipulated by the Labour Law must be followed.

GENERAL PROTECTION AGAINST DISMISSAL

17.18 According to the labour law general protection against dismissal prohibits an employer to dismissing an employee during the period of temporary incapacity (except for cases;(a) where the employee does not perform work due to temporary incapacity for more than six months; (b) if the incapacity is uninterrupted; (c) for one year within three years, if the incapacity repeats with interruptions, excluding prenatal or maternity leave in such period; or (d) as well as a period of incapacity, if the reason for incapacity is an accident at work or an occupational disease). Where the incapacity of the employee is due to an accident at work or an occupational illness, the employer is entitled to give notice of termination after recovery from illness or determination of the disability.

The employer is also prohibited from terminating the employment agreement if an employee is on leave of absence or is not performing duties due to justifiable reasons. For example, case law has established that summoning an employee during leave for one day for the sole purpose of terminating the employment agreement is not a legal justification for dismissal and it cannot lead to lawful termination of employment.[5]

At the same time the employer is not bound by these restrictions if the legal entity is liquidated and it ceases to exist as the employer.

17.19 According to the Labour Law general protection against dismissal ensures that on the written request of the employee, the employer is obliged to grant sufficient time (in contractual working hours) for the employee to look for a new job. This protection applies only if dismissal is based on one of the following reasons:

- the employee lacks adequate occupational competence for performing the contracted work;
- the employee is unable to perform the contracted work due to a health condition, which is evidenced by a doctor's certificate;
- the employee who previously performed the relevant work has been reinstated in their previous position;
- workforce reduction; or
- the employer (legal entity or partnership) is being liquidated.

5 Civil Department of the Senate of the Supreme Court, judgment SKC-288 of February 9, 2011.

17.20 General protection against dismissal includes the rights of an employee to submit a claim against their employer in court in order to establish the validity or otherwise of the termination notice. In some cases the court is entitled to decide to extend the deadline for submission of the claim in court if the indicated reason of delay appear plausible.

17.21 The Labour Law obliges the employer to prove that the termination notice is grounded complies with the procedure for termination of employment.

SPECIAL PROTECTION AGAINST DISMISSAL

17.22 According to the Labour Law special protection in regards to employment termination is guaranteed for pregnant woman, as well as to women with children under the age of one and women who are breastfeeding a child up to the age of two.[6] This protection, however, does not apply if the dismissal was based on the employee's performance (including, breach of the employment contract, unlawful actions during performance of her work duties etc) and liquidation of the legal entity as an employer.

17.23 Special protection against dismissal is also guaranteed for disabled persons. However, this protection does not apply if the dismissal was based on the employee's performance or the employee's inability to perform the work due to their medical condition, which is certified by a doctor, as well as the liquidation of the legal entity as an employer.

17.24 In addition, the Labour Law guarantees special protection to employees, who are members of trade unions. If the person is a member of a trade union an employer is obliged to obtain prior consent of the specific trade union. This protection, however, does not apply if the reason for dismissal is: (i) performance of work obligations while under influence of alcohol, drugs or any other toxic substances; (ii) the employee who previously performed the relevant work has been reinstated in their previous position; or (iii) the liquidation of the legal entity as an employer.

The relevant trade union is obliged to inform an employer of its decision within seven working days from the receipt of a request from the employer. Failing which, it shall be deemed as consent to give notice of termination to the employee. If the relevant trade union refuses its consent and objects to

---

6 In accordance with the amendments of the Labour Law of the Republic of Latvia, that will enter in force on January 1, 2015, the period of protection if the woman is breastfeeding has been limited up to two years, previously it was for all breastfeeding time. After this time period, the woman is not entitled to the special protection under the applicable laws and regulations.

terminations, the employer may, within one month from the date of receipt of the response, bring an action in court for termination of the employment agreement.

WORKFORCE REDUCTION

17.25 Article 104 of the Labour Law states that reduction of the number of employees (workforce reduction) where a notice of employment termination is not based on behaviour or performance of the employee, but is well-grounded on urgent financial, organisational, technical and other commercial events in the company. Workforce reduction according to the Labour Law can be divided into two categories: (i) individual redundancy; and (ii) collective redundancy. Individual redundancy and collective redundancy is distinguished by the number of employees to be dismissed during a period of one month.

17.26 The individual redundancy procedure is commenced when the employer adopts a decision to reduce the number of employees also indicating the particular roles to be eliminated. Concurrently, criteria for evaluating and selecting employees for redundancy should be prepared. It should be noted that such evaluation must be conducted, if there are several employees in a similar position and only one or few of them are to be dismissed. Evaluation of these employees shall be performed according to the provisions established by the Labour Law. Namely, preference to continue employment shall be given to those employees who have performed better and have better qualifications.

If performance and qualification do not substantially differ, preference to remain in employment in cases of collective redundancy should be given to those employees:

- who have worked for the employer long service;
- who, while working for the employer, have suffered an accident at work or have fallen ill with an occupational illness;
- who are raising a child up to 14 years of age or a disabled child up to 18 years of age;
- who have two or more dependants;
- whose immediate partners do not have a regular income;
- who are disabled or are suffering from radiation sickness;
- who have participated in the rectification of the consequences of the accident at the Chernobyl Nuclear Power Plant;
- for whom less than five years remain until reaching the age of retirement;
- who, without discontinuing work, are securing an occupation (profession, trade) in an educational establishment; and
- who have been granted the status of a politically repressed person.

Please note that all the criteria have equal weight.

The employer is prohibited from terminating an employment agreement with the following persons:

- a pregnant woman, as well as a woman during the postnatal period of one year, or, if the woman is breastfeeding, up to two years;
- an employee whilst suffering from temporary incapacity to work (due to illness);
- an employee who is on leave not at work due to other justifiable reasons.

17.27 The Labour Law stipulates two criteria which have to be evaluated in the first instance – **performance** and **qualification**. These criteria carry equal weight and must be objective. Besides it is advisable employees have already undergone regular performance reviews and a decision regarding evaluation is made by a working group consisting of several persons. The law allows the employer to set particular criteria as the employer is in the best position to understand what qualities are most needed for performance of specific duties of the employees who will remain in the company.

17.28 It is advisable to create evaluation score chart if there are several employees who are in the same position. For example, by allocating scores for: the level of education; additional courses; training; performance: work completed in a timely manner; the employee's proposals for improvement of performance; work performed to a high standard; and remarks etc. Upon developing the evaluation criteria specifics of each position must be taken into account.

17.29 Evaluation is focussed on a group of employees within the framework of a specific type of role. It can also be carried out against a group of employees whose specific job descriptions provide for equal or similar work responsibilities and duties. For example, in case of reduction of employees at a company the evaluation should be conducted among cargo handlers whose work comprises the same or essentially similar duties. Evaluation should not be conducted between a cargo handler and a supervisor of a warehouse as their work positions and job descriptions substantially differ.

Practical Tip:

It is crucial to establish effective and lawful evaluation of employees where the number of employees is to be reduced. If a notice of termination based on reduction of number of employees is challenged in court, the employer must explain all related circumstances and provide relevant evidence pertaining to the evaluation procedure.

17.30 After the evaluation has been conducted the employer gives a termination notice to each affected employee – one copy is given to the employee and the other, receipted by the employee, is kept by the employer. The termination notice has to be given to the employee at least one month before actual dismissal. The termination notice must explain that the employment agreement is being terminated due to a reduction of the number of employees and that the employer is not able to offer other work to this employee.

The employer must pay the severance pay to employee in the following amounts: • one month's average income, if the employee has been employed by the employer less than five years; • two months' average income, if the employee has been employed by the employer for five to ten years; • three months' average income, if the employee has been employed by the employer for 10 to 20 years; • four months' average income, if the employee has been employed by the employer for more than 20 years.

17.31 Before decision to dismiss it shall be determined whether the employee selected for dismissal is a member of any trade union; if so, the employer must obtain written consent from the relevant trade union for the termination of employment.

COLLECTIVE REDUNDANCY

17.32 Collective redundancy is a workforce reduction where the number of employees to be dismissed falls within the scope of special regulation on collective redundancy included in the Labour Law. To distinguish between reduction of the number of employees (individual redundancy) and collective redundancy number of the employees to be dismissed in time period of one month is important.

Calculation mechanism in order to determine if the case falls under the category of collective redundancy. The workforce reduction shall be considered as collective redundancy where the number of positions that will be eliminated within a time period of 30 days is as follows: • at least five roles will be removed if the total number of job roles in the company is between 20 and 50; • at least ten roles will be eliminated where the total number of job roles in the company is between 50 and 100; • at least 10% from all job roles will be eliminated if the total number of job roles in the company is between 100 and 300; • at least 30 job roles will be eliminated if the number of the employees and job roles in the company exceeds 300. Note: upon estimating the number of employees to be dismissed, all available options for employment termination must be considered (for example, termination based on mutual agreement).

17.33 The employer is obliged to inform and consult with the representatives of employees on planned collective redundancies, the number of employees to be dismissed, social security matters and the procedure for collective redundancies. Consultation is aimed at ensuring the employee's social protection. However, according to case law non-fulfilment of this obligation is not a sufficient ground for declaring a termination notice invalid *per se*.[7]

Representatives are usually internally elected representatives of employees. If there are no employee representatives, the employer is not obliged to follow the consultation procedure, nevertheless it is advisable to provide employees with sufficient information regardless of the existence of the representatives or trade unions. During the consultation both parties are obliged to evaluate options to prevent collective redundancy or soften the consequences. The Labour Law does not stipulate the period for consultation, however if a dispute arises, the employer will have to prove that consultation has taken place.

17.34 After consultations with representatives of employees the decision on collective redundancy must be given in writing to the representatives of employees stating the grounds for the collective redundancy, the prospective number of employees to be dismissed, term of planned collective redundancy and procedure for calculation of severance pay.

17.35 Thirty days before the planned collective redundancy, the employer should inform the State Employment Agency and local municipality. The notice must contain the grounds for the collective redundancy, the number of employees to be dismissed, their profession and qualifications, the total number of employees employed in the entity and information about the consultation procedure. A transcript of the notice must be sent to the employee representatives (if any).

17.36 The State Employment Agency does not issue a public notice about the planned collective redundancy, but only use it for internal purposes, eg to forecast changes in the labour market.

17.37 In cases of collective redundancy, an evaluation of employees holding the same job role must be performed under the Labour Law. Preference to continue in employment shall be given to those employees who have better performance and better qualifications. The evaluation procedure applied to collective redundancy is the same as of the procedure for individual redundancies.

17.38 Thirty days after informing the State Employment Agency and the local municipality, the employer can start the collective redundancy. In exceptional cases the State Employment Agency can extend the term up to 60 days; where such extension is granted it will be given subject to certain conditions. It must be emphasised that the State Employment Agency cannot

---

7 Civil Department of the Senate of the Supreme Court, judgment SKC-1106 of April 26, 2013.

influence the procedure of collective redundancy. It is not authorised to adopt decisions which prohibit or suspend commencement of collective redundancy.

17.39 Termination of employment can be carried out by the employer's notice to terminate the employment agreement being issued. The termination notice issued by the employer is executed in two copies, one of which is given to the employee and the other shall be signed by the employee and afterwards kept in files of the employer. The employment agreement is terminated after a 30-day notice period.

17.40 Before dismissal it shall be determined whether the employee to be dismissed is a member of any trade union, because if they are, the employer is obliged to obtain prior written consent of the relevant trade union for the termination. The trade union is obliged to provide a written response within seven working days. If there is no response within seven working days it is presumed that the trade union approves termination.

Practical Tip

In cases of collective redundancy, employment can also be terminated on the basis of mutual agreement. In this case the parties are free to agree on terms of termination (termination date, compensations etc).

17.41 On the last day of employment the employer is obliged to pay all amounts due to the employee same as in the case of individual redundancy. Eventually, the employer must notify the State Revenue Service (SRS) of the termination of employment.

NOTICE

17.42 The written termination notice is the main legal instrument used to terminate employment. As mentioned above, the other instruments are: (i)) termination according to mutual agreement; or (ii) the employee's termination notice (resignation). The termination notice is a unilateral written statement from the employer[8] or the employee.

17.43 The rights of the employer to terminate employment agreements are strictly governed by the Labour Law (in particular by Articles 47 and 101 of the Labour Law). The Labour Law provides for termination of employment by the employer, based on performance of the employee, economic, organisational, technical and other measures at the company, such as:

1 an employee has materially breached the employment agreement or the prescribed working procedures without justifiable reasons;

8 Civil Department of the Senate of the Supreme Court, judgment SKC -1352 of December 8, 2010.

2 an employee has acted unlawfully during the performance of his duties and has therefore lost the trust of the employer;
3 an employee has acted contrary to moral principles during the performance of his duties and such action is incompatible with the continuation of the employment relationship;
4 an employee is under the influence of alcohol, drugs or toxic substances during the performance of his duties;
5 an employee has committed a serious breach of health & safety regulations in such a way as to jeopardise the health and safety of others;
6 an employee lacks the required competence for performing the contracted work;
7 an employee is unable to perform the contracted work due to his state of health, which is certified by a doctor's certificate;
8 an employee who previously performed the relevant work has been reinstated to their previous position;
9 workforce reduction;
10 an employer (legal entity or partnership) is being liquidated;
11 where an employee is unable to work due to temporary continuous incapacity for more than six months, or is absent for a total period of one year within a three-year period (except where such absence is due to prenatal and/or maternity leave, or incapacity due to an accident at work or an occupational illness.)

17.44 Article 47 of the Labour Law provides for the right of an employer to terminate employment during probation period (maximum three months) without providing reasons for such termination.

17.45 All permitted/lawful reasons for termination of an employment contracts are prescribed in the Labour Law by inclusion of an exhaustive list of grounds upon which the employer may issue a termination notice. At the same time pursuant to paragraph one of Article 101 of the Labour Law, an employer may, in exceptional circumstances, within one month of good cause arising, bring an action in court for termination of employment. In circumstances where continuation of the employment is not possible due to concerns morality and fairness may be viewed as such cause. The issue whether there is a good cause shall be decided by the court at its discretion.

17.46 If employment is terminated because of the reasons 6–9 outlined above, including workforce reduction cases, the employer is entitled to issue a termination notice only if it is impossible to employ the specified employee in another position in the same or another undertaking.

17.47 Prior to giving a termination notice, an employer is obliged to ascertain whether the employee is a member of trade union and obtain its prior written consent for termination.

17.48 In addition, the employer must notify the employees in writing regarding the circumstances and grounds for the termination notice.

Notice period for employer's notice of termination

17.49 The last day of actual employment of the person is calculated depending on the reason and grounds for termination unless the collective agreement or the employment agreement provides for a longer time period. The calculation is started when the termination notice is handed to the employee. Employment can be terminated with the following notice:

- immediately – if the termination notice is based on the reason 2 or 4;
- ten days – if the termination notice is based on the reason 1, 3, 5 or 7;
- one month – if the termination notice is based on the reason 6, 8, 9 or 10.

Termination of employment during a probation period requires a shorter notice period of three days only.

17.50 The rights of the employer to revoke a termination notice is subject to approval by an employee unless such right is specified in the collective agreement or the employment agreement. The case law has established that such statutory provision has been established to protect employees from inconsequent and indeterminate conduct of their employers.[9] For example, if an employer gives a termination notice to the employee, the applicable notice period starts to run. If the employee finds a better job during the notice period with a different employer, revocation of the notice would violate the rights and interests of the employee, as the first employment agreement would not be terminated due to the revoked termination notice. The employee would be legally bound by the first employment agreement, which would result in removal of legal certainty causing adverse effects for the employee. Therefore, the Labour Law protects the interests of employees by establishing that it is at the discretion of the specific employee to consent to their employer's revocation of a termination notice, once received.

Case law has established that the employee does not have authority to consent or reject a termination notice in cases where the employee has filed a claim in court to invalidate the termination notice and reinstate him/her into his/her previous position. If the employer revokes the termination notice during such court proceedings the revocation will serve as a ground to terminate litigation proceedings as the employee has achieved what they set out to do.[10]

17.51 The employer is obliged to pay severance pay upon termination of employment for reasons 6–11 as mentioned above.

17.52 The employer must show that the termination notice is lawful and complies with the procedure for termination of the employment agreement. In other cases when an employee has brought an action in court for reinstatement to their previous position, an employer must show that, while dismissing

9 Civil Department of the Senate of the Supreme Court, judgment SKC -896 of October 14, 2009

10 Civil Department of the Senate of the Supreme Court, judgment SKC -896 of October 14, 2009.

the employee, the employer has not violated their rights to continue in employment.[11]

17.53 If the termination notice of an employer has no legal basis or the procedure prescribed for termination of employment agreement is not followed, such termination notice shall be declared invalid and the employee shall be reinstated in their previous position based on the court judgment.

17.54 The employee who has been dismissed unlawfully and reinstated later in their previous position shall, in accordance with a court judgment, be paid average earnings for the whole period of forced absence from work. Compensation for the whole period of forced absence is paid also in cases where the court establishes grounds for reinstatement, but the employee prefers and requests termination instead of returning in their previous position.

Restrictive covenants (post-termination confidentiality and non-competition issues)

17.55 The Labour Law provides that an employee is obliged to observe confidentiality in respect of the information that is considered to be a trade secret of the company their employer) and this obligation is indefinite. The employer must notify its employees in writing which information is identified as confidential and protected by the company as a trade secret. Pursuant to the Labour Law the employee shall take precautions to prevent third parties from obtaining such information and refrain from any activities that can lead to unlawful disclosure of this information. The statutory regulation does not prescribe compensation for compliance with confidentiality obligations as such are part of the general duties to the employer.

Practical Tip

A confidentiality clause is usually included in an employment agreement and it is recommended that what constitutes a 'trade secret' is clearly defined. The employer is entitled to include a confidentiality clause in internal rules of conduct as well; more convenient for the employer in case of future changes

17.56 The non-competition agreement is concluded between an employer and an employee in writing and is enforceable after termination of employment agreement. The statutory regulation provides that non-competition agreement shall not provide for restriction of competition for a term exceeding two years after termination of employment and obliges an employer to pay compensation

11 Civil Department of the Senate of the Supreme Court, judgment SKC -1482 of May 8, 2013; Civil Department of the Senate of the Supreme Court, judgment SKC -1275 of November 9, 2012.

for observing restriction of competition (usually in the amount of 30–70% from the monthly remuneration) for the period the restriction is in force.

17.57 The non-competition agreement shall be applied only to the area were the specific employee was employed during their employment and shall be declared null and void if restrictions on the employee's professional activities are deemed unjust in comparison with the aim of the non-competition agreement (for example, a secretary cannot be restricted to work as a secretary in general, but only in particular field).

17.58 It has been illustrated within the current case law that the Labour Law does not directly stipulate an option to include contractual penalties for breach of the non-competition clause, therefore pursuant to the Labour Law, provisions of an employment contract which erodes the legal status of an employee shall not be valid.[12]

17.59 An employer may terminate in writing an agreement regarding the competition restriction at any time prior to the termination of the employment relationship.

BUSINESS SALE, OUTSOURCING/INSOURCING AND OFFSHORING BUSINESS SALE

17.60 Council Directive 2001/23/EC of 12 March 2001 on the approximation of the laws of the member states relating to the safeguarding of employees' rights in the event of transfers of undertakings, businesses or part of undertakings or businesses, has been adopted by the Labour Law of the Republic of Latvia, therefore the core principles embodied in the Directive are directly applicable also under national law.

17.61 When a business is sold, the rights and obligations of the parties involved need to be identified. Pursuant to article 118(1) of the Labour Law, all the rights and obligations that arise out of employment agreements and relations shall be *automatically transferred to the acquirer of the company*. Nevertheless, employees are under no obligation to stay and work for the acquirer, and therefore, according to the principles of freedom of contract, such employee can terminate the employment agreement and relationship with notice.[13]

17.62 Even though the applicable law does not require such measures and also, the State Labour Inspectorate agrees that the consent of the employee in

12 Civil Department of the Senate of the Supreme Court, judgement SKC-6 of January 9, 2008.

13 ECJ case C-51/00, Temco Service Industries SA and Samir Imzilyen, Mimoune Belfarh, Abdesselam Afia-Aroussi, Khalil Lakhdar, intervener, paragraph 37 (please find full text here: http://curia.europa.eu/juris/document/document.jsf?text=&docid=47045&pageIndex=0&doclang=EN&mode=lst&dir=&occ=first&part=1&cid=129006).

case of the business sale is not necessary, it can be recommended to conclude a trilateral contract between the previous owner (seller) of the company, acquirer and each individual employee about the transfer of the employment agreement, therefore also allowing the employee to exercise the right to the freedom of contract. If the employee refuses to sign such an agreement or after receiving of the notice on transfer of undertaking submits an application that he/she does not agree to the transfer, he/she will remain employed by the previous owner (seller) of the company.

17.63 The acquirer of the company must be provided with all the employment agreements, supplements to the employment agreements, relevant communications with employees, collective agreements, internal rules and regulations and other documentation regarding employment relations. These will form a set of rights and obligations that will be taken over by and transferred to the acquirer.

In addition to the respective documentation listed above, the previous owner (the seller) is obliged to disclose all information regarding circumstances where a potential claim could be made; also information on any ongoing or former disputes between the employees and employer must be presented. For example, all the information regarding any disciplinary measures applied to the employees, detailed information on the former disputes, litigation cases or settlements, that would help the acquirer to gain an understanding regarding overall and individual cases, must be disclosed.

17.64 Non-compliance with the obligation to disclose the relevant information that was known or should have been known to the former owner (seller) of the company does not affect the transfer of the rights and obligations regarding employment relations towards the employee. Any claims that arise out of employment agreements and relations after the transfer of rights and obligations can be addressed to the new employer (the acquirer) pursuant to article 118(3) of the Labour Law. The acquirer can later claim damages from the former owner (former employer) if they failed to disclose the relevant information that was known or should have been known on the day of the transfer. Please note that in order to protect the acquirer from any risks, contracting parties (seller and buyer of the company) can individually agree in the contract on sanctions regarding the failure to disclose the relevant information, for example, a contractual penalty or the right to withdraw from the contract.

17.65 The actual date of transfer to the acquirer of the rights and obligations arising from employment relations can be stipulated in the contract, set by the applicable laws and regulations or by the judgment of the court. In accordance with the Labour Law, on the day of the transfer the previous owner (natural or legal person[14]) loses the status of the employer and the acquirer (natural or legal person) acquires the status of the employer.

---

14 In accordance to the Article 4, §1, an employer is a natural or legal person or a partnership with legal capacity that, on the basis of an employment agreement, employs at least one employee.

17.66 In light of the risks, explained above, prior to the transaction, due diligence can be done not only in relation to the employment agreements but also collective agreements in force. It is advisable because, after the transfer of the undertaking, the acquirer is under an obligation to respect and continue fulfilling the obligations set by the collective agreement in force on the day of the transfer until the collective agreement ceases to be in force, another collective agreement must be applied or a new collective agreement has been concluded. It has to be taken into account that the applicable law prohibits the conclusion, within a period of one year from the transfer, of a new collective agreement that would be against the interests of employees.

17.67 If the acquirer plans to reorganise the company, he has to observe certain limitations set by the Labour Law. In the case of reorganisation, including workforce reduction and restructuring, the workforce reduction cannot be justified on the basis of the mere fact of the sale of business; nevertheless, it can be done due to financial, organisational, technological or other measures. The employee is entitled to challenge the reasoning of the termination of the employment agreement and in such case, the burden of proof will be with the acquirer via his status of new employer.

17.68 The Labour Law does not explicitly regulate outsourcing/insourcing and offshoring issues. Employers are free to decide how they organise their business. This includes the right of the company to decide to opt for insourcing, outsourcing or offshoring of its business activities. However, it is necessary for the company to assess whether the structural changes involving outsourcing/insourcing/offshoring could be considered transfers of undertaking. For example, in the event of outsourcing the services and consequent redundancy of employees, it can be argued that transfer of undertaking took place and therefore the former employees should be employed by the service providers. It is highly likely that such conclusion would be adopted by the court.

WORKFORCE REDUCTION IN CONNECTION WITH SHARE SALE OR SHARE PURCHASE

17.69 Share sale or share purchase should not influence the status of employees, but there are situations when a workforce reduction is planned in connection with the share sale and share purchase, therefore in such circumstances, the following procedure should be applied.

17.70 Pursuant to the Labour Law it is clear that the workforce reduction cannot be justified solely on the basis of share sale or share purchase; nevertheless, the law does not prohibit reduction of the workforce, termination of employment agreements and removal of job roles due to financial, organisational, technical or other measures that have resulted from the share sale or share purchase.

In such cases termination of an employment agreement cannot be associated with the individual conduct and their capabilities and the employer, as the person issuing a notice of termination must notify the employee in writing regarding the circumstances that form the basis for the termination notice and removal of the job role.

17.71 According to case law, a decision which specifies the need and inevitability to terminate an employment agreement and remove a position based on organisational, financial or similar reasoning can only be made by the employer and the court does not have the power to review the reasoning behind such a decision (for example, the financial situation of the company). Nevertheless, the necessity to remove the particular job role must prevail over the need to terminate the employment agreement with the employee in question. If the court finds that the position in question has not been removed, while, instead, the employment agreement with the particular employee has been terminated, it will infer that the circumstances do not form grounds for application of Article 104 of the Labour Law regarding workforce reduction.[15] As a result the company can potentially incur financial losses due to actions that were carried out with the purpose of avoiding the initial legitimate procedure and consequences of the termination of the employment agreement.

CHANGING EMPLOYMENT TERMS AND CONDITIONS

17.72 Workforce restructuring might necessitate changes in the employment agreements, collective agreements or any other internal documentation, regulating the terms and conditions of employment.

17.73 The applicable laws and regulations do not prohibit amending or adopting unilateral changes in the documentation regulating employment matters, notwithstanding one of the core principles, regulating this issue states that provisions of a collective agreement, working procedure regulations, as well as the provisions of an employment agreement and orders of an employer which, contrary to applicable laws and regulations, are detrimental to the legal status of an employee, shall not be valid. Nevertheless, terms and conditions that improve the position of employees can be included, for example, parties can agree on longer annual paid leave than required by the applicable laws and regulations. In any case, the employer is under an obligation to ensure that the legal rights of employees are respected and obeyed, therefore the employer cannot claim that the parties have mutually agreed on the stipulations in the employment agreement that are detrimental to the position of employee.

17.74 An employee and an employer may amend an employment agreement by mutual agreement. Pursuant to the Labour Law, subject to giving one month

15 Civil Department of the Senate of the Supreme Court, judgment SKC -145 of April 16, 2008.

notice an employer has the right to terminate an employment agreement unless the employee agrees to continue their employment on the new terms proposed by the employer. This regulation does not mean that the employer has a right to terminate the employment agreement because the employee does not agree to the amendments. General grounds and principles are applicable also in these cases as prescribed by the Labour Law.

The idea of such provision is that, first, an employer has certain grounds for termination, secondly, the employer proposes amendments to the employment agreement; therefore, thirdly, if the employee does not agree to such amendments the employer is entitled to terminate the employment agreement (usually, this is in case of redundancy and change in the positions therefore).

If an employee considers that a termination notice has no legal basis, he/she has the right to file a claim in court, within one month, that the termination notice is invalid.

17.75 In cases, where the parties have opted to conclude a collective agreement, it must be noted that according to the Labour Law, the concluded collective agreement is binding on both parties (the employer and employees) and parties may derogate from its provisions only if the relevant provisions of the employment agreement are more favourable for the employee. In addition, provisions of an employment agreement which, contrary to a collective agreement, are detrimental to the legal status of an employee are invalid.

17.76 In practice, the need to change or amend the terms and conditions of employment often arises after the sale of the business and is initiated by the new owner. It is important to note that according to the Labour Law in case of the transfer of the rights and obligations from one employer to another (for example, in the case of a business sale), after the transfer the acquirer of the undertaking is under an obligation to respect and continue fulfilling the obligations set by the collective agreement in force on the day of the transfer until the collective agreement: (i) ceases to be in force; (ii) another collective agreement must be applied: or (iii) a new collective agreement has been concluded. It should be taken into account that the applicable law prohibits the conclusion of a new collective agreement within one year from the transfer of undertaking that would include any rules and regulations against the interests of employees and would be detrimental to their position.

17.77 The employer can unilaterally adopt changes within internal documentation regarding employment matters (for example, bonus systems), nevertheless it must be noted that the documentation must originally be made unilaterally and adopted by the employer. If the document is concluded between an employer and an employee, the written acceptance regarding amendments must be obtained from each employee.

17.78 In light of the above, it should be emphasised that stipulation of contractual penalties or any other form of penalties in the employment agreements or other internal documentation regulating employment is prohibited due to the special nature of the relationship between the employee and their employer. An application of contractual penalty for breach of competition restrictions is permitted only after termination of the employment agreement and shall be applied in accordance with the applicable laws and regulations.

17.79 In summary, the conclusion is that the rights and obligations arising from the employment agreement and any other internal employment documentation should be in line with the collective agreement and applicable laws in order to avoid any legal risks and situations where important clauses are not enforceable or are recognised as invalid.

USING TEMPORARY STAFF

Fixed term employment agreement

17.80 The Labour Law permits employment of temporary staff by concluding employment agreements for a fixed period of time. Article 44 of the Labour Law states that contracts of this character are concluded for specific short-term jobs, which include:

- seasonal work;
- work, where employment agreements for unspecified periods of time are not concluded considering nature of relevant work or its temporary nature;
- replacement of an employee, who is absent or suspended from work, also replacement of an employee, whose permanent position has become vacant until a new employee is hired;
- casual work, which is normally not performed in employing entity;
- temporary work related to short-term expansion of the scope of work of the company or increase in production;
- emergency work to prevent effects of *force majeure*, an unexpected event or other exceptional circumstances, which adversely affect or may affect the normal course of activities in employing entity;
- temporary paid work for an unemployed person, whose work is related to participation in active employment programmes or implementation of these programmes;
- work of an educational, vocational or academic educational establishment in preparation for a career within a certain field.

The period of employment must be expressly stated in fixed-term employment agreements. Term for such employment agreements may depend on finishing the assigned work, if circumstances indicate that the work is complete.

17.81 Under the Labour Law the same regulation applies both to employees with fixed-term employment agreements and employees, and with permanent agreements are not temporary by nature.

17.82 The Labour Law permits employment agreements for specific periods of time with the members of the management board pursuant to the articles of association and for the period for which they are in office.

17.83 The Labour Law limits a fixed-term employment agreement to a period not exceeding five years. If an employment agreement with the same employer is concluded in the 50 days after termination of the previous one, it is considered as extension of the previous fixed-term employment agreement.

17.84 If parties do not request termination of an employment agreement, after expiration of the fixed-term employment agreement, it is considered that the employment agreement is prolonged for indefinite period of time and the employment is permanent.

Temporary work agencies

17.85 Where the temporary work agency as employer places an employee with the recipient for whose benefit and under whose management the work will be performed, if the entity is located in another state or it performs its operations in another state, the applicable law has set a separate rules and regulations (see para **17.87**).

17.86 In such cases, it is important to identify the status of an employer and employment agreement. The Labour Law clarifies that if an employment agreement is entered into with an employee by a temporary work agency, in order to assign the employee to perform work for the benefit, and under the management, of the recipient, the employer shall be considered to be the temporary work agency. In addition, the applicable law sets obligations which have to be respected by the recipient of the employee as well and balances the burden of obligations.

17.87 In accordance with the Labour Law, if an employee has been posted to perform work for the benefit, and under the management, of the recipient within the scope of the work placement service, it is the duty of the recipient to ensure safe working conditions for the employee during the period of placement according to the requirements of health & safety regulations, except mandatory health examinations. Therefore, it can be concluded that the employer and the recipient are both under an obligation to ensure that the rights of the employee are respected and both of them are performing an important role in the employment of specific employee.

17.88 It shall be indicated in the employment agreement that the temporary work agency is the employer and that the employee, when performing their work obligations, has the duty to follow the work procedure and orders specified by the recipient insofar as this is not in contradiction with orders of the employer. In addition, an employee posted by a temporary work agency has the right to use the facilities, common premises or other facilities of the recipient company, as well as transport services on the same conditions as permanent employees, except where differential treatment may be justified by objective reasons.

17.89 It must be emphasised that even though the employer is the temporary work agency, in accordance with the Labour Law, an agreement which prohibits, or restricts, the posted employee from entering into an employment agreement directly with the recipient is invalid. Therefore the rights to freely enter into direct employment relationship with the person for whose benefit and under whose management the work is performed cannot be restricted and the employee is still relatively free to choose the form of their employment, if such an option is presented. Moreover the Labour Law states that the recipient shall inform the posted employee regarding available work positions within the company where the employee has been posted.

EMPLOYMENT CLAIMS

17.90 Employment claims are governed by the Labour Law, Labour Dispute Law and Civil Procedure Law of the Republic of Latvia. The purpose of regulation is to guarantee just and rapid resolution of employment disputes. Based on the subject matter of the dispute and persons involved (number of claimants), employment disputes are divided into three categories: (i) individual legal disputes; (ii) collective legal disputes; and (iii) collective interest disputes.

17.91 It is important to emphasise that the law prohibits resolution of individual labour disputes in arbitration courts in Latvia. In addition, Civil Procedure Law provides that a claimant is released from their obligation to pay the state duty which is mandatory in other cases to initiate legal proceedings in court.

INDIVIDUAL LEGAL DISPUTES

17.92 Individual legal disputes are disputes between one employee or a group of employees, as one party, and an employer, as the other party, which arises from concluding, amending, terminating or performing the employment agreement, as well as disputes on application or interpretation of statutory regulation, in relation to collective agreement and regulations of working procedure.

17.93 The statutory regulation provides that individual legal disputes should be resolved in negotiations between the employer and its employee whenever possible. The law permits establishing of specific labour dispute commission (reconciliation commission) at the company for resolution of individual legal disputes, if disputes are not settled by negotiation. An employer and the representatives of employees may also agree on a different dispute resolution procedure within the company.

17.94 If an individual legal dispute is not settled through negotiation or any of the parties are not satisfied with the decision of the labour dispute commission, parties can submit a claim in court. The fact that a dispute has not been the subject of settlement discussions does not result in the court rejecting the employment claim submitted in court and review of the case on its merits.

17.95 The employment claims, which are subject to direct jurisdiction of the court without involving the labour dispute commission as the first dispute resolution institution include:

1 Claims on declaring employer's notice of termination invalid and reinstatement of the employee;
2 Employer's claim where the trade union does not agree to the notice of termination of the employment agreement with a member of the employee trade union;
3 Claims regarding the recovery of unpaid remuneration;
4 Claims regarding violation of the prohibition of differential treatment;
5 Claims if the undertaking does not have a labour dispute commission;
6 Claims upon application of an employee or an employer if a third party requests to terminate the employment agreement.

17.96 In accordance with Article 122 of the Labour Law; an employee may within one month from the date of receipt of a termination notice submit a claim in court that the termination notice issued by his/her employer should be declared null and void. In other cases, when the rights of an employee to continue their employment are breached, the employee is entitled to submit a claim in court for reinstatement in their previous position within one month from the date of dismissal.

Case law has established that the claims of employees for reinstatement to their previous position comprise claims for recognition of the termination notice.[16]

If the employee has missed the deadline for submission of their claim in court due to justified reasons, the court may renew the countdown of the timeline on the basis of an application by the employee. The employee must indicate relevant reasons and submit supporting evidence to show that delay was justified. The deadline for submission of such application is two weeks when the reason for missing the time period has ceased to exist, while no later than one year in total.

At the same time as the application for more time, the employee must also file a claim in court to declare the termination notice null and void.

The Labour Law provides that the statute of limitation for all claims arising from employment is two years, unless the statutory regulations provide otherwise.

---

16 Civil Department of the Senate of the Supreme Court, judgment SKC -1352 of March 7, 2012.

17.97 Judicial proceedings concerning employment disputes to declare the termination notice null and void and reinstate the employee into their previous position are adjudicated under an expedited procedure (approximately one year until a judgment of the court of first instance). A court hearing is scheduled no later than 15 days after receipt of written response from the employer or expiry of deadline for provision of such written response. The judgments in such proceedings shall be satisfied without delay (immediately), if an employee has requested such enforcement. If an employer delays satisfaction of a judgment, the employee is entitled to average earnings for the whole period of delay from the date of announcement of the judgment until the day of compliance therewith.[17] In practice the Latvian courts tend to be more lenient towards employees.

COLLECTIVE LEGAL DISPUTES

17.98 A collective legal dispute is based on differences in opinions between the employees (a group of employees) or representatives of employees and the employer, employers (a group of employers), organisations of employers or an association of such organisations, or an administrative authority of the sector. The collective disputes arise from concluding, altering, terminating or fulfilling the employment agreement, as well as from applying or interpreting provisions of statutory regulation, provisions of a collective employment contract or working procedure regulations.

17.99 In the case of collective legal dispute, a party submits an application to the other party indicating its claims. After receipt of the application, the other party reviews and responds to the claims in short notice (in three days). If there is no response or it is negative, the party can approach the settlement commission.

The decision of the settlement commission is adopted by agreement among the members of the commission. The decision is binding on both parties of collective legal dispute and has an effect of a collective agreement.

Within a period of one month the parties to the collective legal dispute can bring an action in the court, if the dispute has not been settled by the settlement commission or no settlement commission is established within one month after submitting the application.

COLLECTIVE INTEREST DISPUTES

17.100 A collective interest dispute concerns differences in opinions between employees (a group of employees) or representatives of employees and

17 Civil Department of the Senate of the Supreme Court, judgment SKC -282 of 2008 (not published).

employer, employers (a group of employers), an organisation of employers or an association of such organisations, or an administrative authority of the sector that arise in relation to collective negotiation procedures determining new working conditions or employment conditions.

17.101 In the case of a collective interest dispute a party submits an application to the other party stating its claims. After receipt of the application, the other party has three days' notice to reviews and respond to the claims. If there is no response, or the response is negative, the other party can approach a settlement commission (composed of parties to the dispute, see para **17.100**).

If a settlement commission cannot reach an agreement, the dispute can be settled according to the collective agreement, by reconciliation (through a neutral and objective third party) or by approaching the arbitration court.

MUTUALLY AGREED TERMINATION

17.102 Article 114 of the Labour Law provides that employment relationship can be terminated on mutual agreement in a written form.

17.103 According to the case law an agreement on termination of employment is an independent, bilateral contract with legal consequences.[18]

An offer to conclude an agreement on termination can be initiated by the employer or the employee. In practice the procedure is initiated by negotiations between both parties, when circumstances, grounds and conditions of termination of employment relationship are discussed. This procedure is not prescribed by the law in detail; therefore it is left to the discretion of both parties.

In addition, statutory regulation does not include provisions of the termination agreement. Therefore parties are free to agree on terms and conditions of employment termination, including compensation (severance pay) or any other bonuses in so far as they comply with the general provision of the law.

The agreement on termination is valid if it has been signed both by the employee and their employer.

17.104 In practice it is possible to enter into the agreement on termination of employment agreement in order to avoid paying severance pay to the employee, eg in the case of liquidation of the company, when termination of the employment relationship is inevitable. The Labour Law does not oblige the employer to pay the severance pay to the employee where the employment is terminated by the agreement. However, parties can agree on compensation and include relevant clauses in the agreement.

17.105 In regards to the collective agreement, pursuant to sub-paragraph one of paragraph 2 of Article 19, it can also be terminated by a mutual agreement

18 Civil Department of the Senate of the Supreme Court, judgment SKC -371 of June 11, 2008.

between parties (the employer and the trade union or the representatives of the employees); nevertheless, it must be directly specified when, or based on what conditions, the collective agreement will no longer be in force.

17.106 Article 226 of the Civil Procedure Law stipulates that parties are entitled to conclude a settlement agreement at any stage of the proceedings governed by the civil law. Therefore, termination of the employment agreement is possible by means of the settlement agreement if an action is brought to the court. The settlement agreement is binding on both parties and constitutes a reason for termination of legal proceedings conditioned that the court has approved the settlement agreement by it decision.

17.107 An employer and its employees are entitled to use mediation in order to reach a settlement in employment disputes. If the legal proceedings are initiated in court and parties agree to use mediation after approaching the court, the claim is left without adjudication and parties are entitled to bring an action in the court again, if no settlement is reached during mediation. The Civil Procedure Law provides for using mediation on the initiative of the court as well. Therefore, a dispute can be resolved by a settlement agreement reached during mediation.

Chapter 18

Workforce Restructuring in Lithuania

Rimantas Stanevicius and Nerijus Patlabys
Valiunas Ellex

INTRODUCTION

18.1 This chapter reviews the main issues relating to workforce restructuring under Lithuanian law. As the Lithuanian Labour Code (the main document regulating this area) contains various protections for employees as well as a number of other requirements and restrictions, it might be considered a strict one. To some extent this aspect is shown in this chapter. However there is also some leeway for the parties to reach their own agreements which in most cases is the best method to fill in the inflexible gaps of legal regulation. In addition, at the time of writing of this chapter the initiative to amend the entire Labour Code has been taken by the Government. However, at this point it is not clear if and when this initiative could result in adopted legal act.

18.2 In this context it may be of interest to note that the level of unionisation in Lithuania is quite low. Therefore, most employers are not under too much pressure from the trade unions. In turn, some companies have works councils established. However, this type of employee representation is usually not as active as one might expect compared to traditional unions. Because of this, the involvement of employee representatives in the workforce reduction process (eg consultation procedures preceding the collective redundancies) is usually a formality and not a challenging bargaining exercise.

18.3 However, when it comes to workforce restructuring itself, this is quite a formal process in Lithuania. It involves adoption of a number of documents and prescribes certain procedures to be followed. At the same time, it leaves quite a narrow window for the employer to decide which employees should be dismissed and which not. Perhaps as a result of this, most employers, as far as they can, tend to prefer mutual termination of employment and only if this fails (ie, if agreement on termination was not reached) will the formal workforce restructuring come into play.

PREPARING FOR A RESTRUCTURING EXERCISE

18.4 As has already been mentioned, workforce restructuring includes a number of steps to be taken, therefore, certain preparatory work is advisable. Such preparation, save for the standard step-by-step plan, usually includes evaluation of:

- the budget for the exercise (since main payments are to be made no later than on the termination date, it may be necessary to plan for or reserve the necessary amount in advance).
- in the context of the budget as well as the applicable procedures, a review of the employment agreements concluded with the target employees should also be undertaken to establish whether they contain non-standard employment termination terms, eg longer notice periods, larger severance payments, etc. This part is especially important in respect of senior management employees;
- additional attention may be paid to the scope of target employees and their level of protection. For instance, certain categories of employees are protected against dismissal without fault on their part (eg employees raising children under three years of age). Therefore in respect of such employees, the simple redundancy process does not apply and alternative measures will have to be used (eg mutually-agreed termination, paras **18.64–18.66**).
- protection of the interests of the employer after termination. This usually includes double-checking if confidentiality issues are duly addressed in the internal documents, whether key employees to be dismissed have signed non-competition/non-solicitation agreements (if necessary), intellectual property issues, etc.

18.5 As mentioned, another advisable preparatory step in any workforce restructuring (even if it affects only a few employees) would be setting up the step by step plan for the documents/procedures involved. Such plan from the legal perspective may include the following main parts:

Preparatory actions (including the ones mentioned in para 18.4 above);	Optional
Information/consultation procedures;	Obligatory
Notification to local labour exchange;	Obligatory in case of collective redundancies

Execution of mutually agreed termination with all/selected employees;	Optional
Adoption of formal decision initiating employment restructuring;	Obligatory
Determination of affected employees and serving of termination notices;	Obligatory
Additional processes in respect of affected employees (eg outplacement services);	Optional
Formal dismissal and full settlement.	Obligatory

EMPLOYMENT STATUS

18.6 In Lithuania only individuals who fall under the legal definition of 'employees' (ie private individuals who work under the employment contract for remuneration) are subject to statutory regulation of employment as well as protection against unfair dismissal in the course of a company's workforce restructuring.

18.7 In turn, from the workforce reduction perspective, temporary employees engaged through temporary employment agencies (see para **18.50**) are not considered as employees. Therefore, even though the law forbids discrimination against temporary employees and in favour of permanent employees, they are not subject to statutory protection against unfair dismissal in the course of a company's workforce restructuring. It should be added that persons working under independent contracts are also not considered as employees who should be protected against unfair dismissal under employment laws.

18.8 When it comes to management of the company, the CEO and other members of the company's corporate bodies are also treated differently from the ordinary employees. Even though the CEO of the company is usually employed under an employment contract, his/her appointment and revocation are subject to different procedures than those applicable to the standard reduction of the workforce. As for other members of the company's management (eg board members) as they are not employees of the company, their status (including revocation and appointment) is even less comparable with the employee status.

GENERAL PROTECTION AGAINST DISMISSAL

18.9 Employment may only be terminated on the initiative of the employer for 'valid reasons'. These reasons are defined in law and include reshaping of the corporate structure, economic/technological reasons, etc. Accordingly, in case of a dispute the employer is obliged to prove that valid reasons existed and that they were sufficient for termination of employment.

18.10 In addition, it is only permissible to dismiss an employee if it is not possible to transfer him/her to other job (subject to the employee's consent). This means that during the entire notice period the employer should offer to the employees to be dismissed all vacant positions in the company for which they might be suitable. Failure to do so (eg not offering any vacant positions and/or employing a third person instead) might result in a claim for unfair dismissal.

18.11 Finally, the entire dismissal procedure (starting from the information/ consultation stage) in a sense may be also seen as a protective measure for the employee. In a dispute the employer has to prove that this procedure was duly followed as failure to do so can lead to a claim for unfair dismissal.

SPECIAL PROTECTION AGAINST DISMISSAL

18.12 In the context of redundancy the following groups of employees are protected from dismissal:

- employees raising a child or children under three years of age;
- pregnant women from the day on which their employer receives a medical certificate confirming the pregnancy, and for one month after pregnancy leave, except for other cases specified by the law;
- employees on sick leave;
- employees on leave;
- employees called up to fulfil active national defence service or other duties of the citizen of the Republic of Lithuania, except for the cases specified by the law.

18.13 Members of bodies of employee representatives (ie trade unions or works councils) who are elected to such representative bodies also enjoy special dismissal protection. Dismissal of such employees during the period for which they have been elected require prior consent of the body concerned. Refusal to grant such consent may be challenged by the employer.

18.14 Finally, it is prohibited to dismiss on discriminatory grounds (eg on grounds of nationality, gender, etc). Also, employees may not be dismissed from work on the grounds of their age. Therefore, there is no mandatory retirement age in Lithuania.

WORKFORCE REDUCTION

Legitimate grounds and procedure

18.15 As mentioned, employment may only be terminated on the initiative of the employer due to 'valid reasons'. Such valid reasons might include employee's qualification, professional skills or behaviour at work. These reasons may also include the restructuring of the company and similar economic/technological circumstances.

18.16 From a practical perspective the majority of employment restructuring arises from the reshaping of the company's structure and a resulting reduction in the workforce. This is the route with the clearest structure, supported by case law. Redundancies on other grounds carries a higher level of risk and uncertainty.

18.17 Based on the foregoing, the main practical aspects of the procedure applicable in case of this type of workforce reduction is highlighted below.

Start of formal process – information/consultation

18.18 Prior to making a decision leading to dismissals or otherwise having material effects on employment conditions, the employer must inform the employee representatives and hold consultations with them. The term 'employee representatives' means either a trade union or a works council active in the company. The aim of such consultations is to reach an agreement between both parties on the anticipated dismissals and the main conditions thereof. Employee representatives do not have the power of veto over the planned restructuring exercise. On the other hand, they may defend their position in other ways, which are not always constructive. Thus, proper dialogue with employee representatives is always advisable as a precaution.

18.19 If there are no employee representatives in the company, the employer should inform the employees directly of their plans. In such cases, information must be submitted either directly to each employee or in a staff meeting. The information to be communicated must cover at least the following:

- dates for anticipated dismissals;
- reason for the decisions on anticipated dismissals;
- legal, economic and social outcomes of such decisions for the employees;
- measures anticipated for the employees.

Adoption of formal decision on workforce restructuring

18.20 A formal decision initiating the workforce reduction is important. This is because it falls within the scope of issues usually reviewed by courts in case of a dispute. In addition, the decision must show that corporate requirements have been met. Therefore, it is important to check such decision against the employer's articles of association.

18.21 At the same time, courts are not normally involved in the economic/business reasoning behind the decision. Therefore, any reasonable explanation of the background to the decision is usually sufficient.

Additional requirements in case of collective redundancies

18.22 Collective redundancies is defined by termination of employment contracts when, due to economic or technological reasons, workplace restructuring, or other reasons not related to a single employee, within 30 calendar days it is intended to dismiss:

Dismissed employees	Number of all employees in the company
10 or more	20–99
Not less than 10%	100–299
30 or more	300 or more

18.23 In the case of collective redundancies the employer must notify the local labour exchange office in writing of the proposed dismissals. This is to be done after consultations with employee representatives and prior to serving termination notices.

Practical Tip

In the case of collective redundancies, consultations with employee representatives (see para **18.18**) together with notification to labour exchange office (see para **18.23**) are important. The law provides that failure to hold these consultations as well as failure to inform the local labour exchange office will prevent dismissal of the employees.

Priority rights

18.24 When it comes to reducing the workforce, some employees enjoy priority rights to retain employment. This is mainly applicable in cases where not all positions of the same type are being eliminated (eg it is necessary to dismiss seven specialists out of ten).

18.25 The first group of employees who in the context of workforce reduction enjoy priority rights is as follows (they are also entitled to a longer notice period, see para **18.31**):

1 employees who will be entitled to receive the full old-age pension within a five-year period;
2 employees who are under 18 years of age;
3 disabled employees; and
4 employees who are raising children under 14 years of age.

According to current regulations, the contracts of these employees can be terminated only if their retention would substantially violate the interests of the employer. Therefore, in a situation where one out of two employees holding similar positions is to be dismissed, if one of them falls within any of the abovementioned categories, that employee should be retained.

18.26 The second group of priority employees includes employees:

1 who sustained an injury or contracted an occupational disease at that workplace;
2 who are raising children (including adopted children) under 16 years age alone or caring for other family members with special needs;
3 whose continuous length of service at that workplace is at least ten years, with the exception of employees who have become entitled to the full old age pension or are in receipt thereof;
4 who will be entitled to the old age pension in no more than three years;
5 to whom such a right is granted in the collective agreement;
6 who are elected to the representative bodies of employees.

18.27 Notably, the priority to retain the job as set in categories 2–5 in para **18.26** above shall apply only to those employees whose qualification is equal to or greater than the qualification of other employees with the same specialism working in that company.

Notice and execution of dismissal

18.28 Once selected for dismissal employees should be notified of the anticipated termination date two or four months in advance (notice and related matters are discussed in more detail in para **18.31**). When this period expires, the dismissal is usually executed by adoption of internal order on dismissal and handing of a document confirming this to the employee on the last day of employment against acknowledgement of receipt by signature. In addition, this process includes filling in the records in the employment contract re dismissal and notifying the social security authority about the termination of employment.

Practical Tip

It is important to possess sufficient written evidence on the date when the relevant termination document (usually the employer's internal order) is served to the employee. This is because the statutory limitation period for filing a claim of unfair dismissal (equal to one month) starts not from the date of the termination but from the date of service of the termination document on the employee (ie on the last day of employment). Thus, if there is no proof of this document being served on the employee, the period during which the claim can be filed might be prolonged.

Settlement with dismissed employees

18.29 Upon termination of employment contracts with employees, the employer is obliged to fully settle payments due with them. Such settlement includes the following amounts that should be paid not later than on the last day of employment (unless agreed otherwise):

- regular remuneration plus bonuses, if any, and similar amounts;
- severance pay (depending on seniority with the company amounting to one–six average monthly salaries, see para **18.30**);
- compensation for accrued, unused holiday entitlement;
- other amounts due, if any.

18.30 The statutory severance payment (in the range from one to six average monthly salaries) depends on the length of service of the employee:

Length of service (months)	Severance payment
up to 12	1 average monthly salary
12–36	2 average monthly salaries
36–60	3 average monthly salaries
60–120	4 average monthly salaries
120–240	5 average monthly salaries
over 240	6 average monthly salaries

> **Practical Tip**
>
> The average monthly salary which is relevant for calculation of severance pay as well as compensation for accrued annual vacation is calculated under the statutory formula. The said formula includes salary and similar payments paid during the previous three months as well as certain bonuses paid during the last 12 months. Therefore, as a rule:
>
> $$\frac{\text{1 average salary}}{\text{1 regular salary}}$$
>
> based on the foregoing in case of, eg negotiations re mutual termination it might be better to use precise amounts, not multiples of salary.

NOTICE

18.31 An employment contract may be terminated subject to two or four months' prior notice. The prior notice of two months applies to all employees except for the following categories of employees, who are entitled to four months' prior notice:

- employees who will be entitled to receive the full old-age pension within a five-year period;
- employees who are under 18 years of age;
- disabled employees; and
- employees who are raising children under 14 years of age.

18.32 The mentioned notice periods should be prolonged for the duration of an employee's leave or sickness leave.

Serving of notice and certain statutory guarantees applicable to employees

18.33 The notice should be executed as a written document and served on the employee against acknowledgement of receipt by signature. Such notice must contain at least the following statutory information:

- the precise reasons for dismissal. Such information should also be sufficient for the employee to understand the level of workforce restructuring so that he/she can effectively defend his/her rights;
- the anticipated date of termination (ie, not less than two or four months after); and
- the process for settlement of payments due with the employee (ie usually not later than on the last day of employment).

18.34 During the notice period the employee must be granted time off work for seeking another job. Such time must correspond to at least 10% of the working hours and it must be paid at the average salary.

18.35 If a decision is made to close the business and liquidate the company, there is no requirement to apply the notice periods, but it would be advisable to provide the information regarding the planned dismissals to the employees as early as possible.

Garden leave

18.36 Garden leave is not explicitly provided for in Lithuanian law and there is no case-law which would clearly confirm that garden leave may be agreed in the contract and applied by the employer. On the other hand, there are no direct statutory restrictions on garden leave, provided that the full salary is paid to the employee.

Payment in lieu of notice

18.37 Payment in lieu of notice is not recognised by Lithuanian law. However, it can be achieved indirectly by signing a mutual agreement to terminate the employment.

BUSINESS SALE, OUTSOURCING/INSOURCING

18.38 In case of business sale or other transfer transactions, employees should automatically be transferred to the purchaser of the particular business (or part of the business). This principle of automatic transfer was transposed into the national legislation from the Transfer of Undertakings Directive 2001/23/EC. Business transfer might occur in almost any type of transactions, including outsourcing respective services, etc. Therefore, in all such cases, provided the transferred business (or part thereof) retains its identity, the following protections apply.

18.39 Transferred employees continue on the same terms and conditions with the transferee of a business as with their former employer. This means that the change of employer cannot serve as a reason to change these employment contract conditions. In addition, obligations under collective agreements, if applicable to the transferred employees before transfer, pass to the new employer as well.

18.40 An additional requirement applicable in the course of an anticipated business transfer is that the employees concerned must be informed in advance about the projected transaction. Such information should be delivered to employees not later than ten business days before the transfer of a business (or part thereof) and it should include all the relevant information (the date of transfer, legal basis, economic and social consequences of such transfer to employees, etc).

18.41 Although, Lithuanian practice establishes that the transfer of employees is automatic, it is possible that the affected employees might still object to the anticipated change of employer. In such case, the employees will remain employed by the transferor of the business (or part thereof), but could instead be dismissed by way of a workforce reduction as described in this chapter if applicable. The objection does not automatically result in employee's dismissal.

WORKFORCE REDUCTION IN CONNECTION WITH SHARE SALE OR SHARE PURCHASE

18.42 Since share deals do not affect the legal status of the employer (ie the company whose shares are transferred), such transaction itself may not serve as a ground for workforce restructuring. However, in practice, the new owner of the company usually decides to reorganise the company which may result in changes to the workforce in accordance with the general procedure described in this chapter.

RESTRICTIVE COVENANTS

18.43 In respect of key employees it may be necessary to observe additional measures for the safeguarding of the employer's business (such as application of restrictive covenants). In turn, Lithuanian courts tend to acknowledge the validity of non-competition agreements and similar arrangements with the employees, provided they meet the following main requirements:

(a) it is absolutely necessary that a reasonable compensation is payable to the employee concerned during the period the restrictions apply. Sometimes employers provide that such compensation will be paid before the termination of employment (although the restrictions will be applicable thereafter). However, given the above requirement such an arrangement may result in invalidity of entire restrictive covenant.

(b) restrictions should be limited in time. While there are no set period requirements, in practice periods of up to 12 months are most common.

(c) restrictions should be reasonable from the perspective of the scope of the restricted activity, business area and territory. In this respect it is, firstly, important not to prohibit activity/territory which is not relevant to the company as well as balance the amount of compensation (see requirement (a) above) with the level of restrictions.

18.44 Restrictive covenants are not regulated in a Lithuanian act of law. Therefore, they apply only if agreed contractually between the parties. An exception may be made in respect of confidentiality obligations, which apply according to the law without additional instruments. However, even in this case recording the extent of confidentiality obligations in an agreement between the parties and in relevant internal documents of the employer to reflect the scope of confidential information is highly advisable.

18.45 Finally, it should be added that having a perfectly drafted restrictive covenant agreement in place does not guarantee success in case of disputes as it is difficult to prove all damages caused by violation thereof. Because of this most employers tend to include bigger or smaller penalties in the agreement applicable for breaches of the restrictions. Even though the courts are reluctant to award significant amounts by way of such penalties, these clauses serve as additional protection/preventive measure in the interest of the employer.

CHANGING EMPLOYMENT TERMS AND CONDITIONS

18.46 As a rule, the terms and conditions of an employment contract may be changed only by the mutual agreement of employer and employee. Such changes should be recorded in writing and signed by both parties. However, where the employer initiates such change due to its inability to satisfy such conditions for objective reasons (eg changes in business environment/processes), the employee's objection may in that context serve to effect his/her dismissal from work (ie under the similar procedure as described in this chapter).

18.47 On the other hand, the work conditions of an employee established via internal documents of the company can normally be changed unilaterally by the employer (unless the changes affect certain important terms of employment, such as bonus payments and similar terms).

Practical Tip

It may be of interest to note that if an employment contract refers to certain internal documents, such internal documents, depending on the reference made, may become a part of the terms of the contract by reference. Accordingly, amendment of such internal documents may become subject to the employee's consent. Therefore, it may be wise to avoid unnecessary references in the contract to particular internal documents or to draft these references clearly stating that they are not intended to incorporate the referenced document into the contract and that the referenced document remains subject to employer's unilateral amendment.

18.48 When it comes to bonuses and similar remuneration issues, such cannot be changed unilaterally even if only recorded in separate internal document (ie without any reference in the employment contract). General practice is such that if bonuses are paid for any achievements of the employees (eg target sales, etc) they are considered to be part of overall remuneration and their amendments are usually subject to the employees' consent. In turn, such bonuses which are not related to performance results and are instead linked to future results of the business, is not considered as a form of remuneration and, therefore, may be changed unilaterally. However, even these bonuses, if they are paid periodically and/or if their share in the entire amount paid to the employee is considerable, might still be considered as part of overall remuneration (ie changed only subject to employee's consent).

USING TEMPORARY STAFF

18.49 Temporary staff in Lithuania may be engaged via temporary employment agencies or, alternatively, the companies might conclude fixed-term employment contracts with temporary employees.

Temporary employment agencies

18.50 Employees engaged through these agencies are not considered as ordinary employees, however they do enjoy certain protection. In general, temporary employees may not be treated less favourably than permanent employees. For instance, it is prohibited to discriminate temporary employees against company's employees performing the same or equivalent functions. In addition, these employees should usually have access to the collective infrastructure and similar benefits as the regular employee.

18.51 It might also be worth noting that:

- assigning temporary employees to perform the functions of a company's employees during strike action is not permitted; and
- entering into a temporary employment contract in order to replace any former employee of a company is not permitted.

Fixed-term employment contracts and their renewal

18.52 The permitted reasons for entering into fixed-term employment contracts are very limited in Lithuania. Such employment contracts can be executed in the following cases:

- when work is not of a permanent nature;

- if work is of a permanent nature but execution of fixed-term employment contracts is agreed and stipulated in the collective agreement;
- if work is of a permanent nature but the employee is employed for the newly established position (temporary option currently available until middle 2015, unless prolonged).

Work which is not of a permanent nature

18.53 The legislation stands silent on the concept of 'work which is not of a permanent nature'. Therefore, in case of a dispute the employer must prove that the work is not of a permanent nature and a fixed-term employment contract could be executed with the employee initially. In practice, fixed-term employment contracts are being executed with employees, who have temporarily replaced permanent employees and in other cases of obviously temporary need of extra employees.

18.54 A fixed-term employment contract may be concluded for a certain period of time or for the period of the performance of certain work, but not exceeding five years. During the fixed-term employment contract, the employer must inform the employee about vacancies and ensure that he/she has the same opportunity to look for permanent employment as other, permanent, employees.

18.55 If an employment contract, upon the expiry of its term, is not extended or is terminated, but within one month from the day of its termination another fixed-term employment contract is concluded with the dismissed employee for the same work, then, at the request of the employee, such contract could be recognised as concluded for an indefinite period of time.

Newly-established position

18.56 The right of companies to execute fixed-term employment contracts with employees for work of a permanent nature in a newly-established position is valid only until 31 July 2015. However, this exception has already been extended several times; therefore it is possible that it could be extended after 31 July 2015.

18.57 The legislation provides for certain limitations that should be taken into account before execution of fixed-term employment contract for a newly-established position, eg that the number of fixed term employment contracts concluded may not exceed 50% of all employment contracts concluded by that employer. In addition, these fixed-term positions should not be similar to previously eliminated permanent positions (ie they should be newly created positions).

EMPLOYMENT CLAIMS

18.58 Individual labour disputes in Lithuania are heard by:

- the labour disputes commission; and/or
- the courts.

18.59 When it comes to disputes on unfair dismissal, such claims are to be addressed directly to the courts. The statutory limitation period for such claims is one month as of the moment the relevant document (eg order on dismissal) was served on the employee.

18.60 Statistically, the vast majority of employment claims are related to and arise from alleged unlawful dismissal. The second most common category of disputes (which might be part of the first group but might be initiated separately) is related to improper settlement with dismissed employees. Such claims can give rise to substantial damages (see para **18.62**).

18.61 The burden of proof in employment disputes usually lies with the employer. The employer is obliged to submit evidence supporting the fact that the dismissal under dispute was executed lawfully, all due amounts were paid on time, etc. In case of such disputes the courts, usually check whether there were valid reasons for dismissal as well as whether the formal procedure was duly followed. The main points which, among other aspects, might attract the courts' attention are as follows:

Procedure/document	Issue of interest
Corporate decision on workforce restructuring	1. If adopted by a competent corporate body; 2. If sufficient basis for dismissal at issue (eg elimination of one department and creation of new one with similar functions might be considered as artificial attempt to create a ground for dismissal of employees from the eliminated department).
Notice	If served against acknowledgement by signature, and if it contains statutory information (see para **18.33**), especially if the reason for dismissal is clearly defined (ie simply 'due to elimination of your position' is usually not adequate information).
Offering of available vacancies	If during the notice period any new employee was recruited, the employer should have valid reasons why the positions were not offered to the dismissed employees.
Selection of employees to be dismissed	If formal selection criteria were met as well as whether there is no evidence of discrimination or other unequal treatment.

Sanctions

18.62 Upon declaration of the employee's dismissal as unfair, the following remedies might apply:

Remedy	Application
(1) employee reinstatement; or (2) statutory severance pay (see para **18.30**) awarded.	One of two remedies will be applied in all cases where dismissal was recognised as unfair. The decision lies with the court and reinstatement is usually not granted where it is obvious that parties are in deep conflict or it is not possible due to economic or similar reasons.
Additional compensation equal to the average salary for the period from the date of termination until the day of execution of the court decision.	Awarded in all cases where dismissal was recognised as unfair.
Additional compensation of non-pecuniary damage.	This is optional (ie not necessarily to be awarded) and is mainly applicable where, in addition to violation of formal requirements, the employer discriminated an employee or took similar inappropriate actions in his/her respect.
Additional compensation equal to the delayed payment (up to the full average monthly salary) awarded for each month until the full settlement.	Awarded if an employer fails to duly pay all amounts to the employee. This sanction is not related to the legality of dismissal. That is, it might be applicable even in case the employee was dismissed fairly, but not all due amounts were paid on time.

MUTUALLY AGREED TERMINATION

18.63 Mutually agreed termination is proved to be the most effective and secure way to terminate employment relationship between the employer and employee. It is difficult to challenge dismissals made in that way, unless the employee succeeds in proving that he/she was forced to enter into the agreement.

18.64 Either party at any time can initiate termination of employment on the grounds of mutual agreement by giving notice in writing to the other. The other party, if the offer is acceptable, should accept in writing within seven days of receipt of the notice. Thereafter, the mutual agreement of the parties regarding the termination of employment will be executed. If the party who received the notice does not respond within seven days, it is considered that the offer is rejected.

Practical Tips

(1) It is not unlawful to sign a mutual agreement on the same day the offer was issued. However, this is often used by the employees as evidence of undue pressure from the employer. Therefore, a gap of at least one day between the submission of the employer's offer and signing of the final agreement is advisable in order to mitigate the above-mentioned risk.
(2) Agreed compensation should be expressed as an amount of money rather than as average monthly salaries in the interests of clarity and simplicity.

18.65 In the event of employment termination by mutual agreement, the amount of severance pay is not regulated by law. Accordingly, it depends on the agreement of the parties. However, as a general rule, the starting point of the negations is often the severance amount provided by law (see para **18.30**) with or without salary for the notice period (see para **18.31**). In turn, the finally agreed amount usually depends on the bargaining power of the respective parties (eg whether or not an additional protection against dismissal is applicable etc).

Chapter 19

Workforce Restructuring in Luxembourg

Anne Morel
Bonn Steichen & Partners

INTRODUCTION

19.1 The legal system in Luxembourg is based on civil law. Luxembourg employment law is based upon EU regulations, the domestic Labour Code which entered into force on 1 September 2006 and which compiles all the pieces of legislation as in force before the implementation of the Labour Code, any contractual arrangements (in the employment contract or any subsequent addendum), case law, collective agreements and under certain circumstances, custom.

When assessing entitlements of employees in dismissal or any other restructuring scenario, it is recommended to first refer to the legal provisions and secondly to ascertain whether the employment contracts contain any derogatory provisions which may to a certain extent be more favourable to the employees than the legal provisions in respect of notice periods, severance pay, voluntary termination indemnities, post-termination restrictions.

PREPARING FOR A RESTRUCTURING EXERCISE

19.2 At the outset of any restructuring exercise it is important to identify the impact of the contemplated measures on the workforce: The most common form of restructuring measure is a reduction of workforce, namely redundancies on an individual or collective basis, but there are other forms of restructuring measures such as redeployments, variation of the terms of employment contracts on an individual or collective basis, outsourcing or integration of workforces, transfer of workforce, use of temporary staff and so forth.

Based on the description of the contemplated measures, it will then be important to analyse the legal obligations triggered by the various contemplated operations, and to identify the relevant legal entities responsible for compliance with such legal requirements, to prepare a timeline and budget on that basis.

Identify the employment relationship

19.3 The first step is to determine which legal entity is the employer of the workforce concerned by the restructuring measures in order to determine the obligations by each concerned legal entity. Although this step may appear, at first glance, simple, it may be difficult in practice to assess within a group of companies, specifically in mobility situations.

Luxembourg law does not provide for a legal definition of an 'employer' or an 'employee'. An employment relationship will be created if the features for a contract of employment are met.

A contract of employment is generally defined as any agreement pursuant to which a person agrees to carry out work subject to the authority of the employer in exchange for monetary remuneration. The contract of employment is primarily characterised by the element of subordination of the employee with regard to his/her employer. The employer issues orders and guidelines, supervises the employee in respect of the performance of his/her tasks and has the authority to impose sanctions for shortcomings on the part of the employee.

Three components are required for a contract of employment: (i) the services rendered; (ii) payment of remuneration in exchange for those services; and (iii) legal subordination. The legal subordination is the most important element as it excludes any other type of contract. It is usually characterised by the following main factors:

- requirement to perform services according to a fixed schedule;
- compliance with daily/weekly working hours;
- duty to report to, and to execute orders given by specific individuals;
- payment of remuneration by the employer;
- registration of the employee with the social security administration by the employer and compliance with the rules applicable to the payment of social security contributions;
- withholding of taxes from remuneration; and
- provision of working equipment.

Collecting important information before the restructuring

19.4 It is no secret that to restructure efficiently takes resources. In order to properly plan and conduct the restructuring process, the employer must keep in mind the costs associated with such restructuring measures.

In order to assess the estimated budget necessary to conduct the restructuring exercise, the first step consists of collecting the relevant employees' data and assessing their pecuniary entitlements and financial risks associated with potential contestations of employees.

The employer shall then seek, amongst other things, the following information:

- any information in respect of the concerned employees allowing to assess their entitlements, such as age, position, length of service;
- pecuniary benefits and entitlements of the concerned employees;
- employees special protection against dismissal (if any);
- derogatory provisions of employment contracts;
- applicable collective agreements (if any).

GENERAL PROTECTION AGAINST DISMISSAL

19.5 In Luxembourg all employees enjoy a minimum protection against dismissal and have the statutory right not to be unfairly dismissed. Luxembourg law provides for precise procedures for both individual and collective dismissals.

SPECIAL PROTECTION AGAINST DISMISSAL

19.6 Luxembourg law provides for a special protection against dismissal/ redundancy in relation to certain categories of employees:

- *Sickness leave*
  An employer who has been duly notified of its employee's incapacity to work on the first day of incapacity, and/or who has received a medical certificate in due form on the third day of absence at the latest, is prohibited from notifying the employee of the termination of his/her contract or summoning the employee to a preliminary interview prior to dismissal when required by law.
  The employer's right to dismiss is suspended for the duration of the incapacity and in case of long and continuous incapacity for a maximum period of 26 weeks following the first day of incapacity. Such suspension applies even in case of gross misconduct.
  Any dismissal during this period protection is deemed to be unfair.

Employees remain entitled throughout this period of protection to their remuneration and to any other benefits accruing during their absence. All employees being on sickness leave are being paid by the employer until the end of the month during which they accumulate 77 days of sickness and by the National Health Fund ('CNS') after that period of time.

- *Staff representatives*

  Staff representatives, as well as their alternates are protected from dismissal throughout their term of office. This protection is extended to former staff representatives for the six months following the end of their term of office, and to candidates for election to such office for a period of three months following the announcement of their candidacy.

  Any dismissal during this period of protection is deemed to be null and void.

  The employer is however entitled to suspend and terminate a staff representative in the event of gross misconduct subject to complying with a specific procedure outlined below:

  – The employer informs the concerned employee of the suspension of his/her contract of employment based on the gross misconduct. During the suspension period, the protected employee will not be entitled to his/her remuneration, unless otherwise authorised by the Labour Court upon the employee's motion.
  – The employer must immediately after having notified the suspension, refer the matter to the Labour Court, which will analyse the grounds asserted by the employer to justify the termination and rule on the termination of the contract of employment based on the grounds of gross misconduct. If the Labour Court rules that the grounds asserted by the employer qualify as gross misconduct, the Labour Court will pronounce the termination of the contract of employment with retroactive effect at the date of the suspension. If however, the Labour Court rules that the grounds do not qualify as gross misconduct, it will order the reinstatement of the employee within the company.

  According to Luxembourg case law however, the protection afforded to staff delegates does not apply in the event of termination based on the complete cessation of activity and closing down of the company[1]. The Courts consider that the protection afforded to staff delegates, which derives from their mission as staff delegates to assist and represent the staff, is no longer relevant in the situation where the whole workforce of a company has been terminated based on the cessation of activity and liquidation of the employing legal entity.[2]

- *Member of the Joint Work Council*

  The members of the Joint Work Council may only be dismissed with the consent of the Joint Works Council of which they form part.

- *Employee who is a member of the board of the company*

  An employee appointed as a member of the board of the employing company cannot be dismissed without the prior consent of the court.

---

1 Order of Labour Disctrict Court 10 February 2009 Docket number 550/2009

2 Order of the Labour Court of Appeal 27 October 2005

This protection is extended to former members of the board for a period of six months following the end of their term of office, and to candidates for election to such office for a period of three months following the announcement of their candidacy.

- *Pregnant employees and employees on maternity leave*
  An employee whose pregnancy has been confirmed by a medical certificate and who has duly informed her employer is protected against any dismissal. This protection is valid throughout the duration of the pregnancy and for a maximum period of 12 weeks following the birth.
  If an employee is dismissed before having informed her employer about the pregnancy, she must provide her employer with a medical certificate justifying the pregnancy within 8 days from the notification of the dismissal.
  Any dismissal during this period of protection is deemed to be null and void.
  The employer is however entitled to suspend and terminate a pregnant woman in the event of gross misconduct under the same terms and conditions as applicable to the staff representatives and as above-described.
- *Employees on parental leave*
  An employer may not dismiss an employee during parental leave. Parental leave may be taken either at the expiry of the maternity leave (the so-called 'first parental leave') or before the child reaches the age of five (the so-called 'second parental leave').
  For the 'first parental leave', the protection starts two months before the beginning of maternity leave.
  For the 'second parental leave' the protection starts six months preceding the beginning of parental leave.
  This protection does not apply in case of dismissal for gross misconduct.
- *Employees on leave for family reasons*
  Employees responsible for a child under 15 years who requires the presence of one of their parents in case of serious illness, accident or other urgent health needs, are entitled to leave for family reasons.
  Employers who have been informed on the same day, of the leave for family reasons are not allowed to inform the concerned employee of the termination with notice of their contract of employment or to summon them to the interview prior to dismissal, when required. However, this protection only applies for the period covered by the medical certificate and does not automatically cover the whole duration of the child's sickness.
- *Employees reinstated within the employing company*
  Any employee who is incapacitated and therefore unable to carry out his/her job owing to health troubles and who is not entitled to any disability benefits under the public social security scheme because he/she may not be considered as disabled, may be subject to a decision of reinstatement by the 'Commission Mixte'.
  The concerned employee is protected against any dismissal from the day when his/her case has been deferred to the 'Commission Mixte' and until the day of the notification of the decision taken by the 'Commission Mixte' with a view to either order the reinstatement of the employee within the

employer ('internal reinstatement') or to place the employee with the Employment Administration ('external reinstatement').
In the event of reinstatement of the concerned employee within the employer, the protection period is of 12 months following the day of the notification to the employer of the reinstatement decision.
The protection over the 12 months following the reinstatement does not apply in case of gross misconduct.

Dismissals notified during the period of protection are deemed null and void.

Protection in case of cessation of the activity and closing down of the Company

According to Luxembourg case law all these protections do not apply when the dismissal occurred after the cessation of activity and the complete closing down of the company. Indeed an employer cannot be forced to pursue its activity in the sole interest of a protected employee.

WORKFORCE REDUCTION

19.7 An employer can terminate the contract of employment at any time, but it must be able to justify by a genuine and serious cause of termination ('cause réelle et sérieuse') and it must comply with the applicable dismissal procedure.

Reasons for dismissal must be supported by demonstrable and explicit facts. By statute, any and all dismissals must be justified by a 'genuine and serious cause' ('cause réelle et sérieuse'). The Labour Code does not provide for a definition of either 'real' or 'serious' cause, or a list of the situations that should be considered as such. The content and scope of this notion has been defined by case law. 'Genuine' means that the cause must be exact, accurate and demonstrable, and 'serious' means that the cause must be of some significance.

There are two major categories of dismissals based on genuine and serious cause:

- dismissal based on the employee's behaviour (dismissals for personal/professional reasons), such as poor performance, the employee's negligence or the employee's inability to work;
- dismissal based on economic grounds (what we will refer to as 'dismissal on grounds of redundancy').

DISMISSALS ON GROUNDS OF REDUNDANCY

Definition of redundancy

19.8 As far as economic grounds are concerned, the Labour Code refers to 'reasons arising from the operating needs of the business, establishment or department'. There is no other statutory definition of the economic grounds/redundancy.

Redundancy requires the elimination of positions and the underlying reason for such elimination of positions may either be motivated by a diminution of work or a reorganisation decided by the employer as part of a cost-saving exercise or reassignment of functional/organisational responsibilities of personnel.

Luxembourg case law clearly rules that the employer may take any measures that he considers as being appropriate and necessary to reclaim a deficit in a business branch. The Court may not assess the opportuneness of the measures decided and taken by the employer.

It is also important to outline that the employer may decide on a discretionary basis which selection criteria he will apply subject to complying with non-discrimination rules and, the courts may not assess the opportuneness of the choice made by the employer, except in case of abuse of rights.

It is however worth mentioning that the Court of Appeal ruled on 1 March 2012 that when the employer contemplating dismissal based on grounds of redundancy, is part of a group, the grounds must be assessed at the level of the group and not only at the level of the Luxembourg company. It resulted in the court assessing the grounds at the group level or at least at the level of several companies of the group even if located abroad and performing the same activity. This decision was based on French case law of the highest court of justice.

The position of the courts had always previously been to limit the assessment to the concerned company/business or undertaking located in Luxembourg but in light of the above-mentioned decision, it is recommended to take into account the whole business to which the Luxembourg company belongs.

Priority to reemployment

19.9 Any employee dismissed on grounds of redundancy may avail of a priority to be reemployed. The concerned employee must address a written request to the employer to inform the employer that he/she wants to benefit from the priority to be reemployed. The employer will be required to inform the concerned employee of any and all vacancies corresponding to his/her qualifications within one year after the employee has effectively left the company. The employee will be in a position to apply for such vacancy but the employer is not under any obligation to effectively reemploy the concerned employee.

Redundancy procedures

19.10 When companies are planning to dismiss employees on grounds of redundancy they must have regard to two redundancy procedures depending on the number of employees concerned by the dismissal: *the individual redundancy procedure* and *the collective redundancy procedure.*

Individual redundancy procedure

19.11 Luxembourg law does not differentiate the procedures applicable to individual dismissals based the employee's aptitude or attitude (non-performance, misbehaviour, etc) and dismissals based on economic grounds. The applicable procedure is the procedure applicable to terminations with a notice period (as opposed to with termination with immediate effect for gross misconduct).

Preliminary interview

19.12 An employer employing at least 150 employees and contemplating dismissing one of its employees must, before taking any decision, convene the concerned employee to a preliminary interview.

The convening notice must contain:

- the object of the convening notice meeting;
- the date of the meeting;
- the time of the meeting; and
- the place of the meeting.

A copy of the notice must be sent to the staff delegation in place, as the case may be, or to the Labour and Mines Inspectorate.

The notice must inform the employee that he has the right to be assisted during the interview by:

- an employee of the establishment or
- a delegate of a representative trade union on the national level represented in the staff delegation.

Such an interview is not however required in the event of dismissal occurring during the probation period.

During the interview, the employer must indicate the reason(s) for the decision to terminate the contract and gather the employee's explanations as well as the objections of the person assisting the employee.

After the interview, the employee must be notified of the dismissal:

- no less than the day following the interview, and
- no more than one week later.

If the employee does not attend the preliminary interview, the employee can be notified of the dismissal:

- no earlier than the day following the day set for the interview and
- no more than one week later.

The Labour Code provides for a formal irregularity in the event of non-compliance with the requirement to organise a preliminary interview.

Notification of the dismissal

19.13 The dismissal is notified either by registered letter or by hand delivery, with the penalty of invalidity applying otherwise. In the event of delivery by hand, the employee must acknowledge receipt of the dismissal letter on a copy of the letter that the employer will keep.

Any employer employing at least 15 persons must notify the 'Secrétariat du Comité de Conjoncture' (within the Ministry of Economy) of any redundancy taking place for any grounds not linked to the employee's aptitude or attitude (dismissal based on economic reasons). Such notification must be carried out at the latest when the employee is notified of the termination.

The employee may request communication of the reasons. Such request must be made to the employer by registered letter within one month of the date of the notification of dismissal. The employer must state the reasons in detail within one further month by registered letter.

Payments to be made in the event of individual redundancy

Notice period

19.14 Notice by the employer must be given as follows:

Length of service	Notice required
Less than 5 years	2 months
5 to 10 years	4 months
over 10 years	6 months

Employment contracts and collective agreements may provide for longer notice periods in case of dismissal.

Notice takes effect only on the first or the 15th day of the month. Notice given before the 15th of the month takes effect on the 15th; notice given after the 14th day takes effect on the first day of the following month.

The contract of employment will effectively terminate on the expiry of the notice period and Luxembourg law does not provide for payment in lieu of notice.

The employer may decide to release the dismissed employee from the obligation to work during the notice period. In the event of a release, the employee will be entitled to take up another salaried activity during the notice period. The employer who has dismissed the employee will no longer have to pay the remuneration during the remaining period of notice if the employee has started to work for another employer. It will however have to make up for any difference of remuneration over the remaining period of notice, if the employee earns less with their new employer. The employer will moreover remain liable to pay the social security contributions on the whole remuneration (including the remuneration paid by the new employer) over the remaining period of notice.

Severance payment

19.15 Any dismissed employee, except those dismissed for gross misconduct, is entitled to severance payment after at least five years of service:

Length of service	Severance grant
< 5 years	No severance pay
5–10 years	1 month salary
10–15 years	2 months' salary
15–20 years	3 months' salary
20–25 years	6 months' salary
25–30 years	9 months' salary
>30 years	12 months' salary

The severance pay is determined on the basis of the average gross salary effectively paid to the employee over the 12 months preceding the dismissal notification. The following are taken into account in the calculation: the sickness benefits, bonus and any recurrent payment, but excluding overtime compensation, premium paid on a discretionary basis and reimbursement of expenses.

The employer must pay the severance payment on the day the employee leaves work. The severance pay is tax exempt (gross = net).

COLLECTIVE REDUNDANCY PROCEDURE

Definition of collective redundancy

19.16 The statutory procedure regarding collective redundancies must be followed, as soon as an employer contemplates dismissing at least 7 employees within a period of 30 days or 15 employees within a period of 90 days.

For the purpose of calculating the number of redundancies provided for in the law, terminations of an employment contract which occur on the employer's initiative for one or more reasons not related to the individual workers concerned shall be deemed redundancies.

Any employment termination further to a pre-pension regime, negotiated termination (which should include negotiated termination by common consent and negotiated resignation) or specific incapacity regimes are also deemed redundancies for the purpose of determining the legal threshold.

Procedure applicable to collective redundancies

Prior information/consultation requirements

19.17 As a first step, as soon as the employer has taken the decision to start collective redundancies, he must comply with the following information/consultation procedure:

(a) inform and consult the staff delegation on any decision which might entail major modifications in the organisation of work and in the employment contracts, as well as on any decision to carry out a collective redundancy;

(b) inform and consult the joint works council on every economical or financial decision that could have a significant influence on the company's structure or the level of employment (production, sales, projects of restriction, extension or modifications in the company's organisation; projects of merger; implementation, modification, abrogation of complementary pension). In principle, information and consultation must occur prior to any decision, except if there is a risk of disturbing the management of the company or compromising an operation. In this case, the employer must give all necessary information and explanations to the joint works council within three days following the decision;

(c) inform and consult the European works council, which has a right to transnational information and consultation on economic and company issues of a transnational and strategic nature that considerably affect employee interests and concern all group companies or at least two group companies in different member states. The Labour code expressly provides that the European works council must be informed and consulted when exceptional circumstances affecting the employees' interests arise, in particular in the event of collective redundancies.

The employer will be able to start the process only after the aforementioned prior information and consultation procedure has taken place.

Negotiation of a social plan (redundancy scheme)

19.18 As a second step, the employer must enter into prior negotiations with the employees' representatives before proceeding with collective dismissals in order to come to an agreement relating to the establishment of a social plan. The social plan is a written agreement signed by the employer and the employees' representatives, which contains the results of the negotiations.

The employees' representatives are either the staff delegation, the joint works council (composed of an equal number of management and employees' representatives) or/and the trade unions if a collective agreement applies to the employer/employee relationship.

The procedure may only start once the employer has set up the legally required employees' representation.

The procedure can be described as follows, outlined below.

The negotiations shall at least cover ways and means of:

- avoiding collective redundancies or reducing the number of workers affected;
- mitigating the consequences of the redundancies by recourse to social measures aimed at, inter alia, redeploying or retraining the workers made redundant; and
- granting financial compensation.

The following matters will notably have to be discussed:

- application of the law governing short-time working;
- implementation of changes to working hours;
- temporary reduction in working hours and participation in training sessions or redeployment of workers;
- training sessions or redeployment within the company or within another company in the same sector;
- application of the law governing the temporary lending of workforce;
- personal support for a change of career, with eventual recourse to external experts;
- application of the legal provisions governing the pre-retirement regime;
- principles and procedures governing the implementation and the follow-up of selected measures.

Companies who put in place an employment safeguard scheme approved by the Labour Minister in the six months preceding the beginning of the negotiations are exempt from the obligations provided by the above-mentioned provisions.

Before negotiations start, or at the very latest at the beginning of the negotiations, the employer must inform the employee representatives in writing of the proposed collective dismissal and must provide them with the following information:

- reasons for the proposals;
- number and description of employees affected;
- number and description of employees usually employed;
- period of time within which the dismissals are proposed;
- method of selecting employees to be dismissed; and
- proposed method of calculating the amount of any redundancy payment.

The employer must send a written notification of the contemplated redundancies to the Employment Administration ('Administration de l'Emploi'), as well as a copy of the above-mentioned notification before the negotiations start. The Employment Administration will then forward the written notification to the Labour and Mines Inspectorate ('Inspection du Travail et des Mines').

The employer and the employee representatives must come to an agreement relating to the establishment of a social plan within 15 days from the start of negotiations.

At this stage, if the parties have come to an agreement, they must sign the social plan. After the signing of the social plan, the employer is entitled to notify each employee of their dismissal on an individual basis.

If the parties have not come to an agreement within the 15-day time period as provided for by the law, the minutes of the negotiations stating the attitude of the parties regarding the issues in negotiation are signed and immediately forwarded to the Employment Administration.

Both parties must jointly refer the matter to the National Conciliation Office ('Office National de Conciliation') within three days of signing the minutes of the negotiations. Within two days of this the President of the National Conciliation Office will summon the joint committee ('Commission paritaire') and within three days of the convening notice, the joint committee will hold a meeting. The committee will consider the matter within 15 days of the first meeting. The minutes of their discussions are forwarded to the Employment Administration and to the Labour and Mines Inspectorate.

After the signature of the minutes by the 'Office National de Conciliation', the employer is entitled to notify the dismissal to each employee on an individual basis. The procedure will then be the same as described for individual redundancy.

Any dismissal notified to the employees before the signature of the minutes is null and void. The dismissals come into effect towards the employees after a period of 75 days, notwithstanding any longer notice period as determined by the law or provided for in the employment contract or in the collective agreement.

Timetable

1st case :

1. Information to the employees' representatives (staff delegation and trade union) on:
   - reasons for the redundancies;
   - number and description of employees affected;
   - number and description of employees usually employed;
   - period of time within which the redundancies are proposed;
   - method of selecting employees to be dismissed;
   - proposed method of calculating the amount of any redundancy payment.
2. Written notification to the Employment Administration of the projected redundancies, giving the same information as above-mentioned.

3. Sending a copy of the mail addressed to the employees' representatives to the Employment Administration.
4. Sending a copy of the mail addressed to the Employment Administration to the employees' representatives.
5. Start of the negotiations. The consultations shall at least cover ways and means (1) of avoiding collective redundancies or reducing the number of workers affected, (2) of mitigating the consequences by recourse to accompanying social measures aimed, inter alia, at aid for redeploying or retraining workers made redundant and (3) of granting financial compensation.
   The following matters will notably have to be discussed:
   - application of the legal provision governing short-time working;
   - implementation of changes to the duration of work;
   - temporary reduction of working hours and participation to training sessions or redeployment;
   - training sessions or redeployment within the company or within another company in the same sector;
   - application of the legal provisions governing temporary lending of workforce;
   - personal support for a change of carrier, in eventually having recourse to external experts;
   - application of the legal provisions governing pre-pension regime.
6. At the latest 15 days after the start of the negotiations: signature of a social plan.
7. Communication of a copy of the social plan immediately to the Employment Administration.
8. Individual notification of the dismissal.

OR

2nd case:

1. Information to the employees' representatives (joint works council and trade unions) on:
   - reasons for the redundancies;
   - number and description of employees affected;
   - number and description of employees usually employed;
   - period of time within which the redundancies are proposed;
   - method of selecting employees to be dismissed;
   - proposed method of calculating the amount of any redundancy payment.
2. Written notification to the Employment Administration of the projected redundancies, giving the same information as above-mentioned.
3. Sending a copy of the mail addressed to the employees' representatives to the Employment Administration.
4. Sending a copy of the mail addressed to the Employment Administration to the employees' representatives.
5. Start of the negotiations. The consultations shall at least cover ways and means: (1) of avoiding collective redundancies or reducing the number of workers affected; (2) of mitigating the consequences by recourse to

accompanying social measures aimed, inter alia, at aid for redeploying or retraining workers made redundant; and (3) of granting financial compensation.
The following matters will notably have to be discussed:
- application of the legal provision governing short-time working;
- implementation of changes to the duration of work;
- temporary reduction of working hours and participation to training sessions or redeployment;
- training sessions or redeployment within the company or within another company in the same sector;
- application of the legal provisions governing temporary lending of workforce;
- personal support for a change of carrier, in eventually having recourse to external experts;
- application of the legal provisions governing pre-pension regime.

6. 15 days later: the minutes of the negotiations stating the motivated attitude of the parties regarding the negotiated issues is signed and immediately forwarded to the Employment Administration ('Administration de l'Emploi').
7. At the latest three days after the signature of the minutes, parties must refer the matter to the 'Office national de conciliation'.
8. Within two days, the President of the 'Office National de Conciliation' must appoint the members and must convene the member of the equal representation.
9. At the latest three days after the convening notice, the 'Office National de Conciliation' must hold a meeting.
10. 15 days after the first meeting, consultations are closed and the 'Office national de conciliation' must draw the minutes.
11. Communication of the minutes to the Employment Administration and to the Labour and Mines Inspectorate.
12. Individual notification of the dismissal.

PAYMENTS

Statutory payments

19.19 The employer will have to make the payments as provided for by the law, the employment contracts and, the collective agreement, if any.

Notice period

19.20 Notice must be given as follows in the event of collective redundancy:

Length of service	Notice required
Less than 5 years	75 days
5 to 10 years	4 months
over 10 years	6 months

The notice period starts either on the first day of the following month or on the fifteenth of the month depending on the day of notification of the dismissal. The notice period will start on the first of the following month if the notification has been done after the fourteenth of the previous month and will start on the fifteenth if the notification has been done before the fifteenth.

The notice pay is paid in the same way as a salary, at the end of each month. The employer is required to withhold taxes and social security contributions.

Severance pay

19.21 Please refer to the severance pay payable in the event of individual dismissal.

Voluntary payments as negotiated between the parties

19.22 Any additional payment is not provided for by the law. The method of calculation of such additional indemnities will exclusively depend on the consultations.

We may provide with the following examples:

(a) Redundancy indemnity
Such indemnities vary with the age, length of service and family situation and they could basically range, as a maximum, from 1 to 8 months of salary taking into consideration the age (from 30 to over 50 years old) plus, from 1 to 16 months of salary depending on the length of service (from 1 to over 25 years of service). Some social plans have considered 1 month of salary per year of seniority.
Those figures are purely indicative and shall exclusively depend on the negotiations. The outcome of the negotiations also greatly depends on the sector of activity.

(b) Increased notice pay
During the notice period, the employer may decide to release some or all employees made redundant from the performance of their work. If the employer decides to have some of them keep on working during part or all the notice period, he usually commits to pay an increased notice pay to compensate them.
In case of release, the employer may provide in the social plan that the payment of the notice pay will cease if the employee has found another job before the expiry of the notice period. The employer may also provide that such notice pay will be paid in any cases, even if the employee finds another job.

(c) Extended notice period
The notice period may also be extended if the concerned employees bring evidence that they have not found another job at the expiry of the statutory notice period. This solution is more expensive for the employer, as it remains liable to pay its part of the social security contributions on the remuneration paid over the extended period of time and the employee keeps their other entitlements to holiday, bonus and so forth.

(d) Redeployment aid/outplacement services
The employer may agree to organise seminars, training courses or to provide employees made redundant with support in finding another job.
A social plan may provide for other types of indemnities as determined by the negotiating parties.

(e) Contestation of the collective dismissal
An employee made redundant on a collective basis has the same rights as an employee made redundant or dismissed on an individual basis. It means in practice that such employee could bring an action against the employer for unfair dismissal and challenge the grounds.
To prevent the employee from filing a request with the court, it is recommended to have each employee made redundant sign a letter mentioning that they are aware of the grounds of termination, that he/she accepts them, that with the implementation of the social plan, all claims against the employer on the basis of the employment contract and its termination have been fulfilled and that they do not have any further claims against the employer.

Tax considerations

19.23 The Luxembourg Tax Code provides that any payment awarded to an employee on account of a total or partial closing of a company or of the decrease of activity duly stated by a Governmental Committee ('Comité de Conjoncture'), is tax exempt up to 12 times the monthly minimum social salary.

EMPLOYMENT SAFEGUARD SCHEME

19.24 Any employer employing at least 15 employees on a regular basis must notify the Comité de Conjoncture of any dismissal, which is not based on the employees' aptitude or attitude, at the latest at the time of notification of the termination.

On the basis of the collected notifications, the 'Secrétariat du Comité de Conjoncture' may request the employees' representatives and the employer to enter into negotiations to come up with an employment safeguard scheme, at any time and at the latest when it involves five dismissals, which are not based on the employees' aptitude or attitude over a reference period of three months or eight dismissals over a reference period of six months.

An employment safeguard scheme must contain the results of the negotiations on various mandatory matters, such as:

- application of the legal provision governing short-time working;
- implementation of changes to the duration of work;
- temporary reduction of working hours and participation in training sessions or redeployment;
- training sessions or redeployment within the company or within another company in the same sector.

POST-TERMINATION RESTRICTIVE COVENANTS

19.25 In Luxembourg, the use of post-restrictive covenants in the contracts of employment is common.

Non-competition covenants

19.26 A non-competition clause is a clause whereby an employee agrees not to carry out, as a self-employed person, similar activities to those carried out by his/her former employer after the termination of the employment contract, so as not to interfere with such former employer's interests.

The non-competition clause is therefore only applicable in the framework of an employment relationship between an employee and an employer, and is triggered by the termination of the employment. The scope of application of such legal provision is moreover strictly limited, as it refers to any activity performed by a former employee as a self-employed person only. Such non-competition clause will therefore not cover situations where former employees carry out an activity as an employee under a contract of employment with a competitor.

Non-competition covenants between an employee and an employer will only be enforceable to the extent that they comply with the legal requirements.

Such a clause must be stated in writing in the employment contract or in any subsequent agreement. Failure to be written results in the non-competition clause being null and void. Moreover, it is deemed null and void, if, at the time of signature of the contract of employment stating the non-competition covenant, the employee is under 18, or if the employee's annual remuneration when they terminate the employment relationship does not exceed €52,843.88 (at current index 775,17). In addition, the non-competition covenant is only enforceable if the restriction:

- applies to a specific professional sector and to similar activities to those carried out by the former employer;
- does not exceed 12 months starting on the date of the termination of the employment contract;

- is limited to a geographical area (which may not extend beyond the territory of the grand-duchy of Luxembourg) where the employee would be in a position to effectively compete with his or her former employer, taking into consideration the nature of the concerned activities and their range.

The non-competition covenant is moreover not enforceable if the employer has abusively terminated the contract of employment with immediate effect or has terminated the contract of employment in breach of the legal requirements governing the notice period.

The contract of employment may provide for pecuniary compensation for damages (equivalent to a penalty clause) in the event of breach of the non-competition clause by the employee, although such practice is unusual in Luxembourg. Failing the provision of a penalty clause, the amount of any compensation for damages will be determined by the courts based on the damages actually incurred as a result of a breach.

Non-solicitation covenants

19.27 Non-solicitation covenants are not specifically regulated by Luxembourg law.

Non-solicitation covenants usually aim at limiting the right of an employee to solicit, interfere with or endeavour to entice away from the employer the custom of any person, firm, or company who, at the date of termination or within a certain time period prior to the termination, was a customer or client of, or in the habit of dealing with the employer, or who at such date was negotiating with the employer in relation to all or part of its business, and to whom the employee personally came into contact during the course of his/her employment. Such provisions are enforceable to the extent that they do not aim at limiting the employee's rights to work as provided for by the constitution, and at circumventing the strict legal requirements for a non-competition covenant as detailed above.

BUSINESS SALE, OUTSOURCING/INSOURCING AND OFFSHORING

19.28 Provisions deriving from the implementation into Luxembourg law of Directive 77/187/EC, as replaced by Directive 2001/23/EC dated 12 March 2001 on the approximation of the laws of the Member States relating to the safeguarding of employees' rights in the event of transfers of undertakings, businesses or parts of undertakings or businesses are included in the Labour Code under Articles L.127-1 to L.127-6.

Such legal provisions shall apply to any transfer of an undertaking, business, or part of an undertaking or business ('Transfer of Undertaking') as a result of a contractual sale, merger, inheritance, division or conversion of a business or incorporation of a company.

Business sales, outsourcing/insourcing and offshoring may amount to a Transfer of Undertaking.

Business Sale

19.29 A business sale may give raise to the application of the legal provisions governing the Transfer of Undertaking. However, the transfer of shares (as well as the reduction of capital within a company) may not amount to a Transfer of Undertaking as such operation only affects the ownership of the legal entity which remains the employer of the concerned employees.

Outsourcing/insourcing

19.30 Luxembourg law does not provide for a definition of outsourcing. Outsourcing activities has become a common feature in a modern economy but has in practice raised various legal issues depending on the way the outsourcing process is carried out. The major legal issue, that has given rise to a certain number of court decisions at national, but also at European level, is the likely application of the legal provisions governing the Transfer of Undertakings.

The first step for the purpose of determining whether such legal provisions apply consists in identifying an undertaking or 'economic entity' in the hands of a seller. The economic entity is described as an organised grouping of resources (persons/assets) facilitating the exercise of an economic activity which pursues a specific objective. The activity may be central or ancillary.

The second step is to assess whether the economic activity has been transferred and has retained its identity after the operation of transfer.

The European Court of Justice ('ECJ') has ruled on a recurrent basis that the existence of a transfer is a question of fact to be determined by the national courts or tribunals, which examine all the circumstances of the case. The ECJ has formulated a number of tests, including assessing the following criteria:

- the type of undertaking or business concerned;
- whether there were tangible or intangible assets to be transferred;
- whether customers or employees were transferred;
- the degree of similarity between the activities carried on before and after the alleged transfer;
- the period, if any, during which those activities were suspended.

These factors are not to be considered in isolation, so no one factor is conclusive in itself.

A different and more restrictive test consists of concluding that there is no transfer of undertaking without the transfer of either significant assets or a transfer of the major part, in terms of numbers or skills, of the previous service provider's workforce.

PROCEDURE TO BE FOLLOWED PRIOR TO A TRANSFER OF UNDERTAKING

Duty to inform and/or consult

19.31

- Any employer must inform and consult the staff delegation on any decision which might entail major modifications in the organisation of work and in the employment contracts, as well as on any decision to carry out a Transfer of Undertaking.
- The employer must inform and consult the joint works council on every economical or financial decision that could have a significant influence on the company's structure or the level of employment including any decision to carry out a Transfer of Undertaking.

Once the decision to carry out the Transfer of Undertaking has been taken in compliance with the legal information and consultation requirements as above-described, the transferor and the transferee shall be required to inform the representatives of their respective employees affected by the transfer of the following:

- the date or proposed date of the transfer;
- the reasons for the transfer;
- the legal, economic and social implications of the transfer for the employees;
- any measures envisaged in relation to the employees.

If there is no staff delegation in an undertaking or business, the employees concerned must be informed in advance of the above mentioned items.

The transferor must give such information to the representatives of its employees in good time before the transfer is carried out. The transferee would be required to give such information to the representatives of its employees in good time, and in any case before its employees are directly affected by the transfer as regards their conditions of work and employment.

The transferor must notify the transferee in due time of all the rights and obligations that shall be transferred to the transferee, so far as those rights and obligations are or ought to have been known to the transferor at the time of the transfer.

A copy of such notification must be sent to the Labour and Mines Inspectorate (the governmental institution in charge of supervising the proper application of labour and employment law within the various employers). A failure by the transferor to notify the transferee of any such right or obligation shall not affect the transfer of that right or obligation or the rights of any employees against the transferee and/or the transferee in respect of that right or obligation.

Consequences of failure to comply with the procedure of information and/or consultation

19.32 The general provisions regarding the staff representatives and/or joint works council provide for civil and criminal sanctions in case of a breach of the information and/or consultation procedure in general.

Effect of the transfer of undertaking

19.33 *Automatic transfer of the employment contracts and protection of employment*

The transferor's rights and obligations arising from a contract of employment or from an employment relationship existing on the date of a transfer shall, by reason of such transfer, be automatically transferred to the transferee by effect of the law. There is no legal need to issue new written employment contracts.

The transferee is required to maintain all the conditions, which result from a collective agreement concluded by the transferor until the expiry date of such collective agreement or until a new agreement is concluded.

After the date of the transfer, the transferor and the transferee shall be jointly and severally liable in respect of obligations, which arose before the date of transfer from a contract of employment or an employment relationship existing on the date of the transfer. The transferor must however reimburse the transferee for any amounts paid to the employee in respect of such obligations, except if that amount had been taken into consideration in a contract between the transferor and the transferee.

Changing terms and conditions of employment

19.34 Where the transferor or the transferee contemplates implementing measures in relation to the transferred employees (for example modifications to terms and conditions), they shall consult the representatives of his employees in good time on such measures with the view to reaching an agreement, notwithstanding the fact that the Transfer of Undertaking may not be a cause of termination for the transferor as well as for the transferee.

The information and consultation shall cover at least the measures envisaged in relation to the employees. The information must be provided and consultations taken place in good time before the change in the business affected by the transfer.

Such obligations shall apply irrespective of whether the decision resulting in the transfer is taken by the employer or an undertaking controlling the employer of an undertaking, business, or part of an undertaking or business.

Termination of employment

19.35 The Transfer of Undertaking shall not in itself constitute grounds for dismissal by the transferor or the transferee. Luxembourg legal provisions have omitted providing that such provisions shall not stand in the way of terminations that may take place for economic, technical or organisational reasons entailing changes in the workforce, as the Directive 2001/23/EC had provided for. Although such provision had been omitted by Luxembourg law, Luxembourg case law considers that a dismissal before a Transfer of Undertaking, even with a view to a merger, is not automatically to be considered as fraudulent, provided that it is based on an economic context triggering the necessity to take reorganisational measures. However, a termination motivated by reorganisation measures directly linked to the transfer, such as redundancy or closure of a position, would be considered as abusive. The sole terminations which would have been made in any case, for instance if the decision had been taken before there was any question of transferring the undertaking, fall within the exclusion.

As a consequence of the foregoing considerations, terminations shall only be possible, if they can be based on:

- grounds linked to the aptitude or attitude of the concerned employees or
- economic, technical or organisational measures not in connection with the merger. In this respect, the closure of position as a consequence of a transfer/merger may not be considered as a valid reason. Terminations could, for example, take place on the basis of organisational measures taken as a result of a cost-cutting policy, or a decrease of the workload/ volume of work, cessation of certain activities, independently of the Transfer of Undertaking.

Objection to the transfer

19.36 Luxembourg law does not provide for a right of the employees concerned by a Transfer of Undertaking to object to the Transfer of Undertaking. If an employee does not agree with a transfer (provided that the contract of employment or its conditions has not been substantially modified after a transfer), they must resign.

VARIATION OF THE TERMS AND CONDITIONS OF EMPLOYMENT

19.37 Contracts of employment may not be unilaterally and substantially modified to the detriment of the employee without the employee's prior consent. The most efficient way for employers to modify the terms and conditions of the employment contract in accordance with Luxembourg law is of course to obtain the employee's express consent to the modification. As a general rule, the parties enter into an amendment to the employment contract reflecting the changes to the terms and conditions as agreed (addendum).

However non-significant changes may be imposed by the employer and it is recommended to provide for some flexibility in the contracts of employment as to any non-significant change to the workplace (for example within the same city or area), of the working hours/schedule of work. It is important to define what is considered by the parties as being substantial to facilitate, as the case may be at a later stage, any assessment process of whether a change is to be considered as substantial and to the detriment of the employee.

However, under certain circumstances, a substantial unilateral variation of the terms and conditions of the contract of employment to the detriment of the employee may be implemented and imposed by the employer (for example, demotion, reduction of remuneration, cancellation of bonus).

In that respect, a specific procedure, similar to the one applicable in case of dismissal must be followed. Failure of the employer to comply with this procedure, would result in the modification being deemed null and void.

The employer must inform the employee of the modification by a registered letter and provide that the modification shall enter into force at the expiry of the notice period. The employee is then entitled to request the employer to provide him/her with the reasons of such modification. Following this request, the employer must provide the reasons of the modification, by a registered letter, within one month.

If the employer complies with the above-mentioned procedure, two hypotheses must be distinguished:

- If the employee continues to work under the new terms and conditions and does not challenge the modification during a reasonable period of time, he/she will be deemed to have accepted it and will be unable to challenge such modification before the courts.
- If the employee refuses the modification, he/she must resign before the entry into force of the new conditions or within a reasonable period of time after the entry into force. The employee may initiate legal proceedings before the Labour Courts and claim compensation for damages as a result of the termination of the employment contract considered to have been initiated by the employer. In such case, the labour court will examine the validity of the reasons put forward to justify the variation of the contract of employment and will award the employee compensation for damages if the variation has not been justified by valid reasons (genuine and serious grounds).

Finally, it should be noted that employees' representatives may not be subject to a modification of their contract of employment during the period of protection (term of office and six months after the end). Such modification is null and void.

TEMPORARY UNEMPLOYMENT

19.38 Employers facing cyclical economic difficulties may want to implement measures with a view to avoiding redundancies.

The current Luxembourg legislative arsenal provides for different measures, temporary by nature, involving temporary unemployment as well as state financial aid.

Such measures, as well as the procedures to be followed, will be described hereinafter together with the conditions to be met in order for each measure to be authorised.

Temporary unemployment due to cyclical economic difficulties ('chômage partiel pour problèmes économiques conjoncturels')

19.39 This measure aims at providing support to companies operating in a sector in crisis and which are consequently facing cyclical economic difficulties. This measure consequently has been set for companies which are part of sectors officially declared in crisis by the government.

The Economy Committee ('Comité de Conjoncture') (at the Ministry of the Economy and Foreign Trade) determines if a given industry is declared in crisis, each time an individual request for temporary unemployment due to cyclical economic difficulties is filed. After analysis of the industry, the Economy Committee proposes to the government, if applicable, to declare as being in crisis, as a whole, the industry of which the requesting company forms part. The concerned company can benefit from temporary unemployment due to cyclical economic difficulties only after such decision is taken.

Finally, such a measure is not applicable to highly competitive industry, such as, for example, the financial and banking industry.

The conditions to be met are as follows:

- it must be proven that following a significant decrease in the orders, the activity rate of one or several economic branches declines compared to the average of the three former years and an important decrease in workforce is expected;
- such difficulties should have a cyclical origin and be temporary;
- the foreseeable trend should allow expecting a resumption of the business and restoring the full employment within a reasonable time period;
- the concerned company must commit to not proceed with any dismissal due to economic reasons.

It should be noted that temporary unemployment may also be granted to companies which are not part of an industry in crisis, when this company:

- faces a reduction of at least 40% of the working hours; and
- has set up either an approved plan to safeguard employment ('plan de maintien dans l'emploi'), or entered into an agreement with the employees' representatives (staff delegation, joint works council or employees).

Temporary unemployment due to structural economic difficulties ('chômage partiel pour problèmes économiques structurels')

19.40 This measure concerns companies facing economic difficulties due to reasons inherent to inappropriate internal structure.

The conditions to be met are as follows:

- it must be proven that, for each company, the decline of the activity rate on a time-period of at least six months;
- such difficulties should not have as origin a general economic recession;
- a resumption of the normal business, allowing the maintenance of the employment in a reasonable time-period, should be uncertain.

This measure is part of a plan to safeguard employment, in addition to other measures, which, if the financial situation of the company requires it, can be cumulated or applied simultaneously.

The implementation and approval of a plan to safeguard employment are the two preliminary conditions to the application of a temporary unemployment measure due to structural economic difficulties.

Prior to introducing a request for temporary unemployment due to structural economic difficulties, the company should contact the secretariat of the Economy Committee to confirm that the problems encountered are indeed structural issues and establish, upon request of the secretariat a plan to safeguard employment.

No maximum time-period to benefit from this measure is provided by the law. However, the company is to renew its request on a monthly basis.

Finally it should be noted that the company may dismiss employees during the temporary unemployment, but solely if the plan to safeguard employment provides for such dismissals.

It should be noted that temporary unemployment due to structural economic difficulties may exceed 50% of the normal monthly work, if this unemployment does not exceed, at the end of the year, ten months of contractual or legal working hours and if a plan to safeguard employment covers the whole period, for which a compensation is paid to the company.

Temporary unemployment due to economic dependency ('chômage partiel en cas de lien de dépendance économique')

19.41 This measure concerns companies facing financial difficulties following the loss of one or several important clients or due to difficulties faced by them.

Consequently, this measure usually applies to companies operating mainly for another company whose orders significantly decrease or which terminated a contract, as well as to companies working for one or several companies which themselves benefit from temporary unemployment in Luxembourg.

The conditions to be met, to benefit from the measure, are as follows:

- it must be proven that there is a significant decrease of the activity due to a proven economic dependency link towards one or several main customers;
- the company must commit to not proceed with any dismissal due to economic reasons.

The Economy Committee will investigate the balance sheets on a case by case basis and will also verify the existence of an economic dependency link.

State aid

19.42 During the application of temporary unemployment measures, the company is to pay the normal wages for the worked hours and at least 80% of the wages for the hours concerned by the temporary unemployment measures (up to 250% of the minimum legal wages, the possible surplus being supported by the company).

The State reimburses to the company 80% of the wages normally received by each employee for the hours concerned by the temporary unemployment measure. It should nevertheless be noted that if employees, during the unemployed hours, attend a continuing vocational training program, they will benefit from an indemnity for temporary unemployment of 90% of the normally paid wages.

Social and tax contributions, deriving from the wages paid to the employees for the unemployed hours, are paid by the company.

USING TEMPORARY STAFF

Agency workers

19.43 Agency workers will be hired when an employer is in need of workforce but does not want to fill in the concerned position on a permanent basis.

A contract for the provision of services is entered into between the temporary employment agency and the user company. The contract may only be concluded for the performance of a specific and temporary task and may not aim at filling in on a permanent basis a position in relation to the normal and permanent activity/business of the user company. A contract must be entered into for each employee and must contain the following particulars:

- the justification for entering into a contract for the provision of services;
- the name of the employee who is replaced, as the case may be;
- the specific features of the position to be filled in;

- the required professional qualification;
- the place of performance;
- the working schedule;
- the remuneration paid to a permanent employee employed by the user company with the same or equivalent level of qualification.

Any clause of the contract providing that the temporary agency worker may not be hired by the user company at the expiry of the assignment is null and void.

A contract of mission is entered into between the temporary employment agency and the agency worker. A contract of mission is similar to a fixed-term contract of employment. This contract is deemed to be a contract of employment. It must contain the following particulars in addition to the one applicable to fixed-term contracts:

- same as above-mentioned for the contract for the provision of services;
- date of expiration of term or minimum period of time;
- duration of probation period, if any;
- renewal clause, if any.

It must state that hiring the temporary agency worker at the expiry of the term is not prohibited.

The contract of mission is only available for a maximum period of 12 months with two renewals included.

Fixed-term contracts

19.44 The employer may enter into a fixed-term contract in respect of specific and temporary tasks. It may not aim at filling in on a permanent basis a position in relation to the normal and permanent activity/business of the employer. The Labour Code lists the cases as follows:

- the replacement of an employee temporarily absent and whose contract of employment is suspended for reasons other than a collective conflict of work or the lack of work resulting from economic causes or inclement weather, as well as the replacement of an employee under an open-ended contract whose position has become vacant until a further employee can be hired to replace the original employee on a permanent basis;
- seasonal work defined by a Grand-Ducal regulation;
- jobs for which in certain areas it is usual not to resort to a contract concluded for an indefinite period of time due to the nature of the tasks carried out or the temporary nature of the job, the list of these jobs being draw up by a Grand-Ducal regulation;
- the performance of a defined and specific task which does not form part of the normal and regular activity of the employer;
- the performance of a specific and temporary task such as is in case of temporary and exceptional increase in the company's line of business or in the case of a start-up or an extension in the size of the company;

- the performance of urgent works made necessary to prevent accidents, such as preparing for failures in equipment and organising emergency measures at company premises or buildings so as to avoid injury to the company and its staff;
- the employment of an unemployed person registered with the Administration of Employment;
- employment intended to support the recruiting of certain categories of job-seekers;
- employment where the employer commits itself to ensuring professional training for the employee.

A fixed-term contract of employment must state the following particulars:

- a definition of its object;
- the expiry date when the contract is concluded for a definite period;
- the minimum employment duration when the contract does not provide an expiry date;
- the name of the absent employee, when the contract is concluded on account of the absence of an employee;
- the duration of any probation period;
- any renewal clause.

A fixed-term contract of employment may be terminated before the expiry of its term only in the event of serious misconduct or by common consent of the parties.

In the event of termination of the fixed-term contract by the employer in breach of the statutory provisions, the employer will be liable to compensate the employee for the damages. The amounts of the damages are fixed by the Labour Code and they amount to the remuneration of the employee until the contractual date of termination of the fixed-term contract but may not exceed the amount payable as a notice period if the employee had been hired under a permanent contract. It means that the amount of the compensation may not exceed the equivalent to two months of remuneration.

Renewal of fixed-term contracts

19.45 Fixed-term contracts may be renewed but not more than twice and the total period of time may not exceed 24 months. If those provisions are not respected the contract will be considered as permanent.

EMPLOYMENT CLAIM

19.46 Employment claims are heard by the Labour Courts composed of the Employment Tribunal for the first instance and the Court of Appeal (Chamber dedicated to employee-employer disputes) for the second instance. Cases may be deferred to the Supreme Court of Justice ('Cour de Cassation') only on a question of law (for example: misinterpretation of the law by the Court of Appeal).

The Employment Tribunal hears disputes between employers and employees arising from contracts of employment, contracts of apprenticeship and complementary pension schemes, even after the termination of the contract between the parties. The action is brought by way of a written brief indicating the name, profession and domicile of the parties, as well as the object of the action and a concise account of the points of dispute. The court summons the parties to a hearing to examine the case, after which it pronounces judgment. The Labour Court usually orders compensation for damages as a result of unfair employment termination, but may order reinstatement of the employee at the employee's request, if the continuation of the contract of service is possible. Either party may file an appeal against the judgment within 40 days from the date of notification of the judgment to the parties before the Court of Appeal.

Summary proceedings may also be initiated before the President of the Employment Tribunal for any urgent matters or for claims that may not be seriously challenged. The judge pronounces an interim order. Either party may file an appeal against the order within a period of 15 days from the notification of the order to the parties.

When proceedings are filed by an employee, the case must be heard by the Employment Tribunal located in the district where the employee performs its tasks under the contract of employment, or where the employer is located if the employee performs his/her tasks in various places.

When proceedings are filed by an employer, the case must be heard by the Employment Tribunal located in the district where the employee resides. Such legal provision raises various issues as a substantial part of the workforce in Luxembourg is composed of cross-border workers commuting from France, Germany and Belgium.

UNFAIR DISMISSAL

19.47 Dismissal is regarded as being unfair if:

- the employer fails to provide the employee with detailed grounds as required by law;
- the dismissal is not founded on valid grounds related to the employee's aptitude or conduct, or arising from the operating needs of the business, establishment or department;
- the reasons are not genuine;
- the reasons are not serious enough;
- the dismissed employee was legally protected against any dismissal (during sickness leave).

If the employee challenges the reasons provided for by the employer in support of the dismissal, the onus is on the employer to prove not only the factual circumstances but, their validity and seriousness.

The employee must act within three months as follows:

- directly bring an action in court for unfair dismissal and claim compensation for damages; or
- address a written claim by registered letter to the employer within three months, claiming that the dismissal is unfair and that he reserves all his rights to claim compensation for damages. In this case, the legal timeframe to bring an action in court is extended to one further year from the date of the written claim.

The three-month period of time starts as follows:

- as of the date when the dismissal letter has been sent out when the dismissal took place for gross misconduct with immediate effect, or with notice if the employee failed to request communication of the grounds within one month following the notification of the dismissal;
- as of the date when the employer has provided the employee with the grounds of the dismissal as requested by the employee within the legal time frame, when the dismissal took place with notice;
- as of the date the employer should have replied to the employee providing him with the grounds of the dismissal, in the event the employee has formally requested communication of the grounds but the employer never replied.

Example:

The dismissal is notified on 12 September, the employee requests communication of the grounds per registered letter sent out on 8 October, and the employer never replies to this request: the employee must either bring an action in court or challenge in writing the dismissal and reserve their rights at the latest on 8 February ie three months after 8 November, expiry date for the employer to reply).

Luxembourg Labour Code does not provide for pre-determined compensation for damages. The judges in Labour Courts have the widest powers to determine at their own discretion the amount of the indemnification. However, compensation for damages is in general determined as follows:

Moral damages

19.48 In the event of unfair dismissal, the following criteria are taken into consideration to assess the amount of the damages:

- troubles raised by the dismissal,
- circumstances in which the dismissal has occurred,
- age,
- length of service.

Compensation for moral damages generally ranges between EUR 1,000 and EUR 30,000.

Financial damages

19.49 Financial damages greatly depend on the professional situation of the employee after the dismissal and are determined on a case-by-case basis by the courts. The courts take into consideration a reference period after the dismissal, which is deemed sufficient for the employee to find another job. The reference period starts at the expiry of the notice period or with the dismissal notification if the employee has been released from the obligation to work during the notice period. The compensation for financial damages is determined on the basis of the difference between the remuneration paid by the former employer and the salary or unemployment benefits paid to the employee after the expiry of the notice period. The reference period is generally set at six months and may be extended up to 12 months, depending on the age and length of service.

DISCRIMINATION

19.50 Any employee, who considers themself wronged because the principles of equal treatment have not been applied to his/her case, may bring before a court or other authority evidence of the facts from which it may be presumed that there has been direct or indirect discrimination. It shall be for the respondent to prove that there has been no breach of the principles of equal treatment.

It must be noted that employees having been subject to a reorganisational measure, do not usually challenge the measures taken against them by alleging that they have been discriminated against.

MUTUALLY AGREED TERMINATION

19.51 An employment contract (either fixed-term or indefinite) may be terminated by the parties by mutual agreement. However, the parties' consent must be stated in writing in two originals and signed by both the employer and the employee, failing which it will not be valid.

It is also common for the parties to a contract of employment to enter into a settlement agreement. A settlement agreement does however not terminate the contract of employment. It therefore means that the contract of employment must be terminated before entering into a settlement agreement, either by means of a dismissal, termination by common consent, or eventually resignation.

A settlement agreement aims at putting an end to a dispute that has arisen between the employer and the employee or at preventing a claim from arising between an employer and an employee. Such situation occurs in practice after a dismissal, where the employee challenges the grounds of the dismissal, considers the dismissal as being abusive and claims compensation for damages. In consideration of the divergences between the parties, they enter into a settlement agreement in order to avoid lengthy court proceedings and usually find a financial agreement without any recognition of liability by either side.

The settlement agreement is only valid if:

(i) it is written,
(ii) the parties have made reciprocal concessions,
(iii) the parties waive rights that had arisen.

As for the timing of entering into a settlement agreement: the parties should enter into a settlement agreement after the employer has provided the employee with the grounds, because the existence of a dispute is a condition of validity of the settlement agreement. Before the employee has had knowledge within the legal timeframe of the grounds justifying the termination, he/she may not claim that the termination is abusive (based on spurious grounds) because he/she does not know the grounds.

In practice, a settlement agreement provides that each of the parties represents that it has performed all obligations arising out of the employment contract and that it does not have any further right, action or claim, whatever legal nature and for whatever reason, against the other party in relation to the performance of the contract of employment and the termination. The parties expressly agree that with the execution of the settlement, all claims that the employee or the employer may have against each other are definitively abandoned, and that they will not start any legal action in connection with their past working relationship and the termination.

The total package that an employer should be prepared to pay generally depends on the extent of the company's exposure to damages in the event the employee is not willing to settle. The settlement indemnity is paid in addition to the statutory amounts. As for the amount of the settlement indemnity, parties usually take into consideration the age, length of service and qualification of the concerned employee to assess the amount of the settlement indemnity payable in addition to the notice pay and severance pay. It ranges from one to half a month of salary per year of length of service.

Chapter 20
Workforce Restructuring in Malta

Dr Josette Grech and Dr Mario de Marco
Guido de Marco & Associates, Valletta

INTRODUCTION

20.1 Malta is a small economy, naturally confined within the geographical limits of its two main islands: Malta and Gozo. The country depends to a large extent on Europe for its imports, exports and tourism. Its main workforce is employed in the public and private sectors, the latter principally concentrated on services and tourism.

20.2 From the 1990s, the Maltese Government has been implementing a policy of privatisation in a bid to liberalise markets and start the journey towards EU membership. This was characterised by substantial reduction in employment in the public sector and in old labour-intensive sectors such as in the clothing and textile sectors and in ship repair. Downsizing the public sector was seen as a key element of the restructuring exercise and was considered essential to encourage the private sector to evolve into a dynamic force of the economy.

20.3 Fresh challenges, triggered by competition following EU membership and further afield, continuously confront companies, necessitating an active reaction in order to secure and safeguard their competitiveness. Companies increasingly respond to the consequences of globalisation, which manifest themselves as structural changes, with operational restructuring measures taken as a result. Restructuring embraces a wide range of form with differing operations objectives such as mergers or takeovers by European or international companies, change in company domiciliation, and outsourcing and insourcing individual company functions. Most of the restructuring resulting in layoffs are generally induced either by the need to downsize the labour force, the relocation of operations and closures.

20.4 This chapter will be looking at the employment laws in Malta with particular reference to workforce restructuring. The legal system in Malta is a 'mixed' system, the product of a long evolutionary legal, political, social and constitutional process. Maltese civil law is based on a codified code deriving from the Napoleonic Code whilst commercial and criminal law are heavily based on common law. Since Malta's membership of the European Union, the legal system has been affected to a notable extent by the implementation of EU legislation.

20.5 In default of a codified employment statute book, legal sources of labour law in Malta can generally be found in primary legislation, adopted through acts of Parliament and secondary legislation consisting of subsidiary legislation enacted under primary legislation. Other important sources are found in sector- or enterprise-specific codes or agreements such as the Public Service Management Code, regulating members of the public service, and collective agreements that regulate the conditions of employment of a significant part of the gainfully employed in the private sector.

20.6 Employment law is essentially based on the contractual agreement reached between an employer and an employee. Employment in Malta is created by means of a written employment contract, although a tacit or implicit employment relationship may still be created even if there is no written employment contract. There is no absolute need for an employment contract to be written down but the employer is legally bound to detail the employment terms to the employee in writing by means of a letter of engagement or a signed statement. There is also the possibility that an individual, nominally carrying the status of self-employed, acquires a presumed status of employment on fulfilment of a number of conditions (para **20.15** below).

20.7 There are statutory conditions and minimum terms for the benefit of employees in primary and secondary legislation that must be respected. As a general rule, the conditions specified by statute are considered to be minimum conditions. For this reason, if an employment contract contains conditions which are less favourable to the employee than those stipulated in legislation, the contractual conditions will not be considered enforceable even if reached with the employees' consent, and the statutory conditions will be deemed to apply instead.

20.8 Contractual agreements generally set out all the terms governing an employment relationship that are left to the parties to agree upon, subject to the said statutory conditions and the reasonableness principle. Therefore, the assessment of employment related issues would be determined by the employment contract in the light of the statutory minimum criteria established at law.

PREPARING FOR A RESTRUCTURING EXERCISE

20.9 A restructuring exercise may prove to be a difficult time for those involved and may be a one-off exercise for an organisation but it has a lasting impact. Sound preparation, communication and sensitivity throughout are key elements for a successful restructuring process. Once the need for a restructuring exercise has been confirmed, an organisation has to analyse how it intends to restructure and reorganise itself to pull itself of financial distress that may have led to such restructuring exercise.

20.10 In the case of workforce planning and restructuring, the organisation may plan to reduce the workforce, change terms and conditions including wages and organisation of working hours, outsourcing and reassignment of duties of the employees.

20.11 The primary objective of workforce restructuring is to identify which employees are to be retained within the parameters necessary to effectively meet assigned and future missions of the company within budget constraints. Restructuring strategies must be closely integrated with planning based on identified workforce requirements.

20.12 Employees in the pool for selection will be identified on the basis of whether their role will no longer exist in the new structure and/or where the corresponding new role is substantially different to the individuals' current role. This necessarily requires the collation of data relating to the job description in respect of any employee potentially impacted by a workforce restructuring exercise. The contractual terms and conditions and any applicable collective agreement are important elements to consider and follow in a restructuring exercise. In the event that the individual is employed without a written contract of employment, the employer must verify the letter of engagement or signed statement detailing the employment terms of the employee. The letter of engagement or the signed statement are a requirement imposed by Information to Employees the Regulations (Legal Notice 431 of 2002) (IER 2002).

EMPLOYMENT STATUS

20.13 Only individuals, who fall under the legal definition of 'employee', are protected under employment law and would be potentially affected in a workforce restructuring purposes. Section 2 of the Employment and Industrial Relations Act, 2002 (chapter 452 of the Laws of Malta) ('the Act'), which is the primary legislation regulating employment law in Malta, defines the term 'employee' as follows:

> 'any person who has entered into or works under a contract of service, or any person who has undertaken personally to execute any work or service for, and under the immediate direction and control of another person, including

an outworker, but excluding work or service performed in a professional capacity or as a contractor for another person when such work or service is not regulated by a specific contract of service'.

20.14 As indicated in the introduction, employment is generally created by means of an employment contract, which can be in writing or tacit. There is also the possibility that a person nominally carries the status of self-employed but is, by virtue of the law, considered to have employment status. A presumed status of employment for individuals whose employment status is nominally that of self-employed is regulated by virtue of the employment status national standard order (Legal Notice 44 of 2012). If five of the following eight conditions are met the individual will be considered to be an employee:

(i) the individual derives at least 75% of his or her income for the year from one source;
(ii) the type and volume of work required are determined by the person to whom the service is provided;
(iii) the tools, equipment and materials required for the work are provided by the person receiving the service;
(iv) the individual is subject to work-time schedules or minimum work periods which are set by the person receiving the service;
(v) the individual cannot sub-contract his or her work to other individuals to act in place of him- or herself when carrying out work;
(vi) he or she is integrated in the structure of the production process, the work organisation or the company's or other organisation's hierarchy;
(vii) the person's activity is a core element in the organisation and of the objectives of the person for whom the service is provided; and
(viii) the individual carries out similar tasks to those of existing employees, or, where work is outsourced, he or she performs tasks similar to those formerly undertaken by employees.

GENERAL PROTECTION AGAINST DISMISSAL

20.15 Dismissal can occur at any time during the term of an indefinite as well as a fixed term contract of employment. The right of an employee not to be unfairly dismissed is statutory and laid down under Maltese law. Unfair dismissal in relation to a worker results when, in the case of an contract of indefinite duration, the employer terminates employment (other than probationary employment) for reasons made solely on the grounds of redundancy, or not for a good and sufficient cause, or which, though made on grounds of redundancy or for a good and sufficient cause, is discriminatory and includes any failure by the employer to re-employ such person when so obliged by law.

20.16 For this reason, from one perspective both the employer and the employer are at liberty to terminate an indefinite employment relationship, subject to notice being given, a termination at the instance of the employer cannot be *ad nutum* but solely based on redundancy, in which case notice is required, or just and sufficient cause, in which case notice is not necessarily required. Although all employees enjoy a minimum notice period by law depending on length of service and, in addition, an employer may be contractually entitled to terminate an employment relationship in line with notice periods set out in the contract of employment, the statutory right of employees not to be unfairly dismissed supersedes, to the extent that the entitlement to notice takes on secondary importance. This is not to say that the contract of employment cannot be terminated summarily. Any type of contract can be terminated summarily and without the need to give any notice to the employee, if good and sufficient cause exists.

SPECIAL PROTECTION AGAINST DISMISSAL

20.17 The test therefore rests on what 'good and sufficient cause' means. Maltese law does not provide an adequate definition or a list of what constitutes 'good and sufficient cause' and therefore the interpretation of the term rests with the Industrial Tribunal set up under the Employment and Industrial Relations Act dealing with a claim of unfair dismissal. Nonetheless it has been established that the cause must be such as to strike at the heart of the relationship and, if not preceded by warnings, be of sufficient gravity to justify summary dismissal.

20.18 On the other hand, Maltese law does include a list of causes that would not be considered as good and sufficient. Thus, under the Employment and Industrial Relations Act, the following are not good and sufficient causes and would therefore constitute automatic unfair dismissal:

- if the employee discloses information, whether confidential or otherwise, to a designated public regulating body regarding alleged unlawful or corrupt activities being committed by his or her employer or by persons acting in the employer's name and interests;
- if the employee at the time of the dismissal was a member of a trade union, or is seeking office as, or is acting or has acted in the capacity of an employees' representative;
- except in the case of a private domestic employee, that the employee no longer enjoys the employer's confidence;
- if the employee marries;
- if an employee is pregnant or is absent from work during maternity leave;
- if the employee has filed a complaint or is participating in proceedings against the employer involving alleged violation of laws or regulations or is having recourse to competent administrative authorities; and
- if the business in which the employee is engaged has undergone a transfer of ownership, unless the employer proves that the termination is necessary for economic, technical or organisational reasons entailing changes in the workforce.

20.19 All of the above are not good causes for termination in themselves, though it may be argued that they are if there is abuse or special circumstances warranting dismissal.

20.20 Good and sufficient cause may arise in the case of proven or actual theft, violence, warnings of poor performance, abuse of sick leave, refusal to obey orders, repeated minor offences or when retirement age is reached.

20.21 The right against unfair dismissal is, however, subject to qualifying conditions and certain exceptions:

(a) Employees who are in their probationary period may not bring an unfair dismissal claim. The first six months of employment constitute probation unless a shorter period has been agreed between the parties. In the case of a contract of service or collective agreement in respect of employees holding technical, executive, administrative or managerial posts and whose wages are at least double the minimum wage established in that year, such probation period is of one year unless otherwise specified in the contract of service or in the collective agreement. Probationary employment may be terminated at will by either party (employer or employee) without stating a reason, provided that a week's notice of the termination of employment is to be given to the other party in the case of an employee who is still in the probationary period but who has been in the employment of the same employer continuously for more than one month. This does not apply in the case of pregnant employees during probation. In such cases, the employer will be obliged to give the employee the reasons in writing, and show that the dismissal is unrelated to the employee's condition.

(b) Employees over retirement age may not bring an unfair dismissal claim and employers may dismiss an employee upon reaching retirement age. Retirement age varies depending on the date of birth of the particular employee. Pension age has seen gradual increases for those who were born after 1952.

(c) Redundancy may potentially constitute a just cause for the employer to terminate the employee's contract of employment as long as the dismissal is wholly or mainly attributable to redundancy. This is particularly relevant in unfair dismissal claims where an employee may allege that the real reason was not redundancy but some other reason.

WORKFORCE REDUCTION

20.22 While the decision to restructure a workface represents an expression of the liberty of economic initiative adopted by employers, the employer must prepare itself to demonstrate and substantiate the reasons behind a redundancy, both from a business as well as organisational perspective. Faced with a complaint by an aggrieved employee, whose employment was terminated on grounds of redundancy, the Industrial Tribunal will verify and ascertain whether the termination of the employment for the reason provided by the employer, was a genuine case of redundancy in terms of law or whether such proposed reason was masking a case of plain dismissal.

20.23 Undoubtedly, in the event that an employer needs to reduce its workforce as a result of a restructuring exercise, the primary obligation is a formal and procedural one in the sense that the employer must communicate to the employee concerned the reason for termination. Additionally, companies that plan to carry out collective redundancies are required to follow the information and consultancy procedures laid down by law (see paras **20.52ff** below).

Definition of redundancy

20.24 There is no statutory definition of redundancy under Maltese law but case law and practice provides a good basis of outlining what redundancy entails. Generally speaking, redundancy refers to a situation whether an enterprise needs to reduce its workforce due to its financial situation. A situation of financial difficulties however is not the only trigger that leads to redundancy. Case law indicates that redundancy can also occur as a result of re-engineering, technological development or change in the work methodology, or for reasons of marketing a reduction of workforce would be necessitated. Case law also establishes that there is a fine balance between the right of an enterprise to regulate the amount of employees necessary for its business operations and the right of the employee not to be unilaterally terminated from its employment.

20.25 It has been established by local jurisprudence, based also on English case law, that the three questions to be positively answered by an employer to prove a case of redundancy are the following:

(a) Was the employee dismissed?
(b) If so, had the requirements of the business for employees to carry out work of a particular kind ceased or diminished (or were they expected to do so)?
(c) If so, was the dismissal caused wholly or mainly by that state of affairs?

In relation to the crucial question in (b) above and in determining whether there is a cessation or diminution of the tasks carried out by the concerned employee, case law suggests that one must not consider only the specific tasks that the concerned employee was performing. The employer must prove that the reason advanced by it for the termination of an employment relationship is genuine, and that the re-employment of the terminated employee under the specific contract tasks or under a diverse, though equivalent, dimension is not possible, considering the re-organisation of the structure under which the employer operates.

20.26 In the case of outsourcing of work, the employer must assess whether the outsourcing exercise will fall to be regulated by the Transfer of Business

(Protection of Employment) Regulations of 2002 (Legal Notice 433 of 2002) which implement Council Directive 2001/23/EC and offer protection to employees in the event that there is a transfer of business by the employer to a new owner (see paras **20.86ff** below).

DISMISSALS ON GROUNDS OF REDUNDANCY

20.27 When companies are planning to dismiss employees on grounds of redundancy they must have regard to how many dismissed employees the exercise of restructuring will entail. This is required in view of the fact that that the collective redundancies (protection of employment) regulations, Legal Notice 428 of 2002, come into play.

Individual redundancy procedure

20.28 As opposed to collective redundancy procedures, there is no established procedure set down by law in relation to individual redundancies with the 'last-in first-out' principle prescribed by section 36(4) of the Employment and Industrial Relations Act, and the re-employment requirement are the only guidelines to go by.

DEFINING THE SELECTION POOL

20.29 Nonetheless, the employer must ensure they have a fair procedure in place once the route of redundancy has been decided. At the outset, the employer must determine the class of employment affected by the redundancy procedure. Identification of the selection pool may be straightforward where there is an entire business or workplace closure contemplated. If the intention is to dismiss one or more employees executing particular tasks, the exercise may be harder.

20.30 In the definition of 'class of employment', the Act states that 'class' when used in the context of a group or a category of employees shall refer to the groups or categories listed in a collective agreement, provided that where there is no collective agreement or where a collective agreement does not stipulate groups or categories of employees, it shall refer to the work performed or expected to be performed independently of the title or name given to the post. An important criterion for the selection of the relevant pool and the delineation of different or similar classes of employment in the context of redundancy is the interchangeability of jobs. Therefore, identifying the relevant pool from which the redundant employees are to be chosen, may not be an easy exercise but in order to comply with the law, the employer cannot be too restrictive in its interpretation of the specific contract tasks where jobs are relatively easily transferable.

> **Example**
>
> Jane Smith had been employed as a teacher with St Paul High School for 37 years. The school terminated her employment on grounds of redundancy claiming that because of a reduction in work due to the diminishing number of students attending the school, it was constrained to terminate the employee on the basis of redundancy. The school then offered the employee an alternative position that would have meant a change in the conditions of her employment, from full-time basis to part-time. The school had however engaged another teacher on a full-time basis and the employee claimed that the said teacher should have been terminated first on the basis of the last in first out principle.
>
> In interpreting the class of employment affected by the redundancy, the fact that the redundant teacher at time of dismissal was teaching a subject which the school was no longer offering to students or there were no students choosing that subject, does not necessarily mean that the class of employment affected by the redundancy are teachers teaching that particular subject. To this extent, the fact that the redundant teacher, at intervals during her years of service, taught other subjects, relieved other teachers for lessons in other subjects, or replaced other teachers in different subject when teachers were on leave or sick leave, meant that the class of employment was not restricted to teachers of that particular subject primarily taught by the redundant employee.

SELECTION CRITERIA

20.31 The employer then needs to identify the number of employees within that class to be made redundant. As previously hinted, the law does not set down any selection criteria except for the last-in first-out principle. Section 36(4) of the Act lays down the rule as to the sequence in which employees may be identified as redundant, and states that:

> '[w]here an employer intends to terminate the employment of an employee on grounds on redundancy, he shall terminate the employment of that person who was engaged last in the class of employment affected by such redundancy'.

20.32 Applying this principle will necessarily entail that the employer identifies from the selected pool the individual who has been last employed. The selection on the last-in first-out principle is qualified in cases where the employer is related to the employee. In cases where the selection process identifies an employee as eligible for dismissal on the grounds of redundancy who is related to the employer (not being a limited liability company or a statutory body) by consanguinity or affinity up to the third degree, the employer may, instead of terminating the employment of such person, terminate that of the person next in turn.

20.33 If the employer deviates from this rule, the termination of employment for reasons of redundancy may be found to be invalid by the Industrial Tribunal, and compensation or re-instatement of the employee may be ordered.

20.34 Upon identification of this individual on the basis of the above criteria, the entitlement to notice kicks in together with any contractual redundancy payments that are in place. A contract of service for an indefinite time may be terminated, by giving either the statutory minimum notice or the contractually agreed longer notice period by the employer on grounds of redundancy.

20.35 Even if an employer complies with a fair redundancy process, the dismissal of an employee may still be discriminatory or unfair. A discriminatory redundancy process may be fair throughout but end unfairly. Such a situation may arise where the affected employees holding a relatively similar situation are treated differently when it comes, for instance, to the amount of termination compensation paid out by the employer. The legal principle upheld by case law is that the method of computation of compensation must be the same in the case of all employees who are being made redundant.

REINSTATEMENT

20.36 Once an employee has been dismissed on the grounds of redundancy and the employee does not challenge such termination, the employer is still duty bound to ensure the re-employment of the redundant employee if the post formerly occupied by the employee is again available within a period of one year from the date of termination of employment. It is a legal requirement that such re-employment is at conditions no less favourable than those to which the re-employed employee would have been entitled if the contract of employment had not been terminated.

20.37 In cases of a transfer of business, the reinstatement rule also extends to the transferee. Employees who were employed in the business or part of the business to be transferred have been made redundant prior to a transfer of business which would have otherwise resulted in the transfer of their employment with the transferee, the transferee has an obligation to re-employ, with the same conditions of employment, such employees if their previous posts become available within one year from the notice of redundancy.

20.38 In cases of collective or group redundancies, the offer of employment should be given in the reverse order that the employee were made redundant, so that the employee with the most years of service with the employer is offered the job first.

20.39 Furthermore, re-employment after dismissal on the basis of redundancy is not considered at law as a fresh employment but the employee who is so employed will, for the purposes of law, be considered to have continued in the previous employment notwithstanding the termination and notwithstanding the lapse of time in which the employee was not reporting for work.

Information and consultation

20.40 Subsidiary legislation has been adopted under the Act to establish a general framework setting out minimum requirements for the right to information and consultation of employees in undertakings, giving into effect the relevant provisions of Directive 2002/14/EC of the European Parliament and of the Council of the 11 March 2002. Although the Employee (Information and Consultation) Regulations (Legal Notice 10 of 2006) are not specific to individual redundancies, the employer is in all cases under a general duty to allow his employees to effectively exercise the right to information and consultation.

20.41 Furthermore, the employer is obliged by law to provide employees or employee representatives with information and to conduct with them a consultation process in specific and limited circumstances. The information and consultation process will involve:

(a) the recent and probable development of the undertaking's activities and economic situation;
(b) the situation, structure and probable development of employment within the undertaking and on any anticipatory measures envisaged, in particular, where there is a threat to employment within the undertaking; and
(c) information and consultation on decisions likely to lead to substantial changes in work organisation or in contractual relations.

20.42 The said information must be given at such time, in such fashion and with such content as are appropriate to enable, in particular, the information and consultation representatives to conduct an adequate study and, where necessary, to prepare for consultation. Besides the information requirement, the employer must also ensure that consultation is conducted in such a way as to ensure that the timing, method and content of the consultation are appropriate;

INVOLVEMENT OF EMPLOYEE REPRESENTATIVES IN INDIVIDUAL DISMISSALS

20.43 The involvement of the information and consultation representatives of employees is either on a trade union level or at employee representative level or both. In the case of undertakings where there is one or more recognised trade union covering all categories of employees, the information and consultation is carried out at trade union level. Where the recognised trade union or unions do not represent all categories of employees, the involvement is with the representative of the recognised trade union or unions, together with the elected or appointed representatives of the workers in the unrepresented categories.

AVOIDING COMPULSORY REDUNDANCIES

20.44 It is good practice that employers, as far as is reasonably possible, take steps to avoid compulsory redundancies. This could be achieved, after an economical and organisational analysis is carried out within the undertaking as part of its restructuring process, by seeking applicants for voluntary redundancy or early retirement, seeking applications from existing staff to work flexibly, terminating self-employed contractors, freelancers and service providers, restricting recruitment, reducing or banning overtime, filling vacancies elsewhere in the business with existing employees, or temporary lay-offs.

20.45 In exceptional circumstances, an employer, in agreement with the employee or union representatives, may provide for different conditions of employment that those specified as a minimum under the Act as long as such agreement is a temporary measure to avoid redundancies and as long as it is approved by the Director of Employment and Industrial Relations, which approval needs to be reviewed every four weeks. This tight control on the application of less favourable conditions to employees that those provided for by law is a recognition of the principle, enshrined in the Act, that if a contract of service between an employee and the employer or a collective agreement entered into between the employer and the recognised union representatives provides for any conditions of employment, including conditions relating to the termination of the contract, less favourable to the employee that those established under the Act, the latter conditions shall have effect such that those conditions less favourable to the employee are substituted with the conditions specified under the Act.

20.46 These alternative solutions to outright terminations on grounds of redundancy are not obligatory, unless stipulated in applicable collective agreements or in contractual redundancy procedures. In such situations, the employee must be made aware of the consequences and acknowledges in writing by way of acceptance or laid down in a compromise agreement.

ALTERNATIVE EMPLOYMENT

20.47 It is also good practice, unless specifically required in a collective agreement or in contractually agreed redundancy procedures, that an employer searches for and, where possible, offers the selected employee alternative employment within the undertaking. With regard to this, the Industrial Tribunal has ruled that it is important that, if and where possible, the employee is offered alternative employment prior to being made redundant. In making such an offer, the employee is typically made aware of what the alternative employment entails and whether there are any changes in employment conditions.

20.48 Although the law is silent in relation to alternative employment offers to employees who return to work after maternity or parental leave, recent rulings of the Court of Justice of the European Union confirm that employers are not able to penalise workers who have taken parental leave when selecting for redundancy. Where a much higher number of women than men take parental leave, any redundancy assessment should cover all staff affected by the changes and identical assessment criteria for all staff are to be used. Employers may dismiss employees who have taken parental leave, as long as they are not dismissed for applying for or taking such leave. It would be unlawful for an employer to transfer an employee who has taken parental leave into a post which it knows is to be abolished. An employer may, in the context of a redundancy situation, proceed with the assessment of a worker who has taken parental leave with a view to transferring that worker to an equivalent or similar post. In addition, an employee who has taken a period of parental leave is entitled to return to the job in which they were employed before their absence or, if this is not reasonably practicable, to another job which is both suitable and appropriate for them to do in the circumstance.

20.49 An employee selected for redundancy following a period of parental leave must be offered a legitimate alternative role within the organisation where it is practical and appropriate to do so.

20.50 As regards those dismissed during injury or maternity leave, the Industrial Tribunal has made it clear that such employees may not be made redundant.

Collective redundancy procedure

20.51 In terms of the Collective Redundancies (Protection of Employment) Regulations 2002 (Legal Notice 428 of 2002), collective redundancy is defined as:

> 'the termination of the employment by an employer on grounds of redundancy, over a period of 30 days, of 10 or more employees in establishments normally employing more than 20 employees but less than 100 employees; or 10% or more of the number of employees in establishments employing 100 or more but less than 300 employees and 30 employees or more in establishments employing more than 300 employees'.

For the purposes of calculating the number of redundancies, termination of an employment contract which occurs on the employer's initiative for one or more reasons which are beyond the control of the individual employees will be assimilated to redundancies, provided that there are at least five redundancies.

20.52 Excluded from the scope of these Regulations are terminations of employment effected under contracts of employment concluded for limited periods of time or for specific tasks, except where such terminations take place prior to their expiry date or the completion of such tasks and the reason for such prior termination is the redundancy of the employees so terminated. Excluded also are persons employed on ships.

20.53 In a collective redundancy situation, the employer has a duty to inform and consult employee representatives within the established timeframes. Where there is a collective redundancy, the employer must also notify the Director responsible for Employment and Industrial Relations (DEIR).

INVOLVEMENT OF EMPLOYEE REPRESENTATIVES IN COLLECTIVE DISMISSALS

20.54 In any restructuring exercise it is essential to establish the identity of the employees' information and consultation representatives. In terms of the Act, 'employees' representatives' for the purposes of collective redundancies means the recognised union representatives and, where there exists no recognised union, the term refers to such representatives of the union representing the employees and in case of non-unionised employees, the term refers to such representatives duly elected from amongst the non-unionised employees, by means of secret ballot called for such purpose by the employer.

20.55 In particular employees' representatives are identified on the basis of the following guidelines:-

(a) the representatives of the recognised trade union or unions, in the case of undertakings where there is one or more recognised trade union covering all categories of employees;
(b) the representatives of the recognised trade union or unions, together with the elected or appointed representatives of the workers in the unrepresented categories, in the case of undertakings where the recognised trade union or unions do not represent all categories of employees.
(c) the representatives of the employees elected or appointed from amongst all employees, in the case where there is no recognised trade union, provided that, if the category or categories of employees who were previously unrepresented by a recognised trade union start being represented by a recognised trade union, the term of office of any appointment or election of information and consultation representatives elected or appointed on behalf of such category or categories is automatically terminated on the date of the granting of recognition of the respective category of employees to the trade union concerned by the employer.

20.56 The information and consultation representatives are elected or appointed by the employees. The employer must make the necessary arrangements for such appointment. There are statutory rules for the election of employee representatives.

ELECTION OF EMPLOYEE REPRESENTATIVES FOR COLLECTIVE CONSULTATION PURPOSES

20.57 The employer must ensure that arrangements are made for the nomination of candidates and for a fair election based on secret ballot. To ensure that this process is above board, the employer is required to supply the DEIR with the procedure to be followed at least one month before the projected date of the ballot.

20.58 Eligible to vote are all employees employed by the undertaking on the date of the ballot. The voting itself must take place, as far as is reasonably practicable, in secret. Once voting is over, the votes given at the ballot must be accurately counted. Eligible to stand as candidate for the appointment of representative in a particular ballot are all employees, namely any employee who is not on probation at the date of the holding of the ballot. In the event that only one candidate presents for the nomination of representative at the end of the period allowed for the submission of nominations, such employee shall be considered to be automatically elected and shall be appointed as representative from the date of the end of the period set by the employer for the submission of such nominations. In the event that no employee submits a nomination for candidature, the employer has the duty to inform the employees, at three month intervals from the initial call, of their right to have a representative to be informed and consulted and to invite them to submit nominations for candidatures to take part in such a ballot within two weeks from the date of such communication.

20.59 Once the election has taken place, the employer is duty bound to inform the employees in writing of the identity of the representative. Elected representatives hold office for a period of three years from their date of election or appointment. Dismissing employee representatives on grounds related to the fact that the employees were representatives or put themselves forward as candidates will automatically constitute unfair dismissals.

NOTIFICATION, INFORMATION AND CONSULTATION REQUIREMENTS

20.60 At the outset of a collective redundancy process, the employer proposing to declare the redundancies is obliged to send a written notification to the employees' representatives, of the contemplated termination of employment.

20.61 Additionally, during the information stage, the employer must provide a statement in writing containing all relevant information to the trade union/employee representatives which must necessarily include the following minimum information:

(a) the reasons for the redundancies,
(b) the number of employees intended for redundancy,
(c) the number of employees normally employed by the employer,
(d) the criteria proposed for the selection of the employees to be made redundant,
(e) details regarding any redundancy payments which are due, and
(f) the period over which redundancies are to be effected.

20.62 The consultation stage commences within a stipulated timeframe. The employer must begin consultation with the employees' representative within seven working days from the day on which the employees' representatives have been notified of the intended collective redundancies.

20.63 The consultation exercise is intended by law to cover ways and means of avoiding the collective redundancies or reducing the number of employees affected by such redundancies and for mitigating the consequences thereof.

20.64 Before these two requirements of information and consultation are fulfilled, the employer proposing to declare the redundancies, cannot terminate the employment of affected employees.

REGULATORY REQUIREMENTS

20.65 Where an employer proposes to make a collective redundancy, a copy of the written notification wherein the employer proposed the redundancies as well as a copy of the written statement setting out the information regarding the redundancies must be forwarded to the DEIR on the same day that it is notified to the employees' representatives.

20.66 Any projected collective redundancies notified to the Director responsible for Employment and Industrial Relations can only take effect after a period of 30 days following the notification of the collective redundancy to the Director. Once the Director has received such a notice, the Director may shorten or extend in exceptional circumstances. DEIR may opt to grant the employer a shorter period within which to make redundancies or lengthen the period of 30 days by adding a further period of 30 days, for a total of 60 days. This extension is granted if the DEIR deems that it will provide further opportunity for the resolution of the reasons for the redundancies or for the identification of solutions to the benefit of those employees contemplated for redundancy.

SANCTIONS

20.67 Non-observance of the Collective Redundancies Regulations including the provisions relating to the information and consultation requirements are tantamount to an offence. The DEIR may prosecute such offences, which are punishable with a fine set at a minimum of €1,164.69 for every employee who is declared redundant. In the event that there are breaches of the information, consultation and notification requirements, the employer can face proceedings in which, on conviction, be liable to a fine of not less than €23.29 for every employee of the undertaking. During such proceedings, the employer cannot raise the defence that the necessary information had not been provided to the employer by the undertaking which took the decision leading to the collective redundancies. In fact, the obligations of the notification, information and consultation apply to the employer irrespective of whether the decision regarding collective redundancies is taken by the employer or the undertaking controlling the employer.

NOTICE

20.68 Employment contracts of an indefinite duration typically provide for the contractual notice period agreed between the parties. The notice period refers to the period of time a party to an employment contract must allow to the other before actually terminating an employment relationship.

Minimum notice period

20.69 In the case of contracts of indefinite duration, the notice period depends on the employee's continuous length of service with his or her employer. The notice periods are laid down by law as follows:

Length of service	Notice period
More than 1 month but not more than 6 months	1 week
More than 6 months but not more than 2 years	2 weeks
More than 2 years but not more than 4 years	4 weeks
More than 4 years but not more than 7 years	8 weeks
More than 7 years but not more than 8 years	9 weeks
More than 8 years but not more than 9 years	10 weeks
More than 9 years but not more than 10 years	11 weeks
More than 10 years	12 weeks

Longer periods may be agreed between the employer and employee in the case of technical, administrative, executive or managerial posts. Note that the established periods of notice cannot otherwise be extended and apply irrespective of an agreement to the contrary reached contractually between an employer and an employee.

20.70 Although the notice period is intended to be worked, both the employer and the employee have a right to terminate the employment relationship ahead of the expiry of the notice.

Pay in lieu of notice

20.71 Employments of an indefinite duration can be terminated effectively with a payment in lieu of notice.

20.72 If the employee chooses to cease work immediately on receiving notice, the employer is obliged to pay the employee a sum equal to half the wages that would be payable in respect of the unexpired period of notice. If, on the other hand, the employee chooses to continue at work until the period of notice expires but the employer precludes him or her from so doing, the employer would be obliged to pay the employee a sum equal to full wages that would be payable in respect of the unexpired period of notice.

20.73 If the employee ceases to perform work during the notice period that he or she has given to the employer, the employee is obliged to pay his or her employer a sum equal to half the wages that would be payable in respect of the unexpired period of notice. If the employee fails to give notice, he or she shall be liable to pay to the employer a sum equal to half the wages that would be payable in respect of the period of notice.

20.74 In the case of contracts of definite duration or for a specified time, the situation is different. Typically, such contracts do not incorporate a notice clause nor are the statutory notice periods made to apply to contracts of definite duration. To this extent, this type of employment contracts are deemed to be subject to earlier termination only where there is good and sufficient cause, in which case the employer is not bound to give notice nor to pay the employee in lieu of notice. On the other hand, jurisprudence indicates that where the reason for termination of a fixed term contract is redundancy, this does not equate to good and sufficient cause and whilst the employer is entitled to terminate the employment during the period of the fixed term contract on grounds of redundancy, the employer would be liable to pay the employee a sum equal to one-half of the full wages that would have accrued to the employee in respect of the remainder of the time contractually agreed.

REDUNDANCY PAYMENTS

20.75 In cases of redundancy, as we have seen, an employer is obliged to observe the statutory or contractually agreed notice period and outstanding pay holiday allowance for accrued vacation. There are no statutory termination benefits or payments for dismissals under Maltese law.

20.76 Nonetheless, redundancy payments may be payable under contract or collective agreement.

Post-termination restrictive covenants

20.77 Maltese law does not contain specific statutory provisions in relation to post-termination restrictive covenants. Therefore, recourse must be had to recent jurisprudence that has delved into the various aspects relevant to the examination of these clauses. Although in Malta there is no doctrine of judicial precedent, in areas where the law is not sufficiently clear, jurisprudence offers a good source as to the obtaining situation with regards to such matters.

20.78 Restraint of trade clauses are generally not accepted insofar as they are intended to restrict the activities that an employee may carry out after the termination of the employment. Insofar as these covenants prevent an individual from engaging in an activity which might potentially prove to be prejudicial to the interests of an ex-employer, they could effectively bar the individual from exercising his profession or trade or employing his expertise and experience to his/her own benefit. In truth, an employee is entitled to terminate the employment relationship and the employee is free to compete thereafter with the former employer.

20.79 The restrictive covenants can be stipulated for a legitimate reason such as to prevent the ex-employee from disclosing trade secrets which he would have got to know about through his employment, particularly where the ex-employee held a position of trust. The situation in this regard is delicate in the sense that a balance has to be struck between the rights of the employer to safeguard his commercial interests and the rights of the employee to pursue his career.

20.80 The requirements that are mandatory if any clause in restraint of trade is to be regarded as enforceable by the court are the following: the clause has to be in writing; there has to be a quid pro quo in favour of the employee; and to this extent adequate measures have to be out in place not only to safeguard the interests of the employer but also the interests of the employee. Failing this test may lead to a court ruling against the restraint. Its limits have to be certain as regards object, time and place. Where the restrictive covenant is such as to limit the working activity of an individual it must be for a determined period of time, which is limited and not unreasonable. In relation to restraint of trade limited in space, regard must be given to the fact that if the clause refers to Malta which is a relatively small island and for this reason, it would not be reasonable to expect the employee to leave his/her country of residence in order to find suitable employment elsewhere. In essence, the test to be carried out here is basically one of reasonableness. The restraint would also be assessed in relation to the nature of the role formerly occupied by the ex-employee, with the restraint being seen as more reasonable in situations where the ex-employee held a high ranking position or otherwise a position of trust.

20.81 One cannot reasonably expect the courts to uphold a manifestly unreasonable clause. It may safely be asserted that clauses in restraint of trade may be impugned under section 985 of the Civil Code which provides that things which are impossible, or prohibited by law, or contrary to morality, or to public policy, may not be the subject matter of a contract.

20.82 In relation to solicitation of existing customers of the employer, an employer is generally speaking entitled to have a limited protection against an ex-employee dealing with existing customers given that direct solicitation of existing customers is deemed to traverse the boundary of acceptable conduct. A covenant can restrict the right to solicit or endeavour to entice away former customers, or to have post-employment dealings with such customers in such a way as to prevent the misuse by the ex-employee of his acquaintance with the employer's clients or customers. Yet, it is likely that such clauses would be acceptable if limited to customers with whom the ex-employee had some dealings as otherwise, the clause can be interpreted as being in restraint of competition.

20.83 In relation to the solicitation or enticement of other employees to terminate their employment with their employer, it is likely that such a covenant would not be accepted as valid on the basis of the recognised right of an individual to work for any employer who is willing to employ the individual. To this extent, a restriction that prevents a person from poaching employees irrespective of their expertise, technical knowledge would be viewed as a restriction against competition.

20.84 In the event that a restrictive covenant is deemed invalid by a court of law, the relevant clause will be held to be unenforceable. For this reason, in drafting a restraint of trade clause, the interest to be protected must be legitimate and well defined and the restraint limited to the protection of that interest. The geographic area covered by the restraint should be limited to that necessary to protect the identified interest and the longer the duration of the restriction, the less likely the courts are to find it reasonable. What is or is not reasonable is considered in the light of the interest to be protected.

BUSINESS SALE, OUTSOURCING/INSOURCING AND OFFSHORING

20.85 The legislation applicable to the various forms of transfer of business in Malta is the Employment and Industrial Relations Act and the Transfer of Business (Protection of Employees) Regulations (Legal Notice 433 of 2002) which implement Council Directive 2001/23/EC ('TUPE'). The previously weak position of employees in the context of a sale of a business was substantially changed as a result of these Regulations.

20.86 When deciding on a transfer or acquisition of an undertaking, business or part there, or when deciding to subcontract an activity or take over an activity previously carried out by a client or another subcontractor, it is important to establish whether such transaction falls to be regulated by TUPE.

20.87 Key consequences of TUPE applying are:

- automatic transfers of employment together with the terms and conditions and collective agreements of those employees transferred such that the contract of employment of each person employed by the transferor shall have effect as if originally made between the person so employed and the transferee and all the transferor's rights, powers, obligations and liabilities in connection with the said contracts of employment are transferred to the transferee.
- special protection against dismissal in connection with the business transfer; and
- mandatory information and consultation requirements, including informing and consulting workers' representatives about the transfer.

Business sale

20.88 A transfer that falls to be governed by TUPE refers to transfer, in whole or in part of an undertaking or economic entity or business which retains its identity as an organised group of resources having the objective of pursuing an economic activity.

20.89 Essentially, in order for there to be a transfer of undertaking in terms of law, the recurrence of two elements is required: (i) the continuation of the business or activity as an economic activity; and (ii) the substitution of the person operating the said business or activity. The transfer of assets, whether capital or otherwise, is not a pre-requisite for the occurrence of a transfer falling under TUPE.

20.90 TUPE does not apply to any transfer of an undertaking, business or part of an undertaking or business where the transferor is the subject of bankruptcy proceedings or in a winding up by the court or other insolvency proceedings which have been instituted with a view to the liquidation of the assets of the transferor and are under the supervision of a court appointed liquidator. TUPE does not apply either in cases of administrative reorganisation of public administrative authorities or the transfer of administrative functions between public administrative authorities.

Outsourcing/insourcing

20.91 Outsourcing/insourcing may constitute a 'service provision change', which by virtue of amendments made in 2012, falls to be governed by TUPE. TUPE regulations cover those situations involving 'service provision changes' which essentially refer to situations in which activities cease to be carried out by an undertaking on its own behalf, or a contractor on behalf of an undertaking and are taken over by a contractor/a subsequent contractor on behalf of the undertaking or the undertaking itself, as the case may be.

Effect of TUPE

Automatic transfer and protection of employment

20.92 Following a transfer, the contract of employment of each person employed by the transferor has effect as if originally made between the person so employed and the transferee. In consequence of this, all the transferor's rights, powers, obligations and liabilities under or in connection with any contract of employment are transferred to the transferee.

20.93 The transferor remains civilly liable to reimburse the transferee for the payment of any statutory bonuses and income supplements in terms of law which relate to the period in employment with the transferor but payment of which becomes due on a date when the employee is employed by the transferee, and payment for the pro rata annual leave entitlement not availed of during employment with the transferor in respect of the period during which the transferor was the employer, whilst the transferor shall have the civil right to be reimbursed by the transferee in respect of any annual leave which had been granted to the employee by the transferor prior to the date of transfer which was in excess of the pro rata entitlement of annual leave till the date of transfer.

Objection to the transfer

20.94 TUPE do not stipulate the need of employees or their representatives to agree to the transfer. The only entitlement that employees and/or their representatives have under TUPE is the right to be consulted. There is no provision at law that entitles the employees to object to a transfer.

Protection from dismissal

20.95 The transfer of the undertaking, business or part of the undertaking or business shall not in itself constitute sufficient grounds for dismissal of employees by the transferor or the transferee. However, termination of employment can be justified for economic, technical or organisational reasons entailing changes in the workforce.

Protection of terms and conditions of employment

20.96 The terms and conditions agreed contractually between the transferor and the transferred employee must be respected by the transferor. Similarly, the terms and conditions agreed in any collective agreement covering the transferred employee must be observed by the transferee until the date of termination or expiry of the collective agreement or the entry into force or application of another collective agreement. Whenever a transfer involves a substantial change in working conditions to the detriment of the employee and this results in the termination of the contract of employment, the employer is regarded as having been responsible for such a termination.

20.97 Furthermore, the employees' right to old age, invalidity or survivors' benefits under supplementary pension schemes are safeguarded. In Malta; employee pension rights are generally provided for by the state under the Social Security Act. The mandatory earnings-related pension scheme provides old-age pensions, survivor's benefits and invalidity pensions and is supported by means tested (non-contributory) welfare programme. The more widespread form of retirement provision is also earnings-related (contributory), providing a pension equivalent to two-thirds of the person's pensionable income. In order to qualify for the latter type of pension, a person must have been employed for at least ten years prior to retirement, have paid the required contribution rate and have paid or been credited with an amount of national insurance contributions each year over the established contribution period. The population is covered under either the contributory or the non-contributory pension schemes. The private pension, whether occupational or personal, is voluntary and this type of retirement provision is less widespread. Complementary occupational pension schemes are generally offered by the larger firms operating in the Maltese market. State pensions are not affected by transfer of business regulations as a person continues to benefit from this type of pension, since it is an earnings-related pension scheme. As regards supplementary company pension schemes falling outside the Social Security Act, relating to old age, invalidity or survivors' benefits receive the same protection on a transfer as other employment rights that transfer, and thus qualify as acquired rights that transfer automatically under national legislation

Information and consultation under TUPE

20.98 Where a transfer is governed by TUPE, both the transferor and the transferee owe a duty of information to the employees' representative, to the Director responsible for employment and industrial relations, and potentially consultation with the employees' representatives. The appropriate representatives to whom the transferor and the transferee owe these duties are either representatives of a trade union recognised for the purposes of collective bargaining and in default, the employee's representatives.

20.99 Very often, commercial agreements dealing with transfer of employees contain conditional clauses relating to the information and consultation process in respect of the transaction contemplated by the transferor and the transferee in such a way that the transaction contemplated will not take effect unless it can be lawfully implemented after the information and consultation requirements have been fulfilled. Additionally, agreements contain indemnification clauses in cases of breach by either party of the duties to inform and consult.

Duty to inform

20.100 Legally, the obligation to inform rests on both parties to a transfer of business agreement. The obligation to inform is satisfied on fulfilment of the following requirements:

- Deliver a written statement to the employees' representatives at least 15 working days before the transfer is carried out or before the employees are directly affected by the transfer as regards their condition of work and employment, whichever is the earlier;
- Include in the written statement the following information: (a) the date or proposed date of the transfer; (b) the reasons of the transfer; (c) the legal, economic and social implications of the transfer for the employees; and (d) the measures envisaged in relation to the transferring employees; and
- Deliver a copy of the written statement containing the said specific details to the Director responsible for employment and industrial relations (DEIR) on the same day that it is notified to the employees' representatives.

20.101 The duty to inform applies irrespective of whether the decision resulting in the transfer is taken by the employer or an undertaking controlling the employer.

Measures letter

20.102 Although there is no legal obligation, the transferee (new employer) is typically required to inform the transferor of any measures intended to be taken in relation to any affected transferring employees. This information is necessary to enable the transferor to be able to fully satisfy the legal requirement to inform.

20.103 There is no definition of 'measures' under legislation. Measures however would cover any action, step or arrangement that may affect the transferring employees and would probably include a change to existing working practices or arrangements such as changes to pay rates, job descriptions, hours of work, place of work, or overtime payments. The fact of the transfer itself is, on its own, unlikely to amount to a measure.

Employee liability information

20.104 The transferor is legally required to provide information about the conditions of employment of every transferring employee, which information shall always include a copy of the contract of employment or written statement containing the terms and conditions of employment. Such information must be provided by the date of the transfer of business. The provision of a copy of the employment contract or written statement containing the terms and conditions of employment is not intended to be exhaustive.

20.105 The intention is to provide the transferee with a full picture of the terms and conditions governing the employment relationship between the employee and the transferor, for instance terms and conditions affecting the employee contained in a collective agreement. Furthermore, such information needs to be full and up-to-date and accurate to enable the transferee to abide by the statutory requirements after transfer in relation to the transferred employees.

Duty to consult

20.106 The duty to consult is separate and distinct from the duty to inform. The transferor and the transferee are both legally required to conduct a consultation process with the employees' representatives where the transfer includes measures affecting the conditions of employment of the transferred employees.

20.107 These consultations must begin within seven working days from the day the employees' representatives have been notified of the intended transfers. The law limits itself to a statement that the consultations are intended to cover the impact of the transfer on the employees' conditions of employment. The law is silent on the procedure that the transferee and the transferor are bound to follow for the consultation procedure to be in line with the law. There is no requirement, however, to reach agreement with the employees during the discharge of the duty to consult.

European works councils

20.108 The European Works Council Regulations 2004 (Legal Notice 324 of 2004) and the European Works Council (Further Provisions) Regulations 2011 (Legal Notice 217 of 2011) (EWCFPR) implement the EU European Works Council Directive (Directive 94/45/EC, the EWC Directive) and EU Directive 2009/38/EC respectively.

20.109 In the case of multi-jurisdictional restructuring or redundancy exercises of EU-wide undertakings, it is the responsibility of the central management of the undertaking to create a European works council (EWC) as an information and consultation procedure where the central management is, inter alia, situated in Malta. It is also the responsibility of the central management of the undertaking to establish a special negotiating body (SNB) to negotiate with the central management for the establishment of an EWC or an alternative information and consultation procedure.

20.110 If the central management, inter alia, fails to provide information about the number of employees employed by the undertaking or group of undertakings as the case may be, or the status of employees, or wilfully obstructs or delays the provision of such information, or fails to establish the SNB, an EWC or an alternative information and consultation procedure, it is liable on conviction to a fine of not less than €23.29 and not more than €116.47 for every employee of the Community-scale undertaking or Community-scale group or in relation to any other offence, to a fine of not less than €1,164.69 and not more than €11,646.87.

Sanctions

Unfair dismissal

20.111 Termination of employment can be justified for economic, technical or organisational reasons entailing changes in the workforce. In all other cases, if an employee's employment is terminated for a reason which is not economical, technical or organisation, the aggrieved employee has the right to seek compensation or re-instatement from the Industrial Tribunal within a period of four months of the date of the alleged unfair dismissal.

20.112 Typically, commercial agreements will commonly contain detailed indemnities in relation to the financial liability for acts and omissions relating to transferring employees. Such agreements will be valid and enforceable to the extent that they do not attempt to contract out of TUPE.

Failure to inform and consult

20.113 The sanctions for failure to abide by TUPE, including the duties to inform and consult, are liability on conviction to a fine of not less than €1,164.69 for every employee that is affected by the transfer.

20.114 The remedy available to the affected employee is the general right provided under the Act in the form of a complaint to the Industrial Tribunal that has jurisdiction to consider and decide on all cases of alleged unfair dismissals and all cases of a breach of a right. The amount of compensation is liquidated by the Industrial Tribunal and there is no statutory capping on what compensation the affected employee is entitled to receive.

20.115 In considering alleged breaches of the information and consultation requirements laid down under TUPE, the defence that such a breach occurred because the information was not provided by an undertaking controlling the employer is not accepted as a justification.

Application of TUPE to cross-border transactions/ offshoring

20.116 TUPE applies to cross-border transactions where, and insofar as, the undertaking, business or part of the undertaking or business to be transferred is situated in Malta.

20.117 In relation to mergers, where one of the merging companies is registered in Malta and the other merging company or companies are constituted and have their registered office or principal place of business within the EU, specific regulations have been adopted to implement in national legislation the relevant provisions of Directive 2005/56/EC of the European Parliament and of the Council of the 26th October 2005 on cross-border mergers of limited liability companies.

20.118 The Employee Involvement (Cross-Border Mergers of Limited Liability Companies) Regulations (Legal Notice 165 of 2008) establish the arrangements for the involvement of employees in cross-border mergers of limited liability companies. In line with these Regulations, representatives of employees are entitled to receive, by the board of directors of the Maltese merging company, and to deliver, within a reasonable time, an opinion on, the report of the board of directors of the Maltese merging company drawn up in terms of regulation 8 of the Cross-Border Mergers of Limited Liability Companies Regulations, issued under the Companies Act.

20.119 In addition to TUPE, in such cases, the rights and obligations arising from contracts of employment or employment relationships between employees of the merging companies and the merging companies and existing at the date on which the cross-border merger takes effect are, by reason of that cross-border merger taking effect, transferred to the company resulting from the cross-border merger on the date on which the cross-border merger takes effect.

20.120 In a cross-border merger of limited liability companies, the right to information and consultation granted to employees under TUPE and the Collective Redundancy Regulations apply. Arrangements for employee participation are to be determined by the merging companies. There is no ad hoc procedure set down in statute for employee participation in cross-border mergers. Reference instead is made to the employee participation procedures contained in the Employee Involvement (European Company) Regulations (Legal Notice 452 of 2004) which are deemed to apply to employee participation in cross-border mergers.

WORKFORCE REDUCTION IN CONNECTION WITH SHARE SALE OR SHARE PURCHASE

20.121 In the case of a sale of shares or where an acquisition occurs by sale of shares, the company, which employs the individuals, does not change in identity. This is owing to the distinction between the company and the shareholders: the company has a legal personality distinct and separate from that of its shareholders. Consequently, the position of the employees does not change with a share transaction and they remain employed by the same entity under the same terms and conditions of employment.

20.122 A share deal does not trigger any employment law consequences. TUPE does not apply to a share transaction.

CHANGING EMPLOYMENT TERMS AND CONDITIONS

20.123 At law, a contract is binding between the parties and cannot be unilaterally changed. To this extent, the terms and conditions laid down in an employment contract cannot be altered except by agreement. After the employment contract is concluded, it is the duty of both parties to fulfil the contract according to the terms and conditions agreed upon and prescribed by law and supplemented by collective agreements which apply to the employee. Consequently the general position is that contracts of employment can only be varied by agreement.

20.124 It is widely accepted that changes to the employment terms and conditions that are occasioned by a change in the applicable law, regulations or collective agreement do not constitute a unilateral change to an employment contract since both parties have a general duty to abide by the law. Furthermore the employer is not under a duty to notify the employee of such a change.

20.125 An exception to this general principle could arise in cases of pressing financial need where the employer may be justified in changing terms and conditions in order to save itself from bankruptcy or liquidation. It is unlikely however that unilateral reductions in employment terms and conditions without the necessary consultation with the recognised union or employee's representatives will be considered as acceptable, even in those circumstances.

20.126 Sometime employers make changes which are the result of management policy rather than a change in the contract of employment. If an employer has a code of practice in relation to a particular procedure, a decision to alter the procedure would not amount to an employment term and condition which the employer could carry out unilaterally.

20.127 In the event that the necessity of a change is not occasioned by a change in the law or is a management policy, which does not affect the employment terms and conditions, an employer should seek to agree the changes with the employees as seeking to vary an employee's contract without the employee's consent is fraught with risks.

Mutually agreed changes

20.128 Amendments to the employment terms and conditions by mutual consent is the cleanest and safest route to take. The parties to the contract can agree on whether there will be any corresponding benefit that the employee may receive in return for the change, although the parties can agree that no consideration will be payable.

20.129 In any event, any such change even if mutually agreed, cannot be less favourable to the employee than the minimum conditions specified in national legislation provided that, in exceptional cases, the employer in agreement with the employee or union representatives may provide for different conditions of employment than those specified in or under this Act as long as such agreement is a temporary measure to avoid redundancies and as long as it is approved by the Director, which approval needs to be reviewed every four weeks.

Unilateral changes

20.130 Notwithstanding the risks involved, the employer may still decide to impose unilateral changes to the employment terms and conditions. In such a case, IER 2002 place an obligation on the employer to notify the employee of any change in the details or the conditions of employment by means of a signed statement which must be delivered to the employee by not later than eight working days from the date when the changes come into effect.

20.131 The legal duty to notify governs the following:

- the name, registration number and registered place of business of the employer and the place of work:
- the date of commencement of employment;
- the period of probation;
- normal rates of wages payable;
- the overtime rates of wages payable;
- the normal hours of work;
- the periodicity of wage payments;
- in the case of a fixed term contract of employment, the expected or agreed duration of the contract period;
- the paid holidays, and the vacation, sick and other leave to which the employee is entitled;
- the conditions under which fines may be imposed by the employer;
- the title, grade, nature or category of the work for which the employee is employed;
- the notice periods to be observed by the employer and the employee should it be the case;
- the collective agreement, if any, governing the employee's conditions of work; and
- any other relevant or applicable condition of employment.

20.132 It is important to note however that the obligation to notify does not mean that the employer has a right to change the conditions of employment as this duty is deemed to be without prejudice to the statutory provisions governing employment and contracts in general. Changing the employment terms and conditions without the employee's consent can give rise to a breach of contract or constructive dismissal.

20.133 An employer may not necessarily require the consent of an employee where the contract of employment itself authorises the change which the employer wants to make. The parties could have expressly agreed on a clause to this effect although if unreasonable it could be regarded as being invalid.

DISMISSING AND RE-ENGAGING EMPLOYEES ON NEW TERMS

20.134 Maltese law does not provide the opportunity for employers who have failed to reach agreement with their employees in relation to a change in the employment terms and conditions to dismiss and re-employ employees on new terms. Dismissal may be considered as being unfair and may be contested by an aggrieved employee unless the employer is able to establish a fair and just reason for the dismissal or redundancy.

20.135 In the case of redundancy, the employer is legally required to follow the appropriate dismissal procedure.

USING TEMPORARY STAFF

20.136 In a reorganisation situation, the temporary need for specific skills may arise. Temporary work can comprise a range of employment relationships including workers placed with an employer by temporary agencies, on-call workers and day labourers or workers who are directly hired on a fixed-term basis by an employer.

Agency workers

20.137 Temporary agency work consists of a relationship between the temporary agency and the undertaking making use of the temporary agency's services. The temporary work agency is considered at law to be the employer of the temporary agency worker to the exclusion of the user undertaking.

20.138 The legal framework is found in the Temporary Agency Workers Regulations (Legal Notice 461 of 2010), which apply to both public and private entities engaged in economic activity, whether or not they are operating for gain and which are temporary agencies or user undertakings or perform the same functions as the latter.

20.139 The Regulations lay down equal treatment obligations with regards to various employment conditions, including, but not limited to, pay, duration of working hours, overtime, rest breaks and rest periods, night work, annual leave, public holidays the protection of pregnant women, women who have just given birth or who are breastfeeding, and equal treatment for men and women. It is a legal requirement that the basic working and employment conditions of temporary agency workers are, for the duration of their assignment at a user undertaking, at least those that would apply if they had been recruited directly by that undertaking to occupy the same job. Employees are thus ensured their basic working and employment rights.

20.140 The Regulations impose obligations on both the temporary agency and the user undertaking. The latter is legally bound to inform the temporary agency worker assigned to it of any vacant posts in the user undertaking so as to give such individual the same opportunity as other workers in that undertaking to find permanent employment. The temporary agency cannot include a clause in the agency workers' contract prohibiting or preventing the conclusion of a contract of employment or of an employment relationship between the user undertaking and the temporary agency workers.

20.141 Temporary workers are also afforded the right to training and to access various facilities. In fact, the temporary agency worker has the right to be given access to the amenities or collective facilities in the user undertaking, in particular any canteen, child care facilities and transport services, under the same conditions as workers who have been employed directly by the user undertaking, unless the difference in treatment is justified by objective reasons. Moreover the temporary worker is be entitled to participate in vocational training programmes provided by or on behalf of the service user in the same manner as workers who have been employed, unless the difference in treatment is justified by objective reasons.

Fixed-term contracts

20.142 Fixed-term contracts can also be used in order to satisfy a temporary need of the employer during a reorganisation exercise. A fixed-term contract is a contract wherein both parties usually agree on its duration and which thus incorporates an expiry date. The end of the contract is determined by either reaching a specific date, or by completing a specific task or through the occurrence of a specific event. These type of contracts are covered by the 'Contracts of Service for a Fixed Term Regulations (LN 51 of 2007) and by the Act.

20.143 By virtue of these Regulations, employees on a contract of service for a fixed term cannot be treated in a less favourable manner than comparable permanent employees, solely because they have a contract of service for a fixed term. However, an employer may differentiate between the conditions of employment of an employee on a fixed-term contract and a comparable employee on a contract of service for an indefinite duration, if such difference arises in view of the recognition of length of service, experience, qualifications or conditions of pay and work attached to the contract of services immediately preceding the contract of service for a fixed term, and such other differences are justified on objective grounds, or the task for which the employee has been employed is specific or is in the nature of a senior management role and includes objective considerations which justify such differentiation.

20.144 The employer must inform employees on a contract of service for a fixed term about vacancies which become available in the place of work and to give such employees the same opportunity as other employees to secure work on a contract of service for an indefinite time within the place of work. The employer may inform the employees by way of a general announcement to be posted up at a suitable place in the place of work. The employer shall endeavour to facilitate access by employees on a contract of service for a fixed term to appropriate training opportunities to enhance their skills, career development and occupational mobility.

20.145 Where either party wishes to terminate a fixed term contract before its predetermined expiry date and there is not a justified reason to terminate the employment relationship, the party who breaches the contract is liable to pay the other party a sum equal to one-half of the full wages that would have accrued had the contract of employment remained in force. In situations of redundancy at the place of work, employees on fixed term contracts are also affected by the procedures of last in/first out in the same category, as other employees on infixed term contracts. Employees who are so affected by redundancy are entitled to be paid compensation as indicated above.

RENEWAL OF FIXED-TERM CONTRACTS

20.146 The employer is not obliged to renew a fixed-term contract that has expired at law, unless the contract terms provide differently or one of the instances stipulated in para **20.147** occurs. Generally, if the employer decides to retain an employee whose contract is about to expire, a fresh contract (of definite or indefinite duration) should be entered into. A fixed term contract can be renewed in accordance with the provisions of the contract itself if the latter establishes a renewal clause. Even where a renewal clause is stipulated in the contract of employment, upon the expiry of the agreed end date and not later than the first twelve working days following the expiry of the previous fixed-term contract, a new contract must be entered into between the employer and the employee. In default, the employee will deemed to be employed on a contract of indefinite duration.

20.147 Termination by operation of the law takes place when fixed-term employment contracts expires. It expires when the specified period ends without the need to provide a notice of termination. However, a contract of employment for a fixed duration may be transformed into a contract for an indefinite duration in any one of the following occurrences:

- the employee has been continuously employed under such a contract for a fixed term, or under that contract taken in conjunction with a previous contract or contracts of service for a fixed term in excess of a period of continuous employment of four years; and the employer cannot provide objective reasons to justify the limitation of a renewal of such a contract for a fixed term, which reasons must be based on precise and concrete circumstances characterising a given activity. Such objective reasons must be indicated in the contract of employment. When calculating a continuous period of service for the purpose of having completed four years under fixed term contracts, after which the contract changes into indefinite duration, the continuous period includes any renewed or subsequent fixed term contract having substantially the same tasks and entered into within six months from the termination of the previous contract.

- If an employee, who was previously employed on a fixed term contract, is retained in employment and is not given a new contract of service for a fixed-term within the first 12 working days following the expiry of the previous contract.

20.148 Employees who have acquired an indefinite status by virtue of the above do not automatically have the right to carry with this status benefits which are particular to fixed term contracts although the terms and conditions of the previous employment will become automatically applicable to the infixed term contract.

EMPLOYMENT CLAIMS

20.149 The first attempt at resolving employment disputes between employer and employee are usually through an amicable process through a compromise agreement that must be made in writing, or through a formal context by using the company's grievance or disciplinary procedure.

20.150 If these measures do not resolve the dispute, an employment complaint can be brought before the Industrial Tribunal, which has exclusive jurisdiction to consider and decide all cases of alleged unfair dismissals and all other statutory employment claims. The Industrial Tribunal can award compensation or reinstatement (in the case of dismissal) or both to an aggrieved employee. The compensation that can be awarded by the Tribunal is not capped. Appeals may be made only on points of law from the Industrial Tribunal to the Court of Appeal (Inferior Jurisdiction). Where there is a question concerning the interpretation of EU law, the tribunal or court may request the Court of Justice of the European Union to give a preliminary ruling.

20.151 Aggrieved employees can also file a report with the relevant body or commission for the conducting of investigation. Where the breach can give rise to an offence under the Act or subsidiary legislation enacted thereunder, an aggrieved employee can file a complaint to the DIER for criminal proceedings to be taken in respect of an offence allegedly committed by the employer. Where the alleged offence is committed by a body or other association of persons, be it corporate or unincorporate, every person who, at the time of the commission of the offence, was a director, manager, secretary or other similar officer of such body or association, or was purporting to act in any such capacity, will face criminal prosecution for a breach in line with the provisions of the Interpretation Act. In order to exculpate himself, a company officer must prove that the offence was committed without his knowledge and that he exercised al due diligence to prevent the commission of the offence.

20.152 Injunctive relief cannot be sought from the Industrial Tribunal but can only be sought from the First Hall of the Civil Court in line with the requirements of civil procedure contained in the Code of Organisation and Civil Procedure.

UNFAIR DISMISSAL

20.153 The right of an employee not to be unfairly dismissed is statutory and laid down in the Act. Unfair dismissal in relation to a worker results when in the case of a contract of indefinite duration, the employer terminates employment (other than probationary employment) for reasons not made solely on the grounds of redundancy or not for a good and sufficient cause or which, though made on grounds of redundancy or for a good and sufficient cause, is discriminatory and includes any failure by the employer to re-employ such person or to re-employ him or her when so obliged by law.

20.154 Any type of contract can be terminated summarily and without the need to give any notice to the employer or to the employee, if good and sufficient cause exists.

20.155 Employees have four months from the effective date of termination to bring a claim for unfair dismissal to the Tribunal.

Remedies

20.156 The employee must first prove that he or she has been dismissed. Termination arises where the employer makes it clear (in writing, verbally or by its actions) that it wishes the employment relationship to end. In assessing the employer's intention, regard may be had to the way in which a reasonable employee would view the employer's actions. When a contract of employment is terminated the employer shall, within four days from the date of termination, notify the Employment and Training Corporation by means of a termination form. This would clearly show that the employer has terminated the employee's employment contract.

20.157 Constructive dismissal of an employee does not necessarily mean that he or she has been unfairly dismissed. Once a tribunal has determined that the employee was constructively dismissed, it must then consider, in the usual way, whether the employee was dismissed for a potentially fair reason and whether the employer acted reasonably in the circumstances.

20.158 An employee unfairly dismissed may lodge a complaint with the Industrial Tribunal, which has exclusive competence to deal with such complaints. The tribunal will generally have regard to the employee's wishes, whether it is practicable to reinstate/re-engage and whether it would be just to make the order. These are discretionary remedies and a tribunal will take into account the disruption that might be caused by reintroducing the employee into the workforce. Failure to comply with a reinstatement or re-engagement order may result in an additional award of compensation against the employer. The Tribunal may also make an award of compensation.

DISCRIMINATION

20.159 An employee may also bring a claim for discrimination in the Industrial Tribunal if the real reason for his selection for redundancy or for dismissal discriminatory on the basis of *inter alia* marital status, pregnancy or potential pregnancy, sex, colour, disability, religious conviction, political opinion or membership in a trade union or in an employers' association. An employee may also be discriminated against, for instance, when redundancy or termination packages are agreed with employees. The employer is not at liberty to discriminate between employees having identical or similar situations.

Remedies

20.160 Victims of discrimination may pursue their claim of having been subjected to discriminatory treatment in relation to their employment under the all-encompassing remedy of referring their complaint to the Industrial Tribunal for redress. This must be done within four months of the alleged discrimination and the Industrial Tribunal will hear such complaint and carry out such investigations as it deems fit. If the Industrial Tribunal is satisfied that the complaint is justified, it may take such measures as it may deem fit. Besides an order for the payment of reasonable compensation to the aggrieved employee, the Tribunal may, in specific cases relating to particular types of discrimination, take such remedial measures as it may deem fit, including the cancellation of any contract of service or of any clause in a contract or in a collective agreement which is discriminatory and an order for the payment of reasonable compensation to the employee.

20.161 In cases of alleged breaches of the principle of equality before the court or Industrial Tribunal, the burden of proof rests on the employer to prove that there has been no breach of the principle of non-discrimination after the employee has established facts from which it may be presumed that there has been direct or indirect discrimination.

20.162 The above remedies are without prejudice to the fact that any provisions contrary to the principle of equal treatment in any individual or collective agreements, internal rules of undertakings are considered null and void.

20.163 In specific cases of discrimination, such as in the case of gender discrimination, the employee has the additional remedy of a complaint in writing to the National Commission for the Promotion of Equality (NCPE), which has the powers to investigate the complaint and may either dismiss the complaint or find for the employee. In the latter case, and where the action complained of constitutes an offence, the NCPE makes a report to the Commissioner of Police for action on his or her part; or where the action complained of does not constitute an offence, calls upon the employer to redress the situation, and mediate between the employee and employer to settle the matter. The findings of the Commissioner, however, are not binding on the employee or on the employer unless they expressly declare in writing to be so bound.

20.164 Reporting the employer to the authorities may also subject the employer to a fine not exceeding €2,329.37 and/or imprisonment for a period not exceeding six months.

MUTUALLY AGREED TERMINATION

20.165 The act does not make specific mention of termination of employment relationships by mutual agreement but focuses on the termination of employment by either party, otherwise than at the wish of both parties. However, it is widely accepted that an employment contract can be terminated by the parties if they mutually agree and under such terms as they may agree between them, in view of the fact that an employment relationship is governed by the law of contract generally.

20.166 In practice, it is not uncommon that on termination of an employment relationship and on the payment of all amounts due to the employee by the employer by virtue of the employee's employment, such as salary till the date of termination, bonuses pro rata to the date of termination, payments for untaken vacation leave till the date of termination, as well as the payment of any additional amounts agreed to between the employer and the employee, the parties sign an agreement declaring that this amount given to the employee is to be considered in full and final settlement and the employee will not have the right to pursue the issue further before the Industrial Tribunal.

Settlement agreements

20.167 An employer may include additional clauses in the agreement relating to the termination of employment relating to undertakings of confidentiality and renunciation of rights in respect of the employment and waiver of claims, rights or actions or proceedings in connection with the employment.

20.168 Compromise agreement in writing may also be reached during pending proceedings before the industrial tribunal. In such event, the employer includes the undertaking that the aggrieved employee cedes the case instituted in the industrial tribunal against the employer within a short timeframe as agreed in the agreement.

20.169 It is common that in such agreements reached between the employer and the employee, the parties agree that the settlement or compromise is not deemed or construed as an admission of wrongdoing or liability on the part of the employer

20.170 There is no specific requirement that the employee has sought legal advice or is assisted by a lawyer during the negotiations leading to or on execution of the settlement or compromise agreement. However, for a contract to be valid under Maltese law, the parties to the contract must have given their consent to bind themselves. Where consent has been extorted by violence or procured by fraud, such contract will be vitiated. A compromise agreement cannot be set aside on the ground of an error of law. Nevertheless a compromise may be set aside, where there has been an error as to the person with whom the contract was made, or as to the matter of the controversy which the parties intended to compromise. A compromise based on documents, which are subsequently found to be false, is void.

20.171 There is no legal requirement for the compromise agreement to be authorised by the industrial tribunal.

Without prejudice and 'pre-termination' discussions

20.172 If an employer intends to enter into negotiations with an employee for a settlement of a dispute between them, discussions are undertaken on 'without prejudice' basis. This principle is recognised in Malta as it enables the parties, with the intention of reaching a compromise, to freely discuss the dispute between them, without fear that what has been stated in the context of the negotiations will be used against them in a court if the compromise does not take place.

20.173 Evidence of what has been discussed or stated in a without prejudice context cannot be used in proceedings that may be instituted by either party if the settlement is not concluded. The rule rests in part upon public policy that encourages compromises. The public policy justification essentially rests on the desirability of preventing statements or offers made in the course of negotiations for settlement being brought before a court or tribunal as admission on the questions of liability. The importance from a public policy perspective results from the obligation imposed by the code of ethics and conduct for advocates, which prevents lawyers from using any without prejudice discussions or negotiations or the contents thereof in a court or tribunal. Although this obligation is imposed on lawyers, jurisprudence has accepted that there is a primary obligation on the parties not to use evidence obtained through discussions conducted on a without prejudice basis.

Chapter 21
Workforce Restructuring in the Netherlands

Frouke Vlaskamp
Vlaskamp Advocaten, Amersfoort

INTRODUCTION

21.1 Various situations can give cause for a restructuring of the workforce. For example, a need to reduce the number of employees due to disappointing results or losses or because of the wish for a different, more efficient structure of the organisation and thus the workforce. In both cases, this leads to layoffs of employees and therefore to a reduction of labour costs. However, a restructuring can also be associated with a different structure of the organisation without any reduction in the workforce. Redundancies are therefore not always on the agenda. A restructuring may also involve a review of functions and proceedings or modification of terms of employment. There may also be a new installation within a group and transfer of tasks within the various subsidiaries. In addition it is possible that tasks are repelled and are placed outside the firm (or the group of which these are part of) through outsourcing or by selling activities. Finally there is the desire of many employers to increase flexibility, which results in increased use of other forms of contract in place of an employment contract. For instance temporary (agency) workers and freelancers who are self-employed under a contract of services.

21.2 Employees working under a contract of employment in the Netherlands enjoy extensive protection against redundancy but also against unilateral modification of working conditions. In order to end the employment contract the employer is required to either obtain the permission of the Employment Insurance Agency (Uitvoeringsinstituut Werknemersverzekeringen, hereafter

'UWV') or request a dissolution of the employment agreement by the district court. The dismissal protection does not apply to employees who are not engaged under a contract of employment but are working for the company, for example in the capacity as a temporary employee (and therefore employed by another employer) or are self-employed.

21.3 A unilateral change in terms and conditions of the contract is only allowed under special circumstances. The employer must demonstrate a compelling need to change the terms noting that the primary employment conditions in principle cannot (or only in very limited circumstances) be customised. Furthermore, in case of changes a thorough process must be followed.

21.4 On 1 January and 1 July 2015, Dutch labour law is undergoing a big change and particularly the legislation on termination of the agreement will change. The following text will be dealing with the new law which came into force on 1 January and 1 July 2015.

PREPARING FOR A RESTRUCTURING EXERCISE

21.5 Before a restructuring exercise can commence, a few things need to be sorted out. As a first step the number of workers and terms and conditions of employment involved with the reorganisation, but also any applicable collective labour agreement should be established. This will impact on the decision as to whether this results in a collective redundancy which should be disclosed to the unions. Secondly it must be clear (if it is not already) what the current organisational structure is and what the new structure will be. This will assist in explaining differences in the organisation. Differences may be identified from a review of an organisational chart or a description of the various functions. Thirdly, the length of employment for all employees should be established. The entire period the employee worked for the employer should be taken into account when calculating length of service. Even any period of work by the particular employee for the employer whilst not in service under an employment contract, for example on the basis of temporary employment or secondment, should be identified. Changing employment between subsidiaries can count as continuous service within a group of companies. This is particularly important to determine the procedure for dismissal. Finally the participation process must be mapped out. The Works Council usually has an advisory right or right of approval in the restructuring process, accordingly an application should be submitted to the Works Council at an early stage (if any influence is still possible).

Identify the employing entity

21.6 As stated, before the restructuring process can start, there should be a complete overview of all employees working in the organisation. The formal employer must be determined, which can be difficult especially in a group of companies. Often a separate legal entity is used to house the personnel who are then seconded to various sister companies to carry out work. The starting point, however, remains the formal employer, ie the company with which a contract is in place.

COLLATING INFORMATION TO PLAN AND BUDGET FOR THE RESTRUCTURING EXERCISE

21.7 Careful preparation precedes a reorganisation. This is also relevant to the question of whether the Works Council should be consulted and whether the unions should be involved. In addition, a clear timetable should be prepared to include the date of the implementation of the new organisation. Furthermore, a proposed date for the redundancies to take effect should be identified.

21.8 As indicated above, the responsible HR department should have a complete overview of the employees in the organisation, including which functions (by level and skill) are comparable, the age and length of service of all employees. Furthermore it should be examined whether there are redeployment opportunities within the organisation for employees provisionally selected for dismissal.

21.9 As to the financial budget of the restructuring, it is wise to make a rough calculation of the compensation that should be paid out to the employees. From 1 July 2015, all employees with more than two years' service should be offered a transition allowance in case of redundancy. Sometimes the applicable collective agreement provides for additional compensations to be paid or such are laid down in a social plan. The employee can also go to court to claim additional compensation, but this will usually only occur in circumstances where the employer has acted in a seriously culpable manner. The costs involved at termination should be taken into account when deciding on the budget for a reorganisation or restructuring and whether such outweighs the exercise.

21.10 As of 1 July 2015, the transition allowance is considered to be the minimum amount of compensation to be paid. This is calculated as 1/6 of a month's salary per six months for the first 120 months of employment and thereafter a ¼ monthly salary per six months. The maximum amount of compensation to be paid is capped at €75,000, or one gross annual salary whichever is more.

21.11 In case of a dismissal that involves several employees, the employer usually prepares a social plan which includes terms of entitlement to compensation, eg whether an outplacement procedure or additional training is being offered. Such a social plan can be agreed upon with the unions but that is not essential.

EMPLOYMENT STATUS

21.12 Only employees with an employment contract are protected from redundancy. An employer who uses temporary workers, freelancers etc is expected to let these employees go first, in case of a reduction of the organisation. An exception to this rule applies, when the employer is able to prove that his market has been subject to significant fluctuations in workload which cannot be served by permanent staff. Also employees on temporary contracts valid for less than six months are to be dismissed before an employee with a permanent contract can be made redundant.

21.13 A managing director or any other member of the board of directors of a company engaged under an employment contract, and not appointed as statutory director, enjoys the same protection as a regular employee.

GENERAL PROTECTION AGAINST DISMISSAL

21.14 In the Netherlands, the most frequently used option for dismissal is with the employee's consent, usually laid down in a settlement agreement. For dismissal without the employee's consent prior permission of the UWV is required. A request for termination of the employment contract can also be made to the district court. From 1 July 2015, an employer can only go through the UWV in case of a restructuring. An exception to this exists when special protection applies against dismissal. In such circumstances the employer can go directly to the district judge. Furthermore, a request for termination can be raised with the district court when the UWV is found to have wrongly rejected the request for dismissal.

21.15 At the UWV an elaborate procedure is in place as to how and which employees can be put forward for dismissal. The employer must be able to substantiate the reason for dismissal, although the UWV recognises that an employer is free to furnish the organisation at their discretion. But, to protect the employee, the UWV ascertains the reason invoked for dismissal. If the dismissal is based on financial reasons (eg decrease of turnover), the employer is to produce financial documents (financial statements of three years); if the termination is based on other reasons justifying the reorganisation (such as decrease of work, automation, etc) these grounds must be evidenced by documents such as prognoses showing decrease of workload, termination of contracts and/or proof of a decision of the board of directors and the advice of the Works Council regarding alternative structure of the organisation.

21.16 If the reason for the reorganisation is justified, the employer must prepare an order of dismissal subject to the rules of the UWV. In principle, this provides that, per age category and per function, the person with the shortest length of service is nominated for dismissal. This will be treated in more detail below.

SPECIAL PROTECTION AGAINST DISMISSAL

21.17 Despite the employer having obtained permission to terminate employment, termination of the employment contract for a few groups of employees is prohibited. These are:

- employees who are ill, during the first two years of their sick leave;
- employees who are pregnant or are on maternity leave;
- employees who perform military service; and
- an employee who is a member of the Works Council or a committee thereof, has been a member of the Works Council or has been on the list of candidates less than two years ago.

Except for employees on maternity leave, the above mentioned termination prohibitions do not apply when the enterprise or part thereof is dissolved. As the enterprise can only be dissolved when the leave has ended any employees on maternity leave will remain in employment for the duration of the leave. Under the changes to the law, as of 1 July 2015, it is possible to terminate employment also during pregnancy (but not if the employee is on leave) or if the employee performs military service, and the reason for dismissal is a reorganisation due to economic conditions or because of effective organisation of the company.

21.18 Further, a number of dismissals for certain specified reasons are prohibited. These are: the employer cannot terminate the contract because the employee is a member of the trade union; because the employee is on political leave or takes parental leave, or because of a transfer of undertaking. However, these conditions will not quickly occur when the employer has obtained permission for dismissal due to restructuring. After all, the presence of that ground for dismissal has already been established. The dismissal prohibitions do not apply if the employee agrees to termination.

WORKFORCE REDUCTION

21.19 In the following only the UWV procedure will be discussed as from 1 July 2015 this procedure will provide the only opportunity for a termination of employment based on economic grounds. Although, it is expected after this date that it remains more common that the employment contract is terminated by mutual consent. Also in case of a reorganisation, the employer can offer employees a settlement agreement, laying down the conditions under which employment terminates. Usually parties will agree to a settlement agreement if the notice period is taken into account and the minimum compensation is paid. If such an offer is made, the procedure via the UWV will not add anything and accordingly there are no reasons not to agree to the employers offer. Thus, the settlement agreement is the most common way of termination of employment in the Netherlands and will most likely remain so after 1 July 2015.

21.20 In a collective redundancy (qualified by having over 20 employees involved in a work area of the UWV within a term of 3 months) the employer has to notify the intention to make such dismissals to the unions and the UWV.

Definition of redundancy

21.21 The UWV dismissal procedure specifies what circumstances are considered economic reasons which give rise to the granting of a dismissal permit. These are the following subcategories:

- poor financial position;
- work reduction;
- organisational change/restructuring;
- technological changes;
- termination of the business in whole or in part;
- business relocation; and
- expiry of (wage) subsidy

21.22 The employer must demonstrate that the alleged reason is present, which is subject to heavy scrutiny by the UWV. The UWV examines the basis for the employers decision to dismiss employees and whether such decision was reasonable on the basis of the stated reason.

Examples of redundancy situations

Suddenly a significant and big client terminates its business or goes bankrupt. If as a consequence there is a decline of work that affects a large portion of the workforce, and it looks like this will not pick up in a period of six months, a dismissal is justified.

Definition of SOSR

21.23 It is possible to dismiss the employee on grounds 'other' than economic reasons. There could be several reasons why the employer wants to dismiss an employee. This may be because circumstances have changed, such as the performance of the employee, but also because a dysfunctional employment relationship between employer and employee has emerged. Even in circumstances when the employer has dismissed the employee spontaneously, it remains open for the employer to request the termination of the employment before the district court.

21.24 Currently employers still have a choice between requesting a dismissal permit at the UWV or go to the district court for a termination of the contract. From 1 July 2015, the employee is obliged to address the UWV for dismissal based on economic grounds and in case of prolonged illness of the employee. Where the employer wants to end the agreement based on personal circumstances the employer has to go to the district court to terminate the employment contract. During the termination procedure, the employer must demonstrate that there are reasonable grounds for the dismissal and it is then up to the judge to determine whether this reason provides justification. Heavy demands are made on the lifting of burden of proof to justify termination.

Example of dismissals on grounds of SOSR

An employer who requests termination due to the poor performance of the employee must demonstrate this adequately. Complaints about performance are to be expressed in a timely fashion, in order that the employee has the opportunity to improve his performance and at the same time, the employer is obliged to support the employee, for example by offering training. These facts and actions must be adequately documented. If the district judge rules that the performance justifies the termination, the district judge will make an order for compensation to be paid by the employer. The amount of compensation is equal to the compensation an employer has to pay when dismissing on the basis of a UWV permit , also referred to as 'transition compensation'. A lessor amount of compensation is ordered when the employee's behaviour is so grave that it indicates a serious act or omission. For more information about the fee, see the section on redundancy payment.

DISMISSALS ON GROUNDS OF REDUNDANCY

21.25 As of 1 July 2015 there is a requirement to follow a mandatory route for dismissal for economic reasons, namely to obtain permission for the dismissal by the UWV. But if the UWV in the opinion of the employer wrongly refuses permission, the employer has the option to request the district court for a termination by way of an appeal. The judge can also be approached directly when termination is not possible due to special protection against dismissal or if it concerns a fixed term contract without the possibility of giving notice. The procedure to be followed for both the individual and collective dismissal is the same, except that there are some additional conditions applying to collective redundancies.

Individual redundancy procedure

21.26 For the sake of completeness, both procedures for individual redundancy are discussed below. Although from 1 July 2015 it is no longer possible to achieve termination at the district court on the basis of economic reasons, it is still possible to go to the district court for other (personal) reasons.

21.27 Up until 1 July 2015, the employer may still request the district court to terminate the employment contract due to economic reasons. The above mentioned special termination prohibitions (such as sickness and pregnancy) do not apply in case of termination by the district court, however the district judge will have to establish whether the request is related to the existence of a specific termination prohibition. For example, there is no question of this when an employee, as a result of a proven need for a reorganisation, is eligible for dismissal. In this case the illness of the employee does not get in the way of termination. Also the employer will have to make the case for prudent dismissal plausible to the district court. The district court also respects the selection criteria (order of dismissal), so these have to be taken into account (see para **21.35**), although it appears from case law that district courts afford themselves some leverage. The district judge will make an order for compensation to the employee at termination, the amount of which depends on the age of the employee, the duration of employment and the degree of culpability on the part of the employer (higher cost) or the employee (lower reimbursement). If the employer can demonstrate a poor financial situation (habe nichts'), the district court may make an order for a lower amount of compensation.

21.28 From 1 July 2015 a dismissal on the grounds of redundancy is only possible based on the route through the UWV. This is described in the Dismissals Decree (Ontslagregeling). In order to terminate the employment contract, the employer requires permission (a license) from the UWV. The UWV will assess the request of the employer including whether the ground for dismissal is reasonable and assess whether the economic reason is plausible, or in accordance with the principle of proportionality the 'right' employee is nominated and whether it is likely that there is no possibility to reinstate the employee.

21.29 The UWV performs an examination of the stated business reason. The degree of examination depends on what subcategory of economic reason (eg, poor financial situation or closure of a business location) is concerned and the employer will have to provide different documents for the different categories. In any case, sufficient information must be provided to justify dismissal. For each subcategory it is determined which documents the UWV considers necessary for the evaluation of the application. As such it is necessary for the subcategory 'bad financial situation' that the employer provides a concrete basis for the minimum amount it needs to save on personnel and that the employer specifies which cost-saving measures have been or will be taken.

21.30 The employer must submit an application for a permit for each and every employee who he intends to dismiss. But the general rationale for the reorganisation can be described in a general explanation which is the same for all employees. In the individual part, the personal data of the employee are included and the explanation why the employment of that employee should be terminated. At this point the employer should examine if there are any redeployment opportunities for the affected employee. If the application is not complete, or when the UWV is of the opinion that more documents are required, the UWV will request these documents from the employer.

21.31 From 1 July, 2015, parties can make agreements on their own UWV procedure in collective labour agreement. To this end, they may set up a dismissal committee who decides on an application for a dismissal permit in the same way as the UWV. The law defines the procedural principles to be taken into account. Where a dismissal commission is appointed it, rather than the UWV, has jurisdiction to take notice of the application.

21.32 Finally, it is important to bear in mind that under certain circumstances the contract cannot be terminated. This applies when a specific protection against dismissal stands in the way, for example because the employee is sick or pregnant. The UWV will then deny the permission from the UWV. This means that even if staff reduction is necessary because of economic reasons, sick employees are still protected against dismissal. An exception to this is when the employee is selected for dismissal due to the termination of the activities of the undertaking or part of the enterprise in which the employee exclusively or predominantly works. In that case, the employer can terminate after obtaining permission, even when the employee is sick or pregnant. From 1 July 2015, a further exception that termination is possible when business activities disappear due to an economic necessity is introduced to permit termination during pregnancy or military service. However, this does not apply to sickness. Sick employees remain protected. In all cases, employees who are on maternity leave are protected. They can therefore not be terminated during their leave, whatever the circumstances.

Defining the selection pool

21.33 The principle of proportionality is the mandatory criterion under which the employer must determine which employee qualifies for dismissal. Until 2006 the principle of seniority (last in, first out) applied, which sometimes led to imbalances in the workforce because the younger employees with the shortest employment were discharged first, while all older workers remained employed. The principle of proportionality changed this and ensured that the dismissed workers are spread across different age groups (15–24 years, 25–34 years, 35–44 years, 45–54 years and 55 years and older). This creates a more balanced spread of redundancies within the workforce.

21.34 On the basis of the principle of proportionality one must differentiate between employees with interchangeable positions within the same business location. Then, within the age group, the employees with the shortest employment are up for dismissal first. The necessary number of redundancies is divided across the age groups, pro rata. For example, the category with 30% of the workforce also provides 30% of the redundancies. The various elements of the principle of proportionality are further elaborated in the Decree, these are treated below ('Selection Criteria').

Selection criteria

21.35 Employees are considered interchangeable if they work in the same position in the same business location. Business location in this context means 'every organisational context acting as an independent entity'. When a company has multiple business locations which do not act as independent entities the proportionality principle should be applied across the whole business. A business location only qualifies as an independent entity if it has separate financial statements (profit and loss accounts) registration at the Chamber of Commerce, its own staff and appearance to the market. Only in these circumstances (which often appear) the proportionality principle can be applied only to that one business location.

21.36 When the scope of the business unit has been determined the next step is to consider the interchangeable positions within the company. Interchangeable positions are defined as functions that 'as to job content, required knowledge and skills and competences required, are similar, at the same level and with equivalent rewards'. For example, secretaries in a notary's office have interchangeable positions, because they all perform almost the same activities.

21.37 Further, the categories of interchangeable positions are divided across five age groups (15–24 years, 25–34 years, 35–44 years, 45–54 years and 55 years and older). In every business location therefore, interchangeable positions are distinguished on the basis of job category and within such also on the basis of age. Once this distinction is made, it can then be determined based on the relationship and seniority which employees are the first in line for termination. The general principle is that the employee with the shortest employment within his age group should be dismissed first.

21.38 Deviation from the proportionality principle is only possible in cases regulated in the BOU and such deviation must be for compelling reasons. Deviation is possible in respect of employees who are considered essential for the business or for those who have a weak position on the job market. The employer will have to adequately substantiate his appeal to deviate from the principle of proportionality.

21.39 Even if only one employee is to be made redundant, the proportionality principle must be applied. For an example on how the proportionality is calculated with collective redundancy, see the example at para **21.51**. As a result of the obligation to apply the proportionality principle, the employer is restricted in which employees he dismisses in case of redundancy due to economic reasons. This can lead to a situation where well-performing employees will be dismissed while sick or under-performing employees must be retained.

Bumping

21.40 When deviation from the principle of proportionality is allowed by the UWV (for example, because an employee is indispensable because he possesses such knowledge and skills that his dismissal would damage the functioning of the company), the next employee in line with the shortest employment history within the relevant age group is eligible for dismissal instead.

INDIVIDUAL CONSULTATION

21.41 The employer is not required to discuss his request for permission to terminate with the employee in advance of applying for a permit for dismissal at the UWV. This is, however, unhelpful as it precludes an examination of whether the employee is willing to agree to a termination by mutual consent. Where there is mutual consent the UWV procedure can be avoided. Accordingly, it is common for employers to discuss the proposed termination with the employee. Failing to do this, does not result in any consequences in the case of the UWV procedure. Where the employer requests termination on personal grounds (bad performance) at the district courts, prior consultation with the employee is required. Otherwise the district court will decide that the employer does not have a reasonable ground for dismissal.

21.42 Once the completed application is received by the UWV, the employee will have the opportunity to respond in writing to the dismissal request. Also, in the case of termination by the district judge, the employee has the opportunity to respond to what is provided by the employer. The employee may be assisted in this case by a lawyer or legal expert, but can also respond to the request by himself.

Involvement of employee representatives in individual dismissals

21.43 When an employee is a member of a trade union he may make use of legal aid offered by this union. There are also many legal expenses insurances in the Netherlands where the employee can get insured voluntarily.

Because the employee – both with the district court as in the procedure at the UWV – is not obliged to have legal representation (although it is to be recommended), there are no consequences for the employer if the employee has no representation.

Avoiding compulsory redundancies

21.44 The employer is obliged to avoid compulsory redundancies if possible. This is inherent to the principle of good employer practice, and is scrutinised by the UWV. If the UWV comes to the conclusion that the employer could have avoided a dismissal then the dismissal will be not be considered reasonable. Furthermore, under Dutch law permanent employees are protected to a (much) greater extent than flexible employees, ie workers who have no indefinite employment contract. In case of forced workforce reduction due to economic reasons, the employer has successively to part first with the 'flexible shell' (agency staff, employees on secondment, employees under contracts with flexible hours etc). For example, the agreement with the agency should be terminated and temps simply (within legal constraints) cannot be called upon. Also employment contracts entered into for a definite period of time with employees which legally end within 26 weeks following the submission of the request, are not to be renewed by the employer. Only then will the employees in permanent employment qualify for dismissal. This way, forced termination of permanent employees can be prevented.

Alternative employment

21.45 Before submitting the application for consent for dismissal for economic reasons to the UWV the employer should verify that there are no opportunities for redeployment of the employee in which case the dismissal can be prevented. The UWV also assesses what the employer has done to prevent the dismissal. If the UWV sees possibilities for redeployment and is of the opinion that the employer may reasonably be required to redeploy the employee, the UWV will reject the application. If the company is part of a group then it would be expected that the employer first examines if redeployment within the group is possible, for example with an affiliate. At the same time it can also be expected from the employee that he endeavours to avoid redundancy, eg by applying for (internal) vacancies.

21.46 The UWV also takes into consideration the interests of the employer, to which the nature and extent of the organisation are relevant. When the employer requests the dismissal of his employee(s) because of the poor financial situation of the company, there will probably not be any possibilities to redeploy because of the necessity to reduce the costs of the company. This is different when, for example, there is a reorganisation, in which the activities in one department are not going well, while other parts of the business are growing (and there is a need for more employees). In this case the employer will have to seriously consider redeployment of employees from one department to another. When there is a suitable position for the employee, but the employee has insufficient training, the employer should examine whether redeployment with training is possible. This way an employer may be required to train his employees, but only if there is a prospect of a suitable position.

Trial periods

21.47 Upon reinstatement it is not possible to agree on a probation period, unless the original contract is terminated and a new contract is offered. But where entirely different skills for the new function are required, a trial period will be justified. The new contract should be an employment agreement of more than six months.

Other considerations

21.48 Finally, the employer must take into account individual appointments made in the employment contract.

COLLECTIVE REDUNDANCY PROCEDURE

21.49 In the case of termination of more than 20 employment contracts (regardless of the manner in which termination is reached) within a period of three months the employer is required to notify the trade unions and UWV in light of the Collective Redundancy Notification Act (hereafter: the 'CRNA'). This means that notification is required when termination is reached by means of a settlement agreement with 15 employees and then within three months for six employees a permission is applied for at the UWV. The termination of the six employees must be notified to the unions and the UWV, as a collective dismissal.

21.50 The employer must notify the unions and the UWV in writing. This also applies in case of a winding-up involving more than 20 employees. After notification the unions can consult with the employer, which brings into play the possibility to achieve a social plan. The unions concerned are those unions of which at least two members are working within the company. The employer must examine which unions to inform and cannot just make assumptions. The unions and the employer will then be given one month to discuss the collective dismissal. The UWV will only take the application for collective redundancy into consideration after the expiry of this period. The obligation to prepare this written notice is based on European law (EC Directive February 17, 1975, EC / 75/129).

21.51 Once the UWV takes the request into consideration the same procedure is followed as for the individual dismissal for economic reasons. The employer will also have to submit an individual application for each employee. The procedure is therefore not repeated here. Because the proportionality principle is also applicable in a collective redundancy, an example as to how to apply this is detailed in the table below. This example concerns a web shop business where profits are declining as a result of which 30 employees in the sales department become redundant. In this sales department the functions are interchangeable and there is a total of 138 people working in this department.

Application of the principle of proportionality in the reorganisation of a shop.					
15–24	25–34 years	35–44 years	45–54	55 years and over	Total
34 sellers	30 sellers	28 sellers	26 sellers	20 sellers	138 sellers
24.6%	21.7%	20.3%	18.8%	14.5%	100%
A total of 30 people become redundant:					
15–24	25–34 years	35–44 years	45–54	55 years and over	Total
24.6% × 30 = 7.38	21.7% × 30 = 6.51	20.3% × 30 = 6.09	18.8% × 30 = 5.64	14.5% = 4.35 × 30	100%
This is rounded to all employees until the total of 30 is reached. These employees are eligible for severance.					
15–24	25–34 years	35–44 years	45–54	55 years and over	Total
7	7	6	6	4	30

Involvement of employee representatives in collective dismissals

21.52 The role of trade unions in collective redundancies is indicated above. The main reason for the consultation procedure with the trade unions is to investigate the establishment of a social plan. Parties are however not under the obligation to reach an agreement. There are three forms of social plans. The first concerns the plan agreed with the trade unions, which is most compelling for the employees to accept. The second is the social plan agreed with the Works Council, which is a little less compelling for the employees to accept. Finally, the employer may establish a redundancy plan and offer this unilaterally to its employees. The employees are under no obligation whatsoever to accept this plan.

21.53 In a social plan the effects of the collective redundancy are regulated for various employees. The aim of the social plan is to prevent compulsory redundancies and to mitigate the consequences of unemployment for the employees. For example the social plan can deal with an outplacement program or a waiver of study costs, but it can also include a different calculation-method for the compensation or rule on the situation where an employee, not redundant, leaves the company of his own accord. The social plan also includes arrangements for those employees who remain employed, such as changes in the workplace and job classification.

21.54 Besides the trade unions, the Works Council is also involved in the restructuring of the organisation. If there is a significant change in the organisation such as a substantial alteration of the manner in which the employer's business is organised, the Works Council becomes involved in an advisory capacity. The employer will have to present his plans for changing the organisation to the Works Council at an early stage, after which the Works Council may deliver a positive or negative recommendation. When the Works Council has given a negative recommendation on the proposed organisational change (which could be the implementation of collective redundancy) the employer must defer the application of the permission for dismissal with the UWV for one month. During this period the Works Council can appeal to the Enterprise Division of the district court of Appeal of Amsterdam. The Enterprise Division can consequently decide that the employer may not reasonably proceed with the intended plan for collective redundancy and can prohibit the execution of the decision. Such a far-reaching decision however only occurs in exceptional cases.

Election of employee representatives for collective consultation purposes

21.55 The employer does not have to institute a Works Council or an employee representative body merely because of the (intended) reorganisation or restructuring. However, if the employer has not instituted a Works Council, but is obliged to do so by law, then the consequences of not having a Works Council come to the account of the employer. Also, the district court or the UWV will be more inclined to deny a request for dissolution or the dismissal permit.

Information and consultation requirements

21.56 In the case of a collective dismissal for economic reasons the employer must provide the following information to the relevant trade unions as specifically as possible:

- the number of employees whose contracts the employer intends to terminate and the time of termination;
- the criteria used for selecting the employees that are to be made redundant;
- the method for calculating possible redundancy payments; and
- the manner in which the employer intends to terminate the employment contracts with its employees.

21.57 When the trade unions agree with the dismissal of employees for commercial reasons, the employer can request a statement from the trade unions that can be provided to the UWV alongside the other documents that are required. The statement made by the trade unions is beneficial for the decision on the applications by the UWV and furthermore the employer does not have to observe the waiting period of one month.

Regulatory requirements

21.58 Representatives and employees of the trade unions are obliged to maintain confidentiality about the reorganisation, if requested by the employer and such request is sufficiently justified. The advantage of confidentiality is that (premature) unrest among employees that usually arises as a result of a collective redundancy can be prevented. Once the UWV invites responses from the affected individuals during its handling of the applications for the employer's requests for dismissal, the confidentiality will become obsolete.

Sanctions

21.59 When the employer has failed to notify the trade unions of the collective redundancy or when the employer has not taken the waiting period of one month into account, the individual employee can file a request with the district court judge for a declaration that the termination of the employment contract is void. This also applies when (whether or not on the basis of the redundancy plan) a settlement agreement has been concluded with the employee to terminate his employment. If the employee becomes aware of the fact that the rules for collective redundancies were not respected, the employee is entitled to request the district court judge to declare the termination or the settlement agreement void. Such claim must be made within two months after the employee became aware and in any event limited to a maximum period of six months after the dismissal. After the expiry of this period legal proceedings against the employer are time-barred. In lieu of the nullification of the termination or settlement agreement the employee may also claim compensation.

21.60 If the UWV is aware of the fact that there is a situation of collective redundancy, the UWV will not handle the individual applications until the duty of the employer to notify the trade unions and the Works Council has been met.

Notice

21.61 The statutory notice period is calculated in months, and notice must be given at the last day of the calendar month, unless the individual employment contract explicitly varies these conditions. The statutory notice period varies for employee and employer. The employee has a minimum notice period of one month from the end of a month, whereas the notice period of the employer depends on the duration of employment. The notice period for the employer will be shortened by the period of handling of the application of permission to terminate by the UWV but a notice period of at least one month will remain.

21.62 Under previous law the notice period does not need to be taken into account when the district court judge terminates the contract. As of 1 July 2015 the district court judge must take into account the applicable notice periods for employer and employee and apply it in the decision. The period of time passed as a result of the involvement of the district court may be deducted by the judge from the notice period, provided that the minimum notice period is always one month. This principle also applies to the notice period when permission for dismissal is requested with the UWV. As an exception to the requirement for a minimum notice period the district court judge may terminate the employment contract without notice in case of serious misconduct by the employee.

21.63 Upon termination of the employment contract by mutual consent and recorded in a settlement agreement, there is no requirement for the statutory notice period to be observed. However, it should be noted that the employee is barred from claiming any unemployment benefits during such period of time where the statutory notice period is not applied. The UWV will look at the 'fictional notice period' and determine the effective termination date as if the statutory notice period had been complied with. The UWV will grant unemployment benefits to the employee no sooner than that 'fictional' date.

21.64 Parties can also extend the statutory notice period in a written agreement. The notice period of the employee can be extended to up to six months, in which case the notice period of the employer must be doubled. Reduction of the notice period can only be done by means of a collective agreement, as well as applying mirror notice periods for both employer and employee.

MINIMUM NOTICE PERIOD

21.65 The Dutch Civil Code prescribes the following notice periods:

Length of Service	Notice by Employer
Less than 1 month	no minimum period
Less than 5 years	One month
Between 5 and 10 years	Two months
Between 10 and 15 years	Three months
15 years OR more	Four months

21.66 A dismissal without observing the prescribed notice period is considered a wrongful dismissal and will make the party who has not observed the notice period liable for compensation. The compensation can be claimed in a separate procedure and comprises of money-based rate of pay for the period that the employment contract would otherwise have continued if the correct notice period had been observed.

Garden leave

21.67 In the Netherlands an employer can put an employee on garden leave or release the employee from the obligation to work only in limited situations. The employee in principle has a right to work and garden leave is often considered a punitive measure. Thus, an employer must generally allow an employee to work until the termination of his employment. However, this is not the case when the employer has a reasonable fear that the employee may cause either intentional or non-intentional damage during the exercise of his work. Despite the legal restrictions, employees are often put on garden leave during the dismissal procedure. Sometimes this is due to there not being any other solution than to put the employee on garden leave, for example because of changes in the organisation resulting in the position of the employee disappearing. This can happen before the dismissal procedure has been completed or whilst the notice period is still running. If the agreement is terminated by mutual consent, and set out in a settlement agreement, then it is preferable to include this in the agreement.

Pay in lieu of notice

21.68 If the employment is terminated without applying the statutory notice period, the money-based rate of pay is always owed in lieu of the notice period (see para **21.67**). In the Netherlands it is unusual to terminate the employment contract without any notice, except in the case of termination of the employment of directors under the articles of association. The advantage of not applying the notice period is that the employment relationship is severed earlier, the employee will for example no longer be entitled to work and as a result the discussion on garden leave is avoided. However, there is no advantage to be found with regard to the calculation of the transition payment. For the purpose of this calculation the district court judge looks at the date of dismissal and the prescribed notice period.

REDUNDANCY PAYMENT

21.69 From 1 July 2015 a lot will change regarding the financial compensation that the employer owes the employee after terminating the employment contract. Previously, an employer who had been granted consent for dismissal by the UWV did not have to pay the employee any redundancy payment.

The only possibility of claiming a payment was if the employee felt that the termination was unfair, the employee could file a claim for compensation with the district court judge.

21.70 Until 1 July 2015, the termination of the employment by the district court judge (whether or not due to commercial reasons) resulted in granting the employee a redundancy payment based on the grounds of fairness. For the calculation of this payment the district court formula was used. In short, the formula (A × B × C) was calculated based on years of service (depending on the age categories, years of service up to the age of 35, weighed 0.5; between the ages of 35 an 45, weighted 1.0; between the ages of 45 and 55, weighed 1.5; and above 55, weighed 2.0 (the A-factor)) multiplied by the gross monthly salary including fixed components (B factor). This is multiplied by a correction factor (C-factor), which depended on the degree of culpability of either the employee or the employer. Generally the C-factor lay between 0 and 2. The latter was based on case law.

21.71 When the employment contract is terminated by means of a settlement agreement then payment of redundancy payment will become part of the negotiations. The district court formula is often consulted for guidance. In case of collective redundancies there was usually a redundancy plan which took into account the district court formula.

21.72 From 1 July 2015, each employee who has been employed for a minimum of two years and who does not voluntarily leave employment is entitled to a transition payment. Accordingly, the employer will be obliged to pay the employee a transition payment regardless of the route chosen (termination by means of the district court judge or the UWV) and regardless of whether the employee is employed for a definite or indefinite period. The calculation of the transition compensation is discussed below.

Statutory redundancy pay calculation

21.73 The amount of the transition payment is calculated on the basis of the number of years of service of the employee and the salary. For the first ten years, the amount due to the employee is one-sixth of the monthly salary for every six months of service, thus one third of the salary for each year of service. From the tenth year of service, the amount due to the employee is one fourth of the monthly salary for every six months of service, thus half a months' salary for each year of service of ten and above years of service. Furthermore, in the case of several succeeding employment contracts the periods of interval do not count as years of service. The transition payment will be subject to a maximum of €75,000 gross, or the gross annual salary where such exceeds €75,000. Any cost of training or schooling by the employer aimed at enhancing employment opportunities or outplacement may be off-set against the transition payment. The financial circumstances of the employer will also be taken into account during the calculation of the transition payment.

21.74 In a collective employment agreement it will be possible to deviate in favour of the employee with regard to the transition payment. In one collective agreement this has already happened and the parties have agreed that costs for training and schooling may never be off-set against the transition payment. Finally, from 1 July 2015 smaller companies (less than 25 employees) will be able to make use of a transitional arrangement to exclude the years of service for older employees. This arrangement expires on 1 January 2020. The main difference is that the C-factor completely disappears from the transition payment calculation. All in all, the transition payment will be considerably lower than the previous district court formula, as the example below will show.

Example of statutory redundancy calculation

An employee is 48 years old and has 12 years of service with his employer. His salary is €2,500 gross per month, including holiday pay.

Redundancy pay based on the (neutral) district court formula:

Years of service ((9 × 1 (years up to the age of 45)) + (3 × 1.5 (years after the age of 45))) ×
€2,500 monthly salary × Correction factor 1 = €33,750, –

Fee based on the transition allowance:

Years of service (((10×1/3) × €2,500, –) + ((2 × 1/2) × €2,500, –)) = €10,833.33

Enhanced redundancy payments

21.75 Previously an employee might claim compensation or reinstatement of employment before the district court judge after consent to the dismissal is granted by the UWV. The employee must however prove that there is an unfair dismissal and that he suffered a loss. In case law some points of reference are given for the manner in which this compensation can be awarded, but the case law is highly inconsistent. As of 1 July 2015 it will no longer be possible to follow this route. As of that date the employee is automatically entitled to a transition payment when the employment is terminated by the employer with consent from the UWV.

21.76 After 1 July 2015 both the employer and the employee can appeal the decision of the UWV to the district court judge. The district court judge may also grant the employee a reasonable compensation in addition to the transition payment in case of 'serious imputable acts' by the employer. This additional compensation will only be granted when reinstatement of the employment is no longer considered a possibility. It is also possible for the district court judge to grant reasonable compensation to an employee whose employment has lasted less than two years (and as such there is no entitlement to the transition payment) and he nonetheless finds it reasonable that some form of compensation is awarded. Future case law will have to establish what will be considered 'serious imputable acts' by the employer. It should be noted that reasonable compensation may also be ordered in favour of the employer, if the employee has committed serious imputable acts. In such event the award will be set-off against the due transition payment, resulting in a reduction (in whole or part) of any transition payment due to the employee.

Finally, parties may also agree in the employment contract on additional severance payment. Such agreed payment will be settled in accordance with the terms of the agreement.

Taxation of redundancy payments

21.77 The employer is obliged to withhold income tax and national insurance contributions over the redundancy payment and to pay this to the Tax and Customs Administration. The rate of tax payable depends on the total taxable income of the employee in the calendar year that the compensation is paid. For 2014 the following rates apply:

- 36,25% on taxable income up to €19,645
- 42% on taxable income above €19,645 and up to €56,532
- 52% on taxable income above €56,532

> **Practical Tip**
>
> Until 1 January 2014, the employee could apply the periodic payments entitlement exemption and request his employer to pay the gross compensation on a special bank savings account or into an account of a private company incorporated for the purpose of making periodic payments. Seeing as this option is no longer available, the only remaining option which provides some sort of tax advantage is to average the income tax over three years. When the income in the form of compensation payment or severance payment is averaged over a period of three years the recipient can avoid a spike in the income which might otherwise result in a higher tax liability in the year of payment. The tax advantage is only at the advantage of an employee.

POST-TERMINATION RESTRICTIVE COVENANTS

21.78 Previously employers could include a non-competition (or non-solicitation) clause in any employment contract for a definite or indefinite period. These clauses are intended to protect the interests of the employer, such as the relationship with customers or particular expertise. Limitations imposed on the employee are often with regard to time (such as validity for one year), geography (such as only in the Netherlands), as well as a job, role or position within a company. The non-competition clause must be agreed in writing with an employee who is not a minor. Failure to adhere to these requirements results in invalidity of the clause. In order to remain valid it is may be relevant to renew the non-competition clause eg when the employment situation has changed. This is, eg the case when an existing non-competition clause limits the employee significantly more than necessary eg change of job role or due to corporate changes due to, eg a merger or take-over. Breach of the non-competition clause can lead to a penalty being imposed on the employee.

21.79 A non-competition clause must balance both the interests of the employer and the employee. Upon termination of the employment, the employer may require compliance of the employee with the non-competition clause; non-compliance results in a penalty being incurred, whilst the only option available to the employee is to seek to have the clause declared void in full or in part. The district court judge will assess whether the employee is unreasonably disadvantaged by the non-competition clause in proportion to the interests of the employer that require protection. The judge can declare the clause void, but can also amend it so that its scope becomes more limited, for example a modification in the duration of the clause or allowing it to be applicable over a smaller geographic area.

21.80 From 1 January 2015 it is no longer possible to include a non-competition clause in employment contracts for a fixed period, unless the employment contract specifies that the non-competition clause is necessary because of substantial business interests. How the courts will deal with the specification requirement is unclear and case law will have to show.

Practical Tip

From 1 January 2015 employers will be required to include a provision in a fixed employment contract detailing to the reason why the non-competition clause is necessary. Therefore, employers will have to identify for which functions a non-competition clause is necessary due to substantial business interests. Such reasoning must consequently be included in the employment contract, without it the non-competition clause is void

BUSINESS SALE, OUTSOURCING/INSOURCING AND OFFSHORING

21.81 In case of a transfer of undertaking the rights of the employees are protected under the Law transfer of undertaking (hereafter: 'LTU') which is included (among others) in the articles 7:662–666 of the Dutch Civil Code. These statutes are based on the European Directive 77/187 of 14 February 1977 (as later amended on 17 July 1998) to protect the rights of employees of transfers of undertakings, businesses or parts of businesses.

21.82 The LTU does not apply to bodies governed by public law where only public officials work, nor does it apply to employers that have been declared bankrupt. The main consequences of the LTU are:

- the rights and obligations under the employment contract between employer and employee will be transferred to the acquiring company (the transferee) by default;
- the former employer will remain jointly and severally liable for all obligations that arose prior to the transfer alongside the transferee up until one year after the transfer of undertaking;
- all employees will become employed by the transferee by default;
- a new trial period may not be agreed upon by the transferee.

Business sale

21.83 There is a transfer of undertaking when one economic entity, while maintaining its own identity, is transferred by means of a contract (sale, merger or division). A sale through a transfer of shares is excluded from the definition because the shareholder merely changes, which is not necessarily the formal employer. Accordingly, in case of a transfer of undertaking all three elements must be met, which are discussed in further detail in the sections below.

21.84 An economic entity is defined as an 'organised grouping of resources which has the objective of pursuing an economic activity, whether or not that activity is central or ancillary'. This definition makes the legal form of the undertaking less important, which is why in cases of transfer of undertaking an entire undertaking, but also a branch of the undertaking and even elements of the undertaking or its branch can be considered an economic entity. Furthermore it does not matter whether the undertaking has a profit motive, because also not-for profit undertakings fall under the scope of the LTU.

21.85 A condition for the transfer is that the economic entity is transferred whilst retaining its own identity. The interpretation of whether the identity of the undertaking is transferred is supplemented by Dutch and European case law. Ultimately the Dutch Court decides whether there is a transfer of undertaking and the court will do so on the basis of all the facts. In evaluating the facts the district court does not merely look at whether the entire workforce or assets have been transferred. The district court judge must take all relevant facts into account, including, but not limited to: the nature of the undertaking concerned; whether tangible assets are transferred and the value of these assets; whether personnel transfers; whether the customer database is transferred; and the extent to which the transferred activities resemble the activities from before the transfer. All these facts are considered a whole and not one fact is decisive on its own. Depending on the sector, certain factors will weigh heavier in the assessment. Also there is a distinction between labour intensive and capital intensive sectors. In labour intensive sectors, the transition of the entire workforce will weigh more heavily in the evaluation than the transfer of tangible assets. In case of the transfer of a branch of the undertaking or a part of the undertaking the district court judge must also determine whether there is a functional link connection between the employees and the activities or assets that are transferred. Thus, all the facts and circumstances must be assessed in its entirety.

21.86 Finally, the LTU is applicable when the transfer of the economic entity is effected by means of an agreement. As determined by case law this requirement must be interpreted broadly. It is therefore not required that the transfer takes place by means of an agreement specifically for the transfer of assets, but an agreement that involves the transfer of the undertaking is considered sufficient. It can also become apparent from the facts that the parties have reached a consensus on the transfer of undertaking. Therefore, even when there is no actual written agreement, on the basis of the transfer it is still possible to argue that there is a transfer of undertaking. This can, for example, be the case when, within a group of companies, one part or branch of a subsidiary company is transferred to another subsidiary company, without there being an actual, written agreement.

Outsourcing/insourcing

21.87 For the purpose of establishing whether there is a transfer of undertaking in case of outsourcing/insourcing it is necessary to examine whether the identity of the economic entity remains after the transfer. There are no separate rules in Dutch law for outsourcing/insourcing. Accordingly, the assessment of whether or not there is a transfer of undertaking is carried out on the basis of the aforementioned criteria and case law. As mentioned above, it is relevant whether the transfer happens in a labour intensive or capital intensive sector. Outsourcing can result in a transfer of undertaking, especially when, in labour intensive sectors, a large part of the staff is taken over.

EFFECT OF THE TRANSFER OF UNDERTAKING

Automatic transfer and protection of employment

21.88 If there is a transfer of undertaking, according to the LTU, all rights and obligations at that time arising from the employment contract are automatically transferred to the transferee. It is not required that such rights or obligations are immediately claimable, only their existence must be proven. This may also involve verbal agreements. In addition to the working hours and the terms and conditions of employment, the seniority claim with regard to length of service is also transferred. An exception to the principle that all rights and obligations are transferred applies to the non-competition clause. This could become void if it turns out that as a result of the transfer the non-competition clause becomes very onerous on the employee. Also, the terms and conditions of the employment that are not agreed upon in the individual employment contract, but derive from the applicable collective agreement or the compulsory declared applicable collective agreement, will also be transferred by default. These terms and conditions will remain applicable until the collective agreement expires, or the transferee becomes bound by a compulsory declared applicable collective agreement. Only then will the collective agreement become applicable to the acquired employees.

21.89 Employees who have been seconded to the undertaking in principle are not transferred, because they are not employed, unless they are permanently seconded.

Objection to the transfer

21.90 The fact that the rights and obligations under the employment contract automatically transfer to the transferee does not mean that an employee can be required to transfer. The employee who unequivocally declares that he does not wish to transfer, shall not be obliged to do so. However, once the employee indicates this, then he will not remain employed with his former employer. The employment contract will be deemed to have been terminated by the employee at the date of the transfer of undertaking.

21.91 For the employee, it may be wise to request, prior to the transfer of undertaking, termination of the employment contract. When the transfer of undertaking has adverse consequences for the employee, he will be entitled to a compensation, as the termination will be deemed to have occurred due to a reason that lies within the control of the employer. However, by unequivocally refusing to accept the transfer and the subsequent termination of the employment contract, the employee risks that he will not be granted unemployment benefits, because the UWV might deem the employee to be voluntarily unemployed.

Protection from dismissal

21.92 As the employment contract is continued with the new employer under the same rights and obligations, a new trial period may not be agreed upon.

21.93 It is also prohibited to dismiss employees because of a transfer of undertaking. However, if the new employer can show that the dismissal is justified and necessary for economic, technical or organisational reasons (also called ETO reasons) and that the dismissal would also be necessary regardless of the transfer of undertaking, then a dismissal of the employee can be justified. The new employer will have to effect the dismissal of the employee in the regular way by means of requesting consent for dismissal from the UWV.

21.94 If the employer requests for consent for dismissal with the UWV, then the UWV does not comment on whether there is a transfer of undertaking, because such review is solely the task of the district court. Therefore it is quite difficult for the UWV to judge the dismissal when parties dispute that there is a transfer of undertaking.

Protection of terms and conditions of employment

21.95 As well as the prohibition on dismissing employees because of the transfer of undertaking, it is also not possible to adjust the terms and conditions under employment or to harmonise them because of the transfer of undertaking. According to European case law an employer is not allowed to harmonise the terms and conditions of employment of its employees (both old and new) just because of the transfer of undertaking. Often employers will argue that this results in a violation of the principle of equal treatment of employees, but they will have no success with this argument. On the basis of the abovementioned ETO reasons an employer may harmonise the terms and conditions of employment, but of course only when the employer proves sufficient cause. In case law it is assumed that the sooner the desire to harmonise follows the transfer of undertaking, the more likely it will be that the two are related and have less to do with the ETO reasons. For more information about how to change the terms and conditions of employment, see para **21.110**.

21.96 There is one exception to the principle that all rights and obligations will transfer by default, which is the pension scheme. If the transferee has a pension scheme for his own staff at the time of the transition, then he can offer the same pension scheme to the employees that were taken over. It does not matter whether this pension scheme is less beneficial than the pension scheme the employees used to have. What is important is that the transferee makes a commitment to the new employees as regards the pension scheme equal to the commitment made to the current employees at the time of the transfer.

INFORMATION AND CONSULTATION UNDER LTU

Duty to inform

21.97 The employer (transferor) is obliged to provide the employee with correct and complete information, so that the employee can make a good assessment of whether he wants to transfer to the transferee or not. The employer must give the employees full disclosure of the state of affairs and must correctly and completely inform them on the transfer of undertaking and its legal consequences. In particular, the employer must inform the employees about the proposed decision to transfer, the proposed date of the transfer, the reason for the transfer, as well as the legal, economic and social consequences for the employees and the measures envisaged with regard to the employees. If the company has a Works Council or an employee representative body then the employer will have to inform them about the envisaged transfer, after which they will ensure that the employees are informed. The Works Council also has the right to give advice on the matter. There is no additional obligation that requires the employer to inform both the Works Council and the employees.

21.98 The transferee also has a duty to inform his employees of the planned transfer of undertaking, but has no obligations towards the employees that are being transferred.

Measures letter

21.99 There is no general obligation for the transferee to inform the transferred employees of the possible measures to be taken as a result of the transfer. The only exception is the already mentioned pension scheme. The pension scheme must be offered by the transferee to the new employees prior to the date of transfer. Sometimes a collective agreement sets terms and conditions that the transferee must uphold, especially in the situation of outsourcing and in case of a change of command (for example, in the cleaning industry). Then there is an obligation under the collective agreement to offer the employee a new employment contract, even if there is no transfer of undertaking and as such no transfer of employees by default.

Employee liability information

21.100 The employees are entitled to information on the transfer of undertaking, but their right to privacy must also be protected, in particular their personal information. Upon the sale of the company or part of the company, the transferee will naturally want to know who will become employed by default, but detailed (personal) data on the employees cannot simply be released. Because of the right to privacy, the data of the employees provided to the buyer is limited to the bare minimum. However, this limitation is in practice not always respected.

Duty to consult

21.101 If a company has a Works Council or an employee representative body, the employer is required to seek advice regarding the transfer of undertaking. However there is no requirement to come to an agreement on the redundancy plan.

European Works Councils

21.102 If a company has a (required) European Works Council then there may also be a requirement to provide information in the event of a transfer of undertaking and collective redundancies.

SANCTIONS

Unfair dismissal

21.105 In case of a transfer of undertaking all the employees employed in the business will transfer with the existing rights and obligations and will enter into the service of the transferee (article 7:662 BW). The transferee is not allowed to dismiss the employees where the principal reason or connected reason is the transfer. This is prohibited in article 7:670, par. 8 BW. If the employer does obtain consent for dismissal from the UWV, he is not allowed to use it. If an employer does give notice, the employee can submit an application at the district court to declare the dismissal void. In that case the employee can claim reinstatement of the employment or a fair compensation.

Failure to inform and consult

21.106 There is no separate sanction for failure of the obligation of informing and consulting employees in a transfer of undertaking, and therefore the general compensation rules of civil law apply. This means that a breach of the obligation to inform and consult may lead to an unlawful act against the workers and on that basis they can recover damages from the employer (Papers II 2000/01, 27 469, no. 5, p. 9). However, there seems to be no case law (yet) in which the employees are actually granted compensation in this matter.

APPLICATION OF THE LTU TO CROSS-BORDER TRANSACTIONS/OFFSHORING

21.107 In a cross-border transfer of undertaking employees can be faced with a foreign employer who is located within or outside the EU. The question is which country's law applies to workers in the event of such a transfer of undertaking. When it comes to transferee within the EU then this employer will also be bound by the European Acquired Rights Directive. In general, within the EU a transfer of an undertaking is subject to the criteria already mentioned above. Although the Directive is implemented by the different countries (in England and Wales a stricter variant applies than in the

Netherlands) the protective scope will be the same. The European case law for each country applies. A company based outside the EU will not be bound by the Directive, but workers would in theory be able to call on the Dutch provisions on transfer of undertaking which applies to their employment.

21.108 In the Netherlands there is only limited case law on cross-border transfers of undertakings. It shows that especially in the border areas, the Dutch district court is fairly quick to conclude that the transfer of undertaking legislation applies. As in all cases of transfer of undertakings a number of factors are relevant, but the key factor is whether the economic entity still exists and retains its identity after the transfer. In this respect it is reasonable to assume that when a company located close to the border moves 30 miles across that border, will be able to retain its identity, but when the company moves much further away, and the legal and social context (eg another language) completely changes, this will not be the case.

WORKFORCE REDUCTION IN CONNECTION WITH SHARE SALE OR SHARE PURCHASE

21.109 As mentioned, the legal framework for transfer of undertaking does not apply if the transfer takes place via a transfer of shares. This is logical because only the company's shareholder changes and thus the employer and the contract does not undergo any change. The new shareholder is of course free to define a different policy regarding the company and can for example decide on a reorganisation. If dismissals result therefrom, the employer will be obliged to follow the regular procedure via the UWV (or the district judge). As an alternative the employer can try to reach a termination of the employment contract by mutual consent.

CHANGING EMPLOYMENT TERMS AND CONDITIONS

21.110 Once an employment contract is entered into, there are only a few possibilities to change the employment conditions. The Dutch legislation assumes that the terms of the contract are respected by the parties and an amendment is only possible in a serious change of circumstances. There are in general three ways to change the employment conditions. The easiest way is to change with the consent of the employee. In this case both parties agree on the change which can be embodied in a new employment agreement. Furthermore, the employer may change the terms unilaterally if a 'unilateral amendment clause' has been included in the existing contract. Lastly, if this is not the case, the terms can be unilaterally changed by the employer on the basis of reasonableness and fairness and good employeeship. The terms under which this applies are explained below.

21.111 First it is important to determine whether the term that needs to be changed is considered to be an agreed term. In general, a term is considered to be agreed if the employee can enforce it. This means that what is incidentally or spontaneously provided to the employee by the employer (such as a discretionary bonus) is not considered a term of employment. Revocation or amendment of such a term can be done easily. When the bonus is provided on a regular basis (without reservation), there might be a vested right, and thus an agreed employment term. In that case, a simple modification is not possible.

Mutually agreed changes

21.112 Changing the terms of the employment contract by mutual consent is possible at any time, provided that the parties act within the limits of the law and – if applicable – the collective labour agreement. Any amendment will only be binding upon parties if there is a clear proposal to the employee that explains the proposed amendment and the results thereof. The employee should be given the time to think about the proposed amendment and if the employee agrees, the employee must accept the amendment clearly. This should be documented, so that it can easily be demonstrated afterwards that the employee's consent has been obtained.

21.113 Please note that certain conditions of employment are covered by the right of consent of the Works Council so that any amendment requires prior consultation (and consent) of the Works Council. Furthermore amendment of terms in a collective labour agreement which is binding on the parties (this varies, not every collective employment agreement is the same in this respect) will be considered void.

Unilateral changes

21.114 When the parties are unable to agree to changes, the employer may decide to impose a change to the terms and conditions unilaterally. Three possibilities arise.

21.115 The first opportunity is when parties have agreed on a so-called 'unilateral amendment clause', in the employment contract or in supplementary employment conditions. This gives the employer the right unilaterally to modify, under certain circumstances, the conditions of employment. The use of a unilateral amendment clause is intended for modification of secondary elements of remuneration for a group of employees (simultaneously) while the interests of workers are protected. As a condition for the use of the clause, the employer must first prove that he has such a substantial interest in the change, that the interests of the affected employees according to the standards of reasonableness and fairness, must yield. There is a legal presumption of substantial interest on the employer's part, if the Works Council or the union have agreed to the change, in which case it becomes much easier for the employer to apply the unilateral amendment clause.

21.116 The employer may also change the terms and conditions, based on the obligation that the employee must act as a good employee. Here it concerns mostly primary elements of remuneration. Based on the principle of reasonableness and fairness the employee can be forced to accept reasonable proposals being made by the employer. Case law provides that this principle can be invoked by the employer if there is a major change in the circumstances of employment. Furthermore, the employer has to make a reasonable proposal, taking into account all conditions, such as the nature of the change, the nature and intrusiveness of the proposal, but also the interests of the employer in the change versus the interest of the employee retaining the agreed terms. Finally, the employer must show that acceptance by the employee may be required in light of these circumstances. This means that the employer must have taken into account the wishes of the employee. Offering a reasonable compensation may also promote the obligation to accept the change. As with the unilateral amendment clause, consent of the Works Council will help the employer to enforce the unilateral change.

21.117 A final option of unilateral change in employment terms is the possibility of applying to the district judge for modification of the contract if it appears that enforcement according to the standards of reasonableness and fairness is not acceptable. The district court may modify the contract if there are unforeseen circumstances, such as conditions that are not (explicitly or implicitly) included in the contract and are not on the account of the employer. This way of change is not easy to achieve and the employer may therefore encounter difficulties.

Dismissing and re-engaging employees on new terms

21.118 The option to lay off employees and then re-engage them under new terms and conditions is available, but not often used. Since it is rather difficult to dismiss an employee in the Netherlands, an employer needs to obtain consent to dismissal by the UWV or termination of the contract by the district court, the scenario of new terms and conditions has been extensively explored on a regular basis. In case parties do not agree on the new terms of the employment contract and the employer is forced to enter into a dismissal procedure, a continuation of the employment relation is usually no longer a realistic option.

Practical Tips on changing terms and conditions

The easiest way to change the terms and conditions of employment, is to obtain the consent of the employee. If this fails, try unilaterally to change the working conditions by proposing a reasonable offer, including compensation, and obtain if possible the consent of the Works Council to this offer. If there is only a small change in circumstances, and the interest of the employer in the proposed change is minor – for example, because the employers' damage is limited by retaining the agreed conditions – it will be difficult to enforce the change. In any case, it is important to document the process well.

USING TEMPORARY STAFF

Agency workers

21.119 The agency contract is a special employment agreement between the agency (the lender) and the worker, where the worker is made temporarily available to a third party (the recipient) by the agency.

21.120 Agency employees do not enjoy the same employment protection as regular employees, but the worker will be entitled to at least the same conditions as apply to employees working in the same job within the same company. This equal treatment standard can be set aside by a collective labour agreement. Generally, the longer an employee works for an employment agency, the stronger his rights become. The main collective labour agreement for temporary workers, the CAO ABU, distinguishes different phases of protection (A, B and C).

21.121 The protection for dismissal of the worker depends on the length of employment of the worker at the agency. During the first phase A, the contract with the temporary worker may be immediately terminated as soon as the recipient ends the assignment with the agency. In accordance with the collective agreement ABU this phase lasts 78 weeks, derogating from the statutory scheme that provides for a maximum period of 26 weeks. The next phase B can last for a maximum of two years (or eight successive employment agreements). During this phase, there is a temporary employment contract for a fixed-term period that ends at the agreed moment (and does not end by the mere ending of the assignment). The last phase C enters when after phase B, a temporary worker is redeployed within 13 weeks by the same agency, in which case the worker receives a contract of an indefinite period of time. In this contract, all the rules of the regular protection against dismissal apply.

FIXED-TERM CONTRACTS

21.122 In The Netherlands, employers may choose to offer an employee an employment contract for a fixed-term or an indefinite period of time. This option will expire at some point, but more on that below (Renewal of fixed-term contracts).

21.123 The rules regarding fixed-term contracts were tightened on 1 January 2015. As already mentioned, from this moment on it is no longer possible to include a non-competition clause in a fixed-term employment contract, unless justified. Also inclusion of a probationary period in a fixed term contract that lasts less than six months is prohibited. In contracts entered into for a longer period than six months a probation period of one month is possible. Also new is that the employer has to take into account a period of notice, for contracts entered into for a longer period than six months. This means that the employer will have to indicate, one month before the expiry of the contract, whether and under what conditions the contract is renewed. If the employer forgets to do so, the contract will still end by operation of law at the agreed date, but the employer is obliged to pay a penalty of one month's salary, or pro rata for the period of delay in communicating this decision.

21.124 In the event of a transfer of undertaking, all employees working on flexible contracts and fixed-term contracts as well as employees working under on-call contracts (such as zero-hour contracts or a min/max contract) will be transferred to the transferee. The length of employment is in this respect not relevant. An on-call contract is an employment contract with a flexible number of working hours (from 0–40), so that an employer can deploy an employee whenever needed. These contracts can be entered into either for a fixed-term or for an indefinite period. The transferee will have to be alert on the rebuttable legal presumption on a minimum range of working hours, which can be invoked by the employee based on the average working hours of the foregoing three (or more) months.

Renewal of fixed-term contracts

21.125 A fixed-term contract ends by operation of law on the agreed date or moment in time. Unless otherwise agreed in the fixed-term employment contract, there is no need for a dismissal of such employee. The so-called chain regulation provides that a fixed-term employment agreement after a certain period of time or number of contracts must be converted into a permanent contract, which results in protection against dismissal. Until 1 July 2015, an employer may enter into a maximum of three fixed-term contracts up to a maximum period of (together) three years, in case the intermission between the contracts is not more than three months (ie: 3 × 3 × 3). If this period or amount of employment contracts is exceeded, such as a fourth fixed-term contract, this last contract shall be automatically converted into a permanent contract. As a result, the employee gets protection against dismissal. In case an employer wants to avoid this, an interval of more than three months between the third and fourth contract is necessary. This chain control is being tightened as of 1 July 2015. From then on, three fixed-term contracts with a maximum period of two years in total, in case the contracts succeed each other within a period of six months (ie: 3 × 2 × 6) are allowed. Fixed-term employment contracts will therefore be more easily converted into permanent contracts. This regulation is also applicable in case of a transfer of undertaking. The new employer needs to be aware of the number and duration of contracts under which the employee has been employed by the transferor, because these contracts count for the aforementioned maximum. The likelihood of the transferee offering a fixed-term contract can therefore be limited.

Practical Tips on fixed-term contracts

Employers must comply with the notice period applying from 1 January 2015. The employee must be informed at least one month before the end of the fixed term that the agreement will not continue. If the notice is omitted, the employee is due a month wages. In a contract of six months or less no probation period can be applied.

EMPLOYMENT CLAIMS

21.126 Employment claims must be submitted to the district court judge. There are 11 district courts located in the Netherlands (geographically distributed). Some courts, however, have several establishments and in total there are 53 locations. The general rule in employment claims is that the district court in the domicile (registered) place of the other party (defendant) has jurisdiction to hear the claim, but the claimant may also choose to bring the proceedings in the jurisdiction of the place of work.

Unfair dismissal

21.127 If permission is obtained from the UWV for termination of the contract, as of 1 July 2015 the employer is obliged to pay a transition allowance. The employee may, within two months after the end of his contract bring proceedings before the district court if he does not agree with the termination. The employee must then prove that the UWV wrongly authorised the dismissal, by eg not having applied seniority rules correctly. The employee must primarily focus on re-instatement of employment but if that is not possible, the district court may award compensation based on fairness. Prerequisite for such compensation award is that re-instatement of employment is not possible due to a cause involving a seriously culpable act or omission of the employer (Article 7: 682 BW).

Remedies

21.128 As of 1 July 2015 an appeal may be brought against the decision of the court for granting re-instatement of employment or compensation in fairness, as well as a termination order, at the Court of Appeal and then appealed to the Supreme Court. This is not possible until 1 July 2015.

The basic award

21.129 From 1 July 2015, the transition compensation will be due in every case of dismissal or termination of the contract initiated by the employer. The only exemption is when the contract is entered into for a limited period of time and has lasted less than two years. The employer must pay the compensation and in the absence thereof, the employee can enforce payment by a court procedure. Until 1 July 2015 another system applies as described above.

The compensatory award

21.130 Under the new rules, it is possible to seek additional fair compensation on top of the transition allowance. The employee is entitled to this if the employer has acted seriously culpable, and this compensation is not limited. It is still unclear what is meant by 'seriously culpable conduct' of the employer since the district courts have not yet dealt with this issue of additional fair compensation. Moreover, the employer may claim reimbursement from the employee (which will be deducted from the transition compensation) if the employee acted in a seriously culpable manner. It is anticipated that additional agreements on this subject will be made in collective labour agreements.

DISCRIMINATION

21.131 Apart from the general prohibition of discrimination on grounds of race, sex, religion etc, direct or indirect distinction between men and women with respect to employment matters is also prohibited. Furthermore there is a ban on discrimination related to working hours and the term of the employment contract. The non-discrimination principles are based on European law (Directive 1999/70/EC). In case of a dismissal in breach of a prohibition of discrimination, the employee may invoke the annulment of the dismissal and claim a restoration of employment agreement, or claim a fair compensation.

MUTUALLY AGREED TERMINATION

21.132 Termination of the employment contract by mutual consent is always possible. The employer can only rely on the consent of the employee if it is clearly and unequivocally stated by the employee. Furthermore the employer must establish whether the employee has understood that he is asked to consent to termination of employment. This applies especially where the employee does not understand the Dutch language very well. The employer, must inform the employee about the consequences of termination, for example, that the employee may lose his pension or may lose his entitlement to an unemployment benefit.

21.133 As of 1 July 2015 the law provides that, if the parties conclude a settlement agreement, the employee has the possibility to invoke annulment of the agreement within a period of reflection lasting two weeks and this possibility should be confirmed in writing to the employee. During this period the employee may revoke his consent to the settlement agreement without reason. If the reflection period of two weeks is not communicated in writing to the employee, this period will be prolonged up to three weeks. After this period the employee can then revoke his consent to the settlement agreement, if he can prove a vitiated consent, such as error or fraud.

Settlement Agreements

21.134 There are no special rules in Dutch employment law with regard to settlement agreement, so the general regime of contract law applies (Article 7: 900 BW).

21.135 In the settlement agreement provisions are made on the date by which the employment agreement will end, the ground for the termination, and financial compensation of the employee. These facilities can include a transition compensation, but also a compensation for any loss of pension, an outplacement program and the costs of legal assistance. It is a custom in the Netherlands that the employer contributes to the legal fees, to a set amount (usually around €1,500).

21.136 Although all rights and obligations of the employment relationship last to the date of termination, it is possible to agree deviations in the settlement agreement. The employee may be exempted from work until the termination date (but then the employee is often considered to have received his holidays). Furthermore, the employee can be obliged to return his work phone and other property belonging to the employer, and be obliged – if he was unable to work due to sickness – to report himself fit at the time the contract ends. The latter is important because of the Dutch social security system which provides for a penalty if the employee is dismissed during sick leave. On the other hand the employer will be held liable for paying the salary and allowances, but the employee may also ask for a testimonial or a good reference. Also, parties can agree on a non-competition or non-solicitation clause, such that it remains in position or that changes are made. Furthermore, the settlement agreement needs to contain a provision that the agreement is in full and final settlement of each party's claims against the other, so that no further claims remain.

WITHOUT PREJUDICE AND 'PRE-TERMINATION' DISCUSSIONS

21.137 In the Netherlands the concept of a settlement 'without prejudice' does not apply. The general rule is that if the negotiations on the settlement have taken place between attorneys at law, the contents of these negotiations are considered confidential. This means that the content of the offered settlement agreement cannot be disclosed in court. However if both parties agree, the judge may be informed of the offered agreement, which in some cases benefits the position of the employer.

21.138 It is often ruled in the settlement agreement that a strict secrecy clause applies, but usually this is exempted by the possibility for the employee to present the settlement agreement to the UWV, in support of his claim for unemployment benefit. It is noteworthy that the employer should never guarantee the unemployment benefit, because the UWV assesses the right to a benefit independently.

Pre-termination discussions

21.139 The concept of 'pre-termination discussions' is not a familiar concept in Dutch law. Usually a negotiation will precede any termination of the employment contract. It is advisable for both employer and employee to seek legal assistance as this stage, in order to strengthen their legal position and to optimise the outcome of negotiations.

Chapter 22

Workforce Restructuring in Norway

Merete Furesund and Lise Berntsen
Kvale Advokatfirma DA
Oslo

INTRODUCTION

22.1 This chapter looks at employment legislation in Norway. The main statute for employment issues in Norway is the Working Environment Act ('the WEA'), which contains provisions regarding the employer's and the employee's rights and obligations. Case law supplements the provisions of the WEA. In addition, collective agreements provide a framework for identifying rights and obligations for employers and employees.

22.2 The WEA stipulates the minimum requirements for the content of an employment contract. It limits the opportunities for the parties to agree terms that deviate from the WEA to the detriment of the employee. Norwegian employment contracts tend to be short and only contain provisions which meet the minimum requirements prescribed by law, as well as provisions restricting the employee's right to use confidential information and intellectual property, and restrictive covenants.

22.3 In a restructuring scenario, it is important to assess the entitlements of each employee affected by the restructuring. This will, among others, include determining the applicable notice period, salary and other benefits, pension and insurance membership schemes, as well as post-termination restrictive covenants, protection of confidential information and IP.

22.4 It is also important to get a good overview of the process that is to be carried out. This includes obtaining an understanding and knowledge of the requirements for conducting a restructuring exercise; eg what conditions must be fulfilled in order to start a restructuring exercise, further understanding and knowledge of each step of the process, the requirements for the process, as well as preparation of the necessary documentation and templates to be used. Such knowledge and understanding must be attained before initiating any intervention in the workforce, including reorganisations and workforce reductions.

PREPARING FOR A RESTRUCTURING EXERCISE

22.5 Several issues may be relevant if a company is to carry out a restructuring or reorganisation. These may include a reduction of the workforce, changing terms and conditions of employment, using temporary staff, outsourcing of or transferring all or parts of the business.

22.6 Before starting a restructuring exercise, the company must compile information and make preparations and assessments for the exercise. It is important to have the correct and relevant information for the specific process that the company desires to carry out. The legislation sets out requirements for the assessments to be made, the process to be carried out and the information to be collected etc. Preparation and planning is therefore of upmost importance. It will also help reduce the risk of disputes, even though there will, in most cases, always be employees challenging some parts of the assessments and decisions of a company.

22.7 Some of the initial key issues are set out below.

Identify the employing entity

22.8 The employer will always be a particular legal entity, and never the group. However, under certain circumstances, two legal entities may be jointly liable as employers. In such cases, it is important to identify who the employer is and may be considered to be, both formally and in reality. Amongst other things, the employer entity will be relevant in relation to the legal entity and body authorised to make decisions regarding a restructuring exercise, the employer's obligation to offer other suitable work before terminating an employment and the employee's preferential right to new employment for one year following the termination.

Collating information to plan and budget for the restructuring exercise

22.9 The company should ensure that it has the relevant information regarding the employees in scope. The employing entity will normally hold such information in the employment contract, personnel handbooks, internal regulations and personnel files. It is essential to ensure that any centralised HR department in the group has (lawful) access to such information.

22.10 In the case of disputes from employees following the termination of their employment, the courts will look closely at what information the company holds for the specific employee, the other employees in scope and the process, as well as the assessments made in the process. Therefore, the documentation collected before and during the restructuring exercise is vital to the process.

Practical Tip

The following constitutes some examples of necessary information which should be gathered in respect of any employee who may be affected by a workforce reduction or restructuring exercise. The list is not exhaustive:

- type of employment (permanent, temporary), whether the employment is part or full time, and the fraction for part-time employment (eg 80 %);
- job role and job description;
- length of service;
- salary and other benefits, both individual and collective (eg compensation for overtime, bonus, pension etc);
- age;
- place of work;
- working hours;
- applicable collective agreement (if any), including the early retirement scheme and the agreement on severance pay included in most collective agreements;
- formal qualifications and other work experience;
- collective entitlements (eg as drawn up in a personnel handbook, internal regulations etc);
- notice period; and
- other provisions relating to terminating the employment (eg restrictive covenants and possible payments for enforcing these)

The same information should also be collected for hired personnel, contractors and consultants. Gathering the above information will assist in preparing an estimate of costs for the restructuring exercise as well as appropriate suitable timetable for the process.

EMPLOYMENT STATUS

22.11 Protection against unfair dismissal is only awarded to people who meet the definition of 'employee' in the WEA. The definition of employee includes full-time and part-time employees, and also permanent and temporary employees. However, due to the nature of the employment, temporary employees are only protected against unfair dismissal for termination of their employment before the expiry of their defined period of work.

22.12 Regardless of the formal arrangement of their engagement with the company, agency workers and contractors may be deemed employees of the company. Whether they are, in fact, deemed employees depend on an individual assessment of a number of factors relating to both the formal side of the engagement and the reality of the relationship. Agency workers or contractors who are deemed employees of the company will enjoy protection against unfair dismissal and must be treated in the same way as the other employees of the company in a restructuring exercise.

22.13 Hired personnel and the use of contractors should be reduced before carrying out a workforce reduction of the employees in the legal entity.

GENERAL PROTECTION AGAINST DISMISSAL

22.14 In Norway, 'employment at will' does not exist. All employees are protected against unfair dismissal. The employer must also follow a specific procedure when dismissing an employee. Only the chief executive of the company may, in a prior and written agreement, relinquish his protection against unfair dismissal in exchange for compensation on termination of employment. Any such contractual termination clauses with other employees will be invalid. Termination of their employment must follow the statutory requirements, including objectively justified grounds for termination and a minimum notice period.

22.15 A dismissal will only be lawful if it is objectively justified on the basis of circumstances relating to the company/employer or the specific employee. The legislation and collective agreements also include requirements for the dismissal procedure which the employer must observe.

22.16 The grounds and procedure for a dismissal must be in accordance with the general lawful requirement of being objectively justified. The employer must be able to document both the grounds and the process. In a reorganisation exercise, this will also include documentation of the assessments that the employer has conducted, including the basis for them and their result as well as the evaluation of one employee against another.

SPECIAL PROTECTION AGAINST DISMISSAL

22.17 Employees in certain types of situations are protected against dismissal:

(*a*) an employee who is wholly or partly absent from work due to sickness cannot be dismissed on grounds relating to the sickness absence for the first 12 months;
(*b*) an employee who is absent from work due to military service or similar national service cannot be dismissed on grounds relating to such absence;
(*c*) an employee who is pregnant cannot be dismissed on grounds of pregnancy; and
(*d*) an employee who has leave of absence due to maternity or paternity leave for up to one year cannot be dismissed during this year.

22.18 Employees as described in (*a*)–(*c*) above may be dismissed on other grounds than the ones described. In such case, the employer must be able to prove that the absence, sickness, military service, or pregnancy has not influenced the decision to dismiss the employee. If a lawful dismissal is given to an employee on maternity or paternity leave during the first year of such leave, the notice period will not run during the leave but start running when the first year of leave has expired. In addition, the grounds for dismissal must be assessed and objectively justified when the year of leave has expired.

22.19 Other examples of dismissals which automatically will be unfair include (but are not limited to):

- whistleblowing;
- membership of a trade union;
- a reason related to a protected characteristic (political views, sexual orientation, age, disability, gender, ethnic origin, national origin, religion, descent, colour, language, ethical and cultural orientation);
- being a part-time employee; or
- claims regarding legal rights (eg working hours, holiday and compensation for overtime work).

22.20 Compulsory retirement due to age is considered as an unfair dismissal and discriminatory before the age of 72. A lower age may follow for certain work, eg 62 years. A company may have established a lower age for compulsory retirement if such age is known by the employees, is practiced consistently and the employee is entitled to a satisfactory occupational pension scheme. In such case, the age for compulsory retirement may be below 72 years but not below 70 years.

WORKFORCE REDUCTION

22.21 Termination of employment as part of a restructuring plan requires the company to have a clear view of the grounds that form the basis for the restructuring plan and dismissals. The grounds must be in accordance with the applicable legislation.

22.22 The company must also ensure that the procedure to be carried out complies with the requirements prescribed by applicable legislation and any applicable collective agreements. Additional requirements for the procedure apply for collective redundancy, ie where ten or more employees have been dismissed or employments have been terminated on grounds not related to their individual during a period of 30 days.

Requirement for objectively justified grounds

22.23 A workforce reduction must have objectively justified grounds relating to the company. There is no statutory definition of the term 'objectively justified grounds', but the legislation sets out certain requirements that must be met in order for this condition to be fulfilled. In addition, the special protection against dismissal, as described above starting at para **22.17**, also clarifies the content of the term.

22.24 The requirement for objectively justified grounds is relevant at several stages. First, the grounds for the workforce reduction must be documented and objectively justified. According to case law, the company's need to minimise loss will fulfil the statutory requirement of the grounds being objectively justified. A wish to reduce costs, even though the company makes a profit, may also fulfil this requirement. The courts will normally only conduct a limited review of the company's decision to implement cost reduction measures which include a workforce reduction provided the assessment and the process prior to the decision is well documented and has been satisfactory. The discussion and involvement of the employee representatives and the employees are crucial in this regard. The company must also be able to document that other, less radical, measures than dismissals have been considered and that these do not achieve the necessary savings for the company. Other measures may be: termination of independent contractors and hired personnel, reorganisation in the company, temporary dismissals and so on. The company must also be able to document the probable rationalisation profit resulting from the dismissals.

22.25 Secondly, the selection pool and the selection criteria used for deciding which employees to be made redundant must be objectively justified. There is no statutory definition of what is required for a selection pool or what selection criteria are considered to fulfil this requirement. However, case law has established some guidelines in this regard. In addition, most collective agreements state that length of service must be the main selection criteria, but this basic principle may in some cases be deviated from.

22.26 Thirdly, the procedure for dismissing the employees must be objectively justified. This includes the involvement of, and discussion with, the employee representatives, as well as the discussions, procedure and assessments towards the individual employee affected by the workforce reduction. The legislation and collective agreements set out requirements for the process, including the assessments which must be carried out and the process towards the employee representatives and the individual employees.

22.27 The legislation also sets out certain requirements for the specific dismissal of an employee during a workforce reduction to be objectively justified. A dismissal due to curtailed operations or rationalisation measures will not be objectively justified if the employer has other suitable work in the company to offer the employee, provided that the employee is qualified for this work. Other suitable work may be a lower position with lower wages. The obligation only encompasses open positions or available work in the legal entity that is the employer. Hence, the legal organisation of a company may have an impact on the extent of the obligation to offer other suitable work. The employer must also perform an individual assessment for each employee who may be made redundant where the needs of the company must be weighed against the disadvantages that the termination causes for the individual employee.

22.28 A company that wants to outsource certain work or functions as part of a restructuring plan must be aware of the additional assessments and risks that this entails. The legislation limits the company's opportunities to dismiss employees, and then re-engage them as self-employed contractors to perform the same services. A dismissal due to the employer's actual or planned contracting out of the company's ordinary operations to a self-employed contractor, will not be objectively justified unless it is absolutely necessary in order to maintain the continued operation of the company. When contemplating outsourcing, the company must also assess whether the outsourcing constitute a transfer of undertaking under the Norwegian TUPE regulations. If so, the employees will have certain rights and the company certain obligations. For further information please see the section below starting at para **22.115**.

22.29 Documentation is essential for the assessment of whether the workforce reduction and the dismissal of employees in that regard are objectively justified.

Examples of how the legal structure of the employer affects the obligation to offer other suitable work

The business of a clothing company is selling fashion clothes from their own shops in Norway. Their business consists of three different shops located in three different cities in Norway: Oslo, Bergen and Trondheim. There are eight full-time equivalents (FTE) in each shop, and an additional five FTEs in the administration located in Oslo. Due to the need for cost reduction measures and after consultations with the employee representatives, the company has decided to close down their shop in Bergen and that this also requires a workforce reduction of five FTEs. The company and the employee representatives have agreed that the selection pool for employees who may be redundant is limited to the shop in Bergen. Provided the conditions for dismissal are fulfilled, all of the employees in the Bergen shop would be dismissed.

If the company is organised as a private limited company (Fashion AS), the obligation to offer other suitable work would apply to any open position in Fashion AS, including in the Trondheim and Oslo shop and the administration in Oslo. Other suitable work comprises all open positions and other available work.

If Fashion AS is a subsidiary of a (larger) group, the obligation to offer other suitable work would still only be in Fashion AS. However, if Fashion AS and another group company (eg Young Fashion AS) are deemed to have shared employer's liability, the obligation to offer other suitable work applies in both Fashion AS and Young Fashion AS.

DISMISSALS ON GROUNDS OF REDUNDANCY

22.30 When a company wants to carry out redundancies, it must follow the relevant procedures. There is one procedure which must be followed in all redundancy processes, and which we for now call the redundancy procedure. It can be summarised as information and discussion with employee representatives and employees, and decision making in the authorised bodies of the company. We will go through the redundancy procedure below, starting at para **22.32**.

22.31 Then, there is an additional procedure, which we for now call the collective redundancy procedure. The collective redundancy procedure will only apply if the process is considered as a collective redundancy. A collective redundancy is when ten or more employees have been dismissed or employments have been terminated on grounds not related to the individual during a period of 30 days. The number includes any dismissal of employees or severance agreements which terminate the employment etc. due to the redundancy process. We will go through the collective redundancy procedure below, starting at para **22.81**.

The redundancy procedure – steps before initiating the individual dismissals process

The decision

22.32 The formal starting point of a redundancy process should normally be a board decision stating the need for cost reduction and providing the administration with a mandate to start investigating possibilities for cost reduction measures. Once such investigations have been conducted and the employee representatives have been involved and presented their views, a new board decision should address the specific cost reduction measure. The decision should also address the required redundancies and the extent of such. The reasons behind the decision should be well documented, including what (alternative) measures have been assessed and why these have not been chosen.

Involvement of employee representatives

22.33 Between the first and second board decision, the employee representatives should be involved. Companies with more than 50 employees are under a legal obligation to consult with employee representatives on issues that regard the employee's employment, including possible redundancies and other measures in that regard. Collective agreements also draw up obligations for a company to consult with employee representatives in these situations. If the company has a European Work Council (EWC), it may also be mandatory to discuss the issue there. The aim of involving the employee representatives in the process and decisions is to secure a thorough and well-considered decision and process where also the employees, through their representatives, have been heard.

22.34 It is mandatory for companies with 50 employees or more to establish a work council (*NO: Arbeidsmiljøutvalg*) consisting of representatives from the employer, employee and the occupational health service. Any plans of rationalisations or redundancies must be discussed in the work council.

22.35 The employee representative should be a representative elected by the employees from among themselves. He/she should also be a person who works in the area of the company that will be affected by a decision to carry out the redundancy process. Hence, if a company is contemplating a redundancy process for its shop activities, the employee representatives in the process should be shop workers and not from administration. Companies that do not have any employee representatives should, for the specific process, ask the employees to elect a representative among themselves. The company may require employee representatives to keep information received confidential, which provides the company with the necessary confidentiality throughout the process and until it is revealed to all the employees.

22.36 Consultations with the employee representatives must, under most of the provisions regulating the issue, be conducted 'as early as possible'. According to case-law and practice, the term 'as early as possible' means 'before any final decisions are made'. This is so that the employee representatives are able to influence the decision to be made by the company.

22.37 There are several issues that need to be discussed with the employee representatives. Before any final decision is made on the measures to be taken, including any workforce reduction, the investigations of the administration and the measures that they consider presenting to the board should be discussed with the employee representatives. Relevant documentation should also be presented to them, and they should be encouraged to provide their views and any proposals that may reduce the damage and number of dismissals. This should be done both in a meeting and in a written statement which can then be presented to the board. The company should make sure to provide their reasons for not accepting a proposal from the employee representatives.

22.38 Further, the scope of the workforce reduction, including the procedure, timeline, selection pool and selection criteria should be discussed with the employee representatives. It is desirable that the discussions regarding selection pool and selection criteria result in an agreement between the company and the employee representatives. Such agreement will normally provide a stronger position for the company should any dismissed employee claim the dismissal unfair on grounds relating to the stated selection pool and selection criteria. The employer and employee representatives can also enter into a readjustment agreement which draw up the restructuring process (NO: *Omstillingsavtale*). The employee representatives should always be informed of the company's planned communication going out to the employees, so that they are able to comment on the information, timing or other relevant issues.

22.39 Once the individual dismissal process has been initiated towards the employees in the selection pool, the employee representatives should be presented with, and be encouraged to comment on, the choices of the company, ie the employees that the company considers to make redundant and employees to whom the company intends to offer other suitable employment. Depending on the type and complexity of the procedure there will normally be other relevant issues which should be discussed with the employee representatives.

Notice to the county authority

22.40 Additional notification requirements apply when a company plans to close down a business with 30 or more employees or plan to dismiss more than 90% of the workforce in the business. The 'business' in this regard is not only the legal entity, but may be a specific department of the company as a whole. For example, a company that has offices in five different counties in

Norway, with 40 employees in each office, will be included in the notification obligations if the company plans to close down one of the offices.

22.41 In such cases, the company must send a written notification containing closer defined information to the county authority. The county authority then summons representatives from the owners, the management and the employees of the company, as well as municipality, Innovation Norway, the Norwegian Labour and Welfare Organisation and other relevant bodies/persons to a discussion meeting. The aim of the discussion is to identify and assess available measures for continuing the operations of the business or other alternatives to closing down the business, and to reduce the negative consequences for the employees and the local community when a business closes down. The discussion must always include any possibilities for compensation or re-adjustments for the employees, and possible measures for the local community.

22.42 The county authority will end the discussions if they find, or think that it is unlikely that the discussions will result in an alternative to closing down the business. The company cannot make any formal decision regarding closing down the business or such (ie the second board decision) until 30 days after receipt of written notification by the county authority, or when the county authority has ended the discussions. In some cases, the county authority may extend the 30 day period by another 30 days, which means that the company cannot make any formal decisions in this prolonged period. Therefore, it is important to assess the notification obligations at an early stage so that the process can be planned accordingly.

European Works Councils

22.43 Provided the company has a European Work Council and the redundancy procedure is a cross-border matter, it is mandatory for the company to inform and consult with the European Work Council.

Selection pool and selection criteria

22.44 The selection pool and selection criteria determine the scope of the workforce reduction and how to choose between the employees in scope respectively. Both the selection pool and selection criteria must be objectively justified. The further content of these has been established through collective agreements and case-law. The company should always try to reach a written agreement on the selection pool and selection criteria with the employee representatives in a redundancy process. If no agreement can be reached, the employer decides the selection pool and selection criteria. If an employee claims a dismissal unlawful, it will normally be harder for the court to deem the selection pool and selection criteria unfair if an agreement exists.

Defining the selection pool

22.45 The selection pool is, as a main principle, the entire company subject to the redundancy process. The term 'company' is limited to the legal entity and, hence, does not include the group or other companies in the group.

22.46 Provided there are objectively justified grounds, the selection scope may be limited to specific parts of the company. According to case law the selection pool may be limited to a geographical restricted area of the company, specific departments within the company and so on. There are several factors in the assessment of whether the selection pool can be limited to parts of the company. These include, but are not limited to

- the size of the company;
- the economic situation;
- the practical challenges with using the entire company as a selection pool;
- whether a large selection pool will make it difficult to keep necessary competence or complicate the securing of safe operations in other ways;
- whether the employee representatives or other representatives from the employees agree on the suggested selection pool; and
- the company's previous practice regarding selection pools.

22.47 It is important for the company to assess whether their proposed selection pool is objectively justified and to be able to state and document such grounds. As described above, the company should aim to reach a written agreement with the employee representative on the definition of the selection pool.

Selection criteria

22.48 Selection criteria are the criteria used to determine who, from the employees in the scope of the workforce reduction, are to be made redundant and who are to receive an offer of other employment. The selection criteria must also be used when the company assesses which of the redundant employees are to receive an offer of new employment in connection with the preferential right to new employment following a redundancy process.

22.49 The selection criteria must be objectively justified and in accordance with practice. Examples of selection criteria that can be objectively justified are

- length of service;
- skills and qualifications, both formal education and work experience, which are relevant for the company;
- personal suitability;
- social aspects, including family responsibility, mobility, particular burdens or debt, possibility to obtain other work; and
- age (special regard to be given to employees above the age of 55).

22.50 It is important to observe the prohibition against discrimination when determining the selection criteria. Also, a criterion which concerns the employee's presence at work should normally be avoided as it will often not be objectively justified to include sick leave, leave of absence to care for a child or in connection with a birth etc.

22.51 According to collective agreements, length of service must be used as the main selection criterion unless deviations from this principle are objectively justified. On this basis, and due to the objectivity of the criterion, length of service is incorporated as the main selection criterion by long practice in Norway, even for companies not bound by a collective agreement.

22.52 In practice, length of service and qualifications are normally used as the main selection criteria. Even though length of service is normally the main criterion for all companies, other criteria may be used as the main one if objectively justified. This condition will normally be easier to fulfil for companies where collective agreements do not apply, than companies where such agreements applies. Qualifications, both formal and work experience, are often preferred as the main selection criterion as the company's need for certain qualifications is a need for the company. In such cases, the qualifications must be relevant for the company and the relevant positions.

The redundancy procedure – steps in the individual dismissals/individual consultations

22.53 If the company fails to have an individual procedure and individual discussions with each employee in the selection pool, this will normally give grounds for a claim for unfair dismissal. All affected employees are entitled to provide their views on a possible termination and their position in relation to the selection criteria.

22.54 The starting point of the procedure in respect of individual employees in a workforce reduction is normally when the board has passed a resolution to carry out a workforce reduction. Up until this point in time, the employee representatives have been the employee's voice in the process. The first step towards involving the employees is to hold a general meeting for all employees who may be involved in the workforce reduction to inform them of the board's decision and what will happen next. Further, all relevant documentation on the employee's employment, benefits and circumstances relating to the selection criteria (eg length of service, formal qualification and work experience) should be collected. Employees not present, but who are assumed to be affected by the redundancy process or included in the selection pool, must also receive this information in some other way, eg by telephone, e-mail or via the intranet.

22.55 According to applicable legislation, a company which contemplates dismissing an employee must hold an individual discussion meeting with the relevant employee before making a decision in the matter. The employee is entitled to bring an employee representative or advisor to the meeting. The aim of the discussion meeting is to discuss the possible termination of employment and it is important to stress that no final decision has been made. It is also important to discuss the employee's information in relation to the selection criteria, including ensuring that the company has all relevant information to make an assessment of termination of employment and that such information is correct.

22.56 For example, if one of the selection criteria is 'formal qualifications', the company must ensure that they have information about the complete formal education of the employee, including education not relevant for the position which the employee has held. If 'length of service' is a selection criterion, it is important to confirm that the company and employee agree on the length of service that the company has registered for the employee, or let the employee disagree, provide their view on the length of their length of service and comment on the reason for this view.

22.57 In the discussion meeting, it is also important that the employee provides information about issues and circumstances that may result in a termination affecting them particularly badly, eg their social situation, if they are a single parent, have a high mortgage, is dependent on continued employment in order to keep their residence permit etc. Such information must be considered by the company in the assessment of termination of employment, as the law prescribes that the needs of the company must be weighed against the disadvantage caused by the termination for the individual employee. This assessment is a factor in the question of whether a termination of employment is unfair or objectively justified.

22.58 The company must carry out individual discussion meetings with all employees in the selection pool. Once all of these are held, the company must gather and compare the information on each employee with regards to the selection criteria. By using the selection criteria, the company must assess what employees are to be made redundant and what employees are to receive an offer of other employment if there are open positions in the company. Employees who are to be made redundant must receive a notice fulfilling the requirements prescribed by law, while the employees who will be offered other employment must receive a formal offer with the new terms and conditions of the new position.

Involvement of employee representatives in individual dismissals

22.59 The employee representatives should always be informed of any meetings which the company is planning on holding for the employees and any information that the company will give them *before* any of this is carried through. For example, the employee representatives should be summoned to a meeting with the company where the company inform them of the board's decision to carry out cost reduction measures and a redundancy procedure that the company will summon the employees to a general meeting and the information that will be provided in this meeting. The aim is for the employee representatives to provide their views and comments for the company to consider, eg the point in time that the company will hold the general meeting. Once this is done, the company is free to summon the employees to the general meeting and provide the information as planned.

22.60 The employee representatives will normally be present in the individual discussion meetings with the individual employee, unless the employee does not want to bring the employee representative or want to bring someone else. Therefore, the employee representatives will normally attend a large number of the individual discussion meetings, and this should be considered when planning the time schedule for such meetings.

22.61 Before sending an offer of employment or notice of termination to the relevant employees, the company must present their proposal to the employee representatives so that they can provide their comments, agree or provide counter proposals. For further information regarding the notice, notice periods, possibilities for employees to challenge a dismissal and other issues arising after the notice is given, please see below starting at para **22.97**.

Avoiding compulsory redundancies

22.62 One of the circumstances that the employer must consider in a redundancy process is whether there are any alternatives to avoid compulsory redundancies (see above at para **22.24**). Such alternatives may include the possibility of using part-time positions, salary sacrifice, changes in personnel benefits including bonus and pension schemes, early retirement or similar. This may reduce the number of compulsory redundancies.

22.63 In some cases, the employer sets up a severance scheme where the employees can submit an application for termination of employment in exchange for severance pay. In such cases, it is important for the employer to emphasise that not all employees who submit an application will be granted a severance pay package. This is to avoid key personnel leaving the company.

22.64 It is up to the employer's sole discretion which of the applications that are granted. However, the employer must not discriminate on grounds of age, political views, membership of a trade union, sexual orientation, disability, age, gender, ethnic or national origin, descent, colour, language, religion and ethical and cultural orientation.

22.65 If the employer grants an application for a severance pay package, the terms and conditions should be drawn up in an agreement for the employer and the employee to sign. It is important to regulate all circumstances relating to the termination. The aim of such a severance agreement is to avoid or reduce the number of compulsory redundancies, and to ensure that the employees who have been granted such an agreement, cannot challenge the termination of their employment at a later stage.

Alternative employment

22.66 In termination of employment on grounds relating to the company, the company must offer alternative employment before dismissing an employee. This is called the employer's obligation to offer other suitable work.

22.67 The employer must identify all open positions and any uncovered work tasks in the company, and provide this information to all the employees at risk of being made redundant. The employer is not under an obligation to establish new positions, or to move an employee not comprised by the redundancy to an open position so that their position will become open for the employees subject to the redundancy process.

22.68 In using the selection scope and selection criteria, the employer must assess which of the employees in scope of the redundancy process are entitled to receive an offer of other suitable employment. For example, if the main selection criterion is length of service, the employees with the longest length of service would be entitled to receive an offer of other suitable employment. The obligation to offer other suitable work also comprises a lower position or a position with lower salary conditions etc.

22.69 If the employee turns down the offer, they may be given notice. The employer must then assess which of the affected employees are entitled to receive an offer of employment for that position. If the notice of termination has been given to all employees who did not receive an offer of other suitable work, the employer must use the selection criteria to assess which of the employees made redundant are entitled to receive an offer of the position based on the preferential right to new employment. For further information on the preferential right to new employment, please see below starting at para **22.112**.

22.70 If the employee accepts the offer of new employment, his old terms and conditions will continue until the notice period has expired. The notice period will start running from (and includes) the first day of the month following that in which the offer was accepted. When the notice period has expired, the new position and new terms and conditions will apply unless otherwise agreed. The company should ensure that the employee signs a new and updated employment agreement.

Trial periods

22.71 If the offer of new employment is for a position which is significantly different from the previous position, the parties may agree a new probation period. The maximum probation period is six months, and the minimum notice period during the probation period is 14 days.

22.72 During the new probation period, the employment may be terminated on ordinary grounds (grounds relating to the employee or the employer). It may also be terminated if the employee is not suitable for the work, lacks skills/proficiency or is unreliable. It is normally easier to terminate an employment due to poor work performance during the probation period than after. If none of these grounds exists or if the employer is unable to document these, the employment continues after the expiry of the probation period.

22.73 In the assessment of whether the conditions for terminating the employment are fulfilled, issues such as providing necessary training to perform the work, adequate guidelines and instructions, regular feedback on performance or skill etc. and that the employee is given opportunity to improve or change skill or performance will be important. It is the employer who has the burden of proof, and who must document that these conditions have been met.

Entitlements under collective agreements

22.74 In redundancy processes, the company must be aware of the rights and/or schemes that collective agreements may provide for the employees. These rights may, amongst other things, impact the selection of employees to be made redundant or make it easier or harder to obtain a voluntarily termination from the employee.

22.75 Two of the relevant schemes in this regard are the AFP Scheme (early retirement pension) and the Severance Pay Scheme. Both of these schemes are embedded in collective agreements and have been established by the main employer and main employee associations in Norway. The schemes are only relevant if the company in question has collective agreements with each of the schemes embedded. Both of the schemes have been revised during the past years, and therefore, the company may have employees who have entitlements under both the old and the new schemes.

22.76 The aim of the Severance Pay Scheme is to provide employees who are between 50 and 67 years old and whose employment is terminated on grounds not relating to them, with economic compensation. Redundancies will normally be a situation which entitles such employees to severance pay under the scheme. The severance pay is tax-free and is paid out by the Severance Pay Scheme if the company has made its payments to the scheme. The scheme is financed by the companies paying a quarterly premiums to the scheme based on the number of employees in the company and the number of weekly working hours for the employees.

22.77 To receive severance pay from the Severance Pay Scheme, the employee must fulfil certain conditions relating to, amongst others, length of service at the company and membership in the Severance Pay Scheme. Different rates for the severance pay, relating to the age of the employee, apply for the employees who fulfil the conditions.

22.78 The AFP scheme in the private sector is a private sector tariff-based pension scheme. It provides an ungraded lifelong supplement to the retirement pension from the Norwegian National Insurance scheme. The AFP scheme is one third financed by contributions from the state of Norway and two thirds by the companies affiliated with the scheme. A company becomes affiliated with the scheme if the AFP scheme is embedded in a collective agreement applicable in the company. Employees who are entitled to and take out early retirement pension under the AFP scheme receive the payments directly from the scheme. If they are entitled to take out early retirement pension from the National Insurance Scheme, the payments are made by the Norwegian Labour and Welfare Organisation.

22.79 Provided the employee fulfils the relevant conditions for taking out pension under the AFP scheme, he/she can start drawing the pension from the age of 62 years. The conditions which the employee must fulfil relate to, amongst other things, length of service and employment at an affiliated company. Some of the conditions must be fulfilled at the time the employee takes out the pension and others at the time the employee reaches the age of 62. A dismissal between 57 and 62 years old may impact the employee's possibility to take out AFP under the scheme. Therefore, it is often harder to dismiss employees who are close to the age of 62, especially if the AFP scheme applies in the company.

Other considerations

22.80 Collective agreements may establish additional procedures for the company, as may other contractual provisions or policies relating to redundancies. The company must ensure that it has a clear view of all of the obligations which apply to it so that all of these obligations can be incorporated in the plans for the redundancy and the information on the employee's entitlements.

Collective redundancy procedure

22.81 Under Norwegian law, a collective redundancy arise when a notice of dismissal is given to at least ten employees within a period of 30 days when such notice is not warranted by circumstances relating to the individual employee.

22.82 The calculation of the number of employees which are to be included in order to assess whether the collective redundancy procedure applies does not only include employees who receive notice due to a workforce reduction, rationalisation or other grounds relating to the company. If at least five persons are given notice due to redundancy, other forms of termination of the employment contract will also be included in the calculation. This includes, amongst other things, termination through mutual severance agreements or termination through agreements regarding early retirement. Hence, the term 'redundancy' in 'collective redundancy' has a wider meaning than in the ordinary use as it does not only include dismissals due to circumstances relating to the undertaking, but also other kinds of terminations that are not warranted by circumstances relating to the individual employee.

22.83 In a collective redundancy process, the employer must inform and discuss the procedure and certain issues with the employee representatives as early as possible, which normally means before the second board decision.

22.84 The employer is also under an obligation to notify the Norwegian Labour and Welfare Organisation (NAV) of the redundancy process. NAV administers a third of the national budget through schemes such as unemployment benefit, work assessment allowance, sickness benefit, pensions, child benefit and cash-for-care benefit.

Involvement of employee representatives in collective redundancies

22.85 In a general restructuring process, the employer must normally identify the trade unions and their employee representatives represented in the company. If these employee representatives represent (all) the employees who will be affected by the planned process, these can be involved in the process. If there are no trade union employee representatives in the company or if not all affected employees are represented by these, the company must ensure that these employees have either a pre-existing employee representative (without connection to a union) or that they elect a representative among themselves. The same principles apply in collective redundancies.

22.86 Collective agreements may also draw up additional requirements for the procedure in collective redundancies.

Election of employee representatives for collective consultation purposes

22.87 If there is no employee representative for the affected employees or for one or more of the employee groups, the company must take steps to ensure that a representative is elected for each of these groups. The representative will then be involved in the collective redundancy so that the company can fulfil their obligations in terms of information and consultation. The company may impose an obligation to treat information confidentially on the employee representative.

Information and consultation requirements

22.88 An employer contemplating collective redundancies must enter into consultations with the employee representatives as early as possible. The consultations must start before any formal decision is made so that the employee representatives have a genuine opportunity to influence the decision which may affect the employees. The employee representatives should be encouraged to provide their comments, suggestions and so on both verbally and in writing so that they can be provided to the entity making the final decision. They are entitled to expert assistance, which normally is through the employee's unions and includes legal experts.

22.89 The consultations must be entered into with a view to reaching an agreement to avoid collective redundancies or to reduce the number of persons made redundant. The employer is also obliged to enter into consultations if the planned redundancies are caused by someone other than the employer who has superior authority over the employer, such as the management of a group of companies.

22.90 If the employer is considering closing down its activities or an independent part of them and this will involve collective redundancies, the discussions must also include the possibility of continued operation of the business that is contemplated to be closed down. Such discussions must include the possibility of employees taking over the activities.

22.91 If redundancies cannot be avoided, efforts must be made to mitigate the adverse effects. The consultations must cover possible social welfare measures aimed at, inter alia, providing support for redeploying or retraining employees made redundant.

22.92 The employer must provide the employee representatives with all relevant information as early as possible and at the latest, at the summoning of the employee representatives to a consultation meeting with the employer. The information must also include a written notification concerning:

- the grounds for any redundancies;
- the number of employees who may be made redundant;
- the categories of workers to which they belong;
- the number of employees normally employed;
- the groups of employees normally employed;
- the period during which such redundancies may be effected;

- the proposed selection criteria; and
- the proposed criteria for calculating of extraordinary severance pay, if applicable.

Regulatory requirements

22.93 The employer must provide the information stated above in para 22.92 in a written notification to the NAV, thereby alerting the NAV that several employees may require their assistance and measures. The employee representative may comment on the information directly to the NAV. The information must be provided to the employee representatives and the NAV at the same time.

Sanctions

22.94 Failure to comply with the provisions regarding collective redundancies will not itself lead to a termination being deemed unlawful. However, it may impact the overall assessment of whether a specific dismissal fulfils the condition of having objectively justified grounds.

22.95 Failure to comply may also lead to a delay in the resignation date as planned collective redundancies will, at the earliest, take effect 30 days after the NAV received the notification. The NAV may also extend this period if necessary in order for the employer and employee representatives to reach an agreement to avoid collective redundancies or to reduce the number of persons made redundant.

22.96 If the employer has not provided any written notification to the NAV, the employees will not be obligated to resign from their positions even if they have been given notice and their notice period has expired. This means that the employee will be entitled to salary if he provides his work for the company.

NOTICE

22.97 An employment contract must state the notice period for each of the parties. The WEA provides minimum notice periods. Other requirements may be drawn up in applicable collective agreements. If the employment contract lacks a notice period, the minimum prescribed by law (or applicable collective agreement) will apply. If the notice period prescribed by law or in applicable collective agreements is longer than the agreed notice period, the first will apply. The notice period for the employee cannot be longer than that of the employer.

22.98 The notice from the employer must fulfil statutory requirements and must be given to the employee in person or sent by registered mail. There are no statutory requirements for notice from the employee, but the employment contract should state that it must be in writing. This will help avoiding any doubts as to whether the employee has given notice.

22.99 The notice period starts to run from, and includes, the first day of the month following that in which notice is given. The notice is considered as given when received by the employee. For example, if the employee's notice period is three months and he receives the notice on 8 December, the notice period starts running from 1 January and expires on 31 March. During an agreed probation period, the notice period starts running from the day which the notice was given (ie from date to date), unless otherwise agreed.

Minimum notice periods

22.100 The table below provides an overview of minimum notice periods prescribed by law. Where the notice period stated in the employment contract is shorter than prescribed by statute the latter will prevail. During the probation period, the minimum allowed notice period to be agreed upon is 14 days.

Length of Service	Age	Notice by Employer
0	N/A	1 month
5 years	N/A	2 months
10 years	N/A	3 months
10 years	50 years	4 months
10 years	55 years	5 months
10 years	60 years	6 months

22.101 The employer and employee's duties and obligations continue unchanged during the notice period. The employee has a right to work and receive his normal salary and the employer is obligated to provide the employee with work in accordance with his position. The employee's duty to remain loyal to his employer, also continues during the notice period.

22.102 In certain special circumstances, the employer may use the right to manage and instruct the employee to not work during the notice period, provided he continues to receive normal salary during this period. Whether this is an alternative will depend on a number of factors in an individual assessment.

22.103 During the notice period, the employee will be bound by the general duty of loyalty in their employment, regardless of whether they work or not. Working for a competitor during this period will be considered as breach of the said duty of loyalty. When the notice period has expired, the employer may prevent the employee from working for a competitor through a post-termination restrictive covenant. For further information please see the post-termination restrictive covenants section below starting at para 22.108.

No garden leave

22.104 In other jurisdictions, garden leave clauses may be a practical measure for the employer. Under a garden leave clause, the employee continue to receive normal salary from his employer during the notice period, but is not obligated or allowed to work for all or part of the notice period. The clause is effective for preventing employees from working for competitors or setting up their own business. Garden leave clauses are not accepted under Norwegian law. However, the chief executive of the company may enter into a prior severance agreement as described at para 22.14, which may include a garden leave clause. If an employment contract contains a garden leave clause and the employer enforces it, it will be deemed void if challenged by the employee.

Pay in lieu of notice/severance agreements

22.105 The employer and employee may enter into a written agreement which deviates from the employee's right and obligation to work during the notice period. Such agreement should regulate all relevant issues concerning the employment and termination, and should be drawn up in co-operation with a lawyer.

REDUNDANCY PAYMENT

22.106 There are no statutory requirements for payments beyond ordinary salary during the agreed notice period, such as for example redundancy payment or severance payment. However, the parties may enter into a mutual agreement regarding such payments. This is normally done if the employee agrees to termination of his employment. In such a case, the agreement should regulate all aspects of termination of the employment, including payments etc. For further information on this regard, please see below starting at para 22.186.

22.107 If a collective agreement with the embedded Severance Pay Scheme is applicable in the company, employees between 50 and 67 years old may be entitled to severance pay. Please see above starting at para 22.74 for further information on the Severance Pay Scheme.

Post-termination restrictive covenants

22.108 The employer may use non-compete or non-solicitation clauses in the employment contract if it is desirable to prevent the employee from working for competitors after the notice period has expired. The Norwegian legislation regulates the validity of such clauses, and this should be considered when drafting such clauses in the employment contracts for each individual employee. For the same reasons, these clauses should be considered in drafting severance agreements.

22.109 As a main principle, a restrictive covenant limiting the employee's possibility to take on work for other (competitor) companies after termination of his current employment will be deemed wholly or partly void if it:

- limits his possibilities of making a living to an unreasonable extent; or
- goes beyond the limits necessary for protection against competition

A restrictive covenant concerning non-solicitation of customers, clients and personnel will be wholly or partly void if it is unreasonable or if it is in conflict with generally accepted business practice to invoke it.

22.110 The period for the restrictive covenant and the compensation that the employee may receive are elements of importance in the assessment of whether a restrictive covenant is deemed wholly or partly void. It is normally harder for a non-solicitation clause to be deemed void than for a restrictive covenant limiting the employee's possibility to take on other employment. The latter will, as a main rule, not be binding if used on employee in a subordinate position (typically an apprentice, a clerk etc) unless the nature of the employment provides the employee with the opportunity to gain knowledge the company's customers or trade secrets which he could use to harm the company.

22.111 At the time of writing, a new proposal regarding the regulation of restrictive covenants has been put forward by the Ministry of Labour and Social Affairs. However, the time schedule for processing this proposal remains uncertain. The proposal include, amongst other things, a maximum period for the restrictive covenants and minimum payments to the employee. There are currently no minimum requirements regarding payment for non-restrictive covenants.

Preferential right to new employment

22.112 The company must also be aware of the preferential right to new employment. An employee whose employment has been terminated due to circumstances related to the company, and who has been employed at the company for the past two years, has a preferential right to a new employment with that company. This means that if a position opens up at the company which the employee with the preferential right is qualified for, the company must offer it to the employee. This also applies for positions for which the employee is overqualified. The preferential right to new employment is valid from the notice is given and for 12 months after the notice period has expired.

22.113 The employee must be qualified for the vacant post that he is offered. If several employees are qualified, as the case may be in a redundancy process, the selection criteria used in the redundancy process must be used when assessing which of them that is to be offered the vacant post. The preferential right to new employment lapses if an employee fails to accept an offer of employment in a suitable post within 14 days from receiving the offer.

22.114 The preferential right to new employment applies to all permanent employees. Temporary employees who are not a replacement for others also have a preferential right to new employment on certain conditions. The same applies to employees who have exercised their reservation right in the transfer of an undertaking. Part-time employees and older employees who have reduced their position may have a preferential right to a larger position on closer defined conditions. The preferential right to new employment for permanent employees will normally have priority. However, when addressing the issue of who to offer a new position, the company must ensure that all employees with a preferential right are included in the assessment.

BUSINESS SALE, OUTSOURCING/INSOURCING AND OFFSHORING

22.115 The EU Directive 2001/23/EF regulates the transfer of undertakings, including the rights of the employees in such situations, as well as the obligations for the transferor and the transferee. The directive has been implemented into Norwegian legislation and, hence, the interpretations of the Court of Justice of the European Communities are relevant when determining the meaning of the regulations. In the following, the Norwegian provisions regarding the transfer of undertakings will be referred to as the 'TUPE provisions'.

22.116 In short, a transfer of undertakings takes place when an undertaking or part of an undertaking is transferred to another employer. Typical situations are out- and insourcing or the selling of all or part of a company. A transfer of undertaking often results in some kind of reorganisation of the workforce at either the transferor or the transferee.

22.117 The key consequences of the TUPE provisions applying are:

- transfer of the employment of the employees in scope to the transferee;
- except for collective agreements and occupational pension schemes, the terms and conditions of the transferred employment are automatically transferred unchanged to the transferee;

- the transferor and the transferee are obliged to consult with and inform employee representatives prior to the transfer;
- the employees in scope by the transfer are entitled to information about the transfer before it takes place; and
- the employees enjoy protection against dismissals due to the transfer.

Business sale

22.118 In order to determine whether the sale of all or part of the business or an insourcing or outsourcing constitutes a transfer of undertaking, three main conditions must be assessed.

22.119 First, the transfer must involve a change in the employer entity, which means that share sales or purchases do not fulfil this condition. Secondly, the transfer must relate to an economic entity which, thirdly, retains its identity after the transfer. An economic entity is an organised grouping of resources which has the objective of pursuing an economic activity. Whether or not this entity retains its identity after the transfer is determined through an overall assessment of the different factors that characterise the transaction, such as tangible assets (ie buildings and movable property), the value of its intangible assets at the time of the transfer, whether or not the majority of the employees are taken over by the new employer, whether or not its customers are transferred and the degree of similarity between the activities carried on before and after the transfer. The type of undertaking or business concerned must also be taken into account.

Outsourcing/insourcing

22.120 Outsourcing means the contracting out of part of a business to a third party, while insourcing is taking the business back into the company. For example, a company may want an external company to be in charge of and responsible for its IT. An outsourcing and insourcing may constitute a transfer of undertaking under the TUPE regulations. Therefore, it is important for a company planning an insourcing or outsourcing to assess the question of transfer of undertaking in the planning stage of the process. The result may impact the company's need for a workforce reduction.

22.121 Dismissals due to outsourcing will normally be considered as dismissals for circumstances relating to the company. This means that the process of workforce reductions as described above must be observed. However, Norwegian legislation has specific provisions relating to and limiting the possibility of dismissing employees due to outsourcing work to self-employed contractors (without any employees). A dismissal due to outsourcing of work to self-employed contractors will be unlawful unless it is absolutely essential in order to maintain the continued operation of the undertaking.

Effect of TUPE

Automatic transfer and protection of employment

22.122 When the TUPE provisions apply, the rights and obligations of the transferred employees are transferred unchanged and automatically to the transferee. It is the rights and obligations in the employment contract and other individual rights ensuing from the employment in force at the time of the transfer that are transferred. If the transferred employee has a claim against the transferor at the transfer date, for example holiday pay, such claim can also be brought against the transferee.

22.123 As a main rule, any collective agreements in force for the transferred employees are transferred. However, the transferee may declare in writing to the relevant trade union that it does not wish to be bound by the collective agreement. In such case, and provided the notification is done within the required time limits, the collective agreements will not be transferred. Individual rights ensuing from collective agreements are, nevertheless, transferred for the relevant employees.

22.124 The employee's membership in of a collective occupational pension schemes is transferred to the transferee unless the new employer chooses to make existing collective pension schemes applicable to the transferred employees. This exception only applies to occupational collective pension schemes, which means that individual pension agreements are transferred unchanged.

Objection to the transfer

22.125 An employee may object to the transfer of his employment to the transferee (the 'reservation right'). It is mandatory for the transferor and transferee to inform the employees who are subject to the transfer of their reservation right prior to the transfer, and set a time limit for exercising the reservation right. The time limit cannot be shorter than 14 days. If an employee exercises his reservation right within the time limit, his employment will cease without further notice on the transfer date, which means that he will be unemployed from such date.

22.126 An employee who exercises his reservation right and who has been employed at the transferor for a total of at least 12 months during the two-year period prior to the date of transfer has a preferential right to new employment.

This preferential right to new employment applies for new or open positions at the transferor for which the employee is qualified. The preferential right applies for a period of one year following the transfer date. The preferential right lapses if the employee fails to accept an offer of employment in a suitable post within 14 days of receiving the offer.

22.127 Case law has also established a right for the employees subject to the transfer to choose that they do not want to be transferred (the 'right to choose'). The right to choose is conditioned upon the transfer involving radical and negative changes in the employment relationship; these conditions are strict. An employee, who exercises his right to choose, remains with the transferor, which means that his employment continues as before the transfer. However, the employee will be vulnerable to any workforce reductions that may be carried out at the transferor after the transfer. If the employee is made redundant, he will have a preferential right to new employment at the transferor as described above, starting at para **22.112**.

Protection from dismissal

22.128 If the TUPE provisions apply in a transfer, the employees enjoy protection against dismissal due to the transfer. This means that a dismissal based on the transfer itself will not be lawful. However, general workforce reductions may be carried through either by the transferor prior to the transfer or by the transferee after the transfer. The grounds for carrying out such process must fulfil the ordinary conditions for workforce reduction, meaning that it must be objectively justified circumstances and not based on the transfer.

Protection of terms and conditions of employment

22.129 The individual terms and conditions of employment of the transferred employees remain unchanged after the transfer. The possibility for the transferee to alter the terms and conditions are the same as for the transferor. For further information on this issue, please see below starting at para **22.145**.

Information and consultation under TUPE

22.130 In cases where employees are transferred in a transfer of undertaking, the transferor and the transferee must inform and consult with employee representatives of the affected employees prior to the transfer. It is also mandatory for them to inform the affected employees about certain factors regarding the transfer prior to the transfer.

22.131 If the employee representatives who represent the employees who will be subject to the transfer are already appointed, the obligation to inform and consult is with them. In other cases, the employees who will be affected by the transfer must be given the opportunity to elect a representative among themselves.

Duty to inform and consult with employee representatives

22.132 The employees at the transferee will, in practice, rarely be affected by a transfer (apart from possible subsequent workforce reductions with the corresponding duty for the company to inform and consult). Therefore the obligation to consult with employee representatives normally concerns the representatives at the transferor. As both the transferor and the transferee have a duty to inform and consult with the representatives, the transferor and transferee should agree on the transferor being responsible for informing and consulting with the employee representatives at the transferor. It is not only the transferred employee representatives who must be informed and consulted with, but also the representatives of other employees who will be affected by the transfer, for example if the transfer leads to a relocation of the workplace or change in the work tasks for the remaining employees.

22.133 As early as possible, meaning before the formal decision which results in a transfer of undertaking, the transferor and transferee are obligated to inform and consult with the employee representatives on the following issues:

- the reason for the transfer;
- the agreed or proposed date for the transfer;
- the legal, economic and social implications of the transfer for the employees (for example change in the place of work; change in the collective occupational pension schemes etc);
- changes in circumstances relating to collective agreements;
- measures planned in relation to the employees; and
- the reservation right and the preferential right and the time limit for exercising such rights.

22.134 In addition, if the transferor and transferee are planning measures in relation to their respective employees, it is mandatory for them to consult with the employee representatives as early as possible on these issues with a view to reaching an agreement. Examples of measures are redundancy procedures, severance agreements to be offered to employees etc. There is no requirement to reach an agreement, only to consult and try to agree. This means that the authority to make decisions lies with the transferor and transferee. The ordinary duty to inform and consult with the employee representatives in a workforce reduction as describe above starting at para **22.33**, will also apply in this situation.

Duty to inform the employees

22.135 It is mandatory for the transferor and transferee to inform the affected employees of the transfer. The information must include all the bullet points listed at para **22.133** above and must be provided as early as possible, which for the employee means as soon as possible after the formal decision resulting in a transfer of undertaking has been made.

European Works Councils

22.136 Provided the company has a European Work Council and the redundancy procedure/transfer of undertaking is cross-border, it is mandatory for the company to inform and consult with the European Work Council.

Sanctions

Unfair dismissal

22.137 A dismissal due to the transfer itself will be deemed an unfair dismissal. For further details on the rights, obligations and possible claims from the employer and employer in unfair dismissal, please refer below starting at para **22.169**.

Failure to inform and consult

22.138 There are currently no statutory consequences if the transferor and/ or transferee fail to comply with the obligation to inform and consult with the affected employee representatives or inform the affected employees. However, it may impact the time limits for exercising the reservation right and/or the fairness in a subsequent dismissal.

22.139 Collective agreements establish a specific sanction where serious breach on the duty to inform and consult can lead to be summoned before a committee which may impose a fine on the employer.

22.140 The information that the transferor and transferee are obligated to provide to the employees is, amongst others, to make it possible for them to assess whether or not they want to exercise their reservation right or right to choose. The minimum time limit that the transferor can set for the employees to exercise their reservation right is 14 days after they received the information as stated in the bullet points above at para **22.133**. If the transferor fails to provide the information or fails to provide sufficient information, the time limit for exercising the reservation right will not start. Neither will the time limit for the right to choose, if such a right exists.

22.141 In addition, failure to provide information as described at para 22.133 may lead to the employees being dismissed in a workforce reduction following the transfer. In such case, the lack of sufficient information may be a factor in favour of the dismissal being unfair and, hence, impact the assessment of whether the dismissal is unfair or not for the specific employee.

Application of TUPE to cross-border transactions/offshoring

22.142 The assessment of whether the TUPE regulations apply must also be considered when a transfer of an undertaking takes place across borders. The provisions regarding choice of law and jurisdiction will have an impact in this regard and should therefore be assessed when planning such transfer.

22.143 If the TUPE regulations apply, the employees are transferred across the border to the transferee on the same work and pay conditions as they had at the time of the transfer. This also includes their place of work. If the transferee wants to change the place of work, it must follow the relevant provisions in relation to changing this work condition for the relevant employees. Provisions regarding choice of law will be relevant in this regard, as the process for changing the place of work may be different in the two countries.

WORKFORCE REDUCTION IN CONNECTION WITH SHARE SALE OR SHARE PURCHASE

22.144 The TUPE rules do not apply to share sales or share purchases as sale or purchase of shares of a company does not result in a change of the legal employer. An employer looking to carry out a workforce reduction may do so provided the ordinary redundancy and workforce reduction process as described above is observed.

CHANGING EMPLOYMENT TERMS AND CONDITIONS

22.145 An employment contract contains individual rights for the employee. The employer is limited in its options to change such individual rights without the employee's consent. The employment contract must always be updated so that it contains the current terms and conditions. An employer wanting to make changes in the employment contract or the employee's position can do so by:

(i) agreement with the employee;
(ii) unilaterally change the contract through the employer's right to manage; or
(iii) dismiss and then re-employ the employee on new terms and conditions (amendment termination).

22.146 The two latter possibilities pose a greater risk of the employee challenging the change and the new terms by legal actions.

22.147 Employees subject to a transfer of undertaking maintain their work and pay conditions as they were before the transfer. The transfer itself will not allow for a change in their work and pay conditions, nor their employment contract. If the new employer wants to enforce any such changes, it must be done within the three possibilities as described above in (i) – (iii).

Mutually agreed changes

22.148 If the employee consents to the changes that the employer has proposed, the employment contract must be re-drafted to reflect the new terms and conditions. The employer and employee must sign the new employment contract. A written amendment, signed by both parties, may be appended to the original employment contract if that appears to be a better way of updating the contract. The same should be done if the employee consents to changes in his job description. Under all circumstances, the new employment contract/amendment should contain the date which the changes enter into force.

Unilateral changes

22.149 Employers who want to unilaterally change the terms and conditions of an employee's employment contract must carry out the necessary assessments before introducing the changes. There is a risk that the employee claims that the change is invalid (by virtue of an unfair dismissal) if it falls outside the scope of the employer's right to manage or if the conditions for an 'amendment termination' are not present. In such case, the employee may be entitled to remain on the original terms and conditions, and may also claim compensation.

The employer's right to manage

22.150 In its role as an employer, the employer is entitled to unilaterally make certain changes in employment conditions (the employer's right to manage). This right to manage is limited through the employment (including individual conditions in the employment contract), collective agreements and other agreements.

22.151 Use of the employer's right to manage requires reasonable grounds in two areas; (i) the circumstances which the change is based on must be objectively justified; and (ii) the procedure making the change must be safe and reasonable. Hence, the employer's right to manage is a right to change individual employment conditions within minor and reasonable limits; eg changing administrative schemes or, in some cases, changing the place of work. However, reducing the salary level will not fall within the employer's right to manage.

22.152 The desired change must be subject to a closer assessment in order to see whether it falls under the employer's right to manage. Relevant factors in such assessment are, amongst other things, whether the change is considered major, whether there is an agreement regulating the term desired to be changed and whether such agreement is clear, the scope of the deviation, whether the employer has an urgent need to implement the change, whether other changes will be made (the more changes, the less likely that the employer's right to manage will justify the change) and whether the change is temporary or permanent.

Dismissing and re-engaging employees on new terms ('amendment termination')

22.153 An 'amendment termination' means that the employer terminates the employment and then presents the employee with an offer of employment on new terms and conditions. It must follow the same procedures as an ordinary termination of employment. This means that the change must be objectively justified by circumstances relating to the employer/company or the employee. Further, the termination process drawn up in the WEA, which includes, amongst other things, an individual discussion meeting with the employee and a notice that fulfils minimum requirements, must be observed.

22.154 The employee may claim an 'amendment termination' unfair, and will, in such cases, have the same rights as in an ordinary and full termination of employment. Amongst other things, he will be entitled to demand and attend a negotiation meeting, and can bring legal action claiming to remain in his position until the dispute is settled. In any case, the change can only be enforced after expiry of the notice period of the employee.

Practical Tips on changing terms and conditions

Any attempt to change the terms and conditions of an employment should be sought in an agreement with the employee. In such case, a signature of the employee is vital in order to document that the employee has consented. This will prevent subsequent disputes with the employee claiming that he had not provided his consent to the change. Bringing up proposal for changes may, strategically, be done in connection with review of salary as the employee may more easily consent to a change if he is also given a salary raise.

If it is impossible to obtain consent, the employer must assess whether the change is within the scope of the employer's right to manage or an 'amendment termination' is required. In both cases, the changes should be discussed with the employee in an individual meeting. Minutes should be drawn up from such meeting.

When drafting employment contracts, the employer should use expressions which do not put limitations on the employer's right to manage. For example, the clause stating the place of work in the employment contract should not only state the place of work, but that 'The *current* place of work is x'. This way, the employment contract will normally not limit the employer's right to manage in relation to changing the place of work. However, please note that changing the place of work may, in some cases, require an 'amendment termination'. An individual assessment of the proposed change should always be conducted so that the right procedure is followed.

USING TEMPORARY STAFF

22.155 The need for temporary staff may arise during a restructuring process. The main principle in Norway is permanent employment and, hence, the situations where a company may use temporary staff are limited. Under Norwegian law, temporary staff can be engaged in the following ways:

(*a*) by employing personnel directly by using fixed-term contracts (temporary employment)
(*b*) by hiring personnel from a temporary-work agency (a company whose object is to hire out labour)
(*c*) by hiring personnel from a company whose object is not to hire out labour

22.156 The WEA draws up an exhaustive list of the situations where fixed-term contracts (temporary employment) may be used, and also regulates the situations where a company may hire a temporary agency worker. For further information regarding a) and b) please see below starting at paras **22.162** and **22.158** respectively. Unlawful use of temporary employment and unlawful hiring of temporary agency workers provides the employee or agency worker with a claim to permanent employment and may also result in a right to compensation. Claims to permanent employment also arise when a fixed-term employee has been employed or an agency worker has been hired for four consecutive years. Such claims may impact the company's restructuring as it may push out other (permanent) employees in the assessment of the selection criteria and who to be made redundant.

22.157 The situations comprised by (*c*) above are very limited. The hired employee must be permanently employed by the lessor and must be engaged within the main areas of activity of the lessor. The possibilities to hire personnel from companies that are not temporary agencies are limited, and will, in borderline cases, most probably be considered as hiring from a temporary-work agency. For further information regarding hiring personnel from a temporary-work agency, please see below starting at para **22.158**

Example

The company Trucks AS produces trucks while its associated company, Cars AS, produce passenger cars. Each of the companies has their own factory as well as their own administrative, cleaning and canteen personnel. Of the 100 employees of Trucks AS, 80 are factory workers, 15 are administrative personnel, three are cleaning personnel and two are canteen personnel. As the sale of trucks has decreased, Trucks AS wants to hire out ten of its employees to Cars AS in order to avoid temporary redundancies of these employees.

The hiring out of ten *factory workers* will be lawful as the main areas of activity of Trucks AS is the work in the factory. Ten employees are only 10 % of the permanent employees at Trucks AS and, thus, well below 50 % of its permanent employees. The main aim of the hiring is not to profit from hiring out personnel, but to avoid temporary redundancies. The hiring out will be lawful.

Sometime later, the market is back to normal, and the ten factory workers return to work in Trucks AS' factory. Trucks AS then employs (permanently) an additional 30 factory workers so that it now has a total of 110 factory workers. All of the 30 new factory workers are hired out directly to Cars AS and other companies. Even though the hiring out takes place within the main areas of activity of Trucks AS, and is below 50 % of all of Trucks AS' permanent employees, the hiring will not be lawful. The main aim of the hiring is not to avoid permanent or temporary redundancies, but to employ personnel to hire out to other companies in order to obtain a profit. For this part of Trucks AS' activity, Trucks AS may be considered as a company whose object is to hire out personnel, and, hence, a temporary-work agency.

Please note that each case depends on an individual assessment based on the circumstances in that specific case, and that the example above cannot be used as advice in a similar situation. For further information regarding hiring personnel from a temporary-work agency, please see below starting at para **22.158**.

Agency workers

22.158 There are three situations where hiring agency workers are lawful. The situations all relate to the end user, which in this case is the company carrying out a restructuring process:

(*a*) For temporary work at the end user when warranted by the nature of the work and the work differs from that which is ordinarily performed in the company (limited possibility despite the wording).
(*b*) For temporary work at the end user as a substitute or temporary replacement for another person or persons being absent from work, eg maternity leave.
(*c*) If the end user is bound by collective agreement, and has an additional written agreement with specific elected representatives stating that hired labour may be used for a limited period of time.

22.159 The European Directive on Temporary Agency Work (2008/104/EU) has been implemented in Norwegian law and provides agency workers with certain rights. It includes the principle of equal treatment of agency workers and the exchange of information to ensure fulfilment of the principle of equal treatment, as well as provisions regulating joint liability for the temporary agency and the end user regarding salary and such.

22.160 The principle of equal treatment entitles the agency worker in a 'given job' to at least the basic employment conditions he would have received had he been recruited directly by the end user to do the same job. It applies in relation to basic pay and working conditions, which mainly includes working hours, rest periods, night work, holiday and salary (including compensation for overtime, other additional benefits and cost coverage). The temporary agency workers are also entitled access in the same manner as permanent employees to the services of the end user, such as canteens, childcare and transport facilities. Pension and collective insurances are not included in the principle of equal treatment.

22.161 The agency workers do not enjoy the same protection with regards to termination of their assignment at the end user as the end user's permanent and fixed-term employees. There are no minimum requirements regarding termination and notice period of agency workers when from the end user (but will be when from the temporary agency, depending on the nature of the relationship between the agency worker and the temporary agency). The contract between the temporary agency and the end user/the call off for the agency worker should contain provisions regarding relevant notice period for termination an assignment.

Fixed-term contracts

22.162 A company can only use fixed-term contracts/temporary employment in the following situations:

- employment of the chief executive of a company;
- when warranted by the nature of the work and the work differs from that which is ordinarily performed in the company (limited possibility despite the wording);
- substitute/temporary replacement for another person or persons being absent from work, eg maternity leave;
- work as a trainee;
- participants in labour market schemes under the sponsorship of or in cooperation with the Labour and Welfare Service;
- athletes, trainers, referees and other leaders within organised sports; and
- certain 12 months' engagements, provided closer defined conditions are fulfilled.

22.163 Unlawful use of fixed-term contracts entitles the fixed-term employees to permanent employment if they so claim. If a person has been (lawfully) engaged on a fixed-term contract for three or four consecutive years (depending on the grounds for using a fixed term contract), he will be entitled to permanent employment should he so claim. Permanent employees enjoy protection of employment under the WEA, including that a termination must be objectively justified on grounds relating to the company or the employee and minimum notice periods.

22.164 A fixed-term contract expires on the end date as stated in the contract. If the fixed-term employment has lasted for more than one year, the employee is entitled to a written notification before resigning from his position. The employer cannot demand him to withdraw until one month after such notification was given.

22.165 A fixed-term employment may be terminated before the end period as defined in the contract if: (i) the fixed-term contract includes a provision regarding notice period during the fixed term, and (ii) if the ordinary grounds for terminating an employment are fulfilled. For further information regarding ordinary grounds for terminating an employment, please see above starting at para **22.14**.

Renewal of fixed-term contracts

22.166 Fixed-term contracts may be renewed, but a renewal will only be lawful if the grounds for renewing the contract fulfil the requirements in the WEA as described above in para **22.162**. When renewing fixed-term contracts, bear in mind that fixed-term employees will be entitled to permanent employment if the fixed-term contract has lasted for four and in some cases, three consecutive years.

> **Practical Tips**
>
> Employers should ensure that the fixed-term contract includes a notice period to use for termination before the expiry of the agreed term. In addition, provisions regulating a probation period and the notice period during the probation period should always be included. If notice is given before the expiry of the fixed-term contract, the notice must fulfil certain minimum requirements prescribed by law.
>
> For fixed-term contracts that have lasted for one year, the employer must notify the employee in writing on month before his fixed-term contract expires.

EMPLOYMENT CLAIMS

22.167 Claims from employees and other personnel engaged by the company are heard at the ordinary district courts in the district where the employee's place of work is situated. The parties are asked to state whether they would like to attend court-sponsored mediation in the district court before their case is brought before the judges in the main proceedings. If so a professional judge mediates between the parties with the aim of reaching an agreement which settles the dispute. Since the introduction of court-sponsored mediation in 2008, a great number of employment disputes are settled in such a way and it has become normal to accept court-sponsored mediation. All information and offers given and discussed in the mediation are subject to confidentiality and cannot be used by the parties later in the dispute. If the dispute remains unsettled, another professional judge will take over the case and hold the main proceedings assisted by two associate judges, one from each side of the social partners.

22.168 Appeal is made to the Court of Appeal and then to the Supreme Court. The parties may agree to attend court-sponsored mediation in the Court of Appeal, but not in the Supreme Court. Disputes concerning the interpretation, validity and existence of collective agreements, cases of breach of collective agreements and the peace obligation and cases of claims for damages arising from such breaches and unlawful industrial action are heard at the Labour Court of Norway in Oslo.

Unfair dismissal

22.169 Any permanent or temporary employee whose employment has been terminated can bring a claim for unfair dismissal. If a dismissal is deemed unfair, the court may, after a claim from the employee, deem the dismissal invalid. The employee will then be entitled to return to his position. In special cases, if so demanded by the employer, the court may decide that the employment shall be terminated if, after weighing the interests of the parties, the court finds it clearly unreasonable that employment continues.

22.170 Employees who want to claim unfair dismissal can demand negotiations with the employer. Such demand must be sent in writing two weeks after receiving the notice. The employer is responsible for holding a negotiation meeting within two weeks after receiving such demand. The employee and employer, as well as their (possible) advisors, attend the negotiation meeting, and they must draw up and sign minutes from the meeting.

22.171 If, after the negotiation meeting, the employee still wants to pursue his claim of unfair dismissal, he must bring legal action within eight weeks after the negotiations ended. If no negotiations have been held, the time-limit starts running from the day he received his notice. If he only claims compensation, the time limit is six months after the said starting points. In redundancy procedures, the employee's claim for unfair dismissal will normally be that, based on the selection pool, selection criteria, and other social circumstances, he should have remained employed by the company while someone else should have been made redundant.

22.172 A permanent employee claiming unfair dismissal can also claim to remain in his position for as long as negotiations are in progress or until the dispute is finally settled by the court, including the appeal courts, should an appeal be filed. This means that the employee will be entitled and obligated to work and to receive normal salary during this period. Such a demand must be put forward within eight weeks after the negotiations ended or he received notice. The employer may demand that the employee leaves when the notice period has expired, but the court will normally not accept this in redundancy processes. The court makes the decision in this matter on the basis of whether it is unreasonable to continue the employment relationship while the dispute is ongoing. The courts often tend to make a decision in support of the employee in redundancy procedures and in support of the employer if the termination is based on circumstances relating to the employee.

22.173 An employee who has been employed at the company for the past two years and who has been made redundant has a preferential right to a new employment with the employer. Please see above starting at para **22.112** for further information regarding the preferential right to new employment.

Damages

22.174 An unfair dismissal may entitle the employee to damages of an amount that the court finds reasonable based on the employee's economic loss, circumstances relating to the employer and employee, and other facts of the case. The damages are normally split into damages for economic loss and damages for non-economic loss

DAMAGES FOR THE ECONOMIC LOSS

22.175 An employee's claim for damages for the economic loss will relate to the loss of salary of the employee from the expiry of the termination and up until the decision from the court. Further, loss of salary in the future until it is reasonable to assume that the employee would get another paid job, normally not more than two years. Income that the employee has obtained during the period in question will normally be deducted. The employee has a duty to mitigate his loss. Any damages for economic loss are deductible for tax as normal salary for the employee.

DAMAGES FOR NON-ECONOMIC LOSS

22.176 Several factors are relevant in the assessment of whether the court grant the employee damages for non-economic loss. They include, but are not limited to, weakness in the employer's handling of the process, the employer's process towards the specific employee, whether the employer has put forward unjustified accusations, whether there have been unnecessary publicity and so on.

22.177 The courts are not known to award large amounts for non-economic loss. The amount is normally within the range of NOK25,000–70,000, but a larger amount may also be awarded, depending on the circumstances in the specific case. Damages for non-economic loss is exempted from tax for an amount up to 1,5 times the at all-time basic amount in Norway. The basic amount is regulated annually and, per 1 May 2015, amounted to NOK 90,068. Any amount beyond 1.5 times the basic amount is liable for tax as normal salary for the employee.

Discrimination

22.178 An employee may also claim that the selection of him to be made redundant was unfair because of the following protected characteristics: political views; membership of a trade union; sexual orientation; disability; age; gender; ethnic origin; national origin; descent; colour; language; religion and ethical and cultural orientation.

22.179 The employee may also submit a complaint to the Equality and Anti-discrimination Ombudsman if he claims that the selection of him to be made redundant was due to a protected characteristic. A decision from the Equality and Anti-discrimination Ombudsman can be appealed to the Norwegian Equality Tribunal. The decision from these authorities will normally state that a matter was or was not contrary to the discrimination legislation. A claim that a decision from the Norwegian Equality Tribunal is invalid can be brought before the ordinary courts.

Remedies

22.180 If an employee succeeds in his claim for discrimination, he may be entitled to damages for economic and non-economic loss regardless of whether the employer is to blame. Damages for economic loss must cover the loss caused by the discrimination and the damages for non-economic loss are determined by the court on the basis of what is reasonable in view of the circumstances of the damage done, the circumstances of the parties and other facts of the case.

MUTUALLY AGREED TERMINATION

22.181 An employer and an employee may reach a mutual agreement regulating the termination of employment for all or some of the employees in a redundancy process. This can be done in several different ways.

Settlement agreements

22.182 Apart from the fact that the agreement must be mutual, there are no legislative requirements for such agreements. There are, however, certain issues that should be covered by such agreements. These include, amongst other things, regulation of the termination of employment, the salary/payments that the employee is to receive, the work he is expected to perform and that, by entering into the agreement, the employee waives his rights to challenge the termination of his employment and claiming an unfair dismissal before the courts. The agreement should be drawn up by the employer's lawyers to ensure that it contains all the relevant provisions.

COLLECTIVE SCHEME FOR SEVERANCE AGREEMENTS

22.183 An employer may draw up a collective scheme where the employees apply for a severance agreement. This way, the number of employees that actually have to be made redundant may decrease, resulting in a reduction of the risk of disputes and claims for unfair dismissal.

22.184 The employer is free to decide the terms of the scheme, but may find it constructive and useful to discuss the scheme with employee representatives. In general, a severance agreement scheme includes conditions which the employees must fulfil in order to be granted a settlement agreement, the calculation of the payment to be made to the employee and the main conditions that the final severance agreement will contain.

22.185 It is normal that the employees eligible for the severance scheme receive information about it and then can decide whether they would like to submit an application. The employer then assesses each application as to whether the specific employee fulfils the relevant conditions and what payment the employee will be entitled to. The size of pay under the scheme is often provided as a formula, eg determined by the employee's length of service, but it can also depend on other factors, provided that the scheme does not constitute discrimination.

Example

After assessing and discussing the situation with the employee representatives, Company AS has found that 50 FTE's have to be made redundant. The company wants to make the transition as smooth as possible for all parties involved, and has therefore, together with the employee representatives, negotiated a severance agreement scheme for the employees. Employees in the x and y department of the company may apply, and will, if granted, receive pay during their notice period and a severance pay based on their length of service in the company or group. Each whole year of employment provides for one month's basic pay, and periods below one year count as one year.

Edward is employed by Company AS and is currently working in department x with a monthly basic salary of NOK25,000. He has been employed at Company AS for the past for two and a half years, and has previously been employed by the parent company for three years. His notice period is three months. If he applies for a severance agreement, he will be granted pay and other benefits as described in his employment contract during his notice period (three months) and a severance pay of NOK150,000 (six months' basic salary).

Amy has been employed by Company AS for one year and nine months and works in the z department. Her basic monthly salary is NOK25,000 and her notice period is one month. She will not be granted severance agreement if she applies.

However, if Amy worked in the x or y department, she would be granted a severance agreement of normal pay and other benefits as described in her employment contract for one month (notice period) and a severance pay of NOK50,000 (two months' basic salary) if she applied.

INDIVIDUAL SETTLEMENT AGREEMENTS

22.186 At any point in the process, the employer may offer a settlement agreement to one or more employees of their choice. If the employee accepts the offer, the parties enter into a settlement agreement terminating the employee's employment. The timing of the employer's (first) offer of settlement agreement to the employee is always a strategic assessment and it is crucial to ensure that the employer is in as good a negotiation position as possible. Some of the main situations where we see such offers are before the redundancy process has started formally, in the individual discussion meetings or in the negotiations meeting/dispute following the termination of employment in the process as drawn up in the WEA.

Chapter 23

Workforce Restructuring in Poland

Renata Warchoł-Lewicka, Iwona Tomaszewska and Natalia Rutkowska
Gorazda, Świstuń, Wątroba i Partner 2Y, adwokaci i radcowie prawni, Krakow

INTRODUCTION

23.1 This chapter looks at employment law in Poland regarding workforce restructuring.

23.2 The legal system in Poland is similar to other continental jurisdictions. The law is codified in a systematic way. Crucial aspects of all legal disciplines are regulated in codes (such as the Civil Code, the Criminal Code, the Labour Code, etc). Details of the main issues are specified in a number of acts and regulations.

23.3 The basic act regulating employment aspects and relationship between employees, employers and trade unions is the Labour Code. The Labour Code specifies, eg: the aspects of conclusion and termination of employment relationship; salary and other financial benefits; employee's and employer's duties; financial liabilities of employees, working time; leave, etc. Details are regulated in a number of acts issued on the basis of the Labour Code and regulations thereto. Furthermore, details might be specified in internal employer regulations.

23.4 When assessing entitlement of employees in dismissal or any other restructuring scenario, the 'first port of call' are the employment contract (or other document confirming the terms and conditions of work and pay) and the Labour Code along with other acts of law implementing its terms and conditions of work and pay. However, the provisions of the employment contract may not offer less favourable term to the employees than prescribed by the provisions of the Labour Code and other acts of law and implementing regulations?.

PREPARING FOR A RESTRUCTURING PROCESS

23.5 In the current economic environment many organisations are experiencing similar issues: having to do more for less; meeting budgets; looking for new growth; and maintaining quality standards. Workforce costs may often represent a significant proportion of the budget, so quite often when thinking of restructuring one of the first thoughts is workforce restructuring. Indeed, very often it is an effective way of meeting new challenges and expectations. However, it is good to bear in mind all risks and disadvantages.

23.6 Once the business goals are identified, any change in the operating environment should be reflected in how the workforce is organised to deliver towards the goals of the business. A correct strategy regarding the whole process should be developed. It is good to know that there are plenty of possibilities to reduce costs of employment without generating cost of its reducing.

23.7 It is crucial to collect as much information as possible regarding the legal relationship with dedicated people before making any decision or announcement.

The key issues to consider are set out below.

COLLECTING INFORMATION TO DEVELOP A BUDGET OF THE RESTRUCTURING PROCESS

23.8 Gathering relevant data and facts on the basis of which a reliable plan and structure of any restructuring process can be developed, is itself time consuming.

Practical Tip

Key data required initially in respect of any employee potentially impacted by a workforce reduction or restructuring exercise includes (but is not limited to):

- **type of engagement** – employment contract or other civil law contract When employment contract:
- **type of contract: for a definite period of time, for an indefinite period of time or for a trial period** (this is crucial information as it influences terms and conditions of work and pay of the termination)
- **date of contract**
- **type of work**
- **place of work**
- **salary** (including all its elements, such as benefits, etc)
- **term of employment**
- **age**

This information is crucial for estimating the overall costs of the restructuring process and for planning the appropriate timetable for executing dismissals.

EMPLOYMENT STATUS

23.9 According to the legal definition the employee is an individual employed on the basis of an employment contract, appointment, election, nomination or co-operative contract of employment.

23.10 Only individuals who meet the legal definition of 'the employee' are protected against unfair dismissal and need to be included in a redundancy procedure for workforce restructuring purposes. It is relevant to remember that there are plenty of individuals engaged that are not employees of the entity, but may be affected by the restructuring (for example agency workers, self-employed freelancers or consultants etc).

GENERAL PROTECTION AGAINST DISMISSAL

23.11 In Poland dismissal is a complex matter, particularly in case of individual dismissals and in any case the dismissal might be supervised by the court. All employers shall take into consideration the fact that in case of any doubts regarding a dismissal an employee always has an option to exercise his/her rights in front of the court. It is free for the employee to bring a claim, but it generates costs and is time consuming for the employer and might present an extra burden for the employer. Therefore, it is crucial to duly prepare the procedure of dismissal to minimise that risk.

23.12 In any case it should be noted that there is an option to terminate the employment contract upon a mutual agreement of the parties. In fact this is the most desirable form. It must be made in writing, but it does not need to specify a reason for the termination of the contract. This option often limits the court's supervision which would otherwise apply (in case of individual redundancies).

23.13 Employees employed for an indefinite period of time, for a trial period and in some cases for a fixed period of time enjoy a statutory notice period (stipulated by the Labour Code). Its length depends on the length of the employee's service with a given employer.

23.14 Furthermore in some cases consultation with trade unions might be required. If trade unions operate at the work premises, the employer must consult them about the proposed termination of the employment contract with or without notice in the following two cases: if the employee being dismissed is a member of a trade union; or if a trade union agrees to represent an employee (even if the employee is not a union member). It must be emphasised that the consultation requirement only applies to employment contracts for an indefinite period of time.

SPECIAL PROTECTION AGAINST DISMISSAL

23.15 It should be noted that in case of termination (either with a notice or without notice) of the employment contract the employer should follow several formal steps to make the termination effective and valid:

- it should be made in writing;
- it should clearly and precisely specify the reason for the termination, such reason should be real and justified (this is not required for contracts for a fixed period of time); and
- it should inform the employee of the right to appeal to the Labour Court.

23.16 Furthermore, certain categories of employees are specifically protected against dismissal. These categories are:

- employees who will reach retirement age in less than four years;
- employees on leave or any other justified absence from work;
- employees on parental leave; and
- pregnant employees.

Generally these employees cannot be dismissed except in some specific situations.

WORKFORCE REDUCTION

23.17 An employer who employs 20 or more employees who it proposes to dismiss as redundant for reasons not related to the employees will have to follow a collective redundancy procedure (see para 23.40) if within a maximum period of 30 days, the redundancy applies to at least:

- 10 employees, if the employer employs less than 100 employees;
- 10% of employees, if the employer employs a minimum of 100, but less than 300 employees;
- 30 employees, if the employer employs a minimum of 300 employees.

The term 'reasons not related to the employees' should be interpreted broadly. Typically such reasons are: restructuring; product reorganisation, or reduction of the number of posts at the work establishment, combined with partial or total business closure.

Definition of redundancy

23.18 In Poland there is no legal definition of 'redundancy'. The Labour Code provides general rules for termination of all types of employment contracts which should be followed in any case of a redundancy.

23.19 The Special Rules for Terminating Employees Employment for reasons not related to the Employees Act, dated 13 March 2003, which implements directive 98/59 (the "Act") uses a term 'termination for a reason unrelated to an employee'. This term should be interpreted broadly.

Dismissals on grounds of redundancy

23.20 In Poland dismissal on the ground of redundancies due to reasons unrelated to the employee obligates the employer (who employs 20 or more employees) to follow a special collective redundancy procedure governed by the Act. The Act generally applies to all terminations for a reason unrelated to an employee. The Act applies to both the private and public sector employer.

Redundancy procedure

23.21 In the case of collective redundancy, a special collective redundancy procedure is included in the Act.

23.22 Furthermore, material rules regarding the termination of the employment agreement are incorporated in the labour code. Additional obligations for the employer might be incorporated in internal regulations, however such cannot be in contradiction with the law.

Individual redundancy procedure

Defining the selection pool

23.23 As the first stage of a fair selection process, the employer will need to identify the group or pool of employees from which those who are to be made redundant will be selected.

23.24 A more complicated procedure applies regarding employees with employment contracts for an indefinite period of time and/or under special protection against dismissal. It is much easier to terminate a contract for trial period and contracts for a fixed period of time (subject to the contract providing for a termination with notice clause).

23.25 The employer should bear in mind that terminating of any contract for an indefinite period of time is governed by formalities (including stating the reasons) and the decision of should be justified.

Selection criteria

23.26 Selection criteria must be objective and should not merely reflect personal opinion.

23.27 Such criteria may not be discriminatory. Furthermore the employer should avoid using other criteria which might be considered indirect discrimination (ie dismissing those employees with higher salaries or higher absence due to maternity leave or illness).

23.28 The selection criteria should be fairly and consistently applied to all staff in the selection pool.

Individual consultation

23.29 A requirement for individual consultation with an employee has not been introduced under the Polish law.

Involvement of employee representatives in individual dismissals

23.30 The consultation with trade unions is provided by Article 38 of the Labour Code (consultation with trade unions). If trade unions operate at the work premises, the employer must consult them about the intended termination of employment contracts with or without notice in the following two cases: if the dismissed employee is a member of a trade union or if a trade union has agreed to represent a given employee (who is not a union member).

23.31 The employer must notify the trade union of the intention to terminate an employment contract and must specify the reason for its termination. The trade union may express its opinion on this matter within five days. The opinion is not binding for the employer and even if it is negative, the employer may proceed to terminate the employment contract. If the above time limit expires and the employer does not receive any opinion, he may proceed to terminate the employment contract.

23.32 Failure to consult trade unions generally renders a dismissal unfair.

Avoiding compulsory redundancies

23.33 Employers should always consider alternatives to compulsory redundancies. Careful consideration should be given to the possibility of part-time working or other changes in the employment terms and conditions. Possible ways of implementing this is termination of the terms and conditions of work and pay under the rules of the Labour Code) or mutual changes.

Alternative employment

23.34 The employer may, but is not obligated to identify and offer alternative employment.

Termination of the terms and conditions of work and pay as an alternative to dismissal

23.35 During any reconstruction process one option for an employer is to modify the terms and conditions of the employment. Under Polish law any change in substantial terms and conditions of the employment contract may be effected by way of the so called 'termination of terms and conditions of work and pay'. The employer may offer the employee a change of the terms and conditions of work and pay and the employee may only object. Should he object, the agreement terminates. If the employee fails to object to the proposed change within a specified time limit, the changed terms and conditions of work and pay become effective. The notice provisions relating to termination of the employment contract apply to the termination of terms and conditions.

23.36 Termination of the terms and conditions of work and pay with notice is considered effective if new terms and conditions of work and pay are proposed simultaneously to an employee in writing.

23.37 If the proposed new terms and conditions of work and pay are rejected by the employee, the employment contract is terminated upon the expiry of the period of notice. Unless the employee rejects the proposed new terms and conditions of work and pay in writing before half of the period of notice has passed, those terms and conditions of work and pay are deemed to be accepted; the employer's notice of termination of the terms and conditions of work and pay should contain an instruction to that effect. If no such instruction is provided, the employee is entitled to wait till the end of the notice period before submitting a refusal to accept the proposed new terms and conditions of work and pay by the end of the period of notice.

23.38 Notice of termination of the current terms and conditions of work and pay is not necessary in cases when an employee is assigned work other than that specified in the contract of employment for a period not longer than three months in a calendar year, if justified by the employer's needs, unless this reduces the employee's salary and is inappropriate considering the employee's qualifications.

Other considerations

23.39 The main risk to the employer when carrying out individual redundancies is whether an employee will be reinstated or awarded compensation. This risk cannot be fully eliminated, but it can be reduced considerably, provided that the termination of the employment contract is duly prepared in legal terms. Polish employees are increasingly aware of their rights in this respect, and thus they request Labour Courts to examine employment termination more and more frequently.

COLLECTIVE REDUNDANCY PROCEDURE

Definition of collective redundancy

23.40 In Poland a collective redundancy occurs when an employer employing at least 20 employees proposes to dismiss as redundant over a period of 30 days a number of employees amounting to:

- 10 employees, if the employer employs fewer than 100 employees;
- 10% of employees, if the employer employs a minimum of 100, but fewer than 300 employees;
- 30 employees, if the employer employs a minimum of 300 employees;

for reasons unrelated to the employee (related to the employer).

The collective redundancy procedure is regulated in the Act (see para **23.19**). It should be noted that the collective redundancy procedure applies not only when the employment contract is terminated with notice, but also when the employment contract is terminated by mutual agreement of the parties. Therefore, the number of employees set forth above may include employees (the number of at least five employees) with whom the employment contract is terminated by mutual agreement of the parties. This procedure does not apply to employees appointed for work and to temporary workers.

Individual redundancy under collective redundancy procedure

23.41 Regulations concerning protection against termination of the employment contract (see para **23.46**), as well as severance pay (see para **23.49**) also apply to an individual redundancy, if the number of employees employed by the employer is consistent with the one indicated in para **23.40**. In the event that the employees subject to individual redundancy effected under a collective redundancy procedure are protected against termination of the employment contract, the redundancy may be effected only if it is no longer possible to employ the employees in their current posts and the employer notifies trade unions. If trade unions object within fourteen days, termination of employment contracts is not possible.

Applicability of Polish law (international aspect)

23.42 It should be noted that the numbers mentioned in para 23.40 above refer solely to employees employed under Polish law, even if the employer is an international company employing people from all over the world.

> Example
>
> The company Blue Moon Limited is a company established and run under the laws of Germany. The company employs 400 employees in Germany, 50 employees in the United Kingdom and two employees in Poland. Collective redundancies do not apply to Polish employees. Employment contracts can be terminated only according to the Labour Code.

Involvement of trade unions or employee's representative

23.43 In a collective redundancy situation, the employer is obliged to consult trade unions (or employee's representatives where there are no trade unions) in matters regarding collective redundancy, including: possibility of avoiding collective redundancy or decreasing its scope, employee issues related to the redundancy (ie the number of employees to be made redundant, period over which the redundancy is planned, workforce restructuring, employee's option regarding new employment, etc).

The employer informs trade unions in particular about:

(a) reasons for collective redundancy;
(b) number of employees and professional groups (categories of employees) in the work establishment;
(c) number of employees to be made redundant and their professional group;
(d) period of time over which the collective redundancy is planned (redundancy schedule);
(e) employees identified for redundancy;
(f) suggestions regarding disputes' resolution; and
(g) calculation of redundancy pay.

Information for a competent National Labour Inspectorate

23.44 Information for trade unions must also be presented to the competent National Labour Inspectorate.

Work regulations

23.45 Within twenty days following the notification, the employer and the trade unions must conclude an agreement regulating the terms of collective redundancy. Should the parties fail to reach agreement, the employer adopts work regulations referring to the terms of collective redundancy.

Special regulations on the protection of employees

23.46 In the event of collective redundancy, special regulations on the protection of employees against termination of the employment contract apply in such a manner, that only termination of terms and conditions of work and pay of work and pay is permitted. Termination of the employment contract is allowed when the protection ceases. Should this termination of terms and conditions of work and pay of employment cause a reduction in salary, the employee is entitled to a compensatory payment. Additionally, when the terms of collective redundancy are regulated in a work regulation adopted by the employer, the employer is obliged to notify the trade unions of the collective redundancy and take their opinion into consideration (not necessarily follow it).

Termination of terms and conditions of work and pay

23.47 Under the Act termination of terms and conditions of work and pay is possible (see paras **23.35** and **23.110**). However, should the proposed new terms and conditions of work and pay be unacceptable to the employee and cause the employee to decide to terminate the employment contract, such termination is still considered to be based on reasons not related to employees and the employee is entitled to severance pay.

NOTICE

23.48 The employer may terminate employment contracts in collective redundancies no sooner than 30 days following conclusion of the agreement with trade union (referred to in para **23.43**) or notification of the trade union (according to para **23.46**). Employment contracts concluded for a fixed period of time or for a period necessary to perform a specific task may be terminated upon a two-week notice period (even if such period of notice was not stipulated in the employment contract).

Severance pay

23.49 An employee made redundant following collective redundancy procedure is entitled to severance pay amounting to:

- a month's salary if the employee is employed by the employer for a period of time less than two years,
- two month's salary if the employee is employed by the employer for a period of time of two to eight years,
- three month's salary if the employee is employed by the employer for a period of time exceeding eight years.

The severance pay may not exceed the amount of 15 monthly minimum statutory salaries. The rules of calculating remuneration by holiday leave apply accordingly to severance pay.

Re-employment

23.50 The employer should re-employ the employees made redundant, should the reasons for collective redundancy cease within 15 months following the termination of the employment contract, if the employees applies for the re-employment in the same post within one year following the collective redundancy.

DISPUTES

23.51 All disputes arising out of collective redundancy are settled by labour courts. In these matters provisions of the Labour Code apply.

EMPLOYMENT ASPECTS OF A BUSINESS SALE/ ACQUISITION (ASSET TRANSFER AND SHARE SALE/PURCHASE)

Transfer of 'work establishment' to another employer

23.52 'Work establishment' comprises a set of tangible and intangible assets, including personnel.

23.53 Transfer of work establishment may be effected by way of eg sale, acquisition, restructuring, privatisation, division of inheritance or division of a company. The type of the legal act forming the basis for the transfer of work establishment is of secondary importance. The factual acquisition of tasks or functions of the work establishment where the employees may perform their obligations is decisive for the transfer.

The transfer does not even have to be final, as it may occur for a fixed term.

LIABILITY FOR OBLIGATIONS EXISTING PRIOR TO THE TRANSFER

23.54 A new employer is fully liable for the obligations under the employment relation which existed prior to the transfer of a whole work establishment.

23.55 Former and new employers are jointly and severally liable for the employment obligations which existed prior to the transfer of a part of the work establishment to the new employer.

LIABILITY FOR OBLIGATIONS ARISING AFTER THE TRANSFER

23.56 A new employer is solely liable for the obligations which arise after the transfer, irrespective of the fact whether work establishment or only the part thereof is being transferred.

CONTINUATION OF EXISTING EMPLOYMENT RELATIONS

23.57 The transfer of work establishment or part thereof is, by law, followed by the transfer of existing employment relationship to the new employer. An employee or a trade union cannot oppose the transfer.

23.58 The continuation of the employment relationship means eg that period of service for the former employer is added to the period of service for the new employer.

23.59 The continuation of contractual relations does not, however, apply to other civil law contracts (eg management agreements) or contracts of outwork (working at home – type of employment not regulated in the Labour Code, but the regulation of the government). Such contracts are not within the scope of the labour law.

NOTIFICATIONS

23.60 Both the former and new employer are obliged to notify the employees in writing of:

- expected date of transfer of work establishment in whole or in part to the new employer,

- reasons therefore,
- the legal, economic and social consequences thereof for the employees, and
- the proposed action with respect to the terms and conditions of employment for the employees, in particular the terms and conditions of work and pay as well as retraining.

23.61 This notification shall be made at least thirty days before the expected date on which the establishment or a part thereof is to be transferred to another employer.

> **Practical Tip**
>
> The date of transfer may often depend on the date of registration of a company entered in the register of companies by the National Court Register. The final date of registration fully depends on a court. Therefore, it is useful to request that the registration takes effect on the indicated date, usually at the beginning of the month. This helps planning notifications concerning restructuring, ie transfer of work establishment.

23.62 The process of notifying is dependent on whether or not there are established trade unions:

- Restructuring by way of transfer of establishment, where trade unions are established, must be followed by the notification of trade unions operating at the existing and new employer.
  In case of planned changes to the terms of employment for the employees, in particular the terms and conditions of work and pay, employer is obliged to negotiate the changes with trade unions in order to conclude an agreement on such changes within 30 days of notification. Should the negotiations fail, the employer may independently decide on implementing the changes with respect to arrangements made with trade unions in the course of negotiations.
- Restructuring consisting of the transfer of establishment, where trade unions are not established should be followed by the notification of employees by both the existing and new employer. Also, any absent employees should be individually notified of the transfer.

TERMINATION OF EMPLOYMENT RELATIONSHIP UNDER EMPLOYMENT CONTRACT

23.63 The transfer of an establishment or any part thereof shall not in itself constitute grounds for termination of an employment relationship by an employer or unilateral changes to the terms of employment. The parties may, however, conclude a mutual agreement in this respect.

23.64 On the other hand, an employee may independently, within two months of the transfer, upon providing notification seven-days in advance, use this opportunity to terminate the employment relationship without further notice.

TERMINATION OF EMPLOYMENT RELATIONS OTHER THAN EMPLOYMENT CONTRACT

23.65 The abovementioned right to terminate the contract may also be used by employees other than those employed under an employment contract (ie appointment, election or co-operative employment contract).

23.66 The new employer may continue the employment contract without any changes of its terms.

23.67 However, on the date of transfer of work establishment or a part thereof, the employer may impose new conditions of work and pay by proposing them to the employees specifying a period, not shorter than seven days from the date of the transfer, by which employees may submit their acceptance or refusal of the proposed conditions. If no agreement is reached as to the new terms and conditions of work and pay, the former employment relationship is terminated upon expiry of a period equal to the period of notice, starting on the date of submission of a refusal of the proposed conditions by an employee or on the date of the deadline by which such statement could have been submitted.

23.68 In the abovementioned cases the termination of an employment relationship by an employee (either employed under employment contract or on a basis other than employment contract) will have the same consequences as those envisaged under labour law for termination of the employment relation with notice by employer, incl. i.a. right to claim benefits, like jobseeker's allowance under the Act on Promoting Employment and Labour Market Institutions or severance pay under the Act (see para **23.19**).

CONTINUATION OF COLLECTIVE AGREEMENTS – GENERAL RULE

23.69 Within one year following the date of transfer of the work establishment or a part thereof to another employer, provisions of a collective agreement apply. A collective agreement is an agreement concluded by the employer and trade unions in a larger work establishment. Such agreement provides for the general terms and conditions of work and pay in this work establishment and these provisions apply equally to all the employees of this work establishment (unless otherwise agreed).

23.70 After one year from the transfer of establishment changes to the terms of employment may be introduced by individual notice to change the terms of employment.

OUTSOURCING/INSOURCING

General

23.71 There are very few regulations which might be applicable in respect to outsourcing/insourcing of employees. Generally, movement of employment is free.

Outsourcing

23.72 Polish law does not provide for any special outsourcing (or offshore outsourcing) provisions, with one exception: the field of banking. The outsourcing agreements are understood as contracts for services, which are governed accordingly by the provisions on mandate specified in the Civil Code.

Bank outsourcing

23.73 A bank may, by a written agreement, entrust an entrepreneur or a foreign entrepreneur with certain bank operations indicated in the Banking Act. Bank outsourcing may be combined with outsourcing of employees.

Unintended transfer of work establishment

23.74 It is common that the tasks of internal departments of a company are entrusted to external specialised entities. Should such division of tasks and functions fulfil the conditions of the transfer of work establishment , it may qualify as a transfer of work establishment. Consequently, the external specialised entity as the acquiring company becomes the new employer of the employees of the outsourced department with all obligations regarding payment of salary and other employment expenses. Such outcome is usually not intended by outsourcing. Moreover, the transfer extends to all employees of the department, even if their occupation was different from the field of the affected department. Therefore outsourcing should be carefully planned.

Example

Transfer of a department dealing with IT services, where not only IT technicians or programmers are employed, but also cleaning or security employees. All of them might be subjected to change of an employer.

Ineffective transfer of work establishment

23.75 Agreements on transfer of employment are concluded in practice. The subject matter of such agreements is the transfer of employees, including transfer of obligations connected therewith such as payment of salary or advances. Should, however, such an agreement not be followed by a factual transfer of work establishment (the factual acquisition of the tasks or functions of the establishment), the transfer is ineffective. Consequently, the former employer remains obliged to pay income personal tax advances and cash allowances on the Social Security Fund for employees as well as is subjected to official controls. In such case the only recourse against the other party of the agreement will be such rights which are set out in the agreement.

Insourcing

23.76 There are also no special regulations regarding insourcing.

23.77 However, insourcing may help to avoid redundancy eg in a case when an employee who has become incapable of working in his previous position due to an accident at work or occupational disease, but whose incapacity for work was not determined within the meaning of the regulations on retirement and disability benefits from the Social Security Fund, shall be transferred to an appropriate position by the employer on the basis of a medical certificate. A post for him may be created by transferring the obligations back from an outsourcing firm to the transferred employee. Should, however, such a transfer be followed by a reduction of salary, the employee is entitled to a compensatory payment for up to six months' salary.

23.78 Insourcing may be very reasonable where the transfer of liability is not possible. This may occur in two situations:

- First, if one party does not want to transfer the liability to an external entity, for example in the IT industry by the development of environment and software.
- Secondly, in the fields where transfer of liability is prohibited by law, such as pharmaceutical legislation around merchandising of medical products. Another example would be the transfer of personal data, or entrusting with bank operations which is under statutory conditions possible, but it does not indemnify the transferring party from liability.

OFFSHORING/IN-SHORING

Employment of Polish employees abroad

23.79 Polish employees may be employed abroad by intermediate employment agencies. The terms and conditions of work and pay of employment abroad are governed and construed according to the rules of employment of the country of employment as well as international agreements.

Employment agencies

23.80 Employment agencies in Poland deal with one or more of the following issues:

- personal coaching;
- work consulting;
- temporary work (see para 23.96); and
- acting as intermediaries for employment of workers.

23.81 There are two types of employment agencies providing assistance and acting as intermediaries in respect of:

- employment in the territory of Poland; and
- employment abroad by the foreign employers, including intermediation in work abroad by foreign employers.

23.82 Employment agencies are registered in the register of entities acting as employment agencies held by a respective Voivodship Marshall (the highest self-governmental executive officer). An official website of the Register of Employment Agencies is available under www.kraz.praca.gov.pl. Registering bodies issue a respective certificate for each registered agency proving its status.

Agreements regarding employment abroad

23.83 Employment abroad by employment agencies acting as intermediaries requires conclusion of two contracts between:

- an employment agency and an employee; and
- an employment agency and a foreign employer.

23.84 Employment agencies conclude written agreements with employees which must fulfil statutory conditions such as details of:

- foreign employer;
- period of employment or other paid work;

- type and conditions of work and pay, as well as social benefits;
- terms of social insurance and the consequences of accidents at work;
- rights and obligations of an employee and an employment agency;
- extent of liability of the parties for non-performance or improper performance of the agreement, including indication of a party bearing costs of arrival and return of an employee;
- the travel costs borne by an employment agency for transport out and back of an employee, issuing visa, translation of documents (only with these costs may an employee be burdened by an employment agency);
- information on conditions of work of foreigners abroad; and
- other obligations of the parties.

23.85 On the other hand, employment agencies in Poland must conclude written agreements with a foreign employer specifying ie:

- number of work posts;
- period of employment or other paid job;
- type and conditions of employment, as well as social benefits; and
- scope of liability of the parties for non-performance or improper performance of the agreement, including indication of a party bearing costs of arrival and return of an employee.

The verified periods of employment abroad must be recognised in terms of the employee's rights as equal to periods of work in Poland.

Employment of a foreigner in Poland

23.86 Generally a foreigner is entitled to work on the territory of Poland if the foreigner:

- is an EU citizen.
- is a citizen of the Economic European Area,
- is a member of family of an EU citizen or a citizen of the Economic European Area;
- has refugee status issued in Poland;
- has a permanent residence permit in Poland;
- has a permanent EU long-term residence permit in Poland;
- has a temporary residence permit; or
- has a work permit and resides on territory of Poland according to ie, a visa.

Work permit in Poland

23.87 The statute provides for plenty of exceptions from the requirement for work permit such as eg having the valid Card of the Pole (the Card of the Pole is a document stating adherence to the Polish nation. The holder of the

Card of the Pole may obtain a long-term visa allowing multiple entry into the territory of Poland, take up legal employment without having to obtain a work permit, run a business in Poland on the same conditions as Polish citizens, The Card of the Pole does not entitle the holder to obtain Polish citizenship or the legal right to reside in the territory of the Republic of Poland).

23.88 Work permits are granted by a respective Voivod (the highest governmental executive officer in the highest level administrative subdivision of the territory of Poland called voivodship) solely on request of an entity giving the work to the foreigner for the time period not longer than three years which may be prolonged. Work permits are granted individually.

23.89 If the work permit is granted for a temporary work, it should additionally indicate a user employer.

23.90 Generally a work permit is required if a foreigner:

- works in the territory of Poland for an entity whose seat, branch, establishment or any other organised form of business is situated on the territory of Poland;
- resides in the territory of Poland for more than six months (during a 12-month period) as a management board member of a company,
- works for a foreign employer and is seconded to Poland to work in a branch or an establishment of a foreign entity or associated entity for the period not exceeding 30 days in a calendar year;
- works for a foreign employer not having any branch, establishment or any other organised form of business on the territory of Poland and is seconded to Poland in order to provide temporary and occasional services;
- works for a foreign employer and is seconded to Poland for the period not exceeding 30 days during subsequent six months for any other purpose than indicated in points 2–4 above.

Posting work abroad with the place of employment in Poland – business trip

23.91 A public sector employee who performs work assigned by the employer away from the location of the registered office of the employer or away from his permanent workplace is entitled to reimbursement of any expenses related to business travel abroad under respective regulations of the Ministry of Labour and Social Policy (for public sector).

23.92 Employees in the private sector shall be entitled to reimbursement defined in a collective agreement or a salary scheme, or in the employment contract (when there is no collective agreement of salary scheme). The amount of per diem travel allowances for business travel in Poland and abroad defined in a collective labour agreement, salary scheme, or contract of employment, cannot be lower than the amount of per diem travel allowances for business travel in Poland defined for employees of the public sector. Should a collective labour agreement, salary scheme or contract of employment contain no provisions in this respect, an employee is entitled to business travel allowances in accordance with the provisions applying to the public sector.

Posting work abroad with the place of employment outside of Poland (within EU)

23.93 An employee may be assigned to work abroad under the directive 96/71/EC of the European Parliament and of the Council concerning the posting of workers in the framework of the provision of services.

23.94 Such posting requires adjustment of work conditions to the specifics of work abroad. The terms of work cannot be less favourable than those applying in the country of work abroad. The obligation to adjust employment contracts arises only if the foreign legislation guarantee employers more favourable conditions than Polish provisions. All changes to the employment agreement should be implemented by the termination of the terms of work and pay or under the mutual consent of the parties.

23.95 The change of the place of employment is the deciding factor when it comes to the application of the European directive. Should the place of employment be Poland, an employee would only be entitled to reimbursement of expenses under the Polish labour provisions.

USE OF TEMPORARY WORKERS

Temporary work

23.96 Use of temporary workers is regulated in the Act on Temporary Employment as a loan of employees hired by special agencies – licensed agencies of temporary work being a type of an employment agency. In case of temporary workers there are two types of employers:

- factual employer – a licensed agency of temporary work who issues work certificates, terminates the employment agreement, pays salary and is liable for damage inflicted to the user employer by the temporary worker according to the provisions specifying liability for property entrusted to the employee. The agency may have the right of recourse against the liable worker.
- user employer – person for whom and under the supervision and direction of whom a temporary agency worker works temporarily.

Agreement on temporary work

23.97 Agreements with temporary workers are concluded with the licensed agencies of temporary work for either a fixed period of time or for a specific task.

23.98 An agreement has to be concluded in writing, unless the licensed agency of temporary work confirms the type of work and its terms to the temporary worker in writing, not later than two days from the begin of temporary work.

23.99 Notification obligations of the respective trade unions or representatives of employees in respect to temporary employment depend on the length of temporary work. Lack of notification does not invalidate the employment agreement.

23.100 An earlier termination of an agreement by either party may be provided in the agreement as follows:

- three-day's notice where the employment agreement is concluded for a period shorter than two weeks,
- one-week's notice where the employment agreement is concluded for a period longer than two weeks.

23.101 The provisions providing an extension of the employment relation until the date of birth of employee's child do not apply.

Restrictions

23.102 Temporary work in Poland is subjected to certain restrictions:

- temporary work is excluded when it comes to: dangerous work, at a post at which within last three months from the begin of temporary work the employment relation with an employee of the user employer was terminated under the Act
- sub-lease of employees is excluded,
  - within 36 consecutive months a temporary worker may work for one user employer for a maximum of 18 months in total, except where covering for an absent employee, up to 36 months. In such a case the 36 months must pass before working for the same employer again
  - the provisions of the Labour Code providing that the third subsequent contract for fixed period of time is deemed as concluded for an indefinite period of time do not apply'
  - any agreement between the licensed agency of temporary work and the user employer to restrict employment of a temporary worker any time after the period of temporary employment has ended shall be null and void; and
  - temporary workers are not subject to the provisions of the Act.

23.103 Another peculiarity is the number of days of holiday entitlement. A temporary worker is entitled to two days of leave for each month, 24 days annually, irrespective of the length of employment.

Licensed agencies of temporary work

23.104 Licensed agencies of temporary work are employment agencies who deal specifically with temporary work employment. Licensed agencies of temporary work are registered in the register of entities conducting agencies of employment held by the Voivodship Marshall for the seat of such an entity.

23.105 Foreign undertakings entitled to and conducting legal business of employment agencies, including licensed agencies of temporary work, within the territory of the European Union or the Economic European Area are not obliged to register, however, such foreign undertakings shall – before commencing activities in the territory of Poland – inform the Voivodship Marshall of their name, registered office, country of origin and approximate place and time of rendering services in the territory of Poland. Should the basic place of rendering services be hard to define, the Mazovian Voivodship Marshall shall be notified.

REASSIGNMENT OF FUNCTIONAL/ ORGANISATIONAL RESPONSIBILITIES OF STAFF

23.106 Reassignment of functional responsibilities of staff may be performed under different conditions. First of all, an employee may be assigned work other than specified in the employment contract for a period not longer than three months in a calendar year if it is justified by the employer's needs and does not lead to reduction of salary or is inappropriate to the employee's qualifications. In such a case, the rules of termination of terms and conditions of work and pay (see paras **23.35** and **23.110**) do not apply. In other words, the employer may assign other work without notice and with no regard to the employee's objection, on condition that the above rules are observed.

23.107 Otherwise reassignment of responsibilities requires a termination of terms and conditions of work and pay made by notice. Such notice is required, even if the conditions of employment remained the same, in case of assigning a new post of work resulting from the change of organisational structure of the work establishment.

23.108 Termination of terms and conditions of work and pay has to be made in writing specifying new terms and conditions of work and pay. The required period of notice is equal to the period of notice of termination of the employment contract. Should the employee refuse to accept new terms and conditions of work and pay, the employment contract will terminate with the lapse of period of notice. The refusal has to be expressed, before half of the period of notice has elapsed (the notice has to contain an instruction in this respect), otherwise approval is implied. If lack of instruction, the employee has until the end of period of notice to refuse.

REASSIGNMENT RELATED TO COLLECTIVE REDUNDANCY

23.109 Reassignment of responsibilities may be executed in order to avoid collective redundancy. The employer who proposes to dismiss as redundant is obliged to consider reassignment and inform trade unions and National Labour Inspectorate about possibility of reassignment.

Unilateral and mutually agreed changes to terms and conditions of work and pay

23.110 There are three options for changing the terms and conditions of work and pay of employment:

- mutual agreement of both parties;
- unilateral change by way of termination by notice; and
- dismissing and re-employing the employee on new terms and conditions of work and pay.

MUTUALLY AGREED CHANGES

23.111 In case of mutually agreed changes to terms and conditions of work and pay an agreement has to be reached voluntarily by the parties, often by way of negotiations.

UNILATERAL CHANGE OF TERMS AND CONDITIONS OF WORK AND PAY OF EMPLOYMENT

23.112 The employer may unilaterally change the terms and conditions of work and pay by way of termination by notice. Provisions of Labour Code related to termination of employment contract apply accordingly to the termination of terms and conditions of work and pay.

23.113 The change has to refer solely to important terms and conditions of work and pay, ie terms and conditions of work and pay agreed by the parties in the employment contract.

23.114 Termination of terms and conditions of work and pay has to be made in writing to be effective and specify new terms and conditions of work and pay.

23.115 The employee may either agree to have the terms and conditions of work and pay changed in the way proposed by the employer or to refuse to accept it. If the employee refuses to accept new terms and conditions of work and pay, the employment contract will terminate upon the lapse of period of notice.

23.116 Only the terms and conditions of work and pay may be changed in the way of termination. Such procedure may not be effected for the purpose of change of type employment contract (eg from an employment contract for a fixed period of time to an employment contract for an indefinite period of time).

EXCEPTION FOR PROTECTED EMPLOYEES

23.117 The notice of termination of terms and conditions of work and pay cannot be given to:

- employee reaching retirement age in less than four years if the length of service entitles that employee to a retirement pension after reaching that age;
- a pregnant employee;
- another employees to whom special protection against termination of employment contract applies;
- an employee during leave or any other justified absence from work, unless the period entitling the employer to terminate the employment contract without notice has expired.

NOTICE

23.118 The notice has to be made in writing and specify new terms and conditions of work and pay. The employee may either:

- accept proposed new terms and conditions of work and pay; or
- refuse to accept new terms and conditions of work and pay.

23.119 If the employee accepts new terms and conditions of work and pay, he should inform the employer. For evidence purposes this should be in writing. Apart from that, a lack of refusal until half of the period of notice elapses is considered as a implied acceptance. Therefore, lack of express acceptance will be deemed as acceptance anyway.

23.120 If the employee refuses to accept new proposed terms and conditions of work and pay, he should express it before half of the period of notice elapses. The refusal is followed by a termination of the employment contract upon the lapse of the period of notice. It should be noticed that in this case the employment contract is considered to be terminated by the employer.

23.121 The employee should be instructed as to the effect of lack of express refusal of new proposed terms and conditions of work and pay. Otherwise, the refusal may be freely expressed until the end of period of notice.

23.122 As far as the salary is concerned, the abovementioned procedure is required only when the salary is to be reduced. When the salary is to be increased, it can be effected by a simple offer and acceptance. Therefore, in case of change related to the salary and its elements, it should always be considered whether it is beneficial for the employee or not. Only in the second case the termination by notice is required.

Example

(1) The employment contract provides for a pay enhancement, deprivation of this element of salary has to be performed by way of termination by notice.
(2) The employer proposes to make bonus an element of salary. Currently the bonus is discretionary. Such a change is beneficial to the employee, the procedure of termination by notice is not
(3) The employer wants a bonus to become a part of salary. Currently the bonus is discretionary. Such a change is beneficial to the employee, the procedure of termination by notice is not required.

Chapter 24

Workforce Restructuring in Portugal

João José Brito
Vaz Serra & Associados, Sociedade de Advogados, rl (vsa) Lisboa

INTRODUCTION

24.1 Continental Portugal and the autonomic regions of Azores and Madeira follow the national employment law, codified since 2003. Until then several laws, decrees and administrative resolutions were the legal base of our employment system, making it very complex for legal practitioners and business professionals. The codification was followed by several substantial changes and adjustments that significantly transformed the regime to create a level of flexibility unthinkable two or three decades ago. Especially since May 2011, after the signature by the Portuguese government of the Memorandum of Economic and Financial Policies with representatives of the International Monetary Fund, European Union and European Central Bank, significant adjustments and flexible policies have been implemented in the domain of workforce restructuring.

24.2 The legal system in Portugal is a typical European civil law jurisdiction. The law is codified in a systematic way and very close to the continental European legal system. The main employment law is the Labour Code (hereinafter LC) revised in 2009 (Law n°7/2009), 2011, (Law n° 53/2011) 2012, (Law n° 23/2012) 2013 (Law n° 69/2013) and 2014 (Law n° 27/2014). LC provides for default employment contract terms that automatically apply. Individual employment agreements may never contravene the basic mandatory employees' rights granted in LC. LC governs issues considered to be of public interest, where employers and employees lose their basic and individual contractual freedom.

24.3 LC is the basic regulation where we may find the entitlements of employees in dismissal or any other restructuring scenario, in respect of admissibility, notice periods, redundancy payments, post-termination covenants, garden leave, corporate change of control, etc.

24.4 Bearing in mind that, as in the other European jurisdictions, the concept of 'employment at will' does not exist; any termination of employment or changes in terms and conditions connected with the transfer will need to be made by reference to the relevant provisions and procedures set out in the LC.

PREPARING FOR A RESTRUCTURING EXERCISE

24.5 In Portugal, as in other EU countries, different types of issues may arise when carrying out a restructuring exercise. This may include the need to reduce the workforce, change terms and conditions, integration and harmonisation of workforces, use of temporary staff, or reassignment of functional and organisational responsibilities of staff.

24.6 It is vital to analyse the existing contractual terms and conditions and data concerning the demographics of the workforce. These elements will be very important when considering the budget for the restructuring plan. The employer must carefully consider and detail the financing of the restructuring and the savings they hope to obtain, and consider a realistic costs/benefit ratio.

The first key issues to consider are set out below.

Identify the employing entity

24.7 The general rule is that the employee's employment is always with a particular legal entity.

24.8 However, there can be an employment with plural employers whenever a reciprocal participation, domain or group relations exist. Even so, when the employer makes a business decision underlying the restructuring and/or any redundancies, each company should be documented separately. The employer company is the one liable and obliged to comply with the legal requirements of the restructuring plan.

24.9 In a 'group' relation, the dominant or parent company may eventually be liable for employee's rights regarding redundancy compensation, where the assets of the employer company are insufficient to cover employment liabilities

COLLATING INFORMATION TO PLAN AND BUDGET FOR THE RESTRUCTURING

Exercise

24.10 A restructuring exercise involving one or more group companies requires careful planning at the outset.

24.11 The employing entity must hold complete data on the employees involved, subject always to the necessary precautions on complying with the rules on data protection legislation.

24.12 Such information as job description, length of service, contractual benefits and entitlement on termination of employment, age, place of work, enhanced redundancy entitlement, applicable collective agreement (if any), and information relevant to determine redundancy selection pool is of great importance for planning the measure to be initiated, for estimating the overall costs of the restructuring exercise and for planning the appropriate timetable for executing dismissals.

EMPLOYMENT STATUS

24.13 Only individuals who meet the legal definition of 'employee' are protected against unfair dismissal and need to be included in a redundancy procedure for workforce restructuring purposes. Agency workers, self-employed free lancers or consultants etc may of course be involved in the restructuring plan, but notice periods and their entitlements etc. will not be governed by the LC.

Statutory directors of companies incorporated in Portugal who are elected after serving as employees (*stricto sensu*) or engaged on the basis of a director's service agreement, are not considered to be employees and will not have the specific level of protection of employees.

GENERAL PROTECTION AGAINST DISMISSAL

24.14 In Portugal the concept of 'employment at will' is not applicable. All employees who have passed the probation period (which can last from 90 to 240 days of service, depending on the grade of seniority and complexity of the functions/post) enjoy a minimum notice period and have the right not to be unfairly dismissed.

24.15 Protection against dismissal comes mainly from the Portuguese Constitution (Article 53 *et seq*) and the LC (Article 351 *et seq)*.

24.16 According to Article 53 of the Portuguese Constitution, 'workers shall be guaranteed job security, and dismissal without fair cause or for political or ideological reasons shall be prohibited'. This is the general principle. Nevertheless, as long as the legal requirements are met, namely in relation to procedure and grounds of dismissal, the employer may dismiss an employee.

24.17 Portuguese law recognises the following types of dismissal:

- Fair dismissal for employee serious misconduct (*despedimento por facto imputável ao trabalhador ou despedimento por justa causa*) Article 351 *et seq* LC – a disciplinary procedure must be set in motion. The dismissed employee is not entitled to compensation.
- Job elimination (*despedimento por extinção de posto de trabalho*) Article 367 *et seq* LC – dismissal by redundancy because of economic, technological or structural reasons. The dismissed employee is entitled to compensation according to basic remuneration and length of service.
- Dismissal founded on the employee's inability to adapt successfully to the changes – technological or others – introduced to his/her job (*despedimento por inadaptação*) Article 373 *et seq* LC – the dismissed employee is entitled to compensation according to basic remuneration and length of service.
- Collective dismissal (*despedimento colectivo)* Article 359 *et seq* LC – collective redundancy based on economic, structural or technological reasons. Dismissed employees are entitled to compensation according to basic remuneration and length of service.

Note that the difference between them lies basically with the motivation for the dismissal, which can be either subjective or objective. While the first is based on the employee's behaviour, the last three are related to the employer company and to economic, structural and technological reasons.

24.18 Once again, it should be pointed out that objective or subjective dismissal must be fair. The only existing exception is dismissal during the probation period (*período experimental*), in which either party may terminate the employment contract without notice or severance payments. It is a kind of temporary 'employment at will'.

24.19 Employers must ensure they provide written reasons for the dismissal decision and that they can show the decision complies with the LC, formally and substantially.

SPECIAL PROTECTION AGAINST DISMISSAL

24.20 Under Portuguese law, there is a general principle of non-discrimination, according to which an individual cannot be discriminated against on the basis of several personal characteristics or religious or political beliefs. Direct or indirect discrimination against the employee or the applicant on the grounds of his or her age, gender, sexual orientation, religion, ancestry, ethnic origin or race, marital status, family condition, economic situation, education, social background, genetic patrimony, reduced working capability, disability, chronic disease, nationality, territory of origin, language, political or ideological convictions, or union affiliation, is expressly forbidden and therefore an employer is absolutely prohibited from dismissing an employee for any discriminatory reasons.

24.21 The Labour Code expressly sets forth that dismissal based on political, ideological, ethnic or religious reasons is unlawful, even when the employer claims a different reason (Article 381).

In cases alleging unfair and discriminatory dismissal, there is a split burden of proof. The employee only has to file a form in court, while the employer has to prove the accuracy of the dismissal, formally and substantially.

24.22 Furthermore, it is important to notice that, like most European jurisdictions, Portuguese law provides a special dismissal protection to certain categories of employees, whose dismissal is presumed to be unfair. The main protected categories are:

- Pregnant employees, employees who have recently given birth, who are breastfeeding or who are taking parental leave (Article 63 of the LC) – pregnancy and maternity can never provide the reason for dismissal even when there are grounds for a fair dismissal, The Commission for Equality (*Comissão para a Igualdade no Trabalho e no Emprego* or CITE) must be consulted in advance, otherwise the dismissal will be automatically unlawful;
- Candidates for trade union associations or employees who are or have been members of such bodies within the last three years (Article 410 (3) of the LC).

24.23 Employers should also be aware that whenever the reason for the dismissal is considered invalid or when the applicable procedure is not followed, the dismissal is considered to be automatically unlawful (Article 381 of the LC). That is what happens, for example, when an employer who wishes to dismiss an employee for misconduct does not hand him over a written declaration in which is clearly stated the accusation and the intention to dismiss.

WORKFORCE REDUCTION

24.24 Workforce reductions are becoming far more common in today's economy. However, an employer who intends to dismiss employees as part of a restructuring plan needs to be fully aware of the legal landscape within which he should act. Careful planning and documentation of the business rationale for the proposed dismissals and effective communication, along with an up-to-date knowledge of the law, are essential if the employer wishes to ensure that the dismissals are carried out on the grounds of the legal and potentially fair reasons and avoid the risk of costly employment claims.

REDUNDANCY

24.25 In Portugal, redundancy can take two distinct forms: collective and individual redundancy.

24.26 Since both individual and collective redundancies are caused by economic reasons, the difference is purely the number of employees who are to be dismissed. Companies with less than 51 employees must follow a collective redundancy procedure whenever they wish to terminate more than two posts. The collective redundancy procedure must also be followed whenever a company employing more than 50 employees wishes to dismiss five or more employees. Finally, in cases where dismissal for economic reasons affects only one employee (or fewer than five employees, in companies with more than 50 employees) individual redundancy applies.

24.27 It is important nevertheless to understand them separately and, most of all, to know when each is applicable, as it will dictate the procedure that the company will be required to follow.

24.28 Even if it is not related to redundancy, dismissal due to the unsuitability of the employee can also be caused by economic reasons, as it is based on the employee's inability to adapt to the new working conditions resulting from technological evolutions or other changes. This type of dismissal is foreseen in Article 373 et seq of the Labour Code.

Individual redundancy (despedimento por extinção de posto de trabalho)

24.29 Individual redundancy, with the literal meaning of job elimination, is the term used to designate one of the two ways in which redundancy may occur under Portuguese legislation.

24.30 In order to dismiss an employee by reason of redundancy, Article 367 of the Labour Code provides that the dismissal must be attributable to economic (or market), structural or technological reasons related with the company. Such reasons may be based on a reduction in the company's activity caused by a decrease in demand or in any other circumstance presented in Article 359 (2) LC, which is applicable for both individual and collective redundancies.

24.31 It is extremely important to notice, however, that the presence of such justifying circumstances is not sufficient to ensure a fair dismissal. In fact, Article 368 LC stipulates that the requirements stated below must also be met:

(*a*) grounds for dismissal may not result from either the employer's or the employee's fault;

(*b*) the maintenance of the employment relationship must be impossible, ie the employer does not have another job role compatible with the professional category of the affected employee;
(*c*) there can be no employees who have been hired on fixed-term contracts to perform tasks similar to those which have been eliminated; and
(*d*) collective dismissal cannot be applicable.

24.32 If there are several employees who carry out work of the same kind and the employer only wishes to dismiss one of them, he needs to decide which employee is going to be dismissed. In order to do so, the employer must apply the selection criteria laid down by Article 368 (2) LC, which has been recently amended by Law n.° 27/2014 of 8 May. Nowadays, it is not up to the employer to define his own selection criteria, but instead the employees must be selected in accordance with the following criteria in this order:
(*a*) those who had the worst performance assessments, in accordance with parameters known in advance by the employee;
(*b*) those who have lower academic and professional qualifications;
(*c*) those who represent higher burdens of maintenance to the employment relationship;
(*d*) those who have less experience in the job role in concern; and finally
(*e*) those with shorter length of service in the company (which is equivalent to the 'last in first out' formula that used to be very common).

Note that these criteria are supposed to be non-discriminatory.

24.33

As stated in Article 372 LC, employees who are dismissed as a consequence of individual redundancy have the same entitlements as those affected by collective dismissal. For further details please see the collective dismissal section starting at para **24.36** below.

Collective dismissal (despedimento colectivo)

24.34 Under Portuguese law a collective redundancy situation arises whenever an employer, with 50 or fewer employees, wishes to dismiss as redundant two or more employees, or an employer, with more than 50 employees, is planning to dismiss at least five employees, all within a three-month period.

24.35 The concept of collective dismissal, provided by Article 359 (1) of the Labour Code, is therefore based on two main elements that will have to be taken into consideration, the first being the number of employees who are going to be made redundant (in relation to the size of the company) and the second the reasons for dismissal.

24.36 Collective dismissal must be justified by the closure of one or more departments or sections of the company, or, as with individual redundancies, by a reduction in the number of employees for economic, structural or technological reasons. Article 359 (2) LC, introduces examples of such reasons. For this purposes, the following definitions apply:

- Economic reasons – a slowdown in business activity caused by an expected decrease of demand for its goods or services; or the impossibility, whether legal or practical, of getting those products to the market;
- Structural reasons – economic-financial imbalance, change of activity, restructuring of the business organisation or replacement of the employer's main product lines;
- Technological reasons – changes in manufacturing techniques, automation of production, control, or cargo-transport, or computerisation of services or automation of the means of communication.

24.37 In contrast with individual redundancies, the Labour Code does not specify the criteria for selecting the employees to be made redundant. This means that the employer has some freedom in this regard as long as the criteria adopted are objective and non-discriminatory. In any case, the employer's selection criteria must be consistent with the grounds for dismissal.

24.38 Employees affected by collective dismissal are entitled: (i) to receive a severance payment of 12 days of basic remuneration and seniority per year of service (Article 366 LC); (ii) to a paid time off to look for another job, while under the notice period (Article 364 LC); and (iii) to terminate the employment contract during the notice period by giving three business days' notice, with the entitlement to receive a severance payment remaining unaffected (*direito especial de denúncia* - Article 365 LC).

REDUNDANCY PROCEDURES

24.39 In order to carry out a fair dismissal on grounds of redundancy the employer must also ensure that the appropriate redundancy procedure is followed. Under Portuguese Law dismissals for objective causes have strict requirements that must necessarily be met. As discussed below, the individual redundancy procedure is very similar to the collective dismissal procedure. Broadly speaking, there are three different stages which are common to both procedures: (i) intention to dismiss; (ii) consultation, information and negotiation; and (iii) decision to dismiss.

Intention to dismiss

Individual redundancy

24.40 When an employer wishes to make an employee redundant he must, in the first instance, communicate his intention to dismiss to both the affected employee and the existing employees' representative body (if any). The employees' representative body may be the works council (*comissão de trabalhadores*), or, in its absence, the inter-union committee or union commission (*comissão intersindical* or *comissão sindical*). If the affected employee is a union representative the respective trade union should be informed as well.

24.41 The notification must be in writing and must include several elements, of which the most important is the description of the grounds of dismissal (Article 369 LC).

Collective dismissal

24.42 An employer intending to proceed with a collective redundancy must notify, in writing, the works council. If there is no works council in the company, the union committee or other employee's representative body should be notified instead. In the absence of the entities referred to above, all employees potentially affected must be notified, and may, within a period of five business days counting from the receipt of notification, form a specific body for this purpose (Article 360 (3) LC).

24.43 At this stage, the employer must provide the following written information:

- the reason(s) invoked by the employer in order to carry out the collective dismissal;
- the staff establishment plan of the company;
- the criteria for selecting the employees to be made redundant;
- the number of the employees who are going to be made redundant and their professional categories;
- the period over which the redundancy procedure will take effect; and
- the criteria for determining the redundancy payment.

24.44 A copy of the notice sent to the works council (or other employees' representative body) must also be sent to the relevant department of the ministry responsible for employment matters – Direcção-Geral do Emprego e das Relações de Trabalho (DGERT).

Consultation, Information and Negotiation

Individual redundancy

24.45 The notification is followed by a mandatory consultation and information period that lasts ten days, where the affected employee, the existing representative bodies, and the respective trade union (whenever the employee is a union representative) may express their opinion on the dismissal and propose some alternative measures to the employer.

24.46 At the request of either the employee or his representatives, the relevant department of the ministry responsible for labour inspections – *Autoridade para as Condições do Trabalho* (ACT) – can also intervene in this stage to check the requirements for the dismissal (Article 370 (2) LC). ACT prepares and sends to the employer and/or to the entity that requested its intervention the response to the inquiry on the matter subject to verification, within the period of seven days after the request.

Collective dismissal

24.47 Within five days of the notification of the intention to dismiss, the employer and the employees' representative bodies must engage in negotiations, with the aim of reaching an agreement not only on the method of carrying out the collective dismissals but also on the adoption of alternative measures to reduce the number of employees to be made redundant, such as the suspension or reduction of work, professional re-training and re-classification, or early retirement.

24.48 Article 362 LC provides that the relevant department of the ministry responsible for employment matters – *Direcção-Geral do Emprego e das Relações de Trabalho* (DGERT) – will participate in the negotiation process in order to support the parties and help to reconcile their interests.

Decision to dismiss

Individual redundancy

24.49 Where an individual redundancy is to occur, the decision to dismiss may be communicated after five days have elapsed from the end of the period for the employee and his representative bodies to issue their opinion on the dismissal, as stated above. Just like the first notification, this communication must be in writing. It must contain the following details:

- the dismissal grounds;
- statement of confirmation that the legal requirements referred to above are met;
- evidence, if objections have been raised, that the selection criteria have been duly observed;
- the compensation amount due, and the place and form of its payment; and
- the date on which the contract is to be terminated.

24.50 The employer shall notify its decision to the affected employee, the relevant representative structures and also the DGERT, observing a prior notice period of at least (Article 371 (3) LC):

- 15 days, for employees with job tenure of less than one year;
- 30 days, for employees with job tenure equal to or above one year but less than five years;
- 60 days, for employees with job tenure equal to or above five years but less than ten years;
- 75 days, for employees with job tenure equal to or above ten years.

Collective dismissal

24.51 Having reached an agreement with employees, or in its absence, 15 days after the initial notification, the employer may issue the collective dismissal final decision. This decision must be sent, in writing and with the same advanced notice as with individual redundancy, to each relevant employee, and must also include the dismissal grounds, the termination date and the amount of the severance payment (Article 363 LC).

REDUNDANCY PAYMENT

Redundancy payment calculation

24.52 Employees who are dismissed by reason of redundancy are entitled to receive a redundancy payment of 12 days of basic remuneration and seniority per year of service (Article 366 LC).

24.53 Bearing in mind what was previously said, there are some legal ceilings that should be noticed. First, the amount of basic remuneration considered in order to calculate the severance payment cannot exceed 20 times the amount of the national minimum salary (if it does, it will be reduced to that amount). Second, the total amount of severance payment due to an employee cannot be greater than 12 times the amount of the employees' basic remuneration and seniority or more than 240 times the amount of the national minimum salary.

24.54 For part years, the amount of severance payment is calculated proportionally.

Example

Mr C and Mr F have both been made redundant from ABT, S.A.
Relevant information about Mr C:

- monthly basic remuneration and seniority = €600
- length of service = 5 years
- Daily remuneration = €600: 30
- Redundancy payment= daily remuneration and seniority × 12 × length of service
  Redundancy payment= 20 × 12 × 5
- Redundancy payment= €1,200

This means that Mr C is entitled to a severance payment of €1,200.
Relevant information about Mr F:

- monthly basic remuneration and seniority = €10,500
- length of service = 2 years

Since €10.500 exceeds 20 times the amount of the national minimum salary, ie €9,700 (20 × €485), it will be reduced to that amount according to Article 366 (2) b) LC.

- Daily remuneration = €9,700: 30
- Redundancy payment= daily remuneration and seniority × 12 × length of service
  Redundancy payment= 323.33 × 12 × 2
- Redundancy payment= €7,760

Mr F is entitled to a severance payment of €7,760. This value does not exceed 240 times the amount of the national minimum salary, ie €116,400 (240 × €485), so it will not be reduced.

Additional information

24.55 Under Article 366 (4 and 5) LC, it is presumed that the employee agreed with the dismissal if he/she receives the redundancy payment. This presumption may however be rebutted as long as the employee hands over to the employer the total amount received.

Taxation of redundancy payments

24.56 Redundancy payments are tax free unless their value exceeds the result of the average salary of the last 12 months multiplied by the length of service (Article 2 (4, 5 and 6) of the Personal Income Tax Code).

GARDEN LEAVE

24.57 Whenever an employer wishes to ensure that the employee does not immediately start working for a competitor during the notice period, he may include in the written employment contract a garden leave clause. These clauses are not specifically referred to in LC but, under the general principle of contractual freedom and on the basis that such a clause does not offend any mandatory rule or principle, they are valid and may be agreed in writing.

24.58 A garden leave clause will assure the employer that in the event of termination of employment: (i) the employee will not attend the work place during the notice period; and (ii) the employee will not start working for a competitor until effective termination of the contract, which happens only at the end of the notice period, even when the employee ends *de facto* his employment.

POST-TERMINATION RESTRICTIVE COVENANTS

24.59 Whenever employers need to ensure that key employees will not materially damage its business after termination of their employment, they must expressly include a non-competition clause in the employment contract. Such a clause limiting an employee's freedom of employment is only valid when the activity restricted may damage the employer's interests. The employer, despite the termination of the employment contract, must pay the employee's salary during the agreed period of non-competition.

PAY IN LIEU OF NOTICE

24.60 Pay in lieu of notice is not legal in Portugal. Employment cannot be effectively terminated with a payment in lieu of notice.

When the employer does not comply totally or partially with a notice period, even when the employee agrees to terminate *de facto* his activity, the employment contract will only terminate at the end of the legal notice period, and the employer must pay all allowances as if the employee was in regular work during the notice period, being such period included in the length of service.

BUSINESS TRANSFER, OUTSOURCING/ INSOURCING AND OFFSHORING

24.61 The European Council Directive 2001/23/CE of 12 March 2001 regulates the transfer of an undertaking by ensuring that the transferee must comply with the exact terms and conditions of employment of the employees affected. In Portugal. This Directive was implemented into the national law by way of Articles 285 to 287 of the LC.

In essence LC protects an individual's employment in the event that the undertaking ('enterprise', 'establishment' or 'economic unity') for which he works is transferred definitively or temporarily by the employer.

In practical terms this means that articles 285-287 of the LC may apply where a business – as a going concern – is sold (definitive transmission) and/or where there is a temporary transmission such as cessation of exploitation of an enterprise, establishment or economic unity.

This regime does not apply to a situation in which ownership of the employing entity changes by way of a share sale.

24.62 Key consequences of this regime are:

- the employment of affected employees automatically transfers to new owner or user;
- the automatic transfer of employment rights, obligations and liabilities relating to transferring staff to the new owner or user;
- the obligation to inform and consult with affected employees individually and with (elected) employee representatives collectively; and
- the protection of employees from dismissal by reason of such transfer.

Business transfer

24.63 A business sale (definitive transmission) constitutes a transfer of affected employees to the new owner, whenever there is a transfer of a stable economic unity which is defined as an organised grouping of resources with the objective of pursuing an economic activity, whether or not that activity is central or just a supporting or ancillary function.

24.64 The same effect arises from any agreement where the exploitation of an economic unit is transferred for a pre-agreed period to a new entity. In this situation the transferor keeps legal ownership of the economic unity's assets to be used by the transferee in the pursuing of its activity.

Outsourcing/insourcing

24.65 The outsourcing of a particular business function to an external service provider does not directly imply the automatic transfer of employment to the new provider. In this situation the transfer of employment of the affected employees requires their previous approval of the transfer to the new employer. This is not a case of an automatic transfer.

Effect of transfer

Automatic transfer and protection of employment

24.66 The employment of those employees employed in the transferring business will automatically be transferred with the business on his existing terms and conditions. Outstanding liabilities (unpaid wages, untaken holiday etc) will be transferred to the transferee. However, the transferor will still be responsible for these liabilities, as a joint obligor, within one year after the transfer.

Objection to the transfer

24.67 An employee may object to his transfer. Following 'Kasikas' jurisprudence, the range of the objection right is to be ruled by the internal law of each EU member state.

24.68 The Portuguese Supreme Court of Justice considers resolution termination of the contract by the employee to be valid where, after getting from the transferor and the transferee all the relevant information, he deems that his interests are going to be materially disadvantaged upon transfer. In practical terms, such termination of employment contract gives effect to the employee's right of objection.

24.69 In such a case, and if the employee shows such evidence, in court, he will be entitled to be compensated by the transferor for the termination of his employment. The amount of compensation will be between 15 and 45 days of salary per each year of length, depending on the seriousness of the failure of the employer.

Protection from dismissal

24.70 Employees do not enjoy any additional layer of protection from dismissal in the event of a transfer. The transferee employer takes full liabilities from the transferor regarding the employment contract such as employee's continuous service length and, therefore, everything will be as if he was the previous employer as regards dismissal.

Protection of terms and conditions of employment

24.71 Similarly, terms and conditions of employment are also protected and may only be varied following a transfer under the basic principles of the LC.

Any changes which are connected to the transfer and for which there is no acceptance of the employee will be void. This will include any attempts to harmonise terms and conditions of affected employees.

Information and consultation

24.72 Where employees are transferred from one employer to another, under Articles 285-287 of the LC, both the transferor and the transferee have duties to inform and potentially consult the appropriate representatives bodies in relation to any of their employees who may be affected by the transfer or by measures taken in relation to them.

24.73 The transferor and the transferee must deliver to the employee's representatives or, if there are no representatives, to the employees involved in the transfer, written information to be delivered at least ten days before the consultation of the employee's representatives.

Duty to inform

24.74 The transferor and transferee are obliged to inform the representatives of their respective affected employees in writing of:

- the fact that the transfer is to take place, when it is to take place and the reasons for it;
- the legal, economic and social implications of the transfer for the affected employees (for example, change in employer, change in work location etc); and
- the measures which the employer envisages it will take, in connection with the transfer, in relation to those affected employees or, if they envisage that no measures will be so taken, that fact.

Measures letter

24.75 The transferee (new employer) is also obliged to inform his employee's representative of the projected transfer before their terms and conditions of employment are affected by the transfer.

24.76 If the transferor and the transferee intend to take 'measures' that may affect their respective employees ('measures' will include any action, step or arrangement in connection with the transfer which has been formulated as part of some definite plan or proposal, such as changes to terms and conditions or proposed redundancies) they must provide employee representatives with written information and are obliged to consult them.

Duty to consult

24.77 The transferor and the transferee only have a duty to consult the employee representatives if either anticipates that it will take measures in relation to any of its affected employees which are connected with the transfer.

24.78 The consultation must be with a view to seeking the agreement of the employee representatives to the measures to be taken. However, there is no requirement to reach agreement. At the very least, the employer should:

- explain the measures which it proposes to take;
- give the representatives the opportunity to make representations about the measures to be taken;
- consider those representations and respond to them in writing; and
- give reasons for any rejection of the representatives' representations.

24.79 The legislation sets out no definite timescale for consultation. Information must be provided ten days before consultation. The duty to consult must be undertaken 'before transfer' and 'in good time' to allow for any necessary information between the parties and the representatives.

European works councils

24.80 Provided there is a European Works Council ('EWC') established within the group of companies affected by a multi-jurisdictional restructuring or redundancy exercise then there may be an obligation to inform and consult with the EWC prior to implementing any such exercise.

Sanctions

Unfair dismissal

24.81 As all employment liabilities transfer to the transferee, dismissal will be automatically unfair where the principal reason for it is the transfer itself or a reason connected with the transfer.

Failure to inform and consult

24.82 The sanctions for failure to inform and consult are not expressly set out in LC. However, whenever the employer fails to inform and consult in compliance with LC, the employee who wants to object to the transfer may present a complaint to an employment tribunal.

24.83 If the employment tribunal declares that the complaint is well founded and the objection justified, it may order the transferor employer who has failed to comply with the duty, to take back the employee (whenever this is possible in practice) or to pay appropriate compensation to the affected employee for the termination of his job. The amount of compensation will be between 15 and 45 days of salary per each year of length of service, depending on the seriousness of the failure of the employer.

WORKFORCE REDUCTION IN CONNECTION WITH SHARE SALE OR SHARE

Purchase

24.84 What is sold in a share sale are the shares of the business, rather than its assets. Consequently the employer does not change at all but only the identity of the shareholder. LC does not apply to a share sale.

24.85 If the new owner (shareholder) wishes to restructure the business post acquisition, then any dismissals must fall under one of the potentially fair reasons permitted by the LC and follow the appropriate dismissal procedure set out above.

CHANGING EMPLOYMENT TERMS AND CONDITIONS

24.86 In general, once an employment contract is entered into, an employer is not entitled to unilaterally change the terms and conditions of employment. Any contractual modification requires the agreement of both parties unless the employer predicted the need to change a particular term in the future and therefore ensured that the contract includes a clause which allows the employer to unilaterally change certain terms and conditions of employment.

24.87 There are however numerous exceptions in the LC that should be carefully taken into consideration.

24.88 To begin with, there are several restrictions on changes agreed between employer and employee. For instance, an employer is absolutely prohibited from reducing the employee's salary during the life of the employment contract (except in the cases provided for in the LC or in an instrument of collective labour regulation) even if an employee has agreed to this (Article 129 LC).

24.89 Moreover, there are some situations in which the law allows the employer to unilaterally change some specific terms of the contract. The two main examples are *ius variandi* and the change of the workplace.

Ius variandi

24.90 Article 120 of the LC establishes that employers are entitled to *ius variandi*, the right to require employees to perform tasks which do not fall within the type of work they undertook to perform under their contract of employment, provided that no substantial change occurs in the employees' position. There must be a clear justification of the company's economic interests that are behind this measure, but as long as the situation is merely temporary and the other legal requirements are met, the employee's consent is not needed.

WORKPLACE

24.91 Under Article 194 of the LC it is possible for the employer to change temporarily or permanently the location of the workplace without the employee's consent. Of course there are some requirements to be met. When it is not caused by a change in the establishment's location, the transfer is only permitted if it represents an important economic advantage for the company and does not involve serious harm or loss to the employee. In any case, the employer is required to pay for any extra costs that the employee may incur due to the transfer.

USING TEMPORARY STAFF

24.92 In a reorganisation situation the requirement for temporary staff may arise. The employer may consider the option of using workers from an agency or directly engage employees on fixed term contracts.

Agency workers

24.93 Using agency workers can be a good solution when a company is in need of some temporary cover at short notice and wishes to avoid engaging in an actual recruitment process.

24.94 Articles 172 to 191 of the LC implement the EU Temporary Agency Workers Directive and provide, amongst others, that agency workers are entitled to the same pay as equivalent permanent staff after 60 days with the user entity. Agency workers are also entitled to receive information from the hiring organisation about any employment vacancies which are available and to access collective facilities and amenities from the first day of starting work with the hiring organisation.

24.95 Agency workers are not entitled, as against the employer, to the same protection that fixed-term employees enjoy. This means that there is no obligation on the employing entity to treat a fixed-term agency worker the same as a comparable permanent employee.

Fixed-term contracts

24.96 Employers may decide to use fixed-term contracts when an individual is required to fulfil a company's temporary need, for instance a specific temporary project, maternity or illness cover, or when the organisation is not yet sure of the demand for a certain position and wishes to start with a fixed-term engagement to assess the requirements going forward. In any case, the contract must be in writing and must include a clause where the justification for the fixed-term clause is clearly stated. This demand is made in order to ensure that the legal conditions are met, preventing employers from using this type of contract as a way to increase probation period.

24.97 A fixed-term contract may be drafted to terminate at a specific date, at the conclusion of a particular project or when its justification is complete. The expiry of a pre fixed-term contract will happen after simple communication of the employer delivered before the last 15 days of service, stating his decision not to renew the contract. There's no need to justify termination. The employer does need to justify the need for the temporary activity for which the employee was engaged, and therefore must be prudent in its justification in the initial contract.

24.98 Failure to justify the legality of the use of a fixed-term contract would give the employee a strong claim for unfair dismissal and the employment court would consider the fixed term clause to be void. The contract would be legally considered as a no term contract.

RENEWAL OF FIXED-TERM CONTRACTS

24.99 Fixed-term contracts are renewed automatically if notice of termination is not given in writing before the last 15 days of service of the initial term or its subsequent renewals. There's a limit of three renewals and in total length the limit of three years.

EMPLOYMENT CLAIMS

24.100 Employment claims are heard by a first instance employment tribunal with jurisdiction in the location of the employee's residence or place of work. Any appeals should be made to the second instance courts (*Tribunal da Relação*) and then to the Supreme Court of Justice (*Supremo Tribunal de Justiça*).

24.101 As specialised tribunals, employment tribunals have exclusive jurisdiction to resolve disputes between employees and employers. Employment tribunals mainly hear disputes arising from the interpretation, execution or termination of individual employment contracts or collective agreements and its negotiations.

24.102 First instance courts are not limited in the amount of financial compensation which they can award.

UNFAIR DISMISSAL

24.103 Employees can bring a claim for unfair dismissal if they believe that the dismissal was unlawful and unfair.

24.104 Employees have 60 days from the effective date of termination to bring a claim for unfair dismissal when this arises from a written decision based on an alleged just cause (subjective reasons), individual redundancy or dismissal founded on the employee's inability to adapt. All the other claims, except the ones related to collective redundancy which have to be filed within six months from the termination of employment, may be filed by the employee or the employer, within one year from effective date of termination. After this delay, reciprocal rights are considered released.

Remedies

24.105 If the employment tribunal finds that the employee was unfairly dismissed he can order the employer to reinstate the individual or award him compensation, at the employee's request. The employee has the right to choose between being reinstated or compensated. However, in micro-companies (companies with fewer than ten employees) or in employments based on personal confidence or at a very high level, the employer may oppose the reinstatement of the employee.

24.106 Compensation for unfair dismissal tends to cover all patrimonial and moral damages:

- a basic award is calculated between 15 and 45 days of salary per each year of length, depending on the seriousness of the failure of the employer.
- in those cases where the employer may oppose to reinstate the employee, the compensation is calculated between 30 and 60 days of salary;
- compensation for alleged moral damages is calculated according to what the tribunal considers to be 'just and equitable' .

THE COMPENSATION AWARD

24.107 Without prejudice to any other compensation, in cases of unfair dismissal, the employer will be ordered to pay the employee's salary due from 30 days before the claim has been filed until a final judicial decision is issued. This amount is deducted from the income earned by the employee in that period, including eventual unemployment subsidy.

DISCRIMINATION

24.108 As previously stated, an employee may file a claim for unfair dismissal alleging discrimination if he believes that the real reason for his dismissal was one of the following protected characteristics: age; disability; gender reassignment; marriage and civil partnership; pregnancy and maternity; race; religion or belief; sex; and sexual orientation.

24.109 Whenever an employee believes he is discriminated because of any of the above mentioned characteristics, he may file a claim requesting the court to rule that the dismissal was unlawful and to award him compensation.

MUTUALLY AGREED TERMINATION

24.110 Unless the employer considers that there is a 'just cause' for dismissal, there are a lot of reasons for him to prefer a mutually agreed termination with an employee by way of a severance or settlement agreement rather than to dismiss the employee unilaterally and risk employment tribunal proceedings.

24.111 Under the terms of such an agreement, the employee agrees to settle the dispute or the potential dispute.

24.112 The agreement must be writing and will then be the cause of termination of employment (it is not a dismissal). Therefore it cannot be litigated in court but can, of course, be enforced in employment tribunals if employer's obligations were not performed in time.

Settlement agreements

24.113 The clauses of settlement agreements are to be agreed between the parties and are not expressly set out in the LC.

24.114 It is not mandatory for a legal advisor to be consulted by any party, but, whenever the clauses of a settlement agreement breach some fundamental rights of the employee, he may file a claim in employment tribunals to request its total or partial invalidity, regardless of his previous acceptance of the clauses that offended 'public interest'.

24.115 Both parties should always obtain legal advice to prevent judicial claims. A settlement agreement should specify the precise legal claims which the employee is waiving. An employer may include additional clauses in the agreement relating to the termination of employment such as provisions relating to confidentiality and references.

24.116 Employees may revoke a settlement agreement within seven days of its signature, if their signature was not attested before a public notary. Therefore, it is prudent to call for notary recognition of the employees' signature.

Without prejudice and 'pre-termination' discussions

24.117 To achieve confidentiality of an offer and prevent it from being used later in court as evidence of admission of any wrongdoing, the proper way is to ensure that both parties are represented by a lawyer. Any lawyer is prohibited from disclosing to the court or third parties any information about the negotiations in the event that they didn't reach consensus.

Lawyers are prohibited from disclosing any information regarding professional participation in any negotiations, and only in some specific cases pre-authorised by the national bar association (*ordem dos advogados*) may such negotiations be disclosed.

PRE-TERMINATION DISCUSSIONS

24.118 In Portugal this legal concept does not exist.

Chapter 25

Workforce Restructuring in Romania

Nicholas Hammond
BWSP Hammond Bogaru & Associates, Bucharest

INTRODUCTION

25.1 The law relating to redundancy in Romania is based on the Romanian Labour Code, Law no. 53/2003 hereinafter referred to as to 'the Labour Code'.

The Labour Code regulates the system of dismissal in relation to the requirements of the market economy, having a special section in the Labour Code entitled 'Termination of the labour contract at the employer's initiative'.

Current legal regulations state the principle that an employment contract may only be terminated in the circumstances and under the conditions set out in the Labour Code. In order to ensure protection to employees, the list of causes and reasons for dismissal are limited. These provisions guarantee the rights at work which are also established by the Constitution, removing the possibility of arbitrary and unfair decisions by the employer. The stability of the labour market is brought about by legally regulating the conditions that can be applied for terminating the employment.

Dismissal is an extreme measure which ends the collaboration between the employer and the employee. The employee not only loses his job, his professional and social status, but in many cases, a dismissal means also the loss of security for him and his family.

The legal grounds for a dismissal are governed by the Labour Code and also by the clauses of each individual employment contract. The legal provisions were revised and improved upon the entry into the European Union. The Romanian legislators have tried as much as possible to harmonise the Romanian law with European legislation.

EMPLOYMENT STATUS

25.2 In Romania the working relationship between the employer and employee is governed by the Labour Code and the Constitution.

Among the basic principles are the principles of liberty, equality, and the right of employees to associate in order to protect their rights and interests.

Romanian law protects all individuals who have an employment contract against unfair dismissal.

Depending on the industry the employee may have different legal rights and obligations. There are some categories of employees that enjoy different rights from the rest of the employees. These are public servants, public dignitaries, military personnel and judges. Their activity is regulated by their own special laws, for example Law no. 188/1999 concerning public servants; Law no. 303/2004 concerning judges and the prosecutors; and Law no. 304/2004 concerning the judicial structure. The dismissal of these categories of employees follows a different procedure.

An employee has rights which are provided for by the Labour Code and employers have to respect the principles, rights and obligations as set out.

GENERAL PROTECTION AGAINST DISMISSAL

25.3 In Romania, employees have a minimum notice period, if the reasons for the dismissal are physical incapacity; professional inadequacy; a reduction in the work force and if the reason for the dismissal is not related to the employee's employment.

It is possible for an employer to conclude a valid employment contract for a fixed period of time. In these contracts, both parties take into account the limited time of the collaboration from the beginning of the employment contract. However, the legislators have tried to restrict the possibility of concluding such contracts to a number of limited instances set out in the Labour Code. A fixed term contract is an exception to this rule and can be completed for a period of up to 36 months. However, the minimum notice period in case of dismissal remains valid for such fixed term contracts.

The employer must prove that the dismissal decision was taken by following both the mandatory procedure as set out in the Labour Code and the formal and substantial requirements provided by the law.

SPECIAL PROTECTION AGAINST DISMISSAL

25.4 According to the Labour Code, certain specified reasons for dismissal are automatically considered unfair, namely:

- the employees gender, sexual orientation, genetic characteristics, age, nationality, race, colour, ethnicity, religion, political opinion, social origin, disability, family status or responsibilities, trade union membership or trade union activities.

- exercising the right to strike, according to the law and granted trade union rights.
- a temporary medical disability for which a medical certificate was issued.
- the suspension of work activity caused by the implementation of a valid quarantine procedure.
- If the employee is a woman and is pregnant, and the employer is aware of this at the time of issuing the dismissal decision.
- legal maternity leave;
- legal parental leave for a child under the age of two years, or if the child is disabled up to the age of three years.
- leave to care for sick children aged up to seven years or if the child has registered disabilities until the age of 18 years;
- working in an official position in a trade union, unless the dismissal is for serious misconduct or repeated acts of misconduct committed by the employee, and
- annual leave

EXCEPTIONS:

25.5 The protection against dismissal given by the law in these situations is not absolute. There are certain legal limitations. Such limitations are provided for by the Labour Code and by Law no. 85/2006 regarding the insolvency procedure of companies. According to 60 Article of the Labour Code, the special protection above do not apply when the insolvency procedure is initiated against or by a company.

REDUCTION OF WORKFORCE

25.6 When restructuring the workforce, the employer must respect and apply correctly the provisions of the Labour Code.

Romanian law provides for two kinds of dismissal. Dismissal for reasons relating to the person of an employee such as serious or repeated misconduct, if the employee is under preventive arrest or house arrested for more than 30 days, physical incapacity, lack of professional skills and qualification and dismissal for reasons not related to the employee. Dismissal for reasons not related to the employee may be of an individual or collective nature.

According to Article 65 of the Labour Code redundancy for reasons not related to the employee, are applicable when the position is cancelled by the decision of the company based on economic reasons, or for any other reasons which are not connected with the employee. The cancellation of the position must be actual, real and serious, without being affected by the person of the employee.

For instance, the employer cannot justify the cancellation of the employment position and the employee cannot be fired if the employer assigns to another employee the duties of the employee whose contract was terminated. In this case, the Romanian jurisprudence and commentators considers that the position is needed and the cancellation is not the real reason for the dismissal. In addition it will not be considered as a justified reason if the dismissal is due to the renaming of the position.

To fall within the above legal norms, an employee`s dismissal must be attributable to economic difficulties. These can be the total or partial business closure, if the employee`s role can be absorbed by other employees, if the business unit is moved to another place different from the location mentioned in the contract and the employee can no longer physically reach the work place.

THE DISMISSAL PROCEDURES

Individual dismissal

25.7 As mentioned above, the dismissal for reasons not related to the employee may be of an individual or collective nature. An individual dismissal can be related to the person of the employee or not.

The dismissal for reasons related to the person of the employee

25.8 This can occur in four situations:

- Serious or repeated misconduct by the employee.
- The employee is under preventive custody or house arrested for more than 30 days.
- Physical or mental incapacity, and
- Lack of professional qualification or skill.

The first situation is when the employee has committed a serious or repeated disciplinary offence related to the personnel discipline rules of the employer or the rules laid down in the individual employment contract, or in the collective labour agreement. The dismissal is a disciplinary sanction;

The employer can dismiss the employee in case of misconduct even when he has committed only one serious disciplinary offence if that act has seriously jeopardised the company's activity.

The employer can apply this sanction, for instance, in the following situations: acts of violence, serious insults, leaving equipment while it is operating, serious negligence, the disclosure of trade secrets including work practices, breach of the laws relating to drug abuse, breach of material clauses in the employment contract and other special clauses.

Any dismissal grounded on a disciplinary offence or misconduct must be preceded by a rigorous investigation and follow a special procedure. In this disciplinary procedure, the employee has the right to be heard, to answer and justify all the allegations made by the employer as reason for the dismissal. He can present evidence in his defence. Following this procedure the employer can apply the disciplinary measure through a written decision delivered to the employee within 30 calendar days from the employer becoming aware of the disciplinary offence, but no later than six months after the date of the disciplinary offence.

The written decision must contain all the information regarding the offence: the description of the disciplinary offence; the description of the provisions in the relevant staff regulations, the rules of procedure and/or applicable collective labour agreement which were infringed by the employee, the reasons for the rejection of the defences presented by the employee during the preliminary disciplinary hearing or the reasons why, no hearing took place, the legal basis on which the disciplinary measures were taken, the date of any deadline for appealing the decision and the competent court where the disciplinary measures may be appealed.

The employee will receive the written dismissal decision, and within 30 days from the moment of its receipt he can appeal in the relevant Court against the measures taken by the employer.

The second situation refers to the situation where the employee who has been taken into preventive custody by the police or similar authorities for more than 30 days. This situation can also take place when the employee is held under house arrest or is held in non-custodial preventative custody under the terms of the Code of Criminal Procedure;

The fundamental condition for the employee's dismissal is his inability to attend his place of work. The decision does not violate the presumption of innocence because it is based strictly on the employee's absence from his place of work. The 30-day period is measured in calendar days including the day from which it started to run and the day on which the 30-day period ends.

Common to both situations is that the employee does not have a notice period stated in his employment contract.

The third case occurs when by a decision of a competent medical examination body or individual an employee is found to be physically and/or mentally unable to fulfil his/her the duties as required by the job description or requirements.

The employee's inability to work is presumed in this case. The legislation refers to the incapacity of the worker to continue his activity, because of his physical or mental state. The employer must offer another vacant job in accordance with the medical state of the individual.

The final situation, occurs when the employee is not professionally qualified to carry out the job in the workplace for which he/she is employed.

The professional unsuitability is established gradually during the performance of the employment contract. For example, the employee's capacity for work has reduced and he cannot cope with the work schedule, even if at the commencement of the employment he seemed perfectly capable.

It will also apply if the law requires further training or learning of new skills or qualifications for the position and the employee is unable to achieve these.

In these circumstances the employer must offer another job if there is a vacant position suited to the professional qualifications of the employee. The employee should be sent an offer to which he must respond within three days of receipt.

If the employer does not have vacant positions in the company, it must request the support of the Territorial Workforce Agency to obtain alternative employment for the employee suitable to his qualifications and to his/her professional background and qualifications or according to their ability to work.

In both the third and the last case described above, the employer shall provide a 20 working days' notice period.

The employer shall issue a dismissal decision containing the reasons for the dismissal; the notice period (at least 20 working days), and also any offer of alternative vacant position suited to the medical condition of the individual, and/or to his professional qualification.

Dismissal for reasons not related to the employee

25.9 A dismissal of an individual is legally permitted where it consists of an act of dismissal (actual and effective) arising from serious and proper reasons. This is the case where the work position is no longer needed and therefore ceases to exist in the company.

Dismissal for reasons not related to the employee cannot take place if the legal request regarding the liquidation of the company is not valid. It is fair to say that simply cancelling the job role and stating that the financial situation of the employer will recover is not a valid reason. The employer is the only one who can decide and initiate all the appropriate measures for its business. The law cannot limit this kind of decisions.

The practice of the courts is to consider real and serious causes, such as:

- a major reduction in the turnover of the company, leading to lower profits;
- The need to limit or reduce costs;
- The need to streamline the company's activities and to improve its financial position, in the knowledge that the activity of any company is to make a profit;
- The company is unable to obtain finance to support the business;
- The need for reorganisation measures are justified by the loss of major contracts; and
- The job role has become redundant because of the loss of a unique client.

The following will not be considered real and serious causes:

- The employer has not eliminated similar unfilled job roles;
- It has only changed the name of the job role, and not eliminated it from the organisational chart; and
- The job role was only suspended as opposed to eliminated.

For instance, a company that deals with the development of film cameras has 15 employee and two production units. Considering that the vast majority of consumers are now using digital cameras and the repair unit is no longer sustainable, the manager must review the business operation and establish why for a long period, the company profits are going down. The employer decides to eliminate the redundant positions, and therefore decides upon the dismissal of four employees.

The selection pool

25.10 In order to establish who will be made redundant, the employer will have to go through a selection process to select the employee who he intends to dismiss. As a consequence of the elimination of the job role, the employer will create a new organisational chart which will not include the job role which has been eliminated. .

The law gives the employer the right to decide freely who it shall dismiss. In the selection procedure the employer can (although he is not forced to) take into consideration some performance criteria. This kind of selection process is mandatory in case of a collective redundancy situation. As we shall see, in case of collective redundancies, the employer is obliged according to the art. 69 para 2, letter. D of the Labour Code, to inform the employees of the selection criteria that have been used to identify the persons to be dismissed.

The selection criteria may be regulated by the collective labour agreement by the internal rules of the company.

Important

25.11 According to Decision no. 60/2011 of the High Court of Cassation and Justice, the employer is not obliged to offer an alternative job role to the employee who is to be dismissed unless the reasons for the dismissal are related to the employee in the form of a physical incapacity, a lack of professional qualification, the court may decide the decision to dismiss is unfair and order reinstatement of the employee. In such case a Court will have concluded that the dismissal was unfair.

COLLECTIVE DISMISSAL

25.12 'Collective redundancies' means multiple dismissals effected by an employer for one or more reasons not related to the employee. This definition it is in accordance to the European Directive 98/59 CE, a Directive which is transposed into Romanian legislation.

In Romanian Labour Code a collective dismissal means the termination of the employment within 30 days of a number of employees, as follows:

- Where there are more than 20 and up to 100 employees up to ten employees are to be dismissed

- Where there are more than 101 and up to 300 employees 10% of the employees are to be dismissed.
- Where there are between 301 or more employees 30 or more employees are to be dismissed.

According to the Romanian Labour Code, the termination of an employment contract which occurs at the employer's initiative for one or more reasons not related to the individual worker, shall be classified as with redundancies, provided that there are at least five redundancies.

Special provisions

25.13 Beside the above mentioned general provisions, there are situations regulated by Emergency Ordinance no. 98/1999 issued by the Romanian Government, which derogate to a certain extent from the general law. These special provisions provide measures of social protection applicable to employees hired under individual employment contracts for an indefinite period and who are facing collective redundancies due to business reorganisation, partial or total closure of the business, privatisation or liquidation of the company, state owned companies and autonomous businesses or other establishments under the control of the central government or local authority, and institutions financed from the state budget.

According Emergency Ordinance no. 98/1999, collective dismissal is defined in the Ordinance as the reduction within 60 days of a number of employees, as follows:

- 10 employees where 20–100 persons are employed;
- 10% of the employees where 101–300 persons are employed; and
- 30 employees where 301 or more persons are employed.

If the employer intends to carry out collective redundancies, it is obliged to initiate consultations with the employee's representatives or trade union, in order to find methods and means for avoiding collective redundancies or reducing the number of employees and to mitigate the consequences of dismissal.

The employer must provide all relevant information and include in a written notice the following:

- The total number and categories of employees employed in the business;
- The reasons for the anticipated redundancies;
- The number and categories of employees who will be affected by the redundancy;
- The selection criteria;
- The measures taken to limit the number of redundancies;
- The proposed measures to mitigate the consequences of dismissal and also the financial compensation to be paid;
- The date or the period over which the redundancies will take place; and
- The period within which the union or, if applicable, the employee representatives may put forward to avoid or reduce the number of the redundancies.

A copy of this notice must be sent to employees and also to the Labour Inspectorate and to the Territorial Workforce Agency. These authorities may suggest solutions to the employment issues. Any proposal must be made within ten calendar days from receipt of the moment of receiving the document, and the employer must respond to any proposals within five calendar days.

After the consultations with the employees' representatives or trade union, the employer shall send a written notice to both authorities mentioned above at least 30 calendar days prior to the date of issue of the dismissal decisions. One copy shall also be sent to the trade union or to the employees' representative.

The Labour Inspectorate and the Territorial Workforce Agency can reply to the employer with their observations, and they can even prolong the periods mentioned for the issue of the dismissal decisions for motivated reasons.

In 45 days from the dismissal, the dismissed employee can be rehired if the job role is re-established. The ex-employee has priority over the other candidates. In addition the law states the fact that he will regain his original position without being subject to passing an exam, or a probation period. The ex-employee must communicate his wish to be re-employed within five days of receiving the notification from the employer.

The entire procedure referred to above is not mandatory if the employee`s company has commenced an insolvency procedure in accordance with the Law no. 85/2014. In this case the administrator is empowered to terminate the employment agreements without following the collective procedure.

The administrator is only required to respect the notice period.

The selection criteria

25.14 In practice during collective redundancies, the employer will identify the group of employees from which those who are to be made redundant will be selected.

The Order no. 1616/2011 issued by the Minister of Labour regarding the amendment of the framework model of the employment contract refers to the right of the employer to set performance goals. If performance goals are included in employment contracts the employer must initially check the achievement of the performance goals of each employee to be made redundant. After that the employer may continue to analyse other criteria, such as those provided for in the collective labour agreement.

In practice, the criteria stated in collective labour agreements are often used as the guidelines. It is common to initially select and terminate the employment of those employees who are receiving a pension in addition to a salary as well as those who are eligible to apply for retirement pension.

Other relevant selection criteria could be to:

- select the employee with the lower wage for redundancy (where the redundancy could affect two spouses working for the same employer);

- select those who do not have children; and
- select on the basis of the principle, last in first out.

The employer must pay attention to the selection criteria, and try to apply them as objectively as possible. A court will not be able to censor the selection criteria, but its role will be to check if the elimination of the job role was for a real and for a proper reason and if the employer has complied with the legal procedures regarding the matter.

The employer unilaterally sets the individual performance criteria of the employee and the staff should not interfere in this process. The employer must assess the individual performance against the job description. The assessment of individual performance is done against the criteria set out in each employer's internal procedures.

Individual consultation

25.15 Whilst there is no general requirement for employers to inform the employees individually about the proposed redundancy, it is advisable to go through this step. The Labour Code establishes that the intention to eliminate job roles must be communicated to the employee's representatives or trade union. Either way, the employee must be made aware of the position regarding their employment.

Examples of collective redundancy situations

25.16 A private factory, which supplies medicines, decides to change its place of business to another city. The reason for this is that its main client (a general hospital) has just been closed down as a result of a decision by the Health Ministry. Faced with this situation the factory management decides to move its business to another location amounting to a reorganisation of the business. As a result, the employer commences the redundancy process by following the legal procedure.

Measures taken by the employer in order to reduce redundancies

25.17 There is useful guidance as to steps to be taken to limit redundancies in Convention 158/1982 of the International Labour Organisation. Romania is not a party to this convention, but it remains useful guidance in practice.

The employer can adopt the following measures:

- limit the new hirings to the minimum necessary;
- stagger the personnel reduction;
- proceed with internal movements, from a department to another one;
- diminish overtime; and
- reduce the normal work schedule.

The dismissal decision

25.18 According to Article 76 of the Labour Code, in case of collective or individual dismissals, the employer must send a written dismissal decision to the affected employees, which must include:

- the reasons behind the dismissal;
- the notice period; and
- the selection criteria;

A dismissal decision takes effect from the date it has been notified to the employee. A dismissal decision arrived at by infringing the procedure provided for in the law is null and void. In the case of employment dispute, the employer cannot put forward in court any other reasons in fact or law other than those mentioned in the dismissal decision.

The decision to dismiss is a unilateral decision, issued by the employer and must be addressed to each individual employee. The law does not give permit the employer to issue a global decision.

An employee can appeal against the redundancy decision within 45 days from the date the decision was communicated and received by him.

The employee may claim in Court:

- the annulment of the Employer's decision;
- reinstatement; or
- payment of all unpaid salaries from the date of dismissal and the date of rehiring or reinstatement.

The relevant Court for deciding such claims is the Tribunal located in the area where the employee is domiciled.

If the dismissal was unfounded or unlawful, the court will order its revocation and will order the employer to compensate the employee with an amount equal to the indexed, increased and updated wages and other rights that the employee would have benefited from if he had not been dismissed.

At the request of the employee, the court having ordered the revocation of the dismissal will put the parties back in the position they were in before issuing the dismissal notice, ie reinstate the employee.

Although the Labour Code does not provide for the employer to make good its own mistake, some books of Romanian jurisprudence recognise this possibility. It is their view that the employer may revoke the dismissal decision on becoming aware that the documentation or basis for which the decision is faulty.

The revocation must be in a written form, and issued by exactly the same department or person who had previously issued the dismissal decision. Revocation of the decision by the employer has no legal effect if is issued after the date of a court decision that confirmed the dismissal decision.[1]

Currently, the courts tend more and more not to recognise this option for employers. Therefore, in order to avoid errors in the process of dismissal it is advisable to carefully follow the legal process.

---

1 p. 456, Ion Traian Stefanescu Theoretical and practical treaty of employment law –, Universul Juridic, 2012,

The notice period

25.19 When the dismissal occurs for reasons for a business reason, the minimum notice period is 20 working days. The same notice period applies in cases when the dismissal is based on reasons related to the employee because of his physical or mental incapacity or of his lack of professional qualifications. Whilst the dismissal decision must contain the notice period, this does not mean that the notice period starts to run at the moment of receipt of the notice. The employee should be informed of his position before the issuance of the dismissal decision.

> **Example**
>
> A company decides to dismiss one of its employees for a business reason. Approximately two years before the dismissal decision, the employee was diagnosed with a disability following a medical examination. The decision to dismiss specifies a notice period of 20 days, in accordance with the provisions of the Labour Code.
>
> In court, the employee points out his disability, and that the employer was aware of this, and even benefited from and obtained some fiscal advantages by way of State assistance due to his disability. In addition the employee shows that he successfully carried out tasks assigned to him.
>
> The employee claims that the correct legal notice period was not adhered to, having provided only 20 calendar days instead of 30 in breach of Law no. 448/2006. Even though Law no. 448/2006 indicates a longer notice period, on appeal the employee`s claim was dismissed on the basis that the employer's failure to provide the correct notice period did not render the notice invalid and went on to merely prescribing amendment of the dismissal notice to reflect an extension of the notice period to comply with the legal requirement.[2]

THE INVOLVEMENT OF TRADE UNION REPRESENTATIVES AND EMPLOYEE REPRESENTATIVES IN THE DISMISSAL PROCESS

25.20 Trade Union activity is governed by the provisions of Law no. 62/2011 and reflects the constitutional right of free association in order to defend the rights and interests of employees regarding work issues.

Trade union activities are less significant during the process of individual dismissal, than during the process of collective dismissal. Trade union

2 [The Appeal Court of Craiova, Decision no. 3104/07.03.2012]

representatives can be on the professional evaluation committee, when the grounds for an individual dismissal of an employee are his professional inadequacy or due to serious or repeated acts of misconduct.

Trade union representatives can give advice regarding the measures that the employer can take during collective dismissal plans and can even represent their members in front of the courts in employment related disputes.

Employee representatives have mainly the same role as Trade Union representatives, except the law limits some of their prerogatives. Their activity is governed by the provisions of the Labour Code, but there are also other legal principles that can be referred to. Employee representatives are elected by the employees when there is no constituted trade union and the employer has more than 20 employees.

REDUNDANCY PAYMENT

Cases of dismissal for reasons not related to the employee

25.21 Based on the provisions of art 67 of the Labour Code employees dismissed for reasons not related to them personally benefit from measures for combating unemployment. They can also benefit from compensation as provided for by law and by applicable collective labour agreement.

In other words, the employer does not have the obligation to make any redundancy payment for a dismissal for reasons that are not related to the employee, unless a special law provides such a right in favour of the employee, or if the employer had assumed such an obligation in the collective labour agreement.

In the private sector, there is no entitlement to redundancy payment by the law unless contained in any agreement between the parties or in any collective labour agreement. Thus, in the private sector the amount of compensation payments and the other conditions for the calculation of these amounts to be paid are set out in the contract or the collective labour agreement. If there is no provision then there is no payment.

25.22 If there is no collective labour agreement, compensation for redundancy will be granted only if the employer's Internal Rules or the individual employment contracts provide such rights to the employees.

Thus, in the case of dismissal for reasons not related to the employee, the employer has the obligation to make redundancy payments if this is provided under a normative act and also if he assumed such an obligation in a legal document concluded in order to implement labour relations such as collective labour agreement, Internal Rules or individual employment contract.

As of 2011 Romania has no collective labour agreement at a national level.

25.23 Based on the provisions of art 128 of Law no. 62/2011 on social dialogue, collective labour agreements can be negotiated at factory/site level, for a group of factories/sites, industry sector level but not at a national level.

As a consequence, the employer has the obligation to make redundancy payments on the redundancy of the employees only if there is a collective labour agreement in place at factory/site level which provides for the payments of these sums, or if such a provision exists in an individual employment contract.

Public system

25.24 Government Emergency Ordinance no. 36/2013 implemented a series of measures for social protection granted to the persons dismissed through a collective dismissal done on the basis of the dismissal plans of state companies.

In this regard, the persons dismissed under the conditions provided for in the Government Emergency Ordinance benefit from the following rights:

- Unemployment benefits (Somaj);
- Monthly supplemental income;
- Redundancy payments paid by the business operators according to the provisions of the applicable collective labour agreements or from the individual employment contracts, concluded at the level of each business operator.

At the cessation of entitlement to unemployment benefit, the dismissed persons benefit under the conditions of the Governmental Emergency Ordinance from a monthly sum equal to the difference between the average individual net salary income for the last three months prior to dismissal, but no more than the national net average income, from the month of January in the year of the dismissal, communicated by the National Statistics Institute, and the level of the unemployment benefit at the date of the cessation of entitlement to unemployment benefit.

The monthly supplementary income is calculated at the same time as the unemployment benefit and is paid based on the seniority of the dismissed persons, as follows:

- 12 months for persons having seniority of between three years and less than ten years;
- 20 months for persons having seniority of between ten years and less than 15 years;
- 22 months for employees who have seniority of between 15 years and less than 25 years;
- 24 months for employees having seniority exceeding 25 years.

Any person who is employed by third parties during the period referred to above receives 50% of the monthly supplementary income only.

An employer who hires or who refused to hire a person who receives the monthly supplementary income has the obligation to notify the employment agencies where the persons were registered within three days, stating the reason for their refusal. Any breach of this obligation is punished with a fine from RON2,500 to RON5,000.

If, during this period the monthly supplementary income is paid the beneficiaries ask to be registered in one of the categories of pensions provided under the Law no. 263/2010 regarding the unitary public pension system, then the payment of the monthly supplementary income ceases at the date the right to a pension is granted.

The payment of the monthly supplementary income also ceases in the following situations:

- An unfounded refusal of an offer of work by a workplace compatible with the employee's training or studies,
- An unfounded refusal to undergo employment and professional training, mediation and counselling services offered by the agency for employment for the persons who are registered, and
- carrying out paid activities without any employment contract.

EMPLOYEES' PROTECTION IN CASE OF A TRANSFER OF UNDERTAKING

25.25 In Romania, the employees' transfer related rights are governed by Law no. 53/2003 regarding the Labour Code, article 173-174 and Law no. 67/2006 regarding the safeguarding of employees' rights in the event of transfers of undertakings, a businesses or part of an undertaking or business.

Law no. 67/2006 transposed the European Union Council Directive 2001/23/EC on the approximation of the laws of the Member States relating to the safeguarding of employees' rights in the event of transfers of undertakings, businesses or parts thereof.

The scope of the law is to ensure the continuity of employment contracts in the event of the employing entity being subject to a transfer.

Under the Law no. 67/2006, a transfer is defined as the passing of an undertaking, of a unit or part thereof from the transferor's ownership into the ownership of the transferee as a result of a transfer or merger, having as its purpose the continuation of the main or secondary activity of the company irrespective of making any profit.

Effects in case of the transfer of undertaking

Enforcement of the automatic transfer

25.26 The rights and obligations of the transferor arise from the individual employment contracts and from the applicable collective labour agreements existing at the transfer date of the undertaking.

Protection from dismissal

25.27 The essential prohibition is that the transfer of undertaking cannot be used as a reason for a collective or individual dismissal of employees by the transferor or by the transferee.

Further, the transferor may not dismiss its employees in order to facilitate the transfer of the undertaking.

This does not mean that the transferor cannot terminate contracts up to the moment of the merger or division or by the transferee after the transfer, but that such a measure cannot have as legal basis the transfer itself.

Only two reasons of dismissal are considered lawful, as follows:

- When economic, technical or organisational reasons determine the employer to implement changes regarding the work-force;
- If the transferor is subject to a judicial reorganisation or bankruptcy procedures.

But, in practice it may be difficult to draft a termination decision so as to exclude any link with the transfer of the business. Therefore, it is recommended that a period of time passes between the transfer and the termination date in order to reduce the risk of having the termination cancelled.

Protection of rights and obligations of the employees

25.28 The transferee is obliged by law to preserve the existing rights of the individual employees as well as any benefits attaching to their employment.

The employees' rights and obligations resulting from the collective labour agreement, in force on the date of the transfer, cannot be unilaterally amended for the entire term of such agreement.

The terms can be re-negotiated with the new owner, but not earlier than one year from the date of transfer.

OBLIGATION TO INFORM

25.29 The law requires the transferor and the transferee to inform and to consult the representatives of the employees affected directly or indirectly by the transfer.

The information to be provided shall include the following:

- The proposed date of the transfer, and the reasons for such transfer;
- The legal, economic and social consequences of the transfer;
- Whether any measures in relation to the transferred employees are to be taken; and
- The conditions of employment.

Romanian law requires that the information and consultation process is to take place at least 30 days prior to the date of transfer.

CONTRAVENTIONS COVERED BY LAW NO. 67/2006

25.30 The law imposes a series of obligations on the transferor or the transferee in the case of the transfer for the purpose of protecting the rights of the employees who are affected by the transfer, as follows:

- the transferor must notify the transferee regarding all the rights and obligations that will be transferred to him;
- the transfer may not be considered as a reason for an individual or collective dismissal of the employees;
- the transferee must respect all the provisions of the applicable collective labour agreement at the date of the transfer and up until its annulment or expiry;
- in cases where the transferor or the transferee expects an impact on its own employees, it must consult with the employees' representatives in order to reach agreement, at least 30 days prior to the transfer; and
- the obligation to inform the affected employees.

Failure by the transferor or transferee to observe their obligations constitutes a breach.

SANCTIONS

25.31 In accordance with art 13 of Law no. 67/2006, breaches are sanctioned with a fine between RON1,500 and RON3,000.

The Labour Inspectorate is responsible for ascertaining the breaches and enforcing sanctions.

UNFAIR DISMISSAL

25.32 The means of available protection in favour of employees in connection with a transfer of an undertaking entitles the employees to apply to the court in the event of dismissal by reason of a transfer of undertaking. Any dismissal ordered which breach the procedure prescribed by law is null and void.

In case of a dispute before a court the employer may only rely on the reasons of fact and law specified in the dismissal decision.

Remedies

25.33 If the dismissal was not lawful the court shall order its revocation and may require the employer to pay compensation equal to unpaid wages, indexed, increased and adjusted and other rights to which the employee would have been entitled during the relevant period.

Unless the employee does request the reinstatement of the position held before the dismissal the individual employment agreement will be terminated with effect from the date of the final and irrevocable court decision.

Jurisdiction for dispute resolution in employment disputes

25.34 The dismissal decision may be appealed within 30 days from its communication to the employee.

The dispute between the employer and employees will be resolved by the competent court in Romania under the Civil Procedure Code. Any application in this matter is exempted from the payment of stamp tax (Court Fee filing fee). According to labour law, the burden of proof in any proceedings is on the employer.

Employment cases will be heard based on an urgent procedure, by one judge, assisted by two judiciary assistants. The judiciary assistants participate in the debate, having a consultative vote, and their separate opinions will be recorded in the judgment.

USE OF TEMPORARY STAFF

25.35 Hiring temporary staff is always an option for companies who do not want to conclude an individual employment contract with an employee for an unlimited period of time. In this respect they can choose to hire temporary employees provided by a specialised agency or to hire directly a person on the basis of a fixed-term contract.

Agency workers

25.36 Temporary staff may be hired by companies that at certain times require additional staff, for example peak production periods or seasonal working. Staff may also be interested in becoming temporary employees if they want to work only for a limited period of time or if they are unemployed and cannot find permanent employment.

Romania has implemented in the National Legislation regarding temporary employment agents the European Union Directive 2008/104/CE on temporary agency work. When considering hiring temporary staff, employers should take into consideration the fact that the rules that govern the status of temporary staff are covered by the legislation.

This process of hiring a temporary worker implies the conclusion of two written contracts: one between the temporary worker and the agency and one between the agency and the company that wants to hire the temporary staff. The company must guarantee to the temporary staff at least the rights that they would have guaranteed to them if they were directly hiring them, as well as the rights that they guarantee to their permanent staff.

A company cannot hire temporary staff in order to replace a staff member whose individual employment contract was suspended due to the fact that they took part in a strike. At the end of the period of the temporary employment the company may hire the employee on the basis of an individual employment contract.

Fixed-term contracts

25.37 Under Romanian legislation, a fixed-term individual contract can be concluded only in the situations provided for under the Labour Code. Employees hired for a fixed-term period cannot be treated less favourably than other comparable employees hired for an undetermined period.

The maximum period of time for which a fixed-term contract can be concluded is 36 months. The employer and the employee can conclude a maximum of three successive fixed-term contracts. If a fixed-term contract is concluded between the parties within three months from the termination of another fixed-term contract, the second one will be considered as a successive contract between the parties and its length cannot exceed 12 months.

The fixed-term contract automatically terminates at the expiry of the term for which it was concluded. In these cases the employer shall issue a five-day written decision from the expiry of the fixed term contract and will communicate it to the employee with five days.

The employer must inform the fixed-term employee if any job within the company is available, or will be available, thereby allowing him to apply in the same conditions granted to the other staff that have permanent contracts.

Under Romanian law, vocational adjustment contract and apprenticeship contracts are fixed-term contracts.

DISCRIMINATION

25.38 One of the fundamental principles contained in the basic rules set by the labour legislation is the principle of non-discrimination. Any direct or indirect discrimination regarding sex, sexual orientation, genetic characteristics, age, nationality, race, colour, ethnicity, religion, political view, social origin, disability, family situation or responsibility, membership of or union activity is strictly prohibited.

The most common forms of employees' discrimination are discriminatory application of the legal provisions related to the remuneration of the employees, the changing of the relationship between employer and employee in a discriminatory manner, acts of harassment in the workplace, the application of discriminatory criteria related to employment, and the application of discriminatory criteria when dismissing employees.

SANCTIONS

25.39 A complaint regarding discrimination will be reviewed by the National Council for Combating Discrimination. A person or company is found to have discriminated against an individual will be liable to a fine of between RON1,000 and RON30,000. If the discrimination is against a group of persons or community then the fine is between RON2,000 and RON100,000. The Territorial Labour Inspectorate may also apply fines for acts of discrimination between men and women. The person or company who has discriminated may also be found liable to imprisonment.

MUTUALLY AGREED TERMINATION

25.40 Under Romanian law the termination of an individual employment contract maybe mutually agreed. This kind of termination is subordinated to the Latin adage '*Mutuus conssensus, mutuus dissensus*'.

This is a simple and fast way to terminate an employment contract that can be initiated by either the employer or the employee. The condition that must be fulfilled in each case is that the parties gave their serious, clear and unambiguous consent.

In practice, if the employee initiates this procedure, he should complete two requests to terminate the contract in a mutually agreed way, one for himself and one for the employer. He should take care that the request is registered in the employer's registers and has been given a proper reference number. For such to have legal effect the employer's representative or the employee's superior should sign the request and acknowledge that they approved the request.

The termination can also be recorded in a joint written decision of both the employee and the employer or it can be contained in a written proposal of the employer. Where a proposal originates from the employer it will only have legal effect if the employee's consent is obtained.

In case a mutually agreed termination of the employment contract the parties do not have to respect any notice period. The parties just agree in a written form (in the request, decision, proposal, etc) the date when the contract shall be terminated.

Chapter 26
Workforce Restructuring in Slovakia

Simona Haláková and Jana Černáková
Čechová & Partners, Bratislava

INTRODUCTION

26.1 This chapter looks at the employment laws in Slovakia. The legal system in the Slovak Republic is a continental European (civil law) legal system, very similar to the legal system of other European Union countries, mainly the Czech Republic with which it represented one single state with shared laws and case-law before 1 January 1993.

26.2 The labour law is codified mainly in Slovak Labour Code (Act No. 311/2001 Coll., as amended) and it provides minimum standard requirements for an employment which may not be deviated from, often not even upon mutual agreement.

26.3 Therefore when preparing for restructuring and assessing the entitlements of the affected employees, the labour laws shall be consulted as a first step.

26.4 As the second step, individual arrangements with the affected employees in employment contracts shall be considered together with any collective arrangement (either in the form of a collective agreement or unilaterally adopted internal guideline of the employer or other documentation).

26.5 One must bear in mind that Slovak labour laws are very formalistic and strict. The Slovak labour law does not recognise 'employment at will' or dismissal without reason by the employer.

26.6 The impact of the formal approach of the Slovak labour laws is most significant in the consequences of failing to adhere to the formal requirements for dismissals and restructuring. Almost any such omission, on its own, may lead, if challenged, to declaration of invalidity of the dismissal by court even if other conditions and requirements for dismissal would be met.

PREPARING FOR A RESTRUCTURING EXERCISE

26.7 As business restructuring is usually intended as a way to reduce the cost base of an employer, preparation for them is crucial, as the restructuring itself may result in increased costs during the short period of its execution.

26.8 As business restructuring includes many formal steps and mandatory time frames to be upheld, it should be carefully planned in order to avoid breaching formal legal requirements resulting in sanctions by the Labour Inspections up to €200,000 per breach.

Identify the employing entity

26.9 Under Slovak labour laws an employment relationship can only be concluded and come into existence with one specific employer entity and not with a group of companies. The employing entity is responsible for compliance with all applicable statutory obligations regarding restructuring and possible dismissals. In the case of collective redundancy which affects a number of employees, it is particularly important to ensure that the correct legal entity is identified as only employees of this particular entity are taken into account when determining whether a collective redundancy occurs or not.

COLLATING INFORMATION TO PLAN AND BUDGET FOR THE RESTRUCTURING

Exercise

26.10 Employers should familiarise themselves not only with the statutory obligations and costs related to the restructuring but also with the contractual obligations and costs determined either in the employment contracts of the affected employees, collective agreement or other documents.

EMPLOYMENT STATUS

26.11 Only individuals in a regular employment relationship with an employer are protected from unfair dismissal. Requirements on redundancy procedures and other termination exercises such as consultations apply only to such individuals.

GENERAL PROTECTION AGAINST DISMISSAL

26.12 Under Slovak labour laws a dismissal by the employer must be for a mandatory reason and there are formal mandatory requirements for such dismissal which must be met by the employer.

26.13 The formal mandatory requirements - include a requirement for a written notice of the dismissal providing detailed reasons for the dismissal; a requirement for prior consultation with the employees' representatives; delivery of the dismissal notice to the employee (primarily delivery in person and, if not possible, then via registered mail); and an offer of a suitable alternative position, if applicable.

26.14 The formal procedural requirements also prescribe a thorough examination of the reasons behind the dismissal and compliance with the non-discrimination rules.

SPECIAL PROTECTION AGAINST DISMISSAL

26.15 There are two types of specific protection against dismissal under Slovak labour laws, protection of specific categories of employees, and protection in specific circumstances.

26.16 Employment representatives are protected against any measures which might harm them, including terminations of employment which are motivated by their status or activity during the term of their office. The protection remains in place for a period of six months after the termination of office as employee representative and/or member of the European Works Council.

26.17 An employer may not issue a termination notice on the basis of organisational reasons (including redundancy) to an employee during the protected period, which includes:

(a) any period of work incapacity of the employee due to illness or injury, except where such incapacity was induced deliberately or sustained under the influence of alcohol, narcotics or psychotropic substances; and during any period from the submission of a proposal by the relevant authority for institutional care or the commencement of medically prescribed spa therapy to the end date thereof;

(b) absence due to being summoned to carry out an extraordinary duty during a crisis from the date the employee was summoned to carry out the extraordinary duty by a call-up order served to him or her or by a mobilisation call or mobilisation notice, or where such extraordinary duty was ordered upon the employee, until the expiry of two weeks following the release from such service; the foregoing shall equally apply to alternative service as referred to in special regulation;
(c) during any period of pregnancy; maternity leave or parental leave, or during which an employee (ie an employee who lives alone and is a single, widowed or divorced) has parental responsibility for a child of three years of age and below;
(d) any period during which an employee has been released for an extended period to pursue public office;
(e) any period during which an employee carrying out night shift work has been signed off by a medical practitioner (in the form of a medical opinion pursuant to the law) as incapable of undertaking night work duties.

26.18 The prohibition on issuing a termination notice during the protected period as described in the previous paragraph does not protect against the issue of a termination notice to an employee due to the winding-up of the employer or part thereof.

26.19 A further exception to the prohibition on issuing a termination notice described in para **26.17** applies to permit the issue of a termination notice in circumstances where the employer due to relocation of the employer or part thereof is having to give notice to either an opposing employee with caring responsibility for a child below three years of age, or to an employee who has been recognised as temporarily incapable of night work duties pursuant to medical opinion.

26.20 Further, compulsory retirement on the grounds of age amounts to a breach of the principle of equal treatment unless it is justified on objective grounds (eg for fire fighters, pilots, etc).

WORKFORCE REDUCTION

26.21 If dismissals occur as a result of execution of a workforce restructuring plan by the employer, the employer shall ensure to document the restructuring plan and as a first step decide which of the organisational changes set below will be adopted.

26.22 Any organisational change shall be adopted by the appropriate body of the employer (usually the general meeting of the company) and in the appropriate form (in writing and in some cases verified by a notary).

Definition of organisational changes

26.23 The following organisational changes are stipulated in Article 63 of the Slovak Labour Code as reasons for dismissal:

(a) the employer or part thereof is being:
  - wound up; or
  - relocated and the employee objects to the change of the agreed place of work;

(b) the employee has been made redundant on the basis of a written decision of the employer or a competent authority to change the employer's function, its technical equipment, or to reduce the number of employees in order to ensure work efficiency, or other organisational changes;

26.24 The organisational reasons can only justify dismissal, where the affected employee performs tasks for an employer or part thereof which is being wound up or relocated (the 'objective organisational reason') or where the employee is selected for redundancy due the reorganisation of the employer (the 'subjective organisational reasons').

26.25 If the reorganisation is adopted by the employer as a part of outsourcing, lease out, offshore or another form of transfer of undertaking in whole or in part, it shall be determined whether the conditions of transfer of the undertaking described below at para **26.102** apply in which case automatic transfer of employment relationships of the affected employees (applicable *ex lege*) will occur.

Examples of redundancy situations

Company A is operating in an old factory while currently being in the process of constructing a new factory in a city 100 km away. Upon completion of the construction it plans to move the whole operation to the new factory. It informs the employees about the move. If some of the employees do not consent to the move and their relocation to another place of work, the Company A is entitled to dismiss these employees on the ground of relocation of the employer. However, Company A cannot use this reason if the employee is willing to relocate.

Company B provides the services of a call-centre as part of a multinational group of companies for its customers in ten different countries with use of 100 employees who provide services to all customers and are not allocated into specific teams for each of the different countries. Upon a corporate decision, the number of countries is reduced to five, resulting in around 50 employees in the service team becoming redundant. As none of the employees can be clearly linked to the countries which are no longer being serviced, the employer is entitled to adopt a written decision on the decrease of the number of employees and dismiss 50 employees of his choice (based on objective, non-discriminatory reasons).

26.26 The Slovak labour law does not prescribe other permitted reasons for dismissal based on reorganisation of an employer.

26.27 Nevertheless, even in case of a reorganisation, the employer is always free to consider whether other forms of employment termination linked with the individual employees, such as loss of prerequisites for the agreed work, breach of work discipline, unsatisfactory performance, etc apply.

DISMISSALS ON GROUNDS OF REDUNDANCY

26.28 Depending on the number of employees to be dismissed, the employer must follow the individual redundancy procedure and, if applicable, also the collective redundancy procedure.

26.29 Where the employer or part thereof terminates the employment due to organisational changes for a reason which does not relate to the employee, the collective redundancy procedure shall apply if during a period of 30 consecutive days such termination affects
(a) at least 10 employees at an employer which employs more than 20 and less than 100 employees,
(b) at least 10% of employees from the total number of employees at an employer which employs at least 100 and less than 300 employees,
(c) at least 30 employees at an employer which employs at least 300 employees.

Redundancy procedures

26.30 An organisational reason for dismissal in itself does not eliminate the risk of an unfair dismissal being established. The employer must also follow a 'fair redundancy procedure' and comply with the formal requisites for the dismissal.

Individual redundancy procedure

Objective organisational reason

26.31 Where the employer or part thereof is being wound up or relocated and the employee does not agree with the relocation, the employer is entitled to dismiss the employees who are affected by this change.

26.32 For this purpose the employer shall identify which employees are affected by the objective organisational change.

26.33 In such instances, there is no need to set and apply other selection criteria as the dismissal reason can be isolated to employees affected by the objective organisational change.

26.34 To effectively and validly dismiss the affected employees, the employer must also fulfil the formal requirements for the dismissal based on an organisational change described at para **26.31** below.

Subjective organisational reason

26.35 The employer is also entitled to dismiss any employee who has become redundant because of a written decision of the employer to change the employer's function, its technical equipment, or to reduce the number of employees in order to ensure work efficiency, or other organisational changes.

26.36 Application of this dismissal reason first of all requires a written decision recording the reorganisation which has been adopted by the competent deciding body of the employer (usually in a general meeting of the company).

26.37 Secondly, the employees who are affected by the decision shall be identified.

26.38 Further, if the number of employees affected by the decision exceeds the number of employees who should be dismissed, a selection procedure shall be performed. There are no statutory criteria for the selection other than the obligation to perform it in a non-discriminatory manner. However, further criteria might be stipulated contractually in a collective agreement or set out in internal guidelines of the employer.

26.39–26.40 The selection criteria shall be objective and non-discriminatory. Although there is no need to inform the affected employees of the selection criteria and their results it is generally recommended where the criteria are being applied by superiors and the human factor is involved.

Individual consultation

26.41 The Slovak labour laws do not stipulate an obligation to individually consult with the employees in cases of organisational change.

Involvement of employee representatives in individual dismissals

26.42 Termination of employment with a termination notice by the employer must be preceded by consultation with the employees' representatives, otherwise the termination of employment with termination notice is invalid.

26.43 The employees' representatives are obliged to consult within seven working days from the date of delivery of the employer's written request. If no consultation occurs during the above time frame (either due to a delay or unwillingness of employees' representatives to consult), consultation is deemed to have occurred and the employer can proceed with the termination.

26.44 Where no employees' representatives operate within the employer, no pre-consultation is necessary.

Avoiding compulsory redundancies

26.45 Even where there are organisational reasons permitting the employer to terminate the employment by termination notice, it remains preferable to avoid compulsory redundancies and terminate the employment by mutual agreement.

26.46 Where organisational reasons permitting termination are present and the employee agrees to terminate the employment by mutual agreement, the employment is still considered to be terminated for organisational changes entitling the employee to statutory severance payments (see para **26.85** below).

Alternative employment

26.47 The employer may serve a termination notice to an employee for organisational reasons only if:

(a) the employer is unable to continue employing the employee in the agreed place of work even for a shorter working hours;
(b) the employee is unwilling to accept different suitable work offered to the employee in the agreed place of work, or to undertake pre-training for such different work (the 'alternative employment').

26.48 The alternative employment is considered to be suitable for the employee if it is suitable with regard to his/her abilities and qualifications and it can be performed in his/her agreed place of work.

26.49 Even alternative employments requiring fewer qualifications are considered to be suitable for the employee if there are vacancies, eg a doctor at a hospital shall be offered the position of a janitor if such position is open at the time the termination notice is served.

26.50 The requirement to offer alternative employment is the prerequisite of a fair dismissal and if it is not met, even if other requirements were met, the dismissal will be declared invalid by court if challenged by the employee.

26.51 Alternative employment is only considered suitable if it is employment with the same employer and at the place of work stated in the employment contract. Therefore, the employer is not obliged to offer the employee alternative employment in one of its subsidiaries or affiliates (although he is free to do so) or to offer the employee an alternative employment at a different place of work (although he is free to do so).

26.52 The offer of alternative employment must be made before serving the termination notice. The employee shall be provided with sufficient information and time to be in an objective position to freely decide on the offer.

26.53 If only one alternative employment is available and there are several employees to be dismissed, the alternative employment shall be offered to all of them at the same time and one who first accepts the offer becomes employed. The other employees may then be dismissed on grounds of organisational changes.

Probation periods

26.54 The Slovak labour law does not recognise a probation period for the alternative employment. The acceptance of the alternative employment results in the automatic change of the job role of the employee.

26.55 The Slovak labour law does not recognise the possibility to terminate the alternative (or original) employment with retrospective effect and if the alternative employment is not appropriate for the employee, a new dismissal notice will have to be served for new reasons meeting the prescribed conditions for such new dismissal.

Other considerations

26.56 Collective agreements or internal policies of the employer usually provide further requirements for redundancy dismissals, eg the category of protected employees is being extended, the method and content of the consultations with employees' representatives are set, etc. Therefore, apart from the above-mentioned statutory procedures, the employer shall always consult the ancillary labour documentation and fulfil contractual obligations thereunder, as well.

Collective redundancy procedure

26.57 As already mentioned, the collective redundancy procedure shall apply when the employer or a part thereof terminates the employment by termination notice due to organisational changes or, if the employment is terminated differently, for a reason which does not relate to the employee's person, during 30 days of at least:

(a) ten employees at an employer which employs more than 20 and less than 100 employees, or
(b) 10% of employees from the total number of employees at an employer which employs at least 100 and less than 300 employees, or
(c) 30 employees at an employer which employs at least 300 employees.

26.58 For the purpose of collective redundancies, a 'part' of the employer shall also include a subsidiary branch registered in the Commercial Register under a special regulation.

26.59 For the purpose of counting the number of employees, fixed-term employees whose employment is due to terminate within the designated 30 days are not taken into account; neither are crew members of boats navigating under the state flag of the Slovak Republic.

Involvement of employee representatives in collective dismissals

26.60 In order to reach agreement, no later than one month before the commencement of collective redundancies, the employer shall consult with the employees' representatives, or directly with the employees concerned (if no employee representatives operate at the employer). Such consultation includes consultation on measures to avoid or limit the collective redundancies, in particular the possibility of placing the employees concerned in any of the employer's other locations, whether with or without training, and measures to mitigate the adverse effects of collective redundancies.

26.61 The employer shall provide the employees' representatives with all necessary information and inform them in writing in particular of:

(a) the reasons behind the collective redundancies;
(b) the number and structure of employees whose employment is to be terminated;
(c) the total number and structure of employees employed by the employer;
(d) the period of time during which the collective redundancies shall be effected;
(e) the criteria for the selection of employees whose employment is to be terminated.

26.62 The employer shall also deliver a copy of the written information, together with the names, surnames and permanent residential addresses of employees whose employment shall be terminated, to the Office of Labour, Social Affairs and Family.

26.63 After negotiation of the collective redundancies with the employees' representatives (or the employees themselves if no employees' representatives operate at the employer), the employer shall deliver written information about the outcome of the negotiation to:

(a) the Office of Labour, Social Affairs and Family;
(b) the employees' representatives.

26.64 The employees' representatives may submit to the Office of Labour, Social Affairs and Family their observations regarding the collective redundancies.

26.65 Following the fulfilment of the consultation and information duties above, the employer may serve a termination notice to an employee for organisational reasons or a proposal for termination of employment by agreement for the same reasons no later than upon the expiry of one month from the date of delivery of the written information about the negotiation outcome to the Office of Labour, Social Affairs and Family. This period may be appropriately shortened by the Office of Labour, Social Affairs and Family. This period does not apply to an employer who has been declared bankrupt by a court.

Sanctions

26.66 Where the employer breaches its consultation and information obligations, the employee whose employment is terminated by the employer as part of a collective redundancy procedure is entitled to salary compensation amounting to at least double their average earnings.

26.67 Further, sanctions by the Labour Inspections up to €200,000 for individual breaches might be imposed due to breach of labour laws.

NOTICE

26.68 The employment relationship does not end at the moment the termination notice is served but only after the lapse of the notice period.

26.69 The mandatory minimum notice periods are set by law. A longer notice period might be agreed in the employment contract, collective agreements or agreements with other employees' representatives, however, such arrangement should not be discriminatory and/or without an objective reason.

Minimum notice period

26.70 The minimum notice periods in case of termination notices due to organisational changes are as follows:

Length of service of the employee	Duration of notice period when notice given by employer
Less than 1 year	1 month
1 year to 5 years (excluding)	2 months
5 years (including) and more	3 months

26.71 Application of shorter notice periods is prohibited; however, if the employee agrees to be employed for a shorter period, the termination notice might be replaced with an agreement on employment termination with a set date on which the employment ceased to exist which might be shorter than the notice period otherwise applicable.

26.72 The notice period starts on the first day of the calendar month following the delivery of the termination notice to the employee and ends on the last day of the particular calendar month.

26.73 The length of service is calculated as of the date of delivery of the termination notice to the employee. This means that the notice period is not included in the length of service of the employee.

26.74 The employees continue to work also during their notice period and they have the right to be assigned work tasks unless the employer decides otherwise.

26.75 Employers sometimes prefer that the employee does not work during the notice period in order to keep him away from sensitive and confidential information or for other reasons. In such situation, the employer might decide to order the employee not to come to work (so called 'garden leave').

26.76 On the other hand, sometimes the employer schedules its business activities taking into account also the notice periods as he counts on having the terminated employees at his disposal during the notice period. To ensure this, the employer may already at the beginning of the employment relationship have agreed with the employee in the employment contract a financial compensation to the employer if the employee does not remain with the employer during the notice period. The financial compensation shall not exceed the product of the employee's average monthly earnings and the length of the notice period. Such financial compensation needs to be agreed in the employment contract, otherwise such arrangement is invalid.

Garden leave

26.77 Although the Slovak legal regime does not recognise garden leave as a legal instrument, it does provide the employer with the possibility of not assigning work tasks to the employee where there are obstacles to doing so.

26.78 The employer may ask the employee not to come to work during the notice period to avoid his exposure to confidential information.

26.79 In such case, the employment of the employee will still be in place also during the notice period and the employee will be entitled to their full salary for the notice period even if they do not work.

26.80 If the employer does not assign work tasks to the employee, the employee is not obliged to come to work.

Pay in lieu of notice

26.81 The Slovak legal regime does not recognise pay in lieu of notice. Therefore any such arrangements will be considered invalid.

26.82 The only way how to lawfully shorten the duration of the employment is to obtain the consent of the employee to replacing the termination notice by an agreement on employment termination where an earlier date will be set as the end date of the employment. The set date may not precede the date of signing the agreement on employment termination.

Notice period comparison table

Type of notice period	Effective date of termination	Benefits	Disadvantages
Employee working during the notice period	The expiry of the notice period	Employee works for his salary.	The employee learns about the latest business decisions of the employer and confidential information. The employee might influence the moral and work efficiency of other employees at the employer.

Type of notice period	Effective date of termination	Benefits	Disadvantages
Garden Leave	The expiry of the notice period.	The employee does not come into contact with the latest confidential information and business. The employee cannot engage himself in competitive activities as his/her employment is still in place.	Employee does not work and therefore does not provide any work for the salary he/she receives.

REDUNDANCY PAYMENTS

26.83 In case of termination of employment due to redundancy or other organisational reasons, the employee is entitled to severance payment (in Slovak '*odstupné*').

26.84 If, after termination of employment, the employee enters into employment with the same employer or its legal successor before expiry of the period determined for the amount of severance payment, the employee is obliged to return the severance payment for termination or a pro-rata portion thereof, unless it is agreed otherwise with the employer. The pro-rata portion of the compensation for termination shall be determined on the basis of the number of days between re-entry into employment and the expiry of the time for which the severance payment was granted.

26.85 On top of the severance payment, in the case of the termination of employment due to redundancy or other organisational reasons is the first termination of employment of the employee after becoming entitled to old-age pension, early retirement pension or disability pension (where the employee's capacity to pursue gainful activity has been reduced by more than 70 %), the employee is entitled to a retirement payment (in Slovak '*odchodné*') in the amount of at least their average monthly earnings, providing the employee requests the provision of the given pension within ten working days of termination of employment.

Statutory severance payment calculation

26.86 The amount of redundancy payment depends on the form of termination (whether termination notice was served or agreement on employment termination was reached) and on the duration of the employment, and is calculated as a multiple of the employee's average monthly salary as follows:

Duration of the employment	Severance payment in case of termination notice	Severance payment in case of agreement on employment termination
less than 2 years	–	1 time
2 years (including) to 5 years (excluding)	1 time	2 times
5 years (including) to 10 years (excluding)	2 times	3 times
10 years (including) to 20 years (excluding)	3 times	4 times
20 years (including) and more	4 times	5 times

26.87 In the calculation of the duration of employment the notice period shall also be taken into account.

26.88 The average monthly salary (the 'average earnings') of the employee is determined on the basis of the amount of the employee's payroll salary for the calendar quarter preceding the quarter in which the average earnings are determined (the 'relevant period') and the time worked by the employee during the relevant period. For the purpose of calculation, the salary shall not include the salary for the inactive portion of on-call duty in the workplace and the time worked by the employee shall not include the time of the inactive portion of the on-call duty in the workplace.

26.89 If the employee did not work at least 22 days or 170 hours in the relevant period, likely earnings are used instead of average earnings. Likely earnings are determined from the salary achieved, or likely to be achieved, by the employee at the beginning of the relevant period.

26.90 Average earnings are determined as average hourly earnings. Average hourly earnings shall be rounded to four decimal places. Where labour regulations require the application of average monthly earnings, average hourly earnings shall be multiplied by the average number of working hours pertaining to one month in the year pursuant to the employee's weekly working hours. Average monthly earnings shall be rounded up to the next euro cent. Where the calculated monthly average earnings are lower than the statutory minimum wage, the average monthly earnings are set at the amount of the statutory minimum wage.

26.91 Where bonuses are paid to the employee in the relevant period for a period longer than a quarter of a year (eg yearly bonuses), only the amount of the bonus corresponding with the quarter is taken into account (eg in case of a yearly bonus only one quarter thereof will be taken into account) when determining the average earnings.

26.92 A more detailed description of the calculation of average earnings might be agreed between the employer and the employees' representatives.

Example

The ABC Company made organisational changes as result of which Mr X and Mr Y became redundant. The length of employment of Mr X is 6 complete years and he was served with termination notice by the employer while not accepting agreement on employment termination. Mr Y's employment with the Company lasted for 11 complete years and accepted agreement on employment termination.

For the purpose of calculation it is assumed that both of them received a monthly salary of €1,800 during the relevant period and were paid a yearly bonus of €7,200 in the relevant period. Further, it is assumed they work standard 40 hours a week.

The average hourly earnings are therefore set as follows: €7,200 (€1,800 × 3 months + 7,200 / 12 months × 3 months) / 160 hours / 3 months = €15 per hour. The average monthly earnings are therefore €2,400 (€15 × 160 hours).

Following this, Mr X shall receive statutory pay of €4,800 (€2,400 × 2 times average monthly earnings) because he worked for the ABC Company for more than 5 years but less than 10 years and his employment was terminated by termination notice.

Mr Y shall receive a statutory pay of €9,600 (€2,400 × 4 times average monthly earnings) because he worked for the ABC Company for 10 years (incl.) to 20 years (excl.) and his employment was terminated by agreement on employment termination.

Enhanced redundancy payments

26.93 The employment contract, collective agreement or an internal policy of the employer may provide for a higher severance payment and/or retirement payment. Such higher redundancy payments, especially if agreed individually in the employment contract shall be set in a non-discriminatory manner.

26.94 In practice the collective agreement most often sets the redundancy payments to be higher than the statutory ones by one average monthly salary.

Taxation of redundancy payments

26.95 Statutory redundancy payments are taxed in the same manner as the regular salary.

Post-termination restrictive covenants

26.96 For the post-termination restrictive covenants to be valid, they need to be agreed as part of the employment contract and under conditions set by law.

26.97 The Slovak labour law recognises only one post-termination restrictive covenant – non-competition clause for the period after termination of employment. The employer and the employee may agree in the employment contract that, after termination of employment, the employee shall not pursue, for a certain period, but no longer than one year, any gainful activity which is competitive in its nature to the subject of the employer's activity.

26.98 The non-competition clause for the period after termination of employment may be agreed only with employees who, during their employment, are able to acquire information or knowledge that is not normally available and the use of which could cause substantial harm to the employer.

26.99 A restriction going beyond the necessary scope might be reduced or cancelled by the court.

26.100 For each month of the duration of the non-competition clause after termination of employment, the employer is obliged to provide at least 50% of the average monthly earnings (the 'financial compensation'). The financial compensation shall be provided at the standard pay dates set by the employer, unless agreed otherwise. In the case of the employer's failure to pay the financial compensation within 15 days of the due date, the employee is entitled to terminate the obligation under the non-competition clause; the termination becomes effective on the date of delivery of the termination notice to the employer.

26.101 A financial compensation due to be paid by the employee to the employer might be agreed for the breach of the non-competition clause by the employee. The amount of this financial compensation shall not exceed the financial compensation payable by the employer for the non-competition clause (mentioned above). The sum of financial compensation proportionately decreases if the employee partially fulfils his or her obligation. Once this financial compensation is paid, the employee's obligation under the non-competition clause ceases to exist.

26.102 The employer may withdraw from the obligation under the non-competition clause only during the employment of the employee; the obligation ceases to exist on the first day of the calendar month following the month in which the withdrawal was delivered to the counterparty, however, no later than the last day of employment.

Practical Tip

The non-competition clause for the period after termination of employment can be a part of standard template of the employment contract as employees are more willing to accept such clause at the beginning of the employment rather than at the end.

If the employer decides not to use the non-competition clause for the period after termination of employment with a specific employee, he can always withdraw from it during the employment, including the notice period.

It is necessary to make sure that the non-competition clause for the period after termination of employment is part of the employment contract and not a part of the agreement on employment termination as such a clause will be invalid and unenforceable under Slovak labour laws.

BUSINESS SALE, LEASE, OUTSOURCING/ INSOURCING AND OFFSHORING

26.103 EU Council Directive 2001/23/EC of 12 March 2001 on the approximation of the laws of the Member States relating to the safeguarding of employees' rights in the event of transfers of undertakings, businesses or parts of undertakings or businesses was implemented in the Slovak legal system as part of the Slovak Labour Code.

26.104 In short, if an economic unit which is the employer or part thereof, or an employer's task or activity, or part thereof, is transferred to another employer (the 'transfer of undertaking'), the rights and obligations from employment relationships towards the transferred employees shall automatically pass to the employer-transferee by the operation of law.

26.105 Key consequences of the transfer of undertaking are as follows:

- employment of affected employees remains effective;
- employment conditions of the affected employees remain unchanged;
- affected employees are protected from dismissal on the ground of the transfer;
- the employer has the mandatory obligation to consult and inform the employees' representatives (affected employees) on the transfer and its impact on the affected employees.

Business sale

26.106 'Transfer' is defined as the transfer of an economic unit, which retains its identity as an organised grouping of resources (tangible, intangible and personnel components), aimed at pursuit of an economic activity, whether it is a core activity or a complementary activity.

26.107 It is crucial to determine whether the transfer of undertaking includes an on-going entity which is in principle independent and might carry out the same activities also after the transfer. Reorganisation of such entity after the transfer is not taken into account when deciding on the independence of such entity.

26.108 Different factors are to be considered when determining whether or not a transfer of undertaking occurred. The presence or absence of tangible, intangible and/or personnel components shall be evaluated with a strong emphasis on the subject of the business. Some businesses can operate only with the personnel components without the need to have any significant tangible assets (eg cleaning services), on the other hand some businesses cannot operate without tangible assets (eg bus transport).

Lease

26.109 The lease represents the transfer of undertaking situation described above as long as the conditions for 'transfer' of an 'economic entity' are met. The rights and obligations from employment relationships of the affected employees are transferred to the employer-lessee.

26.110 If, after termination of the lease of the employer or part thereof, the rights and obligations from employment relationships are not transferred to another lessee, the settlement of claims from employment relationships shall be the responsibility of the employer-lessor.

26.111 The protection under the transfer of undertaking situation does not apply to employees employed by the employer-lessee after the commencement date of the lease.

Outsourcing/insourcing

26.112 It is not clear from Slovak Labour laws whether outsourcing and insourcing represent a transfer of economic entity. The Slovak Labour laws do not specifically mention it as such.

26.113 Following the case-law of the European Court of Justice, if conditions for 'transfer' of an 'economic entity' are met, outsourcing and insourcing can also be considered to represent a transfer of undertaking with the mandatory consequences mentioned above.

26.114 Nevertheless, there is no national case-law in this respect and therefore such approach shall be used with caution.

Effect of transfer of undertaking

Automatic transfer and protection of employment

26.115 Upon transfer of an undertaking the employment relationships of the affected employees, ie the employees who perform work tasks in the transferred undertaking or part thereof, are transferred to the new transferee. The transfer happens automatically under the law and therefore is effective even without being mentioned in the transaction documentation.

26.116 The employment relationships are transferred without any change apart from the supplementary company or intercompany pension schemes outside the statutory social security schemes (generally not transferring under the law) or participations in voluntary share save schemes of affiliated companies of the employer (unless the transferor undertook to cover or contribute employee's participation in such scheme as a part of employee's remuneration – eg claimable benefit – under the employment contract or collective agreement). Such schemes are used in Slovakia only rarely and mainly within companies with a global presence.

Practical Tip

As salaries are paid in arrears, upon transfer of the undertaking, the transferee will be obliged to pay the affected employees salary for work performed during the month preceding the transfer of undertaking.

As such work was performed for the transferor this shall be taken into account during negotiations and the costs of these salaries shall be taken into account when determining the purchase price or compensation of these costs by the transferor might be agreed.

Objection to the transfer

26.117 If the transfer of undertaking resulted in fundamental changes of the working conditions of an employee, the employee is entitled to object to the transfer.

26.118 If the employee objects to the transfer, the employment is deemed terminated by agreement for organisational reasons by the employer at the date of transfer which the employer shall confirm to the employee with a written document of termination of employment. The employee is entitled to a severance payment in the amount corresponding to the severance payment provided where the termination notice is served by the employer in a case of redundancy.

Protection from dismissal

26.119 The transfer of the undertaking shall not in itself constitute the grounds for dismissal by the transferor or the transferee.

26.120 However, the transferor and transferee are still free to make changes in the workforce and perform related dismissals for economic, technical or organisational reasons not based solely on the transfer of undertaking.

Protection of terms and conditions of employment

26.121 The transferee shall respect the employment terms of the transferred employees, as well as any collective agreements agreed by the former employer until their expiry.

26.122 The terms and conditions agreed with the affected employees in their employment contracts shall also be respected.

26.123 The length of employment with the transferor is taken into account when calculating the length of employment with the transferee.

Protection of employees' representatives

26.124 In the transfer of rights and obligations of employment relationships from the transferor to the transferee, the legal status and position of employees' representatives remains unprejudiced until the end of their incumbency, unless it is agreed otherwise with them.

26.125 The transferee shall respect any collective agreements agreed by the former employer until their expiry.

Information and consultation in respect of transfer of undertaking

Duty to inform

26.126 No later than one month before the transfer of undertaking becomes effective, the transferor as well as the transferee shall inform employees' representatives or, if no employees' representatives were appointed at the employer, the employees directly, in writing of:

a) the date or proposed date of the transfer;
b) reasons for the transfer;
c) employment, economic and social implications of the transfer for the employees;
d) planned transfer measures applicable to employees.

Duty to consult

26.127 In order to come to agreement at least one month before the implementation of transfer measures applicable to employees, the employer shall consult those measures with the employee representatives.

26.128 Consultation is a dialogue during which exchange of views occurs. The final approval of the employees' representative of the transfer of undertaking or its structure set by the employer is not necessary, however, the employer shall make demonstrable efforts to reach an agreement with the employees' representatives.

Practical Tip

It is recommended that full, written minutes of the consultation with employees' representatives are prepared by the employer. Such minutes are usually considered a sufficient proof of the consultation duty being duly fulfilled.

26.129 If no employees' representatives were appointed at the employer, no such duty exists.

European Works Councils

26.130 Where a European Works Council was established, it shall be informed about the transfer of undertaking under conditions set in the Agreement on establishment of the European Works Council.

Sanctions

Unfair dismissal

26.131 On the basis of the automatic (*ex lege*) transfer of all employment relationships of the affected employees to the transferee upon transfer of undertaking, any obligations of the employer based on a unfair dismissal by the transferor are transferred as well. For further details on the remedy for unfair dismissal see para **26.162** below.

Failure to inform and consult

26.132 If the employer fails to meet his duty to inform or consult the employees' representative (or employees, where appropriate), such failure does not cause the transfer of undertaking to be invalid.

26.133 Non-compliance with the employer's duty to inform and/or consult might lead to sanctions up to €200,000 being imposed by the Labour Inspection.

26.134 Hypothetically, where fundamental changes to the employment terms and conditions result from the transfer of undertaking and the employees were not aware of them, they may claim compensation for damages caused to them by such failure to provide the information. In such cases the employees shall provide evidence of the existence of damages, their amount, and causal link between the failure to inform them by the employer and the damage incurred.

Cross-border transactions or offshoring

26.135 The conditions for the transfer of undertakings apply also to cross-border transactions or offshoring where the undertaking shall be moved outside Slovakia. Upon the automatic transfer of the employment relationship their governing law remains to be the Slovak law and therefore they will still be protected by the Slovak labour laws.

26.136 Over and above the protection of the Slovak labour laws and in accordance with Rome I, the minimum standards of the law of the EU country to which the undertaking was transferred shall prevail. This applies only to the situation where the place of work is transferred out of Slovakia.

WORKFORCE REDUCTION IN CONNECTION WITH SHARE PURCHASE OR SALE

26.137 By share sale or share purchase only the shareholder of the employer is changed while the entity of the employer remains the same. Therefore, such transaction is not considered a transfer of undertaking under Slovak labour law.

26.138 The new shareholder is free to restructure the workforce as long as the conditions for employment termination set by law are met, ie the termination is reasoned, the consultancy procedures were upheld, etc.

CHANGING EMPLOYMENT TERMS AND CONDITIONS

26.139 Employment terms and conditions are set by:

(a) law;
(b) employment contract;
(c) collective agreement or any other agreement with the employees' representatives;
(d) internal regulations adopted by the employer.

26.140 The changes to the employment terms and conditions might be adopted either by agreement or unilaterally, depending on the source of the terms and conditions.

26.141 Any changes to the employment terms and conditions must meet the minimum standards of the statutory terms and conditions as set by Slovak Labour laws. It is not permitted to set the employment terms and conditions to be less advantageous than the statutory terms and conditions, not even by mutual agreement.

Mutually agreed changes

26.142 The employment terms and conditions set by the collective agreement or any other agreement with the employees' representatives may be changed by mutual agreement with the employees' representatives.

26.143 The employment terms and conditions set by the employment contract may be changed only by mutual agreement with the employee. Such agreement shall be in writing. Although a non-written form of the agreement does not result in its invalidity, the employer is likely to be in a more difficult position to prove that the agreement was reached and what the terms of the agreement are.

Unilateral changes

26.144 Even without mutual agreement the employer is entitled to change the terms and conditions set by him unilaterally in an internal regulation.

26.145 Under the Slovak Labour Code, the employer is obliged to consult or agree on employment terms and conditions with the employees' representatives on several occasions. Therefore, some terms and conditions, even if they are part of the internal regulation might need to be the subject of consultation or agreed with the employees' representatives prior to their change (eg working hours, holidays, etc).

Dismissing and re-engaging employees on new terms

26.146 Although it might be an option to dismiss and re-employ the employees under new terms, this option is highly risky and may be accompanied by claims from the employees for unfair dismissal.

26.147 Further, such an approach might be viewed by the Labour Inspection as circumvention of law by the employer and might result in sanctions being imposed in the amount of up to €200,000.

USING TEMPORARY STAFF

26.148 If the reorganisation requires a temporary increase in the work force, it is possible to use agency workers or conclude employment contracts for a fixed term.

Agency workers

26.149 Agency workers may be used where the employer does not wish to increase its workforce. An agreement with the temporary work agency is signed and the agency provides agency workers to the employer.

26.150 It is necessary to point out that the use of agency workers shall not be misused. Under Slovak laws, a temporary assignment of an agency worker is considered to represent an employment for an indefinite period of time with the employer in case such temporary assignment was agreed between the agency and the employer for this particular agency worker more than five consecutive times within 24 months.

26.151 The employment terms and conditions, including salary terms of agency workers must be at least equally favourable as those of the employer's comparable permanent employees. The employment terms and conditions include:

(a) working hours, breaks at work, rest, overtime work, emergency cover, work at night, holiday and public holidays;

(b) salary terms;
(c) occupational health and safety;
(d) indemnification for occupational injuries or diseases;
(e) compensation during insolvency and protection of temporary employees' claims;
(f) protection of pregnant women, mothers until the end of the ninth month after childbirth, breast-feeding women, women and men who take care of children and young persons;
(g) right to collective bargaining;
(h) catering conditions.

Fixed-term contracts

26.152 If the employer prefers regular employment, and there is only a temporary need for the increase of workforce, fixed-term employment contracts can be concluded.

26.153 Employment for a fixed term needs to be agreed in writing otherwise it is considered to be employment for an indefinite period of time.

26.154 Employment for a fixed term can be concluded for a specific period (up to two years) and for a specific situation (see below).

26.155 A fixed-term employee shall not be preferred or restricted in comparison with a comparable employee as regards employment terms and conditions.

26.156 The employer shall inform, in a suitable manner, the fixed-term employees and the employees' representatives of any available vacancies for employment for an indefinite period.

Renewal of fixed-term contracts

26.157 The employer might conclude an employment for a fixed term without a particular reason. However, in such a case the duration of the employment shall not exceed two years. If a shorter period was agreed, the contract might be prolonged or renewed no more than twice, however, only for a total period of two years.

26.158 Employment contracts for a fixed term and their extension or renewal for a period of more than two years are permitted only if it is necessary for one of the following situations:

(a) substitution of an employee during maternity leave, parental leave, leave immediately following maternity or parental leave, temporary working incapacity or where an employee who has been released long-term for the performance of public office or trade union office;

(b) execution of work that requires a material increase in workforce for a temporary period of time not exceeding eight months within a calendar year;

(c) execution of work that is dependent on the alternation of seasons, recurs every year and does not exceed eight months within a calendar year (seasonal work);

(d) execution of work agreed in a collective agreement;

(e) employment of a university teacher or creative employee engaged in science, research and development is permitted in cases where there is an objective reason resulting from the nature of the activity of the university teacher or the creative employee engaged in science, research and development set out by a special regulation.

26.159 The reason for such extension or renewal shall be specified in the employment contract.

Employment claims

26.160 The district courts in the place of the registered seat of the employer or, alternatively, in the employee's place of work are the competent courts for the proceedings regarding employment claims.

Unfair dismissal

26.161 Any employee, regardless of the length of their employment, can bring a claim for unfair dismissal either because the formal conditions were not met or because the reasons for dismissal are in breach of the law.

26.162 The claim for unfair dismissal must be submitted to the court within two months of the effective date of the termination of employment. This period is preclusive and any such claim brought after the expiry of the two-month period will be automatically dismissed by the court.

Remedies

26.163 If the court considers the dismissal unfair it will declare the dismissal invalid and orders the employer to reinstate the employee and pay them salary compensation.

26.164 Reinstatement of the employee is an automatic result of the dismissal being declared invalid and the only way to rule it out is to request the court during the proceedings to decide that it is not fair to request from the employer to reinstate the employee. Such a request needs to be made by the employer and requests are granted by Slovak courts only in exceptional, well-reasoned cases.

26.165 The salary compensation for the unfair dismissal is provided for the period from the date the employee informed the employer that they consider the dismissal unfair and insists on carrying out their work tasks further until the effectiveness of the judgment on invalidity of the dismissal but not longer than 36 months from the employee informed the employer that they consider the dismissal unfair and insist on carrying out their work tasks.

26.166 The amount of salary compensation is set as average monthly earnings of the employee during the quarter preceding the quarter in which the employment was invalidly dismissed.

26.167 If the total time for which salary compensation should be provided to the employee exceeds 12 months, the employer is entitled to ask the court to proportionally reduce his obligation to provide salary compensation for any time in excess of 12 months or decline award of any salary compensation for any time in excess of 12 months. Such limitation is granted by Slovak courts only in exceptional, well-reasoned cases.

Practical Tip

The meeting of formal requirements on dismissal is checked first by the court. Therefore it is advisable to double check that the prepared dismissal documentation fulfils the statutory requirements and all statutory conditions (including consultation with the employees' representatives) were duly met.

DISCRIMINATION

26.168 If the employee is of the opinion that they were selected for redundancy because of their sex, religion or belief, race, nationality or ethnicity, disability, age, sexual orientation, marital or family status, colour of skin, language, political of other views, national or social origin, property, gender or other status, they might bring discriminatory claims.

Remedies

26.169 Apart from the remedies described above for unfair dismissal, any dismissal based on discriminatory grounds will be considered invalid and it is possible that the employee in such circumstances would also seek appropriate satisfaction or compensation. The amount payable is subject to the employee proving a loss or interference with their rights to non-discrimination which again is subject to approval or variation by the court.

Mutually agreed termination

26.170 The employment might be terminated also with a mutual agreement on employment termination concluded between the employee and the employer.

26.171 If organisational changes, reorganisation and/or redundancy are the reasons for the mutual agreement on employment termination, the reason must be specifically stated in the agreement and the employee is entitled to the statutory redundancy payment (see para **26.85** above) or redundancy payment agreed otherwise (eg in employment contract, collective agreement, etc).

26.172 The agreement on employment termination shall state the date on which the employment terminates. Such date might be set as a fixed date or be described in a manner which allows its setting (eg upon conclusion of a project, etc). However, the date cannot precede the signing date of the agreement on employment termination.

26.173 Employees usually consider the offer to terminate the employment by mutual agreement as the opportunity to negotiate the conditions thereof. Therefore, the finally agreed severance payment might be higher, however, this is not a general rule.

26.174 Although there is no written rule under which the employee must consult legal counsel on the agreement on employment termination, the employee shall be provided with a reasonable time for consideration of the offer made by the employer.

Chapter 27

Workforce Restructuring in Slovenia

Klavdija Erjavec and Ana Lešnik Sitar
Avbreht, Zajc & Partners, Ltd, Ljubljana

INTRODUCTION

27.1 This chapter looks at the employment laws in Slovenia. In April 2013 the new Employment Relationships Act (hereinafter: ZDR-1) came into force in Slovenia. ZDR-1 follows the same principles as the previous act, which regulated employment relationships. The aim of ZDR-1 was to change some sections to reflect decisions of the Constitutional Court, comply with the European Union legislation and with new national legislation, promote employment relationships for unlimited periods of time, simplify the termination procedure of the employment contract and also to take the trend of ageing population into account.

27.2 Slovenia has a continental law system which is based on Roman law. Court decisions in individual cases are important for interpretation of the statute, however the court is not obligated to follow jurisprudence established so far. Importance of jurisprudence is in a way lower as in 'case-law' systems. Directives of the European Union are introduced into Slovenian legal systems mainly via statute.

27.3 If the restructuring requires termination or modification of employment relationships it should be noted, that existing employment contracts are to be respected and that such contracts can only be terminated in the process of restructuring if certain statutory preconditions are satisfied. Unlawful termination of employment contracts can lead to the employer having to pay damages to the employee and very often also the reintegration of the employee.

PREPARING FOR A RESTRUCTURING EXERCISE

27.4 Reasons for restructuring which might result in termination of the employment contract(s), or modifying terms and conditions in the employment contract(s), should be carefully identified. Usually the employer may initiate a restructuring process in case of new market developments (eg stronger competition; lower earnings). Such 'business reason', as defined in ZDR-1, should be carefully documented, in case the employee affected by the restructuring process, challenges the decision. Employers in Slovenia often tend not to document reasons for modifying employment contracts in connection with a restructuring process.

27.5 When making decisions regarding employment relationship(s) the employer should consider, whether termination of employment relationship(s) can be avoided, eg with employment in a different position under different rules.

Identify the employing entity

27.6 Employment relationships are always relationships between employee and employer, the latter usually organised in the form of a legal entity (eg a limited liability company, a sole trader or an independent contractor). Within a group of companies, only one company can be the employer since a group is not a single entity. Transfer of certain competences from one group company to another group company can be a permitted reason for terminating employment relationship(s) in first company.

Collating information to plan and budget for the restructuring exercise

27.7 When planning restructuring it should be noted that employees are understood as being the weaker part of the employment relationship. Consequently the court will decide, in the case of an unclear situation, in favour of the employee.

Employment status

27.8 Generally ZDR-1 protects only employees. However ZDR-1 introduced also certain rights for individuals who are not employed under an employment contract and are consequently not a contractual party to employment relationships. Such special protection was introduced because recently employers have sought to avoid concluding employment contracts. Instead of concluding employment contracts employers demanded, that individuals registered themselves as independent contractors. Consequently a business contract for delivery of services instead of an employment contact was concluded with such individuals.

General protection against dismissal

27.9 In Slovenia all employees have the right not to be unfairly dismissed. Notice of termination of the employment contract should be served on the contractual party whose employment contract is being terminated. The employer may terminate the employee's employment contract only on the basis of a substantiated reason. All employees who have more than one year of continuous service on the day of the notice of termination also enjoy a minimum notice period and have right to severance pay in addition to salary during the notice period.

27.10 The permitted reasons for ordinary termination of a worker's employment contract by the employer are as follows:

- cessation of the need to carry out certain work, under the conditions pursuant to the employment contract, owing to economic, organisational, technological, structural or similar reasons on the employer's side (hereinafter: business reason);
- non-achievement of expected work results because the worker failed to carry out the work in due time, professionally and with due quality; or non-fulfilment of the conditions for carrying out work provided by statute and other regulations issued on the basis of law, for which reason the worker fails to fulfil or cannot fulfil the contractual or other obligations arising from the employment relationship (hereinafter: reason of incapacity);
- breach of a contractual obligation or other obligation arising from the employment relationship (hereinafter: reason of culpability);
- inability to carry out the work under the conditions set out in the employment contract owing to disability in accordance with the regulations governing pension and disability insurance, or with the regulations governing employment rehabilitation and the employment of disabled persons; or
- failure to successfully complete a probation period;

Special protection against dismissal

27.11 In Slovenia special protection against dismissal is enjoyed by the following workers:

- Representatives of workers [member of council of employees; employee's trustee, member of the supervisory board who represents employees, representative of employees in the council of the institute; appointed or elected union representative except with the consent of the employees or employees who elected him or the union, or if he breaches the law, collective agreement or contract of employment, (except if he in case of a business reason for termination of the employment contract rejects appropriate employment by employer or if the termination of the employment relationship is due to the insolvency/dissolution/cessation of the employer is the case)]. Special protection applies for the whole term of exercising the function and additionally one year after termination of the function.

- Employees approaching the age of retirement (currently 55 years of age; this is increased by one year each year until 2017 until age of 58). Special conditions apply in case of dismissal of such workers.
- Mothers are a special protected category during maternity leave, as are parents who have children under the age of one year and in some cases some other categories of parents.
- Disabled persons.
- Workers whose employment contract is terminated for a business reason or for the reason of incapacity and who are, upon the expiry of the period of notice absent from work due to the temporary incapacity for work because of an illness or injury; the employment contract shall be terminated on the day the renewed capacity for work is established and in any event no later than six months after the expiry of the period of notice.

The law additionally specifies which reasons cannot be in any case accepted as reasons for termination of the employment contract. The following shall be deemed as not permitted reasons for ordinary termination of an employment contract:

- temporary absence from work due to inability for work because of an illness or injury or due to the care for family members pursuant to regulations on health insurance, or absence from work due to parental leave pursuant to regulations on parenthood;
- bringing an action, or participating in proceedings, against the employer having alleged breach of contractual and other obligations arising from the employment relationship either before the arbitration, court or administrative authorities;
- trade union membership;
- participation in trade union activities outside working hours;
- participation in trade union activities during working hours in agreement with the employer;
- participation in a strike organised in accordance with the law;
- candidacy for the function of a worker's representative and the current or past performance of this function;
- change of employer;
- race, ethnicity or ethnic origin, skin colour, sex, age, disability, marital status, family obligations, pregnancy, religious and political conviction, national or social origin; or

- entering into a contract for voluntary performance of military service, a contract for performing military service in the Slovenian armed forces reserve, a contract for service in the Civil Protection and voluntary participation in protection and relief in accordance with the law.

WORKFORCE REDUCTION

27.12 Employment contracts can be terminated normally or extraordinarily (gross misconduct). The latter applies in case of eg alleged criminal offences committed by the employee or employer. Extraordinary termination of the employment contract is usually not part of the restructuring procedure and is not discussed in this chapter.

27.13 For the termination of an employment contract a permitted reason must exist. In case of restructuring such permitted reason will be in most cases a 'business reason'. Such business reason exists if need for performing work of a certain worker under the terms from the employment contract ceases to exist. Such business reasons can be economic reasons, organisational reasons, technical reasons etc.

27.14 When a dispute goes to court the employer shall prove existence of the reason for termination of the employment relationship. In such case, the court will not rule on the eligibility of the business decision of the employer, but solely whether such business reason is proven by the employer.

27.15 If the employer concludes that he should terminate employment contracts for a significant number of employees, special procedures apply. What amounts to a 'significant number' depends on the total number of the employees employed by the employer.

Definition of redundancy

27.16 Business reasons for terminating an employment contract exist, if due to economic, organisational, technological, structural or similar reasons on the employer's side, the need for providing certain work under the conditions in the employment contract does not exist anymore.

27.17 The reason must be serious and founded, and shall exclude an option of continuation of the employment relationship. The employer shall prove the validity of such reason.

27.18 An example of a founded reason is reduction in production, which results in termination of the need to perform certain work in accordance with the employment contract. Another example of such a reason, which could be understood as a founded reason, is financial difficulties of the employer which are the result of loss of important clients.

27.19 The procedure of terminating the employment contract is initiated with employers finding that the need for performing certain work in accordance with the employment contract has ceased to exist. Reasons for such a finding of the employer can be economic, organisational, technological, structural or similar reasons on the employer's side.

27.20 Usually the need for reorganisation occurs in the case of rationalisation of the production (eg combining working positions), as a result of the working process not being able to support current cost levels.

27.21 In case of the termination of the employment contract(s) due to a business reason the employer is not obliged to define criteria, which will be used when choosing workers whose employment contract will be terminated. However rules on prohibition of discrimination must still be followed.

27.22 Collective agreements, in force for certain employers, can however place an obligation on such employer, that criteria should also be defined in cases of individual procedures – the dismissal of individual employees.

27.23 Here are some examples of selection criteria for dismissal on the grounds of redundancy of individual employee, if the employer is obliged to provide such selection criteria under the provisions of a collective agreement:

- education of the employee;
- working experiences;
- personal circumstances of the employee; and
- health status

SELECTION CRITERIA

27.24 In the case of the termination of an employment contract with an individual employee, the employer shall define selection criteria only if so required under a collective agreement. On the other hand selection criteria shall be defined in any case, if termination of the employment contract with a 'significant number' of employees is involved.

27.25 What amounts to a 'significant number' of employees depends on the total number of employees. The employer shall prepare a redundancy procedure if it discovers that due to business reasons the following number of employees will become redundant within 30 days:

- At least 10 employees in case of an employer, who employs more than 20 and less than 100 employees;
- At least 10 % of employees in case of an employer, who employs more than 20 and less than 300 employees;

- At least 30 employees in case of an employer, who employees 300 or more employees.

Redundancy procedures

27.26 The 'classical' procedure for termination of an employment contract ('individual procedure') due to business reasons is different from the procedure for termination of employment contracts with 'significant number' of employees. In the latter case, stricter rules shall be followed.

27.27 In the case of termination of an individual employment contract by the employer due to business reasons, the employer shall serve on the employee a notice of termination of the employment contract. Such notice shall provide reasons for termination of employment contract, especially explaining the business reason for terminating the employment contract. The notice of termination shall state the notice period, together with an explanation of which roles will be terminated as well as including terms of the severance payment and a summary of entitlement to appeal such decision.

27.28 As explained above, the procedure for termination of the employment contract is relatively simple in the case of individual termination. The most important element of such procedure is the explanation of the business reason. On the other hand the redundancy procedure where a 'significant number' of employees are affected, as explained above, is more complex. In the latter case a special procedure shall be prepared, as well as selection criteria. Such selection criteria shall be defined in case of individual redundancy procedure solely if a collective agreement requires.

27.29 In case of termination of the employment contract, union and certain other representatives of the employees shall be informed of such termination, if so requested by the employee on whom notice of termination of employment contract is served.

INVOLVEMENT OF EMPLOYEE REPRESENTATIVES IN INDIVIDUAL DISMISSALS

27.30 If so required by the employee, in case of the regular termination of employment contract due to a business reason the employer shall notify in writing the union of which the employee is a member of the intended termination. If the employee is not a member of a union, representatives of employees shall be informed of intended termination of an employment contract due to business reasons, if so required by the employee. The union / representative of the employee can present an opinion on the intended termination of employment contract, however such opinion cannot affect termination of the employment contract.

27.31 Before making the final decision on reducing the number of employees the employer must inform the council of employees and demand collective consultation (even if there is just one termination of a contract). Required information shall be provided by the employer to the council of employees at least 30 days before making the final decision and the deadline for collective council consultation shall be at latest 15 days after the making of the decision. The consultation taking place between the council of employees and employer includes the duty of the employer to inform the council of employees of anticipated decisions in relation to the statutory and HR questions and in relation to safety and health at work and to consult such council and to try to harmonise positions.

AVOIDING COMPULSORY REDUNDANCIES

27.32 The employer can offer the employee a new employment contract in a different working position.

27.33 In the case of the offer of a new employment contract according to the previous point, the new working position must be appropriate. An appropriate new working position is understood to be employment in a working position for which same kind and level of education is required, as for of the previous working position. The place of work on such working position shall not be more than three hours away from the residence of the employee (by public transport or by other transport, organised by the employer).

27.34 With the intention of avoiding the termination of the employment relationship the employer can offer additional education to the employees or retrain employees for employment in another role.

27.35 If the employer cannot provide a minimum of six months' work in each calendar year to the employees, employer can, with the intention of preservation of the employment relationship, order in writing to the employee(s) that such employee(s) shall wait for work at home. In such case employee is entitled to receive remuneration for such 'waiting for work', at a rate of 80% of the net salary of such employee in the last three months. If after six months the employer still cannot provide work for the employee(s), employees are entitled to the remuneration in the amount of 100 % of the average monthly salary in last three months prior 'waiting for work at home' occurred.

27.36 Recently in Slovenia some employers concluded employment contracts with employees for working hours which were shorter than full time in order to preserve employment relationships. In such case employees still have employment relationships, but of course for lower salary since they do not work in the 'full time' regime.

ALTERNATIVE EMPLOYMENT

27.37 During the redundancy procedure the employer is not obliged to assess whether it is possible to employ the employee under modified conditions or in other working position(s). The same applies in relation to the possibility of qualifying the employee for another working position.

27.38 However the employer can (but is not obliged to do so) in process of termination of employment contract(s) offer employment to the affected employees in other working positions/under terms if such new employment is appropriate (one where the same kind and level of education is required). This is to prevent employers from using such an option with the intention to avoid payment of severance payment to the employee concerned.

27.39 If the employee agrees to take up a different role, the new employment contract must be signed within 15 days. If the employee accepts offer of the employer to conclude new employment contract for indefinite period of time, such employee is not entitled to severance payment, however is entitled to demand legal protection of the competent courts. Consequently, such employee can still question the stated business reason before the competent court if she/he believes that such reason is unfounded. If the employee is successful in such court procedure, the previous employment contract (the terminated one) would be reinstated.

27.40 If the employee does not accept the offer of the employer to conclude a new employment contact for an indefinite period of time and the employment relationship is terminated, such employee is not entitled to a severance payment, to which she/he would be entitled according to the legislation in the case of termination of the employment contract due to valid business reasons.

27.41 The employer can offer also so called 'non-appropriate employment' (employment, which is not appropriate as defined above). If such offer is accepted by the employee, the employee is entitled to a partial severance payment, as agreed with the employer. The amount of such severance payment is not regulated in law, but is in practice half of the severance payment, which would be received by the employee.

27.42 According to the legislation another option is the preservation of the employment relationship(s). If the employee concludes during notice period an employment contract with another employer, the previous employer is not obliged to pay a severance payment to such employee, if the new employer undertakes the obligation to respect the duration of the employment relationship concluded with previous employer, when calculating the minimum required notice period and minimal severance payment.

Collective redundancy procedure

27.43 Collective redundancy procedure is a redundancy procedure, in which employment contracts with 'significant numbers' of employees are terminated by the employer.

27.44 'Significant number' of employees depends on the number of the total employees employed by the employer. The employer shall prepare a program of resolution of redundant workers if the employer discovers that, due to business reasons, within 30 days the following number of employees will become redundant:

- At least 10 employees in the case of an employer, who employs more than 20 and less than 100 employees;
- At least 10 % of employee in the case of an employer, who employs more than 20 and less than 300 employees;
- At least 30 employees in the case of an employer, who employs 300 or more employees.

27.45 According to Slovenian jurisprudence only workers whose employment contracts will be terminated due to the business reasons, are to be counted when defining 'significant number' of employees. Consequently employment relationships terminated on other grounds and not on the ground of business reasons are not relevant in this case (eg cancellation of employment contract by agreement).

27.46 The employer must inform any union organised by the employer and the National Institute for Employment about the reasons for termination of the need for the work of employees, the number and categories of all employed employees, and an expected deadline, during which the requirement for the employees will cease and on the proposed selection criteria for making employees redundant. Such notification must be in writing.

27.47 Before accepting a decision on lowering number of the employees, the employer shall inform the council of employees and demand collective consultation. The required information must be provided by the employer to the council of employees at least 30 days before accepting the decision and the deadline for collective council consultation shall be at latest 15 days after accepting the decision.

27.48 Collective consultation of the council of employees and employer represents an obligation of the employer related to the informing the council of employees about anticipated decisions related to the situation as well as HR questions in relation to health and safety at work. The objective of such collective consultation is the harmonisation of the positions.

INVOLVEMENT OF EMPLOYEE REPRESENTATIVES IN COLLECTIVE DISMISSALS

27.49 Where there is a collective redundancy procedure (termination of employment contracts with 'significant number' of employees) the union(s), recognised by the employer shall be informed as soon as possible on reasons for termination of the need for the services of the employees, the number and categories of all employees, the anticipated categories of redundant employees, the anticipated deadline during which the need for work of the employee will cease to exist and on the proposed selection criteria for defining redundant employees. Such notice shall be made in writing.

27.50 Additionally the employer shall, as a first step, with the objective of achieving agreement, consult union(s) recognised by the employer on the proposed selection criteria for redundant employees. When preparing a program to decide upon redundant workers the union(s) shall be consulted in relation to the possible means for preventing and limitation of number of termination of employment contracts and on the possible means for preventing and mitigating adverse consequences.

27.51 A copy of a written notice on the reasons for termination of need for the services of employees, the number and categories of all employees, anticipated categories of redundant employees, the anticipated deadline during which the need for work of the employees will cease to exist and on the suggested selection criteria for redundant employees shall be sent to the national Institute for employment.

27.52 Prior to acceptance of redundancy terms an employee should inform the council of workers and demand common consultation in relation to the HR of the company to include addressing the number of positions by which the workforce is to be reduced. If a council of workers is recognised within the employer company, the employer shall inform such council and demand common consultation with the council of the employees.

27.53 The required information shall be submitted by the employer to the council of workers at latest 30 days prior to accepting the decision and the deadline for common consultation shall be at latest 15 days prior to accepting the decision. Common consultation between council of employees and employer represents a duty of the employer to inform the council of employees about anticipated decisions in relation to the statutory and HR questions and in relation to health and safety at work and to consult such council and to try to harmonise positions.

27.54 If decisions by the employer which are connected with a change of activity, reduction of economic activity, changes in organisation of the production, modification of technology, statutory changes or sale of the company or a substantial part of it leads to the reduction of a 'significant number' of employees, the employer shall acquire within eight days the consent of the council of employees. The council of employees can reject such consent only if the decision on reducing the number of employees does not include a program to resolve the redundancy of employees under the rules on employment relationships or if reasons for the decision on reducing number of employees are not well founded. If the council of employees rejects consent without grounds, such rejection of consent does not have an effect on correctness and lawfulness of the decision of employer.

ELECTION OF EMPLOYEE REPRESENTATIVES FOR COLLECTIVE CONSULTATION PURPOSES

27.55 In the case of the termination of employment contracts of a 'significant number' of employees the employer is obliged to inform union(s) recognised by the employer and which are classified as representative union(s).

27.56 Representative union(s) are union(s), which:

- are democratic and grant freedom of access to the union(s), and proper maintenance of rights and obligations of members;
- have been functioning for at least six months;
- are independent from governmental bodies and employers;
- are financed predominantly from the fees of the members/their other own resources.

27.57 A representative union can appoint or elect a union representative to represent the union in relation to an employer in respect of its members. If a representative is not appointed, the union is represented by its president. Unions shall inform the employer of the appointment or election of a union representative.

27.58 If an employer employs more than 20 employees with active voting rights a council of employees shall be formed. In case of the termination of the employment contracts of a 'significant number' of employees the employer shall inform the council of employees thereof.

27.59 The election of members of a council of employees is confidential and is to be by direct elections of individuals. Each employee shall have one vote. Employees shall vote in person, rather than by proxy.

27.60 Representatives of employees (members of an employer's council, employees' representative, member of a supervisory board representing employees, representative of employees in the council of an institute, or an appointed or elected union's trustee) enjoy special protection against dismissal. If such a person acts according to the law, collective agreement and employment contract (except in the case of termination of employment contracts due to qualifying business reasons) and he rejects an offer of appropriate employment, special protection applies for the period in which such person performs relevant functions, plus another year after termination of such function.

27.61 Membership in the union, participation in union's activities outside working hours and participation in union's activities within working hours according to the agreement with the employer are defined as invalid reasons for termination of an employment contract.

REGULATORY REQUIREMENTS

27.62 The employer shall inform the national Institute for Employment in writing in the following events:

- On it discovering a reduction in the need for the work of a 'significant number' of employees;
- On it carrying out a consultation with a union;
- On the reasons for a reduction in the need for the work of employees;
- The number and categories of all employees;
- The anticipated categories of redundant employees;
- The anticipated deadline, within which the need for the work of the employees will cease.

27.63 After the employer provides such notice to the National Institute for Employment, the employer can terminate employment contracts with redundant employees. The defined program in respect of dealing with redundant employees must be respected, but not prior to the expiration of a 30-day period from the date of service of notice by the employer.

27.64 The employer must give consideration to, and respect, the final suggestions provided by the National Institute for Employment on possible means to avoid or mitigate the number of terminated employment relationships and means for mitigation of adverse consequences of termination of employment relationship(s).

27.65 If so required by the National Institute for Employment, the employer must not terminate the employment contracts of employees prior to the expiration of a 60-day period from serving the notice on the National Institute for Employment.

SANCTIONS

27.66 A council of employees has the right to issue a decision which has the effect of blocking the individual decision of the employer and at the same time prescribes a procedure for resolving the dispute. This applies in the following cases:

- If the employer does not inform the council of employees in advance in accordance with the law before making its final decision on the issues, related to the changes of activities of the employer, the reduction in reducing economic activities, modifications in the organisation of production, the modification of technology, statutory changes or the sale of the company or a substantial part of the company. In such a case the council of employees shall act within eight days from the day on which the council of employees was informed on such issues.
- If the employer does not notify the council of employees, does not respect deadlines or does not institute collective consultation with the council of employees in respect of HR changes, the council of employees should act within eight days of it becoming aware of such facts.

27.67 In either of the circumstances referred to in para **27.67** above, the employer shall not enforce its decision until final decision of competent body.

27.68 A penalty of between €3,000 and €20,000 applies for the employer (whether a legal person or independent contractor) if such employer performs a procedure of termination of the employment contracts of a 'significant number' of employees in violation of the provisions of the legislation. Responsible officers of such an employer is liable to a fine of between €450 and €2,000.

27.69 An employee can file a lawsuit if his employment contract was terminated during a procedure for the termination of employment contracts of a 'significant number' of employees and such procedure was not performed according to the legislation. Such lawsuit must be filed within 30 days from the receipt of the notice of termination of the employment contract with the competent labour and social court.

NOTICE

27.70 A notice period starts to run on the day when written notice of termination of an employment contract is served or, alternatively, on the day which is defined in the program of redundancy. A notice period is the period between serving the notice on termination employment contract and termination of the employment relationship. In this notice period the employee still performs work.

27.71 If in the notice period the employer cannot provide work to the employee, the employer can decide that the employee should wait for work at home. In such a case the employee is entitled to remuneration in the amount of 100 % of his average monthly full time salary for the last three months.

27.72 Both contracting parties can terminate the employment contract within the notice period. The notice period is defined in law and in the employment contract. If the definition of the notice period is in the employment contract, the contracting parties shall respect the minimum applicable notice period, as defined in ZDR-1.

27.73 In a case of the ordinary termination of the employment contract by the employer due to valid business reasons the notice period is:

- 15 days, if the employee was employed by the employer for up to one year;
- 30 days, if the employee was employed by the employer for more than one but less than two years.

27.74 In case of employment for more than two years, the notice period is 30 days plus two days for each completed year of employment by the employee, but with a maximum of 60 days.

27.75 In case of employment by the employee for longer than 25 years the notice period is 80 days, if not defined otherwise in a collective agreement, but in any event not less than 60 days.

27.76 When calculating applicable notice periods the period of employment of the employee by the employer's legal predecessors are also to be taken into account.

27.77 In case of termination of the employment contact by the employer, the employee has the right to be absent from work in order to search for new employment for up to two hours per week with pay. During the notice period the employer shall additionally allow the employee time off from work to look for new employment including attending interviews and/or workshops etc. for a minimum of one day per week. The employer shall pay the employee remuneration for such absence in the amount of his average monthly full time salary in the last three months.

Pay in lieu of notice

27.78 Instead of enforcing the notice period the employer and employee can agree in writing that the employee shall receive remuneration without having to work during the notice period. In practice such remuneration equals the amount, which would be received by the employee if the employee had continued to work in the notice period. In such case the employment relationship ceases to exist on the day agreed in the written agreement.

REDUNDANCY PAYMENT

27.79 An employee, whose employment relationship was terminated due to valid business reasons is entitled to receive a redundancy payment. The basis for calculation of the redundancy payment is the average monthly salary received by the employee or which would be received by the employee, if the employee were to work in the period of last three months before termination of employment relationship.

27.80 The redundancy payment shall be paid by the employer to the employee at the termination of the employment contract, except otherwise provided by collective agreement(s). In practice collective agreement(s) do not provide such alternatives.

Statutory redundancy pay calculation

27.81 The employee is entitled to a redundancy payment in the following amounts:

- 1/5 of the basis identified in para 27.79 for each fulfilled year of the work by the employee, if employment relationship lasted more than one year and up to 10 years;
- 1/4 of the basis identified in para 27.79 for each fulfilled year of the work by the employee, if employment relationship lasted more than 10 and up to 20 years;
- 1/3 of the basis identified in para 27.79 for each fulfilled year of the work by the employee, if employment relationship lasted more than 20 years.

27.82 When calculating applicable notice periods the period of employment of the employee by the employer's legal predecessors are also to be taken into account

27.83 The amount of the redundancy payment is limited. It shall not exceed ten times the amount identified in para 27.81 unless otherwise provided in collective agreements.

Enhanced redundancy payments

27.84 On the basis of a collective agreement, or as mutually agreed at the time, enhanced redundancy payments can be agreed. In this case the limitations above do not apply.

Post-termination restrictive covenants

27.85 Under Slovenian legislation a non-competition clause, which would prevent an employee from working for competing entities after termination of employment relationship is not enforceable/valid if the employment relationship has been terminated for a business reason.

27.86 In the case of a termination of employment relationship due to other reasons (eg termination by the employee, extraordinary termination of employment contract by the employer) a non-competition clause is permitted. It shall not be effective for more than two years from the termination of employment contract and it must be agreed in writing.

27.87 In an employee is prevented by a non-competition clause from achieving earnings comparable with his prior earnings, such employee is entitled to demand compensation from the former employee for respecting the non-competition clause. Such remuneration shall be stated in the employment contract and shall amount to at least one third of the average salary of the employee within the three months prior termination of employment contract. A non-competition clause is not valid if such compensation is not stated in the employment contract.

WORKFORCE REDUCTION IN CONNECTION WITH SHARE SALE OR SHARE PURCHASE

27.88 A change of ownership of the share(s) of the company (employer) does not affect in any way the existing employment contract(s). For example, in the case of the merger of two companies, one company is the general legal successor and therefore all rights and obligations are not modified in any way as a result of the change of ownership.

27.89 Changes in the ownership of a company's share(s) can however eventually result in subsequent termination of employment relationship(s). For example, if the acquirer of a business owns other companies and such acquirer decides that certain activities will be provided by other companies within the group through outsourcing, certain employees could become redundant. Another such example would be, that change in ownership of share(s) could result in organisational changes, what could again lead to the termination of employment relationship(s).

27.90 Another issue relates to a de facto change of employer. In situations where the transfer of the business/part of the business is carried out by operation of law or statutory provision, a business transaction or as a result of a court decision, or due to a merger or de-merger, leads to the actual change in the employer, the rights and obligations from the employment relationship(s) are transferred to the acquirer. In such case the workers employed by the former employer and their employment relationships are deemed to be legally transferred to the new employer, including with all applicable rights and obligations.

27.91 If the employee refuses a transfer in accordance with para **27.90**, the new employer can exceptionally terminate the employment contract concluded with such employee.

27.92 In the case of a situation as described in para 27.90, the rights and obligations under a collective agreement which applied to previous employer, shall be respected by the new employer for a period of at least one year. This does not apply if the collective agreement comes to an end before the expiration of one year or if a new collective agreement is concluded prior to the expiration of the period of one year.

27.93 If, due to objective reasons arising within two years from the date of the transfer, conditions affecting the employment contract worsen or are significantly changed and the new employer terminates an employment contract, the employee has the same rights as if the employment contract had been terminated by the employer due to valid business reasons. The relevant notice period, right to redundancy payment and all other rights are defined by reference to the total length of service with both employers.

27.94 Both employers are jointly liable for claims from employees relating to claims which occurred before the date of the transfer, and also for claims related to termination according to the previous point.

Changing employment terms and conditions

27.95 The employment contract is a two-party instrument, which cannot be unilaterally modified. The law prescribes the mandatory elements of employment contract. Additionally the law defines which modifications of a concluded employment contract are so important that it is not sufficient to amend by way of annex to the employment contract but it is necessary to agree a new employment contract, to replace the previous one.

27.96 Modifications of an employment contract can be suggested by any of the contracting parties. It should be noted that any modification is only legally binding if it is agreed by both contracting parties. As mentioned above in case of modifying certain elements of employment contract a new contract must be concluded.

27.97 No modifications of the law, collective agreements or general acts of the employer can affect those rights of an employee which are favourable to the employee in an employment contract.

Unilateral changes

27.98 Unilateral changes of employment contract are not permitted or binding. Modifications of general provisions (eg rules, accepted by the employer) cannot amend rights of an employee, if the employment contract defines rights of employee more favourably.

27.99 If an employer seeks to modify general provisions but in a manner which denies certain rights to the employee, the employee can nevertheless enforce such unlawfully denied rights through a court order.

Dismissing and re-engaging employees on new terms

27.100 We have discussed above the conditions under which the issue of new employment contracts to existing employees is permitted. In practice, contracting parties to the employment contract define in new employment contract redefines all existing applicable terms. Employees cannot waive certain fundamental rights, even if a new employment contract seeks to include such a provision permitting the waiver of certain fundamental rights.

27.101 As an example of a right which cannot be waived by employees is the right to receive salary, which is appropriately calculated. If an employer seeks to pay to the employee a salary, which is not calculated according to the agreed provisions, the employee cannot waive such right. Even if a new employment contract would include such a provision, such waiver would not be enforceable. Of course it is the employee's decision, whether the employee will enforce such right or not.

USING TEMPORARY STAFF

27.102 Using temporary staff might be questionable if an employer has terminated existing employment contracts due to business reasons. Where an employer terminates one or more employment contracts due to business reasons and later hires temporary staff such as agency workers to perform work in the affected roles, such situation could be treated by the court as 'in fraudem legis agree' (ie acting against purpose of the law but not, formally, an infringement of the law).

27.103 Entering into employment relationship for a definite period of time is also limited by legislation. Generally employment relation ought to be concluded for an indefinite period of time if employee will perform work in the same role. There are certain exemptions from such 'two-year rule' eg workers, who perform work connected with a specific mandate (eg CEO, appointed for four years).

Agency workers

27.104 Agency workers shall not perform work in following circumstances:

- for performing the work of employees who are on strike;

- if the customer of such services terminated employment contracts with a 'significant number' of employees within 12 months prior to hiring agency workers;
- in the case of workplaces where it is determined, on the basis of an evaluation of hazard, that workers at such workplaces are exposed to dangers and hazards, which requires restrictions in the operation of such workplaces;
- in other cases, where a higher level of protection of work is prescribed within collective agreement on the level of activity by reason of the safety and health of workers.

27.105 The number of agency workers shall not exceed 25 % of the employed workers, unless otherwise permitted by collective agreement on the level of activity. When calculating the highest feasible number of agency workers, employees employed for an indefinite period of time shall not be taken into account. The said limitation on use of agency worker does not apply for small employers – ie employers who employ fewer than ten employees.

27.106 If so required by union or council of employees or employees' trustee, an employer of agency workers shall inform them on a yearly basis about the reasons for the use of agency workers and the number of such agency workers.

27.107 The main advantage of agency workers is flexibility, but since such workers are not employed, such agency workers can feel inferior or less motivated.

27.108 Agency workers have the same rights as if they were employed directly by the user. The employer shall ensure that the same working conditions, same payment for same work, same extras, benefits and other payments (remuneration for meals, remuneration for arrival at work, remuneration for annual leave), which are offered to equivalent regularly employed workers are provided.

27.109 Agency workers are not bound by internal rules or collective agreement(s) applying to the employer of such agency worker, but all such rules and collective agreements are applicable to the user. Enlisted agency workers have the same obligations as regularly employed workers.

Fixed-term contracts

27.110 The general approach is that employment contracts are concluded for an indefinite period of time. In certain cases however, prescribed in legislation, an employment contract can be concluded for a fixed-term.

27.111 The contracting parties shall have the same rights and obligations during the course of an employment relationship for a defined period of time as they do in the case of an employment relationship for an indefinite period of time, unless the law prescribes otherwise (the employment contract shall be terminated upon the expiration of the period for which it was concluded, and there is no need to give notice to terminate the contract).

27.112 According to the legislation an employment contract can be concluded for a defined period for time in the following cases:

- for performance of work, which lasts only for defined period of time due to the nature of such work;
- for substitution of temporarily absent employees;
- temporary increase in the business of the employer (eg new projects for a limited period of time);
- employment of a foreign person or a person without citizenship, who has employment permission for a defined period of time, other than where the permission is for personal services;
- management personnel (eg CEO) or proxies (entered on the court register as representative of the company)
- executive workers who manage a business field or organisational unit at the employer and are authorised to conclude legal transactions or to make independent personnel and organisational decisions in the performance of seasonal work;
- workers, who conclude employment contract for definite period of time in connection with preparation for work, training or improvement for work or education;
- employment for a definite period of time during an adaptation period on the basis of a final decision or certificate of the competent body, issued in the process of acknowledgements of qualifications under specific legislation;
- performing public work which contributes to the policy of active employment under the law;
- preparation or performance of work, organised as a project;
- work required during a period of introduction of new programs, new technologies and other technical or technological improvements of the working process or due to the training of workers;
- hand-over of work;
- elected or appointed officers or other workers, whose work is connected to the term of office or officers in local municipalities, political parties, unions, chambers, societies and their networks.
- other cases, defined in the law or in collective agreement on the level of activity.

27.113 A contract for a defined period is concluded for the time that the work is to be performed. An employer shall not conclude one or more subsequent employment contracts for defined periods of time for the same work, if the cumulative period would exceed two years. This does not apply in following cases:

- those prescribed in law;

- the substitution of temporarily absent workers
- the employment of foreign persons or persons without citizenship, who have employment permission for a defined period of time, other than where the permission is for personal services ;
- management personnel or proxies (see para **27.112** above);
- elected or appointed officers or other workers, whose work is connected to the term of office or officers in local municipalities, political parties, unions, chambers, societies and their networks.

27.114 Work is considered as 'the same work' if it is the same working position or type of work as that which is in fact performed under certain the given employment contract.

27.115 An employment contract for a defined period of time for the purpose of a 'hand-over' must be finish within at most one month.

27.116 In case of work, organised as a project, a fixed term employment contract may be concluded for more than two years if the employment contract is for the whole duration of the project.

27.117 If the period between expiration of one employment contract, concluded for a defined period of time, and the conclusion of a second employment contract for a defined period of time is three months or less it is presumed that the employment contract is actually for an indefinite period of time.

27.118 Where an employment contract for a defined period of time is concluded in breach of the provisions of legislation or collective agreements or if an employee continues in the role after expiration of the fixed period set out in the contract, such contract will be considered to have been concluded for an indefinite period of time.

27.119 An employment contract for defined period of time expires:

- at expiration of agreed period;
- on performance of agreed work;
- when reason for which the employment contract for a defined period was concluded, ceases to exist.

27.120 An employment contract concluded for a defined period of time can be terminated early, if so agreed between the contracting parties prior to the expiration of the agreed period or if other legislative reasons for termination of employment contract for a definite period occur.

27.121 Employees, whose fixed term employment contract is terminated due to having expired are entitled to receive severance payment. This does not apply if:

- the employment contract for a fixed term was entered into to provide for the substitution of a temporarily absent employee;

- the employment contract for a fixed term was concluded for performing seasonal work, which lasts less than three months in a calendar year;
- the employment contract for a fixed term was concluded for performing public works;
- the employment contract for a fixed term was concluded under a legislative programme intended to promote an active policy of employment.

27.122 The basis for calculation of severance payment is average monthly salary of employee for full time job in the period of last three months prior to termination of an employment contract for a fixed term.

27.123 If the employment contract was concluded for one year or less, the employee has the right to a severance payment equal to 1/5 of the amount from point 0.

27.124 If the fixed term employment contract is concluded for more than one year, the employee has the right to receive severance payment from point 0 plus 1/60 of said basic for each fulfilled month of work for the employer.

27.125 If after termination of an employment contract for a fixed term such employee continues to work for the same employer on a basis of another employment contract for a fixed term, the severance payment shall be paid for the total period of time during which employee worked for such employer.

27.126 An employee is not entitled to receive a severance payment if the employer and such employee enter into an employment contract for an indefinite period of time during the period of a fixed term employment contract, or after the termination of a fixed term employment contract. The same applies if the employee continues to work on a basis of an employment contract for an indefinite period of time or if the employee does not conclude an employment contract for an indefinite period of time for an appropriate working position, offered by the employer after expiration of a fixed term employment contract.

EMPLOYMENT CLAIMS

27.127 Labour courts decide on labour disputes in the first instance. Four labour courts are established in Slovenia (Ljubljana, Maribor, Celje and Koper). Courts perform duties by hearings in the actual court as well as hearings at separate external divisions of the court.

27.128 Appeals against Labour court decisions are in the first instance heard by the Higher Labour and Social court. Appeals against decisions of the Higher Labour and Social court are heard by the Labour division of Supreme Court of the Republic of Slovenia.

27.129 If a dispute arises and the worker (employee) is the claimant, proceedings must generally be filed in the defendant's (ie the employer's) local court. This is the place where employer has its seat / permanent domicile. Additionally also the following courts shall have jurisdiction to decide on the case:

- the court where work is performed/was performed
- the court where the employment relationship was concluded.

27.130 If the employer is the claimant, such claimant shall issue the action in the court where employee as the defendant has his permanent residence.

27.131 In individual labour disputes related to rights and obligations concerning intellectual property created during the employment relationship, the Labour and Social court in Ljubljana shall have exclusive jurisdiction to decide on such case.

27.132 A Labour court has jurisdiction to decide on the following individual labour disputes:

- on the conclusion, existence, duration and termination of employment relationship;
- on the rights, obligations and liabilities from employment relationship between employer and employee/his legal successors;
- on rights and obligations from relationships between an agency worker and user of an agency worker according to the agreement between the agency worker and the user;
- in relation to the interview and selection procedure in connection with the employment of the employee between employer and prospective employee;
- on rights and obligations regarding intellectual property arising between employer and employee in the course of an employment relationship;
- on performance of work by children aged under 15, trainees, pupils and students;
- on education matters involving the employer and pupil or student;
- on voluntary training periods;
- in other cases, prescribed by law.

27.133 A Labour court has jurisdiction to decide in the dispute on compensation (including where the intervening party is an insurance company).

27.134 A Labour court has jurisdiction to decide in the following collective labour disputes:

- on validity of collective agreements, implementation of such agreements between parties to a collective agreement or between parties to a collective agreement and other persons;
- on competence for collective negotiations;
- on compliance of collective agreements with law, mutual compliance with collective agreements and general compliance of the employer with law and with collective agreements;

- on legality of strike and other industrial actions;
- on participation of workers in management of the company;
- on competence of union in relation to the employment relationship;
- in relation to the appointment of representatives of union;
- in cases defined by statute.

27.135 In the court of first instance the senate shall decide the dispute, unless specified in statute that a single judge shall decide the dispute. A single judge shall decide on individual labour disputes, where the value of the claim does not exceed the value, from which a revision is allowed (currently such value is €40,000).

27.136 Regardless of the value of the claim a single judge shall decide the following disputes:

- In individual disputes, related to the suspension of employment contract, probation work, over-time work, breaks, rests and annual leaves and other absence from work, obligation to perform work due to recognised extraordinary reasons, in cases of a disciplinary penalty, which does not result in the dismissal of the employee, temporary removal from work due to the imposition of a disciplinary procedure and temporary relocation.
- In labour and social disputes senate of the court of first instance is composed of one judge as the president of the senate and two members of the senate as jury. One of such two members shall be elected from the list of the candidate of workers/insured persons and the other from the list of the candidates of employers/institutes. The candidates can propose local representatives, but may also propose organisations with an interest such as clubs or associations registered and operating in the area, with the exception of political parties, which cannot directly propose candidates.

27.137 Revision, on which the Supreme Court of the Republic of Slovenia decides, is allowed in following labour disputes:

- In pecuniary individual labour disputes, in which revision is allowed according to the rules of civil procedure (currently this amount is €40,000);
- In individual labour disputes, related to the existence or termination of employment relationships;
- In collective labour disputes;
- If allowed by the court. Revision will be allowed by the court if it can be expected, that the Supreme Court of Republic of Slovenia will decide on an important legal question, which is important for ensuring legal certainty, unified use of law or for development of law through jurisprudence. Revision will be especially allowed in the following cases:
  - if it relates to a question of law, in relation to which the decision of second instance differs from case law established by the Supreme Court of the Republic of Slovenia; or
  - if it relates to a question of law, in relation to which lack of case law exists or case law of higher courts is not unified and therefore unclear; or
  - if it relates to a legal question, in relation to which jurisprudence of Supreme Court of the Republic of Slovenia is not harmonised.

UNFAIR DISMISSAL

27.138 An employee, who believes that his employment contract was terminated in breach of legislation has the right to initiate within 30 days a court procedure to protect his/her rights. This time starts to run from the date of serving of notice on termination of employment contract or from the time, when such employee became aware of the violation of his/her right(s).

27.139 In relation to the right to be protected from unfair dismissal, the type of employment relationship (definite/indefinite period of time) is irrelevant. Every employee enjoys such a right.

Remedies

27.140 If a competent court rules that an employment contract was terminated unlawfully, the court orders that the employee shall be reinstated and that the employer shall compensate such worker from the date of unfounded termination until the date of the court's decision for all due monthly remuneration of salaries including all taxes and contributions. Consequently the employment relationship between employer and employee continues.

27.141 In certain cases the court can decide that employment should not be re-instated despite termination in breach of the employment contract, if this would not be in the interest of any of the contracting parties. This outcome can be suggested by any of the contracting parties. In this case the court recognises the right to receive remuneration for salaries until the date of the judgment. In such cases, the court decides that employment relationship shall be terminated with effect from the date of the judgment and that the employee shall, due to the termination of the employment contract, receive fair compensation. This 'fair compensation' cannot exceed an amount equal to 18 months' salary of the employee (average monthly salary from last three months prior to termination of employment contract). In practice such 'fair compensation' is between four and six months' salary.

27.142 The court considers the duration of the employment contract, the possibility of the employee obtaining new employment and the reasons for termination of the employment contract when deciding on the amount of remuneration where the employment relationship has been terminated.

27.143 Certain collective agreements recognise the right of employees to demand a contractual penalty in case of a confirmed unlawful termination of an employment relationship. Such amount is defined in a fixed amount or in certain cases in a number of months' salary.

DISCRIMINATION

27.144 An employee can, within five years after termination of an employment relationship or during the employment relationship, take court proceedings to enforce his rights related to the protection from discrimination. In such a case the employee will demand damages incurred due to the discrimination.

Remedies

27.145 In cases of discrimination the rules of civil law on damages shall apply. All forms of damages (including financial damages and damages for injury to feelings) are considered as relevant. When ruling on the amount of the compensation it shall be considered that such amount shall prevent the employer from further or repeated discrimination.

MUTUALLY AGREED TERMINATION

27.146 As in the case of any other contract, an employment contract can be mutually terminated. This leads to the termination of the employment relationship, since an employment contract is basis for employment relationship.

Settlement agreements

27.147 It is important that agreement on the termination of an employment contract is concluded in written form. It is up to each contracting party to decide whether an attorney at law or any other professional advisor shall be asked to provide advice in relation to an agreement on the termination of an employment contract.

27.148 One of the main issues that shall be observed when concluding such agreement is, that concluding such an agreement to terminate the employment contract results in the employee no longer having any rights to claim under insurance policies against unemployment. Part of such agreement on termination of employment contract should expressly state that the employee is aware that conclusion of the agreement on termination of the employment contract will result in the cessation of any rights to claim under an insurance policy against unemployment.

27.149 It is up to the contracting parties, the signatories of such an agreement, which additional issues shall be included in such agreement. In practice often provisions regarding the use of annual leave before termination of the employment relationship is part of such agreement, as well as provisions related to outstanding disputes which arose during the employment relationship.

Chapter 28
Workforce Restructuring in Spain

Sonia Cortés
Abdón Pedrajas & Molero, Madrid

INTRODUCTION

28.1 The main source of employment law in Spain is the Workers Statute (Royal Legislative Decree 1/1995, October 24th), which covers most of the areas of employment. There are however a number of other relevant provisions, including the Gender Equality Act 3/2007, the Unionisation Act 19/1977 and the Act on Temporary Agencies 14/1994, among others. All these provisions are applicable in the same terms in all regions of Spain. Collective agreements are also sources of law. Collective agreements are agreements entered into between employers' associations and trade unions for specific sectors (eg chemical industry, retail trade, metal industry, etc) and for specific territories (national, regional or provincial). Employers and employee representatives may also enter into collective agreements within the scope of the relevant company. Collective agreements complying with the legal requirements of parties' representation authority and formalities (including publication in the Official Gazette) have legally binding effect and thus bind all employers and employees within their scope, whether the employers or employees are members of the negotiating employers' association or trade unions or not. There are close to 5,000 different collective agreements in Spain. Collective agreements are important sources of law that should be borne in mind when preparing a redundancy plan, since they might provide rules that apply to the redundancy plan, particularly with respect to the calculation of the salary for each employee as the basis to calculate severances. There is also a Regulation on collective redundancies (Royal Decree 1483/2012 of 29 October) that should be taken into account with respect to the formalities during the consultancy process and the documentation to be delivered to employee representatives.

28.2 Spain has a civil law system. Spanish employment law has two special features as compared to other civil law countries. The first (as referred to above) is that collective agreements are a source of law with resulting great autonomy of social parties (employers and workers' representatives) to negotiate working conditions. The second feature is the importance of case law.

28.3 It should be noted that Spanish law is mandatory in most aspects, including for severance. Therefore, in a collective redundancy process, any agreement between the employee or employee representatives and the employer providing for a severance below the minimum severance for termination provided by law is bound to be declared null and void. As for non-collective terminations, employee waivers require an actual situation or dispute to be settled – meaning that employee waivers beforehand will be null and void.

28.4 As in the vast majority of European jurisdictions, Spanish law does not admit the concept of 'employment at will' and thus the legal requirements in respect of employment termination should be taken into consideration.

PREPARING FOR A RESTRUCTURING EXERCISE

28.5 During a restructuring exercise there are different types of measures that can be carried out, depending on the specific needs of the business. This may involve the need to reduce the workforce, change employment conditions, use of agency workers or temporary staff, outsourcing and offshoring, or technical changes such as installing new machinery.

28.6 It is important to compile all information related to employee working conditions. This information will be necessary to start planning a restructuring exercise, but it is also needed due to the obligation of the company to hand such information over to the relevant employee representatives.

THE FIRST KEY ISSUES TO CONSIDER ARE SET OUT BELOW.

Identify the employing entity

28.7 In situations where group affiliates have a high degree of interconnection and there is interference among them (for example, with respect to supervisory and disciplinary authorities, reporting lines, financial means, equipment, etc), Spanish courts often declare the joint and several liability of such interfering group affiliates. This usually applies to group affiliates located in Spain, but some court cases have also declared joint liability with respect to companies located in other countries, where the degree of interference is very high. A careful case assessment is required, based on all necessary documentation and information on the day-to-day business organisation, to reduce the risk of null and void redundancy. Indeed, if other group affiliates might be involved as employers, the redundancy procedure will require that information regarding such other affiliates is also rendered to employee representatives and failure to do so might entail an inadequate consultation process that again could render the redundancy process null and void.

Example

The XXX Group has a parent company and two subsidiaries (A and B) in Spain. All three companies use the same premises, which are rented by company B, with no charge to the other two entities and having no agreement among them. Employees work for the three entities in an undifferentiated way. The companies share funds, costs and expenses with lack of transparency or agreement. Subsidiary B has been having heavy losses, whilst the parent company and the other subsidiary are very profitable. The parent company has decided to close company B and to lay off the entire workforce.

In order to comply with the legal procedure for redundancy and to try to justify the grounds, the employing company and the parent company will need to provide employee representatives with information regarding all three companies.

Collating information to plan and budget for the restructuring exercise

28.8 Spanish case law has accepted the possibility of a restructuring exercise carried out across a group of companies. In those cases, when gathering employee information, it is necessary to have the proper consents, thus avoiding any breach of data protection legislation.

28.9 Collecting the relevant information and facts necessary for the restructuring plan and later restructuring exercise, is key to the plan's success. This will enable a decision as to whether a report of an independent expert is required, determining the timing and particularly deciding on the day the collective redundancy is to be announced.

28.10 The information required to be provided to employee representatives will also include information regarding subsidiaries of the same group (those companies subject to consolidation of accounts) where the parent company is domiciled in Spain and where there are credits or debts with the company planning the redundancy plan, or even if not being subject to consolidation of accounts, subsidiaries in Spain with debts or credits with the company planning the redundancy plan which have the same business, or operate in the same sector.

> **Practical Tip**
>
> The initially key data required in respect of any employee that could have been impacted by a work force reduction or a restructuring exercise includes (even though it is not limited to):
>
> - salary, including remuneration in kind, variable salary and benefits;
> - professional group;
> - length of service (the time worked for the company through a temporary agency should be taken into account);
> - age, particularly employees over the age of 50 years;
> - work place;
> - applicable collective agreement;
> - special category (employee's representatives or union representatives);
> - personal situation (pregnancy, maternity leaves, part time working for childcare or care of dependant relatives, disabilities, etc)
> - enhanced redundancy entitlement, eg any collective or individual agreement granting any such right;
> - information relevant to determine the redundancy selection pool, particularly including figures related to gender, union affiliation, work-life balance exercised rights etc;
> - information on justifying grounds for redundancy; and
> - audited annual accounts of the company and all subsidiaries involved.
>
> This information will also allow the estimation of the overall costs of the restructuring exercise.

EMPLOYMENT STATUS

28.11 Only individual employees should be taken into account in the redundancy procedure. However, misclassification of employees as independent contractors has a substantial impact on redundancy plans, since not only may it affect the cost, but also it could change the figures on which the thresholds for individual or collective procedures are assessed. There is a presumption of employment relationship where individuals render personal work within a business organisation and/or under the supervisory and/or disciplinary authority of managers. The nature of the relationship depends on the actual day-to-day relationship. This liability cannot be avoided through contract given that prior waiver of employment rights is null and void. Therefore it is very important to assess whether any relationship with independent contracts may fall into an employment nature. In the event of any such risk, careful assessment of the situation should be taken into account. This is because the implementation of the collective restructuring plan might affect termination rights and could result in claims for employment declaration by any such independent individual contractors.

GENERAL PROTECTION AGAINST DISMISSAL

28.12 Termination requires a formal procedure, including due notice (as is the case for collective redundancy consultation), and justification for termination. If the employer fails to properly evidence the grounds for termination, this can result in higher severance for unfair termination. A termination might be declared null and void (leading to reinstatement with back pay) if the plan is declared discriminatory (eg gender or race discrimination selection criteria) or if the consultation process has not been correctly followed (eg where employee representatives are not provided with the relevant information to assess the grounds for termination or where the company does not consult transparently by replying to queries, considering proposals, etc).

28.13 The company should deliver all relevant documentation to employee representatives and to the employment authorities at least three days before the first consultation meeting takes place.

SPECIAL PROTECTION AGAINST DISMISSAL

28.14 Employees in certain circumstances are protected under Spanish law in the event of redundancy, including disabled employees, employees on parental leave or reduced working hours for child or relative care, pregnant employees, employee representatives, etc. There is a presumption that termination of these employees is discriminatory or resulting from their special circumstance. Such termination is therefore null and void, unless the employer sufficiently evidences that the reason for termination was a valid objective reason. The list below sets out some of these protected situations and their legal consequences in the event of purported dismissal:

- employee representatives: special protection against dismissal and also must be the 'last out' in collective redundancies;
- pregnancy and maternity/paternity leave: dismissals during these periods or within nine months after birth is presumed to be null and void;
- time reduction for childcare and care of sick or disabled close relatives: dismissal during these periods is presumed to be null and void;
- collective redundancies: employer must follow a special procedure involving consultation with employee's representatives where the number of objective dismissals during a period of 90 days reaches a certain threshold; and
- discrimination (age, disability, gender reassignment, marital/civil partnership status, race, religion or belief, sex or sexual orientation) results in a presumption of null and void termination.

28.15 Compulsory retirement based on the grounds of age is not acceptable under applicable law after the 2013 labour reform. It would constitute an unlawful dismissal and is deemed age discriminatory unless the company can objectively justify the dismissal, being in that case the exception and not the norm.

WORKFORCE REDUCTION

28.16 Employers who plan to carry out a workforce reduction as part of a restructuring process will need to take care to document the business reasons for the proposed dismissals, with the only aim to make clear that the dismissals are totally lawful and based on fair and sustained reasons as permitted by the statute. It has a huge importance at this point to be able to identify the business perspective and ascertain the legal grounds for the dismissal (economic, technical, organisational or production reasons).

28.17 Redundancies which affect or may affect a number of employees exceeding the relevant thresholds within a 90-day period are subject to an obligation to implement a collective redundancy, (please refer to Collective Redundancy Procedure section at para **28.17**). This mainly requires consultation with employee representatives. The thresholds involve termination of at least:

(i) 10 workers, in undertakings with less than 100 workers;
(ii) 10% of the workforce, in undertakings with between 100 and 300 workers;
(iii) 30 workers, in undertakings with 300 or more workers; or
(iv) all the workers of the undertaking, provided the number of affected workers is greater than five;

28.18 Redundancies below the above thresholds are subject to the procedures applicable to individuals.

Definition of redundancy

28.19 There is no statutory definition of redundancy in the sense of 'amortisation of work posts'. However the Worker's Statute regulates in a broader sense termination based on objective grounds. Section 52 provides that an employment contract may be terminated due to:

(*a*) Worker unfitness to work in the relevant position occurring after the commencement date of work for the undertaking or previously unknown.
(*b*) Worker's failure to adapt to technical modifications to his work, provided the changes are reasonable and at least two months have passed since they were introduced and the employee has been properly trained.
(*c*) Where there is an objectively justified need to eliminate one or more positions below the thresholds for collective redundancy, due to economic, technical, organisational or production grounds. This is the standard redundancy procedure where we will primarily focus in this chapter.

(*d*) Absenteeism, ie persistent absences from work even if justified, for 20% of working days in two consecutive months provided the employee's absenteeism in the previous 12 months exceeded 5% of working days, or for 25% of working days in four non-consecutive months within a 12-month period. The following are not counted as absence from work for this purpose: absences due to legal strikes so long as such strikes last, legally recognised activities as a worker's representative, accidents at work, maternity, time off and holidays.

28.20 Note that where work is being outsourced it will be necessary to assess if this exercise is covered by the transfer of undertakings provision (section 44 of the Worker's Statute), which prevents termination as a direct consequence of the transfer of an undertaking. However, if the work is being transferred abroad, this will be construed as a collective termination and thus subject to the collective redundancy procedure.

Examples

The company ALPHA, S.A. ('Alpha') is a manufacturer of automotive parts. Alpha has 500 employees, 400 of whom are in the production team. Two production lines require twenty employees for each line for each of the three shifts (ie 120 employees) to operate. Alpha has invested in advanced technology machinery to replace its two old production lines, so as to implement automated processes. Each new production line may be operated by only ten employees per line and per shift, thus only 60 employees. Therefore 60 employees are no longer required and are to be made redundant (technical and organisational grounds).

The company THE HOUSE, SA is a retail chain selling household appliances. The company has 50 stores in Spain. Its annual accounts show that some of the stores result in losses. After comparing the figures of the last three quarters to the same quarters of the previous year, the company's management has decided to close the five stores that are unprofitable due to sales decline in the last three quarters. As a result THE HOUSE S.A is proposing to make all employees in the five stores redundant on the basis that their workplace is closing down (economic and production grounds).

28.21 It is important to note that a *force majeure situation* also justifies redundancy. This is a situation which completely prevents the business from continuing to operate.

Example

The manufacturing plant in Bilbao of the chemical producer Chemist S.L. caught a fire during the night of New Years' Eve. The fire destroyed the machinery and seriously damaged the facilities. Management has decided to close down the plant given that the production cannot be resumed. This will result in the 25 positions in the plant being made redundant out of the total of 28 employees; three employees will be offered new positions in other plants in Spain.

Scope of Economic, Technical, Organisational and Productive Grounds (ETOP)

28.22 Originally the law required the employer to show that the business required restructuring measures to overcome a situation of serious lack of competitiveness and/or lack of feasibility, but the employer was also required to show that the restructuring measures it proposed would directly result in resolving the company's difficulties. Given the courts' very restrictive interpretation, very few restructuring plans were actually deemed justified. The 2012 employment reform (act 3/2012) has removed the need to show the future impact of the measures and softened the degree of justification required to be proven. The employment courts still require some degree of reasonableness and proportionality of the measures to be implemented.

28.23 According to the Worker's Statute, business grounds are referred to as economic, technical, organisational or productive causes, and described as follows:

- **Economic cause:** where the results of the company show a negative economic situation, in cases such as the existence of actual or expected losses, or the persistent decline in sales. In any case, it is understood that the decrease is persistent if for three consecutive quarters the level of revenue or sales each quarter is lower than the revenue for each one of the same quarters of the previous year.
- **Technical cause:** where changes occur, among others, in the field of the means or instruments of production;
- **Organisational cause:** where changes occur, among others, in the field of systems and working methods of the staff or how to organise production;
- **Productive cause:** where changes occur, among others, in the demand for the products or services that the company intends to place on the market.

Example of an objective redundancy plan

The management of a marketing company, SOLUTIONS S.L. is determined to restructure its operations by way of a business reorganisation. A number of roles will be reorganised so as to achieve a more effective internal organisation. To this extent, all administrative services will be concentrated in the main office in Madrid. The smaller offices will be closed down and main resources moved to Madrid. Sales personnel will be reduced by enhancing the use of information technologies. This will result in 100 positions being made redundant out of the total of 700 employees in Spain. The redundancy plan will be justified on organisational grounds.

INDIVIDUAL REDUNDANCY PROCEDURE

28.24 The grounds required for individual redundancy are the same as those for collective redundancy. The difference results from the fact that individual redundancies involve a number of terminations below the number thresholds.

28.25 It should be noted, however, that where the employer implements successive 90-day-period individual redundancies based on similar grounds or there is reason to believe that the employer should be aware that the number of terminations would exceed the thresholds, the law provides a presumption that the redundancies are in fraud because the employer failed to follow the collective redundancy procedure, and thus such linked terminations will be declared null and void.

28.26 Unlike collective redundancy, no consultation is required for individual redundancy. Individual redundancy is subject to the following procedure:

- 15 days' prior written notice to the worker setting out the grounds giving rise to the termination with sufficient detail to allow the worker to challenge the termination in court. Failure to provide sufficient details on the grounds may render the termination unfair, and thus entitle the employee to severance damages for unfair termination (33 days' salary per year of service, capped at 24 months' salary).
- Making the severance available to the worker, upon notice of termination. The severance amounts to 20 days' salary per year of service with a maximum of 12 months' salary.
- The employer should deliver a copy of the termination letter to employee representatives.

28.27 The 15 days' notice can be paid in lieu of notice. If the prior notice is actually given, the employee is entitled to take six hours off per week during such notice period without loss of pay in order to seek employment.

28.28 Individual redundancies are often than not challenged by employees. There is a preliminary conciliation meeting which is usually scheduled within one month after termination. Very often the parties settle the case with a slightly higher severance, ie additional severance of 10–15 days' salary per year of service. If no settlement is agreed, the procedure will continue before employment courts. Any court hearing will be scheduled to take place typically around six to nine months after termination.

28.29 If the courts declare that the grounds for redundancy are not proportionate or reasonable enough to justify termination, or have not been sufficiently evidenced, or that the employer has failed to comply with the relevant formalities (eg making the severance available upon notice of termination), the employee shall be entitled to receive severance damages of 33 days' salary per year of service, capped at 24 months' salary as unfair termination. It should be noted, however that employees with periods of service dating from before 2012 and particularly those before 1996 will be entitled to higher severances based on accrued rights under the old legislation.

28.30 If courts declare that the redundancy is justified, the employee shall not be entitled to any further compensation other than the amount that was made available upon notice of termination (20 days' salary per year of service, capped at 12 months' salary). This severance is fully tax free, although this is subject to review.

28.31 A redundancy may be declared null and void, thus entitling the employee to reinstatement with back pay in the following situations:

- where the dismissal is discriminatory or contrary to the worker's fundamental rights or civil liberties;
- where the employer has laid off a number of employees beyond the thresholds, thus infringing the collective consultation procedure.

28.32 Individual redundancy of an employee representative which is declared to be unfair (eg grounds are not justified or the procedure has not been properly followed), the employee is entitled to opt for reinstatement or for termination with severance damages.

Collective redundancy procedure

28.33 Under Spanish law a collective redundancy takes place where, within a period of 90 days, a number of employees exceeding the following thresholds is terminated:

- ten workers, in undertakings with less than 100 workers;
- ten of the workforce, in undertakings with between 100 and 300 workers;
- thirty workers, in undertakings with 300 or more workers;
- All the workers of the undertaking, provided a minimum of five workers' contracts of employment are terminated.

28.34 All employee terminations are to be taken into consideration when assessing the thresholds, except for disciplinary terminations declared lawful by the court.

28.35 The redundancy is subject to sustained and strongly evidenced economic, technical, organisational or production grounds, through a well justified memorandum and backed by detailed an appropriate documentation. Actual or forecast losses or a sustained reduction in sales are all deemed economic grounds. Forecast losses require however the backup of an independent expert report. In fact, a reduction in sales beyond three consecutive terms is specifically provided by law to qualify as justifying economic grounds. It is strongly advisable to prepare a good report with sufficient evidence and supported by the report of an independent expert, where required.

28.36 During a collective redundancy, the employer has to consult employee representatives in good faith in order to discuss measures to minimise the impact on employment, such as relocation, and to explore possibilities to reach an agreement. The consultation should be held open at least 15 days for businesses with less than 50 employees and 30 days for businesses with 50 or more employees.

28.37 As with individual redundancy, collective redundancy entitles employees to severance of 20 days' salary per year of service.

28.38 The company is also subject to the obligation to pay social security contributions until the age of 61 for all employees being made redundant at the age of 55 or older.

28.39 It should be highlighted that where the company implementing the collective redundancy or its group has had profits for two years and the company or the group have more than 100 employees and the collective redundancy involves termination of employees of 50 years of age or older beyond a given ratio, a contribution is payable to cover unemployment benefits and social security contributions. This is a controversial measure implemented in 2011 (Act 27/2011 of 1 August) which has been subject to several legal amendments. The current legislation is Royal Decree 1484/2012 of 29 October.

28.40 A redeployment or social plan for redundancies involving more than 50 employees has to be made. This implies hiring an outplacement company for a six-month minimum term for outplacement, training and active search support.

The plan may include the following measures:

- measures aimed at avoiding or reducing the effects of the collective dismissal, ie internal replacement (in the same company or companies of the group), etc; and
- measures aimed at diminishing the consequences of the collective dismissal for the employees, ie outplacement, professional training and recycling, etc.

28.41 The collective redundancy is started by the employer calling a meeting with employee representatives or employees (if there are no employee representatives) to inform them of its intention to start a collective redundancy procedure. The workforce is entitled to a maximum term of 15 days (seven days in certain cases) to appoint employees representatives for this purpose, before the consultation process starts. The employer should then deliver certain documentation to the employee representatives and call the first meeting to take place after at least three days from delivery so that they have time to study the documentation. The documentation should include details of the workforce and positions to be made redundant, selection criteria, a memorandum describing the grounds and evidence thereof, a report of an independent expert where required, estimated termination dates, etc. It is important to bear in mind that the information regarding the grounds should also involve other subsidiaries in Spain in the event of consolidation accounts or where the affiliate has debts or credits with the employing company and operates in the same business. A copy of all the documentation should be delivered to employment authorities on the same date. Minutes of consultation meetings should be drawn up and signed. A copy of these minutes should also be delivered to the employment authorities.

28.42 At the end of the consultation process, the company shall resolve on the terms of the redundancy either unilaterally or by agreement with employee representatives, if so. The company's final decision is to be notified to employee representatives and submitted to the authorities. The labour inspection shall issue a report assessing whether the legal formalities have been complied with, particularly including delivery of documentation to employee representatives and consultation process. The company can start implementing redundancies as long as 30 days have elapsed since the date

Involvement of employee representatives in collective dismissals

28.43 Employees are primarily to be represented in the consultation process by union representatives. However, in practice this very seldom takes place. The employees may have elected employee representatives (individual delegates or works council or union delegates for companies over 250 employees). In the absence of such appointment, employees have between seven and 15 days to appoint three individuals to represent them, either from the employees themselves or from union personnel. A number of rules apply for appointment of representatives in the event that the redundancy plan is to involve several worksites. It is of the utmost importance to ensure employee representation is appropriate and has been properly documented so as to avoid risks that the procedure or any agreement might be declared null and void for lack of appropriate employee representation.

Information and consultation requirements

28.44 The following information must be provided in writing by the employer to employees' representatives as part of the information stage:

(a) the aim(s) of the proposed redundancies;
(b) the number and description of employees proposed to be dismissed;
(c) the number and description of employees during the last year;
(d) the period proposed in which the dismissals will take effect;
(e) the proposed method of selecting employees;

(f) copy of the company's notification to the workforce or employee representatives informing of its intention to start the collective redundancy procedure;
(h) memorandum setting forth the grounds for the collective redundancy; and
(i) the relevant technical or financial reports by independent experts if required.

28.45 Where the company is part of a group of companies and obligated to draw up consolidated accounts and where its parent company is domiciled in Spain, certain accounting information of the parent company must be provided. Where such obligation of drawing up consolidated accounts does not exist, accounting information of the parent company must also be provided as long as it is domiciled in Spain, belonging to the same activity or sector and having trade balances payable and receivable and financing operations with the company that starts the procedure.

28.46 The main reason for consultation is to try to reach an agreement between the two legitimate forces, the employer and the appropriate representatives. Agreements during consultation are directed to avoid as many dismissals as possible, or as a last resource try to reduce their negative effects (eg offering outplacements and careers guidance or a higher severance payments).

28.47 The consultation period should be used by the employee representatives to bring new proposals and therefore adequate information should be provided to them. The employer should also respond to any questions or fully consider any employees' representation proposal. Case law establishes that the employer should always enter into such consultation or negotiation in good faith and with the aim of reaching a fair agreement.

28.48 Typical mistakes for employers include not delivering the mandatory information to employee representatives or engaging in passive conduct, not considering employee representatives' proposals or not acting in good faith (eg increasing the number of employees affected by redundancy as a result of a strike).

28.49 The procedure for collective redundancy may take around two months, including document drafting and preparation, consultation, and termination. Once the term for consultation is over, the company should inform employee representatives and the employment authorities on its decision within 15 days of the last consultation meeting.

28.50 After this, the company may start terminating employees by notifying them in writing with a summary of the grounds and by giving 15 days' notice or payment in lieu of notice.

Sanctions

28.51 The plan may be challenged in court by employee representatives collectively or by employees individually. The new legislation has provided a very relevant change to this situation; given that if courts find that the plan was not justified, the only implication is that severance pay rises to same level as severance damages for unfair termination (see below).

28.52 However, the plan may be declared null and void and thus entitle employees to reinstatement in the following two main situations:

Failure to follow the formal procedure
The plan may be declared null and void if the company has failed to follow the relevant procedure, namely to have followed the appropriate consultation process or to deliver sufficient information to employee representatives. Therefore it is important that the company plays an active role in the consultation process.

28.53 *Discrimination or Infringement of fundamental rights.*
If the plan is challenged for being discriminatory or against fundamental rights, then employees involved are entitled to reinstatement or the plan is declared null and void, depending on the extent of the infringement. This would be the case if the selection criteria shows discrimination with respect to fundamental right protections, ie a disproportional number of protected employee terminations as compared with the workforce or discriminatory selection criteria, including women, employees known to be affiliated to unions, pregnant women or employees on maternity or paternity leave, employees working reduced hours for child care, employee representatives, handicapped employees, sexual orientation, age, race or other protected condition etc.

28.54 Therefore, it is strongly advisable to follow consultation actively and to check the above issues when selecting employees so as to avoid the unwanted consequences flowing from the plan being declared discriminatory or infringing fundamental rights.

REDUNDANCY PAYMENT

Statutory redundancy pay calculation

28.55 The amount of the statutory redundancy payment is of 20 days' salary per year of service, capped at 12 months' salary.

Example

Mr Garcia and Mr Martinez have been made redundant from pintaplus S.L. on 21 June 2014. Mr Garcia has been employed by the Company from 13 March 2012 and his salary is €36,000pa. Mr Martinez has been employed by the Company from 12 January 1995 and his salary is €60,000 pa.

The sum of €7,323.29 is the statutory redundancy pay that Mr García is entitled to receive (his daily salary is €98.63 – €36,000/365- and the total worked days are 799, that is to say, 2.19 total worked years – 799/365-, and rounding up months is 27 months, that is to say, 2.25 round up years, so €98,63 x 33 x 2.25 = €7,323.29)

The calculation of Mr Martinez' statutory redundancy pay will be calculated in two rounds as follows:

- his employment from 12 January 1995 to 11 February 2012 will entitle him to €126,416.44 (his daily salary is €164.38 – €60,000/365- and the total worked days are 6,239, that is to say, 17.09 total worked years – 6,239/365-, and rounding up months is 205 months, that is to say, 17.08 round up years – 205/12-, so 164.38x 45 x 17.09 = €126,416.44),
- the period from 12 February 2012 to 23 July 2014 (his daily salary is €164.38 – €60,000/365- and the total worked days are 892, that is to say, 2.44 total worked years –892/365-, and rounding up months is 30 months, that is to say, 2.50 round up years – 30/12-, so 164.38x 33 x 2.50= €13,561.64.

In conclusion, Mr Martinez is entitled to receive a total sum of €139,978.08 as statutory redundancy pay.

Enhanced redundancy payments

28.56 Spanish law provides a statutory redundancy severance payment, although often the severance is improved as a result of the consultation procedure. After the 2012 Employment Reform, the improvement is in the region of 35 days' salary per year of service or in the worst case scenario up to 45 days' salary per year of service.

Taxation of redundancy payments

28.57 Statutory redundancy payment used to be fully tax free up to the legal severance amount, ie 45 days' salary per year of service, capped at 42 months' salary. However a tax reform enacted as of January 2015 has limited the tax exemption to severances up to €180,000.

Post-termination restrictive covenants

28.58 Spanish law accepts non-competition obligations for a maximum term of two years after the employment agreement is no longer in force for whatever reason. This is subject to the employee receiving an 'adequate' compensation, which should be paid after termination or expiration of the agreement.

28.59 The law has given very general indications of what 'adequate' means. In general terms, compensation in the region of 40–50% of the employee's salary should be acceptable.

28.60 It is also subject to the employer having an actual business interest in preventing the employee from competing. This requirement could prevent enforcement of a non-competing obligation by a former employee in an area where the employer does not operate.

> **Practical Tip**
>
> Enforcement of non-competition obligations is difficult under Spanish law, particularly as regards evidencing the employee's breach. In order to discourage executives from breaching this obligation and given the difficulties to enforce these provisions, a high penalty clause should be inserted.
>
> Non-competition obligations should however be adequately compensated. In order to avoid having to pay a considerable amount after termination, it is useful to assign part of the employee's remuneration during employment to compensate for such post-termination non-competition obligations. This can be made either as a percentage of the executive's remuneration or as a fixed amount (eg covenant payment).

BUSINESS SALE, OUTSOURCING/INSOURCING AND OFFSHORING

28.61 The ARD (Acquired Rights the European Council Directive 77/187 of 14 February 1977, amended by the European Council Directive 1998/50 of 29 June 1998 and its ruling Directive 2001/23 of 12 March 2001) was implemented in Spain by 12/2001, of 9 of July 2001. This implementation is reflected in article 44 of the Workers Statute ('TUPE').

28.62 In essence TUPE protects an individual's employment in the event that the undertaking for which he works is transferred by the employer to a new owner. In practical terms this means that TUPE may apply where a business – as a going concern – is transferred (sold, etc). TUPE does not apply to a situation where ownership of the employing entity changes by way of a share sale.

28.63 Transferred employee are entitled to continue having the same employment rights and terms of employment, including pension rights, unless the relevant procedure is implemented to change employment terms (including justifying grounds, formal notice, consultation and prior written notice).

Business sale

28.64 To assess if a business sale constitutes a Transfer of Undertaking in accordance with article 44 of the Workers Statute, the relevant definition in the regulations considers whether the business unit being the subject of the transfer is a stable economic entity and whether it retains its identity after transfer. The Workers State defines an economic entity as an organised grouping of resources with the objective of pursuing an economic activity, whether or not that activity is central or just a supporting or ancillary function.

28.65 The main question is whether the economic entity is still in existence and to what extent it is carrying out the same or similar activities post transfer. When carrying out such an assessment, a number of factors will become relevant, including whether the assets are sold as part of the transfer of a 'business' as a 'going concern' and whether the purchaser is planning to use the assets with the intention of carrying on 'business' of the same kind as the seller (whilst not necessarily identical). Whether or not goodwill has been retained (ie whether any customers have been transferred) may be included as a determining factor, similarly factors such as the resemblance in activities pre and post transfer and the degree of any disruption to such activities may be considered. Spanish case law follows the European Court of Justice case law.

28.66 Spanish law provides for a joint liability of the transferor and the transferee of a business for a three-year term for liabilities generated before the transfer, unless the transfer is declared to be a criminal offense (eg a collusion to deprive employees from employment and severance protection by causing bankruptcy).

28.67 Transferor and transferee are under an obligation to notify employees of the transfer in proper time, by providing the relevant information regarding the purpose of the transfer, the implications for the workforce and the intended date of the transfer.

Outsourcing or insourcing

28.68 *Outsourcing or insourcing* may constitute a transfer of undertaking in the same terms and subject to the same requirements as a transfer of undertaking, ie transfer of a stable economic entity that retains its identity post transfer, economic entity defined as an organised grouping of resources with the objective of pursuing an economic activity.

Effect of Transfer of Undertakings according to Art 44 of the Workers Statute (WE)

Automatic transfer and protection of employment

28.69 In the event of transfer of undertaking under article 44 WE, those employees being transferred will keep their existing employment conditions. This is the case, provided they were entirely or mainly assigned to work for the transferring business, including access to an occupational pension scheme where this was a benefit prior to the transfer unless otherwise agreed with employee representatives, typically by providing certain minimum pension provisions.

Objection to the transfer

28.70 Employees are not entitled to object to the transfer insofar as it meets the requirements for a transfer of undertaking. Should they refuse to transfer, they could be deemed to have resigned or their employment could be terminated.

Protection from dismissal

28.71 Termination of employees upon a transfer of undertaking may be declared unfair and entitle the employees to severance damages, or even null and void entitling such employees to reinstatement.

Protection of terms and conditions of employment

28.72 In the event of transfer of business, both the transferor and the transferee are jointly liable for three years for employees' rights before date of transfer.

Duty to inform

28.73 In a transfer of undertaking under article 44 WE, employees representatives (or in their absence) employees themselves are entitled to be informed of the following:

- expected date of transfer;
- reasons for the transfer;

- legal, economic and social implications for employees ;and
- measures to be implemented with respect to employees.

Duty to consult

28.74 If as a consequence of the transfer, the transferee intends to implement any measure that may affect employees, particularly including collective redundancies or collective relocations or changes to employment terms (working hours, office move, etc), employee representatives should be consulted in good time for a 15-day term.

28.75 The transferor should inform employee representatives that they have the opportunity to issue a report regarding such measures.

28.76 Consultation should include details and evidence of the business grounds justifying any such measures and any discussion on measures to reduce the impact of such changes.

28.77 The relevant documentation regarding employee transfer should be submitted to the social security and employment authorities, together with the relevant forms, so as to register employees under the new employer.

28.78 It is advisable to inform employee representatives that the transfer process is complete.

Failure to inform and consult

28.79 Failure to inform employees or to consult where applicable may expose the employer to administrative sanctions and could entitle employees to compensation for damages for infringement of union rights.

European works councils

28.80 Where the transfer affects a group of companies across the UE, there might be a European Works Council ('EWC') to inform and consult. For further details please refer to the separate chapter on European Works Councils.

Unfair dismissal

28.81 Any dismissals directly resulting from the transfer will be declared unfair, unless the company can show a strong argument that this is a result of productive or organisational measures, ie reorganisation after the transfer.

Null and void dismissal

28.82 If the transferor terminates a number of employees exceeding the thresholds before the date of transfer, such terminations will be declared null and void for failure to have implemented a collective redundancy procedure. Since the transferee becomes bound by all transferor employer obligations with respect to the transferring employees under article 44 WE, the transferee shall be liable to reinstate those employees.

WORKFORCE REDUCTION IN CONNECTION WITH SHARE SALE OR SHARE PURCHASE

28.83 A workforce reduction in connection with share sale or share purchase is subject to the rules for individual dismissal or collective redundancy depending on whether the number of terminated employees exceeds the thresholds or not.

CHANGING EMPLOYMENT TERMS AND CONDITIONS

Functional or occupational mobility: transfers of employees between work posts

28.84 As general rule the employer is entitled to move employees to other positions within the same professional level as defined by the applicable collective agreement.

28.85 Temporary demotions are only acceptable for limited period of time and subject to there being sustained economic, organisational, technical or productive reasons, duly notified to the employee and evidenced. The employee who is temporarily performing lower duties is entitled to the same pay as before.

28.86 Promotions also require justifying grounds unless obviously the employee would not object to them. A move to a position of a higher level entitles the employee to the higher salary if he has performed these tasks for more than six months within a one-year term or for more than eight months within a two-year period. The employee performing more senior duties is entitled to the salary for those senior duties.

28.87 The parties may enter into agreement regarding moves to other positions and in fact agreements are very common.

Geographical mobility: relocation

28.88 The relocation of employees to a different work centre that does not require employees to move their usual place of residence (domicile) is not subject to any requirement and thus can be implemented with no special procedure, although a prior notice is expected for good order. The case law has clarified that this is the case where the new work centre is within a 25–30 Km distance from the current work centre and there are no special circumstances that may imply a considerable longer time to commute, eg communications are appropriate.

28.89 Temporary detachment to a different work centre is also not subject to restrictions, insofar as this does not exceed 12 months within a three-year period and that it is not discriminatory or abusive.

28.90 However, a relocation that implies employees' need to move their domiciles is subject to the specific procedure and requirements described below, which vary depending on whether the number of affected employees is beyond the thresholds (collective procedure) or is below the thresholds (individual procedure).

28.91 If employees decide not to relocate, they are entitled to terminate their employment with severance of 20 days' salary per year of service, capped at 12 months' salary.

Individual relocation

Thresholds and grounds

28.92 Relocations affecting a number of employees below the threshold are also subject to there being sustained economic, technical, organisational or production grounds. Grounds justifying the relocation are deemed to occur when the measures contribute to improve the company's situation through a more appropriate organisation of its resources, which favours its competitive position in the market or gives a better response to market demands. It is strongly advisable to obtain all relevant evidence to justify the decision, including economic, commercial, marketing, production and any other relevant studies and reports.

Procedure

28.93 Individual relocation requires at least 30 days written notice to employees and employees' representatives. The letter should provide all the details and attached evidence on the grounds justifying the decision.

Collective relocation

Thresholds and grounds

28.94 A relocation is collective when it affects a number of employees exceeding the following thresholds within a 90-day period:

- ten workers, in undertakings with less than 100 workers;
- ten of the workforce, in undertakings with between 100 and 300 workers;
- thirty workers, in undertakings with 300 or more workers; or
- all the workers of the undertaking, provided the number of workers affected is greater than five.

28.95 Relocation may only be carried out if justified on sustained economic, technical, organisational or production grounds. Grounds justifying the relocation are deemed to concur when the measures contribute to improve the company's situation through a more appropriate organisation of its resources, which favours its competitive position in the market or gives a better response to market demands. It is strongly advisable to obtain all relevant evidence to justify the decision, including economic, commercial, marketing, production and any other relevant studies and reports.

Procedure

28.96 Collective relocation is subject to consultation with employee representatives for a 15-day period. Such consultation should be a good faith active discussion on the reasons for the decision and the possibility to reduce or avoid its effects, as well as on measures to mitigate the consequences of the relocation.

28.97 If no agreement has been reached with employees' representatives, employees can also challenge the decision to relocate through a collective or an individual procedure. Collective challenges prevent the company from implementing the relocation plan until a court decides on the matter.

28.98 The employee may also challenge the decision to relocate through an individual procedure. This however does not have the effect of preventing the company from implementing the relocation and thus the employee has to relocate during the litigation process.

Substantial modification: changes to employment terms

28.99 Spanish law is based on the principle of acquired rights. Therefore, any benefits that the employer has given to its employees may create employee rights to continue receiving such benefits.

28.100 In order to avoid such acquired rights, employers should carefully draft specific documentation to show that such benefit is given on a one-off basis or on specific circumstances or criteria (eg as a reward for ten completed years of service, when a specific business growth is achieved, etc) and thus does not raise acquired rights, other than as described.

28.101 No acquired rights are created when the benefit has been granted on the basis of a collective agreement, given that such benefit will stop upon the expiry of the collective agreement and thus the parties shall have to re-negotiate new terms.

28.102 Although the employer is entitled to take decisions, when the benefit has created an acquired right, the amendment of employees' substantial employment conditions is subject to a strict legal procedure. Working hours, remuneration, tasks, shifts, work system and performance system are deemed substantial employment conditions.

28.103 Substantial employment conditions may only be changed either by the employee's express consent, or when there are proven economic, technical, organisation or production reasons that justify such change. This is so when the measures contribute to the improvement of the situation of the company through a more appropriate organisation of its resources, which favours its competitive position in the market or gives a better response to the requirements of demand. Given that Spanish courts are reluctant to accept any conditions that may provide less favourable terms, it is very important that the employer obtains all relevant evidence to justify the decision, including economic, commercial, marketing, production and any other relevant studies and reports.

Individual procedure

28.104 In the event of individual change, the employer should notify the employee of its decision, giving at least 15 days' notice before the effective date.

28.105 Where the change damages the employee's rights, they are entitled to leave the company by earning a tax free severance pay of 20 days' salary per year of service, up to a maximum of nine months' salary. The employee may alternatively challenge the measure. If the challenge is successful, the employee shall have the right to continue working on their former conditions.

Collective procedure

28.106 The procedure varies if the change is deemed to be individual or collective. It is individual when within a period of 90 days the measure affects fewer than:

- ten workers, in undertakings with less than 100 workers;
- ten of the workforce, in undertakings with between 100 and 300 workers;
- thirty workers, in undertakings with 300 or more workers; or
- all the workers of the undertaking, provided the number of workers affected is greater than five.

28.107 A collective change of substantial conditions requires a prior period of consultations with employees' representatives (workers' council or delegates) of at least 15 days.

28.108 Consultation shall be based on the grounds for the change and possible alternative plans or other measures to minimise the effects. Once the consultation period is over, the employer shall notify the employees of its decision, which shall take effect at least seven days after notification.

28.109 Even if workers' representatives have not agreed to the change, the change becomes effective after this period of seven days. However each employee retains the right to:

- leave the company by earning a tax free severance pay of 20 days' salary per year of service, up to a maximum of nine months' salary; or
- challenge the change through a collective litigation procedure, although, given that the change is enforceable, this is subject to the employee submitting to the change during litigation.

28.110 If the Work Council or employee's representatives have agreed to the change, the employee is still entitled to challenge the decision individually.

Changes to working terms provided for in collective agreements

28.111 The recent labour reform has also introduced a substantial reform regarding the modification of the conditions provided in the Collective agreement. The law now includes a provision which allows the employer to change the terms of the CBA when there are economic, technical, organisation or production reasons.

28.112 The conditions that can be modified are the following:

- working day; working schedule timetable and time distribution;
- shift work regime;
- remuneration system and salary;
- working systems;
- functions or workplace, when this exceeds the limits for functional mobility provided by Article 39; and
- voluntary social security contributions payable by the employer

28.113 The procedure to perform such changes is similar to the previously mentioned collective procedure to change terms of employment. It requires an agreement between the employer and the employee's representatives. However, if such agreement is not reached, both the employer and the employee's representatives can refer to the Joint Committee of the Collective agreement for a solution.

USING TEMPORARY STAFF

28.114 Companies may not use temporary staff to cover for strikes or to replace indefinite term employees who have been terminated. Indeed, if the employer contracts fixed term contracts or agency workers during the redundancy process, this would result in the redundancy plan being declared unfair, thus exposing the company to higher severance payments or even null and void, thus resulting in reinstatement.

28.115 It is also worth mentioning, that where the employer intends to implement a collective redundancy plan, it should make sure that no temporary layoff plan is in place, since this would render the redundancy plan unlawful, as has been declared by case law. A temporary layoff plan is a plan where employees do not work for a given period of time (days, weeks or months) based on business grounds and are entitled to receive unemployment benefit.

Agency workers

28.116 Agency workers can only be hired to cover typically temporary positions, eg replacement of employees on sick or maternity leave etc, to cover unexpected increase of workload or to implement a short term project or to cover a position during a recruitment process. However, the management should bear in mind that agency workers have certain minimum rights that must be complied with by both the agency and the hiring company.

28.117 If the contractor merely provides workforce to the principal, rather than actually rendering a service, this may be deemed unlawful. Spanish law applies different penalties to unlawful assignment of workforce, depending on the seriousness of the infraction (damages to employees' rights, number of employees, period of time during which this situation has taken place, etc). The penalties may involve the following:

Employment penalty

The contractor and the principal would be jointly liable for the contractors' labour and social security rights, including the salary and contributions to the social security (unemployment subsidy, health coverage, etc. In Spain this is currently about 30% of the salary). The contractor's employees would be entitled to opt to have a labour relationship with the principal or with the contractor.

Administrative penalty

Fines may range from €3,005.07 to €90,151.82. Again the criteria described above are taken into account, among others, to determine the amount of the fine.

Criminal penalty

If the unlawful assignment is found to be a criminal offence (only in very serious cases), then the contractor's directors may be subject to imprisonment ranging from 6 months to three years and to fines. The declaration of a criminal offence is very uncommon, except in very serious cases, eg involving danger to employees' safety, discrimination, damage to human rights, etc.

Fixed-term contracts

28.118 Fixed-term contracts can only be hired to cover typically temporary positions. Management should bear in mind that fixed-term workers have certain minimum rights that both the agency and the hiring company must comply with.

28.119 The following are the grounds for fixed-term employment contracts:

(*a*) Where the employee is contracted for a specific temporary task which is not within the company's ordinary business, eg to install particular software.

(*b*) Where the employee is contracted to help to cope with an exceptional increase in workload, even within the company's ordinary business. The term of these agreements will range between 6 to 12 months, unless the collective agreement provides for a longer term (of up to 18 months).

(*c*) Where the employee is hired to replace employees who are entitled to reinstatement, including maternity leave, leave for child care, union or public duties, employees on partial retirement, etc. The term of these agreements last for as long as the replaced employee is entitled to return to his job.

28.120 Temporary contracts should be in writing. In the absence of a written contract, there is a presumption that the worker has been hired on a permanent basis. This can only be overturned by showing that the contract was in fact of a temporary nature. Permanent status is also granted automatically if the circumstances legally justifying the entering into of a temporary contract did not in fact exist.

28.121 Expiration of temporary employment agreements entitles employees to a severance pay of 12 days' salary per year of service or pro-rata.

28.122 Temporary contracts can be full-time or part-time.

28.123 Courts tend to be very restrictive in interpreting whether the requirements for temporary relationships are met and thus court decisions declaring indefinite term relationships are fairly common. Still, in practice the number of temporary jobs in Spain is extremely high.

Renewal of fixed-term contracts

28.124 Temporary employees who have been hired for over 24 months within a 30 month period of time for the same job through two or more temporary employment agreements for specific temporary tasks (see para **28.119**(a)) or for exceptional increase in workload (see para **28.119**(b)) shall be deemed indefinite in time. This applies even if the employee is hired through a registered temporary work agency. This provision was implemented in December 2006 in order to avoid the common abuse of temporary employment contracts which diminished employees' rights to indefinite term contacts.

Practical Tips

Where the employee is contracted for a specific temporary task the specific date of expiry need not be specified in the contract, an approximate date is sufficient because gradual finishing is acceptable as a reason for the cessation of the employment. This is allowed because different employees can be contracted for a specific task but the reasons for the assigned task are different.

Where the employee is contracted to help to cope with an exceptional increase in workload, even within the company's ordinary business, this should not be recurrent seasonal work, since if so, this would be treated legally as an indefinite term seasonal relationship.

EMPLOYMENT CLAIMS

28.125 Employers and employees can obtain a remedy for breach of their employment rights from specific labour courts. Employee representatives and trade unions may also start collective claims where a number of employees are affected by an employer decision. Decisions by labour courts can be appealed to the appellate courts of the relevant autonomous regions and, in certain cases, judgements may be appealed to the Supreme Court.

Individual termination challenges

28.126 In individual termination cases, the time limit within which the employee has to challenge termination is of only 20 working days from the effective date of termination. A preliminary request for conciliation before an administrative conciliation public entity is scheduled within one month (approximately) from termination. It is very common to settle at conciliation. If no agreement is reached at this stage the worker can then seek a remedy before the courts.

28.127 A termination may be declared unfair or null and void. There are two main reasons why an employee could claim for an unfair dismissal. One reason is that the actual cause for the dismissal does not constitute a cause for fair dismissal as established in the Workers Statute. The other, is that the employer did not follow the legal procedure to implement a business grounds termination.

Remedies

28.128 The effect of a court decision that a termination was unfair, is that the employer must pay a higher severance damages (unless he agrees to reinstate the employee with back pay). Severance for unfair termination amounts to 33 days' salary per year of service, capped at 24 months, although employees hired before February 2012 are entitled to severance of 45 days' salary per year of services for the seniority prior to such date with different caps applying according to the date of hiring.

28.129 The employee may claim for reinstatement with back pay in the event of infringement of fundamental rights, eg discrimination or termination during maternity leave.

Discrimination or infringement of fundamental rights

28.130 An employee may also bring a claim for discrimination (e..g by arguing that he was made redundant because of his age; disability; race; religion or belief; sex, sexual orientation etc) or for infringement of fundamental rights (eg privacy). There is a reversion of the burden of proof and thus the employer needs to evidence that the grounds for termination were other than those infringing fundamental rights and that these grounds were sufficient and sustained so as to justify termination.

Remedies

28.131 In the event that an employee is successful in a claim for discrimination or infringement of fundamental rights, the employee is entitled to reinstatement with payment of back wages and also compensation by way of damages.

> **Practical Tip**
>
> Where an employee brings a claim for discrimination or infringement of fundamental rights, there is a reversal of the burden of proof so the employee must only bring some prima facie evidence thereof and the employer must prove the dismissal was not based on any discriminatory reason or infringement of any fundamental right.

Collective redundancy challenges

28.132 Employee representatives or union representatives (in the latter case with sufficient representation in the company) may challenge the collective redundancy through a collective claim. The challenge may be based on the following:

- redundancy is not (or is not sufficiently) justified on the business grounds set forth by the company;
- infringement of the procedure, ie consultation, delivery of documentation etc;
- redundancy is implemented in fraud, bad faith, coercion or abuse; or
- redundancy is discriminatory or infringes fundamental rights.

28.133 If the redundancy plan was agreed with employee representatives, these also must be sued so that they have the opportunity to defend the agreement.

Remedies

28.134 Redundancy will be declared null and void and thus lead to reinstatement in the event that the employer has not properly implemented the procedure (consultation or delivery of appropriate documentation) or is discriminatory or infringes fundamental rights

28.135 Redundancy shall be declared unjustified if the business grounds set forth by the company are not sufficiently evidenced or justified, in which case the employer will be liable to pay the higher severance for unfair termination (33 days' salary per year of service capped at 24 months' salary; or in the case of longer periods of service, 20 days' salary per year of service, capped at 12 months' salary).

28.136 Employees may also individually challenge the collective redundancy plan after the collective claim or time limit based on individual reasons, eg if the employee has not taken into account their preferential right to the position (eg employee representatives), but also based on employer's failure to implement the collective consultation procedure.

Mutually agreed termination: settlement agreements

28.137 An employer might be interested in reaching a mutually agreed termination with an employee by paying him severance damages and entering into a settlement agreement. However, in order to make such settlement agreement effective, it should be reached within an actual dispute rather than beforehand, since such waivers made beforehand are invariably null and void. Therefore, the employer should first terminate the employee and settle on conciliation either at the preliminary administrative conciliation meeting or settle in court any time before the hearing.

Without prejudice and 'pre-termination' discussions

28.138 There are no without prejudice discussions under Spanish law. Without prejudice status will only be achieved through discussions between lawyers.

Chapter 29

Workforce Restructuring in Sweden

Anna Stenso
Flood Herslow Holme, Stockholm

INTRODUCTION

29.1 This chapter focus on the employment laws in Sweden. There are several legal rules which regulate employment in Sweden and an employer planning a workforce restructure must consider both the codified provisions in law as well as case law and, in many cases, the applicable collective agreement. A good place to start is the Swedish Employment Protection Act (1982:80) and the Swedish Co-Determination in the Workplace Act (1976:580) which regulate the relationship between the employer and the employee, and between the employer and the employees' organisations.

29.2 In Sweden there is mandatory legislation and semi-discretionary legislation when it comes to employment law. The semi-discretionary rules may be deviated from by a collective agreement. Such a collective agreement could therefore replace or deviate from the provisions of, eg the Swedish Employment Protection Act.

29.3 Many of the rules protect the employee and the rights of employee. A provision in an employment contract between an individual employee and an employer which leads to poorer protection of or benefits for the employee than those in statute, is thus non enforceable.

PREPARING FOR A RESTRUCTURING EXERCISE

Identify the employing entity

29.4 In order to prepare for a workforce restructuring process the employing entity has to be identified. The employment agreement is a starting point when determining which legal entity the employer is. According to case law the employer is the natural or legal person who has entered into an agreement with another party for the performance of work under such circumstances that an employment relationship can be established.

COLLATING INFORMATION TO PLAN AND BUDGET FOR THE RESTRUCTURING

Exercise

29.5 There are several pieces of information in relation to the relevant employees to be gathered in order to plan and budget for a workforce restructuring. Such information includes (but is not limited to):

- length of service;
- position and job description;
- place of work and operational unit,
- applicable collective agreement (if any); and
- information relevant to determine if the employee can be relocated.

EMPLOYMENT STATUS

29.6 The protection under the Swedish employment protection act includes both public and private employees. However, the following employees are excluded from the Swedish employment protection act:

- employees who, by virtue of their duties and conditions of employment, may be deemed to be in a managerial or comparable position (usually the CEO),
- employees who are members of the employer's family,
- employees who work in the employer's household; and
- employees who are employed for work with special employment support or in sheltered employment.

The employer shall provide written information to the employee of all the terms and conditions that are of material relevance to the employment contract or employment relationship no later than one month after the commencement of work by the employee. However, it is not required that the employment contract is in writing in order for a person to be considered to be an 'employee'. If the employment contract is verbal or if the parties have actually acted as if they had an employment contract, eg when a person starts to work and the company pays a salary, he/she could be protected against dismissal in accordance with law.

Other individuals engaged in the employer's business, for example agency workers or consultants, must also be identified when planning a workforce restructuring exercise.

OBJECTIVE GROUNDS

29.7 An employer planning to reduce the number of employees has to make sure that such planned dismissals are based on reasons as are permitted by statute. According to Swedish law termination of employment must be based on 'objective grounds'. Objective grounds are shortage of work or personal reasons.

29.8 A termination of employment can never be considered to be based on objective grounds if it is reasonable to expect the employer to transfer the employee to another available position within the company.

29.9 The obligation to transfer the employee includes available work within the whole company. The 'whole company' means the legal entity. The obligation is not applicable to other companies within the company group. The employer must investigate whether there are any vacancies available to the employee and if there is any opportunity to relocate the employee to such an available position. However, the employer is not obligated to create a new position.

SHORTAGE OF WORK

29.10 The term 'shortage of work' refers to any termination of employment that is not due to personal reasons. Shortage of work is always about positions, never about individuals.

29.11 Shortage of work may for example arise when a company loose a customer and there will no longer be enough work for all current employees, or if the employer decides to wind up part of the company, when new technology or new machines are introduced and the need for manpower is thereby reduced, or when the employer decides to replace certain positions with consultants etc. Shortage of work may arise even if the company is profitable.

29.12 It is common that termination of employment due to shortage of work includes several employees, but it could also be limited to one person. However, if an employee can reasonably show that the termination was really made because of personal reasons and that there in fact are no relevant personal reasons the employee can claim damages for wrongful termination.

First in last out

29.13 In the event of notice of termination on the grounds of shortage of work, the employer shall observe an order of priority. The guiding principle is 'first in last out'. The employees with the longest aggregate period of employment with the company have priority for continued employment over employees who have been employed for a shorter time. In the event of equal employment times, priority shall be given to the older employee. For example, one employee's position is disappearing due to a re-organisation ('Employee A'). Employee A has been employed for three years but instead of dismissing Employee A as redundant the employee moves Employee A to another position to carry out another employee's work ('Employee B'). Employee B has been employed for one year and Employee B is made redundant as a result.

29.14 Where it is only possible to offer continued work to an employee with the employer following a re-location of the employee, priority shall be conditional on the employee possessing satisfactory qualifications for the continued work. A period of up to a couple of months of training paid by the employer - but not re-education - may have to be accepted.

29.15 If the employer has several operational units, the order of termination shall be determined separately by place of business. A place of business is a physical unit.

29.16 If an employee has his/her workplace at his/her home that is typically not considered to be a separate operational unit.

29.17 If the employer is (or is usually) bound by a collective agreement, a special order of termination shall be established for each agreement sector.

29.18 An employer with a maximum of ten employees may exempt a maximum of two employees who, in the opinion of the employer, are of 'particular importance for the future activities'. The said employees have priority for continued employment. When calculating the number of employees at the employer, employees which are not protected by the Swedish Employment Protection Act (eg the CEO, consultants, employees who are members of the employer's family) shall not be included.

29.19 The employer and employee organisations may agree upon deviations from the order of priority. This is rather common and such deviation from the Swedish Employment Protection Act shall be made in writing through a collective agreement. If the agreement has not been entered into or approved by a central organisation of employees, it is required that a collective agreement entered into or approved by a central organisation of employees applies as regards other issues between the parties or that such a collective agreement is temporarily inapplicable.

29.20 The employer should ensure that an employee affected by the dismissal due to shortage of work cannot be said to have been selected because of discrimination.

29.21 As a consequence of the principle 'first in last out', an employee entitled to continued employment may not necessarily always be the best suited for that particular work. It can be difficult – or impossible – for the employer to be able to choose which specific employees will be laid-off and which specific employees will continue their employment.

29.22 Where an employee declines an offer of re-employment that they should reasonably have accepted, any right to priority is lost.

Right to re-employment

29.23 An employee who is given notice due to shortage of work has priority to re-employment provided that the period of employment has exceeded 12 months during the latest three years. This right is valid during the period of notice and the nine months subsequent to that. The right relates to available work within the place of business for which the employee has the required qualifications.

29.24 The right to re-employment means that an employer who wishes to employ new employees must first offer the new position to the previous employee, provided that the employee possesses satisfactory qualifications for the new employment. If there is more than one employee who have rights of priority for re-employment, priority among these previous employees shall be determined by their individual accumulated length of employment.

PERSONAL REASONS

29.25 The term 'personal reasons' refers to any termination that is due to the individual. Such reasons could be related to the behaviour or lack of performance of the individual employee. However, the behaviour must be severe to constitute objective grounds for dismissal and it is normally difficult to terminate an employment due to personal reasons.

29.26 Personal reasons that could lead to a dismissal include absence without leave (for more than an insignificant period of time and in a manner that indicates nonchalance), refusal to accept orders, serious breach of the employment agreement, disloyal behaviour, criminal offences, such as theft, violence or harassments against the employer or against colleagues.

29.27 The employer must normally have informed the employee of the unacceptable behaviour and the employer also must have made efforts to try to correct it. For instance, the employer could provide the employee support in form of practical advice and guidance. Furthermore, the employee must have been given a reasonable chance to correct his/her behaviour.

29.28 An employer who wishes to terminate an employment due to personal reasons shall inform the employee of this at least two weeks in advance. If the employee is a member of an employees' organisation, the employer shall at the same time notify the local organisation to which the employee belongs.

29.29 Notice of termination due to personal reasons may not be based solely on circumstances that were known to the employer for more than two months before notice of termination was given. However, the employer may base the notice of termination entirely on circumstances known to the employer for more than two months where there are extraordinary reasons for invoking such circumstances.

29.30 The Swedish rules on termination of employment due to personal reasons are complex and the interpretation is based on case law. Employers who ignore or are unaware of the relevant legislation or recent court cases can easily make mistakes. Errors can result in a liability to pay economic compensation or punitive damages. It is therefore essential that employers and their management have a comprehensive and up-to-date knowledge of these matters before making any decisions.

SUMMARY DISMISSAL

29.31 In very serious cases of misconduct the employer may terminate the employment without any notice period by summary dismissal. The procedure for a summary dismissal is in many aspects similar to the process for a termination due to personal reasons.

29.32 An employer who wishes to summarily dismiss an employee shall inform the employee of this at least one week in advance. If the employee is a member of an employees' organisation, the employer shall at the same time notify the local organisation of employees to which the employee belongs.

29.33 The Swedish rules on summary dismissal are complex and interpretation is based on case law. Employers who ignore, are unaware of the relevant legislation or the recent court cases can easily make mistakes. Errors can result in a liability to pay economic compensation or punitive damages. It is therefore essential that employers and management have a comprehensive and up-to-date knowledge of these matters before making any decisions.

REDUNDANCY PROCEDURES

Notice and information to the Swedish Public Employment Service

29.34 In accordance with Swedish Act Concerning Certain Measures to Promote Employment (1974:13), as amended up to Act (SFS 2009:414), any employer contemplating a closure of business entailing redundancy must give the relevant Swedish Public Employment Service (*Arbetsförmedlingen*) prior notice as follows:

- at least two months' advance notification where at least five but not more than 25 employees are to be affected;
- at least four months' advance notification where more than 25 but not more than 100 employees are to be affected; and
- at least six months' advance notification where more than 100 employees or more are to be affected.

29.35 Further, if at least 20 employees to be affected during a period of time of 90 days, the Swedish Public Employment Service must be given prior written notice.

29.36 The employer must provide the following information in accordance with the Swedish Act Concerning Certain Measures to Promote Employment:

- the reasons for the planned dismissals,
- the number of employees to be affected and the employment categories to which they belong,
- the number of employees normally working at the employer and the employment categories to which they belong; and
- the planned timetable for the redundancies and information on when the dismissals are intended to take effect.

29.37 In addition to the information set out above, the employer shall inform the Swedish Public Employment Service at least one month before the dismissals, as to which employees will be affected and relevant information on negotiations with regard to redundancy with the applicable employee organisation.

29.38 In the event that the employer could not have predicted or foreseen the circumstances which have led to the redundancy, and if the employer therefore has not been able to give notice to the Swedish Public Employment Service within the time limits as set out above, the employer shall give notice 'as soon as possible'.

Negotiations with the employees' organisation

29.39 In accordance with the Swedish Co-Determination in the Workplace Act (1976:580) an employer shall, before it makes any decision regarding significant changes in its activities, on its own initiative, negotiate with the employees' organisation to which the employer is bound by a collective agreement.

29.40 The obligation to negotiate does not include the day-to-day management of the employer's business. However, downsizing, redundancy and dismissal due to shortage of work are, among other issues, considered to be a 'significant change in activities' and negotiating with the employees' organisation is often the first step to take in any redundancy procedure. This often means that no information can be given to the employees before the negotiations.

29.41 The employer shall also negotiate with the employees' organisation prior to any decisions by an employer regarding significant changes in working or employment conditions for employees who belong to the organisation.

29.42 Only in exceptional circumstances may the employer make (and implement) a decision before the employer has fulfilled its duty to negotiate with the employees' organisation.

29.43 Furthermore, even if the employer is not bound by any collective agreement, the employer shall be obligated to negotiate in the event that a matter specifically relates to the working or employment conditions of an employee who belongs to an employees' organisation. Hence, the employer shall negotiate with that organisation.

29.44 Where an employer is not bound by a collective agreement, the employer shall negotiate with all affected employees' organisations in all matters relating to termination of employment as a consequence of insufficient work or the transfer of an undertaking, a business or a part of a business subject to Section 6 b of the Employment Protection Act (1982:80). However, this shall not apply, where the employer is only temporarily not bound by a collective agreement.

29.45 The term 'negotiation' means an obligation to inform, to consult with and listen to the employees' organisation before the employer makes any decision. The employer shall put forward a reasoned proposal for a solution to the employees' organisation and the employees' organisation shall get an opportunity to present its point of view. The employer shall summon the negotiation with the relevant employees' organisation or organisations and it is often possible to set up a date for a negotiation with about one or two weeks' notice. Negotiations are most often held through a meeting in person, but can also – if both parties agree to do so – be held by telephone or sometimes by e-mail.

29.46 The employer shall in good time notify the employees' organisation in writing of the following matters:

- the reason for the planned dismissal/dismissals;
- the number of employees who will be affected by the dismissal and the employment categories to which they belong;
- the number of employees who are normally employed and the employment categories to which they belong;
- the planned timetable for the redundancies and information on when the dismissals are intended to take effect; and
- the method of calculation of compensation to be paid (if any) in addition to that which is required by to law or applicable collective agreements.

29.47 After negotiating, the employer is free to make its decision and the employer is not obliged to reach an agreement with the employees' organisation. The negotiation is consequently not an obstacle to the employer´s decision-making, since the power to make the decision stays with the employer.

29.48 If the employer makes a decision without prior negotiations, the employer is in breach of its duties according to the Co-Determination Act and may be liable to punitive damages to the relevant employees' organisation or organisations. The employer should therefore always start the negotiations by sending an invitation in writing and also make sure that there are written minutes from the negotiations.

Practical Tip

Negotiations with the employees' organisation shall take place *prior* to any decisions on dismissals due to redundancy.

Negotiating with the employees' organisation is mandatory if: (i) the employer is party to a collective agreement; or (ii) any employee – who is to be expected to be made redundant – is a member of the employees' organisation.

Hence, in case of (i) or (ii) negotiations shall then be carried out even if the employer will only let off one employee.

Alternative employment

29.49 An employer must examine the possibility of offering suitable alternative employment to affected employees within the company (see paras **29.15–29.16**).

Other considerations according to employment contracts

29.50 When planning a workforce restructuring process the employer should review the employment contracts and/or any applicable policies in order to determine if there is any provisions which stipulates extra remuneration or extra protection which has to be considered.

NOTICE

29.51 Notice of termination is deemed effective when such notice is received by the employee. The notice period is the period of time between such notice and the actual last day of employment. Employment contracts often refer to the notice period set out by statue or for a notice periods of between one and three months' notice to be observed by the employee.

Minimum notice period

29.52 The minimum notice periods under statute are set out below. If an employment contract stipulates a shorter notice period, the minimum notice period shall be observed when notice is given by the employer:

Length of Service	Notice by Employer
Less than 2 years	1 month
At least 2 years but less than 4 years	2 months
At least 4 years but less than 6 years	3 months
At least 6 years but less than 8 years	4 months
At least 8 years but less than 10 years	5 months
At least 10 years	6 months

29.53 Note that if the employer is a part of a collective agreement, the notice period could be longer than the minimum notice period under statue. For instance, there are collective agreements in Sweden which stipulates that employees who are 55 years or older at the time of the termination due to shortage of work and have been employed by the employer for ten years, could be entitled to a further six months' notice period, ie in total 12 months' notice period.

29.54 The minimum notice period for an employee is one month.

29.55 For employees who are on parental leave at the time of being given notice of termination due to shortage of work, the notice period begins only when the employee resumes work or when the employee was supposed to have resumed work.

29.56 During the notice period, the employee is entitled to receive all his/her regular employment benefits. This applies even if the employer cannot find work for the employee who has been given notice. It is possible to release the employee, by an agreement, from his/her duty to work. However, in some cases there is a possibility to make wage deductions if the employee obtains work from another employer during the notice period.

29.57 An employee who changes employment by transferring from one employer to another may, with respect to the second employment, also be credited with the period of employment with the former employer if, at the time of the transfer, both employers belong to the same group of companies.

29.58 An employee who changes employment as a result of the transfer of business from one employer to another, may include the period of employment with the former employer in the calculation of the period of employment with the subsequent employer. This also applies in connection with change of employment in conjunction with bankruptcy.

Termination form

29.59 A termination notice shall be in writing and must contain certain information, for example information regarding what steps an employee must make if he/she does not accept the termination and information whether the employee has rights of priority concerning re-employment or not.

29.60 The employer must state the procedure to be followed by the employee in the event the employee wishes to claim that the notice of termination is invalid or to claim damages as a consequence of the termination.

Practical Tip

The following information could be inserted in a written termination notice:

You have rights of priority for re-employment in the business in which you were previously employed, unless you and the company agree otherwise. Such right to priority shall apply during a period of nine months after the date that the employment ceased.

If you intend to initiate proceedings to have the notice of termination declared invalid you shall notify the employer of such intention not later than two weeks after receiving the notice of termination. Where negotiations have been demanded within this two weeks period according to the Employment Co-Determination in the Workplace Act (1976:580), or by a collective agreement, proceedings must be commenced not later than two weeks after the conclusion of the negotiations. Otherwise proceedings shall be commenced within four weeks after notice of termination was given.

> If you intend to claim damages you shall notify the employer of such intention not later than four months after receiving this notice of termination. Where negotiations have been demanded within this four months period according to the Employment Co-Determination in the Workplace Act (1976:580), or by a collective agreement, proceedings must be commenced not later than four months after the conclusion of the negotiations. Otherwise proceedings shall be commenced within eight months after notice of termination was given.
>
> If a notice has not been given or proceedings have not been commenced in respect thereof within the periods stated above, your right to any claim will lapse.

REDUNDANCY PAYMENT

29.61 Employees who have been given notice are entitled to pay and other employment benefits during the notice period, as well as other contractual entitlement the employee may have under his or her employment contract or an applicable collective agreement. However, the employees are not entitled to any additional statutory redundancy payment.

Post-termination restrictive covenants

29.62 It is common that employment contracts for key employees include post-termination restrictive covenants.

29.63 As a starting point, a non-compete clause where an employee undertakes to not engage in a certain type of business, or undertakes not to be employed with a company conducting such a business, shall not binding on the employee giving it to the extent that the undertaking is more extensive than may be considered *reasonable*.

29.64 If a non-compete clause is considered extensive it is possible that the clause is unenforceable by the employer and, as a result, the employer ends up with no protection at all.

29.65 If an employee is in breach of the post-termination restrictive covenants the employer may apply to court to demand the employee not to compete in order to prevent the employee from any further breaches of the restrictions and also claim for damages.

BUSINESS SALE, OUTSOURCING/INSOURCING AND OFFSHORING

29.66 The European Council Directive 77/187 of 14 February 1977 was implemented in Sweden by way of Section 6 b in the Swedish Employment Protection Act (1982:80). In short, this Section 6 b regulates the protection of an employment in the event of a transfer from one employer to another.

29.67 Key consequences of Section 6 b applying are:

(*a*) In conjunction with the transfer of an undertaking, a business or a part of a business from one employer to another, the rights and obligations under contracts of employment and employment relationships that existed at the time of the transfer to the new employer shall also be transferred.
(*b*) The previous employer shall, however, be liable to the employee for any financial obligations that are related to the period prior to the transfer.
(*c*) A transfer of undertakings according to Section 6 b does not constitute objective grounds to terminate employments, ie the employer, is prohibited from terminating employment contracts if this is a result of the transfer.
(*d*) Section 6 b does not apply to a situation where ownership of the employer changes by way of a share sale.

Effect of Section 6 b

Automatic transfer and protection of employment

29.68 In the event of a transfer of a business or a part of a business where Section 6 b applies, the rights and obligations of those employees employed in the transferring business will automatically transfer to the new employer. Outstanding liabilities related to the period prior to the transfer of business will also transfer.

29.69 The transfer of an undertaking, a business or a part of a business under Section 6 b shall not, per se, constitute objective grounds for giving notice of termination of employment. The above-mentioned prohibition shall not, however, prevent an employer from giving notice of termination of employment as a consequence of economic, technical or organisational reasons that include changes to the workforce.

Objection to the transfer

29.70 An employee may object to their transfer under Section 6 b. However, if an employee objects, their employment will continue with the previous employer (ie the seller). Since the business has transferred to the new employer (ie the purchaser) and there may be shortage of work within the previous employer it is often unlikely that an employee exercises this right.

Negotiation with employees' organisations under Section 6 b

29.71 Where employees may be transferred from one employer to another under Section 6 b, both the transferor and the transferee have duties to negotiate with the relevant employees' organisation before any decision is made with regard to the potential transfer.

WORKFORCE REDUCTION IN CONNECTION WITH SHARE SALE OR SHARE

Purchase

29.72 If a business is sold by a share sale, and not by a sale of the assets, the employer does not change. Hence, the employee will still be employed by the same legal entity (the employer), even if the shareholder of that legal entity has changed.

29.73 If the new owner wants to restructure the business of the employer, then any termination of employment must be based on those objective grounds (shortage of work or personal reasons) permitted by statute and the employer will need to follow the appropriate dismissal procedure as set out above.

FIXED-TERM CONTRACTS

29.74 According to Swedish law contracts of employment are valid for an indefinite term (permanent employment). Contracts of employment for a fixed term may, however, be entered into under certain circumstances specified in the Swedish Employment Protection Act. An employer may for instance decide to use fixed-term contracts for temporary substitute employment or seasonal employment.

29.75 The employer may also use a so called 'general fixed-term employment' in accordance with the Swedish Employment Protection Act. Such general fixed-term employments are allowed without having to specify a reason or cause.

29.76 If an employee has been employed for a period of five years by an employer either for a general fixed-term employment for in aggregate more than two years, or as a temporary substitute for in aggregate more than two years, the employment is transformed into indefinite-term employment (permanent employment).

29.77 A fixed-term contract is normally automatically terminated without notice at a specific date or at the conclusion of a particular project.

29.78 An employee who is employed on a fixed term who will not be given further employment when the employment ends, must be notified to this effect by the employer not less than one month before the expiration of the period of employment. Entitlement to such notification shall be contingent upon the employee, upon the expiration of employment, having been employed by the employer for more than 12 months during the past three years. Where the period of employment is too short for notification to be given one month in advance, it shall instead be given upon the commencement of employment.

29.79 Where a seasonal employee, who at the end of the employment has been employed by the employer for a specific season for more than six months during the past two years, will not be given further seasonal employment at the beginning of the new season, the employer must notify the employee to this effect at least one month prior to the commencement of the new season.

29.80 Whatever the reason for using fixed-term contracts, employers should be aware that the EU Fixed-term Work Directive has been implemented by the Swedish Prohibition of Discrimination of Employees Working Part Time and Employees with Fixed-term Employment Act (2002:293) and that as a result fixed-term employees enjoy certain rights. An employer may for instance not disfavour an employee by applying less beneficial pay or other terms and conditions than the employer applies for other employees.

29.81 The employer shall provide employees in fixed term employment with information about indefinite-term employment and probationary employment vacancies. The information may be provided by it being made generally available at the workplace.

29.82 The rules on fixed-term employments are semi-discretionary and there may be collective agreements which replaces or deviates from the Swedish Employment Protection Act and the information set out above.

DISCRIMINATION

29.83 An employee may bring a claim for discrimination if they believe that the real reason for their selection for redundancy is unlawful discrimination in accordance with the Swedish Discrimination Act (2008:567).

29.84 There are different grounds of discrimination prohibited by the Swedish Discrimination Act. These are discrimination due to:

- sex;
- transgender identity or expression;
- ethnicity;
- religion or other belief;
- disability;
- sexual orientation; and
- age

29.85 Discrimination is also prohibited with regard to membership of or participation in an employees' organisation and benefits that any such organisation provides to its members.

29.86 An employer may not discriminate an employee (including trainee, temporary staff or persons employed by an agency but hired to the employer). The term discrimination includes direct discrimination, indirect discrimination, harassment, sexual harassment and instructions to discriminate.

29.87 If an employee has not been promoted or selected for education or training for promotion, the applicant shall, upon request, receive written information from the employer about the education, professional experience and other qualifications that the person had who was selected for the employment interview or who obtained the job or the place in education or training.

29.88 By violating the Swedish Discrimination Act an employer may have to pay compensation for the discriminatory behaviour. The employer may also be liable to pay compensation for any losses suffered by the employee (eg lost income) if an employee lost his employment due to discriminatory behaviour.

29.89 In addition to the Swedish Discrimination Act there is a protection for employees on parental leave according to the Swedish Parental Leave Act (1995:584). An employer may not disfavour nor treat an employee unfairly for reasons related to parental leave. This protection includes situations when the employer decides on an employment issue, promotions, or applies pay or other terms of employment, or when the employer manages and distributes work, or gives notice of termination, summarily dismisses, lays-off or implements other significant measures against an employee.

29.90 If an employee is given notice of termination or is summarily dismissed solely for reasons related to parental leave, the termination or summarily dismissal shall be declared invalid, if the employee so requests.

29.91 An employer who violates the Swedish Parental Leave Act may be obligated to pay damages for any losses suffered by the employee and for any infringement that occurred.

TERMINATION WITHOUT OBJECTIVE GROUND OR AGAINST ORDER OF PRIORITY

29.92 An employee who is given notice without objective ground or against order of priority can claim damages. Damages can be high and depend on the length of employment.

29.93 Employees can also bring a claim because the appropriate dismissal procedures were not followed by the employer.

29.94 An employee can claim economic damages for lost income. In addition to the economic damages an employee can be entitled to general damages as compensation for the violation of their rights according to the Swedish Employment Protection Act.

29.95 An employee who is given notice without an objective ground can also claim that the termination of employment shall be declared void. If there is such an ongoing dispute concerning the validity of a notice of termination, the employment shall not be considered to be terminated until the dispute is finally settled by court. Such court proceedings may take up to a year or more and the employee will then be entitled to salary and benefits for the entire duration of the employment. This is, however, not possible due to breach against order of priority and the employee will therefore not remain employed during the dispute if a termination is challenged solely on the grounds that it is in breach of the rules regarding priority.

Remedies

29.96 The economic damages covering lost income are determined in accordance with the employee's total period of employment with the employer at the time of termination of the employment relationship. The economic damages are capped and are limited to the following amounts:

- 16 months' pay for less than five years of employment;
- 24 months' pay for at least five years but less than ten years of employment;
- 32 months' pay for ten or more years of employment; and
- in the event the employee has been employed by the employer for less than six months, the amount assessed shall correspond to six months' pay.

29.97 The amount for general damages vary due to seriousness of the violation but can be estimated to be between SEK50,000–150,000.

Chapter 30

Workforce Restructuring in Switzerland

Marcel Aebischer and **Manfred Küng**
Küng Lawyers, Gossau/Zürich

INTRODUCTION

30.1 This chapter looks at employment laws in Switzerland with regard to workforce restructuring. The Swiss Confederation (Latin: Confederatio Helvetica; CH) comprises four main linguistic regions: French in the west, Italian in the south, German in the east and the Romansh-speaking valleys of the canton Grisons. The English language is often used as a lingua franca in commerce. The law permits English to be used as a language in contracts or in correspondence, however it is not an official language used in courts. Therefore documents in English have to be translated into German, French or Italian if someone has to submit a case to court.

30.2 The legal system in Switzerland is not a common law system: the law is codified in a systematic way. The Federal Act on Work in Industry, Crafts and Commerce (called 'the Labour Act'/'Arbeitsgesetz') contains rules about health, safety and working hours. It warrants a minimal standard and its rules are mandatory. The source of the rules governing employment contracts is the Federal Act on the Amendment of the Swiss Civil Code (Part five: the Code of Obligations; art 319 CO). The law provides an 'employment at will' concept. Protection against employment termination is very limited, however the courts tend to widen the protection in favour of employees. Furthermore, in some lines of business the mandatory rules of a Collective Employment Contract or the rules of a Standard Employment Contract are effective and applicable. The company has to check if such a contract is applicable and, if so, what it says about the dismissal of employees.

30.3 The Swiss Confederation consists of 26 cantons. Although employment law is based on federal laws, each canton has its own constitution, its own government, its own parliament and its own courts. Each canton has one, two or three official languages. Until 2010 each canton had its own Civil Procedure Code. Since 2011 rules about civil procedure have been unified in the Swiss Civil Procedure Code (CPC). However in some courts some old habits may still have an impact on the practice in procedures. The court at the domicile or registered office of the defendant, or where the employee normally carries out his or her work, has jurisdiction to decide actions relating to employment law. If a job applicant or an employee brings an action based on the Recruitment Act ('Arbeitsvermittlungsgesetz'), the court at the place of the business establishment of the recruitment or hiring agent with whom the contract was concluded, also has jurisdiction. In planning a restructuring exercise, the company has to consider the possibility of the involvement of different national jurisdictions and courts.

30.4 At the beginning of the restructuring proceedings, the first source of information is the employment contract. It is also necessary to check if the rules of a collective employment agreement are applicable.

30.5 The Workers Participation Act ('Mitwirkungsgesetz') provides a right to information and consultation. In companies with at least 50 employees there is a right to employee representation. But there is no right of participation of employees in the board of directors. Switzerland is not a member of the EU. Therefore there are no legal provisions to implement EU-Directives on works councils into Swiss law. The works council representatives have to be informed on a business sale or workforce restructuring. Trade unions have a limited influence in Switzerland. Therefore a substantial number of companies do not have a works council.

PREPARING FOR A RESTRUCTURING EXERCISE

30.6 At the beginning of the restructuring proceedings it is necessary to gather all relevant demographic data of the affected workforce (age, education, opportunities on the job market etc.). Based on this information and based on a first legal analysis, the company will then be able to estimate the costs of the restructuring proceedings.

Identify the employing entity

30.7 The employee's employment is always with a particular legal entity. In most cases, the relevant legal entity is stated in the employment contract. In business correspondence, on order forms, invoices and in official communication, the business or other name registered in the commercial register must be given in full and unamended. The registrar is obliged ex officio to ensure that the interested parties comply with the statutory provisions regarding the composition of business names. Therefore, the company is obliged to use the registered business name on all official documents. It is easy to check the business name on the internet (www.zefix.ch).

> **Example**
>
> The 'iuni GmbH' runs a homepage containing legal knowledge (www.iuni.ch), but the registered business name is 'I.U.N.I. GmbH' (www.zefix.ch: searching iUNI).
>
> Do not provoke unnecessary legal disputes by providing documents with incorrect or incomplete written business names.

COLLATING INFORMATION TO PLAN AND BUDGET FOR THE RESTRUCTURING EXERCISE

30.8 If the restructuring exercise concerns different group companies and possibly a number of different jurisdictions it requires careful planning. The employing company should be holding all the necessary data on the relevant employees.

30.9 If the company with the employee data has its domicile in Switzerland but the HR department of the group is not based in Switzerland the question of a cross-border disclosure of data arises. The Federal Act on Data Protection ('FADP'/'Datenschutzgesetz') is the source of the applicable rules and provides that: 'personal data may not be disclosed abroad if the privacy of the data subjects would be seriously endangered thereby, in particular due to the absence of legislation that guarantees adequate protection' (art. 6 FADP). In certain cases the federal data protection and information commissioner must be informed of the safeguards on data protection by cross-border transactions.

EMPLOYMENT STATUS

30.10 If the company engages agency workers, self-employed free lancers or consultants, the contracts of such individuals should be analysed carefully so to understand the true nature of the status of the individuals so engaged. When assessing the form and terms of a contract, the true and common intention of the parties must be ascertained without dwelling on any expressions the parties may have used either in error or by way of intentionally disguising the true nature of the agreement. If the interpretation of the contract concludes that the relationship is one of employment, employment law is applicable, even if incorrect classification expressions have been used by the parties.

30.11 Employment is assumed where an individual, by means of an individual employment contract, undertakes to work in the service of another (the employer) for a limited or unlimited period and the employer undertakes to pay him a salary, basically based on an hourly wage rate or a monthly wage. Furthermore the contract distinguishes between full-time and part-time work. A contract whereby an employee undertakes to work regularly in the employer's service by hours, half-days or days (part-time work) is likewise deemed to be an individual employment relationship.

30.12 In a workforce restructuring case an agency worker, a self-employed freelancer or a consultant might be qualified as an employee by the court. Crucial is the independency-test: the individual is not part of the organisation, is not subject to directives of the management and the company does not pay social insurance contributions, but the individual charges VAT on any fees.

30.13 Except where the law provides otherwise, the individual employment contract is not subject to any specific formal requirements to be valid. It is deemed to have been concluded where the employer accepts the performance of work over a certain period in his service which in the circumstances could reasonably be expected only in exchange for salary. Where an employee performs work in good faith for the employer under a contract which is subsequently found to be invalid, both parties must discharge their obligations under the employment relationship as if the contract had been valid until such time as one party terminates the relationship on grounds of the invalidity of the contract.

30.14 Once the employment contract is entered into it is difficult to vary the contract without the employee's consent.

TERMINATION OF EMPLOYMENT

Overview

30.15 Employment contracts can be terminated by mutual consent. They also end by lapse of time (fixed-term contracts), by death of the employee or upon expiry of any notice of termination given by one of parties to the agreement. There are two different types of notices of termination: ordinary termination with notice and extraordinary termination for cause without notice.

30.16 In Switzerland the employment at will-doctrine in general is applicable: a permanent employment contract may be ordinarily terminated by either party for any reason at any time by observing the notice period.

30.17 Both employer and employee may terminate the employment relationship with immediate effect (extraordinary termination) at any time for good cause. These are circumstances in which trust and confidence is undermined to such an extent that the party giving notice cannot be reasonably expected to continue the employment relationship. Therefore, only severe breaches of the contractual duties entitle to terminate the employment extraordinarily. Ultimately, if the dismissal is challenged, a court will determine at its discretion whether there has been good cause. In case of an extraordinary termination the employment relationship ends with immediate effect.

30.18 The party giving notice of termination must state the reasons in writing but only if the other party so requests. Therefore a notice of termination must neither be in writing nor set out the reasons for termination with immediate effect in order to be effective.

30.19 A business wishing to change the terms and conditions of its employee's employment contracts, but no express clause allowing this exists in the contracts, has the options of: agreeing the changes with the employees, seeking to unilaterally change the contract or dismissing and re-engaging the employees on the new proposed terms and conditions (so called 'Änderungskündigung'). Following the employment-at-will-doctrine the so called 'Änderungskündigung' is lawful as long as notice period is met.

Garden leave

30.20 After giving ordinary notice to an employee an employer may require that the employee stays absent from the workplace while continuing to pay the salary during the applicable notice period (garden leave). If the employer does not state otherwise in the notification of garden leave, the employee is entitled to start a new job. The employer remains bound by the employment contract and the duties imposed by the contract (garden leave clause).

30.21 Garden leave prevents the employee given notice working for a competitor or from incorporating an own business, because the employee stays employed during notice period, although the employee is not obliged to perform any work. This way the employee is not able to utilise the information the employee has about the employer before notice period has expired. Another benefit of garden leave is to bar the employee from being an unproductive or disruptive presence in the workplace.

30.22 Generally, garden leave is permitted by law. During garden leave, all contractual rights of the employee persist. He is entitled to receive ordinary remuneration including pension entitlements. Therefore base salary, variable salary and bonus (if any) must be paid as if the employee worked during notice period. However, in certain cases a garden leave can create a breach of the contractual obligations of the employer, namely if a full release from duties violates the employee's personal rights, eg in case of a very long garden leave.

No general protection against dismissal

30.23 Regarding the employment-at-will-doctrine it can be said that there is no general protection against dismissal in Switzerland.

30.24 However, Swiss law does have some restraints in the following instances:

- cases of mass redundancies;
- cases of wrongful termination;
- cases of transfer of employment relationship (business sale); and
- cases of a termination at an inopportune juncture (see following chapters).

TERMINATION PROTECTION

30.25 After the probation period has expired, the employer may not terminate the employment relationship:

- while the other party is performing Swiss compulsory military or civil defence service or Swiss alternative civilian service or, where such service lasts for more than 11 days, during the four weeks preceding or following it;
- while the employee through no fault of his own is partially or entirely prevented from working by illness or accident for up to 30 days in the first year of service, 90 days in the second to fifth years of service and 180 days in the sixth and subsequent years of service;
- during the pregnancy of an employee and the 16 weeks following birth; or
- while the employee is participating with the employer's consent in an overseas aid project ordered by the competent federal authority.

30.26 Any notice of termination given during the proscribed periods stipulated in the preceding paragraph is void; by contrast, where such notice was given prior to the commencement of a proscribed period but the notice period has not yet expired at that juncture, it is suspended and does not resume until the proscribed period has ended.

WRONGFUL TERMINATION

30.27 Notice of termination is unlawful where given by one party (employer or employee):

- on account of an attribute pertaining to the person of the other party, unless such attribute relates to the employment relationship or substantially impairs co-operation within the business;
- because the other party exercises a constitutional right, unless the exercise of such right breaches an obligation arising from the employment relationship or substantially impairs co-operation within the business;
- solely in order to prevent claims under the employment relationship from accruing to the other party;
- because the other party asserts claims under the employment relationship in good faith;
- because the other party is performing Swiss compulsory military or civil defence service or Swiss alternative civilian service or a non-voluntary legal obligation

Further, notice of termination given by the employer is unlawful when given:

- because the employee is or is not a member of an employees' organisation or because he carries out trade union activities in a lawful manner;
- while the employee is an elected employee representative on the staff council for the business or on a body linked to the business and the employer cannot cite just cause to terminate his employment;
- in the context of mass redundancies, without his having consulted the organisation that represents the employees or, where there is none, the employees themselves.

30.28 The protection against termination of employment afforded pursuant to an employee representative on the staff council for the business or on a body linked to the business whose mandate has ended as a result of transfer of the employment relationship continues until such time as the mandate would have expired had such transfer not taken place.

30.29 An unlawful notice of termination is not void and the employment ends with it. But the wrongdoing party may be liable to pay compensation.

30.30 Unless the law provides otherwise, the burden of proving the existence of an alleged fact shall rest on the person who derives rights from that fact. The burden of proof of an unlawful notice of termination is imposed on the employee. However if an employee has difficulties concerning proof of evidence about the motivation of the employer the courts accept the proof of utmost probability.

30.31 A party who terminates the employment relationship unlawfully must pay compensation to the other party. The court determines the compensation taking due account of all the circumstances, though it must not exceed an amount equivalent to six months' salary for the employee. Claims for damages on other counts are unaffected.

30.32 In certain cases the compensation may not exceed two months' salary for the employee. In other cases the compensation may not exceed six months' salary for the employee. Important factors for the judicial discretion are the age of the employee, duration of the employment or the circumstances of socially deprived persons. Therefore the six months' salary per capita is the criterion for calculating the risk of litigation in cases of an unlawful notice of termination.

30.33 A party seeking compensation must submit his objection to the notice of termination in writing to the party giving such notice not later than the end of the notice period. This time limit qualifies as a preclusion period.

30.34 Where the objection has been properly submitted and the parties cannot reach agreement on the continuation of the employment relationship, the party on whom notice was served may bring a claim for compensation. The claim becomes time-barred if not brought before the courts within 180 days of the end of the employment relationship.

TRANSFER OF EMPLOYMENT RELATIONSHIP (BUSINESS SALE)

30.35 Where the employer transfers a business or a part thereof to a third party by way of an asset transfer, the employment relationship and all attendant rights and obligations pass to the acquirer as of the day of the transfer, unless the employee refuses such transfer.

30.36 The same rules are effective in the case of a merger, a division, a partial division or a transfer of assets governed by the Federal Merger Act.

30.37 These rules are not applicable in case of a change of the legal form of the company (eg where a limited liability company changes into a company limited by shares) because no modification and no transfer of the employment contract occurs. The same applies to a purchase of shares of a company, where the employer does not change, but only the identity of the shareholder respectively the ownership of the company.

30.38 Where the transferred relationship is governed by a collective employment contract, the acquirer is obliged to abide by it for one year unless it expires or is terminated sooner.

30.39 In the event that the employee refuses the transfer, the employment relationship ends on expiry of the statutory notice period; until then, the acquirer and the employee are obliged to perform the contract.

30.40 The former employer and the acquirer are jointly and severally liable for any claims of an employee which fell due prior to the transfer or which fall due between that juncture and the date on which the employment relationship could normally be terminated or is terminated following refusal of the transfer.

30.41 Moreover, the employer may not transfer the rights arising from an employment relationship to a third party unless otherwise agreed or dictated by the circumstances.

30.42 Where the employer transfers the company or a part thereof to a third party, he must inform the organisation that represents the employees or, where there is none, the employees themselves in good time before the transfer takes place of: the reason for the transfer and its legal, economic and social consequences for the employees.

30.43 Where measures affecting the employees are envisaged as a result of such transfer, the organisation that represents the employees or, where there is none, the employees themselves must be consulted in good time before the relevant decisions are taken. Unless the employer complies with these duties to inform and to consult, any dismissal based on the transfer of business is deemed abusive.

30.44 If the company or part thereof is transferred during a debt restructuring moratorium, in the course of bankruptcy proceedings or under a composition agreement with assignment of assets, the employment relationship with all rights and obligations is transferred to the acquirer if this has been agreed with the acquirer and the employee does not object to the transfer. In addition, the rules as aforesaid apply the same way.

WORKFORCE REDUCTION

30.45 On 1 January 2014 new regulations regarding mass redundancies came into force: bigger companies (250 employees or more) must negotiate a social plan before carrying out mass dismissals. Regulations regarding the instrument of a social plan have only been introduced recently, but only apply to mass redundancies (definition, scope of application, procedure). These provisions were brought in to legislation as part of a revision of the debt collection and bankruptcy legislation. The legislator wanted to simplify the process of restructuring of companies which have difficulties meeting their payment obligations.

Definition of mass redundancies

30.45 Mass redundancies include notices of termination given by the employer to employees of a business within 30 days of each other for reasons not pertaining personally to the employees and which affect:

- at least ten employees in a business normally employing more than 20 and fewer than 100 employees;
- at least 10% of the employees of a business normally employing at least 100 and fewer than 300 employees;
- at least 30 employees in a business normally employing at least 300 employees.

30.46 An agreement to terminate a contract with an employee or the termination of the employment by the employee excludes the application of the rules of mass redundancies.

30.47 The provisions governing mass redundancies apply equally to fixed-term employment relationships terminated prior to expiry of their agreed duration.

They do not apply in the event of cessation of business operations by court order or in the case of mass redundancies due to bankruptcy or under a composition agreement with assignment of assets.

30.48 Individual notices of termination are considered abusive by statute, if such notice was given in the context of a collective dismissal and if the employer breached the following consultation obligation. In such case, the employer is legally bound to pay an indemnity up to an amount equivalent the employee's salary for two months.

Consultation requirements

30.49 An employer intending to make mass redundancies must consult the organisation that represents the employees or, where there is none, the employees themselves. The consultation should be initiated as soon as the mass dismissal is intended, even before the final decision, the display at the employment office and giving notice of the dismissals.

He must give them at least an opportunity to formulate proposals on how to avoid such redundancies or limit their number and how to mitigate their consequences.

He must provide the organisation that represents the employees or, where there is none, the employees themselves with all appropriate information and in any event must inform them in writing of:

- the reasons for the mass redundancies;
- the number of employees to whom notice has been given;
- the number of employees normally employed in the business;
- the period in which he plans to issue the notices of termination.

He must forward a copy of the information to the cantonal employment office.

30.50 An employer intending to make mass redundancies who does not consult the organisation that represents the employees or, where there is none, the employees themselves risks that his notice of termination is qualified by court as unlawful. Therefore the rules of wrongful termination apply.

30.51 The rules of wrongful termination apply also if the employer gives false motivation for the mass redundancies.

Procedure

30.52 The employer notifies the cantonal employment office in writing of any intended mass redundancies and forwards a copy of such notification to the organisation that represents the employees or, where there is none, to the employees themselves.

30.53 Such notification must contain the results of the consultation with the organisation that represents the employees and all appropriate information regarding the intended mass redundancies.

30.54 The cantonal employment office seeks solutions to the problems created by the intended mass redundancies. The organisation that represents the employees or, where there is none, the employees themselves may submit their own comments.

30.55 Where notice to terminate an employment relationship has been given within the context of mass redundancies, the relationship ends 30 days after the date on which the mass redundancies were notified to the cantonal employment office unless such notice of termination takes effect at a later date pursuant to statutory or contractual provisions.

Social plan

30.56 A social plan is an agreement in which an employer and employees set out measures to avoid redundancies or to reduce their numbers and mitigate their effects. It must not jeopardise the continued existence of the company.

Social plans basically contain benefits to the employees, such as severance payments, additional contributions to their pension schemes, assistance in finding new jobs or financing transition arrangements (such as schooling) etc.

30.57 The employer must hold negotiations with the employees with the aim of preparing a social plan if he:

- normally employs at least 250 employees; and
- intends to make at least 30 employees redundant within 30 days for reasons that have no connection with their persons.

Redundancies over a longer period of time that are based on the same operational decision are counted together.

The employer negotiates:

- with the employee associations that are party to the collective employment contract if he is a party to this collective employment contract;
- with the organisation representing the employees; or
- directly with the employees if there is no organisation representing the employees.

The employee associations, the organisation representing the employees or the employees may invite specialist advisers to the negotiations. These persons must preserve confidentiality in dealings with persons outside the company.

30.58 If the parties are unable to agree on a social plan, an arbitral tribunal is appointed. The arbitral tribunal issues the social plan in a binding arbitral award auf.

30.59 The provisions on the social plan do not apply to mass redundancies that occur during bankruptcy or composition proceedings that are concluded with a composition agreement.

Severance allowance

30.60 Swiss law does not provide for mandatory severance payments in case of a dismissal (individual and collective dismissals).

30.61 A statutory severance allowance is only paid out in the following case: Where an employment relationship with an employee of at least 50 years of age comes to an end after 20 years or more of service, the employer must pay the employee a severance allowance. If the employee dies during the employment relationship, such allowance is paid to the surviving spouse, registered partner or children who are minors or, in the absence of such heirs, other persons to whom he had a duty to provide support.

30.62 The amount of the severance allowance may be fixed by written individual agreement, standard employment contract or collective employment contract but may never be less than two months' salary for the employee.

30.63 Where the amount of the severance allowance is not fixed, the court has discretion to determine it taking due account of all the circumstances, although it must not exceed the equivalent of eight months' salary for the employee.

30.64 The severance allowance may be reduced or dispensed with if the employee has terminated the employment relationship without good cause or the employer himself has terminated it with immediate effect for good cause or where the payment of such allowance would inflict financial hardship on him.

30.65 The severance allowance is due on termination of the employment relationship, but the due date may be deferred by written individual agreement, standard employment contract or collective employment contract or by court order.

30.66 Where the employee receives benefits from an occupational benefits scheme, these may be deducted from the severance allowance to the extent that they were funded by the employer either directly or through his contributions to the occupational benefits scheme. The employer is likewise released from his obligation to make a severance allowance to the extent that he gives a binding commitment to make future benefits contributions on the employee's behalf or has a third party give such a commitment.

3067 There is no statutory severance allowance for younger employees. However in a social plan such payments can apply on a collective agreement.

Index

[all references are to paragraph number]

N

Sweden, 29.72–29.73